YENNE

The Great Works of

COMPILED, TRANSLATED AND

Joachim

VELT

Jewish Fantasy and Occult

INTRODUCED BY

Neugroschel

PUBLISHED BY POCKET BOOKS NEW YORK

The author wishes to express his deep gratitude to the YIVO for the tremendous help given him in his studies of Yiddish language and literature.

The spelling of Yiddish names and words follows the YIVO transliteration system, except for those that have become part of the English language or might be misread by American readers. In problem cases, the author has used his own discretion.

WALLABY

POCKET BOOKS, a Simon & Schuster division of
GULF & WESTERN CORPORATION
1230 Avenue of the Americas, New York, N.Y. 10020

Copyright © 1976 by Joachim Neugroschel
Published by arrangement with Stonehill Publishing Company

ISBN: 0-671-79006-4

First Wallaby printing April, 1978

Trademarks registered in the United States and other countries.

Printed in U.S.A.

1   2   3   4   0   9   8

CONTENTS

Foreword   vii

THE FIRST DAY

Ansky   *The Tower of Rome*   3

Mendele Moykher-
  Sforim   *The Wandering of a Soul*   21

From *The Mayse-Book*   *The Rabbi Who Was
                                 Turned into a Werewolf*   31

Der Nister   *At the Border*   44

Y. L. Peretz   *The Three Wedding Canopies*   60

THE SECOND DAY

Ansky   *The Penitent*   107

Y. L. Peretz   *Three Gifts*   114

Der Nister   *The Fool and the Forest Demon* 123

I. J. Trunk   *The Jewish Pope—a
                                 Historical Tale*   128

Moyshe Kulbak   *The Wind Who
                                 Lost His Temper*   157

Yudl Rosenberg   *The Golem*   162

THE THIRD DAY

From *The Mayse-Book*   *The Conversation
                                 of Two Ghosts*   229

Ansky   *A Good Laugh*   231

From *The Mayse-Book*   *The Possession*   241

Dovid Bergelson   *At Night*   243

Der Nister   *In the Wine Cellar*   246

Rabbi Nakhman of Bratslev	*A Tale of a King and a Wise Man*	265
Moyshe Kulbak	*The Messiah of the House of Ephraim*	268

THE FOURTH DAY

Rabbi Nakhman of Bratslev	*A Tale of a Prince*	349
Ber Horovitz	*The Dybbuk*	353
Y. L. Peretz	*A Passion for Clothes*	364
From *The Mayse-Book*	*King Solomon and Ashmedai*	371
Rabbi Nakhman of Bratslev	*A Tale of a Rabbi and His Only Son*	377
Y. L. Peretz	*The Conjuror*	381
A. B. Gotlober	*The Gilgul or The Transmigration*	386

THE FIFTH DAY

From *The Mayse-Book*	*Haninah and the Frog*	437
Rabbi Nakhman of Bratslev	*A Tale of a Menorah*	446
Ber Horovitz	*The Legend of the Madonna*	448
Der Nister	*A Tale of Kings*	460

THE SIXTH DAY

Mendele Moykher-Sforim	*The Mare*	545

AND ON THE SEVENTH DAY

Rabbi Nakhman of Bratslev	*The Tale of the Seven Beggars*	667

NOTES   697

Foreword

Fantasy is a subjective notion. The various ways we define it and respond to it are determined by so many cultural attitudes—religion, science, mysticism, rationalism. Our concepts run a gamut of precarious and unstable categories.

Dovid Bergelson's terse story "At Night" sums up all such energies of fantasy and skepticism.

A train is hurtling through a rainy night across the wastes of Russia, a dark void that is really the modern era which has terminated the absoluteness of previous life and set up a system of rational and relative values, emphasizing skepticism and inquiry.

Inside the train, the narrator, the "I," is suddenly confronted with a stranger, the "Night Jew," a mysterious and omnipresent individual, who is always to be found on trains, but who appears quite suddenly out of the darkness, as though not previously there. He asks the narrator: "Where are you going, young man?" And the narrator never replies; he doesn't know. The train is still hurtling through the void. But everyone is asleep. Only a baby is crying nearby.

A baby can cry in hunger, but a male baby cries at the circumcision ceremony, which is the first rite of passage, initiating a newborn Jewish male into (Jewish) life. The next rite of passage in Jewish existence is the bar mitzvah, the initiation of the Jewish boy into adulthood, into the right to take part in a minyan, the quorum of ten male Jews required for a divine service in synagogue. And this adolescent rite of passage takes place: A young Jewish boy suddenly emerges next to the Night Jew, and the latter teaches him the Bible, starting with the Creation and pausing at Noah's Flood and the subsequent salvation and grace of humanity. This instruction replaces the ten years of study that an orthodox Jewish boy traditionally undertakes at the age of three until his bar mitzvah. Afterward, the study of the sacred texts of Judaism remains his daily activity and is the key to his, and his wife's, salvation.

The teaching in Bergelson's story stops with the destruction and salvation of the world, as symbolic of the end and beginning of humanity, foretelling a messianic era. It is autumn in Russia, the Jewish year has only just begun. Every week Jews read a portion of the Pentateuch in synagogue, and now, in mid-autumn, they have reached the portion narrating the Deluge and the survival of Noah and his family. Hence: the story of Noah in this train that is hurtling through the autumnal void, which is really the early part of the year, and not the closing part as in the Christian calendar. Likewise, the Jewish day begins at sunset. The deep of night is the first part of the twenty-four-hour cycle, and not the end, as in the Christian day. And the concept of grace, although not traditionally Jewish, brings in a mythic component that is fused with Noah through cabbalistic *gematriah*, i.e., the reckoning of the numerical values of the Hebrew letters. The two Hebrew letters spelling Noah's name, when reversed, spell *khein*, the Hebrew word for "grace." This integral cabbalistic touch likewise betokens the reintegration of mysticism and mythology into religion, which, at certain points, must be revitalized by literature and the imagination.

The ignoramus, the Jewish youth who was never instructed in the religion, has now been initiated, and the old man, the Night Jew, who performed the rites of passage in the speeding train, turns out to be Noah himself, both an archetype and an avatar, reincarnated to bring divine grace into the fearful void of modern life.

This assurance of grace, this promise of the future beyond the deluvian wastes outside the train, this sense of progressive life from the squalling baby, through the adolescent, up to the old man, is a perfect example of messianic belief, revitalized by poetic energy.

Noah saves the world, just as poetry and the imagination save religion and reincarnate it in an aesthetic that is turned toward the divine and the eschatological, without truly resolving the questions voiced throughout the story.

It would seem as if what we call "fantasy" is often an attempt at understanding what rational and daily experience fails to grasp: forces, notions, possibilities frequent in our everyday life, often at remote points in our coordinates of infinity and eternity.

Jews obviously did not regard their Bible and Talmud as "fantasy." For them, the Scriptures, especially the first five books, were millenial objects of study, and a portion of the Pentateuch was read each week in synagogue, thereby forming an annual cycle. The Bible and the Talmud were the basis of a national constitution, a code of laws, a way of life, at the core of acting and thinking, particularly outside the Holy Land, and imbued with the promise of a messianic future.

The Cabbalah, a medieval Jewish mystical movement, may have brought mythology into the Jewish religion and into Jewish history. But the "fantasies," the "fairytales," the "fables" in the Bible, and in the post-biblical commentaries and exegeses in the Talmud and what came after, were not really regarded as fantasy by the Jews themselves, until perhaps the Haskalah—the rational movement in nineteenth-century Judaism.

It is the legacy of that era and of the West European Enlightenment that makes us talk about fantasies and fairytales. The polarity of the rational and irrational in regard to such literature does not historically exist for Jews, at least not in the way we regard existence as rational and practical on the one hand and fantastic and irrational on the other: a clean split, which literature and the occult movements try to bridge and turn into a dialectic.

It is this retrospective attitude that lets us seek out "fantasies" among Jewish stories, just as the Haskalah satirists attacked the irrational and mystical traditions in Judaism, from the Bible and the Talmud, through the Cabbalah and its Eastern European offshoot, Hassidism, which has become a major religious force. By seeking out fantasies, we are actually tearing existence into two parts: the "rational" and "pragmatic," the "irrational" and "mystical." We are destroying the oneness of experience and imagination, earthliness and divinity.

Yet such fantasies and fairytales, such mystical stories, actually preserve the unity of human life. They show that divine and supernatural forces are quite human and natural; or vice versa: that the human and the natural are really integrated in a cosmos that allows for anything in the human or divine imagination.

In modern life, the need for such a reintegration of human thought has led to the worst and best, from the inhuman myth and mysticism of fascism to the most daring exploits of poetry and science.

And it is this need for a reintegration of all experience, for a synthesis of all apparent contradictions between rationalism and fantasy that has produced such exciting literary adventures. For Jews, the ultimate synthesis would be the Messianic Age, the advent of an era in which such polarities or dialectics once again become meaningless.

The presence of these contradictions is steady and inevitable, and often spells a secularization of messianism, as evidenced by the rationalist satires that made use of fantasy and the occult, giving them more credit than intended. Skepticism and inquiry belong to the tradition; after all, they also generated the Cabbalah and thus, curiously, added a mystical rather than rational energy to Judaism.

The messianic thought, the doleful and cheerful expectation of that nearby and distant era, imbues all levels of these stories, from the anguish of frustration at the human condition to the sometimes happy endings that prefigure the ultimate Happy End, which is really a Happy Beginning. Moyshe Kulbak's *The Messiah of the House of Ephraim* shows the anguishing side of messianism. Peretz's *The Three Wedding Canopies* is an ambiguous inquiry into the very concept and its possible realization on earth. Der Nister's *A Tale of Kings* points out the arduous road to earthly fulfillment. And Gotlober's rationalist satire *The Gilgul or The Transmigration* is a hilarious and pessimistic exposure of both human folly and the inadequacies of traditional religion in aspiring toward messianic goals.

The two traditions, rationalism and fantasy, are so intergrown as to point out a recurrent theme: the attempt to reintegrate mysticism and messianism into religion and practical experience.

This will become obvious throughout the anthology. The works are matched and contrasted along those lines. The arrangement according to the seven-day cycle refers both to the start of cosmic life, the Creation of the Heavens and the Earth, and to the ultimate promise of messianism, the ultimate Sabbath, anticipated in God's first Sabbath, the promise of that ultimate age, which is mystically reiterated once a week in Jewish life. However, the true nature of the ultimate and eternal Sabbath is still beyond our ken. Thus, the Sabbath story terminating this collection could only be Rabbi Nakhman's "The Tale of the Seven Beggars." A beggar came every day of the week, and then on the Sabbath ... ? The story, and the anthology, has to end with a question rather than an answer. So far, fantasy and skepticism are still dialectical. They will only be fused into one when the Messiah comes.

The First Day

The Tower of Rome

A fearful and wondrous tale about a magic tower with four portals and an iron crown and blades of grass that did not wither

1.

Ages and ages ago, in Rome, the capital of the land of Edom, there stood a huge tower of indescribable beauty. The tower had four portals facing the four sides of the world. And these four portals were shut, and bolted with iron bolts, and locked with iron locks, so that not a living soul could enter the tower. And no one knew what was on the inside.

Now there was an ancient custom that as soon as an emperor was crowned, he had to hang a new lock on each portal. No one knew why this had to be done, but every emperor rigorously observed it, for it had been going on since the dawn of time, from generation to generation.

One day, the emperor of Edom passed away. So there was a gathering of the lords, the princes, the stargazers, and other important men to pick a new emperor.

In those days, there lived in Rome a man of common descent, who had raised himself from the dust to the highest rank and become a great nobleman. And all the others followed his words for he knew how to rule human hearts. And when the mighty of the realm gathered to choose a new emperor, they decided to put the man of common descent on the imperial throne.

And the princes, lords, and stargazers went to this man, bowed to him, and said:

"Long live our lord! We have chosen you to rule us as emperor."

And the man replied:

"I will agree to become emperor over you only on one condition: That you will promise me, and confirm it with your seals and signatures, that you will fulfill what I ask of you."

They said to him:

"Tell us what you will ask of us."

Whereupon the man said once again:

"I swear by your heads that I will not open my lips until you give me your word and confirm with your seals and signatures that you will carry out my request to you."

And they agreed. And they put the man on the imperial throne, and placed a golden crown on his head, and bowed to him and knelt before him, and shouted:

"Long live our emperor, forever!"

And they prepared a great feast, and they ate and drank and made merry.

The next day, the emperor called for all his princes, lords, and stargazers, and said to them:

"It is my will to know what is inside the tower with the four locked portals. Therefore, I command you to open the portals so that I may enter the tower and find out what is on the inside."

The princes, lords, and stargazers were terror-stricken by these words and they all answered at once:

"We are terribly frightened of fulfilling the request of our ruler! Since the dawn of time, no man has dared to open the portals of the tower. Indeed, every emperor has hung new locks upon them. And if we now transgress against the orders of our fathers, we will bring the greatest misfortune upon ourselves and our land."

When the emperor heard these words, he angrily shouted:

"Didn't you yourselves promise and confirm with your own seals and signatures that you would do anything I asked of you? If you refuse to carry out my desire, then your blood will be upon your heads!"

Seeing that the emperor stood fast in his wish, the princes, lords, and stargazers most humbly answered:

"It shall be as Your Majesty desires."

And they sent for the finest locksmiths and told them to undo the bolts and unfasten the locks on one portal of the tower. And when they had done so, the emperor with his courtiers and servants went to the tower and entered through the portal. But the instant he crossed the threshold, the portal banged shut, and none of the men escorting the emperor could follow, so he remained alone in the tower.

And he raised his eyes and saw a huge garden flourishing in front of him, like the Garden of Eden, and it was filled with trees that were pleasant to the sight and good for eating.

The emperor walked on, and in the middle of the garden he saw a pool filled with a thick, red liquid, and he realized that this wasn't water, but blood. And on the surface of the pool, he saw an iron crown, and all around it, there were human hands reaching from the ground to the crown, so many hands that they looked like a young grove. And many of the hands were interwoven, like the roots of an ancient oak tree.

And the emperor walked around the pool, and he was amazed at what he saw, for he couldn't understand the meaning of the reaching and interwoven hands or how the iron crown could stay upon the surface of the pool rather than sink to the bottom, which an iron crown would do.

He went back to the portal and tried to leave the tower, but the portal wouldn't open. So the emperor angrily shouted at the portal:

"I, the emperor of Rome, order you to open immediately."

And the portal opened.

The emperor stepped out of the tower and went back to the royal palace. But he didn't tell anyone what he had seen.

The next day, the emperor once again assembled the princes and lords and stargazers and demanded that they open the second portal of the tower for him. Once more they were afraid, and again the emperor used harsh words with them, and so they did as he wished.

And the emperor entered the tower through the second portal, but he couldn't see what was happening around him, for here there was a deep darkness, like the darkness of Egypt.

At his first step, the emperor felt human bodies beneath his feet. He bent down and felt them and realized that they hadn't lost their warmth. And the bodies were lying next to one another wherever his feet might step. And he was amazed that the bodies lying here for so many years were still warm and did not give off a stench, as corpses do.

And he waited to see what would happen.

After a short while, a host of candles burst into flame, and the space became bright as day. And the emperor saw that he was in a temple of wondrous splendor, and its cupola rose to the very heavens. And the emperor realized that this was a temple to the Jewish God. And the instant it became light, the bodies, which had been lying as dead, awoke and hastily rose to their feet and began praying with great fervor. And the emperor listened, and he realized they were praying to the Jewish God. And their ardor and enthusiasm were so great that their faces began to blaze and sparks flew from their lips, and when the prayer reached its peak, there were flashes of lightning, and the cupola opened, and the emperor saw angels hovering in the heavens and floating down to the temple. And he saw that the angels were carrying in their wings a splendid man in white garments and with a radiant face. When the prayer came to an end, and all that was left was the final *Amen*, the people fell to the ground, as dead, and the cupola shut, and the candles went out, and the space was filled with darkness again.

And when the time came for evening prayers, everything happened all over again. And in the morning, it happened again. But the emperor did not wait until the end of the prayer. It was still light when he left the tower.

On the third day, the emperor commanded that they open the third portal for him, and he entered.

And there he saw a circular room, and the walls were inlaid with black stone, and in the middle stood a golden coffer, its workmanship more wondrous than any human eye had ever seen. The emperor wanted to open the coffer, but it couldn't be opened. So the emperor shouted:

"I, the emperor of Rome, command you to open!"

And the top of the coffer rose by itself.

The emperor saw that the coffer was filled with all kinds of blades of grass, torn out by the roots. And the grass was green and fragrant, and the roots were fresh and lush. And all the blades were bound in sheaves of ten.

And the emperor counted them up, and there were sixty thousand sheaves. He couldn't understand why the uprooted blades of grass hadn't lost their green color and their fragrance and their lushness years and years ago. And he was greatly amazed, and he left the tower.

On the fourth day, the emperor commanded that they open the fourth portal. And he entered and saw a palace of red marble. And he stepped into the palace.

Inside, there were rooms decorated with gold and silver, with pearls and precious stones. And the emperor walked through six rooms and came into the seventh, and the seventh was more beautiful than all the others. And at the end, there stood a royal throne carved out of pure sapphire. And in the middle of the room, there stood silver tables covered with golden cloths. And they were set with the finest foods and the choicest wines, yet there wasn't a living soul anywhere in the palace.

However, when the sun went down, a loud noise could be heard, and the blare of trumpets, and shouts of joy, and the stamping of feet, and the clatter of horsemen. And the emperor realized that many people were coming and he hid behind the royal throne to see what would happen, without his being noticed.

And the doors of the palace opened wide, and a swarm of soldiers tramped in, and captains, and princes, all of them armed and wearing gold-embroidered garments. And at their head marched a man in royal attire with a crown on his head. And all of them paid great homage to him and addressed him as emperor. And they came into the seventh room and sat down at the tables, and ate and drank and made merry.

After the feast, the emperor sat down on the royal throne, and all of them fell to their faces before him and shouted:

"Long live our god the emperor of the whole world!"

And everything the emperor ordered was carried out with great haste and servility. And when midnight came, the emperor stood up from his royal throne and called in a loud voice:

"I command you to bring the iron crown and place it on my head!"

And no sooner had he uttered these words than the soldiers and captains and nobles leaped upon him and dragged him from his royal throne, tore off his royal attire, and ripped him to shreds. And in the very same instant, the soldiers and the princes all vanished, and the pieces of the emperor, who had been ripped apart. And the hidden emperor came forth from his hiding-place and was amazed at what he had seen because he couldn't understand what it all meant.

And he left the tower.

2.

After all these events, the emperor summoned all the magicians and stargazers and other wise men, and told them everything he had seen in the four parts of the tower. And he said to them:

"My wish is that you explain everything I have seen. And if you do not obey my order, I will condemn you to the sword."

And the magicians and stargazers and wise men bowed to the emperor and replied:

"Long live our emperor, forever! We are ready to do your will. But the things you saw in the tower are very wondrous. Those are events of olden times, and it will be hard for us to explain them right away. We therefore ask you, give us thirty days, so that we may have time to work our magic, ask our gods, gaze at the stars, and consult the innards of animals."

And the emperor agreed and said:

"It shall be as you say. I will give you thirty days' time. And if, by the end of thirty days, you fail to reveal the secret of the tower, then your blood shall be upon your heads."

And the stargazers and the magicians and the wise men left the emperor and went to their temples and asked their gods, and worked their magic, and consulted the innards of beasts and animals. But the secret of the temple was not revealed to them.

And when the thirty days were drawing to an end, the magicians, stargazers, and wise men went back to the temples of their idols, and they wept and wailed and tore their clothes and covered their heads with ashes, for they saw that the wrath was poured upon them and that their end was at hand.

At this time, there lived in Rome a very old stargazer, and he had seven sons, all of them magicians and stargazers. And it was their custom to have one of them visit their father every day to take care of him and wait on him. But on the last of the thirty days, none of them came to the old father. And he was greatly surprised. And with his last strength, he took his crutches and hobbled off to see his eldest son. And when he came to his house, he asked:

"Why is this day different from all other days of the year? Why did none of my sons visit me today to take care of me and attend to my needs, as always?"

And the eldest son answered his father:

"Oh, father! A dreadful misfortune has come upon the heads of your sons. They know that before the sun ends its daily course, the threads of their lives will be snapped. And so as not to grieve your heart with bitter sighs, none of us came to you today, as we always do."

And he told the father everything that had happened to them.

The father listened to his son's words, and then he said:

"Grief has muddled the thoughts of my sons, and the desire to honor their old father has blinded their sight. Have you all forgotten that I am a stargazer too? I, along with all the others, must come before the emperor. And this is my paternal commandment: Tomorrow, my sons are to take me to the emperor so that I may stand in their ranks. And who can tell what the coming day will bring! Perhaps fortune will smile upon me, and I will keep the sword away from your throats and turn your grief into joy and your sighs into song."

And the son answered with great respect:

"It shall be as our father has ordered."

And the next day, when the morning star had emerged, and the stargazers, magicians, and wise men had gathered at the royal court with the nobles of Rome and many of the people, there also came the seven sons of the old stargazer, carrying their father on their shoulders.

And the emperor came out to the gathering and said:

"The thirty days that I gave you for stargazing and magic have come to an end with the rising of the morning star. You must now reveal to me the secret of the wonders that I saw in the tower."

And the greatest of the stargazers stepped forward, and fell upon his face before the emperor, and said:

"Long live the emperor, forever! Your humble servants, the magicians and stargazers, have forfeited their heads to you. We have worked our magic, asked our gods, done sorcery with the stars, and consulted the innards of beasts. But we have not succeeded in unveiling the secret of the tower. And now, do with us as you see fit."

And the emperor's anger blazed up, and he shouted:

"I swear by my head that your eyes will never again see the stars over which you have no power, and your lips will never again babble incantations which have no meaning. Before the rising of the evening star, your bodies will be torn by wild beasts and tattered by bloodthirsty birds!"

Now the aged stargazer stepped forward. He bowed to the emperor and said:

"Oh, almighty emperor of Rome! May the blaze of your anger be stilled, and may your sword be stayed, which you have wielded over the heads of your humble servants. The stargazers and magicians are not at fault for their ignorance. They know, Your Majesty, that the tower with the four portals was built by the greatest wizard, who knew the course of the ages. And in order to hide his magic tower from the stars and the demons, he built it in those moments when one day speaks its words to the next, and one night whispers its dreams to the other. In such moments, the rays of the stars die out, and the rule of the demons over the world is weakened. And everything done at such a time remains hidden from the wisest and deepest magicians and stargazers."

And when the emperor heard the words of the aged stargazer, he said:

"Aged man! Your words prove that you are wiser than all the magicians and you are aware of things that are hidden from their eyes. And if the secret of the tower is revealed to you, then you must know who built it and what is hidden in its stony interior."

And the old stargazer answered.

"Oh, almighty emperor of Rome! In your great wisdom, you have foreseen that I know secrets concealed from the eyes of others. Know, then, that since the dawn of time, the secret of the magic tower has been entrusted to only one stargazer. And when the hour of his death arrives, he hands down his secret to the greatest of those surrounding him. Exactly one hundred years ago, an old stargazer in the desert, while dying, handed down the secret of the tower to me.

"But now the time of my death has arrived and I choose you to be the guardian of the secret until you pass it on to someone else. Your Majesty, order all the people standing here or elsewhere in the palace to move far away from your imperial throne to a distance of a gunshot. And then my lips will open."

And the emperor ordered all the people standing before his royal throne or elsewhere in the court to move away to a distance of a gunshot.

And when this had been done, the aged man began to tell his story.

3.
The Aged Stargazer's Tale

You must know, emperor of Rome, that the tower with the four portals was built by Emperor Nimrod, and not with human hands, but with the power of witchcraft.

When Nimrod conquered the entire world and became ruler over all living beings, he said to himself:

"I am God!"

And all had to bow and kneel before him and bring offerings.

And fearing that after his death, another man would rule the earth and destroy the altars raised to Nimrod, and that this man would wipe out Nimrod's name from human memory, he put all the strength and power of his world-wide rule into his iron crown. This made the crown so heavy that the strongest of men could not move it even a hair's breadth. And Nimrod raised a tower around the crown, and put in four portals facing the four sides of the world, so that the tower would be open to everyone and the man who crossed the threshold could not say: "I have entered the tower and it belongs to me now!"

However, in order to safeguard the crown against many human gazes, Nimrod cast a spell, so that the portals could only open to kings and rulers of nations.

And when Nimrod died, a rumor spread through all countries that whoever could lift up Nimrod's iron crown and put it upon his own head, would become ruler over the entire earth.

And now, kings and rulers started coming to Rome from all over the world and eagerly seized the crown to lift it up. But not one of them had the strength to move it, and their efforts were so tremendous, that each man who tried to lift the crown began sinking into the earth, at first up to his ankles, then until his waist, and finally over his head, and all that remained above ground was his hands, which still eagerly clutched at the crown and clung to its edge.

And thus much time wore on, and many kings and rulers perished. But this did not lessen the number of those who were drawn to the iron crown.

Now it came to pass that the land of Edom was ruled by an emperor with a strong will and without fear, and his name was Nero. And he, like other men, also went into the tower to lift up the iron crown. But upon seeing so many stretching hands around the crown, he realized in his great wisdom that hands were not strong enough to lift it.

And so, from the land of Egypt, he summoned the greatest sorcerers and gave them the loveliest presents and asked them to reveal to him what strength was needed to lift the iron crown.

And the sorcerers cast their spells, and then they answered Emperor Nero:

"Through our spells we have determined that Nimrod concealed the secret of the iron crown from the stars and demons and hid the secret inside a rock. He wrote the secret on a tablet and, flying up to the highest peak of the Mountains of Darkness, he chopped out a hole in a crag on the mountain. There, he inserted the tablet and, with magic, he rolled the heaviest rock in the world upon it. And so that no one may hurl the rock off the tablet, he put the strongest wind in a cave and laid a spell upon the opening, so that the wind could not leave and carry the rock away from the tablet."

Upon hearing this, Nero shouted:

"I must get hold of the tablet and find out the secret written upon it."

And the sorcerers said to him:

"There is only one way you can get the tablet. Order your men to catch an eagle of the high mountains. Prepare strong ropes and a long pole. Bring a man who has been condemned to death and have his head chopped off. Then, mount the eagle between the wings, stick the severed head on the point of the pole, and stretch out the pole in such a way that the eagle keeps seeing the eyes of the head in front of him. And the eagle, lusting to peck out the eyes, will fly after the head. And you must guide his flight to the highest peak of the Mountains of Darkness. And when you arrive, do not let go of the eagle, but take him along. And when you come to the middle of the mountain peak, you will see a cave which is covered with a spellbound door. There, the wind is held captive. Tie yourself to the peak of the crag with the rope so that the wind won't carry you away. And then speak the incantations that we will tell you and remove the spell from the door of the cave. And the wind will dash out, the wind that uproots mountains, and it will sweep the rock away from the tablet. And you will take the tablet, and mount the eagle, and, using the pole with the head at its end, you will guide the flight of the eagle back to the earth.

And Emperor Nero obeyed the sorcerers and did as they told him, and he obtained the tablet. And when he returned to the imperial palace, he took out the tablet, and on it were written the following words in the language of Babylon:

"From me, the God of all creatures and the Most Omnipotent Ruler of the entire world, Nimrod, to the Emperor of the land of Edom, Nero: Peace unto you!

"Know, Emperor Nero, that my crown cannot be lifted with the strength of hands or the might of swords, but only with fraud, falsity, and deceit.

"In order to obtain my iron crown, send forth messengers to the kings and rulers of the seventy nations of the world. Write flattering letters to all of them and praise their might and wisdom. And propose to every king, that together with you, but unbeknownst to all the other rulers in the world, he lift up the iron crown, and the two of you share the dominion of the world. Use great cunning, and take care that no king discovers that you are sending your messengers to other kings as well.

"And when the rulers of all the seventy nations gather here, take each of them in turn into the tower. And lead each of them along a separate way to the iron crown. And when all the seventy kings and rulers shall come together at the same time, they will not try to lift the crown. Instead, they will all attack one another and clash with their swords, and all of them will fall down dead. And the blood they shed will become a bloody pool around the crown. And the crown will float up to the surface, and then you will stretch out your hand and lift up the crown effortlessly and place it on your head and become ruler over the entire world."

As soon as Emperor Nero had read the inscription on the tablet, he did everything it said. And he did it all with great shrewdness and deception. And when all the kings and rulers had gathered in the tower and clashed swords with one another so that the blood they shed became a pool and the crown floated up to the surface, Emperor Nero went into the tower and reached out for the crown.

But he couldn't move it, for even though it was on the surface of the pool, it felt as if it were shackled fast, and it was as heavy as ever.

And Emperor Nero once again assembled the sorcerers of Egypt and asked them why the inscription on Nimrod's tablet had not come true and why the iron crown had remained heavy and unmovable, as before.

And the sorcerers cast their spells and gave Nero the following answer:

"Know, Your Majesty, that it is all your fault that the crown has not lost its weight. For you did not fulfill everything that was written on the tablet."

Emperor Nero was surprised, and he asked:

"What did I omit of what was written on the tablet? Tell me, and I will correct my mistake."

And the sorcerers answered:

"You were told to gather the rulers of all the seventy nations of the world. But you neglected one nation and failed to invite its ruler."

Emperor Nero began to inquire. And he saw that it was written that he had gathered together the rulers and kings of only sixty-nine nations, and he counted them up and realized he had forgotten the people of Israel.

And Emperor Nero called for the sorcerers and said to them:

"The words of your lips were justified. Truly, I did not gather together all the kings and rulers. I forgot the people of Israel. But how can I invite the ruler of that nation, since it has no country of its own and wanders among the nations with no king of its own?"

And the sorcerers replied:

"Know, Your Majesty, that even today the people of Israel is still ruled by the House of King David. Therefore we say to you: Gather together ten Jews who descend from the House of King David and take them to the crown in the tower. And the moment they reach for the crown, it will lose its heaviness, for thus will be completed the count of the seventy nations of the world."

And Emperor Nero ordered his servants to find ten men descending from the House of King David. And they found them and brought them to the emperor. And Nero spoke to them with the same flattering words he had written to the rulers of other nations. And he tried to persuade them to lift up the iron crown with him.

But the ten men answered in one voice:

"Because of our sins we were driven from our land and exiled from our soil. And now with all our hearts and souls we ask our Almighty God to send us the Messiah, who will restore the greatness of the House of Jacob. Our souls do not yearn for a crown of dominion over the entire world. We yearn for peace and friendship between men and nations. Therefore, Your Majesty, we will not go into the tower and we will not stretch out our hands to the iron crown."

And Emperor Nero tried to persuade them with flattering words. But when he saw they wouldn't budge, he became angry, and forced them to go into the tower, and shackled them near the bloody pond with copper chains, for he hoped that by seeing the crown they would yearn for it and reach out their hands for it.

But instead, the men of the House of David ground through their chains and fled to the western side of the tower, and begun praying for the Messiah to come. And their prayer was full of great ardor and enthusiasm. And their blazing fervor created walls around the ten men and the cupola of a temple like the Temple of Jerusalem. And this synagogue was beautifully decorated, and many candles were lighted. And when the prayer reached its peak, the cupola came apart, and the heavens opened above it. And angels were hovering, singing hymns. And the angels flew to the Messiah and, surrounding him, they carried him on their wings to the open cupola of the temple. But since the Messiah's hour had not yet struck, the worshipers, upon reaching the final *Amen*, fell to the ground as dead, and the cupola closed, and the candles went out, and the Messiah returned to his solitude.

But when the time came for the second prayer, the men of the House of David awoke, and everything happened all over again, like the first time. And thus it has been happening ever since then, three times a day.

Emperor Nero waited for a certain length of time, and then he entered the tower to see whether the stubbornness of the men of the House of David had been broken. But when he saw that instead of stretching out their hands to the crown, they had surrounded themselves with the walls of a temple and were absorbed in fervent prayers, his wrath blazed up.

And Emperor Nero once again gathered the sorcerers of Egypt and asked them to show him how to break the will of the men of the House of David.

And the sorcerers answered:

"There is no way of overcoming the children of this nation for they are a stiff-necked people. Therefore listen to our advice. Forget about forcing the men of the House of David to reach out for the iron crown, in order to fulfill the number of the seventy nations of the world. Instead, wipe out their people to the very last one, so that not a single Jew survives. There shall then be sixty-nine nations subject to your rule. And then the iron crown will lose its weight for your hands.

And the advice of the sorcerers found favor in the eyes of Emperor Nero, and he asked:

"With what power can I wipe out this nation to the very last one?"

And the sorcerers replied:

"Only a member of this nation can reveal the secret of how to wipe out the people of Israel. Know, Your Majesty, that on the eastern border of your country, there is a land in which the people bow to the severed head of a Jew. In distant countries, they look for a Jewish priest who is the first-born of first-born for seven generations. And with fine words and all kinds of promises, they trick him into coming to their land. And then they chop off his head and put a magic formula under his tongue. And the severed head lives for seventy years and speaks prophesies. And the citizens of the country bow to the head and bring offerings and burn incense to it. And when the seventy years draw to an end, the head loses its power, and the citizens of that country, upon finding another priest who is the first-born of first-born for seven generations, throw the old head to their dogs.

"Now this is our advice, Your Majesty. Go to that eastern country, bring an offering to the severed head, and ask it to tell you how to wipe out the people of Israel unto the very last one."

And Emperor Nero listened to the advice of the sorcerers, and he went to the eastern country, and found the mosque, where the severed head was perched on a pulpit, and he brought an offering, and asked the head to prophesize for him.

And the lips of the severed head opened, and they began to prophesize:

A man has come from Edom,
A mighty emperor of the city of Rome,
He has come to seek my words
To hear my prophecies
And learn how to level the House of Jacob,
And destroy the people of Israel.
How can I keep silent
If the spell lies under my tongue?
How can I hold back my words
If my lips speak against my will?
Listen to what I say, son of the land of Edom,
Hear my prophecy, man from the Goat Mountain.
The people of Israel
Is scattered among the nations.
It is like sprouting grass
Over the face of the earth.
There is no border to the scattering of Israel,
It grows and blossoms and withers.
But when the sun goes up
It lives again and it blossoms afresh . . . .
But know, then, son of Edom,
Lend your ear to my words, Emperor of Rome . . . .

And the severed head went on speaking:

"Every one of the children of Israel has his blade of grass in the world, and as long as the blade grows and stays green and has its lovely scent, then the Jew is alive and sound. But when the roots of the blade go dry, and it bends and turns yellow, and loses its scent and sap, then at that same moment the life-spirit leaves the body of the Jew, and his flesh is like dust.

"And know also, Emperor of Rome, that the blades of grass of the children of Israel have a special appearance that makes them different from all other grass. And if you want to wipe out the people of Israel to the very last one, you must hunt out the blades of grass of the lives of their children. Look for them in high places and in low places, on fruitful fields and in desert wastes, on mountain peaks and in cracks of rocks. And when you find them, tear them out by the roots, and save them, and keep an account of their number. And when you have gathered sixty-times-ten-thousand blades of grass, then you will know that the number is full. For that is the number of the children of Israel. And when all the blades are faded and yellow, and the sap dries from their roots, then that shall be the end of the House of Jacob, and silence shall fall on the tribes of Israel.

And when Emperor Nero heard the prophesy of the severed head, he returned to his country and sent out his men to all four corners of the world, men who were familiar with the plants of the fields, and he told them to hunt down and tear out by the roots the blades of grass of the lives of the children of Israel. And he told them by what signs they could recognize them.

And when a certain length of time had gone by, his men came back with piles upon piles of grass. And Emperor Nero began counting the blades, but he couldn't count them up.

All at once, however, the blades of grass began coming together on their own and put out thin threads and tied themselves up in sheaves of ten. And Emperor Nero was overjoyed that it would be easier for him to count. And when he had counted sixty thousand sheaves, he knew that he had wiped out the life-roots of the people of Israel to the very last one.

And he sent for the loveliest and costliest golden coffer from the imperial treasury, put all the sheaves of grass inside it, and brought it to the tower. Then he came back in the best of spirits for he was certain that the people of Israel was now destroyed and that he would soon be ruling the entire world.

He waited for a year. And when the year drew to an end, he went into the tower to look at the faded grass. But when he opened the coffer, he saw that all the blades of grass were green and fragrant and had not lost the sap from their roots, as if they had never been torn from the earth.

And when he saw this, he shouted out with a fiery anger:

"Now I see that the severed head spoke prophecies, and I swear by my soul, I will wipe out Israel with my sword so that not even a memory will remain."

And he sent out his armies over the land of Edom and all other lands in the world and ordered them to destroy the nation of Israel, men, women, and children, unto the very last one, and to leave their belongings to pillage. And their destruction began, and many were destroyed, and they melted like wax at a flame.

And when the final destruction of the people of Israel was at hand, hosts began appearing before Emperor Nero's imperial throne—hosts of spirits in the shape of armies and officers and princes. And with a loud peal of trumpets they announced to Emperor Nero that his wish had come true, for they had conquered the entire world for him. And with great honor, they led him into the tower, into a palace of red marble which they had built. And they brought him to the last room, where a feast had been prepared, and where there stood a royal throne hewn out of sapphire. And they ate and drank and praised Nero, the emperor of the entire world. Then they put him on the royal throne and worshiped him like a god and shouted:

"Long live the ruler of the world, Emperor Nero!"

And when midnight came, Nero stood up from the throne and shouted:

"I order you to bring me the iron crown and place it on my head!"

And now all the soldiers and officers and princes leaped upon him, dragged him from the royal throne, pulled off his royal garments, and tore him into little pieces, and then they all vanished.

And this is repeated every night . . . .

Now the princes and lords in Nero's court saw that the emperor had gone into the tower but had not come back. And they understood that something terrible had happened to him. So they decided that to keep the same thing from happening to future emperors, they would lock all four portals of the tower. And they also decided that every new emperor should put a new lock on each portal. And the sorcerers and stargazers, reading Nimrod's tablet, decided that forever after, the secret of the tower and everything that had happened in it should be known to only one sorcerer. And he would pass it down before his death to the finest of his friends. And that was what they did.

4.

And when the aged magician finished telling the story to the emperor of Rome, he fell ill and began to breathe his last. But the emperor spoke to him, aroused him, and asked him to reveal why the grass of the lives of the people of Israel had been torn out by the roots and yet had remained fresh and lush. And he asked him what he could do to make them fade and wither.

And the aged stargazer, in great agony, opened his lips and mumbled with great effort:

"The blades of grass have not lost their greenness and lushness because they were bound in sheaves. If Emperor Nero had separated them . . . ."

And with these words, the old man fainted and died.

And the emperor of Rome hurried from his imperial throne and quickly entered the third portal of the tower, and came to the golden coffer, and opened it, and reached out his hand to the grass.

And when he began tearing off the threads binding the sheaves of grass, a two-headed calf leaped out of the coffer, and he was fearsome to behold. And fixing his fiery gaze on the emperor of Rome, the calf let out a deafening bellow, like the roar of a lion. And upon hearing this roar, the emperor of Rome fell down dead. And the tower filled up with smoke, and the bloody pool began rocking furiously with crashing waves, and the iron crown turned over and plunged to the bottom.

And from the temple of the children of King David came the final *Amen*.

Thus ends the tale of the tower
with the four portals
in the city of
Rome

The Wandering of a Soul

It was the time (and I don't mean our time, God forbid!) when boy-husbands were boarding with their in-laws, fathering, and sitting with folded arms in the synagogue. I say (he says) that I don't mean our time because the words "it came to pass," as our sages say, always herald a lot of trouble. Our trouble is that young husbands in those days were not as smart, except in their own matters, as young husbands in our time. Nowadays, young husbands do not know their own goals as they did in the past, and they are useless; quite simply because they need the kind of things that impractical idlers, much to our distress, and whether earlier or later, are lacking; and no one is prepared to speak out and berate them for it. It would be like making fun of a pauper for not closing some great business deal, or making fun of a mute for not talking, or a lame man for not dancing, or a cripple for not standing straight. But useless to themselves (maintain the moderns), those of the past couldn't even pin a tail on a donkey, that is to say, lie down for the nation of Israel. They couldn't pursue their own goals, and, woe to them and to their lives, they never gave a second thought to, never moved heaven and earth for, the goals of the Jewish people! ... They were lazy and moldy, they never formed groups or unions, they never tried to hold assemblies, not at their own expense, coming or going. They had feet, but not for walking; mouths, so to speak, but not for talking or sermonizing. May such sluggishness befall our worst enemies! What did they understand, what did they know? . . . Stocks and bonds?—No!—Funds?—No.—"Culture"?—Forget it!—Well, then what? Nothing!

They yawned, went to synagogue, rose for midnight prayers, lamented the destruction of Jerusalem, peered into holy books, studied the Scriptures, and learned how to be broken Diaspora-Jews with their fine, high-falutin' Friday-night prayers: "How beautiful . . . !"

"Because of our sins we were driven out."

It was for all these things that the wrath was poured out on those poor creatures. The beginning of all wisdom is: Get wisdom. But today, the beginning and end of all wisdom is to hell with the fathers, the past. "Ugh!" they say. "Ugh!" for old, bygone days! That is the entire wisdom, really quite Jewish, in the manner of a wise and intelligent people, the "People of the Book,"—and *that*, I'm afraid, is the trouble! . . .

But that, says the author, is neither here nor there.

And we can believe him, for, as it turns out in the end, his intentions really do lie elsewhere.

What I'm after, he says, is to tell what happened to me once in those days, when, as is the custom of sons-in-law, I was rooming and boarding with my mother- and father-in-law. My father-in-law, a simple man, fine and well-to-do, took me in, like a rare and precious thing, an earnest student, took me from the yeshivah for his one and only beloved daughter, the apple of his eye. It's hard to say how old I was because there was so much confusion about my age, and there was no way of untangling it. My mother counted my years after a great conflagration at the time of my birth. My grandmother, however, calculated after some great panic, and my aunts had different reckonings altogether. But whatever it was, and be that as it may, all I know is that when I got married, my face was pale, smooth, and beardless, like a boy's.

During the first few years of our marriage, nothing much happened . . . . All I knew how to do was pray, eat my mother-in-law's meals, and study. It never even occurred to me to do the tomfooleries that people sometimes do—and my wife didn't get any children . . . . In the beginning, I would simply come home to eat and drink—and that was all. Not to hear a nasty word, not to notice a nasty grimace. But then a slight change took place. I noticed peculiarities about my mother-in-law, a wry face, a pouting, and I was supposed to know what it was all about. But what I didn't know didn't hurt me—I merely went about my business and ate heartily. Little by little, the reason for her pouting was explained to me. First, by way of hints, *allusions*, insinuations, that is to say, she meant—*children!* How could a Jew not have children! ... And next, my mother-in-law told me in so many words, with a simple straightforward *explanation*: "Listen!" she argued, highly excited, as though I had stomped on her toes. "Listen! You've been married for two whole years already and—nothing! ... Husbands who got married at the same time as you have been fathers for ages already, some with one child, some with two. They're mature and responsible, they know what their goals are .... How happy they are, and how happy their parents are! And you? A fine husband you are!"

And next, they worked around this matter *in secret*. I would often find my mother-in-law sitting with other women—neighbors, wives of rabbinical managers, women who administered the ablutions to women at the bathhouse, and my own wife in the middle, with downcast eyes red from weeping, and all the women whispering, winking at one another. An old Gentile woman (if you'll excuse my mentioning her in the same breath) also joined them a couple of times. It turned out that they were sitting there, wondering why my mother-in-law hadn't gotten any grandchildren from her daughter, that is to say, my wife. And they were using household remedies on her. Naturally, the old Gentile woman and the local healer had their fingers in the pie, along with the women who had been mothers many times over.

But I never thought about any tomfooleries. I ate heartily and studied heartily.

Now since *allusions* didn't help, and *explanations* didn't help, and *secret*s didn't help, my mother-in-law finally resorted to *homiletical discourse*, i.e., sermons. She was a marvel at sermonizing. The minute she opened her mouth, out came pouring, as from a sack full of holes, a preacher, a torrent of speech, helter-skelter, higgledy-piggledy, hugger-mugger, Gentile sayings all mixed up with (please excuse my mentioning them in the same breath) Talmudic quotations (it sounded moronic) spiced with the bittersweet language of Yiddish prayers for women, so that it would have the proper Jewish flavor.

Her sermons about me were based on the verse: "My son-in-law is indecent." And she demonstrated at length that it was indecent of me to do this, and do that .... Indecent, like the peasant's proverb "Neither fish nor foul," which in Yiddish goes: "No bah, no moo, no cock-a-doodle-doo!" So what was I then? A dummy! That's what! And a further indecency: Any other father-in-law would take his son-in-law to the rebbe of Khandrikev—long may he live!—and if not personally, then through one of his followers, to turn the son-in-law into a decent human being .... And he would prosper, with "children and money,"—as it says in the Sabbath prayer. But as for me, she would exclaim—glaring at her poor husband, who had to put up with everything from her: As for me, oh God in heaven! It should happen to her worst enemies! I simply wasn't decent, amen, amen! ...

When I hear the sermons of preachers nowadays, they fit me like a six-fingered glove. I merely look at them in pity, these poor people affecting wisdom, no doubt knowing very well, as well as I do, that their wise sayings are bogus, a swindle, a put-on. But my mother-in-law's sermons hooked into my heart like leeches, they sucked out my blood. I still ate her food as heartily, I still studied heartily, but it just didn't taste quite right anymore. Something was itching, nibbling in my head, and I would sometimes daydream for minutes at a stretch, with bulging eyes, at random. But still, I was all right, there was no danger. I couldn't botch up my youth, until the time came for me to decide on one of the Jewish professions: teaching Hebrew school, running a store, keeping a tavern, for instance, and thereby become my own boss. But then a dybbuk got hold of me, the Evil Spirit himself, in the guise of a Hassid, and tried to talk me into the devil knows what, lead me off to the devil knows where ....

My Evil Spirit, the Hassid, was an ugly little mannikin with all the gestures, all the charm befitting such a person. His way of speaking was exquisite, he could talk holes into your head. For telling stories, there was never a creature like him, there isn't now, and there never will be, in all the world. The skies were open to him, he could do what he wanted to there, the gates of hell and of paradise stood open for him. Angels and demons were his servants, fire and water his playthings .... His stories could capture a person's soul. If he wanted, his stories could cast a sweet sleep on a person, a warmth flowed through all parts of your body, and you felt a delicious scratching. If he licked his fingers and smacked his lips—you would get an urge to drink, simply to have a sip of spirits . . . .

That was my Evil Spirit, the one that caught hold of me (may all Jews be spared the like).

"Listen, shlemiel!" the Evil Spirit would start reproving me. "Just how long are you going to stay a shlemiel anyway? What can come of all this studying, day and night? Talmud—Shmalmud! You can brood over the Talmud all you wish, like a mother hen, but you won't hatch any children—and what's the sense of it anyway? You're a grown man, you shlemiel! . . . What a pity, I swear, such a young man. . . . I wouldn't care if you were a rationalist, an old recluse separated from your wife, a bookworm with a beard—to hell with him, the heretic! Keep sitting, keep swaying, get hemorrhoids, go through the Forty-nine Steps of Uncleanliness, and so much for you, you'll never get out! But you shlemiel, you're still a boy, you've still got time to exorcise the rationalist in you and become a decent man, a gifted person. Get on the right path while you still have time, and follow me, don't lag behind other young husbands, children of good families, don't lag behind, I tell you, and come . . . come . . . . Others may say to you: Come to Kandrivek, or come to Yehupets, to the rebbe of Yehupets, but I say to you: Boiberik! There are lots of rebbes around, you know, all of them alike, none of them, thank God, in any way sluggish about Jewishness—may they be healthy and strong! But all of them together are nothing but a garlic peel compared with the rebbe of Boiberik, long may he live. —Come, I tell you, come to Boiberik, he'll be able to help you. He's really an expert in barren women, the rebbe of Boiberik. Besides, your eyes will open when you look at his radiant face. 'You will warm yourself in his light,' you frozen yeshivah-student, you cold rationalist you. Like the noble children of Israel, you will see the Shekhinah, the Divine Radiance, upon his face, and you'll be so enthusiastic that, like them, you will eat at his court and drink . . . . You've got the possibility now, you're boarding with your in-laws, you haven't touched your wife's dowery yet. Later on, I hope, you'll pawn something, you'll steal your wife's last bit of jewelry—and you'll take a wagon, or you'll walk, to Boiberik! . . ."

That was how the Evil Spirit talked, and how he talked me into things. And when he saw he hadn't gotten very far, that moralizing didn't help, he tried getting to me with alcohol. He would smack his lips wordlessly, and so tantalizingly that I got a yen for a shot of brandy. It began with drinks on anniversaries of people's deaths, and then one drink led to another, brandy to conclude a section of the Talmud in synagogue, a celebration here, an anniversary there, to sanctify the new moon, to usher in the new month, a holiday here, a Sabbath there, a social drink, and then finally, a brandy-for-its-own-sake drink. As a result, I went so far once that I was literally out if my skin, that is to say, my mind left my body, it leaped out of my flesh, I was intoxicated, in seventh heaven!

The things that I, or, more precisely, my soul, heard and saw if it were humanly possible, in heaven, can scarcely be described in human speech. I'll try anyway, as far as I can, only for the sake of my readers really, because my readers are very curious, they're dying to know about what goes on in heaven, in the world to come.

First of all, I was welcomed by an extremely long nose, as thick and swollen as a mountain, fiery red, slightly dazed, like a flame of burning alcohol, and studded over with warts, and moistened by wellsprings of sweat. After the nose came its owner, reeling, barely keeping himself on his feet, just barely . . . . Lot—the chief cup-bearer of the wine reserved for the righteous at the coming of the Messiah—Lot, in all his glory, more in the spirit than in the flesh, and then an oracular voice boomed out as from a huge, empty barrel: "Make way, make room, for our guest, Ployne the son of Sosye! . . ." Upon hearing this voice, I was overcome with trembling, like a woman in childbirth. The chief cup-bearer smeared my lips, and poured a hundred-proof bitter drop into my mouth, and I felt like a new man!

"I know," he said to me, "what you want, and why you've come. The voice of your mother-in-law, praying for her daughter, your barren wife, is rending the heavens. The healer's incantations are moving heaven and earth. I was ordered to welcome you, fortify you with a bit of liquor, and lead you to the first division of our judicial apparatus, or as you call it down there, the first tavern, and since you're a bookworm and thereby under the supervision of the Angel of Study, we'll have to appeal to him, and he'll make sure your request goes to where it has to go. . . . Well, have another drink, and come along!"

And then he actually took me and carried me, the way a demon carries a scholar, so fast that my head swam. All at once, he threw me, *pow*! I landed on my feet all alone and suddenly there was

light throughout my body. And I looked up and saw a palace before me five hundred leagues high, all of marble and fine gold. And
the palace had five hundred enormous gates, and each enormous
gate five hundred tiny gates. Between them stood the Angels of
Wisdom, the Angels of Intelligence, the Angels of the Talmud, the
Guardian Angels of Hassidism, the Guardian Angels of Enthusiasm,
the Guardian Angels of Religious Ecstasy. And I saw something
like two fearfully long flashes of lightning crackle out of the palace,
and a shape of a hand clutched a heap of black fire and made
crowns for the letters in the Torah. My ankles buckled in terror
and I collapsed on my face. I felt a hand touching me, and I heard a
voice calling me: "Please stand up, you mortal. The Guardian Angel of Study has heard your mother-in-law's prayer!" And I could
feel a frost run over my whole body, my teeth were chattering
with cold, and, getting to my feet, I saw a cold angel before me, a
hunk of ice!

"It is I," he said, "your angel, the Angel of Rationalist Scholars
and Yeshivah Students, the Overseer of the Guardian Angels of the
Talmud. Come, I shall take you, as I have been ordered, to the
Guardian Angel of Conception, that is to say, of Pregnancy."

And the cold angel took me and carried me so fast, the way a
demon carries a scholar, the cold devoured me, and I fainted dead
away. Suddenly—*pow!* I was standing on my feet, and a delicious
warmth was pouring through all my parts. I raised my eyes and saw
a palace of five hundred stories, constructed of all kinds of gems
and jewels, in a beautiful garden with all sorts of plants: roses,
flowers, and trees—a delight for the eyes. And above them, a dark
blue curtain was spread with a golden moon in the center and diamond stars, all looking like a lovely summer night. The garden was
full of thousands of paths running every which way, both open and
concealed, and there were angels strolling about in couples, kissing
one another, pouring out a sweet, tender song. Amuriel, the
Guardian Angel of Love, armed with a bow and arrow, was
shooting, and playing with cherubs, like children, lying hidden
among dense branches. And his arrows hit their marks. At each
shot, a cherub would spring from his hiding-place . . . . It was delightful to stand there watching. Something lured me on, as when
you recite the Song of Songs. And then I heard Amuriel's voice calling my name:

"Ployne the son of Sosye!"

"Here I am," I said, "I'm ready!"

"If you're ready, then fine! I've been expecting you and I'm about to fulfill your request."

Having spoken these words, he turned to another angel and said: "Go and open the treasury of souls and bring me a lively little soul for this man." The angel hurried off on his errand, but soon he came back empty-handed.

What was wrong? They couldn't open the treasury, the key was gone!

There was an uproar, the angels scurried about in alarm, seeking high and low, until they found out, alas, that the rebbe of Boiberik had the key! Opening the hole in heaven through which the prayers from Boiberik came, they pleaded with the rebbe: "Damn it, give us the key for a barren woman!" But they were wasting their breath, he stuck to his guns: "No—let the woman come to me! . . ."

Amuriel became furious at the rabbi of Boiberik and poured out his anger on me and on all Jews: "You Jews are simply impossible! You grab the keys to all treasures, and you want to make us guardian angels your servants. You push in everywhere, and no rage in heaven is complete without you . . . .

"Where are you crawling?" he yelled at me. "Your place is down there in the Jewish district with the other Jews! What's a Jew doing up here? Kick him out!"

I got punched and kicked so much that I lost my senses. And when I opened my eyes, I found myself lying in bed in my own little cubicle, with the family standing around me, all talking at once: "He's come back from the dead! He's alive again!"

What was wrong? Can you imagine, I had been lying in a coma for three days!

A person lying in a coma looks dead, as everyone knows. His body is here in this world, but his soul is gone, it's hovering in heaven, as they say. There, they decide his fate: Should he come, should he go? Is he a goner, a newcomer. Should he come back to earth, where he came from, should he go on to the world to come? While they cast lots for his coming and going, the man's soul wanders freely around heaven, seeing wondrous sights. Very marvelous tales from olden days are told or else can be found in ancient tomes. These tales were told by people who had gone to heaven in a coma and then come back. Rabbi Joseph, the son of Joshua ben Levi (says the Talmud) was very ill and fell into a deathlike coma.

When he regained consciousness, his father asked him: What did you see there? And the son told him that he saw something topsy-turvy—the lowered were raised, and the raised were lowered.... His father asked him: What about sages and scholars, how do things look for us up there? And the son replied, short and sharp: The same (so to speak) as here! ... And he told him other, similar things.

Thus, if the whole matter of a coma is so important, no one will be surprised that people, big and little, young and old, fell upon me like locusts when I regained my strength, they were dying to have me tell about what was happening in heaven, and what was new up there. They were so eager that they drooled as they gazed at me in deep respect. If I had been smart, I would have known which side my bread was buttered on, in fact, I could have earned my bread and butter like many other heavenly people among us, who made an income from their comas. Like them, I could have told tales, vast exaggerations, and if the fools had heard them they would have loved them, and I would be swimming in gold. But I was a raw youth, boarding with my in-laws, I knew only the Talmud and little of the bitter taste of earning one's living at hard work. So, fool that I was, I stuck to the truth, and only told people what I knew. I told the same thing to our rabbi, Lord preserve him. He asked me, as a scholar: "How are things for us Jews up there?" I replied: "They don't want us."

It was dreadful to see his face, the poor man, as he heaved a deep, heartfelt sigh.

And now, after all these things, my Evil Spirit, the Hassid, urged me all the more strongly with his dishonest gestures:

"So you see, simpleton, how revered and venerated *he* is up there, may God preserve him! C'mon, say something ...."

"It should only happen to our worst enemies," I muttered under my breath, remembering the abuse I had heard.

"So what!" he said, "what's the difference if they talk among themselves? But he *is* powerful, he *does* hold the world in his hands, and he does have the key to the treasures, and he can make decisions .... Just go to Boiberik! I simply don't understand what's eating you."

And something was really eating me! Boiberik was eating me! To me and to everyone around me, it seemed absolutely weird! And Jewish stubbornness was eating me, and having to put aside the Talmud, to which I had been accustomed ever since childhood. But on the other hand, I have to admit that, except for the reason that forced me to go there, I got to like Boiberik, it grew on me. Weird as the people of Boiberik may appear, if you look hard, you'll find a few virtues in them. They're very devout. Gloom and worry are sins, ugh! The rabbi of Boiberik said people should be merry. All of them, young or old, rich or poor, maintain a comradely tone with one another. They're not so dry, not so cold, with somber troubles, like the Jews in my town. They can sometimes have a drink and dance a jig, not necessarily at Purim or the Feast of the Torah, but on an ordinary weekday. I was all prepared to follow my Evil Spirit, when suddenly something happened . . . .

My wife—can you imagine!—got pregnant without the Boiberik rebbe and she up and gave birth to twin boys!

This weakened my Evil Spirit a bit. Boiberik became less important to me, and I stood there like a Jew on the Sabbath, with one foot inside the prescribed Sabbath area and one foot outside it—I didn't know whether I was coming or going! I was neither here nor there!

The Rabbi Who Was Turned into a Werewolf

This story really happened.

Once there was a rabbi, a man of distinction, who lived in the land of Uz. He was very rich and he knew all the seventy languages. The rabbi kept a great yeshivah, which was attended by many fine students. He also paid for the education of a number of boys. All in all, there were some hundred young men in the yeshivah.

He also supported an organization for the poor, and there were many paupers who frequented his home. In a word, the rabbi was a pious Jew, with all the virtues befitting a Jew.

His wife, however, was a wicked woman, who looked askance at his good deeds. She couldn't bear the presence of any poor people in her house.

How does the proverb go? When the rope is too taut, it snaps.

And that was what happened with our pious rabbi. He lost all his wealth. Now, he could no longer help the poor, the students, and the little boys. He thought to himself:

"Oh God, what should I do? I've devoted all my life to charity for the sake of the Lord. But now, sinful creature that I am, I have become a pauper. What can a man do? I'll bear this without protest from God's hand, for everything He does is righteous. Who knows? Perhaps I committed some sin!"

And he mused:

"Well, what's the use of complaining? There are people who gloat over other people's misfortunes. I'll do something about it. I'll leave town secretly so that no one will know what's become of me."

He called together his fine students in the yeshivah and said:

"Dear students, you know how devoted I've been to you all this time. I've provided you with food and clothing, and studied with you. But now I have to tell you a secret, and I hope that you will do toward me as I have always done toward you."

The students answered together:

"Dear Rabbi, tell us your secret. And we promise that we will be true to you as long as God gives us life."

The rabbi told them he had to leave town, he couldn't understand why he had become a pauper. And he asked them to come away with him. "I still have a few ducats in my pocket, and we can live on them together. Who can tell? Perhaps some day the Good Lord will make me rich again, and then you can board with me for the rest of your lives."

The students answered:

"Dear Rabbi, we will gladly do everything you ask of us. And whatever we own, whether money or clothes, we will share with you."

And so the rabbi went away with fifty of his yeshivah students, and no one in the community knew about it. When the poor people found that the rabbi was gone they were deeply frightened, just like the boys he had raised at his own expense, and the other students, who remained in his house with his wife.

But the rabbi was off with his students. And because he was famous, he was greatly honored wherever he went, as befits such a great man. No one was surprised that he had left home, people assumed that he and his students were traveling to a yeshivah to study the Torah.

After they roamed about for a year or two, their clothes became tattered, and they ran out of money. Now they had to go begging. And there were fifty of them. Wherever they came, people shut the doors in their faces and refused to let them in. No one could tell whether they were yeshivah students or ne'er-do-wells.

At last, they became tired of their life of wandering, and they said to the rabbi:

"Dear Rabbi, what's going to become of us? How much longer

can we roam like this? We have no money and no clothes. There's nothing we can do about it. Wherever we come, people close their doors and take us for ne'er-do-wells. Perhaps we ought to go home to our parents. We're growing older, we want to get married. But we won't tell anyone what you're doing, or where you are."

Upon hearing this from his students, the good rabbi pondered for a while, and then he said:

"My dear students, what greater praise can I speak of you than your loyalty, which you have been showing me all this time. I therefore want to ask you: Stay with me another four or five days, until after Sabbath. Then, with God's help, I'll let you go. Perhaps the Good Lord will grant us some luck, and we'll be able to go home together."

The students answered:

"Fine, dear Rabbi, we've been with you so long, we'll stay together for a few more days."

And so they wandered on until they came to a clump of saplings. Here the rabbi said to his students:

"Go on ahead, I have to relieve myself."

The students walked on, discussing and disputing.

After relieving himself, the rabbi wanted to wash his hands. He caught sight of a spring not too far away. He took some water and washed his hands. Just as he was about to go farther, he sighted a little weasel dashing past, with a lovely golden ring in its mouth. The rabbi began to chase the weasel, until the beast dropped the ring. The rabbi picked it up. He saw it was worthless. But then he noticed an ancient writing on the inside, which he was able to read. It said: "Though I look ugly, I am invaluable."

The rabbi was very wise and he realized there was something special about this ring, and he pondered and pondered. "What kind of virtue does the ring have. What makes it so invaluable? Perhaps it has the magic power to grant any wish that a man might desire. I'll try it."

And he wished: "May God let me find a moneybelt before me." Scarcely had he uttered his wish when he saw lying before him a belt full of gold. He was overjoyed again. And upon returning to his students, he said:

"Dear students, you can make merry. We will soon arrive in a place where a friend of mine lives. He is a wealthy man, and I'm sure he will lend me money, he doesn't yet realize that I'm poor.

With the money, I'll be able to buy you all new clothes and send you home."

He didn't want to tell his students about the ring. He feared they might take it away, or else report him, and he would lose it. So he didn't say a word.

When the students heard they would soon be getting new clothes, they were overjoyed, and they asked no further questions. They believed everything he told them.

And so, they arrived in the next town.

On the very first day, the rabbi began dressing his students in the finest velvet and silk. And he bought himself the same kind of clothing he had worn before. He remained in this town for a week or ten days, studying hard with his students. The citizens paid him a good deal of respect, as was proper, for he was a great Torah scholar and very learned.

He went into the city and bought a beautiful coach, fit for a prince, and he told his students:

"Dear students, come here, and I will pay you back for everything you did for me while we were roaming about, and then we shall go home."

The students merely thought that the wealthy relative in the town had lent him a thousand ducats, just as the rabbi said to them, so that he might return home in honor. And they started back. And the people who had once closed their doors to them, now opened them wide and welcomed the travelers warmly.

However, while the rabbi and his students were away from their home town, the people were miserable. But then they found out that the rabbi and his students were coming back, and there were shouts of joy. And who was as glad as the poor people in town?

When the rabbi arrived, everyone gave him a warm welcome, for nobody realized he had gone out into the world because he had been poverty-stricken. People thought he had gone away to study. And the rabbi acted as he had always acted before. He gave charity, opened his yeshivah and brought up little boys to study. On Sabbath afternoons, following his nap, he would interpret the hard critical glosses of the Talmud for his students.

One Saturday afternoon, he went to sleep with his wife. Some time later, his wife started nagging him:

"Dear husband, how come you have so much money all at once? We were so poor earlier that you left town."

Her husband answered:

"The Good Lord sent me some luck during my travels."

But his wife didn't believe him. She kept tormenting him, as women do, until he gave in and told her the secret. That was very foolish of him. King Solomon once warned that a man should never tell a secret to his wife, for she will betray him. This happened to the good rabbi, as you shall hear. If the rabbi had refused to tell her the secret, he would have spared himself a lot of trouble. But because he told the secret of the ring, which made all wishes come true, he soon had to suffer terribly.

The moment that shrew of a rebbetsin heard about the ring, she thought to herself:

"If only I can get the ring out of him, he'll never see it again."

She was simply dying to get the ring, but she knew she couldn't get it without his consent. So she said to him:

"Dear husband, give me the ring for a while, I want to see it."

But the rabbi knew how wicked she was, and he wouldn't let her have the ring. So she started yelling, and said:

"I can see you don't love me anymore. Otherwise you wouldn't be afraid to trust me with the ring."

And she put a flea in his ear, until he had to give her the ring.

The moment she had it, she stuck her head under the cover and said: "I wish that God would turn my husband into a werewolf and let him run around in the forest with the wild beasts."

Scarcely had she uttered her wish when the good rabbi leaped out of the window and dashed off into the deep forest, the Bohemian Woods.

Here, he started devouring people in the forest. He caused so much havoc that it was worth your life walking through the forest. Everyone was scared of the werewolf. He built himself a dry den to live in. And he caused so much terror that the charcoal-burners all ran away from the forest because they were frightened of him.

But now we'll leave the wolf for a time and write about what was happening in his home with the students.

When the time came, that Sabbath afternoon, for the rabbi to do his lesson with the students, his wife, damn her soul, said to them:

"The rabbi won't be able to give his lesson today because he doesn't feel well."

The students believed her and went back home. The next day, they came for their lesson again, and the wife said:

"The rabbi has gone traveling again, but he didn't tell me where he was going. But I think that when four years are up, he'll return."

And she made believe she was very sorrowful. But in reality, damn her soul, she was very glad.

Now, when poor people came, she wouldn't let them in the house. This was a dreadful time for the poor, and they were very miserable because of the rabbi's absence. The wicked shrew grew rich, as we can well imagine. She got herself everything she desired, and there was no end to her wealth.

But no one could understand what had become of the rabbi and where he had suddenly vanished to. Nor could anyone find out. People only hoped that he would finally come home, as he had already done once before.

But now we'll leave the shrew for a while and describe the condition of the poor rabbi, who was running around in the shape of a wolf. He caused terrible suffering and tore apart people and other animals. For there is no animal stronger than the werewolf. The town sent for the charcoal-burners and asked then whether they would be willing to go after the werewolf and destroy him. The charcoal-burners refused, saying the werewolf was stronger than a lion, and as smart as a human being.

Hearing this, the king went hunting for the werewolf in the forest, but he couldn't catch him. They dug pits in the forest, but nothing helped.

However, there lived a charcoal-burner in the woods, whom the werewolf never bothered. On the contrary, he became friendly with him and always hung around his hut, although other men had to keep clear of the forest because they were so frightened of him.

One day, the king issued a proclamation that whoever would overcome the wolf and capture him, dead or alive, would marry the king's daughter and inherit the kingdom. The king had an adviser who was unmarried, and he was very strong and heroic, and had displayed his might in tournaments. This adviser said to the king:

"Your Majesty, if you intend to keep your word, then I will undertake to kill the wolf. You know that I've fought in a lot of wars and shown a great deal of strength and always carried the day in my fights. And now I want to try my luck again."

The king promised he would keep his word. The adviser took his weapons and armed himself well, for he was convinced he would kill the wolf.

First he went to the charcoal-burner, who was friendly with the wolf, and said to him:

"My friend, show me where the wolf's den is or where he hangs about."

When the charcoal-burner saw that the royal adviser was intent on killing the wolf, he was deeply alarmed, for he was fearful for the adviser's life since he himself had almost been killed by the werewolf.

So the charcoal-burner said to the adviser:

"My lord, what are you doing here in this forest? When the wolf sees you, you will be doomed no matter how great you are."

The adviser said:

"Never mind. Just show me where he is. I came here to try and kill the wolf."

The charcoal-burner said:

"My lord, I beg you, do not go on, or you will be doomed."

The adviser said:

"Don't hold me up! This is what has to be!"

So the charcoal-burner said:

"Then God have mercy on your soul!"

And he led the adviser to the place where the wolf was running about. With his musket and spear in his hands, the adviser slowly crept up toward the werewolf, thinking he would kill him as soon as he saw him up close.

But when the wolf saw that his life was in danger, he leaped to the side and sprang upon the adviser's throat. He flung him upon the earth and was about to kill him.

When the charcoal-burner saw what was happening, he chased the wolf away from the adviser. But the adviser wouldn't stop. He still wanted to kill the wolf. The charcoal-burner wouldn't allow it. When the adviser tried to attack the wolf a third time, the wolf became so fierce that he wanted to tear him to shreds. The adviser pleaded with God to save him from the wolf. He swore he wouldn't go after him anymore. The wolf let go, and began wagging his tail, quite humanly, the way one man tries to flatter another. He wouldn't stay away from him, and he trotted after him the way a loyal dog trots after his master. The adviser wanted to get rid of him for he was terribly frightened. But the wolf kept running after him.

The adviser took his belt off, and used it as a leash for the wolf. In this way, the wolf became his steady companion in the woods, and, whenever a wild beast appeared that might harm the adviser, the wolf would kill it. If he saw a hare or fox running by, he would catch it and bring it back to the adviser.

Finally, the adviser led the wolf back to the king in town. The king and his advisers were terror-stricken. They had heard enough rumors about how the wolf had torn people to shreds. The king asked the adviser to get rid of the wolf. But the adviser said:

"Your Majesty, don't be afraid! He won't harm anyone if nobody bothers him. I'll put my head on the block for that. Why, he's even caught various animals for me."

And so, the adviser kept the wolf at his side and did a lot of good things for him. He told everyone that the wolf had taken pity on the adviser and allowed him to live, even though he certainly deserved to be torn to shreds, because he had tried to kill the wolf three times. That was why the adviser was now treating the wolf so well, giving him food and drink, the very best and not the very worst. Whenever the adviser went hunting, he always took the wolf along, and when the wolf sighted an animal, he caught it and brought it back to his master.

As we already know, the king had promised to let his daughter marry the man who captured the wolf dead or alive. Now the adviser certainly deserved her hand. The king did indeed keep his word and gave him his daughter for a wife as well as half his wealth. And when the old king died after a time, the adviser took his place and ruled over the entire land. He always kept the wolf at his side and was unwilling to part from him as long as he lived. This was because the wolf had saved his life, and helped him become king. And thus he took care of him, for it was only just.

One winter's day, when it was snowing heavily, the young king went out hunting, and he took along the wolf. As soon as the wolf was outside, he began wagging his tail and kept running on ahead, as though he were tracking down something. The king rode after him and saw him, from afar, grubbing in the snow with his paw. When the king arrived he saw some words written in the snow. The king was astounded and said:

"There's something wondrous here—a wolf that can write! Perhaps he's really a human being under a curse! Such things have happened in the past!"

But no one could read the writing. So the king sent for scholars, but none of them could read the script. However, among the king's advisers, there was one who knew Hebrew, and he said:

"Your majesty, that is the script of Jews."

And he began to read:

"Dear king, remember our friendship and do not forget the good I did you when you came to my den in the woods. I could have torn you to shreds for I overpowered you three times. You certainly deserved it. But nevertheless, I spared your life. In the end, you became king. Know then that I have a wife in that town" (and he mentioned the name of the town) "and she put a spell on me. If I don't get the wishing-ring back very soon, I'll have to remain a wolf for the rest of my days. But if I can get back the wishing-ring, I can become a human being again like everyone else. Therefore I beg of you, recall my loyalty to you. Ride to that town, take the ring from my wife and bring it back to me for the sake of our friendship. Otherwise, I will kill you." There was also a sign showing what the ring looked like. And all this was written clearly in the snow.

Upon hearing this, the king said:

"I want to help him even if I have to risk my life."

With no further ado, he started out with three servants and rode and rode until he came to the town where the rabbi had said that his wife lived. Here, he announced that he wanted to buy lovely rings and old-fashioned jewelry. Nothing was too expensive for him. He would pay the full price. He also summoned the Jews of the town and asked them whether they had any old-fashioned gold or rings or perhaps even gems. The Jews said to him:

"We are poor people, but there is a woman here in town who owns a lot of beautiful jewelry and many gold rings."

He asked them to take him to the woman. They did so. But they didn't realize that this was the king himself. They took him for an ordinary merchant who dealt in gold and all kinds of precious stones.

Upon coming into the woman's home, the king said to her:

"Listen, my good woman! I've been told that you own old rare objects and old golden rings, some with and some without jewels, but with lovely, old-fashioned work. If I see something I like, I'll pay you a good price."

He took out many lovely rings from his pouch and told her he had bought them en route.

The woman said:

"I will be pleased to show the lord my old gold."

She went into her chamber and took out quite a number of precious objects. The king had never seen anything so beautiful in all his life. He was astounded at finding a Jew with such lovely things. But then all at once, he caught sight of a string of rings, and among them was the gold ring that the wolf had described. The king thought to himself:

"How can I get the ring?"

He took hold of the rings and said to himself:

"If only my wolf had the ring he desires."

And to the woman he said:

"How much would you charge for such rings?"

But he didn't point to the magic ring.

The woman said:

"So-and-so-many hundred ducats."

My good king came to terms with her two rings, and he stole the wishing-ring, but the woman didn't even notice. He paid, took his leave, and went home.

By the time he came home, the woman realized that the wishing-ring was gone. But what could she do? She didn't even know who the merchant was. She was as miserable and grief-stricken as a widow, and no one could console her.

When the king arrived home, he gave a great banquet and invited all the lords of the realm. As he sat at the table, merry and joyous, he sent for the wolf. Coming in, the wolf was so overjoyed that he wagged his tail flatteringly, for he knew the king had gone out to get the ring. The wolf kissed the king and caressed the king. When the king saw this, he took the ring from his bag and showed it to the wolf. If the king had known about the true power of the ring, he might not have given it away so readily. But now he took the ring and put it on the wolf's paw. And a naked man stood before them.

When the king saw him, he quickly threw an expensive cape over him to cover his nakedness. The lords of the realm were terrified. The king said:

"Don't be afraid! The man standing before you was the werewolf."

Now the man leaped up in great joy and said to the king:

"Dear king, I beg you, give me permission to go home again, for I haven't been there for three or four years. Do me the great favor and let me go."

The king said:

"My dear friend, if you wish to go, you may do so. But if you prefer to remain with me, you can live here and eat at my table for the rest of your life. I'll never be able to repay the good things you did for me."

And so the rabbi took leave of the king and went home. The king wanted to give him many presents, but the rabbi said:

"Your Majesty, you have seen for yourself that I have money enough at home. Therefore, I don't need your money. You've done me a big enough favor by getting me the ring. Without it, I would have had to remain a werewolf all my life."

Of course, if the king had known the secret of the ring, he would not have been so quick to return it. Even though the king had no dearth of beautiful objects, he still did not possess such a prize as the ring, whose value was beyond estimate.

And so, the rabbi took some food for the journey and started out. On the way, he once again gathered fifty students and bought them clothes of black velvet, and they came to his town. But before he even set foot there, he said:

"I wish to God that my wife, damn her soul, would turn into a donkey. Let her stand in the stable and eat from the trough with the other beasts."

Meanwhile, the news had spread through the town that the rabbi was arriving with fifty students, all dressed in velvet. The whole community gave the rabbi a hearty welcome.

They wanted to know where he had been for so long, but the rabbi said:

"It would be better if you didn't ask. I won't tell you where I've been."

The rabbi acted as if he didn't know what had happened to his wife, although he fully realized she was in the stable. Nevertheless, upon coming home, he did ask his servants:

"Where is my wife? I don't see her anywhere! She won't be able to look at the fifty students I've brought back with me."

His servants said:

"Dear Rabbi, please don't be frightened, and we'll tell you the whole truth."

The rabbi said:

"I won't be frightened."

So they began:

"Dear Rabbi, as soon as we heard that you were coming, we ran to tell your wife the wonderful news. But we couldn't find her anywhere. And we don't even know what's become of her."

The rabbi wasn't the least bit frightened and he continued to affect ignorance. He said:

"I think that if she stays away as long as I did, she'll still come back in the end."

Meanwhile, the rabbi started acting as he had always acted. He distributed alms to the poor, kept up a yeshivah, did good deeds and kind actions. Everyone rejoiced.

A short time later, he gave a large banquet and invited the entire town. Sitting there in high spirits, he said:

"Friends, since the Good Lord helped me to come home safe and sound, I swore an oath to build a beautiful house of worship. The bricks we need for the construction will be hauled by the donkey."

This donkey was his wife. But the others didn't know he had transformed her. They said:

"Dear Rabbi, may the Good Lord help you and enable you to carry out your wish in peace and health."

Meanwhile, the donkey had been eating a lot and gotten fat. And in front of people, she had no sense of modesty, she coupled openly like all animals. But when the rabbi made her haul bricks on her back, she became very scraggy. The rabbi saw that she didn't want to move, so he kicked her in the ribs and said:

"You wicked shrew! What ordeals you inflicted on me—the devil take you!"

And the rabbi made the donkey work until she grew very, very scraggy. This took a long time, and no one wondered where his wife had gone.

As soon as the synagogue was built, the rabbi gave another great banquet, inviting all his wife's kith and kin. When they were all tipsy, the rabbi told them the entire story, everything that had happened to him, the terrible troubles his wife had caused him, until the Good Lord had helped him and he had recovered his human form:

"That's why I turned her into a donkey, and that's what she'll remain for the rest of her days."

When her kith and kin heard this, they were terrified and felt pity for her. They pleaded with the rabbi to forgive her, assuring him she would never do it again. But the rabbi wouldn't trust her.

Not long after that, the rabbi passed away, leaving his children a vast wealth. But the wishing-ring had vanished, and his wife remained a donkey as long as she lived.

That is why King Solomon said that one should never entrust a secret to one's wife. For if the rabbi had not told his wife the secret of the wishing-ring, he would have been spared his ordeal and not have had to run about in the woods. But in the end he paid her back what she deserved. For, as it is written in the Book of Psalms:

"He made a pit, and dug it, and he has fallen into the pit that he made."

At the Border

On the border between the settlement and the desert, there is some sort of creature, a monster, walking about, keeping watch and guarding the border, and always absorbed in watching and guarding.

What is she awaiting from the desert?

"Someone has to come and appear from there," she says.

Who?

She refuses to say . . . . But if someone urges her, toward the end of the day, when she's weary of watching and walking, and exhausted from strenuous expectation, and she sits on a rock and turns her worried and mournful face to the desert; if someone then sees her and goes to her rock and sits at her feet, and inquires who she is waiting for—she turns her face to the inquirer's face and stares at him, and then turns her eyes back to the desert, turns away, and speaks from within herself:

"Who am I waiting for? The camel with the two humps from the desert."

And what is the camel bringing?

"No rider, no rein-holder, no goods and no load; just two candles on his humps . . . ."

What does that mean?

And the creature tells her story:

Deep in the desert now, beneath a gigantic mountain of sand, there lived a giant, the last of his kind. The giant had sworn he would find the way back to the tribe of his fathers, he would dig out their graves and their temples, he would bring them back and restore them to power. But he wandered through half the world, in vain, until he found himself in the desert, until he made his way to that mountain .... He was told that the gods are living on that mountain, and he was informed that on certain evenings when the mountain is darkened and shrouded in night, in the midst of a storm, a nocturnal tempest in the desert, you can see them on the high peak, leaning on their staffs and wrapped in their cloaks.

And so he settled beneath the mountain, staring and staring up at the peak, and he still has never caught sight of them. And fervently he yearns for them and eagerly he waits for them, and every evening he kneels at the mountain, at its foot, with his head turned up high, and stares his eyes out, and not the least stirring goes past his hearing or bypasses his ear. But in all this time, he has never seen them and never heard them.

It was only once, it was an evening, after long staring and the long strain of kneeling, that he heard a voice from the peak of the mountain and the highest height, and the voice said:

"Giant, you will never bring your gods back to rule, and never restore your father's tribe, until you find yourself a mate, and the two of you have a new generation . . . ."

The giant heard these words, and he wondered:

Where could he ever find a mate if he were the last of his giant race, and to whom could he turn if his kind had died out, and no one was like him in the villages, and they looked on him as an ancient thing from the furthest bygones, a vestige of the most distant times .... And whenever he strode through a settlement, his head would hide the sun from the people, and whenever he trod through a settlement, his feet would leave havoc and ruin: and he stomped on forests and trees, and trudged on towns and fields, and turned men into mites, and the people would hide in holes in the ground and cracks in the rocks.

And he wondered:

Where could he turn, and whom could he ask?

And the voice of the mountain, it only spoke once, and he never heard the voice again. He was full of sorrow. And he looked all around, on all sides of the desert: perhaps somebody might come to him, after all, and perhaps somebody might emerge in the distance, after all. But the desert was— desert and nothing else. So he sat there, lonesome, in his place, and kept his eyes in the remoteness, and he found nothing outside himself, and outside the skylines and the heavens, in all that vastness he didn't even sight a bird.

Again he waited for a while, until one day, sitting there, uneasy and stubborn and gloomy, he suddenly heard, aloft and overhead, something like wings, a rustle. He lifted his head and saw: A bird, enormous, high overhead, swooping and wheeling, around and around, gliding, and holding himself as in a prescribed circle, and then, descending from his height, and pausing low, and stopping its flight. And the bird called out:

"Giant, don't worry. Giant, don't grieve. Your mate is ready for you now, your mate is waiting for you, but your mate is very far from you. And to her, and the place where she is, this letter will lead you . . . ."

And the giant saw, from the bird, down to his feet, a letter fall, sealed and shut, and drop to the earth. He bent down and picked it up, and broached the seal and began to read, and this is what the giant read:

To the last of the giants: Wherever he may be and wherever he may find himself, whether at sea, or on land, in a settlement, or in the desert: Peace, and blessings, and affection. We come to inform him that at the edge of the waste, there where the desert comes to the sea, on the shore and on the rocks, we have a relic, a ruin from the past. Our fathers ruled there for eons, until they died out, wiped one another out in battle. All that remains of our giant tribe is one daughter: and there she lives in the ancient tower, with three windows, one facing the sea, one facing the land, and the third— facing high to the heavens aloft. And she has her say, and she has her way: over the water, and the fish in the water—in seas; over the earth and the creatures of earth—the dry land; and over the winds and the gales and all manner of birds—in the air, aloft, and all of

*them listen to her, and they heed all her orders, and she herself
obeys her gods and observes their commandments.*

*Now the gods have said to her: Why should she sit there, and
just sit and sit, for she is the last, and the imperial tower is growing
older, and no one will fix it, and wood-worms have gnawed into its
walls, and all its parts are full of holes . . . . And she still is young,
but her youth is vanishing in vain, and her body is strong, and her
womb could give birth to a race of giants.*

*So they counseled her: They knew for sure that a giant is left—at
sea or on land, but somewhere for certain, and he is in the same
situation, and he too is all alone, and longing for a second half, and
looking, and not finding a mate—why not seek him out and bring
him back to the tower?*

*She heeded the gods, and addressed all the birds, the speediest and
the canniest, she asked them and she questioned them:*

"Who will try to find the giant?"

*One bird, the most skillful, called out and took the mission.
The emperor's daughter gave him a letter, to fly through the
world and seek the giant, in oceans, in lands, and not miss any
place—and now to you, who are reading this letter, to you, at
whose feet the letter has fallen, it comes from your only mate, from
the giant daughter, and the giant daughter says: Come to me . . . .
Love and affection wait for you, for you and your coming, for
you, the only one, and the long awaited.*

Having finished reading, the giant again looked up at the
bird and his place, and the bird was gliding around his place,
and so the giant asked him a question:

"How can I reach the giant daughter?"

"On foot."

"And in what direction shall I turn my feet?"

"There where the bird shall fly away."

And the bird soared up from flying low and made several
wheels around his head, and then, having wheeled, he flew
off to one side, toward a point on the horizon—and flew
away. And the giant stood up from where he was sitting,
turned, and then, before his first step, he turned for a last
time to the mountain, to its height and its peak, and he
looked and said:

"Mountain, I promise and I swear: As I have rested

beneath you and at your feet, thus will I have my gods rest above, on your highest heights, and I give you my word and I swear an oath, that the first-born son, the first child to emerge from my loins, shall be given to you as an anchorite, as the first priest and devoted servant on the mountain . . . ."

Having spoken, the giant put down his foot—the giant did a day's walking—and the second foot—a second day's walking—then the first foot again—and in the middle of the desert, the giant stumbled upon a tent . . . of poles and sticks and sheets and rags. . . . And the whole construction looked like a frail booth hugging the earth, and in the middle of the desert and in great loneliness it aroused pity . . . . The tent was very small, and the giant wouldn't even have noticed, but then a manikin appeared at the door and at the hole, crouching as though emerging from earth, and shrouded he was and wrapped in a dark cloak, from head to foot and back again, and no face and no eye came into sight, and the giant was amazed: Who can this be and what is he doing here in the desert? He bent over, and called down, and cried out:

"Who's there?"

"The leper," a voice from the ground, dull and faint, from under the wrapping of cloak, replied.

And what was he doing here in the desert?

There was no place for him in the settlement.

And how had he gotten his leprosy?

From the giant daughter, at the edge of the desert.

What was he saying?

Let the giant bend over, let the giant bend down to him, he had no strength, he couldn't shout.

And the giant bent over to him, lowered half his body and his head, and the leper told him:

At the edge of the desert, on the shore of the sea, there is a palace, and a giant daughter lives there, the last one, left over from the giant race. She lives there lonesome, without a mate. Her youth is passing in grief and solitude, she spends her time alone with the walls, wanders about, and her life is bleak, from day to night, and she doesn't know what to do with herself . . . . But she still has hereditary power, and say

and sway over all the birds, and they listen to her as they did
to her parents, and serve her and carry out her commands.
And she called them together and sent out the best and the
nimblest, to go and fly and bring back her promised mate,
her giant, from the ends of the earth.

So the bird flew and flew, and sought and sought, but
found no one, and just as he was about to turn back, he ran
into me on a road. At the time, I was young, and a giant too,
and I was looking for my mate, and I was seeking—my other
half. The bird liked me, and he suggested and praised his
mistress, and told me a great deal about her, and about her
life and loneliness in the palace—so I agreed and followed the
bird, and I came to her, to her youth and her home, and she
welcomed me lovingly, and I settled there and I stayed with
her, and I got to know her, and prepared to become her husband and master.... And then at last I became her husband.
It happened one night, when the moon was ruling the sky
and the sea, and the moon was shining into our rooms, and I
was together with her, and no other creature but us in the
palace. I saw her then: in the moonlight, and on the bed, and
I was terror-stricken, and she stared in silence, and her eyes
were cold and her face was thoughtful, and she looked as if
she were somewhere else, and didn't notice me at all....
And then I turned to her and I asked: What was she thinking, and what was she musing? But she didn't reply. So I
asked again: What was going on in her and why did she
look like that and whom was she thinking about? She
answered: "About another and a better one, and not about
you, who are lying here."

"What do you mean?" I asked her.

"Just that!" she answered reluctantly, and ignoring me.

"Why?"

"You're small and leprous."

And so it was! As she spoke, and I looked at myself, I saw
how small and trivial and useless I was at her side, unnecessary and alien, as though somebody had left me behind there.
And she was beautiful and extraordinarily calm, and she lay
there quietly, and I lay at her side, covered with leprosy....

And I leaped up and left the bed and left her lying. And I
looked at her and at her indifference and at her aloofness,

and her repulsion and her it's-all-the-same-to-me at my leav-
ing. I stared at her for a while, stared and understood: A
sorceress! A sorceress had bested me. I left the room, and I
left the palace, and came out into the open, and walked
down to the sea, and stood before the sea and the moon's
domination. I looked at the sea: By the shore, where the
water wasn't deep, a camel was standing with all fours in the
water, up to his knees, and his head turned away, silently
gazing, his mouth not chewing, absorbed in himself and in
his thought.

I walked over to the camel. In my misery, I found him as
a friend, and in my sorrow—a kin in water. I asked him
then:

"What do you think, camel?"
"I think it's not the first time, I think you're not her first."
"What can I do?"
"Go into the desert."
"And then?"
"Keep others like you from coming here, from taking this
road."

And I listened to the camel, and I got on his back, and he
took me from the sea and the shore, and off to the sand, and
to the desert. And I settled here in a tent, and I warn all the
wayfarers and travelers going there—I warn all of them.

And the leper finished his story, and the leper fell silent,
remaining in the shroud of his cloak, and in his stillness and
concealment, and with his head drooping, and with his body
and his muteness, he waited for the giant who stood overhead.

"And what would you tell me to do now?"
"Don't go."
"And the bird who's calling?"
"He's her messenger."

Silence and several minutes. And the giant straightened up
from his bending, and turned his head toward the horizon, to
where the bird had taken its course. He looked for him and
his eyes peered out, but the bird was nowhere and didn't appear. And then time passed. And the bird came flying from
far away, flying and circling around the giant.

"What did you want, giant?"

"To know the truth."

"About what?"

"About the giant daughter and your mission."

"It's the truth."

"And what about what the leper said?"

"What can a leper say?"

"And proof?"

"The camel."

"Where?"

"Here."

And a camel appeared next to the giant, in the desert and in the middle, and the camel's neck was craned, and his head and face were turned toward the edge of the sky. And the camel was pensive and seemed to be ready for something, waiting for the giant, for his questions, to reply and respond.

"And you, camel, what do you have to say about the leper?"

"I don't know him."

"And who brought him here?"

"Not I, nor my like, nor my kind."

"Leper!" screamed the giant, lifting his foot to the leper's head and body, and holding him ready: "Leper!" His voice screamed louder, and all at once, with all his strength, he brought down his foot.... And the leper was wiped into nothingness, and the giant brought down his tent and booth, and his rags and his poles as his tombstone and—let him lie there, and never tell lies again, and the giant set out again on his journey.

And when the giant had walked in the desert a day or two, encountering no one, and the desert didn't end, with no issue in sight, he sat down one evening on the road, lay down on the sand, and called out and invited the bird, his escort, guide, and harbinger, for the evening: "Bird, appear!"

The bird emerged from a remote edge of the sky and from flying back, in the darkness and with weary wings, and keeping low, in the final glow of the desert, he flew over to the giant, flew up and asked:

"What do you want, giant?"

"To ask how far it still is to the giant tower."

"It's not so far, you can start preparing."

"For what?"

"For the night and for bed. Lie down."

And when the giant lay down, stretching his legs and limbs the length of the desert, closing his eyes and slowly yielding to sleep and the thoughts of sleep, and slowly dozing off, he began to dream:

The mountain abandoned by the gods was coming to life again. On the height and on the peak, a temple appeared, new and reconstructed, and refurbished, and opened as for a festivity . . . . And now the night was coming on, and outside there was darkness and gloom, but inside the temple was bright and radiant, and through the windows the festivity was shining upon the mountain and through the night . . . . And for the moment, the temple was empty. But then a man appeared on the threshold, a servant, and he opened the portal, and opened the temple, for those who were to come and enter—let them in. And now they were coming from the mountain, from all its sides and from the bottom, over stairways and footpaths, and all with candles in their hands, shielding the lights from the wind and from snuffing.

The people went up and came to the temple, and gathered at the entrance, and quietly stepped indoors. And the climbers increased, and women and children, and the old were led by the young, and they all went into the temple's brightness, and they all gathered with their candles. And then, in the temple, at pulpit-height, by the eastern wall, facing the entrance, an old priest appeared, dressed in white. He quietly stood before the crowd, stood there and spoke to the crowd:

"In the name of the temple and in the name of the gods of the temple, I herewith proclaim that this temple is open and new again! We owe it to one of us, a last and remaining one of our race, this was his wish, he yearned for this renewal, and thanks to his wishing, thanks to his yearning, we now have gathered together, we have assembled here. I say unto you: Honor the temple."

And the worshipers listened to the priest, and with their candles in their hands they fell to their knees, and the priest raised his hands over them, and the priest softly prayed over them, and they knelt there in silence, and took the prayer and its stillness upon themselves and upon their heads . . . .

"And now," said the priest, "stand up and listen."

And the crowd got up from its kneeling, the worshipers got to their feet, and all of them gazed at the priest and waited for his words. And the priest went on to say:

"In the name of the temple, and in the name of the gods of the temple, we shall give our benefactor a gift now, we shall give him a present for his wedding night, two unlit candles, for him and for his spouse, for him and for the giant daughter, his chosen bride."

And now the priest took from the pulpit table, which was covered with burning candles, two unlit candles, two candles that weren't burning: large and long, waxen and freshly wicked, and he took them in his hands, and held them out to the crowd, and then he went on to say:

"Let him come and let him take them, our benefactor, our temple-rebuilder, for his wedding, and for his night, his first, and when he and his beloved, he and his spouse, shall unite, then the two candles and wicks shall blend, each one kindling the other, and becoming one fire, and they shall be sent down to men, and men shall see the candles and they shall know: An ancient race has been restored, and ancient gods have come back to life, and the giants and their dynasty have been restored to power and might . . . ."

And the giant listened to all these words, for he was in the crowd, and then he walked over to the old priest and the pulpit and stretched out his hands to him and took the candles and walked back.

And as the giant walked back with the lights, he saw: The brightness in the temple grew dark and went out. The festivities died out, and a grief drew across the walls and a shadowy shroud descended on the people, and they all remained in the darkness, and the candles in their hands faded and died, and the candles at the pulpit—flickered and shrank. And the temple grew still. On the pulpit they saw: The priest was gone and in his place stood a man, shrunken, and shrouded in some kind of cloak, and his face was concealed, and so was his body, and his head was covered, and his voice emerged from beneath his cover, faintly emerged, as he spoke these words:

"And the giant shouldn't think and he shouldn't assume that what he sees now is really seen, and what happens now before his eyes is truly and really taking place .... It's all a dream, a figment, it's all a fancy of his, a wish fulfillment, and right is he who is speaking now, and right was the leper, and he says he stamped him out but not his truth, he wouldn't listen, but truth is truth!"

And then everything, the entire temple, and all that filled the temple, vanished from before the eyes of the giant, and the crowd was gone, and the mountain was as deserted as once, and silent in the night and on the mountain peak, silent stood the leper's tent .... And the giant trembled, and the giant awoke.

"Bird!" he shouted. "Where are you?"

And when the giant opened his eyes with his shout and cast his eyes around far and wide, all that he saw was a graying, dawning, a silent desert dawning, and no one was near his bed, and no creature appeared in the distance, and all the world was drowsing still, and everything was deathly silent. The giant called out to the bird again, called out, and the bird called back to him, and came flying to him from drowsiness and grayishness, and sleepily flew up to him, and asked him what he needed.

"I've had a dream."

"I know."

"Explain."

"It's nothing."

"And the two candles?"

"Here they are!"

And the bird pointed to his side, and the camel was already standing there, ever since dawn, for such a long time, and on his two humps there were two candles, two long, large candles, waxen and never kindled, and standing opposite one another, straight and tall and sparkling at one another, and the camel, silently holding them, camellike, the candles on his humps, and staring at the giant and waiting for the giant's standing up from the ground, and for his standing straight, and the camel waited for him to start out.

And the giant stood up, and shook off the night and his lying, and the bird flew off into the distance, and the camel stirred from where he was, and the giant walked off from where he was, and started off into the day and into the further part of his journey.

And for the third time, and the last, the leper came in the giant's way. And this is what happened:

When the giant had been walking a while, and had strode across most of the breadth of the desert, and was coming close to the end of the sand and the start of the ocean, and to the tower by the sea, he suddenly saw in the bright broad day a mirage in the desert. The sun reflected and brought to the giant, before his eyes, in the desert: an enormous city, filled with walls and houses, and filled with streets, and people scurrying to and fro, and people avoiding one another in haste, and people deeply absorbed. Suddenly, a square in the city opened, a large square, a giant square, enough for an enormous crowd. But the square was empty and abandoned, and filled with a void, and no one appeared. However, people started coming, from all sides and from all streets, and from all corners, and from all alleys. One by one, and hugging the ends, and then more and more, and into the middle, and slowly, slowly, filling the square, and growing into a huge assembly. Now the square was thronged and black with people, and a black throng filled it out. Next, a high place appeared at the center—of wooden boards, or a pile of sand, it was hard to say which. And there in that place that stuck out of the crowd, a man emerged and stood out above the assembly. For a while, the man waited for the crowd, for a moment or two, looked around as he waited, and then, to attract their attention he held up his hand, stretched it out and called to the people:

"Great and mighty assembly, a holiday has been proclaimed for us today. A great event has called us together. Know that a giant has appeared in the desert, till now he lived in loneliness, he was the last and alone and a leftover, and now at last he has found his mate, and today he will go to mate with his mate; and he means to create offspring like himself and his ancient forebears, and giants will emerge from his loins and giants will come to the settlements now, and a new power shall rule over our heads. And the giant's dominion shall be lofty, and it shall reach to the very sky, and the lofty sun will reach from the heavens to crown his head. And you shall be shielded and protected by the giant crown. And no enemy shall attack you and no hostile armies shall cross your borders .... Now listen to every word I say, listen and be joyous at what I say!"

And the people listened to everything, and they listened in silence, and when the man was finished speaking, the people wouldn't stir from the square and no one spoke and no one roused a cry of joy. The people stood hushed, waiting, and waiting, and all at once—a voice cried out from the throng, a single voice that carried across the square, carried its shout:

"We don't need him! We don't want him! We aren't waiting for him to eclipse the sun ...."

"We don't need him! We don't want him!" came from all sides and all ends and from the great center and from all mouths—"We don't need him, he's foreign to us, the giant, he will tread over our heads, he will wreck our houses, he will eclipse the sun and send darkness to us—We don't need him!"

All of them bent down and all of them picked up clods of earth and dust and stones and turned to the man who was standing on the height, and they shouted:

"Where is he?" they all shouted and hollered as one.

"There!" said the man, pointing to the giant who stood in the desert. "There he is! Do what you will! There he is! He's in your hands!"

And the people began to fling stones and cast dirt, and an uproar arose in the throng, and people stampeded one another, and pushed and jostled one another, and thronged and crowded and attacked one another, and came closer and closer to the giant—and all at once:

The vision vanished, the crowd was gone, the square was empty. Abandoned and deserted, and not a soul in sight, and only one man, on the high place, the crier, face to face with the giant, silently they eyed one another, the two of them alone on the square. He was alone now, the crier, and he looked sad, and forlorn, and after his silence, he spoke to the giant:

"Giant, where are you going, where are your steps directed?"

"Toward the place where the bird is calling!" replied the giant.

"Why?"

"To arouse the strength of the old giants and to bestow power on the settlements."

"Who wants it?"

"I want it, and I shall do it!"

"And what about the people?"

"They belong to the leper!"

And now the man who stood before the giant began to cover and hide his face, and buried his head in his cloak . . . . And now it was the leper before the giant, his old friend, shrunken and covered, and the giant strode over to him, and the giant, in disgust and fury, trod over to him . . . . And the leper was gone, and the vision in the desert disappeared from the giant and the giant's eye, the city was gone, and the streets of the city, and every last trace of the city was gone, and then—the evening came to the desert, and when the giant, striding and treading to the leper, looked around, and opened his eyes, he saw the desert and the way out. And he sniffed the ocean, and soon he caught sight of the shore of the ocean, and a tower was standing on the shore, an old and ancient tower, with windows facing the sea and the desert . . . . It was evening already, and a flag was fluttering on the steeple, and calling out, and inviting him into the tower, and the giant walked over, and turned his steps toward the tower . . . .

And he saw: The bird flew over to one of the windows, and rapped on the glass with weary wings. The window opened. A head came out, huge and rare, the head of the daughter of the tower, waiting for someone from the desert. The head appeared and was radiant, and turned to the new-comer, welcoming. The giant saw the head, and the sea was calm, and at the shore, along the sand, stood the camel who had come from the desert, stood with the candles on its humps, the large and silent candles, the waxen and never-ignited candles.

The giant entered the tower.

And when he encountered the daughter of the tower, no one could see, and when they met, no one was present, because she had a room in a room, and she never went into that room, and that room was always locked, and only waited for this to happen. And a lamp and a table were standing there, and the lamp was never lit, but now it was burning for to-day, for this meeting.

They entered the room, and an hour went by—and they were silent, and after an hour—they still remained. And the night arrived and the stars emerged in the heavens, and the night covered the world, and the tower and the lamp of the tower were radiant with festivity. And it was late at night, and the sea was talking in its sleep, and the camel was standing on the shore and listening to the talking sea, and the camel wet his feet in the water, waiting for the tower and for the lamp in the tower . . . . And at last, the lamp was snuffed . . . .

And all was still, and the tower stood there, old and ancient, and the darkness was as if reborn, and it had never been so dark. And the sea was sighing, and breathing with all its might. And the camel was standing still, waiting for the night to end. And finally the night *did* end.

The morning star emerged in the heavens and peered down upon the sea and the desert, and blessed them both with its gaze and its favors . . . . And then in the tower, a window opened, a window facing the sea, and a voice could be heard on the shore and the water:

"The night is past, and the night was blessed, and now is the time for the candles on the camel's humps . . . ."

And then the candles on the humps leaned toward one another, came toward one another, and the morning star was watching, and the morning star was shining from the sky, and both wicks lit up, and both wicks joined in one fire and—the camel emerged from the water and walked away from the ocean shore, and he turned to the dawn, the quiet daybreak, turned his face toward the desert and walked into the desert, intending to walk beyond the desert and bring the light and the tiding to mortals . . . .

"And that's who I was waiting for, the camel, and that's who I keep looking for, at the border, and it's been so long since he entered the desert, and it's been so long since he's been coming."

And that was the creature's tale.

The Three Wedding Canopies

First Part

FIRST CHAPTER
The palace—The king and the princess—The king's worries.

Far, far away, beyond the Mountains of Darkness, on the other side of the Sambatyon River, there is a country known as Wonderland, where the red-haired Jews dwell, the descendants of the Ten Lost Tribes. And in that country of Wonderland, in the city where the king lives, in Faithstone, the royal residence, there once stood a high, white, marble palace. And it was beautiful, that high, white, marble palace, standing in a green, luxuriant park as in a green ocean, with its hundreds of golden columns and its thousands of diamond windows.

And at the foot of the white marble palace, a small, clear, crystal river murmured softly and flowed dreamily, and the little river was lined on both sides with the finest flowers and the noblest plants. And in the small, clear, crystal river, there were thousands of golden fish, dancing and flashing about, and on top, on the blue surface of the water, there were swans floating about, snow white, full of myriad charms, and with thin, long, white necks and long, sharp yellow bills . . . .

It was a fascinating sight!

But it was most beautiful at night, when the moon was shining . . . . The marble palace was reflected in the river along with the moon and the stars . . . . The flashing golden fish merrily hopped and danced, springing from one golden column to the next, from one diamond window to the other, and the white swans gravely and majestically swam about from one silvery patch of fog to the next, from one golden star to the other . . . . And trembling, as if deeply in love, they wove around all these things the finest, most wonderous shadows of the flowers and plants that blossomed along both sides of the water . . . . And the song of the nightingale could be heard among the branches, which were bending under the weight of golden fruits. Anyone might think that there was no garden here, no palace here—that it was all a dream, an enchanted dream . . . .

And yet it was *not* a dream.

At that time, the king of the Red Jews, in the country of Wonderland, was Solomon XXVII, our King Solomon's great-great-great-grandson; and he lived in the palace, with his only daughter, Princess Shulamite.

For fifteen years now, the king had been a widower, but he never remarried, because he didn't want to bring a stepmother for the apple of his eye, his second soul, the princess.

And the princess was worthy of his great love.

She had all the qualities and virtues of her father, the king; in addition, God graced her with a beauty that dazzled all eyes.

And because the princess did not resemble her father or her dear departed mother, people thought that the queen had stared at an angel in heaven when about to give birth . . . .

Shulamite's beauty was famous throughout Wonderland, but the people loved her for her goodness, her kind heart, kind eyes, and deep piety.

Every day, people would gather in front of the white palace, the poor, the old, and the sick, and all those in need of help, and the princess would come to them with her friend Deborah, the daughter of Joab the grand vizier. The two young women listened to everyone, gave them gifts and presents, helping and healing . . . .

So that the princess wouldn't need to ask for money every time, the king, her father, had a second golden key made for his treasury, and presented it to her; and in front of his treasury, he put a trained parrot, who, upon seeing the princess, would call out:

"Take, angel, take! Take with full hands, and give with a full heart!"

And the king's treasury did not shrink; on the contrary, it was blessed. The more the king and the princess gave away, the fuller the treasury became, and this was a sign that their charity was having an effect.

Yet in spite of all this, King Solomon XXVII was not happy.

On his golden bed, under the silk canopy, the king would lie awake all night, never closing his eyes, listening to the soldiers walking up and down on their watch.

In Wonderland, a person's conscience is a ruler that won't let you sleep; but this was not the case with Solomon XXVII.... And in the second chapter we will find out why he couldn't sleep.

SECOND CHAPTER
The cuckoo—The sorceress and the princess's oath.

One day, on L'ag Bomer, a spring holiday that Jews celebrate with outings, the princess and her friend Deborah went strolling in the nearby forest.

When the birds caught sight of them, they began to sing more freely and merrily. The birds didn't realize that one of the girls was a princess and the other the grand vizier's daughter. All they knew was that these were the lovely girls, the golden girls, that gave them food whenever they appeared at the palace.

These were the girls who fed them all year long with royal white bread, on the Sabbath with challah and gravy, and, on the special Sabbath when Moses' song is read, with the finest honey cake.

And in honor of the lovely girls, they sang a rare concert.

"C'mon, brother, c'mon!" they called from branch to branch. "In honor of the golden girls, in honor of the lovely girls."

The flowers, usually hiding in high grass in the shade behind the trees, and trembling in terror at an empty hand or a heavy tread—the flowers heard them and thought to themselves:

"If birds praise, then it must be so! Birds never flatter! So we needn't be afraid of the girls!"

And the flowers stuck their lovely heads out of the deep, green grass; and they breathed freely and merrily, so that the whole forest was filled with the finest fragrances!

And the stags and does, who at the slightest rustle, hide in the intertwining branches, emerged and looked at the girls with faithful, loving eyes, as only stags and does can look!

Now the happy princess also felt like singing; her young heart was so full. No sooner had she opened her coral lips than all the birds fell silent, they wanted to hear the golden girl sing . . . .

One cuckoo stopped too late, and Deborah, the grand vizier's daughter, was the first to see him.

She went over to the cuckoo and, half in earnest, half in jest, asked him:

"Cuckoo, how old is my future husband now?"

The bird began to call: "Cuckoo! Cuckoo!" over and over again, and Deborah mirthfully counted five hundred and eighteen years. And her voice tinkled like a silver chime.

The princess heard the cuckoo, she also came over and asked him:

"And tell me, how long will I live, you tree sage?"

And the bird again called out: "Cuckoo! Cuckoo!"

And who can say how many years he would have numbered off if the princess hadn't got tired of counting.

She interrupted him and asked:

"And how many years has God provided for my good father?"

The good princess wanted the cuckoo to call and call and not stop calling, as before.

But the princess stood there petrified, the cuckoo wouldn't emit another sound.

The frightened girls made up their minds to consult the sorceress living in the woods and ask her whether the cuckoo was merely being rude or whether this signified some disaster.

No sooner had they thought of it than a mass of little animals appeared, small, merry, wonderful, multicolored animals, that began dancing and jumping and running on ahead, leading the way to the sorceress.

The sorceress was surrounded by rabbits and squirrels, whom she was feeding, she was old and shrunken, but her eyes were so kindly that the girls weren't the least bit frightened, and they drew nearer. The princess was too saddened to speak, and so the grand vizier's daughter spoke for her:

"Listen," she asked, "how long will her father live?"

She didn't want to tell her that her friend was a princess, so that the witch wouldn't be afraid to speak the truth.

"How's that?" asked the witch.

And Deborah repeated the question, pointing at the princess.

But the witch was obviously stone-deaf, and she misunderstood Deborah's pointing her finger. She was accustomed to girls who asked when their wedding day would be.

So she replied:

"Who? This fine young daughter? Ahh! She's so beautiful! She's so marvelous! Suitors will come to her from the East and the West! And soon she'll get married. Very soon!"

Deborah had to stand on tiptoe and shout her question into the sorceress's ear.

This time the sorceress heard her and replied:

"Her father will live—to see her get married!"

The princess let out a terrible cry. And at that moment the witch and her animals disappeared.

The stags, the deer took refuge. The birds and flowers vanished.

All that could be heard in the hushed forest was the gnawing of the woodworms in the hearts of the trees, and the princess swearing *that she would never marry*. Her father would live, he would out-live her!

Then she begged Deborah to keep all this a secret.

We will see how they kept their word.

THIRD CHAPTER
*A gathering of suitors—A conversation between the king
and the princess—The white dove and her advice.*

Now there came a gathering of lords and princes.

They were all invited to the palace . . . . First they went hunting in the woods. Naturally, when a Jewish king goes hunting, the sportsmen only shoot at beasts of prey and poisonous snakes. After the chase, they had a royal banquet.

The food, strictly kosher, was plentiful. Old wines, also kosher, were fit for a king . . . . When a bottle was uncorked, a bouquet as of the most precious perfumes wafted through the hall. The princess ate, drank, talked, and discussed all sorts of wise topics and faraway lands and countries. All eyes were hanging on the beautiful and radiant face of the princess.

Every man was hoping to see a smile on her lips, a good omen for himself!

The princess, however, was equally friendly to all, and yet refused each one.

The king asked the entire company to leave the dining hall and then said to the princess:

"Shulamite, God is with you! Today, the greatest and the highest and the finest men in the world were here! Princes from the greatest countries came here and sat at our table . . . . And you have turned them down!"

The king went on:

"And they came to you from the East and from the West! They were brought here by your renown, they were dazzled by your beauty."

And tears could be heard in the king's words.

"What's wrong with them? If you're not certain of their intelligence, then give them riddles to solve. You know so much, I've taught you so many things!

"Aren't they rich enough?" the king went on. "Some of them have wealthier countries than I, greater treasuries than I! And all of them swear that they love you!"

The king continued:

"Daughter, my dear devoted daughter! Look! My old head is already covered with snow! Look at my beard, it's as white as milk . . . . And when God calls me, whom shall I leave you with, daughter? What do you desire? They love you so much, they swear they do!"

The princess's heart was weeping at her father's unhappiness, but she couldn't tell him the truth.

So she said she didn't believe their oaths.

"I'm rich, father dear, and I'm your only daughter! How can I tell whether they want me or my wealth? Do they desire me or, after you pass away, your kingdom, father dear?"

And she offered some evidence for her words:

"Look," she said to the king, her father, "isn't my friend Deborah more beautiful than I, finer, smarter, and more learned than I? Yet why don't suitors gather to ask for her pure hand? Why hasn't a single prince fallen in love with her?—Because I'm *your* daughter! Because I'm the princess!"

The king didn't want to say that he didn't believe anyone could be lovelier, smarter, or finer than his daughter, so he replied:

"Goodness knows! Your flashing red hair, your deep, blue eyes,

attract them, and her silken, flaxen hair and deep, honest eyes don't
attract them . . . . Every person has his own fortune . . . ."

And in his heart, he thought: "Oh me! Isn't this sadness a legacy from great-great-grandfather Solomon: Such a fresh little
apple, and already a worm is gnawing at it."

That same instant, a milk white dove appeared at the window.

The princess thought it was one of her doves and turned to it so
that it would perch on her shoulder.

But the dove refused.

The milk white dove flew into the room and alighted on the table
in front of the king.

She bowed three times and began cooing to the king.

Now, you must know, that in the land of the Red Jews, they observe the old Jewish custom that a man sitting in the Sanhedrin, the
highest tribunal, has to know all the seventy languages of the world,
and a king, like Solomon in his day, must even know the languages
of beasts and birds.

And the white dove churred to the king:

"King, great king! Do not worry, everything will turn out for
the best. You will reap pride and happiness from your daughter . . . .
But don't force her to take any of the princes who are asking for
her hand. None of them is her destined bridegroom, nor does he
live in Faithstone, her one and only."

And the king replied in dove language:

"Good dove, wise dove, tell me where her destined bridegroom
lives, I will have my servants harness the finest horses to bring him
here. Whether he's a prince, or the lowliest pauper, or the hardest
laborer, I shall give him my only daughter and my crown—or my
name isn't Solomon XXVII!"

And the dove answered:

"King, great king, may you be healthy and live long! But I was
not told to tell you that. Your princess wants to be certain that the
man who swears he loves her, wants only her, and her alone, not
the treasury, not the kingdom. The good, pious heart is afraid, so
we'll have to calm her fears."

"But how, wise, white dove?" asked the king.

And the dove replied:

"Great king, wise king, may you be healthy and strong and live
to see your grandchildren! Tell her to pick the poorest clothes that
her heart desires, for you and for her, Your Majesty, and the two

of you shall wander away from the places where people can easily recognize you. And when her destined bridegroom desires her in filth and poverty, then the princess's golden heart will not tremble or be afraid."

"I am ready to do everything you say," he replied to the dove, and she hopped back and forth and bowed three times, like a Jew after reciting the eighteen blessings, and then she flew out the window.

The princess had no excuse for not going along with the dove's advice. So, for their wanderings, she picked out the clothes of rag-pickers.

She thought the following: "In such dirty clothes, I won't attract anyone."

But man proposes, and God disposes.

While the king and the princess were talking about their traveling clothes, Joab, the grand vizier, was standing behind the silken curtain, eavesdropping.

Only a bad, false man would do such a thing, and that was what he was.

The populace was murmuring against him. But the king was beguiled by him.

Nations and children have a keen eye, that is to say, they can recognize at first glance things that the wisest sages fail to see. Their very first impression tells them who is truly good, honest, and pious, and who is wearing a mask on his face—and has hell in his heart.

This man should not have been the grand vizier of Wonderland.

He had come into the palace by chance. The queen, may she rest in peace in Paradise, died in childbirth, and they needed a wet nurse for the baby. As fate would have it, they chose Joab's wife. Through her, he gained entry into the palace.

One day, King Solomon noticed him and asked him who he was and what he wanted.

He said he was the husband of the princess's wet nurse, and all he desired was permission to sate his eyes on the radiance of the king's face.

Flattery is to a king as a hook to a fish.

Joab remained in the palace. His power grew from day to day, and in time he became grand vizier.

He was intelligent, like Ahitophel in his time, and he played his pious and honest role so cleverly that the people who murmured couldn't show that there was anything wrong with him.

The princess couldn't stand Joab, the grand vizier. Whenever he looked at her, she felt as if a cold, slimy worm were slithering across her face. But she never mentioned it because of her wet nurse, Joab's dear departed wife, because of the king, her father, and perhaps most of all because of Deborah, in whom she had a devoted and beloved sister. So she controlled herself, and spoke a kind word to him from time to time.

The evil man however misinterpreted the kind word. He wanted to use it for his own ends and become the king's son-in-law!

Joab was no spring chicken, but he tried to look young. He dyed his hair and beard so that everyone forgot how old he was.

The ladies-in-waiting all winked at him, and so he thought that Shulamite too . . . . Only a false and evil man can think such things.

Just to make sure, he bought love potions from all kinds of sorcerers and secretly put them into everything the princess ate and drank.

Wise Joab didn't realize that all these drops help only when the person using them really and truly loves, whereas all that Joab had in mind was the kingdom.

Now when the princess turned down all the princes, he regarded this as a good omen for himself. And to make more certain of his plans, he kept spying and eavesdropping on the king and the princess.

And when, standing behind the silken curtain, he heard that they were planning to wander away in poor clothes, he didn't lose heart at all. In fact, it even raised his hopes falsely.

He thought that the princess, who had swallowed so many love drops, had suggested the match herself, and that they were going off in disguise to test whether he was worthy of being a king and to hear what the people thought of him.

He was afraid that people would say nasty things about him to the king and especially to the princess, that he sent out spies to follow them everywhere and write back daily in code where they were and what they were doing.

The first few letters he received from the spies didn't surprise him. The king and the princess were wandering and wandering, never stopping. But later on, when his spies informed him that they had crossed the border, the grand vizier was delighted. He hit upon a different and much easier plan for getting the kingdom!

He would have both the king and the princess killed! And he could do so abroad, with no fear whatsoever!

He sent for two cutthroats and said to them:

"I, the grand vizier, and now regent, know very well that you two are robbers and murderers and that I should have you strung up in the middle of the marketplace and then cut into pieces, and have the pieces sent to all parts of the kingdom. It is up to you to be saved from the gallows and make something of yourselves.

"If you do what I tell you, and keep it a secret, I shall make one of you prime minister and the other the head of the Sanhedrin."

The cutthroats fell to the feet of the grand vizier, and he made them swear, as they knelt, that they would do what he wanted!

The cutthroats swore: One, by all the wild and deserted ruins where demons and devils dwell, and by all the unburied remains of robbers and murderers:

"If ever I fail to keep my word, may all the demons of forests and ruins, and all the evil spirits of lost bones, wreak vengeance on me."

And the second cutthroat also swore the same oath, and added that he swore by his secret—by his father's mouth which he kept in a bladder full of vinegar.

The evil grand vizier said:

"You have sharp swords, and I'll give you naked spears. I'll also give you horses, the best in the royal stables, they fly like eagles and they soar over the wind.

"Ride out into the world. And when you meet two ragpickers, an old man as gray as a dove and a young girl whose face shines out of her dirty clothes like a sun from behind a leaden winter cloud—then stop them!

"Kill the old man on the spot! And as for the daughter, you will do the following: Ask her whether she's willing to keep it all a secret and return to become my wife. If she agrees, and if she swears by the soul of her dead mother, then let her live and bring her here.

"Otherwise: Kill her! And then bury them on the spot. And as a sign that you've done everything properly, bring me back their clothes. I'll be able to recognize them!"

The murderers agreed, and he gave them money for traveling expenses, armed them from head to foot, put them on horseback, and sent them out into the world.

The evil man was certain that his plan would work.

He would become king!

And the moment he became king, he would know what to do.

He would fortify the kingdom! And he would emulate Ahasuerus! He would give a royal banquet—a banquet for all Wonderland.

He would set up golden tables in a great garden. And they would groan under the weight of the choice foods, and the choicest wines would flow like water.

And all players, and all dancers, and all singers in the entire country would come to play and sing and dance.

It would be a festive day, a rejoicing for all Wonderland!

And they would eat and drink for seven days and seven nights, and they would celebrate for seven days and seven nights.

And the most beautiful girls in the country would come.

And he would go from table to table, looking and choosing.

And the most beautiful girl would be his wife, his queen.

FOURTH CHAPTER
Deborah has to escape—She says goodbye—The witch's cavern.

Deborah, the grand vizier's daughter, was very unhappy ever since the princess left. She was all alone.

Her father had never loved her. He hadn't rejoiced at her birth. He was poor at the time, and didn't look forward to another mouth to feed. When the baby was a few weeks old, he suddenly began hating it, he complained it wasn't *his* child but a changeling. Later, after coming to the king in the palace, he concealed his hatred and played the same false role toward his own daughter as toward everyone else.

No sooner had the king and the princess gone away, however, than he pulled the mask from his face.

The first thing he did was to drive all the sick and the poor from the palace and make Deborah give him the key to the king's treasury.

She was even unhappier when she saw what her father was doing to the country. He immediately discharged all the honest veteran generals, all the veteran officials of the towns and hamlets, and all the honest judges and policemen, from the lowest to the highest senators in the Sanhedrin. He replaced them all with evil and dishonest men, with flatterers and spongers, who were prepared to help him with all evil plans.

Deborah tried to reason with him, but she only made matters worse. He decided once and for all to get rid of his daughter. He would have had her killed but he was afraid of the inhabitants of the country, who were as fond of Deborah as of the princess. Instead, he decided to marry her off to someone living abroad and he looked for a bridegroom among the rich lords of other countries who came to Faithstone on business.

There was one such businessman whom he liked. He was a big, fat man with sharp, grim eyes. He, thought the grand vizier, won't let go of her so easily. He called for him in the marketplace where he was standing with his wares, brought him back to the palace, and presented him as a bridegroom to his daughter.

She wrung her hands, a wellspring of tears came gushing out of her eyes. Her legs gave way beneath her. She knelt down before her father and threw her arms around his legs. But he kicked her away.

"You're getting married tomorrow!" he snapped and walked out.

That same night, Deborah escaped from the palace.

The soldiers on guard felt sorry for her and didn't stop her, and a pale, merciful moon lit the way through the park to the remote paths.

As she fled, Deborah couldn't help it, she kept stopping at different flowers, saying goodbye and kissing them. And her tears remained on several rose-petals or lily-petals like drops of fresh dew.

"Who knows whether I'll ever see you again!" she called to the flowers, the trees, and the golden fish in the river, waking them with her light steps, and to the birds, who were swaying among the silent branches.

And a soft, barely audible rustle passed from branch to branch, from tree to tree, as though saying: "Quiet! Shhhh! The good, the golden girl is running away, running away from her fine palace, from her bad father, her nasty father . . . . Shhh! Don't wake them up, don't wake them up . . . ."

From the park, she slipped into the forest.

At the first tree in the forest, three strange beasts were waiting for her, as white as milk, with golden stripes, two of the animals each had a horn of tortoise shell and one had a horn of ivory.

Deborah stopped and asked them:

"Oh, you good animals with your white skins, golden stripes, and tortoise-shell or ivory horn! Please take pity on me, and show me the way to the cave where the good sorceress lives."

She told them she had never been in the woods at night before, everything looked different in the moonlight, she might easily go astray, and bad people could find her and bring her someplace where she shouldn't and mustn't be . . . .

The animals apparently understood every word, they nodded their heads, and lowered their horns several times.

This was a sign that they considered it right and that they would show her the way.

And the animal with the ivory horn stepped out of the row and stood in front of her; the two with the tortoise-shell horns—to her left and her right.

And they started to walk.

And they walked and they walked, downhill and uphill, through intertwining branches, until Deborah caught sight of a fine golden beam shining from the earth.

The animal with the ivory horn knocked upon it softly.

"Who's there?" someone asked from underground.

Deborah recognized the sorceress's voice and wondered how the deaf woman had heard the soft knocking of the little horn.

"I, I, I," the animal kept knocking—it couldn't speak. But that same instant, there was a noise in the branches of a nearby tree, a white dove appeared and called out in a human voice:

"Auntie, open up! Deborah's here! Deborah with the big, black eyes, and hair like flax . . . . Open up, Auntie, it's high time . . . ."

The cave opened, and Deborah stepped in and found the old woman sitting and plucking feathers, which she threw into a large pot.

"Good evening," murmured Deborah. And gaping at everything that was going on in the cave, she forgot to ask whether she could come in.

There was a tiny lamp in front of the old woman, lighting up the entire cave. In the middle of the space, there was a bed with fine linen, and she recognized it, her own bed, with her bedding, with her silken, gold-embroidered quilt.

"Good evening to you," replied the sorceress. "I knew you were coming, and I sent out my crows to steal your bed from the palace. It's not so nice sleeping on a strange bed."

Deborah remained silent and even more amazed.

And the old woman went on:

"You're tired, Deborah, get undressed, go to bed. Tomorrow, you'll know everything."

Deborah obeyed, and when she fell asleep, the old woman got up quietly and took a snow-white wing, like a swan's, and fanned it through the air in all directions, muttering softly:

> Good dreams, come,
> From all sides, come
> To the lovely girl,
> To the pious girl,
> To the darling girl,
> To Solomon's daughter.

And white doves came flying from all sides, with snow-white chrysanthemums and lilies in their beaks, and flew over Deborah's bed softly and quietly.

FIFTH CHAPTER
A morning in the cave—What's going on in the other half of the cave?—The story of a great soul—How it was born and fell asleep.

And it was evening and it was morning. And in the morning, when Deborah awoke, she noticed that the cave was divided by a curtain embroidered with all sorts of flowers and birds; she was unable to remove her eyes from them.

"What? Do you want to know," the old woman asked her with a smile, "what's going on in that half of the cave?"

"No, Auntie, if you don't tell me of your own accord, I won't ask."

"Since you're so good," replied the old woman, "I'll tell you. Meanwhile the milk that I've put on for your breakfast will heat up."

And the old woman told her the following story:

"Once God looked down at our poor world and saw that things weren't going so well, there were tiny little souls that couldn't devise anything and if they ever did devise something, then they couldn't carry it out. So God sent down a single soul, a proper one—a large, tall soul.

"And somewhere, a child was born with such a soul. It was a boy, and when he opened his big eyes upon the world, he became full of sorrow and pity.

"But as he grew up, he couldn't devise anything either because he had no time to think.

"There was so much unhappiness all around him, so much helplessness, so much sorrow.

"And he started helping, giving advice, doing good things.... If someone fell, he would help him up. If someone was drowning, he would reach out a branch. If someone couldn't carry a load, he would give him a hand. If someone needed some good advice, he would think it over and then give it to him.... And if none of this helped, he would take out his harp, and sing and play.

"Now the harp had a sweet tone, and his voice was even sweeter than the sound of the harp, and sweetest of all was the song he sang.

"He sang about later, happier times.... When all people would be helped, when all tears would be dried, all illnesses wiped out, all wrongs done away with, and all people, even the weakest, would be happy."

"Is that a true story?" asked Deborah.

"Oh my! How your eyes lighted up!" answered the old woman. "Is it a true story? I don't know. He sang and people believed him, and that alone made life easier for them.

"Little by little, he became famous throughout the land, and the more famous he became, the more poor, helpless, and unhappy people needed his help.... And yet he was just one man, all alone.

" 'God,' he once argued with heaven, 'why did you create me all alone? How can I help all people by myself?'

"And an oracular voice replied from heaven:

" 'I created an Adam, and the world descended from him. Look for your Eve.'

"And he abandoned everything and started looking.

"But he didn't find her. A true woman is hard to find. Authentic, genuine, not childish and foolish and greedy. And then after a time he argued with God again: 'I can't find her,' he said.

"And from heaven there came an answer:

" 'Since you can't find her, wait until she looks and finds you.'

"And he was put to sleep, here in the cave. And he has been sleeping for a long, long time. I was told to watch over him so that no harm would come to him while he slept."

"How long has he been sleeping, Auntie?"

"Over a century now, even longer. Would you like to see him, Deborah?"

Deborah trembled all over, unable to speak a word.

The old woman tugged on a string, the curtain drew apart, and in the second half of the room, a young man appeared, he was asleep, and as lovely as the dream of an innocent young girl.

Deborah sprang up and dashed from the cave into the woods. The old woman peered after her with a smile, and then she stuck her old head out of the cave and whistled. The three animals appeared at the edge of the cave the very instant she whistled.

"What is your wish, soul of the forest?" they asked.

And the old woman looked at Deborah who could still be glimpsed among the trees, running farther.

"What happened to her?"

"A dream," smiled the old woman benevolently, "was born in her girlish heart, and now it's carrying her as if on wings. Watch over her and bring her back to the cave this evening."

"Fine!"

And the animals disappeared.

SIXTH CHAPTER
The second night in the cave—Deborah wakes up uneasily—What she sees and hears.

The second night, Deborah slept uneasily. The dream was growing in her girlish heart, spreading its wings. But that wasn't the only thing that woke her from her sleep. What disturbed her even more was worrying about Princess Shulamite and her father King Solomon.

She awoke and, with her eyes still closed, she thought:

"Where are they? Where are they wandering now? Why did they leave the kingdom in bad hands—unhappy and poor ... without help?"

Once awake, she couldn't say anything nasty against her father.

In her heart she knew how bad her father was. It did no good to fret and reproach herself for not loving him! She couldn't love him—He was a bad person, very bad! She knew that if Solomon, the real king, didn't return, then her father would destroy Wonderland, and turn Faithstone into a Gehenna. Generals and judges would be thrown out of office, and honest men would be chained up and thrown into dark holes.

And what would become of Shulamite?

Deborah's heart was full of fear and trembling. She opened her eyes.

A few burning embers in the fireplace were shedding a bright, reddish glow over the entire cave. The walls were covered with green branches and flowers of all colors, and all these things appeared to be growing in the reddish light. The curtain fluttered softly, quietly, dividing the niche with its sleeper from the rest of the cave. And in the red glow, the large birds and tiny flies embroidered in the curtain seemed to be alive, trembling and moving their wings. They quivered and struggled as though trying to tear themselves loose from the curtain and soar off into space!

She could not tear herself away from the curtain!

Oh, how she wanted that curtain to move a lot more, open a bit, reveal a tiny crack so that she might see him again! If only one light ray could reach her from his radiant face!

But what good did it do! It was not for her that heaven had put him to sleep. If only Shulamite had been here!

All she wanted to do was see him, merely see him! See him!

She was frightened by her own thought as though it were sinful, and she looked around for the old woman.

The old woman wasn't asleep.

She was sitting on the three-legged stool in a corner of the cave. A marvelously white shimmer arose, like an airy crown, over her silvery hair. With her head bowed, she looked down at her lap. She looked so earnest, so deep!

Deborah saw that balls of different-colored threads were lying at the old woman's feet, and the balls were stirring as though of their own accord, the different-colored threads slowly rose, very slowly, up to the old woman's lap, weaving themselves into a frame, a flashing golden frame.

Was she awake, was she dreaming?

"Auntie, aren't you sleeping?" she asked, a bit frightened.

"No, daughter! I'm not sleeping. I never sleep! After all, I'm the soul of the forest, you know, the soul of the forest, yes indeed! And I'm a watchwoman! I simply can't sleep. The forest would fall asleep altogether. And you would find barkless trees tomorrow, withered flowers and leaves, and dead animals.... Everything would turn into refuse and carrion if I fell asleep! And he, the man behind the curtain there, would never awake again."

Deborah was scared.

"But then what do you do, Auntie?"

"I, daughter? I don't do anything, not for the time being! I merely look! I look and I see what's happening! When the time comes, I will do something, do what I have to, by all means.... My thread will also weave in!"

"In what, Auntie?"

"In the things that are happening."

"What is happening, Auntie?"

"Do you want to see, daughter?"

"May I?"

"A little. Come! Get behind me, quick! While the coals are still burning!"

And Deborah sprang down from the bed and got behind the old woman to look at what was weaving on her lap.

"I don't see anything, Auntie!" she exclaimed in disappointment.

"Look harder, wipe your eyes three times."

Deborah did so and screamed in joy:

"I can see, Auntie, I can see!"

"Shush! We mustn't wake the forest! What do you see, child?"

"I see a square, a quiet marketplace, it looks like a frame of small, hushed houses."

"A marketplace!"

"A quiet marketplace."

"Empty?"

"Wait, Auntie.... I can see ... two figures ... poor people, tattered, with ragged clothes...."

"Ragpickers?"

"They look like ... an old man and a young girl...."

"Look harder, maybe you'll recognize them!"

"Oh my God!" Deborah leaped up. "Shulamite! The king!"

"Shush! ... It's not time yet to wake up the man behind the curtain."

"What are they doing, Auntie?"

"They're wandering .... Soon they'll be crossing the border of Wonderland .... Just as the dove advised them to do."

"But they're standing ...."

"King Solomon is a bit worried."

"Why? Is it hard for him to wander in his old age?"

"No, child. He's noticed that someone is riding after them."

"Bad people, Auntie?"

"Cutthroats!"

"Do they want to hurt them?"

"They want to— But their threads are weaving out of the frame .... It doesn't matter!"

"And Shulamite, is she afraid too?"

"She doesn't know about it, child."

"She's standing and thinking."

"She's staring."

"At what, Auntie? She looks as if her entire soul were staring out of her eyes ...."

"Look to the left of the frame. What do you see, child?"

"I see a window .... The window of a small house, like a green-covered hut in the Feast of Huts ...."

"And in the window?"

"Someone's sitting, a young man .... He's embroidering ... embroidering on pressed velvet with golden threads .... He's embroidering an eagle .... He's working on the wings now .... Just look at the wings, those golden wings, growing under his nimble, white, alabaster white, hands .... Golden wings .... But the radiance of his deep, blue, pure eyes is even more golden .... A river is like that at times, blue, and clear like the sky, and deep, very deep .... Just look at his eyes glow! ..."

"With pride!"

"Pride over what?"

"With the pride, with the joy of God creating the world .... Whoever creates, is radiant like that .... And the light of the eyes weaves into the thing one creates .... And the radiance remains in the work forever, in the creation, and if anyone else looks at it, then the pride and the joy radiate into his soul .... Do you understand me, child?"

"I can *feel* it, Auntie. But why are his lips trembling?"

"He's singing, daughter. Whoever works and creates in his work, he sings! The song is magically transformed into the work!"

"When the Messiah comes, everyone will work like that."

"Do you like it, daughter?"

"Yes . . . very much . . . . Only, that other man . . . . I like him more."

"The one behind the curtain?"

"Yes."

"Goodness, how hot your breath is. It smells hot, it's very hot! That's how a rose trembles sometimes, a sweet rose . . . . Yes, child, what else do you see."

"Shulamite looking at him! Is that her destined bridegroom, Auntie?"

"Perhaps!"

But Deborah remembered something and exclaimed in fright:

"Make her go away, Auntie! Make her run away! She mustn't, she swore she wouldn't!"

"You talk too much!" the old woman exclaimed, laughing.

That same instant, the embers faded, the weaving disappeared, and the cave was aglow with the morning that rushed in through the opening at the top.

"If you want to see, you have to keep quiet," the old woman reproached her kindly.

Second Part

FIRST CHAPTER
*Wandering through Wonderland and toward the border of
Wonderland—Working here, and there—Feelings
about foreigners abroad—"Help yourself"
and "Begging is prohibited"—
The princess's certainty.*

At ease again, Deborah closed her eyes and fell asleep, or else, still awake, continued spinning the sweet dream in her quiet soul about the man in the second half of the cave. We'll take advantage of the time and see what's happening with the king and the princess.

The hardest thing for us Jews, the punishment that a Jewish penitent has to suffer for the worst sins—wandering, "the sorrows of exile"—was a very easy matter in Wonderland and brought a great deal of pleasure.

In a land where people are good, everything is good. You feel at home anywhere.

Whatever you look at gives you joy and peace; it welcomes you with a smile. From the tiniest blade of grass in the forest to the loftiest, sky-high pinetree, the strongest spreading oak—everything welcomes you cheerfully! Thousands of different colorful mushrooms nod to you with their fine caps. The flowers stick their heads out of the grass and call out to you: "Good morning!" Towering trees embrace you in their shadows for a sweet rest.

If you meet a lumberjack in the woods, he puts his axe aside the moment he sees you, walks along with you, and shows you which tree offers a refreshing sap, where a living wellspring gushes forth, which tree contains a beehive with honey. Anything your heart desires!

And the field where the peasant sings as he works is equally good to you. He greets you heartily and shows you his basket of milk and bread hidden from the sun. "Have a bite," he says. And overhead, singing flocks of birds are flying about. He doesn't drive them away, he doesn't begrudge them anything, God's blessing is for all, and they soar around him and sing to him as he works . . . . The birds promptly realize that you are a stranger, and they greet you and sing for you—a greeting from home: "We were just there, everyone's fine, thank goodness!"

And wherever you lay your head, on white moss of fine gold, on the bare earth, on a hard-looking stone, you sleep calm and sound. Balmy breezes play around your face, whispering the loveliest dreams into your ears, wishing you: "Sleep, you good man, sleep. No harm will come to you here."

And it's just as good in the city.

The houses are open, like the hearts of the inhabitants! You walk through the streets, and the people working in doors and windows accompany you with kind gazes, with friendly words: "Have a good trip!" or "Get there safe and sound!" And they'll share their last crumb with you, their last drop of water.

But even Wonderland comes to an end. Solomon XXVII and his daughter, the princess, both disguised as ragpickers, passed across the border.

Those were the words of the dove: Far, far away from the land; in a foreign country, no one would recognize them!

And they wandered farther and farther away from the border, and the journey became harder and harder, more and more arduous. Different towns, different fields and forests, everything changed. Bad and cunning people live in these towns, and they have locked themselves up in their homes as in prisons, barring and bolting their doors!

Every door is guarded, at every gate people glare at you suspiciously, eyes and mouths ask: Who are you, who do you have here?

They glare most harshly of all at garbage-pickers! Everyone steps away so as not to get dirty.

"Hurry, hurry! There's garbage behind the town, old women are picking the old rags! Go on, go on!" And they drive them from the city.

"Our garbage isn't for foreigners, it's our property. Our own people barely have enough!"

And the king and the princess wandered and wandered, farther and farther . . . .

And the woodsman glared at them nastily, and the peasant in the field retorted to their greetings with an ugly curse.

"Daddy," asked Shulamite, "why are they so nasty?"

"Because they work hard and joylessly. If your soul isn't in your work, you won't succeed. Thorns grow among the sheaves and all sorts of evil seeps into the mind! They are accursed. Their work is accursed, their fields and forests are accursed . . . . Their woods are full of predatory beasts. Their fields are full of thorns and their hearts full of curses; they are thorns themselves, burning brambles!

"No free birds can be seen in the air, they shoot them down for the most trivial uses, or merely for fun, out of pure nastiness, to vent their spleen, or show off. So the birds flee, they flutter past in mute, cloudy nights, and no human ear has heard them sing for a long, long time . . . .

"And you can't see any flowers. They are all torn out. Useful things are sown instead. And they've killed and devoured all the pets and cattle.

"A man without flowers, birds, and pets may be smart, but he won't be good. Each of them thinks of nothing but himself. And if a man can't get along on his own and starts falling, then he falls, and no one here will reach out and hold him up, no one will offer him a crumb of food to keep up his strength, or a drop of water to keep his lips from burning!

"And whoever falls, falls down and dies by himself, or else gets up to kill others in his place.

"And the highways are crawling with murderers and robbers, and with soldiers and policemen hunting them down.

"And the air is full of cursing and shooting instead of singing."

The king and the princess kept wandering here, disguised as rag-pickers. Their money ran out, and to make matters worse, they lost their way. When they asked about Wonderland, people laughed at them: "There's no 'Wonderland' in any geography book! Old women used to ramble about Wonderland, scholars of ancient history once came upon some old children's songs about an imaginary place called Wonderland. But today, all those things are forbidden. You're not allowed to tell such falsehoods to even the youngest child. All that counts is truth, pure, bare truth.

"They're crazy!" And people would shake their heads.

If they had been local people, the others would have locked them up in a madhouse. But they didn't want to lodge and feed foreigners, so they drove them away: "Get along with you, you crazy foreigners! C'mon, get moving!"

And their disguise became a reality.

The king and the princess became real ragpickers.

As long as it was summer, they didn't complain about their lot. "The dove knew what she was saying, everything will turn out for the best," thought King Solomon, and Shulamite comforted herself with her only thought: "My father will live, he'll live! Praised be God, no one wants to look at me!"

But at times she did sigh. Was she homesick or, as her father smiled at her kindly, was she unable to forget the embroiderer by the border? But her sighs were light.

In winter, however, things were different.

A hard winter, such as never comes to Wonderland, covered the earth. It came abruptly, attacking like a wild murderer, and its first breath brought down a rain of frozen birds.

And everything was rigid with cold.

And a heavier punishment fell upon Solomon XXVII than upon his great-great-great-grandfather.

In tattered clothing, he wandered about with his daughter Shula-

mite, starving, freezing. He might have called out: "I am Solomon."
But he knew that the people here not only didn't believe in Solomon, they didn't even believe in his kingdom—in Wonderland.

Begging was illegal. There were gilded signs on all the doors and gates: *Begging is prohibited.* Once, the old man held out his hand, and a kind-hearted lady didn't report him to the police, she mercifully handed him a pamphlet, a very intelligent pamphlet. Its title was: *Help yourself!*

And he helped himself as best he could. He bent over the garbage behind the city, grubbing around with his frozen hands. His old bones were cracking. A free world! And when you're a garbage-picker you really believe it!

And the princess stood across from him, her hands were weak, her delicate skin was cracking in the frost, the spade was pushing holes into her flesh.

She dug, and drops of blood ran from her wounded hand and froze to the spade.

The old king couldn't just watch indifferently.

He burst into tears.

"You have sinned, daughter!" he exclaimed bitterly. "And this is our punishment!"

"Sinned?" stammered Shulamite.

"Yes, daughter. You had pride in your heart, great pride! You wanted to be certain of your happiness, and hold it in your hand. But God doesn't want it that way! Happiness isn't a bird to keep in a cage! God wants human beings to hope and have faith! Each one should follow his star, his fortune, with half-closed eyes. That is what God wants!"

Shulamite remained silent, and Solomon went on:

"This is God's punishment. We will have to remain here. We will never see Faithstone or Wonderland again!"

Shulamite likewise thought that this was the end.

"Now," she thought, "I can tell him everything, everything, at least we can leave the world with no secrets between us, with open hearts! So that my father won't accuse me wrongly."

And she fell upon her father, embracing him, kissing him, holding him tight, and told him everything.

She hadn't been proud, she had feared for his life.

The cuckoo and the sorceress had said . . . he would only live to see her get married.

With cold, cracked lips, old Solomon kissed her.

"Don't be afraid," he exclaimed joyfully. "If that's so, then God will help us! He won't abandon us!"

That same moment, a dull sound came from the earth, and far off in the distance, two horsemen loomed into sight on wild horses, flying like eagles, and they held swords in their hands.

"There they are! There they are!" one called to the other. "And this will be their end!"

"Murderers!" Solomon yelled in terror, casting about in vain for a place to escape, to hide—but it was an open field, with no caves and no trees.

"Then let the earth swallow us up!" he shouted. "It's better than falling into their hands.

SECOND CHAPTER
A lucky moment—A hanged man's mouth—What the earth threw out.

If Solomon XXVII and his daughter, Princess Shulamite, had died at the hands of the murderers, God forbid!, then there would have been no story, or at best a bad story, and bad stories are told only by bad, embittered people.

Solomon called out his wish at the right moment: "Let the earth swallow us up! It's better than falling into their hands!"

It was a lucky moment. The earth split open under their feet, and he and his daughter fell in. A red, flaming glow poured out like red lightning, vanished, and the earth closed up again.

The two robbers halted, stunned.

Coming to their senses, they realized this was no easy matter.

"What can it be?" one murderer asked the other.

"I'll soon find out," the other one replied. "I always have my hanged father's mouth on me. He was hung for committing fourteen robberies in one week, and anything I ask it will be answered."

Having said these words, he took out the mouth and began asking it.

"Mouth! Mouth! You mouth of my hanged father, may he rest in peace! What's going on here?"

And the mouth answered with a muffled voice as though from underground: "It's a cave belonging to a rich dwarf."

"And what was the flame?"

"The reflection of the mountains of gold that he has gathered in his cave. He has whole treasuries of gold!"

The eyes of both murderers were ablaze with lust for gold.

"Should we break into the cave?" one asked the other.

"No!" he replied. "First of all, the earth is too frozen for us to split it open. Secondly, I'm scared of dwarfs, they're all wizards. And thirdly, anyone who wants to work will never be a thief."

"What else can we do?"

They decided to stay there until the earth split open again. A thing that happens once can happen once more.

And the two thieves made up their minds to keep watch until something appeared.

Meanwhile, the evening came on, and to keep from falling asleep, they resolved to keep talking all night long.

Naturally, thieves do not talk about religious commandments and good deeds.

First, they spoke about themselves, praising their murderous strength and their cunning robberies. Next, when they ran out of their own thieveries and robberies, they began talking about other criminals. But even this subject wasn't enough for a long winter's night. And finally, one of them yawned wide, and then asked:

"Do you know, brother, why dwarfs collect gold?"

"I know why," the second one replied. "I once asked my hanged father's mouth, and it told me the reason."

"What is it?"

"Wait, it's a long story."

They lit their small pipes. Now they were two red dots in the silent, white-flashing winter night.

And the cold heavy air cut through the robber's voice:

"Once, my dead father's mouth told me, there were two kinds of people in the world—two human races.

"One race had small bodies and big souls—"

"The students, the unworldly scholars and teachers!" remarked the other one, his voice full of shame.

"And the other race had small souls, but big strong bodies."

"They're the ones we're descended from!" said the other with pleasure.

"Don't interrupt, it's a long, long story!"

"I'm doing it on purpose, so I won't go to sleep!"

"You won't go to sleep. Listen!

"The two races never lived in peace with one another."

"That's obvious."

"The two races never intermarried. They never ate at the same table, they never drank together, they never even did business with one another."

"That was silly! You can do business even with your worst enemy."

"They always fought wars with one another, merciless and ruthless, killing and killing! And so much blood was shed that all the rivers and all the oceans turned blood-red. They sailed on blood, they drank blood from the wells. And the earth couldn't soak in so much blood, and the fleshless bones of wild beasts and wild birds drifted around in blood.

"They didn't even bury the corpses. Occasionally, a famous man, perhaps a king!

"And finally, when men started fearing a deluge of blood, both sides made up their minds—they would have an arbitration before a rabbinical court!

"Justice, and not the sword, would decide who was right.

"But who would judge them? No one came down from heaven, and here on earth only human beings could speak and judge, but all men were at loggerheads with one another.

"So they resolved to find an intermediary man, that is to say, a man with an in-between body and soul. He wouldn't be biased.

"And they had an armistice for a while, to look around for an in-between man. They found him and took him to a high mountain, had him sit in the shade of an old, sacred tree, and said to him: 'Be our judge!'

"They spanned a canopy of white silk over his head, and a pressed velvet carpet under his feet, as is proper for a great judge, and they gave him three days to hear the arguments and reach a decision!

"And both sides swore they would abide honestly by the decision.

"But this in-between man, who wasn't biased at first, became biased, he allowed himself to be bribed!"

"Who by?"

"Our forefathers, the ones with big bodies and small souls. It never even occurred to the people with the big souls!

"For a fat cow and two calves, the in-between man pronounced a fine judgment: Both races of man would have to divide the earth between them, fifty-fifty! Only, the people with large bodies and small minds were to live *above ground*, and the people with large souls and small bodies—*underground*."

"Aha! A fine judgment. And so that's who the dwarfs are!"

"That's right!"

"And why do they need gold under the earth?"

The two robbers had been sipping liquor, and the one who knew everything from his hanged father's mouth, continued his story:

"This is what happened:

"In time, the men with big bodies and small souls were no longer satisfied with the area above ground. They began digging into the earth, deeper and deeper. They looked for iron, copper, gold, and silver.

"And the dwarfs (according to my hanged father) realized what was happening. *They* were gathering treasures. The dwarfs thought to themselves: There'll be a war. That will settle it. We'll see who's stronger, the body with its *strength* or the soul with its *ideas*. And if it comes to another arbitration, they'll gild the judge!"

"It's unbelievable," replied the second robber. "It was too smart of the scholars with the great souls."

"Could be," replied the first robber. "My father, God bless him, never spoke a true word in all his life."

"But it's quite plain," exclaimed the second one. "Maybe they collect everything that glitters—gold, diamonds, all precious stones, because it's so dark in their caves! They long for the sun, the daylight, the things they lost through the in-between man who was bribed, and so they gather radiant metals . . . . God knows!"

That very same instant, the earth split open again, spewing out the poor clothing that Solomon and the princess had been wearing; then it closed up again.

"Look!" the robbers shouted joyfully. And at the break of day, they saddled their horses to ride back to Faithstone. They were going to tell the grand vizier that they had carried out his orders and killed both the king and the princess and were bringing back their clothes as a sign!

And they wouldn't get lost. At every parting of the roads, they would halt and ask the hanged man's mouth.

THIRD CHAPTER
In the cave—The white dove—The black eagle—
Royal clothes again—Presenting the dwarf—
The dwarf sets the table and tells
who he is.

When the earth closed up over King Solomon and his daughter the princess, they both remained stunned and dazzled, no less than the robbers up above.

In the reddish golden light that was blazing from all the walls of the cave and all its niches, white, flashing rays were twisting and flaming—from all the precious stones among the gold that was lying around the walls.

Solomon and Shulamite were dazed, they didn't even notice their old friend—the white dove, who had just arrived and was flying overhead with a cheerful cooing.

She began descending, hovered before their eyes, and said in a human voice:

"Don't be frightened. You've followed my advice, and everything will turn out for the best.

"Meanwhile," she went on, seeing that Solomon and Shulamite were so surprised they couldn't answer, "meanwhile, you're safe here in the dwarf's cave. Soon, you'll be redeemed and you'll be happy."

Solomon shook his head sadly, and the princess exclaimed with a sigh:

"No, my good, white dove! There's no happiness possible for me!"

"Have hope and faith!" replied the dove. "Your happiness is spinning and weaving in a small window near the border of Wonderland."

"No, no!" screamed Shulamite.

"Have hope and faith!" continued the dove. "Your happiness shall not hurt a single hair on the gray head of Solomon XXVII!"

"Is it possible? The cuckoo . . . the sorceress . . . they all said . . . ." Shulamite stammered.

"I am the cuckoo, I am the dove, I am the sorceress, and I am the one to tell you."

And as she spoke, the dove turned into a cuckoo and then back again into a dove, and then into the sorceress, whom we know from the forest behind Faithstone, and then the sorceress turned back again into a white dove.

"God's miracles!" exclaimed Shulamite, overjoyed. "Is it magic, or the hand of God?"

"Magic is also godly!" the dove answered with a smile. "But we don't have time to talk about it now, the dwarf will be here soon, and you'll have to change your clothes before then."

Solomon and Shulamite were surprised. Where would they get new clothes? They looked around, but couldn't see a sign of clothing anywhere. At that moment, a black eagle with huge, wide wings came flying into the cave and threw an enormous bundle down in front of them. As it fell, it opened up by itself, and Solomon and Shulamite were even more amazed: they recognized their clothes, their royal garments, which they had left in the palace at Faithstone when they disguised themselves as ragpickers!

"Hurry up!" warned the dove. "I can already hear the dwarf's footsteps. Let him find you in your own clothes.... I'll fly off to get some food for you."

The white dove flew out of the cave, and the dwarf appeared at the entrance to a niche.

He was tiny, awfully tiny, but his long, silver beard was huge. He had to hold the ends of it so as not to trip over them.

And huge were his two deep, blue eyes which he riveted upon Solomon and Shulamite.

"Welcome!" the dwarf greeted them with a sweet voice, "Welcome! Solomon XXVII, king of Wonderland, in whom the Messiah is sleeping and will soon awaken and redeem the world.... Welcome, Shulamite! I can see a golden star lighting up over your head—your good fortune is beginning to glow!"

And he clapped his little hands, careful not to drop the ends of his beard, and three golden chairs came down from the air.

He invited them to sit down, and all three did so.

He clapped his hands again, and four lions appeared; they loped along slowly, carrying an onyx tabletop decorated with mother-of-pearl and set with crystal dishes. The lions halted in the middle of the cave between the three golden chairs.

"Go to sleep!" the dwarf commanded the lions. And they settled

on their back legs, drew in their tongues, closed their eyes, and remained petrified, like lions of copper or bronze.

The dwarf turned to Solomon and Shulamite.

"The table," he said, "is set, we only have to bring the food from
aloft, from above. We don't have any ritual slaughterers down here.
And before the food arrives, let me introduce myself. If you want
to be saved, and save others along with you, you have to have full
trust in me, you have to have *faith* in me!"

"I have faith in you!" the words came rushing out of Shulamite's
heart.

"The fortunate star is twinkling above you, its rays are in your
heart already, but you have to get to know me more closely. There
are a lot of things we have to do together!"

"Tell us," said Solomon, "I don't even know what to call you."

"As you can see," the dwarf began to talk, "I live in a cave, like
all dwarfs, I gather gold, silver, and precious stones, like the others.
I certainly look like a dwarf, and yet I was not born of one. I was
once a simple human being, living above the ground, I had a wife
and children. How many? I can't even remember . . . ."

"Was it that long ago?" asked Solomon in surprise.

"About six centuries ago!" replied the dwarf.

"It was in Baghdad," he continued, "I was a small person, a
shames in a synagogue, a poor beadle in a poor synagogue, in a poor
back street.

"And in the same city of Baghdad there lived a rich and powerful young man, a relative of the royal family and a descendant of
priests. A divorced woman caught his fancy, and he wanted the
chief rabbi to perform the wedding ceremony, even though Jewish
law forbids a descendant of priests to marry a divorcee. When the
rabbi refused, he informed against him falsely, and the authorities
drove the rabbi out of the city, and out of the country. The rich
man issued a proclamation that if any scholar would grant him a
dispensation and perform the ceremony, he, the rich man, would
use his power and make that scholar chief rabbi of Baghdad! The
burghers remained silent, they were all afraid of the rich man.

"There wasn't a single rabbi in all the land who was ready to
take such a sin upon himself. No judge had the courage to do it. So
the rich man turned to learned men, to scholars—not one was willing. He went down to the beadles of synagogues and houses of

study, but not a single beadle, no matter what his job and income, was prepared to sell his soul—until he came to me!

"And with me, he was in luck.

"I was very poor, and my wife and children were sick.

"And my sick wife talked me into it, she led me astray, and I worked out a false dispensation. We talked about the rich man's mother, saying that after all there was no proof that he was actually descended from priests.... I performed the ceremony, and a rabbinical certificate was already lying in the rich man's pocket for me. A rabbinical certificate signed by all the burghers who were dependent on the rich man.

"The wedding canopy was embroidered with gold, and all around us hundreds of twisted wax candles were burning and torches were blazing .... And the rich clothes of the wealthy were glittering with gold and precious stones. It was dazzling!

"On earth it was very bright, very, very bright. But up above, the sky was very dark, a dark heaven, moonless, starless, and suddenly, from the dark heavens, came God's burning wrath! A storm began, a sudden wild torrent came pouring down, and one peal of thunder chased the next, burning flashes of lightning flew by like serpents—The heavens and the earth were shuddering!

"And suddenly, the wedding canopy was torn from the hands of the attendants and rose like an umbrella on the wind. The guests ran away, screaming dreadfully, driven by the thunder and lightning, lashed by the torrent!

"I alone was struck by lightning.

"And in the other world, a judgment was pronounced:

"Because I had wanted to be great, so great—I was to become smaller than small, my spirit was to pass into the body of a dwarf, and I was to live like the dwarfs, under the earth ....

"And because I had wanted to become rich and have gold and silver, I was to gather gold for centuries, and silver, and precious stones, not for myself, but for men or women worthy of it."

His eyes alighted on Shulamite.

But she didn't notice.

"How awful!" she exclaimed, her voice full of compassion.

"But God's grace is enormous!" replied the dwarf. "I will be saved along with you. And this is how—"

He broke off.

A soft rustle could be heard.

"The dove's coming," said the dwarf. "We'll talk about the rest after we've eaten."

FOURTH CHAPTER
The meager breakfast—Who is the dove?—
The way kings hear groans—
The day is blasting—
Off to Faithstone!

It really was the dove, and she was bringing a meager breakfast: A pot of rice.

"Have you brought this meager breakfast from the palace?" asked the dwarf.

"It's enough for me," Solomon broke in. "I haven't had meat for a long time."

"And Shulamite," said the dove, "will certainly like this breakfast when she hears where it comes from."

This was probably the first time that anyone sitting on golden chairs before crystal dishes had eaten such a poor and scant repast.

And the dove related where she had gotten the breakfast:

"I wasn't in the palace!" she said. "Ever since Joab has been in charge, things aren't strictly kosher! I wasn't even in Faithstone. Things aren't quite right there either. Bad morals are spreading from above! I got the rice at the border of Wonderland.

"There's a little town by the border, a quiet little place, and there, in a small window, an artist is sitting, an embroiderer!"

"I noticed him!" remarked Solomon, and Shulamite blushed silently.

"He works so beautifully, the young man! And the picture he's finishing is so lovely! And with what marvelous eyes he looks at the picture he's finishing on the velvet! You know him Shulamite! You must have looked deeply into his heart, for he's embroidering your portrait from memory!"

Shulamite lowered her eyes.

"But he's pale, the young man is! His dark, burning eyes have a moist film over them. He must be sick."

"Sick?" Shulamite exclaimed in fright.

"He looks sick! An old woman was standing at his side, stroking his hair, asking him to eat—from this pot of rice, which she put in front of him. And he asked her: 'What for?' She told him that if people don't eat they can't live, and he replied he had nothing to live for. . . . The woman he could have lived for appeared to him once and then vanished, like a dream . . . . He looked for her, he said, on hills and in valleys, in villages and towns, but he hasn't found her."

The dove fell silent and was delighted to see Shulamite's face changing color, her young bosom heaving. The dove finished abruptly:

"And while he was weeping out his heart to the old woman, I flew over and bought the pot of rice from him."

"You bought it?" Shulamite sprang up with flashing eyes.

"Of course!" the dove replied laughing. "And I paid quite a bit for it. I told him where he can find the woman he's looking for."

"He's coming here?" asked Shulamite.

"Oh no! I told him the following: In a few days he's going to hear that Joab, false, evil Joab, who stole the kingdom, wants to get married. And Joab is going to give a banquet, like Ahasuerus in his time. They're going to slaughter countless fowl and kill countless birds in the forest, they're going to unyoke bulls and bring them to the slaughterhouse, they're going to take the last remaining lamb from every pauper and prepare it for the feast. And wine, and all sorts of liquors, will flow like water.

"And players, singers, and dancers will come together from the East and from the West, conjurors and jesters.

"And the most beautiful girls in Wonderland will be invited, and the one he desires (so he thinks) will become his wife, the queen of Wonderland!

"And when he hears this (I said to the young man), he should join a group of singers or players—he can sing and play, you can see it in his eyes, you can tell by every gesture of his—and he should come with them to the wedding.

"Come, Shulamite," the dove concluded. "I'll whisper the rest into your ear."

Shulamite and the dove went out into a side cave.

"May I," said Solomon to the dwarf, "ask who the dove is?"

"I'd be glad to tell you. She was once human, a beautiful girl, and then a young wife. But love is blind, and she couldn't see her young husband's fault—it's a hard thing to recognize. Just as it's hard for the king to tell who is truly loyal to him and who is merely licking his boots.

"And by the time they had a child, a little girl, he had already wasted everything they had, they didn't even have hot water for the mother giving birth, not a single piece of linen to cover the baby. But then fortune smiled on them. The palace was looking for a wet nurse for the princess, and they found the young mother to be the loveliest and the best . . . .

"With a sorrowing heart she left her own child without a cradle, and went into the palace to nurse the princess for the country.

"She sent her salary and all the presents she got to her husband.

"And yet when she came back after a few weeks to see her child, she found it sickly and starving.

"Now a bad thought came to her. She decided to exchange the babies! Not for long—she would exchange them again afterward. Once the sick child was well again.

"But then she couldn't change them back.

"In the course of time, both children were thriving. Her own child, in the royal cradle, grew golden flashing hair; the true princess got hair as fair as flax!

"When did this happen, and where?" asked Solomon in dismay.

"In Wonderland," replied the dwarf, "it happened in Faithstone, and Shulamite and Deborah are the changelings."

Solomon lowered his gray head under a burden of thoughts.

"Was she afraid to tell the truth?" he asked, "or didn't she know that I forgive anything for the truth?"

"She couldn't. Joab had become important in the meantime. For the sake of his wife they had let him into the palace, he was given rich presents, and he thanked the king! That was all he needed to do, he beguiled him with flattery, stole into his heart, and became more and more important every day.

"When his wife completed her service, he locked her up in a cellar. And there she died. She screamed and called for help, but no one could hear her voice behind the thick walls!"

"I deserved this exile!" exclaimed Solomon. "I have sinned gravely! At times, strolling about my palace, at night I thought I heard someone groaning, but I proudly said to myself: No one could be groaning in my palace, it must be the wind rushing out of the cellars."

"That's it! A king's ears are keen for any flattery, but dense to the groans of poor people. It's always the wind."

"But now," said the dwarf, "your exile is ending, you will be redeemed. But this must remain a secret. Shulamite will remain princess."

"What about my daughter Deborah?"

"She'll be happy. All the treasures of the cave will be hers.

"She will be richer than any king and any emperor. She'll know what use to make of the treasures."

That same moment they heard a blast, as from a trumpet.

The dwarf stood up:

"It's beginning," he said. "Our redemption is beginning. My aunt is blowing the trumpet in the forest of Faithstone. It's the sign for daybreak, our pure, bright day!"

That instant, Shulamite and the dove returned.

And the dove merrily said to the dwarf:

"Shulamite believes. I swore to her once again in my name and in his name that she will be happy, and that not a single hair will be harmed on the head of Solomon XXVII. And she will trust me with her appearance.

"Thank the Lord!" exclaimed the dwarf. "The eagle is waiting in front of the cave!"

At that moment, Shulamite and the dove exchanged appearances! The dove, in the guise of Shulamite, left the cave, and Shulamite, in the guise of the dove, flew up and perched on Solomon's shoulder.

The dwarf clapped his hands, the cave opened, and Solomon saw an enormously strong eagle carry the dove, in the guise of Shulamite, into the air.

"She's flying off to Faithstone," said the dwarf. "We'll be right behind her, our eagles are waiting too."

And the cave closed up again.

FIFTH CHAPTER
*The ray—The sorceress's blessing
—Deborah's dream.*

A pale, late-winter morning crept in through a crack in the cave within the forest of Faithstone. Caressing the face of the sorceress, it woke her up.

The old woman simply loved the ray that the morning had sent into the cave—it was as if it were bringing her good news from heaven.

She shook her old head merrily, a billow of silvery hair parted on either side of her, and a smiling face with shining eyes appeared.

Her lips quivered, she was saying the morning prayer of thanks. Next, she washed her hands, lifted her eyes, and said in a soft, trembling voice:

"I thank thee and praise thee, Creator of the world, for this new morning, for the golden ray, for the good news it has brought me, for the redemption beginning for myself and my people.

"I was so tired, oh Lord, I was already yearning for my rest. A crow doesn't want to live so long!"

Then she cast a hard glance at the curtains behind which the enchanted young man was sleeping.

"Praised be the Lord, may His Name be exalted! The boy's sleep is light now, his breathing is stronger, the curtains are stirring! It's time to waken him!"

She got to her feet and walked over to the second half of the cave, to Deborah's bed. She put her hand on Deborah's forehead and awoke her with a kiss.

"A very hearty good morning to you, my child."

Deborah awoke, half-frightened, and looked about in surprise.

"Where are you coming from, daughter? Where did the angel of dreams take you?"

Deborah hugged the old woman and said:

"A terrible and wonderful dream!"

"Can you tell it to me?"

"Certainly, Auntie, I don't have any secrets from you!"

The old woman sat down on the edge of Deborah's bed, and the girl told her the following:

"I was sitting somewhere in a foreign country, in a completely unfamiliar city, in a remote and narrow little street, between two rows of dark, closed, weather-beaten houses.... I was sitting on a rock, all by myself, trembling with fear.

"And overhead, a black sky was coming down upon me, brooding and angry—as if covered with clouds, and it lay heavy and wrathful over the lifeless street. And I was sitting and thinking: Who am I? What am I doing here? Who has abandoned me here?

"And I felt as if I had to go somewhere and do something, so that the cloud would rip apart, so that a serene summer sky would burst forth, so that the dead street would come to life again, so that the tiny houses would start growing and growing toward the sky like the loftiest palaces and holy places, and a singing, a shouting of happiness, should arise from the palaces and holy places—a glad tiding should fly from home to home, house to house . . . .

"And I only had to walk several steps and do some trifling thing. But I couldn't remember where to walk or what to do!

"And my heart ached terribly! I remembered that something had to be done before the poor, accursed street could awake. I felt that otherwise it would awake with a sinful anger, awake like a predatory beast, roaring a curse on foaming lips. And it would be too late. The sky would turn even darker, and God would nail the gates shut and never let out another morning star, another sun . . . . There would only be endless night.

"And everything turned to me, and I forgot everything!

"And suddenly I saw a floating white spot under the black sky.

"It drifted toward me from the east, coming lower and lower.

"And it was a white dove.

"She perched on my lap, and I saw that she had a letter on her neck, and that she offered me her snow-white neck so that I might remove the letter.

"And I untied the red string from the white throat and opened the letter, but I couldn't read, it was too dark!

"Yet at that moment, a star blazed overhead in the sky and shone upon the letter."

Deborah paused as if to catch her breath.

"And what did the letter say?" asked the old woman.

"It said . . . it said that I . . . I, I . . ." Deborah began stammering.

"Let *me* tell you what it said!"

"You? Do you know, Auntie?"

"I know everything! The letter said that you are not the daughter of wicked Joab, that you are the princess! That you had been exchanged with Shulamite!"

"Yes!"

"It also said that you must hurry back to the palace of Faithstone, to a great feast—Joab is giving a huge banquet—and Solomon and Shulamite will also be there, and Solomon will be redeemed from his exile and be crowned king again. At that point (says the letter), you should take Solomon by the hand and lead him to the portrait of the dear departed queen and show him whom you resemble!"

"That's what the letter said!"

"And you shall be princess."

"Yes, yes . . ."

"And what did you say?"

"I? I tore the letter into little pieces and threw them into the wind. They flew apart like tiny white wings . . . ."

"Why did you do that?"

"Because I knew that the path I have to take does not lead to Faithstone, and that what I have to do is not put a crown on my head. I have other things to do and other places to go to. Though in the dream I couldn't remember what or where . . . ."

"And now?"

Deborah's face flamed like a rose.

"May I?" she asked with trembling lips.

"Wait, a little later. Just tell me the end of the dream first. What happened then?"

"Then? The dove flew away, and the star came down and settled like a crown on my head."

"That is your fortune, Deborah," the old lady joyfully kissed her. "Stand up and come into the forest with me."

SIXTH CHAPTER
The ram's horn blows—Ahasueras's feast—
Quick! Quick!—Wake them up.

There was a breath of spring in the air, yet all the forest of Faithstone was blanketed in snow. The trees looked like topsy-turvy tassels with white flowers, and on the snowy carpet covering the forest floor, billions of snowy diamonds were glittering toward the rising sun.

The sorceress and Deborah emerged from the cave, and the old woman had a shofar, a ram's horn, hanging on a long golden chain from her neck. She halted and put the shofar to her lips: "*Tekiah!*"

The blare of the shofar was still trembling in the air, and Deborah could feel the ground quaking with thousands of treading feet.

The shofar had aroused the sleeping deer, who were gathering from all parts of the forest in a single file to the right of the sorceress.

Was this a dream? Deborah heard the sorceress greeting them with a cheerful "Good morning," and the deer, who were trembling with cold, answered with an equally cheerful: "Good morning to you!"

And again the sorceress put the shofar to her lips:

"*Teruah!*"

It echoed through the air again, and with trembling hides, wakened stags came running from all parts of the forest and gathered in single file facing the deer, to the left of the sorceress.

"Good morning, stags!"

"Good morning to you, Auntie!"

And the old woman put the shofar to her lips yet a third time. And she blew it yet a third time, and the white crowns on the trees began to quiver, heaps of snow burst open all over the forest, and little animals came springing out, running, racing through the forest —squirrels half-asleep, rabbits, hares and bunnies, tiny yellow foxes, and all kinds of little creatures, with silver whiskers, and silvery and ivory horns, came running and formed a line across from the sorceress.

"Good morning, animals!"

"Good morning to you, Auntie!"

And then for the fourth and last time, the old woman blew the shofar, it blared even louder in the air, and under the sky, floating white and black and colored spots began appearing, and there was a loud rustling, a humming, a fluttering of wings, and a whole cloud of birds and fowl were floating through the air and wheeling around the old sorceress's head.

"Good morning!" And "Good morning to you!" And the old woman said to them:

"First of all, please forgive me for waking you up and calling you together so early this year! Next year, when God gives you life again, you'll be able to rest longer to make up for this time. But now you have to do something for me!"

"We'd love to! We'd love to!" they shouted from all sides. "Whatever your heart desires!"

"All of you," said the sorceress, "all of you who jump, hop, dance, run, and fly! All of you are to go this very instant to Uncle Dwarf's cave, over your usual roads, in your seven-league boots. Tell him that I said: 'Good morning!' And take his treasures and bring them to the palace of Faithstone! Each stag should carry a

hundred pounds of gold, each doe fifty, and each little animal—
twenty-five! And the white birds should wear black strings of
pearls, and the black birds white strings of pearls, and the colored
birds—all sorts of corals and precious stones!"

The old woman paused for a moment and then turned to Deborah:

"What would you do, child, if they turned over the entire wealth
to you?"

Deborah thought for a while and then answered:

"I would abandon it, so that gold would lose its value, and all
envy, hatred and rivalry would stop."

"Fine, fine," smiled the old woman. "That sounds like a good
possibility."

And turning back to the birds and the animals, she went on:

"Take all those things, and fly, run, and dash to the palace of
Faithstone. Joab is giving—"

"False Joab!" broke in the animals and birds.

"Mind your business!" the old woman snapped. "Joab is giving a
feast!

"And a feast," the old woman continued with a peculiar smile,
"like Ahasuerus in his day! He wants to choose a queen! He wants
the most beautiful girl in the land!"

"The pig!"

"Shush!" The old woman stamped her foot. "This is his daughter!"

"That's not his daughter!" The noise swelled up. "We know, we
know!"

"It's a wise child that knows its own father!" laughed the old
woman. "But silence is golden!"

Her face became earnest again and she said:

"And the feast will be absolutely royal. It will last for seven days
and seven nights! A thousand colored lanterns will burn in the
palace and in the garden. Countless tables will be groaning under
the weight of food and wine, hundreds of orchestras, hundreds of
choruses of singers and musicians will be scattered throughout the
rooms and garden paths. Songs will waft over from golden, ivory,
and mother-of-pearl skiffs gliding over the blue surface of the
water, every bouquet of flowers will emit singing and playing . . . .

"An embarrassed yellow moon will float in the sky, and not a star
will be visible. The stars will be hiding out of envy.

"There'll be more beautiful ones below! All the stars of Wonder-land—the loveliest women in Wonderland will pass before the throne. And Joab will be sitting on the throne, Joab with his old, wizened face, with glassy eyes, with a gaping mouth, like a fish. And he'll gawk and gawk and try to choose a queen."

"Ugh!" all the animals yelled and whistled.

"Shush!" called the old woman severely. "Bring the treasures to the palace! I'll take care of the rest!

"And now," she continued, "get moving! Walk, fly, dash! Joab's hunters are coming! They're looking for wild game! Let no arrow strike you, no bullet hit you! Hurry! Hurry!"

The birds and the animals vanished, and the old woman hugged Deborah, kissed her, and said:

"Now, in God's name, go and wake you know who!"

SEVENTH CHAPTER
What the old crow knew and told.

During these last few days, the forest of Faithstone was uneasy.

No sooner had the wakened birds and animals flown and dashed away than whole masses of hunters appeared in the forest. They began shooting and chasing. They shot and chased single creatures and whole flocks, and they killed the last few lazy animals, sleepy-heads, who hadn't heard the sorceress calling and blasting, or else they had heard her but merely turned over and gone back to sleep. The huntsmen woke them and killed them as game for Joab's feast.

Now the guests came walking, riding, and rolling from all corners of the country, in all sorts of conveyances, drawn by all sorts of animals.

Players and singers and conjurors—on foot, or else a whole bunch rumbling along in one farm wagon—hitchhikers! Heavy carriages were trundling along, carrying the loveliest village maidens—merry eyes glittered by, particolored ribbons wafted past, cheerful ditties sounded through. Coaches, carriages, cabriolets showed up. With glittering windows, with gold-and-silver harnesses, and expensive horses . . . .

No animals snorted, no birds warbled, yet the woods were filled with noise and song, and the earth underfoot was shaking from the many people walking, galloping, trundling.

And when all the noise reached Faithstone, the forest remained silent, dreadfully silent.

The snow was trodden and slushy, the earth full of wheel ruts and footprints.

Only a few crows were left on a white tree, and the oldest was telling the younger ones what had happened in Faithstone.

She was in the middle of her tale:

"An enormously long line of beauties filed past Joab.

"They walked slowly, marching step by step, to a soft, sweet, magical music. All the bands were playing at the windows of the palace, all the choruses were singing, and the parlor was aglitter with diamonds and adamantine eyes.

"Clothing of all colors was dazzling and blinding.

"And old Joab sat there, hunched over, with a pale face and bulging eyes, gaping and gaping . . . .

"Suddenly, not far from the throne, he saw a handsome young man with a white dove on his shoulder. What was he doing? He looked to the left and saw his own daughter, Deborah, with a brightly shining star, like a crown, on her head, and standing next to her was a young man who looked at everyone with eyes like two stars. And in front—he saw Shulamite coming in . . . .

"Only it wasn't really Shulamite, it was just her shape.

"Shulamite, in the guise of a white dove, was perching to the right, on the shoulder of the famous embroiderer; and, in the guise of Shulamite, the spirit of Joab's wife, whom he had tortured to death in the cellar, was coming over.

"And in the distance, Solomon appeared, dressed once again in his royal garments.

"Joab was so frightened he fell from his chair and crawled over to Shulamite on all fours, that is to say, to his departed wife, who had disguised herself as Shulamite.

"He crawled over, fell down, and put his white lips to the hem of her dress, croaking:

" 'I did all this because I loved you. Please forgive me, Shulamite, be my wife!' "

"The old fool!" called out the younger crows.

The old crow kept right on talking:

"That moment the miraculous thing happened.

"Shulamite and the white dove exchanged their shapes.

"The true Shulamite stood next to the famous embroiderer, and the white dove changed her appearance again and for the last time, and Joab, insane with lust and terror, saw his dead wife before him. She was standing there in her shroud, and she put her dead white hand on his head . . . .

"That same moment, three doors opened, in front, and to the left and right.

"Four white bears came in from the right, four white bears carrying four golden poles of a red velvet wedding canopy, embroidered with pearls and diamonds, and the four bears stopped next to the famous embroiderer and Shulamite and took them under the canopy.

"And four white bears came in from the left and took the second couple under such a canopy: Deborah, Joab's daughter, with the bright star on her head, and the young man with the radiant starry eyes . . . .

"And in the front, four black, terribly black, crows flew in, with a black, black wedding canopy and halted in the air above Joab and his wife . . . .

"And our aunt also appeared.

"Our old aunt with white hair, burning eyes, and the shofar on the long golden chain.

"And Uncle Dwarf appeared in black velvet clothes and in a fur cap—a black fur cap with long, long silver rays—he was going to perform the ceremonies under the red canopies.

"And the old woman blew her shofar. Broken sounds came out. And the four demons in the guise of crows flew up with the black canopy and soared off with Joab and his wife, with whom he had once again stood under the wedding canopy.

"And as they flew, the crown dropped from Joab's head and rolled over to Solomon XXVII's feet.

"And the ceremony began at the red canopies, and soon other animals and birds appeared and laid the dwarf's treasures at Deborah's feet.

" 'Here is your dowry!' they said."

"Instead of the kingdom," said the young crows and asked: "What happened next?"

But the old crow called to them: "Listen, listen!"

A soft noise passed through the woods, quiet steps were heard.

A troop of tiny, very tiny, people, dwarfs in black velvet clothing, golden belts with glittering diamond ends, small, silvery fur-

edged hats, the kind worn by Jews on high holidays, and eyes that
outshone everything else, appeared in the forest and marched
through, calm and quiet.

The crows peered after them until they vanished.

"What was that?" the young crows asked the old crow.

The old crow replied: "I know and I'll tell you.

"That is a delegation that the dwarfs have sent to Solomon
XXVII. These people of small bodies and large souls want to make
peace with the people of large bodies and small souls."

"You mean they've never tried before?"

"Goodness! They know that until now the people in command
over those with large bodies and small souls were the men who
loved war. Each victory was a new diamond in their crowns.

"But the little people are certain that Solomon XXVII will not
wage any more wars. He has suffered through exile and he has lived
with a dwarf under the earth. He'll listen to them and understand
what they have to say."

"Why didn't they try with Solomon the First? He never fought
any wars and he was wise."

"They did visit him three times, but they never found him in. He
never had time for them.

"The first time he was bringing back Pharaoh's daughter as his
thousandth wife, and for her sake, and for her pleasure, he left the
kingdom for a whole year.

"The second time—someone was bringing him a stable of horses
from Egypt, so he had even less time, and the people of Jerusalem
made fun of the little visitors!

"The third time, it was even worse. The Queen of Sheba was visiting Solomon.

"It seemed to be a matter of heavenly intervention! They probably didn't want peace there, and the dwarfs began to doubt
whether Solomon was really all that wise! It didn't matter what the
world said!"

The old crow fell silent and wistfully pecked at her tail.

"Will they succeed this time?" asked the young crows.

"Who knows? The present Solomon is honest and decent. The
famous artist is his son-in-law. Deborah's husband with the star-
bright eyes is to become grand vizier . . . ."

The crow began musing again and pecking at her tail.

The Second Day

The Penitent

1.

Once upon a time, in a village, there lived a wealthy farmer and his wife. They had a full measure of everything, both grain and live-stock. All that they lacked was children. And this made them very unhappy. But then God took pity, and when they were old, a son was born to them. The wealthy farmer and his wife were over-joyed, and they spoiled the child. They gave him the best things to eat and drink and the softest bed to lie in. When the boy was growing up, they wouldn't let him do any work. Their neighbors asked the wealthy farmer why he wouldn't accustom his son to working, and he answered:

"Let poor people force their children to labor. I don't have to. My wealth and property will be enough for my son for all his life. He can lie on the oven and be idle."

The neighbors shook their heads, but they didn't argue with him. After all, who wants to provoke a neighbor—especially if he's rich?

The wealthy farmer's son grew, not by the day, but by the hour. He became big and tall, healthy and husky, and no one dared to op-pose him in anything. He had a will of his own, never heeded his father and mother, and always talked back to old people.

One day he left the village for a walk and wandered deep into the forest. All at once, in a clearing, he came upon a gang of young men sitting around a cauldron. They were eating, drinking, and singing merry songs. So he walked over and said:

"God be with you, friends!"

The men looked up at him in surprise, and one of them exclaimed:

"God isn't with us, and we're not very friendly.... And just who are you?"

The farmer's son replied:

"I'm from the nearby village, my father is a wealthy farmer .... And who are you?"

Another in the gang answered:

"We're merry people. We stroll along the highways and look for fine visitors. If we run into a fat little landowner or a rich little merchant, we dispatch his soul to God. And in exchange for our troubles, we take everything we find in his wagon .... Do you get what I mean?"

"It's not hard to get! You're robbers," answered the farmer's son. "I've been looking to find people like you for some time now. I wanted to meet you."

The robbers looked at him astonished. They were no weaklings, but he looked stronger than any of them. They thought to themselves: A fellow like him is just right for our gang.

One of them said:

"We have a merry life. We don't till and we don't sow, but we always have a rich harvest. Now sometimes, one of us gets his head chopped off. But we don't mourn him, we have a fine memorial service with rich food and choice wine. Just a few days ago, some landowners got their hands on our captain and they did him in. So now we're having our memorial service. Why don't you join our gang. If you turn out to be stronger and braver than the rest of us, we'll make you captain."

The farmer's son agreed on the spot. They shook hands, and the farmer's son said he would go home and then come back and join the gang in the morning.

He went home, went into the orchard, and carved himself a thick club from a pear tree, the kind of club that robbers use.

He entered his house with the club. His mother was there all alone, and he said to her:

"Goodbye, mother! I'm leaving home forever!"

"Where are you going, darling?" asked his mother, terrified.

"I've joined a gang of robbers and I'm going robbing with them."
The mother burst into tears and began pleading:
"Who are you leaving us for, darling? And where? Don't go!"
"No, mother dear! I've given my word and I'm going."
The mother threw herself upon him, grabbed his arm, and wouldn't let him go. He tore himself away and screamed:
"Leave me alone! Or I'll kill you!"
But she wouldn't let go. So he struck her on the head with his club. And she fell down dead.
He went off. At the edge of the village, he met his father, who asked him:
"Where are you going, my son?"
"I'm leaving you, father dear. I've joined a gang of robbers and I'm going robbing with them."
His father grabbed him and begged him not to go off with the robbers. The son tore himself loose and shouted:
"Leave me alone, father! Mother wouldn't let me go, so I killed her. If you don't let me go, then I'll kill you too!"
But the father clutched him all the harder. So the son killed the father too with his club.
And he went to join the robbers.

2.

The robbers liked the farmer's son, and they made him their captain. He stayed with them for thirty years, robbing and killing on the highways, and he shed a great deal of human blood.
The robbers in that gang were all unschooled, they couldn't read or write. Why should a robber bother knowing how to read? But there was one who *could* read. And the captain noticed that he went off deep into the woods every night, and no one knew what he was doing there. The captain's curiosity was aroused, and one night he followed him. He saw that the "reader" had gone deep into the woods, sat down under a tree, lit a candle, and started reading a book aloud. The book described every punishment in the afterlife for every sin—for robbery, for murder, and for other misdeeds.
The captain was deeply troubled and he went over to the robber. When the robber saw him, he was terror-stricken, he thought the

captain was about to kill him for reading such a book. But the captain put him at ease and said:

"Read the book to me from beginning to end. I want to know everything it says."

And thus they sat in the forest all through the night, until daybreak. One man read, and the other man listened.

In the morning, the captain went back, called together all the robbers and said:

"For thirty years now, I've robbed and killed with you. But from this day forward, I am no longer your captain. All the gold and silver that I've stolen is yours now. You can do as you think best. If you like, repent. If you like, go back to the village and live as you did before. If you like, remain robbers.

"But I am going out into the world to seek penance for my sins."

3.

The captain took his club and went off into the next village. Right at this time, mass was being celebrated in the church. When it was over and the priest was leaving the church, the captain went over to him and said:

"Father, I am a great sinner. I've come to ask you to put a penance upon me."

"What is your sin?" asked the priest.

"My sin is that I have killed my father and my mother, robbed and murdered for thirty years, and shed a great deal of human blood."

The priest thought about it and replied:

"Your sin is great. There is no penance for it."

"Think it over, Father! Perhaps you'll find some penance for me, no matter how harsh!" the robber begged.

"No! There's no penance for you, no redemption! Get away from me, you sinner!"

The robber picked up his club and killed the priest.

He went off to the next village and asked the priest for a penance.

"What is your sin?"

My sin is that I have killed my father and my mother, robbed and murdered for thirty years, and shed a great deal of human blood, and killed a priest because he wouldn't give me a penance."

The priest thought about it and replied:

"Your sin is great. There is no penance for it."

"Think it over, Father! Perhaps you'll find some penance for me, no matter how harsh!" the robber begged.

"No! There's no penance for you, no redemption! Get away from me, you sinner!"

And the robber killed him.

He went off to a third village and saw the priest. But the priest wouldn't give him any penance either. So he killed him too.

All in all, he went to eleven villages and killed eleven priests.

When he came to the twelfth village, he found a young, learned priest. The priest also asked him:

"What is your sin?"

"My sin is that I killed my father and mother, robbed and murdered for thirty years, shed a great deal of human blood, and killed eleven priests because they wouldn't give me a penance. If you don't give me a penance, I'll kill you too."

The priest thought about it and replied:

"There is a penance for you . . . . Come with me."

He took the robber home with him, told his servant to harness a horse and wagon, climbed into it with the robber, and drove deep into the woods. There they got off and the priest asked the robber:

"What did you use to kill your father and mother, and rob and murder for thirty years, and kill the eleven priests with?"

"With this club. I carved it out of a pear tree."

"Take the club and plant it deep in the earth," said the priest.

Then he got back into the wagon with the robber and drove down to the river. There he told the robber to climb out, and he said:

"Get down on your knees, fill your mouth with water from the river, and crawl back to the woods on all fours, to the place where you planted the club, and water it with the water in your mouth. Then crawl back on all fours to the river, fill your mouth with water again and go back to the club and water it. Keep doing this day after day, year after year, until the pear tree blossoms, and is covered with leaves and then pears. And then, when all the pears are ripe and fall down—your sins will fall from you too."

Having spoken, he turned his horse around and drove home.

The robber remained alone and began carrying out the penance that the priest had put upon him. He crawled on all fours from the woods to the river and the river to the woods, and kept watering the club.

Months wore by, and years. The penitent lived on berries and mushrooms and herbs, and he spent the winters in a tent of branches. And thus thirty years passed by. The penitent had become very old and weak. The crawling had worn away the flesh on his knees to the very bone. But he did not stop carrying out the priest's commandment.

In the thirtieth year, the pear tree blossomed. Many pears grew on it. By the end of the summer, all the pears dropped off, except for two, the largest ones, which remained hanging on the tree.

The priest remembered the penitent he had left in the woods and he went to visit him.

When he saw the blossoming pear tree, from which all the pears but two had fallen, he said to the sinner:

"All your sins have been forgiven except the sin of killing your father and mother. Keep doing your penance, and God will take pity and forgive you for that sin as well."

And he drove back to the village.

4.

The penitent crawled back to the river on all fours. All at once, he saw a boat moving over the river, and there was a man sitting inside it. For thirty years, the penitent had not seen a living soul, and now he saw a man in a boat. He was amazed.

And the boatman was also amazed at seeing a man crawling on all fours to the river and taking water into his mouth. He rowed up to the shore and asked:

"Who are you? And what are you doing?"

The penitent replied:

"I am a penitent, and I am redeeming my great sin . . . . And who are you?"

"I am an informer," replied the boatman.

"What is an 'informer'?"

"The landowner has hired me to spy on his peasants. I eavesdrop under the windows to find out what they're saying about the landowner, I watch what they do, and I report everything to the land-owner. He severely punishes the peasants who think badly of him. And he rewards me very well. He gives me food and drink and presents. So I lead a fine life."

When the penitent heard this, his blood boiled.

"Even if I have to crawl on all fours and water the tree for an-other thirty years, I'm going to kill him and free a whole village from its murderer!" he decided to himself.

He looked at the boatman and asked:

"I've been sitting in these woods for thirty years without seeing a living soul. I'd like to go rowing a bit on the river. Let me have your boat and your oar for a while."

"You don't even have the strength to stay on your feet. How are you going to row?" said the informer.

"Just wait! Give me the oar and you'll see."

The informer handed him the oar. The penitent got to his feet and struck the oar so hard over the informer's head that he fell into the boat dead.

The penitent pushed the boat off with his foot. Then he filled his mouth with water and crawled back to the tree. He thought to himself that he would have to water the tree for many more years to redeem the new sin. But he did not regret what he had done.

When he came back to the tree, he saw that the last two pears had dropped off . . . . He was so overjoyed that God had forgiven all of his sins that he died.

That same night, the priest had a dream:

"Go and bury the penitent in great honor. All his sins have been forgiven."

And the priest buried him in great honor.

Three Gifts

1.
By the Scales

Once, generations and years ago, a Jew passed away.

Well, a Jew passed away—you can't live forever—and he was given his due, a decent Jewish burial.

The grave was closed. The bereft son spoke the prayer for the dead—the soul flew up, to judgment, the celestial court . . . .

When he arrived, the scales were already hanging before the court. To weigh the good deeds and the bad.

The dead man's defender came—his former Good Spirit—and stood with a snow-white sack in his hands to the right of the scales . . . .

The dead man's accuser came—his former Bad Spirit, his seducer, and stood with a filthy sack in his hands to the left of the scales . . . .

The snow-white sack contained the good deeds, the filthy sack— the bad deeds.

The defender poured out the good deeds on the right-hand scale. They wafted like perfumes and sparkled like the stars in the sky.

The accuser poured out the bad deeds on the left-hand scale. They were (may you be spared!) coal black and stank like pitch and tar.

The poor soul stood and gazed and gaped. He had never imagined there was such a difference between good and bad. Down below, he had often been unable to tell them apart, mistaking one for the other.

And the scales rose slowly, up and down. Now one pan, now the other . . . . And the pointer trembled in the air. Shifted a hair's breadth to the left, a hair's breadth to the right . . . .

Only a hair's breadth . . . and not all at once! He had been a simple Jew, with no great crimes, nor any martyrdom. And thus— tiny virtues, teensy peccadillos. Bits and pieces, specks of dust . . . . Some barely visible to the naked eye.

But still, when the pointer shifted a hair's breadth to the right, the higher worlds resounded with joy and pride. When it shifted to the left, heaven forbid, a sigh of melancholy passed through the air, all the way up to the Throne of God.

And the angels poured slowly, with devotion, bit by bit, speck by speck. The way simple people at a charity auction bid penny by penny . . . .

But every well runs dry. The sacks were empty.

"Are you through already?" asked the court attendant, a very busy angel.

The Good Spirit and the Bad Spirit turned their sacks upside down. That was all! The attendant went over to the pointer to see where it had stopped, right or left.

He peered and peered and saw something that had never happened since the creation of the heavens and the earth . . . .

"What's taking so long?" asked the presiding judge.

The attendant stammered:

"It's even! The pointer is right in the center! . . . The good deeds and the bad deeds are perfectly balanced."

"Perfectly balanced?" they asked at the celestial bench.

The attendant peered again and replied: "On the dot!"

The celestial court deliberated and then issued the following verdict:

"Since the sins do not outweigh the virtues, the soul shall not go to hell . . . .

"On the other hand, the virtues do not outweigh the sins, and so we cannot open the gates of heaven for him.

"Hence, he shall be a vagabond . . . .

"He shall fly about in the middle, between heaven and earth, until God remembers and takes pity and summons him with His grace."

And the attendant took the soul and led him out.

The poor soul bewept and bewailed his fate.

"Why are you crying?" asked the attendant. "You won't enjoy the delights of paradise, but you won't know the pains and torments of hell. You're even!"

But the soul couldn't be comforted:

"The worst torments are better than nothing! Nothing is awful!"

The attendant felt sorry for the soul and gave him some advice:

"Fly down, little soul, and hover about the living world. Don't ever look at the sky, what will you see? Only stars! And they're bright but cold creatures, they have no sense of pity, they won't do a thing for you, they'll never remind God of you . . . .

"The only ones who can intercede for a poor homeless soul are the saints in paradise . . . . And they, my little soul, they like presents . . . lovely gifts . . . . That," he added bitterly, "is what saints are like nowadays!

"So fly, my little soul," he went on, "hover low around the living earth and watch life, watch what happens. And if you see anything of extraordinary beauty and goodness, grab it and fly up. It will be a gift for the saints in heaven . . . . And with that gift in your hand, knock and announce yourself in my name to the angel at the window. Tell him I said it was all right!

"And once you've brought them three presents, you can be sure that the gates of paradise will open for you. The gifts will do the trick. At the Throne of Honor, they don't like the high-born, they prefer those who make it on their own."

And with these words, he mercifully pushed the soul out of heaven.

2.
The First Gift

The poor soul flew low. Hovering around the living earth. Seeking presents for the saints in paradise. He flew and flew, over villages and cities, wherever Jews could be found. Through burning rays in the worst heat spells. Through raindrops in wet seasons. Through silver gossamer that drifted in late summer, and snows that fell in winter. He looked and looked, and he looked his eyes out . . . .

Whenever he sighted a Jew, he hastily flew down and stared into his eyes. Was he about to sacrifice himself for God?

Wherever a light seeped through a crack in a shutter at night—
the soul was there. Were God's fragrant blossoms growing in the
quiet house, secret good deeds?

Alas! Usually the soul sprang away from eyes and windows, terrified and trembling . . . .

And as the seasons and years wore on, he was stricken with melancholy. Towns had already become graveyards. Graveyards had already been plowed up as fields. Forests had been cleared. Stones
near water had turned into sand. Rivers had changed their courses.
Thousands of stars had fallen. Millions of souls had flown upward.
And the Good Lord did not remember this one soul. And the soul
found nothing of extraordinary beauty and goodness . . . .

He thought to himself:

"The world is so wretched, people are so mediocre, their souls so
gray and their deeds so small . . . . How can there be anything 'extraordinary' about them? I'll be a homeless outcast forever!"

But as he was thinking, a red flame caught his eye. In the middle
of the dark, dense night, a red flame.

He looked around. The flame darted from a high window.

Bandits were attacking a rich Jew, bandits with masks on their
faces. One was holding a burning torch to light their way. A second one was holding a shiny knife against the rich man's chest, and
saying: "One move, Jew, and it'll be your last! The blade of my
knife will come out your back!" The rest were opening chests and
closets and looting them.

The Jew stood there with the knife at his chest and watched
calmly. Not a lash twitched over his clear eyes, not a hair stirred in
the white beard that reached down to his loins. Why should he
care? "The Lord giveth, the Lord taketh away," he thought,
"blessed be the name of the Lord! You're not born with it, and you
can't take it with you," his pale lips whispered.

And he watched quietly as they opened the last drawer of the
last chest and hauled out bags of gold and silver, sacks of jewelry
and all kinds of valuables. And he kept silent.

Perhaps he was glad to be rid of them!

But all at once, when the robbers reached the last hiding-place
and yanked out a small bag, the last one, the best concealed, he forgot himself, shuddered, his eyes blazed, he reached out his right
hand to stop them and tried to scream: "Don't touch that!"

But instead of a scream, a red torrent of steaming blood shot out of his mouth. The knife had done its work. It was his heart's blood, splashing on the bag!

He dropped to the floor and the bandits tore open the sack. This would be the best, the most valuable!

But they were bitterly mistaken. The blood was shed in vain. There was no silver, no gold, no jewelry in the bag. Nothing that was precious or had any value in this world! Just a little soil. From the earth of Palestine, for his grave. And that was what the rich man wanted to save from thieving hands and eyes and splashed with his blood . . . .

The soul grabbed a bloody speck of soil from Palestine and took it to the window in heaven.

The first gift was accepted.

3.
The Second Gift

"Remember," the angel called out as he closed the window behind the soul: "Only two more gifts!"

"God will help!" thought the soul hopefully, and he cheerfully flew back down.

But in the end his optimism waned. Years and years wore on, and he saw nothing of extraordinary beauty. And again he was haunted by the dismal thought:

"The world emerged from God's will like a living source, and keeps running and running in time. And the further it runs, the more dust and earth it takes in, the muddier and murkier it becomes, the fewer presents one can find in it for heaven . . . and the smaller the people grow, the pettier the virtues, the tinier the vices, and the good deeds cannot be seen with the naked eyes! . . .

"If God," he went on to himself, "were to weigh the good and bad deeds of the world, the pointer would barely stir, barely quiver . . . .

"The world cannot go up or down either . . . . It too is a homeless vagabond between radiant heavens and dark abysses . . . and the defender and the accuser would grapple over it forever, the way light and darkness, heat and cold, life and death, grapple on and on . . . .

"The world balances, but it can't move up and it can't move down, and there will always be marriages and divorces, circum-

cisions and funerals, festivities and mournings . . . and love and hate
. . . forever and ever . . . ."

There was a sudden blare of trumpets and horns . . . .

He looked down. A German city (of long ago, naturally), slanting roofs edged the square in front of the town hall, the area was
filled with people in particolored garb, the windows were crowded
with heads, people were lying on the roofs, some of them perched
astride the wooden beams that stuck out of the walls beneath the
roofs, and the balconies were packed . . . .

In front of the town hall stood a table covered with green cloth
and lined with golden fringe and tassels. The magistrates were
sitting there in velvet garments with golden frogs, and sable hats
with white feathers and diamond buttons. Above them, by himself,
sat the presiding magistrate. A gluttonous eagle fluttered over his
head.

Off to the side, a Jewish girl stood all bound up. Not far from
her, ten servants held a wild horse. The magistrate rose, turned to
the marketplace, and read a verdict from a document:

"This Jewess, this child of Jews, has committed a grave sin, a sin
so grave that even God in his vast mercy could not forgive it . . . .

"She stole out of the ghetto and went about our pure streets during our sacred holiday . . . .

"Her shameless eyes sullied our holy procession, our holy images,
which we carried through the streets with hymns of praise and a
beating of kettledrums.

"Her accursed ears took in the singing of our innocent white-
robed children and the beating of our holy drums. And who can
tell whether or not the devil, the filthy devil, who assumed the
shape of this Jewess, this daughter of an accursed rabbi—who can
tell whether or not the devil touched and soiled some purity of
ours?

"What did he desire, the devil in that beauteous shape? For I cannot deny it—she *is* beautiful, beautiful as only a devil can make
himself— Just look at those eyes radiating insolence under the silken
lashes that she lowers so chastely . . . . Look at the alabaster face,
which has only gotten paler rather than darker during her long imprisonment! Look at her fingers, her long, slender fingers,
transparent in the sunshine.

"And what did he desire, the devil? To tear a soul away from its
devotion in our procession . . . . And he succeeded!

" 'Look at that beautiful girl!' one of our knights exclaimed, a member of one of our most illustrious families! . . .

"And that was too much! Halberdiers noticed her and seized her. He didn't even resist, that devil! And why? They were pure, absolved of any sin, and so he had no sway over them.

"And this is the judgment for the devil in the shape of the Jewess:

"Her hair, her long diabolical braids, shall be bound to the tail of the wild horse . . . .

"The horse shall gallop away and drag her through the streets like a corpse, the streets that carried her feet against our sacred law.

"Let her blood bespatter and scour the stones that her feet have defiled!"

A wild scream of joy tore from all throats, and when the wave of ferocious shouting had washed by, the condemned woman was asked whether she had any final wishes.

"I do," she replied calmly. "I would like some pins."

"She's crazy with terror!" said the magistrates.

"No," she retorted, cold and placid, "that is my last wish and desire."

They brought her some pins.

"And now," commanded the presiding judge, "tie her to the horse!"

Halberdiers strode over and with trembling hands they tied the long black braids of the rabbi's daughter to the wild horse, which they could barely restrain.

"Make way!" the magistrate shouted to the crowd in the square, and there was an uproar. The people hugged and massed along the house walls, and all of them held up their hands, some clutching a whip, some a rod, others a cloth, all of them ready to egg on the wild horse, their breath bated, their faces ablaze, their eyes flashing. And in the turmoil no one noticed the condemned woman bend over quietly and fasten the hem of her dress to her legs, sticking the pins deep, deep into the flesh, so that her body would not be exposed when the horse dragged her through the streets . . . .

It was noticed only by the homeless vagabond, the soul . . . .

"Release the horse!" came the command of the magistrate. The servants leaped back, and the horse tore forward. And a scream whirled from all the mouths, and there was a whirling and whistling of lashes, rods, and cloths, and the terrified horse dashed across the marketplace through streets and back alleys and out of the town . . . .

And the soul, the homeless vagabond, had already pulled a bleeding pin out of the condemned woman's leg and was flying up to heaven with it.

"Just one more gift," the angel at the window comforted him.

4.
The Third Gift

And down flew the soul again, he needed only one more gift.

And more and more seasons and years wore on, and again he was stricken with melancholy, the world seemed to be getting even smaller, tinier people and tinier actions, both good and evil . . . .

Once, the soul thought: "And if God, praised be His Name, should ever stop and judge the world as it is, all at once, and if there should be a defender on one side, pouring out the bits and specks from a white sack, and an accuser on the other side, pouring out his shreds and pieces—it would take years and years for the sacks to empty. So many trivia, so many!

"But if the sacks were ever empty, what would happen?

"The pointer would stay put in the center!

"With so many trivia, so many trivia, neither side can outbalance the other. And then what? Another tiny feather, a wisp of straw, a speck of chaff, a mote of dust?

"And what would God do? What would His judgment be?

"Back to the primal chaos? No. The sins do not outweigh the virtues.

"Redemption? No again! The virtues do not outweigh the sins.

"Then what?

" 'Keep going,' He would say. 'Keep flying between hell and heaven, love and hatred, tears of pity and smoking blood . . . between cradles and graves . . . on and on!' "

But the soul was destined for redemption. A roll of drums aroused him from his brooding.

Where was he? When?

He couldn't tell the place or time . . . .

All he could make out was a square in front of a prison. The rays of the sun played and flashed along the iron bars and the tiny windows. They sparkled on the weapons stacked along the wall. The soldiers held—rods in their hands.

They stationed themselves in two long rows with a narrow passage between them. To run someone through the gauntlet.

Who?

A little Jew with a tattered shirt on his scrawny body, a skullcap on his partly shaven head.

Now they led him in.

Why was he being punished? Who could say! A matter of olden times. Perhaps a theft, perhaps a robbery or murder, perhaps he was the victim of a blood libel. Those were olden times!

And the soldiers smiled and thought: Why did they order so many of us out here? He won't even endure half of it!

But now they pushed him into the passageway between the two rows. He walked straight and did not stumble and did not fall . . . . He was lashed and he endured it . . . .

A fury took hold of the soldiers! He was still walking, still walking!

And the rods whistled through the air like demons and swished around his body like snakes. And the blood from the scrawny body splashed and splashed, and didn't stop splashing!

All at once, a soldier struck out too high and lashed the skullcap from the victim's head. He only noticed it after a few steps. He stopped, deliberated, made up his mind, and spun around. He would not go bare-headed, he strode back to the skullcap, bent over, straightened out, turned around, and walked on, placid, blood-stained, but with his skullcap on his head, walked until he dropped.

And when he dropped, the soul flew over and grabbed the skullcap, which had brought the victim so many unnecessary lashes, and he flew up to the window of heaven.

And the third gift was also accepted!

And the saints interceded for him. The gates of paradise opened up for the soul after the three gifts!

And the oracle, the "light and truth," said:

"These are really gifts of beauty, extraordinary beauty . . . but rather useless. Not practical, but beautiful—extraordinarily so."

The Fool and the Forest Demon
A Beginning

For years on end the fool lived in the wild forest, serving the forest
demon. He chopped his wood, he carried his water, escorted him
wherever he went, followed whatever orders he gave, no sooner
said than done, smiling and holding his peace. But one day, it was
summer, the kind of hot and bosky summer day when there's nothing to do, when everything has been done for the day, and the day
is still huge and the forest is languorous—from the sun itself and
the day and from standing—and the forest demon felt null and
void, and wearily and summerly and in the bright daylight, he
climbed into his ancient linden tree to rest. It was the time of
day when sunny shadows crouch by trees that stand in the forest
that lies with quiet birds and nests that are quieter still. On such a
day the fool would go off to his faraway known-only-to-him place,
the quiet place hidden behind low trees and dense leaves. There was
an old, old stone there, covered with moss. And the fool would
come and sit down next to it with his back to the stone and his face
to where he had come from, and for the rest of the day he remained lost in his own and in bosky thoughts. All alone in this
place, with the day's peace upon his head and with no one about, he
would sit there, and sometimes a smile could command his face and
come to his lips, a clear smile and a joyous one, a pure smile from
his inmost being, and he would beam and radiate, by himself and to

himself, fine and more than fine, and thus, joyously, he would remain in his fine and foolish mood for a long, long while.

At dusk, however, when the sun was setting, when shadows were creeping forth all around, settling on the forest and on the trees, the fool would get up, would turn to the stone, would stand before it for a long time, staring at it, and then say to it before he left: "I've sat near you all day long, stone, believed in you all day long, thought, like all the other times, that today at last you would open by sunset, and pull a sun out of yourself, and give it to the evening, and make night impossible . . . . I was hoping for it today, and more than once it seemed to me as though the power were coursing through you to open you at last, and inside myself I laughed aloud, but now I've got to double back, and serve the forest and the demon again, and keep waiting for you, stone, and I, the fool, I have to leave . . . ."

And the fool would turn and leave the stone in its hiding-place and thicket, alone in the woods, and return with dusk and sunset, and softly and late, in the evening, in the darkness, come back to the forest demon and his linden tree and find him lying there and sleeping.

"What time is it?" after a while, from the trunk of the tree, a husky voice would emerge:

"It's late, and time to get up."

The demon would first stick out his head and horns, and then crawl out with bones and skin, and stretch and yawn, and crack his bones and lean on the fool's shoulder, and the fool would hold him up, his body and his heaviness, until the demon felt demonic and refreshed. Then he started looking about, nocturnal and cheerful, as to where and on what side he would do something at night, where and what was in store for him tonight . . . . He thought, and thought it out, he would at last, with a commanding forefinger, order the fool to get the pots together for supper. He went along with him, and off they went, off to the side . . . .

That's how it was, that's how it went, for years, and years on end. And the demon was master, the fool was his servant, and changes were none.

But then one day, after an afternoon of sleeping and an evening of getting up, the demon and the fool went off into the deepest woods. That night, a summerly and moonly one, a clear and radiant night, they were walking and walking, till at last they arrived at some kind of midpoint. And there they saw that they had never been in this place before, that they had never noticed a place so overgrown with grass below, so overshadowed by trees above, and never so wild and never so strange, never so dusky and never so bright. Long, gigantic trees were standing in their tallness and fullness, their trunks alive with healthy saps, their roots in earthly security, the tops in brightness and the branches at their heads, and never noticing, in their might and their height, the demon and the fool at their roots. Tiny and trivial, the two of them moved about the trunks, their heads tilted up and away, gaping at the treetops, unable to remove their eyes or cease their wonder.

"Where are we?"

"I don't know," the fool replied.

"I don't recognize these woods."

And then the demon gave the fool an order: He was to unpack their things, and build a fire, they had to spend the night, they had to reconnoiter. The fool obeyed: He quickly built a fire in the grass, and put on the evening meal, and started cooking it. He sat there, staring at the fire, and from time to time he added fuel to keep it going, and it flared and flamed. While the fool was staring at the fire, the demon was wandering about and away, reconnoitering the place, and still not leaving and then staying by the fire. But then when the smoke was storming the sky, the demon came over to the fool and said to him: "Fool, I am leaving you alone, to sit by the fire and keep it going, and to keep yourself awake. Just let the smoke keep rising . . . . I'm leaving you now, I have to leave and get to know this place: It's not good for a demon, whose woods are his province, to find a place he doesn't know . . . ." No sooner said than gone.

The fool remained alone at the fire. He sat and he sat, in silence and, as was his wont in woods and grass, in the forest light, he was lost in thought. And he softly laughed, for long and longer, like the simpleton he was, quietly and joyously, as was his way. But having laughed his fill to himself and for his pleasure, he turned back to the fire quietly, and with his final smile, he built it up. The smoke rose higher and higher up the trees, straight, in smoky columns, so still and so long, so dusky and unperceived, till the dusk had fully deepened and midnight came along, and the demon didn't come, and the fool felt like sleeping, and he started drowsing off, and moved closer to the fire, and he cuddled up and, sitting there, his head upon his chest, losing it and dropping off.

And just as the fool was falling asleep down below, up above, in a high strong tree, at the very top, a branch began to sway .... A young woman, a forest creature, appeared in the tree and started staring down at the fool asleep by his fire. She stared and she swayed, and sylphlike, sylvan, and barely visible, she kept swaying up and down, until her swaying stopped, and she stopped the branch with her body, and weightless and breathless, and after staring and staring, she finally shouted down: "Fool, why are you sleeping? I come from the stone, the stone's not alone, the stone has split open ...." Shouted and waited for the fool and his awakening. No use! So she shouted down again: "Why are you sleeping, fool? This is your final night for serving the demon, go, they're waiting at the stone, they're watching out for you ...." And still the fool would not awake. So she took a huge, dry, hard nut and aimed it straight and true, and hit the fool right on his sleepy head:

"Get up!"

And as the fool awoke he found the demon, who had come back and was standing before him, his head tilted up and turned aloft, gazing and staring at the top of the nearby tree, surprised and asking upward:

"Who's there?"

"Me," came the answer back down.

"Who's me?"

"The forest creature."

"What do you want?"

"I want to redeem the master from bondage."

"Who do you mean?"

"Him!" she pointed down at the fool.

And when the demon turned to look him in the face, he found him, as was his wont and his way, with his head bowing down to the ground, stooping and standing ashamed, quiet and good-natured and smiling, embarrassed and abashed as though guilty of something. The demon gave him a more serious stare, awoke him and harassed him in his shamefaced standing:

"Who! Fool!"

"Yes," the fool replied, raising his head and barely looking him in the eyes, "we're going our separate ways."

And the demon held his tongue.

And the fool gave the demon his evening food. He stood alone and aloof, like a servant, waiting for the demon to finish eating, then he put the dishes and silver away, and quietly and together with the demon, he left that place and he left that night to go back, to go home. And when they arrived, the fool went over to the tree and quietly, after the quiet events, he stood and faced him, holding his tongue and standing at the trunk, and then he knelt down, with his face to the ground, and lay before him, still and long. Knelt and stooped, so long and before his tree-filled earth, until he stood up before him and his property, and went over to the demon and looked in his eyes, and then he tersely said to him:

"The fool is grateful to you."

"For what?"

"For all these long and many years, for my being here and my having been . . . ."

And waiting for nothing, no speech and no words, he turned around and he turned away, from the demon and from serving the demon, and left his place and his tree forever.

I . J . T R U N K

The Jewish Pope—
a Historical Tale

CHAPTER ONE
Let Us Go to the Bookshelves and Open the Old
Parchments

Our sages have said: Jewish troubles are as lasting as the world. And they knew what they were saying. Today, we Jews are still living in a dreadful world. "Israel is a scattered flock," said Jeremiah. Specks of dust in a hurricane. And even now, the world is bringing us no end of hardship. Today's Jews are not the only ones to have suffered in our history. Sorrow is nothing new for us.

Thus, from time to time it doesn't hurt to go to our old bookcases and open the dusty parchments. To have a look at bygones, to see how our grandfathers and grandmothers lived long ago.

We leaf through these bygones—and what do we see? Old wine in new pouches.

Scholars try to persuade us that time is a carriage drawn by fiery steeds. Galloping headlong. And the world sits in this carriage like an aristocrat and drives on. But believe me, my dear readers, that's nothing but a fairy tale. In reality, we are stuck knee-deep in the mud of the Dawn of Creation. We merely dream that we are dashing along in a carriage.

At times, Jews aren't even allowed to dream that they are driving in a carriage. Jews are still caught in the mud of the world, at the very outset of existence.

And so, dear readers, let us look at an eternal present, at which all clocks have stopped. Let us turn back several centuries and see how Jews once lived and worked in such a renowned city as Frankfort on the Main.

CHAPTER TWO
Jews and Christians in Frankfort on the Main

In those days, Frankfort was one of the richest cities in Germany. A city of prince electors, bishops, and patricians. The austere and colorful plenty of the Christian Middle Ages was poured out on its houses and districts, on the behavior and dress of its Christian inhabitants. It was the stiff and stern splendor of medieval worldiness.

Off to the side of this imperial and episcopal city, lay the Jewish ghetto like an enclosed and secluded darkness. Not even the sun was permitted to give its radiance to the Jews, or the air to blow its freshness here. The alleys of the ghetto were narrow and dingy. The houses poor and shabby. They couldn't expand on the ground, so they stretched and grew upward, consumptive and bloodless. The new generations of Jews had to squeeze into these dark, close cages. One generation atop another. No expansion was allowed. The Christians kept the area of the ghetto bound off, like an abomination.

And even this miserable abomination had been thrown to the Jews by the citizens of Frankfort like alms to a beggar. You Jews can live and die right here. But not a step farther.

Yet the ghetto hummed like a beehive.

During the six workdays of the week, a stranger at first sight would have been flabbergasted: What was all the commotion about? What was all the hustle and bustle in this cramped darkness? He would have thought he had come to a place of the worst paupers and beggars. The men went in rags and tatters. The women were shrouded in poverty. Why, then, were the Jews hurrying and scurrying?

Eventually, the stranger would have realized that business was buzzing in these ruins of existence. Jews dealt in old clothes. You could see the expensive knightly garments which, worn outside in the Christian Frankfort on the Main, had shone at balls and palaces, in the light and incense of Catholic churches and cathedrals. And now, perhaps it was the way of the past, they lay in heaps through-

out the darknesses of the Jewish ghetto. And Jews drove their trade
with these Gentile bygones. Made a good living. Jews also did
business with valuables. With gold, silver, and precious stones. And
their coffers held golden ducats. The nobles and patricians of
Frankfort came into the Jewish darknesses to buy and sell. And to
borrow the golden ducats that lay in the Jewish coffers.

Next to the Jews who did commerce with gold in the con-
finements of the ghetto, there were also Jews who dealt in the gold
and gems of the highest worlds. Jews who were Talmudists, Cabbalists, scholars. The Jewish ghetto was small and close, and so everything fused into one. Wordly talk and spiritual dialogue were
coupled like the harmonies of some dark, profound symphony of
the world.

The Jews could show no strength like that of their Christian
neighbors outside the walls of the ghetto. Thou worm, Jacob! Jews
were weak from the eternal darkness and old from the eternal burden. Even the weapons they had in the ghetto were junk—good
only for hawking and not for war.

But their age-old experience teaches Jews how to use everything
as a parable. The whole world is nothing but a parable. In the bottomless depths one can play with clouds. And so they knew how to
use the "tune of trumpets" in the fighting of armies.

Now their wars had no bloodshed, God forbid! Their troops
were wooden figures. And with these armies, they fought many
battles with the nobles and patricians of Frankfort on the Main.
The powerful Gentiles were often beaten on the battlefield, and
suffered defeat at the hands of the Jews.

It was the battlefield of chess.

The human soul is like a flowing river. When the current is ob-
structed along one bank, it overflows on the other bank. And its
force is greater there. The accounts of human desires have to be
balanced somewhere. And substance and spirit are on the same level
here. Man—who by nature cannot renounce anything—merely
changes his fields òf action and desire. Whatever he loses in substance he tries to make up for in spirit. And vice versa, unfortunately. The Good Spirit and the Evil Spirit are most likely one and
the same angel. An angel who acts in Purim skits. A rascal and a
rogue, who merely dons the cape in which we wish to see him.

And the Jews enclosed in the ghetto of Frankfort on the Main
would in no wise forgo anything that their powerful neighbors and

oppressors enjoyed outside the walls. They merely pursued it in other worlds. They drew the pleasures and fantasies of this life from the Talmud, the Cabbalah, and from other sacred books.

Nor did they wish to do without wars and knightly jousts—and they absolutely wanted to fight a great battle with their powerful neighbors.

The chessboard was the only battlefield on which the ghetto Jews were transformed into knights in armor.

For all their hatred and scorn of the Jews in the cramped ghetto, the Gentiles of Frankfort on the Main could never cease to admire their mastery at chess. These men without rights showed genius and sharp reasoning in their strategies with the wooden figures. Patricians, priests, and bishops would often summon the Jews to their palaces. To lock horns in a quiet, intricate war—and to suffer defeat and downfall.

The Jews kept buying and selling in the palaces. Lending golden ducats, taking collateral. Doing a generous business.

CHAPTER THREE
Simon Barbun and His Renown

In those days of long ago, there lived in the ghetto of Frankfort a Jew named Simon Barbun. He was a great teacher, a Cabbalist, and a sharp scholar. A fine figure of a man. Tall and with a beautiful long beard. His Judaism shone like a good name. He was a God-fearing Jew, endowed with all the virtues. He not only devoted himself to religious studies but also to doing good deeds and helping his fellow Jews. His business was old coins—valuable ones. And through this trade, he came into contact with the foremost men and nobles in Frankfort on the Main.

But his wide renown among Christians was mainly due to his skill and acumen in the ways of chess figures. Whenever Simon Barbun sat down to a game of chess, he looked as if his mind were crackling and sparkling with sharp, hidden bolts of light.

Offhand, it might have seemed as if the amazing thing about this Jew was his embodiment of that Talmudic sentence about the union of learning and wealth. What more could a Jew desire than a good name in all his accomplishments?

His measure of honor became full when the elders of the community came and asked him to be rabbi of the Frankfort ghetto.

Simon said "No!" to the elders. "When I play chess with the Gentile nobles and beat them, I can request more favors for Jews than if I were to sit on the rabbinical throne."

CHAPTER FOUR
He Shall Not Flourish With the Jewish Trees

There is a shadow behind every light. The sun has spots. Perfection is to be found only in the Maker and not in a mortal. A human being is only dust and ashes. His days are a passing shadow like the instants that flash by us.

To make a long story short: Simon (may all Jews be spared the like) was childless.

Let us again take up the parable of the stranger entering the ghetto of Frankfort on the Main. He would have seen the confinement. The darknesses. He would have seen the shabby Jews walking about like wan shadows. The stranger might even have thought to himself:

"These poor Jews in this prison of darkness—why are they so eager to have children? And even more children? They won't be allowed any room to spread out in. Why do they need so many offspring for this confinement? New generations for Jewish misery? Isn't it a stubborn madness to call forth new Jewish generations for the future?"

If the stranger had only been a keen observer and managed to find his bearings in the darkness of worldly thought, he might have realized that what he saw in the ghetto wasn't all there was to know about Jews. It *was* dark here, to be sure. But dark like the twilight before a new radiance about to reach across the world. And it is this coming light for which Jews prepare their generations.

A Jew without offspring is like a tree that shall not bloom when a new springtime comes over the world.

"He shall not flourish with the Jewish trees!" That was the great sadness in the life of Simon Barbun, supposedly the happiest Jew in the ghetto of Frankfort on the Main.

CHAPTER FIVE
A Dream in Three Parts

It was a Minor Day of Atonement, the fast observed by Jews on the eve of the new moon. Simon Barbun was in the thirty-fifth year of his life. Coming home from synagogue, he couldn't understand why he was wearier than he had ever been after a fast. He could barely keep his eyes open.

Simon Barbun had a bite. But he was so racked with fatigue that he ate very little and went to bed.

No sooner did his head touch the pillow than he fell asleep. He dreamt that his wife Glikl had given birth to a boy and he was celebrating the circumcision.

In the twinkling of an eye—Simon Barbun, in his sleep, was amazed at how the years flash by like instants in a dream—it was thirteen years later. He was already celebrating his son's bar mitzvah. His son was renowned as a prodigy. Any Jewish mother would desire such a son.

His joy woke Simon out of his sleep. His eyes opened. The room was dark. Off in a corner, a tiny candle stub was flickering in a nightlamp.

Simon Barbun fell asleep again, and again he had a dream.

In the dream, he heard the pealing of many bells. He was in a large square. The sun was shining. His son, a handsome young man in his twenties, was standing at the center of the square. He had a strange pointed crown of gold on his head. The crown was sparkling in the sunshine. The square was crowded with thousands and thousands of people. They were all kneeling before his son in the golden crown. Simon Barbun wanted to walk up and ask his son: "Who are these people and why all this ringing and kneeling?" But Simon was driven away with cracking whips.

He was so dismayed at being driven away from his own son that he began weeping piteously in his sleep. The sobbing woke him up.

His eyes opened. And behold, it was a dream. The room was dark. The tiny candle stub flickered in the nightlamp.

He fell asleep again.

And again he dreamt:

His son was dressed like a Jewish pauper. He had ashes on his head. Sackcloth on his loins. He was sitting on the ground next to a glowing stick of wood, and his broken voice was reciting the 102nd Psalm. The prayer of an afflicted man, who poured out his woe to God . . . .

Terror-stricken, Simon Barbun woke up from his sleep.

The room was dark. In the corner, the tiny candle stub was flickering in the nightlamp.

CHAPTER SIX
The First Part of the Dream Comes True

The world says: A dream is a fool. Who believes a fool? Simon Barbun tried to forget his dream, which was so peculiar. So joyous. So mournful. And slowly it slipped out of his mind.

But it often happens that a fool speaks the deepest wisdom and a dream reveals the greatest truth. Before three months were up, Simon Barbun's wife Glikl announced the glad tiding: "Husband, I am with child."

Simon trembled with joy. The dream suddenly emerged from oblivion. He saw all three scenes, clear and sharp before his eyes. He shuddered at the three parts of the dream that an unknown hand had written on the darkness of night—like a *menetekel.*

He was joyous. Hopeful. Saddened.

The nine months of pregnancy flew by. Glikl gave birth to a boy who simply filled the cradle with light. Again the months flew by. They saw the boy growing, a delight for any Jewish mother's heart. Beautiful and intelligent. He was the talk of the ghetto of Frankfort.

At three, like all little Jewish boys, he started attending the *helyder,* the traditional Jewish school. The teacher was beside himself with admiration for the sharp little mind. He said the boy would grow up to be a great man in Israel.

When he was thirteen, they couldn't find any more teachers for him. He outshone them all.

At his bar mitzvah, he received a rabbinical certificate from the greatest rabbis in France and Germany. The wealthiest Jews throughout the world sent marriage brokers to Simon Barbun. They showered him with gold, trying to get that rare prodigy Joseph Barbun for a son-in-law.

Simon Barbun was the envy of all Jews. But his heart was filled with trembling and sinister expectations. The first part of the dream has come true, he thought to himself, who can say whether the other two parts will not come true—God forbid!

At night, when no one was listening, he opened a window. Looked up at the stars. His lips softly whispered the 102nd Psalm, "the prayer of an afflicted man . . . ."

CHAPTER SEVEN
Joseph Barbun Goes to Bathe in the Main

Our wise men have said: Between heaven and hell there is only a thin partition. As fine as a hair. This fine partition also stands between fortune and misfortune. It stands between our good and our bad deeds. It stands between our hopes and blights. Most likely, it also stands between death and life.

It was a day of rejoicing in Simon Barbun's home. A wealthy Jew, a prince in Israel, who was also a great scholar, a certain Don Menakhem from the city of Orleans in France, was supposed to visit Frankfort on the Main and see the famous prodigy Joseph Barbun. He would talk to him and study with him and then draw up a contract of betrothal between him and his only daughter Terza, an unusually learned and beautiful girl, who had no peer in all the world.

The joy was boundless. Simon even forgot the dream that always gnawed at his heart.

It was the middle of summer. The great Don Menakhem was expected at dawn, God willing. The ghetto was stifling. The young prodigy Joseph asked his parents if he could go outside the city to bathe in the River Main. Naturally, at a place where Jews were allowed to bathe.

Because of the foul heat in the ghetto, the parents gave him permission. They sent along a servant to guard him.

CHAPTER EIGHT
"Joseph Has Been Torn to Shreds!"
Simon Barbun Battles with the Winds

That was in the morning.

It was noon. It was evening. The sun was setting. Over Frankfort on the Main. Joseph Barbun and the servant still weren't back.

It was night.

The weeping of Simon Barbun and his wife Glikl filled the ghetto, the men sighed along. The women wept along. Others tried to comfort them: Perhaps they had just gotten lost. Perhaps the gates of the ghetto had been closed and Joseph and the servant had to spend the night out.

And it was dawn.

All words of solace turned out to be false. They hunted wherever Jews might hunt. Simon Barbun hired Christian fishermen. They sailed their skiffs across the Main and cast their nets into the deep. Perhaps God would take pity. Perhaps they might still find some trace of the lost boy.

But no voice and no answer. The river kept its silence.

A month later, a traveling beggar found Joseph's hat on the bank of the Main. The hat was full of sand.

Simon Barbun grabbed the hat with both hands. In great dread he shouted: *"Joseph has been torn to shreds!* Joseph is dead. My eyes will never see him again. Oh, you dreams," he shrieked, "you're all a pack of lies, whether you're happy or whether you're sad!"

Simon Barbun and his wife Glikl sat down for the seven days of mourning. All the Jews in the ghetto came to comfort him. The tragedy reached the ears of the nobles in Frankfort, the Gentiles who did business with Simon and played chess with him. Some of them felt the stirrings of pity. They thought to themselves: In unhappiness, all people are alike, both Christians and Jews. Fate makes no distinctions.

And the nobles of Frankfort came to Simon's home. Spoke words of comfort to him.

But how could human beings comfort him if the years could not? Even time could not close the wound. Though it is in the nature of time to heal all pains. Glikl went blind from her constant weeping. She walked about, groping the air, calling: "Joseph!" Simon hunched together and became as gray as a pigeon. He stopped plying his trade, he no longer had a mind for valuables and old coins.

Reluctantly, he became rabbi of the ghetto in Frankfort on the Main.

He renounced all the worldly delights that a Jew is allowed to enjoy. In his grief, he no longer felt the least pleasure in bodily desires.

There was only one thing he couldn't give up—chess.

When he sat down at the chessboard, his sharp mind soon blazed in a war between the wooden figures. Simon played with passion. Pleasure. He wanted to fight, and he did fight. Against whom? The winds or destiny?

CHAPTER NINE
Twenty-three Years Have Flown By

Twenty-three years flew by.

In the ghetto of Frankfort on the Main, the Jews were preparing for Passover. They were cleaning and scrubbing in the Jewish darknesses. They were baking matzoth. Rabbi Simon Barbun went from house to house with a large handkerchief, collecting money for poor Jews who didn't have enough for the holidays.

A few days before Passover, he received a visit from Zalman-Ziskind, the head of the community elders. His eyes were red with weeping. In a broken voice, he informed the rabbi of a bitter tiding.

CHAPTER TEN
Zalkind the Synagogue-Crier Beats His Drum in the Streets
The Jews Fast

"Rabbi," said Zalman-Ziskind, the community elder, "a time of trouble has come upon the Jews. This morning I received an order from the electoral bishop. Within six weeks all Jews must leave the Frankfort ghetto. If we stay even a day longer, they will strip us to our skins—and the elector's lansquenets will drive us out with hounds and whips."

"The Christians have been quiet for a long time," said Rabbi Simon with a deep and bitter sigh.

"You'll have to make the effort," said Zalman-Ziskind, "of personally going to the electoral bishop. He's always had a great deal of respect for you, Rabbi. When you were young, you played no end of chess with him. We've always thought of him as a fine nobleman and a friend of the Jews. His heart must have suddenly spun around."

"Such an awful decree," Simon couldn't stop sighing. "The way I remember the bishop, he was a good and pious Christian. Perhaps, Zalman-Ziskind," Simon suddenly cried out to the community elder, "perhaps a fellow Jew has committed some sin against the ruler—God forbid!—or perhaps he deceived one of the noblemen and gave him counterfeit money! You know how it is, Zalman-Ziskind, when Gentiles say 'Jew' they soon mean all Jews."

"I would offer the following advice," Simon went on. "Zalkind the synagogue-crier should immediately take the community drum, go through the streets and declare, under pain of ban, that whoever has done any wrong to the nobles should come to synagogue for afternoon prayers and speak the truth. And like Jacob and Esau, we shall become friends anew. The truth might help to soften the hearts of the rich Gentiles outside."

And thus it was. Zalkind, the synagogue-crier went about through the ghetto and beat his drum and called out the decree of the court of justice.

Afternoon prayers in synagogue, no one confessed to even the slightest peccadillo.

Rabbi Simon ordered the Jews to fast the next day and pray for forgiveness.

He himself put on the pointed Jewish hat, took the staff with the silver knob, and went off to the palace of the electoral bishop.

CHAPTER ELEVEN
The Electoral Bishop

When Rabbi Simon came to the Episcopal Palace he was received very cordially. The bishop had him ushered into his cabinet. He even walked over to welcome Rabbi Simon. Held out his hands to him, inquired after his health.

"Your Eminence," said Rabbi Simon in a gloomy voice, "has any Jew offended or, God forbid, deceived a Christian? 'One man has sinned, and you intend to pour out your wrath on a whole community.' " The rabbi quoted this biblical verse to the bishop, but in a pure Church Latin.

"God forbid, Rabbi!" said the bishop, trembling. "None of you has done anything whatsoever to me. My heart bleeds at the thought of treating you with such cruelty. It is also a loss to the city of Frankfort. We have had a large revenue from the Jews. You have enriched the city with your trade and commerce. But what can I do? The expulsion decree has come from the hands of the pope in Rome. His Holiness has issued the order himself. I would advise you to go to Rome personally, fall on your knees before the Holy Father, and beg him to rescind this bitter decree."

"I know your good heart, Your Eminence," said Simon, "but how can a Jew reach the papal throne all by himself? Could you possibly give me a letter that would open the doors of the Vatican and let me come to the feet of His Holiness."

"I would be honored to do so," said the bishop happily. "Not only will I give you a letter, but I'll also write to the Vatican that you are a great chess player. The Holy Father loves to play chess. Believe me, Rabbi, at the chessboard you will have a much greater influence in getting His Holiness to rescind the decree."

The bishop wrote a long letter to the pope in Rome. And handed the letter to Rabbi Simon.

Simon Barbun thanked the bishop on behalf of all the Jews in the ghetto of Frankfort. When he stood up from the chair and was about to take his leave, the bishop held Rabbi Simon's hands for a long time and suddenly asked him whether he had ever heard any news about his lost son.

Rabbi Simon Barbun heaved a deep sigh.

"We never can tell, Rabbi," said the bishop, holding Simon's hands. "The world is huge in its expanse and wondrous in its occurrences. One should never despair. Never stop hoping."

Simon Barbun lowered his head. He thought to himself: What do the Gentiles know about faith?

CHAPTER TWELVE
Simon Barbun and the Three Elders Set Out for Rome

As soon as Simon Barbun came back to the ghetto, he called together the community elders for a meeting. He told them about his conversation with the bishop. They absolutely had to go to Rome immediately and petition the Holy Pontiff himself. And three of the community elders would have to accompany Rabbi Simon. Let it look like a delegation from the Jews of Frankfort. That is what Jews have always done whenever they went to plead with the mighty of the world to rescind a terrible edict.

They drew up a precise account of the expenses. The journey would cost them more than a thousand thalers.

Several rich Jews in the ghetto together contributed the thousand thalers.

Rabbi Simon Barbun proclaimed a general fast. On the evening of the fast, before the Torah was read in the great synagogue, Rabbi Simon gave a long sermon. Both the men's and the women's sections were packed. A crowded mass of Jews. The huge candles were melting. The rabbi spoke words of reproof. The men wept. The sobbing of women could be heard from the balcony.

The day after the fast, Rabbi Simon and three of the community elders set out on the long journey to the Vatican in Rome.

CHAPTER THIRTEEN
They Travel Through the Jewish Communities

The journey from Frankfort on the Main to Rome took many weeks.

The Jewish communities through which Rabbi Simon and the three elders passed were all atremble. Jews everywhere had heard about the terrible papal decree expelling the holy community of Frankfort on the Main. The Jews were sighing. The rabbi and the three elders were received with great reverence in all the ghettos. In their honor, the Jews recited psalms and liturgies in synagogues, so that the Good Lord would take pity on the children of Israel in Frankfort on the Main.

And thus, traveling through the many communities, the four Jews at last arrived at the gates of Rome.

CHAPTER FOURTEEN
Four Jews in Pointed Jewish Hats on the Streets of Rome

When a Jew sees a cross, he knows what's in store for him.

When the four Frankfort Jews walked through the streets of Rome, they were filled with dread. Rome looked like an everlasting Holy Thursday. It was right after Easter. The warm blue heavens resounded with prayers. The streets were dark with the cassocks of thousands of priests. Amid the black cassocks were the burning scarlet gowns of cardinals. Barefoot monks walked by. Their heads were shaven. Their loins girded with rope. There were processions everywhere. The people were carrying holy images of gold and marble. Babbling prayers. Amid the bustle of cassocks and processions, they could see rich carriages. Inside them sat great beauties dressed in splendor and luxury. Later, the elders of Frankfort discovered that the beautiful women in the carriages were well-known Roman courtesans and hetaerae. Many of them were the mistresses of high-ranking cardinals and even had great influence in the Vatican.

The four Jews in their pointed Jewish hats felt like specks of dust in raging winds. From all sides they could feel gazes of hate and scorn.

The Frankfort Jews just barely pushed their way to the ghetto of Rome. They didn't breathe freely until they found themselves among Jews again.

CHAPTER FIFTEEN
How Comely Are Thy Tents, O Jacob!

The Jewish ghetto of Rome lay right by the valley of the Tiber, behind the ruins of the Roman Empire, near the remains of an ancient Roman arena, the Circus Maximus. In the time of the Destruction of Jerusalem, huge mobs of Romans came here to watch the games of gladiators and the fights between men and beasts. The ghetto wasn't far from the Capitol (the Roman mountain of the gods), the ruins of the Forum Romanum, and the Arch of Titus, on which there was engraved for all time Titus' triumphal procession with the holy vessels from the Temple of Jerusalem and the last captive Mourners of Zion.

Roman Jews never pass through this gate.

The Jewish ghetto of Rome was like a living fragment of Titus' Arch of Triumph. If Rome was known as the Gateway to the World, then the Jewish ghetto was the mournful spot on the victorious Gateway.

From the vast splendor and luxury of the processions with crucifixes, burning candles, and babbling prayers on the streets of Rome, the Frankfort Jews came into the ghetto as into the ramshackle booths of the tents of Jacob. They thought to themselves: How comely are thy tents, O Jacob! The world is truly large. Strange. Mighty. But we see our own Jews everywhere, thank goodness!

Again they found the same eternal darknesses as in the ghetto of Frankfort on the Main. The streets were filled with pale, shabby men and women. Again they found the heaps of strange junk lying about everywhere, wandering from Christian Rome into the Jewish ghetto. Jews were arranging Christian bygones, mending them, and doing business with them.

There was only one thing that came as a great surprise to the four Jews of Frankfort.

Inside the ghetto walls, by the entrance, not far from the deserted ruins of the Circus Maximus, there stood a small white Christian house of worship. No bell rang in its tower. Its doors were closed. No one was babbling prayers in it. There were no processions around it, and no one carrying gods of marble and gold. The powerful Catholic deities had abandoned it. It stood mournful and sinister among the Jews. The temple had somehow strayed here into the darkness of Jewish exile. Around it walked the pale, shabby Jews, carrying bundles of Christian bygones.

A pagan temple among Jews? The four visitors from Frankfort were deeply amazed.

"Look, Rabbi," said Zalman-Ziskind the community elder, pointing his finger.

Under the black cross of the church, a marble tablet was nailed to the wall. It bore the following verse in Hebrew from the book of Isaiah:

"I have spread out my hands all the day unto a rebellious people, which walketh in a way that was not good, after their own thoughts."

CHAPTER SIXTEEN
Looking for a Solution
Jews Stop Up Their Ears and Converse in Sign Language

Simon Barbun and the three elders of Frankfort immediately went to the rabbi of Rome, Sampson Froscati. He lived right next to the synagogue.

Rabbi Froscati had already heard about the edict of expulsion. There were no telegraphs in those days, but Jewish troubles were carried by the winds on the rooftops above or the vagabonds and beggars below as they strode through all the Jewish communities in the world. Tramps and wanderers brought news to and from Jews.

The rabbi of Rome greeted the visitors with a cheerful face and bitter sighs. The visitors were also sighing. There was no need to ask any questions. Everything, alas, was fully obvious.

"I never realized," sighed Rabbi Sampson Froscati, "that the pope was such an enemy of the Jews. On the contrary: Here in Rome, he has always left us in peace—thank goodness."

Rabbi Froscati said that the elders of the holy community of Rome would soon be here. They would then think about what they could do and figure out which of the cardinals could be bribed to let the Jews into the Vatican, so that they could deliver the bishop's letter to the pope and try to get him to rescind his edict.

Meanwhile the Jews slowly appeared to forget about their troubles. Rabbi Sampson Froscati and Rabbi Simon Barbun launched into a brilliant discussion full of new interpretations of the Torah.

A pitched battle unrolled between two knights of the Torah, who had come from remote corners of the Jewish exile and met in the ancient city of Rome. The arrows of their casuistry whizzed through the air. The spears of speculation. It almost appeared as if the two debating Jews had forgotten (God forbid) the reason why they had come together here, had forgotten that it was of the essence to find some strategy for reaching the Vatican.

The knights of the Torah didn't quiet down until the elders of

Rome arrived, greeted the visitors from Frankfort, and began to think of solutions.

Solomon ibn Eter, a pure Sephardi and the chief elder of the Roman community, started listing the names of cardinals who could be approached with a tidy sum. He even included the names of famous Roman courtesans. They had an influence on powerful cardinals. Money could accomplish a great deal. Rabbi Simon listened. During the conversation, Solomon ibn Eter mentioned that they would have to find a good interpreter who could speak Latin, so that he might accompany the Frankfort Rabbi into the Vatican. "Latin is the only tongue spoken in the Vatican," he said.

"You don't have to worry about that," said Rabbi Simon. "I can speak Church Latin just like one of them."

Several hours of talking elapsed. Evening came on. The men said the evening prayers.

Then the community elder Solomon ibn Eter exclaimed to the town rabbi Sampson Froscati, "We have to go to *that place* today, Rabbi."

The rabbi of Rome heaved a deep sigh and told Simon Barbun a dreadful story:

"Ages ago, when the Christians set the Jews here apart and secluded them by the Tiber, they also erected an abomination by the gates of the ghetto. It is locked up all month long. But once every month, on a Wednesday evening, it opens like a doorway to the netherworld. All the Jews have to go inside and listen to a Christian cleric who tries to seduce them and dissuade them from the living God. The papal sbirri come with whips in their hands and search all the homes to make sure that not a single Jew has hidden rather than going to the sermon."

Rabbi Simon trembled. He lowered his head, and his heart was silent. He felt sorry for the Roman Jews, the poor wretches, who didn't have the strength to sacrifice themselves for the glory of God.

Rabbi Sampson Froscati must have sensed what Simon was thinking, for he went on:

"Jews, thank the Lord, are a stiff-necked people. They manage to find ways of not going astray from the One God. All the men and women, young and old, who have to go to that terrible place and hear the clergyman speak, put pieces of cloth into their ears and become stone-deaf. Not the tiniest smidgen of a priestly word ever reaches a Jewish ear—heaven forbid!"

That very instant, the rabbi's wife Esperanza walked in with a large tray. There were little bits of cloth lying on it. All the Jews put cloth into their ears. Rabbi Sampson Froscati showed Rabbi Simon and the three elders of Frankfort how to stop up their ears with the cloth. Because foreign Jews who happened to be visiting the ghetto also had to attend the pagan house of worship.

The Jews couldn't speak. No one could hear anyone else's voice. All further conversation was carried on with the fingers.

CHAPTER SEVENTEEN
The Cleric Speaks to Deaf Jews

When the rabbis and elders of Frankfort and Rome came outside, the streets were full of shabby men and women. It was already well into evening. Here and there, an oil lamp was burning on a wall. The darknesses were dimly lit.

Rabbi Simon saw that all the Jews were going the same way. All waggling their fingers. Conversing in sign language.

"A dear stiff-necked people," Rabbi Simon Barbun thought in the deafness of his ears.

They were approaching the white temple at the gates of the ghetto. The doors were wide open. A wan light came from within.

When they stepped indoors, the place was already filled with Jews. All of them were waggling their fingers. Talking in sign language.

None of the clerics had as yet arrived. Two white tapers were burning on the "altar." Between them, a high black crucifix was visible behind the altar. A figure hung down the full length of the cross. He looked like a scrawny, melancholy Jew. He was stark naked. He had a small thin beard. His eyes were glassy. His head was twisted to one side and it bore a cap of thorns. Above the cap, on a small board, there were several words written in black Hebrew letters: *THE KING OF THE JEWS.*

That poor starving King of the Jews stared vaguely with his glassy eyes and smiled vaguely and bitterly at the shabby men and women sitting in the musty darkness of the church—and conversing in sign language.

Before long, a barefoot monk stepped up to the altar. His head was clean-shaven and he had a rope around his loins. His face was fat and full. His belly was dangling in his robe.

He began to talk. The Jews sat there with stuffed ears. None of them heard him. They could only see his eyes sparkle. He raised his fists and threatened the deaf Jews. They stared at him in silence. Behind him, on the cross, hung the naked, tortured Jew with the cap of thorns on his head. The King of the Jews likewise stared in silence. Whenever the monk raised his fists and threatened, he looked as if he weren't just threatening the Jews in the darkness of the church, but also the Jesus hanging behind his head.

The monk on the altar screamed. The Jews in the darkness stared at him, deaf. A few dozed off.

Upon leaving the church, the crowd of men and women took the pieces of cloth out of their ears. They could hear again.

On the way home, Rabbi Simon Barbun and Rabbi Sampson Froscati launched into sharp and dazzling casuistry on the laws concerning idol worship.

CHAPTER EIGHTEEN
The Courtesan Imperia

Early the next day, the Roman community elder, Solomon ibn Eter, began petitioning cardinals he knew to find some way of obtaining a papal audience for Rabbi Simon.

At that time there lived in Rome a world-renowned courtesan named Imperia. Cardinals and bishops lay at her feet. She drove about in a golden coach. Her palace was as beautiful as the most beautiful palaces in Rome. The greatest men danced attendance at her doors. Begged for a glance.

Jews in those days were no experts in feminine beauty. But she was the talk of Rome. Whenever Imperia drove by in her golden coach, the way was lined with mobs of Christians. Staring after her. It was said that any cardinal or bishop who sinned with her could not wish for a better paradise in the hereafter. The Christians claimed there were satanic forces in her beauty. A fallen angel must have coupled with her mother.

Solomon ibn Eter knew how to gain access to this courtesan Imperia. He brought her a present, a pair of old and rare earrings—from the precious objects that Jews bought and sold in the ghetto. The courtesan couldn't take her eyes off the beautiful earrings.

She received Solomon ibn Eter in the morning as she sat at a large golden mirror. Her maids were combing her hair. She spoke amiably with the Jew, and he told her about the edict expelling the Jews from Frankfort. Imperia was moved to pity. She promised to do whatever she could to help Rabbi Simon Barbun obtain an audience with the pope.

CHAPTER NINETEEN
Rabbi Simon Barbun Drives Away His Gloomy Thoughts

Every evening, Solomon ibn Eter would come to see Rabbi Simon and tell him what he had managed to accomplish with the dignitaries of the church. Overjoyed, he added: "I can see divine help clearly. I am certain that the edict expelling the Jews from Frankfort will be rescinded." Never in all his years of trying to intercede for the Jews had doors opened so readily for him as this time. The cardinals were simply promising him everything. The Jews were practically at the pope.

Rabbi Simon Barbun raised his eyes to heaven and recited the 102nd Psalm, "a prayer of an afflicted man." In a time of trouble, his lips almost spoke the psalm by themselves. He never doubted for a moment that if the Good Lord was punishing Jews, He was only doing it to prepare them for a grand, radiant day. A human being has to be purged to attain the highest levels. "And if you go through water, I am with you, and if you pass through rivers, they shall not overwhelm you; and if you go through fire, you shall not be burnt and no flame shall singe you." Simon Barbun was positive that Jews were borne by a great mercy.

But what about his own wound, which had never closed? When had God shown mercy to him, to Rabbi Simon Barbun?

The rabbi sighed amid the great joy of the tiding that everything would turn out well for the Jews of Frankfort.

He drove away the gloomy thoughts about his own fate. And he spoke the evening prayers with great fervor.

CHAPTER TWENTY
Jews in Pointed Jewish Hats Walk Through Papal Rome

Before long, Solomon Ibn Eter came to Rabbi Simon Barbun and told him to prepare for the papal audience. The pope was ready to receive the Jewish delegation from Frankfort on the Main.

The day before the audience, the Frankfort Jews fasted and recited the proper prayers.

Only the three elders of Frankfort with Rabbi Simon Barbun at their head went to the Vatican. The elder of Rome, Solomon ibn Eter, accompanied them to the gates of the Vatican. There he was supposed to turn them over to a priest, who would take them to the pope. He would then have to wait outside—until they came back safe and sound from the Holy See.

They traveled the entire distance on foot. In silence. Solomon ibn Eter led them through many streets and squares. There were churches everywhere. Palaces. Statues. On the squares they saw large and extraordinary fountains of white, red, and black marble. The fountains were populated with a plethora of fantastic stone figures and masks. Some of the figures had human heads—but the bodies of rearing horses or wild buffalo. Columns of water splashed aloft in all kinds of shapes. It looked like a thicket of water. And all the stone creatures and masks had water gushing and pouring out of their faces as though they were yelling and roaring with watery voices.

The pale Jews in the pointed Jewish hats looked like terrified strangers in the world of palaces, churches, and marble fountains. A world in which even the stones were laughing and enjoying themselves with a lusty and rutting pleasure.

They arrived at the shore of that stretch of the Tiber which separates the Vatican from the city of Rome. Here, Solomon ibn Eter lifted his finger and pointed at a round gray tower. The black maws of cannon were glaring down from it. Guards holding halberds were striding up and down.

"That is the tomb of Adrian the Evil," said Solomon ibn Eter.

The heads with the pointed Jewish hats turned up. Gazed at the round tower of the tomb of Adrian the Evil.

CHAPTER TWENTY-ONE
At the Holy See

They soon arrived at Saint Peter's Square in front of the Vatican. It was flooded with sunlight. Rabbi Simon Barbun trembled. Years and years ago, he had seen this very square in the second part of his dream.

Solomon ibn Eter led them through long rows of columns and pillars.

They came to a small gate. In front of it stood a guard of papal lansquenets. They wore yellow velvet and were holding halberds. Solomon ibn Eter called out the name of a cardinal. One of the lansquenets vanished behind the gate. He came back shortly, accompanied by a wan plain priest in a black cassock.

The priest did not greet the Jews. He was rigid. He pointed a finger at the Frankfort delegation.

Rabbi Simon Barbun and the three elders of Frankfort went off with the priest.

He took them along stairways and dark and light corridors. Through rooms that were covered with paintings by the greatest masters. Each room was like a different world. Some of the rooms were rich and prosperous like the dwellings of the most powerful kings on earth. And some were dark and bare—like the Christian afterlife. Candles were burning in high candelabras of gold and marble. And all sorts of oil lamps were burning over wooden and golden crosses—lighting up the faces of all kinds of Jesuses.

At last, the priest stiffly opened a door.

It was a middling room with bare white walls. An oil lamp was burning over a large black crucifix. Near a table that was plated with copper sat the pope.

The pope was dressed in white. Everything on him was white. He wore a white stole on his shoulders and a white skullcap on his head. However, on his feet, he wore scarlet slippers. And on the slippers two golden keys were embroidered.

The four Jews bowed deep.

The pope lifted his head. Gazed at the delegation from Frankfort. He stared at Rabbi Simon Barbun for a long time. At length, he softly asked in Latin:

"What do you wish?"

Simon Barbun was holding the letter from the electoral bishop of Frankfort on the Main. With his head lowered, he approached the white figure on the chair. Handed him the letter.

The Pope tore open the seal and began reading.

He read for a long time. Smiled. Kept raising his eyes. Looked at the Frankfort Jews and most of all at Simon Barbun. Finally, he folded the letter and said:

"Rabbi Simon Barbun, the electoral bishop writes that you are one of the greatest scholars among Jews and also an extraordinary chess player."

Simon Barbun lowered his head.

"A chess player," the pope repeated. "I love to play chess, and I would very much like to challenge you on the chessboard."

Suddenly, the pope turned to the Frankfort Jews and said impatiently:

"You shall receive an answer tomorrow about the expulsion from Frankfort. You may go and wait in one of the rooms outside. But meanwhile your Rabbi Simon Barbun will remain with me. I want to play a round of chess with him."

CHAPTER TWENTY-TWO
Joseph in Egypt

And so, it came as the pope desired. He remained alone with Rabbi Simon. The priest in the black cassock brought in a chess set of old ivory. The figures had the faces of knights and lansquenets. The king and queen were masterpieces of carving.

The pope asked Rabbi Simon to sit down with him at the table, and then he made the first move. Rabbi Simon responded with a move on his part. He forgot who was sitting across from him and became absorbed in the course of battle. He even held his beard suavely. Softly hummed a Sabbath hymn. The movements of the figures became more and more intricate.

Suddenly the pope made a move.

Rabbi Simon Barbun trembled. His hand hung motionless over the chessboard.

"Why aren't you moving, Rabbi Simon?" asked the pope, seemingly nonchalant.

"That last move, Your Holiness," Rabbi Simon spoke faintly, "was very surprising. It's a move unknown to any chess player in the world. The only place you'll find it is in an ancient Hebrew manuscript in my home."

"You've never shown it to anyone, Rabbi Simon?" asked the pope.

Rabbi Simon let out a deep sigh.

"I only revealed it to one person in the world." Simon had tears in his eyes. "That person is no longer among the living. Many, many years have flown by. The wound will not stop bleeding. 'Joseph has been torn to shreds,'" he said almost to himself, in Hebrew. Involuntarily, he withdrew his hand from the chessboard. Remained sitting with a drooping head before the pope.

For a while, there was a hush.

"Joseph has been torn to shreds," the pope suddenly said in Hebrew.

Rabbi Simon shuddered.

"The world is wondrous in its distances and its occurrences," the pope went on in a pure classical Latin. "Perhaps he'll come back to you, your lost son Joseph."

Rabbi Simon began to weep.

The pope abruptly got up from his throne. He fell upon Rabbi Simon's neck and burst into sobs.

"I am your son Joseph," he said in a choked voice.

The call of blood resounded in the old Jew. And he instantly recognized Joseph. He wanted to raise his eyes to heaven and cry out his utter joy. But he gazed at the white pope and the black crucifix hanging on his throat—and the father's lips closed. Joseph was a renegade! The call of paternal blood was drowned by the voice of the ancient people of Israel. A voice pronouncing all the temptations and that wondrous stubbornness that is Jewish history in the world.

"Joseph is a renegade!" he said to himself. "He has deserted the old tents of Jacob!"

Rabbi Simon kept his eyes closed. His lips were as pale as death and locked as if with a thousand locks. Involuntarily, he could only feel them inaudibly whispering the 102nd Psalm: "The prayer of the afflicted man when he is overwhelmed . . . ."

"The second dream has come true," he thought. "Will the third one come true as well?"

The chess game on the table stood like a silent observer amid the great battle.

The pope stood next to the broken Jew and lovingly stroked his hair.

CHAPTER TWENTY-THREE

Joseph Tells His Story

Simon Barbun sat there with his head bowed low. Next to him stood the pope, quietly speaking a plain Yiddish that Jews spoke in the ghetto of Frankfort on the Main. Holding his eyes shut, the rabbi felt as if distant, distant years were present occurrences. He could hear their voices with his eyes.

"It was a hot, putrid day, and I went to bathe," Rabbi Simon Barbun heard Joseph's voice: "You sent a servant to accompany me. I didn't know my way around the edge of the city. The servant took me into a narrow street between two gray churches, which were both closed. He went up to a small door. Yanked a rope. The door opened. Out came a nun's head.

"It took only a second. Several powerful hands dragged me inside the church. The door slammed shut behind me. I was surrounded by a strange silence. There was no one in sight. I looked around. I was in a small rectangular courtyard which was lined with columns. In the middle of the courtyard there was a stone well with a chain hanging from it. There were several pigeons perched on the lip of the well.

"I sat down next to the well. And began weeping.

"I wept and wept until at last I fell asleep.

"When I awoke, I found myself in a small monastic cell. The walls were white and bare. The only furnishings were a hard bed, a wooden table, and a hard bench. The only lifelike thing in the cell was the crucified figure on the black cross. They soon brought me some food and drink. I didn't want to eat any forbidden food, and so I lived on bread and water. I was afraid to lie on the bed, the blanket might be a mixture of linen and wool. I slept on the cold stone floor of the cell.

"Gradually they began talking to me. They praised my great abilities. They said it was too bad that I would have to squander them among Jews. I could some day become world-famous. What would I become among Jews? A junk dealer with a pointed Jewish hat or possibly a rabbi. The words slowly fell on me like drops of water on a stone. My ears began to open to the glory of this world, and also to my Jewish abjectness. I had a choice to make. I slowly began to waver. What were Jews? An everlasting darkness. An everlasting game with temptations. What would become of this bloody Jewish game? Who can say? Here, a free and radiant morning was beckoning to me from the window of the monastery.

"I saw two ladders before me. One ladder led to honor, glory. A power to which all nations bow and are subject like a flock of lambs. The second ladder—it also led somewhere. The Jews of Frankfort were climbing it. The shabby tattered Jews with sacks of junk on their shoulders and with pointed Jewish hats on their heads. And the nations of the world were also standing under that second ladder, which the Jews were climbing. But they weren't like lambs, they were like wild lions and leopards, screaming for blood, ready to tear their victims apart.

"I slowly began to delve into the Christian books. To listen to the conversations of the priests. My ears opened. Gradually, I forgot the ghetto of Frankfort and its darknesses. I started out on the path of success and worldly power.

Fortune carried me on its wings. I rapidly climbed higher and higher. Now I sit on the throne of the highest power in the world. The nations bow before me."

CHAPTER TWENTY-FOUR
Rabbi Simon's Lips Are Sealed With a Thousand Locks

Rabbi Simon Barbun was still sitting there with a lowered head and closed eyes. His heart was being torn to bits in a storm of contradictory feelings. He wanted to stretch out his arms and fling them around Joseph. Burst into tears and forgive him for everything. A human being is just a weak creature, he thought, the Lord is a gracious and compassionate God. But then—everything within him shouted: Run, Simon! What is a Jew without temptations? A mote of dust in the winds. How comely are thy tents, O Jacob! A Jew who cannot bow his head and wait in the darknesses—he is a tree that shall not flourish on the last day of the world. The day of doom and justice. Your Joseph is a renegade. Stop up your ears, Si-

mon, like the Jews you saw in the Roman ghetto. What is a Jew
without great trials?

He felt Joseph's hands upon him. They were lovingly stroking
his hair. He shut his eyes tighter and lowered his head deeper and
deeper.

Simon Barbun's lips were sealed with a thousand locks. After
long inward struggles and torments he barely managed to ask, almost at random:

"What will happen with the Jews in Frankfort on the Main?"

"Not a hair on their heads shall be touched. The whole edict was
merely a trick to make you come to Rome and talk to me."

A broken man, with his eyes shut, Rabbi Simon Barbun got up
from the chair. His hands trembling, he groped the air like a blind
man. He himself didn't know whether his arms were seeking his
Joseph, or the door through which he could escape from his inner
tortures and once again forget everything.

The pope stopped speaking. Rabbi Simon felt someone gently
leading him from the room. The door closed softly behind him.

When Simon Barbun opened his eyes, he saw the three elders of
Frankfort before him. Because of the rabbi's palor, the Jews
thought he had not succeeded in getting the pope to rescind the
decree. They too turned deathly pale, and their eyes filled with
tears.

"Everything is all right, the Lord be praised! The decree has been
revoked," said Rabbi Simon Barbun with feigned self-assurance.

The Jews asked no other questions. Silently they left the Vatican.
Outside, Solomon ibn Eter was waiting for them. The five Jews
walked back to the ghetto.

CHAPTER TWENTY-FIVE
Rejoicing in the Jewish Communities

Before the five Jews even reached the ghetto on foot, a special
papal messenger had galloped to the Roman Rabbi Sampson Froscati and handed him a sealed document from the papal chancelry,
declaring the expulsion of the Jews from Frankfort on the Main
null and void. The glad tiding quickly spread through the ghetto.
One can imagine the rejoicing. When the five Jews walked through

the gates of the ghetto, Jews were standing near the white closed church, raising their arms to herald the good news.

Simon Barbun joined in with the rejoicing of the Jews. But in his heart, the storm was still raging.

The next day, the Frankfort delegation started back home. The Roman Jews took a fond farewell of them and wished them all the luck in the world. The same rejoicing prevailed in all the ghettos through which the delegation passed. And thus they gradually made their way back to Frankfort on the Main.

CHAPTER TWENTY-SIX
In a Stormy Night

In the Jewish darknesses of Frankfort on the Main, the Jews went back to their old clothes and moneylending.

Rabbi Simon Barbun withdrew more and more into seclusion. The Jews were surprised that he also gave up the one worldly delight he had enjoyed: chess. He no longer wanted to sit down at the chessboard with anyone.

They could see the lamp burning in his library all through the night. People wondered when he slept. On very quiet nights, they could even hear him murmuring like a mournful dove. It was said that he was absorbed in the Cabbalah and was preparing to leave Frankfort and go to Safad in the Holy Land—to stretch out and pray on the sacred tombs and wait for the last day of his life among the great Cabbalists of Safad.

And then one stormy night—

Rabbi Simon Barbun was sitting on the ground with ashes on his head. Reciting the midnight prayers in memory of the destruction of Jerusalem and for the restoration of Israel. All at once, a violent gale swept up outside. Thunder boomed fearfully. The darknesses were shredded by sharp, penetrating lightning. The storm grew worse from minute to minute. Peals of thunder, bolts of lightning. Wild gales roared through the night. Every so often, a crack of lightning would illuminate Simon Barbun's window as though someone were peering through it.

Then a torrent came down.

Rabbi Simon Barbun silently kept his eyes shut and wept over the destruction of Jerusalem.

In the midst of the storm, he heard a knocking at his door.

"Probably a poor wayfarer looking for shelter in this deluge," thought Simon Barbun to himself.

He stood up from the mourning chair and went to open the door.

A strange vagabond, in rags and tatters, was standing at the threshold, a sack on his shoulders.

Thunder crashed. A jagged flash of lightning lit up the darkness and the face of the strange vagabond.

Rabbi Simon Barbun shuddered. In the sharply illuminated storm, he saw, standing before him, his own son Joseph.

Simon Barbun put his finger to his lips. He took his son Joseph's hand. Made him sit down next to him on the floor.

The storm outside grew stronger. The darknesses were shredded by bright jagged lightning.

Rabbi Simon Barbun spoke the 102nd Psalm, the prayer of the afflicted man, as he stroked the head of the strange vagabond, his prodigal son Joseph.

MOYSHE KULBAK

The Wind Who Lost
His Temper

The old wind dragged wearily over the snowy fields. He had been
through many towns and villages without resting anywhere. He
passed over all the rooftops, knocking his long, cold fingers on the
windowpanes and whistling in the chimneys.

But then a sudden thaw came to the towns, and the wind barely
managed to climb out of a chimney where he was lying and singing. He made a narrow escape into the meadows.

The snow sparkled white in the fields, the sky was blue, and the
worn-out wind passed on, seeking a place to rest. All at once, he
caught sight of an oak tree looming on the far horizon by the edge
of the meadow.

The wind thought to himself: "I'll lie down and rest under that
oak tree." And barely managing to reach it, he collapsed exhausted
under the leaves.

He lay there, the wind, and his eyes closed from fatigue, and just
when he was about to fall asleep, he suddenly heard the oak snap
into the air with a gruff voice: "What kind of strange creature has
gone to bed down there? The cold is cutting to the very tips of my
roots."

The wind replied:

"Don't be so cruel, dear oak tree! I'm an old wind, a vagabond. I
wanted to spend the winter in the towns, but there was a sudden

thaw. I had such a hard time breathing that I just barely managed to escape into the meadows."

The oak tree said in a more mellow tone:

"Dear wind, my heart isn't doing so well. This very winter, I remained bare, my branches were all leafless, and if I hadn't kept my roots in the earth, who can tell whether I would have survived till spring. Dear wind, please go a bit farther. You'll find a rock by the side of the road. You can sit down on him and rest."

So the old wind got up and set out to find the rock.

He went on and on until, by the side of the road, he spied the rock, huge and mute. He sat down on it, tucked his hands in his sleeves, and was about to doze off. But the rock felt someone sitting on his back, and let out a deep grumble:

"Who's there?"

The wind replied: "I am."

The rock asked: "Who is 'I'?"

The wind answered: "I, an old wind, a vagabond. I wanted to spend the winter in the towns, but there was a sudden thaw. And I had such a hard time breathing that I fled into the meadows. I wanted to lie down under an oak tree, but the oak tree said I was too much weight on his roots, and his roots are as dear as life to him."

"Roots? Who gives two hoots about roots!" The rock was a nasty creature and he cut him off in the middle. "If you want to sit down on somebody, you ought to ask permission first. You can't just throw yourself down like that! I'm cold and dry inside too, I'm on the point of bursting. And now you come along and jump on top of me! Have you ever heard of such a thing!"

The rock hated anybody that could move and the wind didn't realize this.

What was the wind to do? He went on. Meanwhile evening had come. The sun had set. In the west, something kindled, like a great fire. The white snow turned rosy, and white, pink, and blue snowflakes were glittering on all the fields.

The wind wandered along the road for what must have been an hour, and by now he was totally feeble. But then he sighted a large inn with a large red porch. The wind's eyes were all aglow. But he was afraid to sit down on the porch without asking first. He thought to himself: "I'll ask the innkeeper if I can rest on his porch." And he went to the door and knocked.

"Innkeeper!"

There was no answer, and so the wind pleaded in a tearful voice: "Innkeeper!"

Again there was no answer. The innkeeper was lying asleep on the stove. After all, the peasants always go to the market in town on Mondays, and today was Tuesday, so the innkeeper had thought to himself: "Since no one ever comes on a Tuesday anyway, I'll just lie down on the stove and go to sleep."

The wind slowly opened the door and stuck his head into the house. He wanted to see what was inside.

But now a cold draft blew under the innkeeper's collar. Furious, he leaped down from the stove and yelled:

"Oh my goodness! A draft! The door is open!"

The wind barely pulled his head out of the door, he ran breathlessly down the road, while the innkeeper yelled and cursed behind him.

The wind lost his temper at the whole world. No one would let him rest when he felt bad. He stopped, just like a giant, in the middle of the field, rolled up his sleeves, girded his loins, and, in his misery, began blowing with all his might. The snow rose up from the earth and, like silvery flour, started pouring back down upon the earth . . . .

The wind kept blowing with all his might. Then he started whistling, blowing and whistling, whistling and blowing. There was a snowstorm and a blizzard, a whistling, a moaning. And the snow whirled and raged, like white towels flying through the air. And the wind began to weep. He wept like a little child, without stopping. Then he began howling like a dog, and howled and poured snow, and yelled, and there came a darkness, and all that was visible was the white snowflakes. And the white snowflakes poured through the darkness, poured from the sky to the earth and from the earth to the sky. And the wind began meowing, weeping, meowing and weeping, like cats in the dark of night. And a great blizzard came. The wind covered all the roads with snow. The draymen driving along the roads had to rein in their horses. They couldn't see the way. Standing by their wagons of goods, they hopped up and down and slapped their hands under their armpits, amazed at the blizzard:

"What a tempest!"

"What a whirlwind!"

"There's never been such a snowstorm!"

Around the towns and villages, the mountains were covered with snow. Dogs stood by their dens, stretching their necks and howling. Everywhere, the people closed their shutters, locked and bolted their doors. But the wind banged in the doorposts, he stopped at the chimneys and wept so that the whole world might hear. People couldn't fall asleep in their beds, and even the adults didn't know what to do.

Now somewhere, in a poor house at the edge of the town, there lived a poor woman with two children. The wind covered the entire little house with snow. The children snuggled in with their mother. They were terrified at the wind. The mother stroked their hair and tried to lull them to sleep. But the wind banged on the windows and wouldn't allow the children to go to sleep.

"Mother, please ask the wind not to bang so loud on the windows!"

The wind stood behind the wall. He heard what the children had asked the mother. His heart bled. But the good wind had lost his temper at the world.

"Mother, please ask the wind not to weep so loud in the chimney."

The wind wept even harder. He was grief-stricken at spending all his life like a dog, always on the outside, with little children afraid of him.

"Mother, please ask the wind not to lose his temper!"

The mother quickly put on her kerchief and opened the door. It was dark outside. She stood at the threshold and spoke into the darkness:

"Wind, wind, please don't lose your temper!"

The wind wouldn't listen. He only got angrier and blasted a whole pile of snow into the mother's face. The mother wiped the snow from her face and told the wind a second time:

"Wind, good wind, just look at what you're doing!"

Again the wind wouldn't listen. But he didn't blast any snow into her face.

This time the mother addressed the wind with tears in her eyes:

"Wind, dear wind, just think of the little children!"

The wind quieted down. The snow gradually stopped falling. Behind the corners of the house, there still could be heard a stifled weeping, softer and softer, until it stopped altogether.

The wind had made up with the world.

The next day, all the boys pulled their hats down over their ears, put on thick mittens, picked up shovels, and cleared away the snow that was blocking all the doors.

The Golem
or
The Miraculous Deeds
of Rabbi Liva

An historical description of the great wonders that the
world-renowned *gaon*, Rabbi Liva of Prague, performed
with the golem, which he created to wage war against the
Blood Libel.

Foreword

Dear readers! I am giving you a rare and precious treasure, which
has hitherto been lying in a library for three hundred years. Jews
have always been thinking and talking about this treasure, and some
have actually come to deny the whole story, claiming that Rabbi
Liva never even created a golem, that the tale is fictitious, a mere
legend. The truth of the matter is that when the great scholar
Rabbi Ezekiel Landau was rabbi of Prague, he did, in fact, confirm
that the golem was lying in the attic of the old great synagogue.
The day he found the golem, the rabbi fasted and took his ablutions
in the ritual bath. Then, donning his prayer shawl and phylacteries,
he asked ten of his disciples to recite psalms for him in the
synagogue, whereupon he mounted to the attic of the old great
synagogue.

The rabbi lingered there for a long while and then returned in great terror, saying that from now on he would reinforce Rabbi Liva's decree forbidding anyone from venturing to go up there. Thus it once again became known that the story of the golem is true.

But then several decades went by, and a number of people once again began saying that the story is merely a legend. This happens, of course, because there is no precise account of the whole story in Jewish history books. But truth will out. And thus you see that the entire story was written down by Rabbi Liva's son-in-law, that great scholar Rabbi Isaac (a true priest, blessed be the memory of that righteous man). However, the manuscript lay hidden for so many years in the great library of Mainz, where so many of Rabbi Liva's writings can be found. I had to devote a great deal of labor and expense to having this manuscript printed. And thus I hope that every intelligent person will be grateful to me for my work, and I am certain that every Jew will soon give this valuable treasure a place on his bookshelf.

—Yudl Rosenberg

The Birth of Rabbi Liva

Rabbi Liva was born in the city of Worms in Germany, in the year 5273 [or, according to the Christian calendar, 1513], on Passover evening during the seder. His father Rabbi Bezalel (blessed be the memory of that righteous man) was a great saint.

Right after Liva's birth, the Jews were saved from a great disaster. Christians were persecuting the Jews, claiming they used Christian blood to bake unleavened bread at Passover. And almost no Passover went by in the lands of Moravia, Bohemia, Hungary, and Spain without someone smuggling a dead Christian into the home of a wealthy Jew so that he might be falsely accused of committing murder for religious reasons. And thus, for that Passover in Worms, a Blood Libel had been prepared.

A Christian put a dead Christian child into a sack and set out with it, intending to plant the corpse in Rabbi Bezalel's home by throwing it through a basement window. Bezalel's wife was in her seventh month. Sitting at the seder that first night of Passover, she suddenly felt sharp pangs. The others in the house began shrieking and they dashed out to find a midwife.

At this point, the Christian with the dead child in his sack wasn't very far away, and when he saw all those people running toward him with a yell, he was convinced they were after him, and he turned and took to his heels. He was so terrified that he dashed toward the Jewish district, past a police station. The police, seeing a man race by with a sack over his shoulders and a crowd running after him, thought he was a thief being chased. They stopped him and found the dead child in the sack. The Christian had to confess and name the people who had hired him to plant the corpse for a Blood Libel.

Rabbi Liva was born that very same moment, and his father prophesied: "This child will comfort us and ward off the Blood Libel." And he was named Judah Liva, the Lion, for he would be like a lion who does not permit his cubs to be mangled.

The Wondrous Story of Rabbi Liva's Betrothal

In the city of Worms, there lived a Jew named Shmelke Reich, a wealthy and honored man from a fine family. When Rabbi Liva was fifteen, Shmelke Reich took him as a prospective bridegroom for his daughter Pearl. The future father-in-law sent the youth to the yeshivah of Przemysl to study with a *gaon*.

But then Shmelke Reich lost all his wealth and was unable to provide a wedding or a dowry for his daughter.

When Rabbi Liva turned eighteen, Shmelke Reich wrote him a letter saying that the sages maintain eighteen is the right time to marry, but since he, Shmelke Reich, had lost all his wealth and was in no position to keep his promises, he didn't want to hold the youth to the engagement contract. They were willing to release him so that he might find another bride, whomever he wished.

Rabbi Liva sent back the following answer to his future father-in-law: He, for his part, was unwilling to break his word, he agreed to wait and look forward to help from the Lord God. So if Shmelke Reich wanted to cancel the contract, he ought first to find another match for his daughter, and then he, Liva, would know that he was released from his vows.

But unfortunately, Shmelke Reich's business affairs didn't get any better, on the contrary, he kept losing more and more money.

When Pearl, the bride-to-be, saw how unhappy her father was because of his livelihood, she rented a tiny store and began selling bread and baked goods to help out her parents. She thus burdened her youth for some ten years. And Liva likewise didn't want any other betrothal, and he spent those ten years studying the Torah and the Talmud, day and night. And because he was a bachelor, people nicknamed him Liva the Bachelor. And the *gaon* used to say that a verse from the Psalms had come true with Liva the Bachelor. For Liva's soul had a spark of King David.

Now this is what happened with the betrothal:

At the time, the country was in a state of war, and many soldiers were passing through Worms. These soldiers were followed by a cavalrist, and as he rode past the little store where Pearl was sitting with her baked goods he speared up a large loaf of bread on the end of his pike and then seized the bread.

The young girl ran out to the horseman and tearfully begged him not to rob her for she was just a poor girl trying to support her old, weak parents. The horseman shouted: "How can I help you? I don't have any money to pay you, but I'm famished for a piece of bread. There's only one thing I can do for you. Since I'm sitting on a double saddle, I'll give you one saddle for the bread."

And with these words, he pulled out a saddle from under himself, hurled it into the store, and then galloped away.

When the young bride went to have a look at the saddle, she was terribly frightened at seeing that the saddle had burst on one side and several golden ducats had fallen out. She realized that the saddle was stuffed with ducats. With a great deal of effort she managed to lift up the saddle and hide it. Then she hurried to tell the news to her parents. Her father wrote to Rabbi Liva, asking him to come for the wedding, for the Good Lord had miraculously helped him, and now he was in a position to pay for everything and to give the wedding in great honor, as was fitting for him.

Rabbi Liva used to tell this story whenever he had to settle a case concerning a prospective father-in-law who was unable to pay in accordance with a betrothal contract. The rabbi never liked to get involved in such cases. But if it happened that the rabbi couldn't get the two parties to agree on the marriage, he would send them to his assistant judges, so that they could settle the case in their homes but not in Rabbi Liva's house.

Rabbi Liva's Struggle Against the Blood Libel

Rabbi Liva moved from Posen to Prague in the year 5333 [1572, by Christian reckoning]. He was famous throughout the world for being wise and learned in all branches of knowledge, and for speaking many languages. Because of this, he was very popular among Gentiles too, and greatly respected by King Rudolf of Hapsburg. He was thus able to fight against the enemies of the Jews, who besmirched Jewish honor with the Blood Libel. He finally conquered them, and King Rudolf promised him he would permit no more Blood Libels against Jews in his lands.

When Rabbi Liva first arrived in Prague, the Blood Libel was making life very difficult for the Jews, and much innocent Jewish blood had already been shed because of that foul accusation. Rabbi Liva proclaimed he would struggle with all his might against the Blood Libel and rid the Jews forever of that foul accusation.

Rabbi Liva Engages in a Disputation with the Catholic Priests

Rabbi Liva immediately wrote a petition to Cardinal Jan Sylvester, requesting that he be summoned for a disputation to prove the falsity of the Blood Libel against Jews. The cardinal did not wait to be asked twice. He called together three hundred great priests for the debate. The rabbi informed him that he could not possibly debate with three hundred priests at one time. He asked that the debate last for thirty days, and that ten new priests every day submit their arguments and questions in writing to the cardinal. He, Rabbi Liva, would then come to the cardinal to examine their submissions and reply to them in writing.

The cardinal agreed. At every dawn of those thirty days and in every synagogue, the Jews of Prague recited the entire Book of Psalms, and they fasted on Mondays and Thursdays.

The Disputation

The disputation produced so many questions about Judaism and Christianity that they filled an entire history book. The major controversy turned around the following five questions:

1. Is it true that Jews need Christian blood for Passover?
2. Are the Jews guilty of the murder of "Christ"?
3. Does Jewish law require Jews to hate Christians because it regards Christianity as idol-worship?
4. Why do Jews hate a person who converts from Judaism and why do they strive to wipe him off the face of the earth?
5. Why do Jews consider themselves greater than other nations because of their Torah? After all, other nations can be even prouder of being honest and decent, since they haven't been urged to be so with a great and difficult Torah.

In reply to the first question, Rabbi Liva quoted the Bible and the Talmud to demonstrate how greatly Jews regard blood as an unclean thing. Jews are strictly commanded to avoid blood even more than fat, for the Torah calls blood an abomination.

In reply to the second question, Rabbi Liva demonstrated: "Firstly, the only Jews guilty of the murder of Christ were the priests in league with King Herodotus and the Roman government, who ruled Jerusalem at that time, and deeply hated Christ because they feared he wanted to liberate the Jews from the Roman yoke by means of an uprising and have himself crowned King of the Jews. But most of the Jews, particularly the Pharisees and the Essenes, who all despised the priests and Herodotus, refused to have any part in the judgment against Christ.

"Secondly," Rabbi Liva went on, "any man who wishes to take over for God and accuse the Jews of murdering Christ is a true heretic and has no belief whatsoever in God. Let me tell you a parable. An emperor had only one son and that son was condemned to death for rebelling against his father, and his father knew that the accusation was a lie. Now, they were about to carry out the sentence and execute the son before his father's very eyes, and the father only needed to say a single word to have his son set free. But the father refused to interfere and watched them kill his only beloved son gratuitously, merely for his own glory. Who then is more guilty of the murder? The emperor who clearly knew that the accusation was a lie, or the judges who, by virtue of their discernment, felt they had to act for the emperor's glory. Certainly, everyone realizes that, more than anyone else, the emperor was at fault.

"Now, let us examine the story. Christianity says that Christ was God's only beloved son. And the judges falsely accused him of rebellion against his father, the God of all the universe, and gratuitously condemned him to death, only for the glory of God. How could the Father allow them to kill His only beloved child gratuitously, before His very eyes, for His glory? Let us assume further that the Father, God, did not have the power to prevent the execution or else did not know about it. One could only conclude that this Father was not God. Thus, anyone pursuing that course would have to be a complete heretic. But what else can you Christians assume except what Christianity tells you, namely that Christ had to be killed. His death was to atone for the sin of Adam so that anyone accepting Christianity would not suffer in hell, but go straight to heaven. One would therefore have to conclude that those who carried out the sentence of death on Christ did the finest of deeds for Christians and according to the Christian viewpoint this was certainly in fulfillment of God's decree and Christ's good will. So how can anyone accuse the Jews?"

As to the last three questions, Rabbi Liva replied with an ingenious parable:

"Let us closely examine the way an emperor deals with his armed forces. An emperor has, serving under him, generals, colonels, majors, lower officers, and the rank and file. The rank and file have to obey the officers, the officers the majors, the majors the colonels, and so on, but only when the emperor is not present. When the emperor himself visits the army, then everyone, from the bottom to the top, has to show due honor to the emperor alone. And any request that a man may have must be submitted to the emperor personally. If a simple soldier directs his request to an officer before the emperor's eyes, paying tribute to the officer instead of to the emperor, he will be regarded as rebelling against the state and handed over for a court-martial.

"The same is true of the nations. According to Jewish law, we regard as pagans only those nations who do not pray to the One Creator of the universe, who worship and serve the stars and the constellations. Such nations are despised in the Talmud. But those nations who address their prayers to the One Creator of the universe cannot be counted among the pagans, and they are not discussed in the Talmud.

"And as for converts, the Talmud heaps scorn only on Jews who become pagans and no longer believe in the Sole Creator of the entire universe. But a Jew who converts to Christianity isn't even mentioned in the Talmud. However, today, Jews do despise a convert to Christianity, just like an emperor who rules in this world and passes judgment on his armies. His armies consist of different branches. There is an infantry, a cavalry, an artillery, a corps of guards, and a navy. Furthermore, in the great kingdoms, there are various kinds of soldiers who serve from the day they are born. For example, in Russia, the Cossacks, or the Circassians. Now, what happens when a soldier runs away from his company and joins some other branch of the armed forces, serving the same emperor? Isn't he regarded as a criminal? Isn't he punished? And isn't this even more true of the born soldier who tears himself away from his roots, his sources, and joins another branch of the army under the same emperor? He is certainly punished even harder and despised by his brothers.

"The same is true of converts, even if they become Christians rather than idol-worshipers. As a born Jew, who tears himself loose from his roots, he brings shame upon his own brothers, which is why he is hated by Jews and regarded as despicable. And any intelligent man will understand that such hatred is a natural thing, like all natural things. But this is not the same hatred and the same laws that the Talmud directs against the Jew who converts to paganism and denies the existence of the One Creator of the entire universe.

"Now, as for the question of why Jews consider themselves greater than any other nations because of their great Torah and why they say, 'Thou hast chosen us among all the nations.' There is no reason for other nations to feel resentment or envy, or to attack the Jews.

"Let us assume that in an imperial residence there are two regiments of soldiers and the emperor has assigned a great task to one of those regiments, physical labor and mental labor, to keep the soldiers occupied all day long with serving their emperor. The other regiment has been given greater freedom and assigned only light tasks.

"Now one day, the two regiments began arguing. The soldiers with the greater task claimed that they were superior, that the emperor loved them more, and that they were the emperor's guard. A proof of this was that he was willing to entrust his teachings only to them and not to the other regiment. And that was why he gave the other soldiers more freedom, because he did not consider them suitable for and capable of his service and his teachings.

"However, the soldiers in the regiment with greater liberty shouted that the very opposite was true, the emperor loved them more, and they were the emperor's guard. A proof of this was that the emperor was considerate of them and unwilling to overtask them, for he also regarded them as decent and orderly men. But he imposed such enormous work on the other soldiers because he realized that if they were to become better men, decent and orderly soldiers, they would have to devote their entire days to service and study. The judgment reached the minister of war, and he in turn issued an order that this judgment should not be the cause of any discord and rivalry among the soldiers. Each regiment had the right to be proud of its service and to proclaim that the emperor loved it more than the other. In fact, that would make their service more enjoyable. As for the question of which regiment was more beloved by the emperor and was considered the emperor's guard, they could only determine that later, on the basis of two pieces of evidence:

"First, they would see which soldiers the emperor would reward more generously at the end of their service. Second, when the emperor went out into the world, they would see which regiment would have the honor of escorting and surrounding him wherever he went. These soldiers would then certainly be recognized as the emperor's guard.

"Now, it is obvious how that parable applies to Jews and the other nations."

That is a summary of Rabbi Liva's answers to the five questions. And then came twenty-five more questions, Rabbi Liva had a fine answer for each one, and they were all set down in a special tome.

The cardinal was very pleased with the rabbi's answers to the thirty questions, and he heaped great honors upon him. But Tadeus, the renowned priest of Prague, who was a great anti-Semite, still had his heart set on disputing against Rabbi Liva. He argued that there were still a lot of fanatics among Jews who were uneducated and thought that a Jew needed Christian blood for the unleavened bread at Passover. How, then, could Rabbi Liva assume responsibility for all the lower classes of Jews?

Afterward, the entire disputation was presented to King Rudolph. The king was very pleased with the rabbi's responses and issued an order to have Rabbi Liva come to court.

Rabbi Liva Is Presented at the Court of King Rudolph

In Shebat [January], at the new moon, the king sent a carriage to Rabbi Liva, summoning him to court. The rabbi left immediately and was received there with great honor. The audience lasted a full hour, and no one knows what they spoke there. Rabbi Liva came home in a fine mood and said:

"I've managed to destroy more than half of the Blood Libel, and with God's help I hope to remove this foul lie fully from the Jews."

Ten days later, a royal decree was issued: In a trial concerning a Blood Accusation, the tribunal was not to prosecute any outside person, but only those parties whose culpability in the murder could be adduced by proper evidence.

And the king issued a second decree. The rabbi of the city was to be present at any trial concerning a Blood Accusation. And the tribunal's judgment was subsequently to be submitted to the king for his signature.

Jews now began living a bit more freely. But their troubles were not completely over. Whenever a Christian felt any hatred of a Jew, he could plant a dead child in his home. How could the Jew be left free, if the corpse were found on his premises? But most of all, Rabbi Liva feared the priest Tadeus, who was a terrible anti-Semite and a magician as well, and who was bent on waging war against Rabbi Liva and driving him out of Prague altogether. The rabbi told his pupils that he would not ordinarily have been so afraid of the priest. But he, the rabbi, had a spark of King David, and the priest had a spark of the Philistine in Nob, who so relentlessly persecuted King David. The rabbi decided to put all his efforts into battling against the priest, his antagonist.

How Rabbi Liva Created the Golem

Rabbi Liva directed a dream question to determine how to wage war against the priest, his antagonist. And the answer came out alphabetically in Hebrew: "*Ah*, *By* *Clay* *Destroy* *Evil* *Forces*, *Golem*, *Help* *Israel*: *Justice*!" The rabbi said that the ten words formed such a combination that it had the power to create a golem at any time. He then revealed the secret to me, his son-in-law, Isaac ben Sampson Ha-Cohen, and to his foremost pupil, Jacob ben Khaim-Sassoon Ha-Levi. It was the secret of what he had to do, and he told us he would need our help because I was born under the sign of fire, and the pupil Jacob ben Khaim-Sassoon Ha-Levi, was born under the sign of water, and Rabbi Liva himself was born under the sign of air, and the creation of the golem would require all four elements: fire, air, water, and earth. He also told us to keep the matter secret, and informed us seven days ahead of time how we were to act.

In the Jewish year 5340, in the month of Adar, [corresponding to February 1580 in the Christian calendar], all three of us walked out of the city early one morning until we reached the shores of the Moldau River.

There, on a clay bank, we measured out a man three cubits long, and we drew his face in the earth, and his arms and legs, the way a man lies on his back. Then, all three of us stood at the feet of the reclining golem, with our faces to his face, and the rabbi commanded me to circle the golem seven times from the right side to the head, from the head to the left side, and then back to the feet, and he told me the formula to speak as I circled the golem seven times. And when I had done the rabbi's bidding, the golem turned as red as fire. Next, the rabbi commanded his pupil Jacob Sassoon to do the same as I had done, but he revealed different formulas to him. This time, the fiery redness was extinguished, and a vapor arose from the supine figure, which had grown nails and hair. Now, the rabbi walked around the golem seven times with the Torah scrolls, like the circular procession in synagogue at New Year's, and then, in conclusion, all three of us together recited the verse: "And the Lord God formed man of the dust of the ground, and breathed into his nostrils the breath of life; and man became a living soul."

And now the golem opened his eyes and peered at us in amazement.

Rabbi Liva shouted in Hebrew: "Stand on your feet!"

The golem stood up and we dressed him in the garments that we had brought along, the clothes befitting a beadle in a rabbinical household. And at six o'clock in the morning, we started home, four men. On the way, Rabbi Liva said to the golem:

"You have to know that we created you so that you would protect the Jews from harm. Your name is Joseph, and you will be my beadle. You must do everything I command, even if it means jumping into fire or water, until you've carried out my orders precisely."

The golem was unable to speak. But he could hear very well, even from far away.

The rabbi then told us he had named the golem Joseph because he had given him the spirit of Joseph Sheday, who was half man and half demon, and who had helped the Talmudic sages in times of great trouble.

Back home, the rabbi told the household, in regard to the golem, that he had met a mute pauper in the street, a great simpleton, and that he had felt sorry for him and taken him home to help out the beadles. But the rabbi strictly forbade anyone else from ever giving him any orders.

The golem always sat in a corner of the rabbi's courtroom, with his hands folded behind his head, just like a golem, who thinks about nothing at all, and so people started calling him "Joseph the Golem," and a few nicknamed him "Joseph the Mute."

The Golem Carries Water at Passover

Rabbi Liva's wife Pearl, may she rest in peace, was unable to contain herself, and on the day before Passover Eve, she broke her husband's prohibition against giving orders to the golem. She asked him to bring some water from the river and fill up the two kegs standing in a special, festive room. Joseph promptly grabbed the two buckets and hurried down to the banks. But no one watched as he poured the water into the kegs. Joseph the Golem kept bringing back more and more water until the room was flooded up to the threshold. And when the water began pouring into the other rooms through chinks and cracks, the people saw what was happening and raised such a hue and cry that the rabbi, upon hearing it, came running in terror. He now saw what was going on and he smiled at his wife:

"Dear me! You've certainly got yourself a fine water carrier for Passover!"

Then he hurried over to the golem, took the two buckets away from him, and led him back to his place.

From then on, the rabbi's wife took care not to give the golem any orders. The whole incident gave rise to a proverb in Prague: "You know as much about watchmaking as Joseph the Golem about carrying water."

Joseph the Golem Goes Fishing at New Year's

The kind of help that Pearl, the rabbi's wife, got from Joseph the Golem's water-carrying for Passover was the kind that the rabbi got himself when he sent Joseph fishing at Rosh Hashanah [New Year's]. The incident took place several years after the golem was created.

There was a shortage of fish for Rosh Hashanah because of great winds and a cold wave. It was the morning of the day before New Year's, and there wasn't even a minnow in all Prague. Since it is a good deed to have fish on Rosh Hashanah, Rabbi Liva was extremely upset, and so he made up his mind to order the golem to go fishing.

Rabbi Liva told him to bring a net and then go to the river outside the town and catch fish. Since the rabbi's wife didn't have a small bag to give him, she handed him a large sack instead, for holding the fish he would catch. Joseph the Golem paid no heed to the bad weather. He grabbed the equipment and dashed over to the river to catch fish.

Meanwhile, someone brought the rabbi a present, one scant fish from a village near Prague. As a result, they were less concerned about Joseph and his fishing, and they forgot all about him, because on New Year's Eve Jews are usually busy with other matters. Twilight was coming on, and it was time to go to synagogue for evening prayers. The rabbi needed Joseph for something and asked where he was. He was told that the golem hadn't returned from the river yet, and everyone assumed that he still hadn't caught anything and didn't want to come back empty-handed. But since Rabbi Liva needed him urgently, he sent out the other beadle, Abraham-Khaym, to call him home. And in case he hadn't caught any fish and refused to come back, then Abraham-Khaym was to tell him that the rabbi said to forget about the fish and just come home right away.

Abraham-Khaym the beadle left for the river immediately. He arrived at the top of the riverbank and shouted down to Joseph the Golem that it was time to go home. Joseph held up the sack and pointed out that he only had to net a few more fish to fill it up. He motioned that he couldn't start back until the sack was full. Abraham-Khaym shouted down that the rabbi had ordered him to forget about the fish and just return home right away, because the rabbi needed him. The golem, upon hearing these words, grabbed the sack and dumped all the fish back into the river. He slung the net and the sack over his shoulders and ran home. When Abraham-Khaym the beadle returned, he told them what a fine thing Joseph had done! Everyone had a good laugh and Rabbi Liva told us in secret that he now realized the golem was good only for saving Jews from misfortune but not for helping them with good deeds.

What Rabbi Liva Used the Golem For

Rabbi Liva used the golem only for saving Jews from misfortune, and with his help he performed a number of miracles. Most of all, he used him to fight against the Blood Libel which hung over Jews in those times and caused them great difficulties. Whenever the rabbi had to send him to a dangerous place and didn't want him to be seen, he gave him an amulet to make him invisible.

Around Passover, the rabbi would have Joseph the Golem put on a disguise. He gave him Christian clothing to wear, and a rope around his waist. He looked just like the Christian porters.

Rabbi Liva told him to spend each night wandering up and down the streets of the Jewish quarter, and if he saw anyone carrying something or transporting it in a wagon, he should hurry over and see what it was. And if he saw that it was something for bringing a

Blood Accusation against the Jews, he was to tie up the man and
the object and lug them over to the police at city hall to have the
man arrested.

Rabbi Liva's First Miracle With the Golem

There was a wealthy Jew living in Prague, a community leader
named Mordecai Mayzel, who lent money on interest. A Christian
butcher owed him five thousand crowns, and Mordecai Mayzel was
dunning him to repay the debt.

The slaughterhouse was outside the city, and the butcher always
drove the meat into town through the Jewish section. Being unable
to pay back the money, he decided to bring a Blood Accusation
upon Mr. Mayzel, which would keep the moneylender so busy he
would forget about the butcher. A few days before Passover, one
of the butcher's neighbors lost a child and it was buried in the
Christian graveyard. That same night, the butcher dug up the dead
child and killed a hog, taking out its innards. Next, he cut the
child's throat to make it look as if the poor thing had been slaughtered, stuffed the corpse into the dead hog, and then drove to town
in the middle of the night to plant it somewhere in Mordecai
Mayzel's home. He was driving down the street, and just as he
stopped not far from Mr. Mayzel's house, along came Joseph the
Golem. He ran up to the wagon and, upon seeing what it was, he
took his rope and tied the butcher and the hog to the wagon. The
butcher was a strong man; he fought and struggled with the golem,
and tried to break loose. But Joseph wounded him several times and
finally overpowered him, for the golem's strength was greater than
natural force. Joseph climbed into the wagon and drove off to city
hall.

Upon his arrival, a great hubbub began in the courtyard, policemen came, and other people, but meanwhile Joseph the Golem
slipped out of the crowd and returned unmolested to patrol the
Jewish streets.

In the courtyard of city hall, they lit torches and saw before them
the butcher, bloody and maimed. Upon seeking further, they found
the dead child in the belly of the hog. Since it was wrapped in a
Jewish prayer shawl, the butcher couldn't worm his way out, he
had to confess everything he had planned to do to Mordecai

Mayzel. When they asked him who had brought him here against his will, he replied that it had been a mute Christian, who was more like a devil than a human being. The butcher was locked up and sentenced to several years in prison. No one in town knew who that mute Christian could be, and the enemies of the Jews were stricken with fear.

But Tadeus, the renowned priest, knew very well who was behind it, and he began spreading a story that Rabbi Liva was a magician. He hated the rabbi more than ever, and bent his entire heart and soul on a war against Rabbi Liva and all the Jews of Prague.

The Wondrous Tale of the Healer's Daughter

There lived in Prague a Jewish healer named Moritsy. And even though he had strayed far from Judaism, he nevertheless considered himself a Jew. The healer had a daughter, fifteen years old, who became rather licentious and allowed herself to be talked into converting to Christianity. During Passover Week, she ran away from home and took refuge with Tadeus, the famous priest, who was known far and wide as an anti-Semite. This incident was connected with another.

There also lived in Prague a Christian woman from the country who lit the fires in Jewish homes on the Sabbath, and thus she was known to all the Jews in the city. Before Passover, the servant-girl had an argument with her employer and ran away that same night, so that no one knew what had become of her. Her employers did not make a big to-do about it, they assumed she had gone back to the country, but they didn't know for sure where she was from.

Tadeus the priest took advantage of this opportunity. He knew that Rabbi Liva had a strange beadle, Joseph the Mute, who helped him shield the Jews from the Blood Libel. Now the priest was intent on capturing both of Rabbi Liva's beadles, for it would then be easy to get his hands on the rabbi himself.

When the healer's daughter came to his closed church, he made her promise that when the cardinal asked her why she wanted to convert, she would say it was because she couldn't comprehend the ferocious customs of the Jews, who had to kill a Christian soul every Passover and use the blood to bake their unleavened bread. The priest instructed her to bear witness that prior to Passover she had personally seen both of Rabbi Liva's beadles, one of them an old man with a gray beard, and the other a young mute man with a black beard. They had come to her father at night and given him a small flask of blood, and he had paid them well and then used the blood in his unleavened bread. She had been disgusted at the very thought of eating the matzoth, and simply had to run away from home and totally renounce the Jewish faith. The priest also instructed her to say that according to what she had heard, the victim was the heating-woman who had vanished around Purim.

At the baptism, the cardinal did ask the expected question, and the girl answered just as the priest had instructed her. However, she requested them not to bring charges against her father because he had been forced to act upon the wishes of Rabbi Liva, who was highly respected among Jews, and every Jew was afraid to go against his orders.

The things the healer's daughter said made the rounds of the city lightning-fast, and the cardinal had to take down her testimony, even though at heart he cared little for her denunciation. But he could not hush it up because of Father Tadeus. He promptly sent word to Rabbi Liva about the matter so that he might hit upon some way of proving the truth.

Meanwhile, Father Tadeus wrote down the girl's testimony, but in a dreadful way: She claimed that she had witnessed Jews putting blood in the unleavened bread for Passover, that the blood had come from the Christian woman who used to light the stoves for Jews on the Sabbath, and that the men behind it were Rabbi Liva and his two assistants.

When Rabbi Liva heard about this testimony he realized they would come for his two beadles in the middle of the night, which was the way they usually did it. He hit upon a plan. It was clear to him that the convert wasn't really acquainted personally with Joseph the Golem. Now there was no lack of mutes among the vagabonds in Prague, and so the rabbi secretly sent for one who was about the same height as Joseph and had a black beard like his.

As soon as they brought back a man of that description, they concealed Joseph the Golem so that he wouldn't sleep by the stove in the rabbi's courtroom. They put the other mute in his place, dressed him in Joseph's clothing, and served him a good glass of spirits and a decent supper. He was very satisfied and fell sound asleep in Joseph's bed.

In the middle of the night, the police surrounded the home of the old beadle Abraham-Khaym, took him out of his bed, and led him off to jail. At the same time, other policemen surrounded Rabbi Liva's house and woke up the groggy mute, who had been sound asleep on the golem's bed, and didn't grasp what was happening. They helped him throw on the golem's clothes and took him off to jail. The next morning, the town was in a turmoil over the dreadful news that there was a new Blood Accusation against the Jews, but no one could think of any solution except to weep, wail, and recite psalms. The trial was to take place in another month. Rabbi Liva was called to the trial, in accordance with King Rudolf's new law. Meanwhile, never resting for a moment, he labored with might and main. He had several intelligent men out, thoroughly investigating the house where the heating-woman had stayed, in order to determine exactly where she came from, since she might have gone back there. They also investigated the intrigues against her, since presumably those intrigues had made her so angry that she ran away. Rabbi Liva finally narrowed down the search to two villages and two towns, which were several miles from Prague. He then secretly sent out eight men, two for each place, to wander about and try to locate the Christian girl.

Twelve days elapsed, and all eight messengers came back empty-handed.

The rabbi went about with an aching heart. Three days later, Rabbi Liva sent for Joseph the Golem late at night and asked him if he was personally acquainted with the Christian heating-woman, who was supposed to be the victim in the Blood Accusation because she had disappeared. Joseph nodded that he knew her very well and would be able to recognize her among a thousand people. Then the rabbi wrote a letter in German on behalf of the head of the house where the girl had been staying. He said he was deeply sorry about the intrigues and the injuries done to her in his home. He begged her forgiveness and was sending a special messenger, a mute assistant, with money for her to rent a wagon and return to Prague. He earnestly beseeched her, upon receipt of the letter with the money, to rent a wagon immediately and return to Prague with the mute messenger. And he assured her that she would have a decent life in his home.

Rabbi Liva put the necessary sum into the letter and sealed it. He explained to Joseph the Golem that the Christian woman was in one of those four places, and he gave him strict orders to start out that same night and spend several days in those places, hunting carefully until he found her. He was then to give her the letter and come back to Prague with her immediately. He also commanded him to make sure to return within the two weeks remaining until the trial.

Next, he dressed Joseph in Gentile clothing and gave him provisions, and just before dawn the golem left Prague.

The two weeks flew by, the day of the judgment came closer and closer, and Joseph the Golem still wasn't back. The rabbi was in the throes of despair. On the day before the trial, Rabbi Liva ordered the Jews of Prague to observe a fast. And at dawn of the day of the trial, Jews were reciting the entire Book of the Psalms in all the synagogues of the city.

A huge mob, mostly Christians, began collecting at the gates of the enormous stone building of the court. The judges assembled. Father Tadeus and the convert arrived in a closed carriage. The two beadles, in chains, were brought from the prison, escorted by a strong guard. Next, Rabbi Liva drove up, accompanied by Mordecai Mayzel, a leader of the Jewish community in Prague.

The trial got underway.

The presiding magistrate asked the old beadle, Abraham-Khaym, whether he owned up to the crime of distributing Christian blood for Passover among the Jews of Prague.

The beadle replied that he had no idea what they were talking about.

Next, they questioned the mute by means of sign language. The presiding magistrate showed him several vials filled with red water. He made signs with his hands and his head, asking the mute whether he knew anything about the matter. The mute thought they were offering him little bottles of sweet brandy. He smiled and nodded his head, pointing at his mouth.

There was an uproar in the courtroom. Father Tadeus got to his feet and said that the mute was an honest witness, he had admitted in sign language that the Jews had indeed made use of such bottles of blood for their Passover food. But others understood what the mute really meant, and they burst out laughing.

The defense attorney walked over to the mute, took a small knife out of his pocket, and drew it across his throat the way one man kills another. He pointed at Rabbi Liva and asked the mute whether he knew anything of such a matter. The mute turned deathly pale and shook his head violently.

Father Tadeus stood up again and said the mute thought they were asking him whether he wanted to kill the rabbi. That was why he had gotten so pale and shaken his head. The defense attorney began arguing with the priest, but then the judge asked for order in the courtroom, and told the convert to reveal what she knew about the case. The convert quietly began telling the very same story that had already been taken down: A few days before Passover, the two beadles, whom she was personally well acquainted with, had come to her father at night. There was no one else in the house but herself and her father, and the old beadle had said to her father that the rabbi of Prague was sending him a bottle of Christian blood for the unleavened bread and asking him to pay a good price for it. Her father handed the money to the old beadle, who then made a sign to the second beadle, the same mute, and he took a small bottle of blood out of his pocket.

"My father called me over and quietly told me to take the bottle from the mute and hide it well. So I took the bottle from the mute's hand and I hid it. And when they were leaving, the old beadle said goodbye to my father and spoke the following words to him:

" 'Don't worry, Mr. Moritsy, by the time it gets cold, the Good Lord will send us another victim, a heating-woman.' "

The defense attorney went over to the convert and asked her whether she recognized the two beadles.

She replied with a laugh: "I would recognize them in the dark."

The defense attorney now asked that her father be summoned. The presiding magistrate answered that they had already sent out word to the father to appear at the trial, but a note had come back, saying that the healer had moved away from Prague two weeks earlier, and no one knew where he was. However that wasn't sufficient reason to delay the trial.

No sooner had the presiding magistrate spoken than a loud noise and a yelling could be heard from the mob in front of the court building. All the people in the courtroom jumped to their feet, shouting: "What's that? What happened?"

It was truly miraculous. Joseph the Golem had suddenly driven up in a wagon with the Christian woman, the one who heated ovens on the Sabbath. He had found her with her family in a village.

When the wagon had gone down the street where Rabbi Liva resided, Joseph had halted, jumped down, and gone into the rabbi's study. He had thrown off his peasant clothes, put on his Sabbath garments, and run to announce that he had brought back the Christian woman—only to discover that the rabbi wasn't home. He had been told to hurry to the big court building, and there he would find Rabbi Liva.

Joseph the Golem dashed back out, leaped on the wagon, and drove the horses in a wild rush to the court. The mob had burst into screams, some of the people were fearful of being run over, others were shouting: "Hooray! Hooray!" For they quickly recognized the real Joseph and the Christian woman. They were aghast and wondered where the two of them had come from, and they immediately realized that a great miracle had happened to the Jews. The people were so overjoyed that they yelled and clapped their hands. It didn't take long for those inside the courtroom to grasp what was happening outside. The real Joseph the Golem and the Christian woman were brought in, and the golem bounded over to the rabbi and informed him with his bizarre gestures that he had found the woman and brought her back.

Father Tadeus and the convert were terror-stricken. The convert was so frightened that she fainted. But she was promptly revived.

Now the presiding magistrate summoned Rabbi Liva and asked him to explain what was going on. The rabbi submitted to the judges the work he had done to prove the truth. Heaven had assisted him in revealing the truth so that no innocent blood would be shed. The judges called over the Christian woman and also the man for whom she had worked and they established that she was indeed the same woman.

The presiding judge kissed Rabbi Liva on the forehead and thanked him for his energetic labor and great wisdom, which had prevented the judges from falsely convicting pure souls.

The defendants were instantly released. But the convert was sentenced to six years' imprisonment for bearing false witness. Father Tadeus drove home in a fury, like Haman, with his head downcast. And, like Shushan in ancient Persia when Queen Esther saved the Jews, the city of Prague "rejoiced and was glad."

The Wondrous Tale That Was Widely Known as the Sorrows of a Daughter

There lived in Prague a very wealthy wine merchant named Mikhel Berger. You could get the choicest wines only from him. All the priests and all the officers would buy their wine only from Mikhel Berger.

This rich wine dealer had a daughter who was sixteen years old, and very beautiful and learned. She spoke several languages and was a perfect merchant because she could talk to people of any class.

Father Tadeus, who was infamous for his hatred of the Jews, would also come to the wineshop to buy wine. The priest cast an evil eye upon the daughter, he wanted to get her to his home and talk her into converting to Christianity. He had already ruined a number of Jewish girls in this way. But this time, there was no way of getting to her, she was a decent girl with pious parents and a fine lineage. She never even went for a stroll.

The priest hit upon a plan. He began taking wine on credit, and then always paid in full, reckoning that at some point there would be a conflict so that the girl would have to come to his home.

And Tadeus' plan really worked.

Usually, the servant would bring the bill to the priest, and the priest paid punctually. But one day, when the servant presented the bill, Father Tadeus claimed that he was being overcharged for ten bottles of wine, and he angrily accused the servant of trying to get too much money out of him. He demanded that the wine merchant's daughter accompany the servant in presenting the account. She was to bring the ledger, and he would prove to her that he was in the right.

The girl didn't even think twice about it because the servant was escorting her. When they arrived at the priest's home, the priest demanded that the girl write out a correct bill from the ledger. But the bill copied from the book tallied with the figure that the servant had presented. The priest cried out! He remembered now what the mistake was, he hadn't noted down ten bottles they had sent him a few weeks earlier because he hadn't wanted to accept the wine, it was as sour as vinegar. He added that it wasn't right for such a large business to try and cheat him.

The girl exclaimed that it just couldn't be, she was certain that they had always sent him the choicest wines. So the priest told his butler to bring the ten bottles up from the cellar, they were in a basket.

When the butler brought up the basket, the priest asked the servant to open any bottle he wanted to, the girl could taste it and she would see that he was right, they must have made a mistake and sent him vinegar instead of wine. The servant uncorked a bottle and poured out a glass for the girl to taste.

The girl was so wrought up she didn't stop to think that she mustn't even taste the wine. After a few sips, she saw that the wine was perfectly good. She told the priest there was nothing wrong with the wine. The priest had a taste for himself and then said that the girl was right, there was nothing wrong with the wine, he must have been mistaken.

With these words, he offered the girl his hand, asking her to shake hands with him and forgive him for offending her. Even though the girl was always careful not to give any strange man her hand, she didn't want to be impudent to the priest and so she gave him her hand, saying there were no hard feelings, and that they were still friends.

The priest paid her the full sum, and now he began speaking more and more familiarly with her. The girl, for her part, had drunk some of the priest's wine, which was a pagan liquor forbidden to Jews, and when she had given him her hand, she had been virtually poisoned with a lewd venom.

Her character changed, she entered into a long conversation with the priest and felt more and more drawn to him. And when she left his house to go back home, she shook hands of her own accord and very amicably said goodbye to him, which gave the priest the opportunity of asking her to visit him more often.

And that was indeed what happened. She began secretly corresponding with the priest and would sometimes visit him alone late at night, until one night she didn't even come home to sleep. She vanished like a stone in water. Her parents wept and wailed, the girl was their only child, all they had. They questioned lots of people, until they finally had a clue: That night, the girl had gone into the street where Father Tadeus' church was located. The miserable parents ran weeping to the priest, but he was furious and told them he didn't know what they were talking about. Weeping and broken-hearted, they returned to their home, and at the mere sight of them everyone joined in their tears.

Father Tadeus had locked up the girl in the courtyard of the church, in a place where no one could possibly get to her. He made sure that she lacked nothing in the way of pleasure, and he kept telling her that she ought to accept baptism. Each time he visited her, he would study something of the Christian religion with her.

But one day, the priest saw that she wasn't very cheerful sitting all cooped up like that. He realized he couldn't make her happy until he got her a proper bridegroom. The priest assured her that he would find someone, and thus he became a matchmaker.

Not far from Prague there lived an old, rich duke, and he had an only son, who was eighteen years old, handsome and educated. Father Tadeus was friendly with the duke, and it occurred to the priest that the duke's son would be a fitting husband for the girl.

The priest went out to visit the duke and presented the idea to him, heaping praises upon the girl. His words made a strong impression on the old duke and his young son. It was decided that the duke and his son would come to the church in Prague that Sunday and have lunch with the priest, and the priest would present the girl to them.

On Sunday, they came to Prague, and Father Tadeus prepared a huge lunch for them. When they were drinking wine, the priest sent for the girl. She had already been informed of the visit and so she made herself very beautiful for the presentation. The young man was greatly taken with her, and he and his father spent the night in the priest's home.

The next day, the priest threw a grand ball, and from the very start of the evening the girl sat next to the duke's son, she was in high spirits as though they were already engaged.

At the second ball, it was decided that the cardinal himself should baptize her in two months, and that her marriage to the young duke would take place on the same day, right after the christening.

The duke and his son drove home, and the bridegroom gave the bride a going-away present, a valuable ring with his name engraved in it.

The girl's parents, however, hadn't slept all that time. They did all they could to get their child back from the priest, but to no avail. Next, they went to a close relative, the great scholar Jacob Gintzberg, who was the rabbi of Friedburg, and they asked for his help. The great scholar replied that the rabbi of Prague, Rabbi Liva, was in a better position to help than he, and he gave them a letter to Rabbi Liva, asking him to do everything in his power to rescue the girl because it was a blow to his family honor.

The parents drove back to Prague and delivered the letter to Rabbi Liva. The rabbi was deeply upset by the letter because he had preferred to keep clear of this matter rather than battling with Father Tadeus. But he had to be hospitable for the sake of the great scholar Jacob Gintzberg. There were a number of people present when the parents gave him the letter, and the rabbi said out loud that he couldn't help the parents and that he didn't want to get involved in the matter.

But that night, Rabbi Liva secretly sent the old beadle, Abraham-Khaym, to summon the parents, and they came immediately. The rabbi told them he intended to do something about the whole business, but nobody was to know about his participation. He also told them that as of the next day they were to have a carriage with a pair of good horses in their courtyard, along with a good driver and two strong men, all in secret, and to be ready to escape with the girl as soon as he succeeded in getting her home. And he asked the parents if they had some distant place where they might take their daughter. The father answered that he had a brother, who owned the largest wine business in Amsterdam, and he was very wealthy and learned. His name was Khaym Berger. His home would be a good place to bring the girl. The rabbi agreed, and he ordained that the father and mother should fast for three days, starting tomorrow, and read the entire Book of Psalms with tears every single day, and to eat only at night. He told them to go home and not let anyone know that they had been to see him. The parents went home and did everything exactly as the rabbi had ordained.

During those three days, the girl began to feel a deep longing for her parents, and she looked wretched. The priest asked her why she looked so wretched. She said she felt a bit under the weather, but it didn't matter.

At the same time, many priests were gathering in Cracow for a conference and they summoned Father Tadeus. Before he left, the priest ordered his servants not to allow anyone into the courtyard of the church.

When Rabbi Liva discovered that Tadeus was also going to the conference, he summoned Joseph the Golem secretly at night and gave him the amulet of invisibility so that no one could see him. Next, he wrote the following words on a slip of paper:

"I, your grandfather, have come down from the other world to rescue you. Get into this sack and I will carry you home."

Rabbi Liva took a large sack and handed it to Joseph along with the note. He ordered him to leave at the crack of dawn and go to the church. There, he was to wait at the small iron door, and as soon as someone opened the door to go in or out, he was to slip through quietly. Then he was to go around the courtyard all day long, find out exactly how to open the door from the inside and figure out where the girl was. As soon as he knew these things, he was to creep into her room and hide there until late at night, when all the servants and guards were asleep. Now he was to wake up the girl and place the sack and the note in front of her. When she had given sufficient thought to the message, he was to open the sack, let the girl climb in, and take her home to her parents.

Rabbi Liva knew that the small iron door leading to the courtyard of the church could be opened from the inside, but not from the outside, yet not everyone knew how to work it.

Joseph the Golem took the difficult task upon himself, and he succeeded in doing everything exactly as the rabbi had ordered. By two o'clock in the morning, Joseph the Golem was already back with the girl in her parents' home.

One can scarcely imagine the joy and weeping when the parents saw their only child again. The daughter fell at their feet and tearfully kissed them and begged their forgiveness. But then the father recalled the rabbi's instructions, he ordered his servants to prepare the carriage, got into it with his daughter and the two men, and hurriedly left Prague for Amsterdam.

When they asked the daughter who had rescued her, she showed them the note: Her grandfather had come down from the other world and brought her here. And the parents likewise believed that this was what had happened.

The next morning, in the courtyard of the church, the lackey let out a yell when he saw that the girl had run off. He was terrified that the priest would accuse him of helping her to escape. We would never have known what the lackey did; but a later story, which can be found after this story, tells us that he went down into the cellar of the church, took some human bones, and put them on the girl's bed. Then he started a fire, and by the time the firemen arrived, the whole room was destroyed, and they found the charred remains of a human being.

The police reported that a stranger who happened to be spending the night there had been burnt up, and the name was supplied by the lackey and the priest.

The lackey informed the authorities that the priest had violently forced a girl surnamed Berger to accept baptism, and she felt so wretched that she set fire to the room in which she was imprisoned.

Naturally, when the priest came back from Cracow, he had to keep silent. But he really assumed that the lackey had let the girl go for money, and Father Tadeus took revenge on the lackey, which is described in the other story.

When the priest saw the duke he told him that while he had been at the conference in Cracow, the room in which the girl was sleeping had caught fire at night and she had been burnt up, and all they had found of her was her bones.

When the young duke heard the terrible news that his beloved fiancée had been burnt up, he was overcome with grief and fell into a deep melancholy, he couldn't eat or sleep, and he looked wretched. His father tried to put his mind at ease with all kinds of pleasures and asked marriage-brokers to find him a fitting bride. But the young duke didn't care for any of the proposals after the beauty and nobility he had seen in the Jewish girl. He decided he would only take a Jewish wife, and since he realized it would be difficult to get a Jewish girl to accept baptism for him, he resolved to go to another country and convert to Judaism without his father's knowledge. However, he understood that he would need a lot of money for this and so he suggested to his father that since it was so hard for him to forget his fiancée here and he felt he might lose his mind, the best thing for him would be to go and study in Venice for a few years. By the time he finished the university, he would forget his sorrows and come home and marry. The old duke had to consent. He gave his son all the money he asked for, and the young duke left for Venice.

When he got to Venice, he rented himself a private room and registered as a traveling merchant. The room was to be constantly vacant and ready for him so that he could use it at any time, even though he might only come a few times a year. He also gave instructions that if any letter were to arrive for him, it was to be placed promptly in his room, because he knew his father would write him in Venice, and in this way he could come there any time to get the letters and write back.

Now at this time, the great *gaon* Jacob Gintzberg of Friedburg was renowned through the world and was regarded as second only to Rabbi Liva of Prague. So the young duke made up his mind to go and ask the *gaon* to initiate him into Judaism.

The young man went to him and made a very favorable impression on the *gaon*, and before long the *gaon* converted him and began studying the Torah with him, and he changed the young man's first name to Abraham and gave him the last name of Yeshurun, which is the poetic name of Israel.

Now Abraham Yeshurun had a very able mind, and he quickly absorbed everything he studied with the *gaon*. But the *gaon*, being the rabbi of the city, was extremely busy and couldn't give up that much time to him. So he sent the young man to the great yeshivah of Amsterdam with a letter to the head of the school, saying that Abraham was a relative of his and asking the head of the yeshivah, to welcome him and take special care of him.

Abraham Yeshurun tearfully took leave of the *gaon*, and the *gaon* gave him his blessing and assured him he would find his destined bride in Amsterdam. And by way of proof he told him that if the marriage they proposed to him would be with a member of Rabbi Gintzberg's family, he was to agree. The *gaon* also instructed him not to reveal who he was, but to say that his name was Abraham Yeshurun, and that he came from the city of Bucharest and was a relative of the *gaon*, all of which could be checked with the Rabbi of Friedburg.

Abraham Yeshurun journeyed to Amsterdam, and there he called upon the head of the yeshivah. He told him who he was and showed him the letter from the Rabbi of Friedburg. The head master welcomed him as a friend and began studying the Torah with him. Abraham Yeshurun worked hard and became a great scholar, his fame spread and he was known as the young prodigy of Bucharest.

Meanwhile he kept going to Venice to get his father's letters and answer them, so that his father would think he was studying there and not worry about him.

Abraham Yeshurun studied in the yeshivah for two years, and then the headmaster told him to return home and get married. Abraham replied that he preferred to remain in Amsterdam because it was a more pious city than Bucharest, and he would rather marry a girl from Amsterdam. He added that money was no problem, he could get all the money he needed from his father, who was a very wealthy man, and had no other child but him.

It soon became known throughout the city that there was a rich yeshivah student here who wanted to marry a girl from Amsterdam. And the marriage-brokers started visiting him. He turned down many offers until one marriage-broker suggested the girl who was staying with her wealthy uncle Khaym Berger and who was kith and kin with the great *gaon* Jacob Gintzberg, and as for her family, the matchmaker explained that according to her reputation in Amsterdam she was an orphan from a distant city and her inheritance was very large.

As soon as Abraham Yeshurun heard that she was related to the *gaon* Jacob Gintzberg, he realized she must be his destined bride and he agreed to the match. The betrothal was carried out in great dignity. The bridegroom deceived the bride in regard to his background because he didn't want anyone to find out that he was a convert to Judaism. The bride, in turn, deceived the bridegroom, as well as the whole city of Amsterdam, in regard to her background because she was afraid the people might find out about her bad reputation in Prague, where she had very nearly converted to Christianity. The girl did look familiar to the boy, but it never occurred to him that this was the same girl who had been burnt to death in the courtyard of Father Tadeus' church two years ago.

A few weeks after the official engagement, the bridegroom bought some costly presents for the bride, among them two diamond rings. When she tried on the diamond rings, she had to remove the gold ring she had been wearing ever since her arrival from Prague, the one she had gotten at the ball from that very same bridegroom, the young duke. The moment she put the gold ring on the table the bridegroom began inspecting it and he promptly recognized it as his own ring for his name was still engraved on it. The young man was so startled and upset that he fell into a swoon. They revived him but he was unwilling to explain why he had fainted. Now he came to realize that the bride was the same as the girl in Prague.

The bridegroom could no longer control himself, and he asked the girl in secret to tell him the whole truth as to who she was and where she had gotten the ring, she needn't be afraid to tell him everything. The bride was so frightened that she too fainted. He revived her, but now she was unable to keep her secret anymore. In short, they revealed themselves to one another and both of them burst into tears of joy.

The young man went out and told the entire story to the head of the yeshivah and to the bride's uncle, and he also repeated the blessing and the parting words of the *gaon* of Friedburg. The headmaster was overjoyed and said: "It is obvious that this marriage was made in heaven, and that something which was nearly unlawful has been done in a lawful manner."

A short time later, the wedding took place in Amsterdam with great honor. And not long after that, the old duke died, Abraham Yeshurun and his wife inherited all his property and they decided to settle near Prague.

When the young couple arrived at their estates, Father Tadeus was no longer in Prague. He had been sent away after a great trial, as we shall hear in the next story.

A few days later, Abraham and his bride gave a grand ball and invited her parents, Mikhel Berger and his wife, as well as Rabbi Liva and other prominent Jews of the city.

At the ball, the entire story was told from beginning to end, and now they saw that it wasn't the grandfather from the other world who had carried off the girl inside a sack. It really was Rabbi Liva, who had gotten Joseph the Golem to do the trick.

A few years later, old Mikhel Berger died, and soon his wife followed him. And Abraham Yeshurun donated his father-in-law's house to be used as a synagogue. And it was named the Yeshurun Synagogue. The couple did many charitable deeds in Prague and lived very happily.

A Very Wondrous Tale About a Blood Libel
Which Spelled Final Defeat for Father Tadeus

This wonderous tale took place in the year 5345 [or 1585 according to the Christian reckoning].

In Prague, not far from the great synagogue of the city, there stood a large, old mansion, which looked like an ancient royal palace. The old building was known as the Five-Sided Palace because it had five walls facing five streets; in front of each wall there were five columns; and in between the columns there were five windows. On top of the mansion there were five large towers with ancient figures, which were obviously from the days when men worshiped the sun. Now because there was no owner and the mansion belonged to the government, it fell into greater and greater disrepair, and only beggars lived in it.

Underneath the building there was a large cellar, but the tenants were afraid to go down into it. They said the cellar had been defiled by demons who had settled there and constantly terrorized the beggars, and it was rumored that a number of people had already been harmed down there. That was why there were so few tenants in the Five-Sided Palace, which looked like an ancient ruin.

Now one day, during preparations for Passover, after the ceremonial search for unleavened dough in Jewish homes, Rabbi Liva was in the synagogue to pronounce the Annulment of Leaven for this Feast of Deliverance. He was about to begin when the candle went out. Since it was the rabbi's custom to read from the prayerbook rather than recite from memory, he motioned to the beadle to relight the candle. The beadle lit it over and over, but it merely went out again each time.

The rabbi turned deathly pale, and the worshipers were likewise terrified. Rabbi Liva had to interrupt the service. He asked the old beadle Abraham-Khaym to take the prayerbook over to the candle burning in the sconce and to read the Annulment aloud word by word; the rabbi would repeat it from memory word by word.

The beadle did as he was bidden. Terror-stricken he went over to the candlestick on the wall and began to read: "All the leaven that I have ..." But when he came to "have," he thought it said "five," and that was what he read aloud for Rabbi Liva.

The rabbi paused and then cried out to the beadle: "Well? Well?"

The beadle was even more terrified and began all over again, and when he came to "have" he repeated "five."

Rabbi Liva snapped his fingers, which he always did when something surprised him, and he exclaimed: "Aha! Now I understand! 'It is a time of trouble unto Jacob, but out of it shall he be saved.' Our enemies want to put out the Jewish light. Now I know the meaning of the dream I had the night of the Great Sabbath, before Passover."

The rabbi hurried over to the candle and climbed up on a chair because the sconce was high on the wall. He read the prayer from the book, and then he told everyone else to go home. No one remained except for his son-in-law the *gaon* Jacob Gintzberg (blessed be the memory of that true priest and righteous man), the old beadle Abraham-Khaym, and Joseph the Golem.

When they were alone, Rabbi Liva told the others what he had dreamt on Friday night: The Five-Sided Palace was burning furiously, and the flames were leaping into the windows of the great synagogue, which was packed with Jews. Rabbi Liva screamed in his sleep and woke up in dread.

He realized now what his dream signified. Someone in the Five-Sided Palace was preparing a Blood Libel, a calamity for the Jews of Prague, and they would have to remove it just as they got rid of all leaven on the Eve of Passover.

At this point, God had sent those words into the beadle's mouth. They signified that the Jews had to remove and destroy the leaven in the Five-Sided Palace, where someone had prepared a disastrous calumny against the Jews of Prague.

Rabbi Liva desperately tried to figure out what kind of catastrophe someone could be planning in that building. He asked about all the tenants, but the beadle went through each of them in his mind and he felt that not one of them could be suspected of any evil. However, one thing that the beadle said came as a great surprise to Rabbi Liva. The beadle recalled that when he was a child the little boys used to tell one another stories they had heard at home about the Five-Sided Palace. Their parents had said that once upon a time a king had lived in the palace and he would never show himself to the people of the city. Whenever he wanted to attend church, he would go to the Green Church by way of a cavern running underground from the cellar of the palace to the cellar of the Green Church. And that was the church in which Father Tadeus lived, the priest who was an infamous anti-Semite.

Upon hearing these words, Rabbi Liva realized that Tadeus had prepared a great Blood Libel in the cellar, something he could easily do because of the underground cavern that ran from the cellar in the church to the cellar of the palace. The rabbi knew quite well that the priest was stealthily waiting for a chance to take revenge on him because the rabbi prevented any Blood Libel from succeeding in Prague. And the priest was even angrier because he was fully aware that Rabbi Liva had somehow helped to ruin his plans for baptizing Mikhel Berger's daughter. Afterward, in the courtroom, it turned out that the priest had assumed that his lackey had given the girl back to her parents for a sum of money while he, the priest, was in Cracow, and that the rabbi had been behind it all, and that the fire had merely been a decoy. That was why the priest had made up his mind to settle accounts with the lackey and also with Rabbi Liva.

And the truth of the matter was that a dreadful Blood Libel had indeed been prepared in the cellar. This is what happened:

The priest's lackey had a wife and several little children. The priest's house stood in the courtyard of the church, and on the other side there was a large orchard surrounded by a wall. Inside the wall there was an iron gate which opened onto a path outside the city.

Two weeks before Passover, when the weather was turning warm, the lackey and his wife began doing a bit of work in the orchard every day, and their young children ran around in it, each child playing with whatever it could, and while the parents were working in the orchard they had to open the iron gate and throw out the unnecessary things which had gathered during the winter, and then some or all of the children would dash through the gate and start playing outside.

Father Tadeus knew about this, and he wanted to take this opportunity to carry out his revenge against the servant and start a Blood Libel against Rabbi Liva. The priest waited until the lackey and his wife were busy with their work in the orchard while some of their children were scattered around the orchard and others were running around outside the gate. When no one was looking, the priest lured one of the children to come along, and then killed the child. He poured his blood into several small vials, on which there were labels with Jewish names—the names of Rabbi Liva, his children, and his sons-in-law, and the names of three leaders of the Jewish community, and some of the richest and noblest men in Prague.

Then he took the vials from his cellar through the cavern leading to the cellar of the Five-Sided Palace, and he hid them there so that on the Eve of Passover he could invade the Jewish quarter, launch an investigation, and then have Rabbi Liva, his children, and all the leading Jews of the city put in prison.

The priest made his preparations on Friday, the eve of the Great

Sabbath before Passover. And that night, Rabbi Liva had the terrible dream described above.

With darkness coming on, the lackey and his wife wanted to stop work in the orchard and go home. They started calling their children together, and then they saw that one was missing. They hunted it for a long time, but in vain. The child was gone. At the crack of dawn, they went to the priest and told him what had happened.

The priest said that it seemed to him the child must have run out through the iron gate and wandered off somewhere. He added that they had reason to worry because it was close to the Jewish Passover, and the Jews were on the lookout for Christian blood to use in their matzohs. For all they knew, the child might have fallen into Jewish hands by now. There was little they could do except notify the police. And the priest instructed the mother to say that last night, when they were about to go home and she was closing the iron gate, she had seen a Jew in the distance, carrying something in a sack on his shoulders, and the sack had been shaking. Tadeus told her to weep and wail and plead with the police to make a thorough search of the Jewish Quarter. And she was also to ask the police to take Father Tadeus along on the investigation.

Hearing these words, the mother began to weep and wail, and then she hurried to the city hall and notified the police just as Tadeus had instructed her to do. The police in turn told her not to worry. The next day, which was the Eve of Passover, they would start out early in the morning and make a thorough investigation everywhere in the Jewish Quarter, together with Father Tadeus.

However, it is written in the Psalms: "Behold, he that keepeth Israel shall neither slumber nor sleep." This means that the Good Lord never sleeps, He watches over His Nation, the Jews.

Rabbi Liva had gotten the tiding from heaven that a disaster was threatening the Jews, and he wasted no time. He said it was certainly dangerous to go down into the cellar, but he girded himself with the Talmudic saying that "a man sent on a pious mission shall meet with no evil."

This was the night of the Inspection for Leaven. And after midnight prayers Rabbi Liva set out with the old beadle Abraham-Khaym and Joseph the Golem. They took along a tinderbox and three of the twisted candles used in the ceremony closing the

Sabbath, and then they stole over to the Five-Sided Palace, and very quietly so that no one would notice them.

When they were about to go down the steps into the cellar, they kindled a fire and lit all three candles. Then they opened the door and stepped inside, and at once a wind arose and dust whirled about, and they heard the barking of dogs as the wind tried to blow out the candles. But the Rabbi told his beadles to recite "He who dwells in secret . . ." three times, and then everything began quieting down and grew perfectly still. The three men kept going.

But now stones began dropping from the vault of the cellar, and they were afraid that the vault would cave in upon them. Rabbi Liva and the old beadle Abraham-Khaym stopped, but the rabbi ordered Jospeh the Golem to go on alone with the candle in his hand and to inspect the cellar carefully, and if he found any suspicious object he was to bring it back and show it to the rabbi. Joseph the Golem set about his task.

It wasn't long before he came back to the rabbi with the murdered child wrapped in a prayer shawl and a small basket containing some thirty vials of blood, and on the vials there were labels with Hebrew characters, the names of all the leading Jews in Prague.

Rabbi Liva ordered Joseph the Golem to take the dead child through the cavern leading to the cellar of Father Tadeus' home and to hide the body carefully among the kegs of wine which the priest had standing there, and then Joseph was to come right back.

Joseph the Golem did as he was told and carried out the rabbi's instructions precisely. A half hour went by, and Joseph the Golem was back again.

Now the rabbi ordered him to take stones and smash the vials, and then dig a hole in the cellar and bury everything in it. When it was done, they all went home in high spirits. Rabbi Liva told them to keep it all a secret, no one was to say anything about it.

At ten in the morning, on the day before Passover, the police suddenly appeared in the Jewish Quarter with many soldiers, accompanied by Father Tadeus. The soldiers dashed into the Jewish homes, two to a house, and searched them thoroughly. First they went into the great synagogue, then Rabbi Liva's home, and then the homes of all the community leaders and many prominent men.

When they came past the Five-Sided Palace, the priest cried out that they ought to search the palace as well. Naturally, they searched it thoroughly, taking longer than anywhere else, but, as it is written in Exodus, "If he come in by himself, he shall go out by himself." They went home empty-handed.

Meanwhile, alas, a deathly fear took hold of all the Jews in Prague. However Rabbi Liva said to pass the word that the Jews had nothing to fear, they were to have a happy holiday because the Lord God had worked secret miracles to rescue the Jews from false accusations.

The dead body lay well concealed among the wine kegs in the cellar, and after a few days it began to smell. The Catholic holiday of Easter was approaching, and the priest ordered his lackey to put the cellar in order, and to see how much wine there was so that they would know how much more to buy for Easter. The lackey went down into the cellar, and as usual his dog followed him everywhere. But then the dog smelled the stench of the dead body and ran over to where it was hidden, and there he began barking and pawing the ground. The lackey realized something was wrong, and he hunted carefully until he came upon the dead child, whom he recognized at once.

The lackey ran out of the cellar and brought the police back with him. Everyone understood that this was the priest's doing because he had always been plotting to bring a Blood Accusation against the Jews. The priest tried to deny the whole story, he said he knew nothing about it. But in the face of so many facts he finally had to confess that it was indeed his work. He had wanted to get even with his servant, who had taken a precious soul away from the Christian faith, a girl who had been staying with him for several weeks and who had been ready to accept baptism. But the servant had helped her go back home in exchange for money. And he, the priest, had also wanted to get even with the Jewish rabbi, who had most surely been behind the escape, and so he had planned a Blood Accusation against him, using the child, in order to settle accounts with both the rabbi and the lackey.

The lackey, however, said it wasn't so, the priest had tricked Mikhel Berger's daughter into coming to him and had been forcing her to accept baptism. He had done terrible things to her and made her life wretched, and so she had set fire to her room when she was alone.

The priest was arrested at once, and he was tried and banished forever.

In regard to these events, Rabbi Liva repeated the Hebrew: "He wanted to protect the worthy woman," by which he meant that God wanted to protect the holy Shekhina, the divine emanation, "and her children as well,"—the Jews. And the holy Shekhinah had sent the word "five" to his lips so that he would know enough to search the Five-Sided Palace.

This Is the Wonderful and Miraculous Tale of What Rabbi Liva Did for the Two Beryls Whose Children Were Exchanged by a Midwife

There lived in Prague a man who taught elementary subjects to young Jewish children, and he was known as Tall Jacob. One day, two poor little boys came to him, two orphans from Rumania, and the teacher hired them as assistants. Both of them were named Beryl but one had dark hair and so he was known as Black Beryl and the other had a ruddy face and so he was known as Red Beryl.

The two Beryls loved one another, they lived together and shared their food with each other. They were liked by the teacher and also by the people of the city because they did their work with honesty and devotion. And little by little, they saved up some money for their marriages. Both of them married women from Prague, and since the two men couldn't live without one another after their weddings, they decided to go into business together.

Their first business as partners was a slaughterhouse and a meat shop. Their business prospered and little by little they became wealthy. Then they closed up their meat shop and began dealing in cattle. They continued to prosper, they became great cattle dealers, and their wealth was renowned throughout Prague.

Now they bought a large mansion in Prague, and the two Beryls lived in it, next door to one other.

But there was one thing in which they were not equals: their children. Red Beryl had both sons and daughters, all of whom survived. While Black Beryl had only daughters, and not all of them survived.

Both wives of the two Beryls had the same midwife, and her name was Esther. Black Beryl's wife felt a keen envy of Red Beryl's wife. But because she was a very noble person with a noble character, she did all she could to contain herself and not show any rivalry with the other wife. Esther the midwife fully realized what was happening, and she felt a great pity and sympathy for Black Beryl's wife. She began wondering if there was something she could do for her so that she might also boast to her husband that she had given birth to a son.

One night, both wives went for a ritual immersion, and the midwife found out. She made up her mind that if both women were to conceive tonight, and Black Beryl's wife had another daughter, and the other wife a son, and both children were born at the same time, then she, the midwife, would exchange the babies, with no one the wiser.

And that was exactly what happened. Both wives began moaning at the same time, but Red Beryl's wife had her baby first, and she bore a son. Esther the midwife wished her joy for her daughter. She thought to herself that even if Black Beryl's wife had a son, she would still exchange them because Red Beryl's children were stronger and hardier than Black Beryl's children, and she would tell Red Beryl that she had wished his wife good luck for a girl in order to ward off the evil eye by not saying aloud that it was a boy.

The next day, Black Beryl's wife also had a baby, and it too was a boy! Esther the midwife wished Black Beryl all the luck in the world for his son, and the joy was very great. Then, Esther the midwife told Red Beryl that his wife had also had a boy, but since Black Beryl's wife was about to give birth herself, the midwife had been afraid of an evil eye and so, to ward it off, she hadn't wanted to say aloud that the child was a boy. He took her at her word.

A few nights later, when everyone was asleep, Esther the midwife switched the two children and no one was the wiser, she told no one what she had done. She did however write in her diary that at this time on this day she had taken the two boys that had just been born to the Beryls and exchanged them in secret, for a hidden reason. But who ever looked into her diary? The whole thing remained as secret as a stone in water.

The two boys thus grew up and became adults. Esther the midwife died. Her diary passed into the hands of a daughter, who followed in her mother's footsteps and became a midwife too. But since she never had any cause to look into her mother's diary, the book was stored in the cellar along with other useless things.

The two Beryls began marrying off their children and they

found wonderful matches for them. Now since Black Beryl still had two daughters and an only son (the one the midwife had exchanged), and Red Beryl had four sons and two daughters, plus the last son (the one the midwife had exchanged), the two fathers never arranged a match between their own children.

But as the years went by, a number of marriage-brokers suggested that Black Beryl's only son should marry Red Beryl's youngest daughter, who was just one year his elder, and everyone agreed it was a fine match.

The marriage contract was drawn up with great rejoicing, which is customary among the wealthy, and then the wedding day arrived. The two Beryl's insisted that Rabbi Liva perform the ceremony, just as he officiated at all the rich weddings in Prague.

But something peculiar happened at the wedding. When Rabbi Liva took hold of the wine glass to pronounce the first blessing, it tumbled out of his hand. People thought it had been knocked out of his fingers because the synagogue was so crowded. The guests were asked to stand back so that there would be more space, and the glass was filled with more wine. But as soon as Rabbi Liva said "Blessed art thou . . . ," the glass tumbled out of his hand again. The rabbi turned pale with grief, and all the onlookers were bewildered and frightened.

Meanwhile, there was no wine left in the bottle for a third glassful. So the old beadle Abraham-Khaym cried out to the mute beadle Joseph the Golem to run quickly and bring up another bottle from the rabbi's cellar because the rabbi would never use any other wine for a blessing.

Joseph the Golem dashed over to Rabbi Liva's home, which wasn't far from the great synagogue, where the wedding was taking place. But just as Joseph the Golem came to the rabbi's door, he halted abruptly, and the people saw that he seemed to be talking to someone. From afar, the wedding crowd began shouting at Joseph the Golem to hurry up with the wine. But Joseph the Golem didn't even go down into the cellar, instead he calmly walked into the rabbi's office and wrote some Hebrew words on a piece of paper: *THE BRIDE AND GROOM ARE BROTHER AND SISTER.* And instead of the wine, he hurried back with the note and handed it to Rabbi Liva.

The crowd wanted to tear Joseph apart, but they knew better than to fool around with him.

When the rabbi read the note, he became very frightened and he cried out: "Oh dear God! Brother and sister!"

The other people were also terrified, they realized that something awful was happening.

Rabbi Liva asked Joseph the Golem: "Who told you the bride and groom are sister and brother?"

Joseph the Golem pointed at the window of the synagogue to show who had said those words to him and told him to repeat them to Rabbi Liva. The rabbi took a few steps from under the wedding canopy and stood facing the window that Joseph had shown him. The rabbi peered up at the window and then went back to the canopy. The whole crowd peered up at the window, but no one saw anything.

When Rabbi Liva was back at the canopy he said that the wedding could not take place today because there would first have to be a thorough investigation. He told them to distribute the entire feast to the poor.

That same night, after midnight, Rabbi Liva called over Joseph the Golem and said something to him quietly, and gave him his staff. Joseph the Golem hurried off, and came back an hour later. Afterward, people found out he had been sent to the graveyard to tell Esther the midwife she was to appear at Liva's rabbinical court the next day.

Early in the morning, the rabbi told his servants to prepare a place for himself and his two assistant judges, a few cubits away from the northeast corner of the synagogue, and to set up a wooden screen forming a triangle with the corner. Next, he asked them to call out that all the men praying in the synagogue should remain after prayers rather than go home, and should gather on the other side of the reading desk, toward the western wall.

After the rabbi finished praying, he and his two assistant judges sat down at the table in their prayer shawls and phylacteries. He sent the old beadle Abraham-Khaym to summon the families of the bride and groom, the two Beryls with their wives, and the bride and groom themselves.

When they arrived, Rabbi Liva asked them to stand on the other side of the table, toward the south, and he questioned the two Beryls and their wives about everything concerning them, to the last detail, but it did not come out that the children had been switched, so far as anyone knew.

Next, Rabbi Liva called over Joseph the Golem and handed him his staff, saying: "Go to the graveyard, Joseph, and bring back the soul of Esther the midwife so that she can clear up this matter for us."

The others were terrified, but Rabbi Liva rose to his feet and said in a loud voice: "Do not be afraid, I beg you, for nothing bad shall come of this."

The people calmed down a bit.

A half-hour later, Joseph the Golem returned to the synagogue and gave the rabbi back his staff. Then he pointed at the screen to show that the person they were waiting for was on the other side.

There was a deathly hush in the synagogue. No one had the heart to look at anyone else.

Now Rabbi Liva said: "We, the Earthly Court, decree that thou, Esther, shalt explain in detail why the bride and the groom are brother and sister."

The dead midwife began to tell the whole story.

The crowd in the synagogue only heard a faint voice, but the court, the parents, and the bride and groom clearly heard the dead midwife tell the story of how she had switched the two children. And she added that in the twelve years since her death she had known no rest and would not know any until she righted the wrong she had done. On the wedding day, she had been empowered to prevent the marriage of a brother and sister from taking place, otherwise she would be doomed to Gehenna forever.

When she ended her story, she burst into tears, pleading with the court to have mercy on her soul, and to set the matter aright and switch back the children, and she begged the families and the children to forgive her. In the end, she added that if they didn't believe her, they could go and find her diary, which was in her daughter's home, and which listed all the children she had brought into the world. And if they checked the day and year when the children were born, they would see her entry, which said she had exchanged the two children. And if she had been in her right mind at death, she would have corrected the matter herself before dying. But because she had died of a sudden, severe illness, which had made her lose her mind, she had been unable to set things aright.

With these words, they could hear the sound of weeping.

When Rabbi Liva had heard the story, he sent both his beadles to the midwife's daughter, asking her to come immediately with her dead mother's diary. It took them a good hour to locate the half-rotted book in the cellar. But they did find it, and they did find the entry in the diary.

The court ruled that first of all, the dead midwife would have to ask forgiveness of the bride and groom for having shamed them. And if they were willing to forgive her with all their heart and soul, then she would be free of her sin. Now they heard the weeping voice from the other side of the screen:

"I, Esther, ask you, brother and sister, for forgiveness."

They answered that they forgave her with all their heart and soul.

Now the rabbi and the two assistant judges got to their feet and spoke: "We, the Earthly Court, exempt you, Esther, from any manner of punishment. Go in peace and rest in peace until all is peace."

Rabbi Liva then called the entire crowd in the synagogue and said it had been clearly proven that the youngest sons of the two Beryls had been exchanged by the midwife Esther, so that the two children would have to be switched back again, and both the bride and groom would have to be registered as Red Beryl's children. The youngest son of Red Beryl was the only son of Black Beryl.

The rabbi added that if the fathers-in-law agreed then it would be fitting and proper for the real son of Black Beryl to marry the same bride, and the wedding would take place the following week.

The fathers-in-law and the children promptly agreed to the rabbi's proposal, and a new marriage contract was drawn up in the synagogue. Spirits and cakes were served to everyone, and Rabbi Liva blessed them all.

The rabbi then asked for the book of records. When it was brought to him, he briefly set down the full story, and the judges all signed their names.

Rabbi Liva then gave the new couple his best wishes for a happy marriage and told the people that they could go home. He asked his beadles to take a board from the wooden screen and nail it up in the corner as a reminder. The beadles did as he told them.

The following week, the proper wedding took place with great merriment. Rabbi Liva himself performed the ceremony, and he was overjoyed that heaven had stayed his hand from uniting a brother and sister in wedlock. The young couple lived to a ripe old age in Prague, and their life together was very happy.

The Tale of the Torah That Fell to the Ground on Yom Kippur

In the year 5347 [or, by Christian reckoning 1587], on Yom Kippur, when Rabbi Liva was attending evening prayers at the great synagogue in Prague, someone went to roll up the scroll of the Torah after the reading of the Law, only to drop the Torah on the ground.

Rabbi Liva was greatly upset and confused by what had happened. The first thing he did was to proclaim that all the worshipers who had seen the Torah fall upon the ground were to fast throughout the day before the Eve of the Feast of Tabernacles. The rabbi understood that this was not enough, something like this did not just happen at random, without cause. But he couldn't find the reason, and he went about very gloomy.

On the day of the fast, Rabbi Liva asked heaven in a dream to reveal why the Scroll of the Law had fallen to the ground. But an unclear answer came from heaven. The Hebrew words were such that the rabbi failed to grasp their meaning.

Rabbi Liva was at a loss to figure out what these words were hinting, and he made up his mind to use Joseph the Golem once again.

He wrote out each letter of the words on a separate piece of paper and then asked Joseph the Golem to put the letters in the proper order. Joseph, without thinking, laid them out in a certain order, and Rabbi Liva saw that these letters were the initials of the words in a line of the evening prayers that had been read from the Scroll of the Law for Yom Kippur. These words were: "And thou shalt not lie carnally with thy neighbor's wife to defile thyself with her."

Rabbi Liva realized that the man who had gone to roll up the Scroll of the Torah had committed adultery with another man's wife. The rabbi sent Joseph the Golem with a note to the sinner, asking him to come immediately. And when Joseph the Golem went for someone, that person knew he had to come, for if not, it had often happened that Joseph the Golem would take the unwilling man and throw him over his back like a sheep, and then carry him back to the rabbi through the streets.

The man he sent for left immediately with the golem, and when he came to Rabbi Liva, the rabbi took him into a private room and asked him in a kindly tone to confess the sin that had caused him to drop the Torah on Yom Kippur. The man saw that no amount of lying would help, and he confessed that for a long time now he had been sinning with his partner's wife.

Rabbi Liva put a penance upon the man, and righted the matter in accordance with the Law.

The Attack on Joseph the Golem

During the years when Rabbi Liva was rabbi of Prague, the inhabitants of Prague would use a dreadful word to one another if ever they got into a fight. This word was *nadler*, a slanderous accusation that the other man did not have pure Jewish blood flowing in his veins. It came from the expulsions from Spain and Italy when many Jews accepted baptism and then returned to Judaism upon finding refuge in Prague. The slanderous word *nadler* was sometimes hurled at their descendants in a quarrel.

Rabbi Liva wanted to do away with this slander, because it brought a great deal of harm to the Jewish community. So he called together a great number of rabbis, and they decreed with a blast of the ram's horn and with the burning of black candles that any Jew who insulted another Jew with the word *nadler* would be placed under a ban.

The decree worked very well, and the Jews took care never to utter the word. However, there were three porters, impudent fellows, who, only a few weeks after the proclamation of the decree, again began insulting other Jews with the word *nadler*. They were reported to Rabbi Liva.

The rabbi was very angry and sent for the most impudent of the porters, the first one to flout the decree. But he merely laughed at the beadle Abraham-Khaym and told him to tell Rabbi Liva that he didn't have the time, and he would come as soon as he could make the time for himself.

This made the Rabbi even angrier. He called in a few strong young men and asked them to prepare a bundle of rods and a rope. Then he summoned Joseph the Golem and ordered him to go over to the porter right away and bring him back by force on his shoulders. Not losing a moment, Joseph the Golem went over, snatched up the porter by the scruff of his neck, and carried him through the streets like a sheep. The porter was no weakling, everyone was afraid of him. But there was nothing he could do against Joseph the Golem.

As soon as the golem delivered the porter to Rabbi Liva, the rabbi had his men tie up the culprit and give him a good whipping to bring him to his senses.

The men did as they were told, and Joseph the Golem went to work with a vengeance, like a slaughterer with a bull. When they had carried out the sentence, they ordered the porter to take off his boots and go to Rabbi Liva in stocking feet to receive his reprimand. He obeyed and then barely dragged himself home, and once there, he had to lie in bed for two weeks until his wounds were healed.

But a fire of vengeance burnt in the porter, and he made up his mind to get even, especially with Joseph the Golem, whom he planned to wipe from the face of the earth.

The porter had a secret talk with his cronies to hit upon a way of dealing with Joseph the Golem, and at last they devised a plan of attack that could be carried out easily. And this was their plan:

At the close of every Sabbath, after the blessing, Rabbi Liva would customarily have someone bring a pitcher of water from a deep well, and the water was used for brewing his tea. Normally, other people performed this task, but when it was dark and slippery outside, he would send Joseph the Golem, who brought back the water safe and sound. Little by little, he got used to doing it, so that right after the closing of the Sabbath, he would hurry out and bring back the pitcher of water.

The porter and his cronies got ready to carry out their plan.

At the closing of the Hanukkah Sabbath, several powerful young men hid near the well. As soon as Joseph the Golem came by and lowered the pail into the well, bending far over the rim as usual, the men ran up to him, grabbed his legs, and sent him hurtling headfirst into the well. The pole with the bucket sprang back out.

Joseph the Golem got a good dunking, and when he came to the surface, he began to splash about with his arms. The men had planned ahead and prepared some heavy rocks, which they threw in the well to make the golem sink and drown. The rocks crashed upon his head, wounding his eye and his nose. He sank down and they kept hurling rocks at him. But then he rose to the surface once more and remained floating on the water.

In Rabbi Liva's home, they were waiting and waiting for the water, until at last the old beadle Abraham-Khaym and two other men went out with lanterns to look for the golem. When they arrived at the well, they caught sight of Rabbi Liva's pitcher near it. They realized something had happened, so they peered into the well with their lanterns. The moment Joseph the Golem spied them, he began clapping his hands, and they saw it was really Joseph down there. They lowered the bucket into the depth and hauled him out. He was bruised and bloody. They took him home and changed his clothes, and they washed and bandaged his wounds.

Rabbi Liva examined him and said he would be all right. They put him into his warm bed, and he fell asleep. But it was a while before he could get out again. By the third day, however, he was up and about.

The rabbi called him in and asked if he knew who had attacked him. Joseph the Golem replied by writing down what had happened, saying he recognized one of the attackers, the porter who had been whipped. The golem asked Rabbi Liva to allow him to get even with the porter. The rabbi answered he would not allow him to do so, adding that the porter would be struck down by heaven.

Not long after that, the porter fell ill with a black mange, and they had to cut out pieces of his living flesh. The porter now confessed the whole story. He and three friends of his, powerful fellows, had thrown Joseph the Golem into the well and hurled large rocks at him. He sent his wife to plead with Rabbi Liva for forgiveness. But it was no use.

The porter died a horrible death.

Afterward, the other three bullies came to Rabbi Liva to ask his forgiveness for participating in the attack on the golem. They defended themselves, saying that the porter had incited them and given them money, but now they deeply regretted what they had done, and they wept bitter tears. The rabbi required them to pay a fine, which went to his yeshivah, and to fast forty days throughout that year, and to recite the entire Book of Psalms every Sabbath.

The three men did everything he told them, and they remained alive.

The Dreadful Tale About the Deserted House Near Prague

Outside of Prague, on a road leading into the city, there stood an old ruin, which at one time had been a factory for gunpowder. And because the building stood on the roadside and had become too old, they moved the factory farther from the town, to the huge barracks of the imperial fort. And thus, the building went to wrack and ruin, standing there for a long, long time.

It slowly became dirtier and filthier, terrifying anyone who passed it at night. Many claimed they had heard a band playing there in the darkness. And some people said they had seen a pack of several hundred black hounds milling about the walls. One Jew swore that while walking by one night he had sighted a soldier standing on the roof and blasting on a trumpet.

All these stories made people wary of going near the ruin at night.

Now one night it happened that a Jewish courier was coming home from a small village by Prague. Unmindful, he walked along the side of the road near the ruin. All at once, he saw a huge black hound, who came running out of the building and barked at the wayfarer. The hound ran around him and then dashed back inside. The courier was so terror-stricken he scarcely made it back home. Upon his arrival, he told his family what had happened.

That night, the Jew began barking in his sleep like a dog. The rest of the household woke him up in alarm. He was exhausted and drenched with sweat. He told the others he had dreamt he was riding on a black hound along with many other people, like a troop of soldiers, and since all the other hound-riders were barking like dogs, they also forced him to bark like a dog. And they warned him that if he didn't bark, then the dogs would devour him alive, and so he barked along with them.

The rest of the household told him not to worry, it was only a dream, he had been thinking about the ruin when he fell asleep, and the best thing for him would be not to think about it.

The next night came, and the same thing happened. And night after night, the man kept barking in his sleep. He started growing weak and losing weight.

The man and his wife decided that only Rabbi Liva could help.

They took along their few children and went to the rabbi, weeping bitterly as they told him the whole story. They begged him to take pity and help them in their plight. For the man supported the entire family with his work as a courier, and now they might starve.

First, Rabbi Liva inspected the fringes on the Jew's undergarment, worn in accordance with God's commandment, and he saw that they were blemished. Next, he examined the man's phylacteries, and he found that the phylactery to be worn on the head was blemished. The rabbi said that this was why the Jew had not been protected and had fallen into an impure mire. For it is written that "every Jew is accompanied by angels who guard him on every road," and the angels are created by his fulfilling the commandments of the phylacteries and the fringes. As proof, we need merely rearrange the letters of that verse in Hebrew and we get another sentence meaning: "Thus, the phylacteries and the fringes."

Rabbi Liva told the courier to fix the phylacteries and the fringes immediately and then go to the ritual bath. Next, he told his scribe to set down a biblical verse on a slip of paper and put it in an amulet: "But against any of the children of Israel shall not a dog move his tongue, against man or beast." The amulet with the verse was tied around the Jew's forehead every night before he went to bed. And for seven nights, at the rabbi's bidding, he slept in the rabbi's home, in Joseph the Golem's bed, while Joseph slept in the courier's bed.

They did everything that Rabbi Liva told them to do. The Jew slept peacefully in the golem's bed, and no longer barked.

On the seventh night, the rabbi summoned Joseph the Golem and gave him his staff, and told him to go into the ruin at midnight with two bundles of straw and fuel, and to kindle the straw, so that the entire building would burn down. Joseph the Golem followed the rabbi's orders, and the entire ruin was burnt to the ground.

From that night on, no more evil things were to be seen in that place, and the courier fully recovered.

The Wondrous Tale of Duke Bartholomew

A few leagues east of Prague, in a large village, there once lived a rich duke, who owned ten villages. In the middle of his large park there stood a tiny castle topped with a peaked tower and ringed by a thick wall, and around the wall there lay a deep moat filled with water, and a narrow iron drawbridge spanned it on one side.

The castle is empty now, but there are two headstones marking the graves of a mother and a son. And the story about this mother and her son is indeed wondrous.

Once there was an old duke living here, and his name was Bartholomew. He had only one child, a son.

The old duke was very fond of Jews, and there were many Jews living in his ten villages, and taking care of his many businesses. After his wife died, he would take his son and visit the Jews in his village, just to feel at home. Most of all, he liked going to them on the Sabbath. He would have some fish in one house, some pudding in another, and so on.

In the village where the duke resided, there lived a wealthy Jew who leased land from the duke. The Jew had a learned daughter, a beauty, and she was the same age as the duke's son. The son liked her very much and spent long hours talking to her.

One day, the old duke said to his Jewish landholder: "Listen to me. If your daughter were willing to become Christian, my son would marry her and you would never have to pay for the land you lease from me."

The Jew tried to laugh it away, and answered that such a marriage wasn't worthy of the duke's son, he could find a far more beautiful wife in a ducal family. The Jew realized however that he couldn't take the matter lightly, and he was afraid that the duke's proposal might become an awful truth. So he quickly engaged his daughter to a Jewish scholar from Prague. The bridegroom was an orphan, but he was a fine young man, and the wedding took place soon thereafter. A year later, the young wife bore a son.

But soon, an epidemic struck that region, claiming many victims, even whole families, and a great number of people fled into other countries, losing complete sight of one another, not knowing who had perished and who had survived. The epidemic raged through the villages of the old duke. And the young wife lost her parents and husband both, she was left alone with the tiny baby and had nowhere to flee.

She finally took refuge in the castle park. The old duke and his son found out she was there and felt great pity for the young wife and her child, so they offered her a private apartment and took care of her every need.

In Prague, as in the ducal villages, people assumed that the entire family of the Jewish landholder had perished. Meanwhile, the young widow forgot about her troubles. The duke's son felt a stronger love for her than ever, and so they decided to marry with no one realizing who she was.

They sent her and the child to Venice in secret, and there they gave the child to a wet-nurse. Shortly thereafter, the wedding took place in the same city. Back home, the duke announced in the village that his son had married the daughter of a Venetian senator and would return with his bride in a year.

Meanwhile, the young couple were living happily in Venice and journeying to other lands. It wasn't until a year and a half later that they came back to the old duke's village. No one was aware that the young aristocrat was actually the Jewish landholder's daughter. The young couple announced that they had already had a baby in Venice, they had given him to a wet-nurse and would bring him back as soon as he was weaned. It wasn't long before the old duke died, so that all his property and his title passed down to the son.

After a time, the baby was weaned and brought to the village, and since his Hebrew name was Jacob, he was registered as the duke's son with the name of Jakob Bartholomew.

The young duke led a good life with his Jewish wife, and she bore him two lovely daughters. Now the duke felt that since the son was born of a Jewish woman he would be strongly drawn to the Jewish religion, for everything is drawn to its own roots. So the duke made an effort to pour a hatred of Jews into the boy's heart, and he hired tutors who despised Jews. Little by little, the hatred that the boy felt in his heart for Jews kept growing, so that in the end he wouldn't even speak to a Jew.

The three children grew up in the ducal castle. They were endowed with beauty and learning, and all three of them made brilliant marriages. The two daughters went off with their husbands, and only the false son and his wife, who was a general's daughter, remained with the duke.

At the age of sixty, the duke went to his reward, and all his property and his title passed down to the false son, Jakob Bartholomew, who lived with his mother, the daughter of the Jewish landholder.

As soon as the new duke, Jakob Bartholomew, took over all the property and began to rule in the villages, he set about oppressing the few Jews who lived there, and did terrible things to them, making sure they stopped earning their livelihoods. He did all he could to get rid of them. Many Jewish families were left without a crust of bread. When they saw how bad things were, they came to Rabbi Liva, begging him to help them. The rabbi answered that for the moment he didn't know what to do, but he hoped that heaven might reveal some plan to him. He asked them to come back in a week.

That very night, when Rabbi Liva was dreaming, the duke's father came to him from the other world and bitterly lamented. The dead man told Rabbi Liva the whole story. Duke Jakob Bartholomew was born a Jew, and he, the dead man, was his father. His name was Isaac ben Aaron Ha-Levi, of Prague, and he was the son-in-law of the Jewish landholder and had died during the epidemic. The duke's mother had been his wife, and after his death she had married the duke. Her Jewish name was Rosa, the daughter of Moses. And when his son Jacob, known as Jakob Bartholomew, had taken over the title of duke, he had started oppressing all the Jewish inhabitants of his villages, and their tears had flowed up to heaven. These tears had brought him, the dead man, great suffering, and he was not allowed a moment's peace. The dead men added that he had come to his son in dreams to reveal to him that he was a Jew, for he was circumcised after all, and he had asked him not to do any harm to the Jews. But the son paid no attention to dreams!

Thus, the dead man lamented bitterly, and he pleaded with Rabbi Liva to take pity on his soul and lead the duke away from his evil path. The dead man then said to the rabbi that he had heard in the True World that only the rabbi could help him with his wisdom.

The next morning, Rabbi Liva asked his old beadle Abraham-Khaym to go to the village where the duke resided and find out whether a landholder named Moses had really lived there and had had a daughter named Rosa, and whether there had ever been a boy named Isaac ben Aaron Ha-Levi in Prague and whether he had married the landholder's daughter.

Abraham-Khaym the beadle found it was all true. Whereupon Rabbi Liva said: "Well, if all this is true then what was said in heaven must also be true—that I can be of some help. I'll have to devise a plan."

And this was the plan that Rabbi Liva carried out:

Rabbi Liva knew that Duke Jakob Bartholomew drove to Prague

every Sunday to attend church. The rabbi wrote the following letter.

> My dear child,
> You must know that I, Isaac ben Aaron Ha-Levi, of Prague, am your real father. I was the first husband of your mother Rosa, who lives with you, and she was a daughter of the Jewish landholder Moses, who dwelt in the village of the deceased duke's father. And I and my father-in-law died in the epidemic. The name I gave you was Jacob.
> And now I have come from beyond the grave to ask you not to do any harm to the Jews who have lived in these villages for so many years.
> I have come into your dreams several times to reveal that you are a Jew by birth, but then I saw that you paid no attention to your dreams. Thus I had to descend myself to give you this letter so that you might realize the truth, for I have had no peace in the next world ever since the tears of the Jewish families began flowing into heaven. You can tell that you are a Jew because you are circumcised, and if you repeat these things to your mother Rosa, she will surely confirm what I have said. If you wish to know what to do, place your trust in the rabbi of Prague.
> Your father, Isaac ben Aaron Ha-Levi

That was the content of the letter. And early in the morning of the day that duke Jakob Bartholomew was to attend church in Prague, Rabbi Liva handed the letter to Joseph the Golem as well as the amulet that made him invisible. The road that the duke was to take went uphill as it neared the city. Rabbi Liva ordered Joseph the Golem to station himself there with the letter and wait for the duke. As soon as the duke came and started driving slowly uphill, Joseph the Golem was to go over to the carriage and drop the letter into the duke's lap.

Joseph the Golem carried out the plan exactly as told. When the duke saw the letter, he turned pale. He peered all around carefully but couldn't see anyone, and so he really believed it had been his dead father.

When the duke arrived home, he questioned his mother thoroughly and showed her the letter. His mother confessed that it was all true and told him not to oppress the Jewish families who were their brothers and sisters.

The next day the duke sent out his carriage for Rabbi Liva. The rabbi accepted his invitation at once and drove to the castle, where he stayed for a day and a night. Rabbi Liva never repeated what had taken place. But people did find out that Duke Jakob Bartholomew had given the rabbi a large sum of money, which he used to found the great yeshivah of Prague, and it was named the Yeshivah of the House of Jacob in honor of its patron Jakob Bartholomew. As for the Jewish families that lived in his villages, they all remained of course, and were given great concessions.

Some time later, Duke Jakob Bartholomew built the well-known little castle at the center of his park and the two tombs, one for his mother and one for himself, so that in death they could lie apart rather than in the Christian churchyard.

The Last Blood Libel in Prague During Rabbi Liva's Lifetime

For three years now, Prague and the surrounding region had been resting from the hardships caused by a Blood Libel. And their rest was due to Rabbi Liva, whom everyone feared for his powerful mind which revealed all secrets.

But in the year 5349 [1589], a terrible Blood Libel occurred in Prague. This is what happened:

There lived in the city a wealthy man named Aaron Ginz. His home was truly Jewish and rich. "Learning and affluence in the same place," as the Talmud says. He had three sons-in-law boarding with him, and they spent their days studying the Torah and the Talmud. He also had three sons and a daughter who weren't married.

Aaron Ginz's business was a leather tannery. The entire household lived in town, in a brick house, but the tannery stood outside the city. There were twenty workers employed there, twelve Jews and eight Christians. And since these men had already been working there a number of years and were always together, the Christian workers came to speak Yiddish as well as the Jews.

Now, there were three brothers among the Christian workers, and they came from a village some four leagues from Prague. Their father had died long ago, but they still had a poor old mother, who lived in a hut away from the village.

The two older brothers were named Karl Kozlovsky and Hendrikh Kozlovsky. At the tannery, people didn't quite know the name of the youngest brother, but everyone called him Kozilek, because when he had first come to the tannery he had been as young and as wild as a *koziol*, a billy goat. His two older brothers were unwilling to tell people his real name. They were ashamed of him and didn't allow him to use their family name because their mother had given birth to him two years after the father's death and without a legal husband. So he was registered as a child born out of wedlock, with the first name of Yan, the son of Yadviga (their mother).

The two older brothers were already married, and they had been living in Prague for some time now. Since the mother was a widow and earned a meager living taking in wash, she pleaded with her two older sons to take their youngest brother into the tannery as a worker like themselves. And she asked them to watch out for him. They agreed for her sake and asked the owner.

When the "billy goat" started in the tannery, he was fifteen years old. He worked hard for three years and was already getting good pay.

One day, Kozilek, the billy goat, was jumping and playing around. All at once he tumbled into a deep vat full of unclean water where the hides were soaking. He was fished out more dead than alive. And two fingers on his right hand were so badly hurt they had to be amputated. Kozilek was laid up for several weeks. He barely regained his health, and he was no longer able to do the same work as before. For not only had he lost two fingers, but he became very sickly after his accident, and sometimes he spit blood.

The owner wanted to let Kozilek go since he was of no use for the work. But the two older brothers wouldn't hear of it, they flatly demanded that he be allowed to remain and receive the same salary as earlier. But if the owner laid him off, he would have to give him a good sum of money. The two brothers had several arguments with the owner about it, and in the end the owner agreed to keep him on, they would use him for hauling and cleaning, but as for pay, he would receive only half as much as before.

From that time on, the two brothers harbored a grudge against the owner, Aaron Ginz, and they started thinking of a way to get even with him, for they saw that Kozilek the billy goat was badly treated. He had to sweep and clean everything, and he had to carry and lug the heavy loads. Besides his chores in the tannery, Kozilek also had to work for the owner at his home in town. He had to sweep, and clean and scrub, and on the Sabbath he had to heat the stoves. In the end, Kozilek became consumptive and constantly spat blood. His life was a living death, and he made up his mind to escape from work even if it cost him his life.

Purim came, and at the banquet in Aaron Ginz's home there were many guests. The company made merry as they always did at Purim, to celebrate the victory of Queen Esther in Persia, who had overcome Haman and prevented him from massacring the Jews. The guests drank a great deal of wine from silver goblets, after which Aaron Ginz and his entire household fell asleep.

Kozilek took advantage of this opportunity. He sneaked into Aaron Ginz's home and took off with ten silver goblets, a dozen silver knives and forks, and Aaron Ginz's watch. And that same night, he fled with all the booty to his old mother by the village, so that no one knew what had become of him.

In the morning, when they saw that there had been a robbery and that Kozilek was gone, they realized it was his handiwork. Aaron Ginz promptly sent for Kozilek's two brothers and told them what he had done, and he accused them of talking him into the robbery and hiding him and his booty. The two brothers argued with their employer, saying he had no right to accuse them, they knew nothing about the robbery, and they certainly couldn't know where he was, because he had no parents.

They didn't want to tell about their old mother because they were sure that Kozilek had fled to her. If they said anything, then Aaron Ginz would certainly go to her hut to look for the booty.

Aaron Ginz reported the robbery to the police, and had them make a thorough search in the home of the two brothers. But nothing was found. As a result, the hatred of the two brothers for Aaron Ginz grew even greater, though they worked in his tannery and earned their living from him. All the same, they agreed to get even with him.

On Friday evening, the two brothers went out to their mother's hut by the village to see what was going on. When they arrived, they found Kozilek dying. He had fled Prague at night a few days earlier and gone out to the country on foot through a terrible cold, so that his consumption grew worse. He was losing a good deal of blood and lay in bed all through the night. At daybreak he died.

The two brothers decided to bury Kozilek on Sunday, in the village graveyard. Now, since they had no money to pay for the funeral and the rites, they took along the watch that Kozilek had stolen from Aaron Ginz, and they brought it to the village priest. They told the priest that their half-brother had just died, and since their mother was very poor, they had no money for the funeral and the ceremonies. The only thing they could give him was the watch that the old widow had as a memento of their deceased father. And they asked the priest to accept it and let them bury their brother without rites.

The priest took the watch and carried out their wishes. Kozilek was buried in the village graveyard, quietly and without ceremonies, and no one in the village noticed.

The brothers took the rest of the stolen silver articles and sold them to someone in the village, giving the money to their old, poor mother. And Sunday afternoon, they went back home to Prague.

On Monday morning, the two brothers didn't come to work until midday, for of course they were tired from their trip. Aaron Ginz was annoyed at this, and upbraided them and treated them very harshly. He yelled that they had probably been drinking all day and all night on what they had robbed from him. The two brothers deeply resented this, they were so angry they couldn't reply. But they made up their minds that the time had come to get even with the owner.

The two brothers worked out a plan. No one knew what had become of their brother Kozilek, and even the people in the village where he was buried didn't know he had died. The two brothers wanted to take this chance to organize a Blood Libel against the owner of the tannery, using the dead body of their Kozilek.

On a certain night, the two brothers stole out to the village where Kozilek was buried. They took the corpse out of the grave, and then put the empty coffin back, and set up the wooden cross again, so that no one could see what had happened. Next, they cut the dead man's throat as in a ritual slaughter, pulled off his clothes, and wrapped him in a blood-stained white sheet.

They then brought the corpse back to Prague, to the Jewish cemetery, and took it to the side near a road that led from Prague to a neighboring village. The road was traveled by many Christians driving their wagons out to the country. The brothers dug out a grave under the wall surrounding the cemetery and waited until some Christians drove by in a wagon, on their way out to the country.

The brothers started burying the corpse, and kept laughing and speaking loudly in Yiddish so that the passers-by would ask them what was going on. And when the Christians asked them what they were doing, the brothers laughed and answered that they were burying a Jewish Gentile, who was neither Jewish or Christian, and thus not worth burying except near the wall in the darkness of night. The Christians who passed by took them at their word and continued driving home.

The two brothers then took Kozilek's clothes and boots, which were well known to all the workers at the tannery, and they stuffed them into a sack. They drove home, and as soon as it was night, they smuggled the clothes into the cellar of Aaron Ginz's home in Prague. There, they buried the sack in a pile of sand when no one was looking.

The next day, in various parts of the city, the two brothers claimed they had heard that some Christians from the nearby village had seen two Jews at night, burying a Christian under the wall of the Jewish cemetery. The brothers remarked that it could only be a Christian victim who had fallen into the hands of the Jews before Passover, for they needed Christian blood in their matzohs.

The rumor quickly spread throughout Prague, and there was certainly no lack of anti-Semites spreading it further day by day. Some of them even started going about, inquiring whether any Christian had vanished during the past few days.

The two brothers stealthily did their share in spreading the rumor, and finally claimed that the victim was no other than the Christian known as Kozilek, who worked in the tannery. During the past few days he had suddenly vanished, like a stone in water, and it must have been because he was sick, and the owner, who wanted to get rid of him, had turned him over as a Passover victim, and to avert any suspicion he had spread a rumor that Kozilek had robbed him and run away.

The rumor circulated by the two brothers grew and grew from day to day, until at last it reached the ears of the police commissioner. And since so many inquiries were coming to him from so many places, he had no choice but to launch an investigation.

The commissioner and the police went over to the nearby village and summoned the Christians who had witnessed the scene. He then took them back to Prague so that they could show him the exact location of the grave.

As soon as the commissioner came home, he asked the leaders of the Jewish community, and Rabbi Liva, and the gravediggers to explain whom they had buried there. But they all flatly denied knowing anything about such a burial, and said it was a falsehood and slander.

Finally, the commissioner, the police, and several Jews went out to the Jewish cemetery and began to search it until they found the grave. They took the dead body out in front of all the people.

Meanwhile a crowd of people from the city had gathered at the cemetery. Kozilek's two brothers were there, along with several other Christian workers from the tannery. As soon as the corpse was unwrapped, they saw that it was really Kozilek. The best proof was that two fingers were missing from his right hand. At once, the two brothers stepped out of the crowd, weeping and wailing, and they mourned their brother.

Turning to the crowd they yelled: "See what those damned Jews do to us! See how that Jew from the tannery, Aaron, slaughtered our young brother!"

The whole mob of Christians became all worked up by his shouts, they wanted to tear apart the few Jews who were there, but the police prevented the murders. Still, several of the Jews had stones hurled at them. The Christians were on the verge of launching a pogrom, but Rabbi Liva hurried over to the city hall and begged the authorities not to let any such dreadful thing happen until the matter was thoroughly investigated. And thus the Jewish quarter was saved from a pogrom.

But the two brothers wouldn't let the matter rest there. They asked the police commissioner to make a thorough search of Aaron Ginz's cellar, for it could well be that they might find their brother's blood in small vials, prepared by the Jews for Passover. The commissioner followed their suggestion, and together with a huge squad of policemen he broke into Aaron's home and undertook a thorough search of the cellar until they found the bundle of Kozilek's clothing, which the two brothers and the rest of the Christian workers from the tannery immediately recognized. The police promptly arrested Aaron Ginz and his two sons-in-law and the women and children and took them all to prison. The house and the tannery were locked and sealed.

The next day, they put the clothes back on Kozilek's dead body, and a large crowd of Christians, with many priests, carried the corpse to a church with all possible ceremonies. The priests mourned the deceased and sermonized against the Jews. Then they informed the police commissioner that they couldn't bury Kozilek until the Jew who had killed him confessed at the victim's side and sewed his throat together again. The commissioner had to do as they said, and they brought Aaron Ginz in fetters, guarded by a huge number of soldiers, to the church.

The most important priest said to the Jew: "Your hands shed this pure blood and severed the throat. You must therefore make good your crime. Beg the dead man's forgiveness and sew his throat together again."

Aaron Ginz, as pale as death, replied: "Since I did not sever the throat, I shall not sew it together again!"

The crowd in the church wanted to pounce upon Aaron Ginz and tear him to shreds. But the soldiers surrounding him held the Christians back.

Again, the priest addressed Aaron Ginz with these words:

"You can see that your sin was revealed as clear as day. And you will most surely be judged and sentenced to death. So if you confess your crime to the dead man and sew his throat together again, you shall do much good for your soul. And when your soul comes to the afterlife, it shall not be so sinful, if you confess your sin and name the people who incited you to such a crime."

To this, Aaron Ginz retorted:

"I do not have to do any good for my soul, for it is innocent of this crime."

When the priests saw they couldn't do anything with him, they told the soldiers to take him back to prison. Then, they buried the victim with great honors. A terrible fear and gloom came upon all the Jews of Prague. They were afraid to show themselves in the Christian streets. *And the city of Prague was perplexed.*

Rabbi Liva himself was horrified at this Blood Libel. He went about in a state of bewilderment, and he had lost the good graces of the rulers, for what could he say in Aaron Ginz's favor? The rabbi realized it was a libel, but it was so cunningly organized, that for the moment he had to hold his tongue.

It was the month of Nissan, and the rabbi did not wish to ordain any fasts. However, he issued a decree that the entire city should rise very early every morning and recite the entire Book of Psalms, until after the trial for the Blood Accusation.

The crisis brought on another crisis. The priests of Prague proclaimed that the Christians were not to purchase anything from Jews, for they were not sure of their lives with the Jews.

When Rabbi Liva saw that the crisis was worsening and that he still hadn't hit upon a solution, he decided to consult his dreams, and he received seven Hebrew words as a clear answer. They meant: "Investigate, inquire thoroughly, they shall be released." The rabbi felt stronger now and comforted his community, saying there was hope, and the truth would out.

The day of the trial arrived. It was the new moon of Sivan, in early summer. Rabbi Liva was present in court. But there was nothing he could offer by way of defense. Aaron Ginz and his three sons-in-law were sentenced to fifteen years at hard labor, the four wives to six years imprisonment, and only the little children were allowed to go free. The city was shrouded in gloom.

However, Rabbi Liva was not asleep. He knew very well that Kozilek had suddenly died of consumption where he had taken refuge, that he had been buried there and then dug up again and smuggled in with his clothes. But how could it be proved?

For one thing, they didn't know where he had died, because they didn't know where he had sought refuge. And secondly, how could they find out, if they didn't even know his real name, which was registered in the book of the deceased, "Kozilek" being only his nickname.

The first thing Rabbi Liva did was to bend all his efforts to discovering where Kozilek could have died and been buried. Now, since it made sense that he had sought refuge in his native town, the rabbi began investigating where the three brothers came from. By questioning the workers of the tannery, he managed to ferret out that they came from the large village four miles from Prague.

The rabbi sent capable men to that village, to find out about the Kozlovsky family. They did discover where the mother lived, but they couldn't get any information out of her. She stuck to the story that she hadn't seen hide nor hair of her youngest son ever since he had gone away to his two older brothers.

The rabbi's men came back to Prague empty-handed. But when Rabbi Liva heard there was a Christian cemetery in the village, he said that now there was a way to bring forth the facts, but they would have to depend on a higher power. He explained that during the first year of a person's death, the soul remained by the grave because it was still somewhat attached to the body; but if a body wasn't in the grave, they wouldn't see the soul above it. Now a dead man's soul could only be seen by people on a high level or by cattle, beasts, and birds. And Joseph the Golem could see a soul as well as cattle, beasts, or birds could.

Thus, Rabbi Liva demanded that the authorities allow him to send two men to look upon all the graves of the last three months in the Christian cemetery of that village. They would determine whether there was any empty grave from which a dead man had been unlawfully removed. He also demanded that city hall give him two policemen. The commissioner yielded to the rabbi's request and sent him two policemen, together with an order that the gravediggers of that cemetery should show them all the fresh graves of the last three months.

Rabbi Liva assigned the task to Joseph the Golem, and gave him a capable man, and they went to investigate the cemetery. There, the golem paused at a grave, and motioned that it was empty. They sent word to Prague, and the commissioner came with several policemen, and the rabbi with several intelligent men accompanied them.

They dug up the grave and took out an empty coffin.

The commissioner sent for the priest and had him bring the book of the deceased and tell them who had been buried in that grave. The priest came with the records, and they discovered that just a few days before Purim, the gravediggers had buried a man named Yan, the son of Yadviga. They already knew that this was the name of the old mother of the two brothers.

Now the commissioner realized that Kozilek had actually been buried here and that the body had then been stolen. The commissioner questioned the priest closely to make him remember the men who had asked permission to bury the corpse. The priest recalled that they were the two brothers of the dead man. They had paid him no money, but had given him a watch, which he had in his pocket. The priest showed the watch to the police commissioner.

The others remembered that Aaron Ginz had been robbed of a watch, and so the commissioner sent a horseman to town to ask Aaron Ginz whether this was indeed his watch. Aaron Ginz identified the watch as his at a distance and with the help of a hidden sign. The horseman quickly rode back to the village and told the commissioner how Aaron Ginz had identified the watch.

The commissioner and his men broke into the old woman's hut. The old woman kept denying everything, but then, after two hard slaps, she began crying and pleading, and said she would tell them the whole story, and she gave them a correct account of what had happened, and she even told them where the rest of the stolen articles had been sold in the village.

The police commissioner ordered a thorough search of the village and they found the rest of the stolen articles. The commissioner promptly arrested the old woman and the man who had bought the valuables, and they were taken back to Prague.

Next, the commissioner entered the home of the two brothers, because the man who had bought the stolen articles told the police he had gotten them from Yadviga's two older sons. However, the two brothers were no longer in Prague, they had made their escape. Now the authorities finally realized the truth about how the Blood Libel had been organized, and they quickly released Aaron Ginz and his two children, and *the city of Prague rejoiced and was glad.*

Rabbi Liva wrote down a full protocol of exactly what had happened, from start to finish, and sent it to King Rudolph with a request that the king allow him to present himself at court. The king gave Rabbi Liva the permission, and on a certain day, the royal palace sent two generals after him in a coach.

When the rabbi appeared before the king, he tearfully begged the ruler to put an end once and for all to the Blood Libel, so that such a trial would never again be repeated in any court of justice anywhere in the land, for the sin of accusing innocent souls falls upon an entire kingdom.

The king had a long conversation with him. Rabbi Liva never cared to reveal what was said. But afterward, the king issued an order that no more Blood Accusations were to be made against Jews in his kingdom.

How Rabbi Liva Removed Joseph the Golem

After King Rudolph's law was put in effect, and another Passover went by with no incidents, Rabbi Liva summoned his son-in-law Isaac and his pupil Jacob Sassoon Ha-Levi, who had both participated in the creation of Joseph the Golem. The rabbi said the golem was no longer needed because there would be no more Blood Libels in this country. This was the night of Lag b'Omer in the year 5350 [or 1590 according to the Christian reckoning].

Rabbi Liva ordered the golem not to lie down on his bed in the rabbi's home, but rather to take his bed to the attic of the synagogue and to go to sleep up there. Joseph the Golem did as he was told when no one was watching. After midnight, Rabbi Liva, together with the *gaon* and his pupil Jacob Sassoon, mounted the stairs up to the attic of the great synagogue. Before going, the rabbi had a thorough discussion with his son-in-law to decide whether a Cohen could be in the same room as a corpse like the golem's, since such a thing was forbidden to a descendant of priests. Rabbi Liva demonstrated that such a corpse is not really a defilement.

Rabbi Liva had given Abraham-Khaym, the old beadle, his permission to attend and told him to stay back a bit with two candles in his hands.

When they reached the attic, the three men stood in positions opposite to the ones they had taken when creating the golem. First they stood at the head of the prostrate golem and faced his feet. Next, they began circling him along his left side to his feet and then along his right side to his head, where they stopped and said something. They did the same thing seven times.

After the seven encirclements, the golem was dead. He lay there like a piece of hardened clay. The rabbi then called over the beadle Abraham-Khaym and took hold of the two candles, and they stripped the clothes off the golem, leaving only his shirt on him, and since there was no lack of old prayer shawls in the attic, they wrapped him up in two old prayer shawls and bound him well. Next, they shoved him under the mountain of stray leaves from holy books so that he was fully hidden from sight.

Rabbi Liva told Abraham-Khaym to take the bed and the clothes downstairs and burn them up slowly without anyone seeing him. Next, they all descended and washed their hands.

The next morning, it was announced that the beadle Joseph the Golem had gotten angry and departed that night. The mass of Jews believed it, but some of the community leaders knew the truth.

A week later, Rabbi Liva proclaimed a ban against going up to the attic of the great synagogue. He forbade any further storing of loose pages in the attic. They said the prohibition was due to a fear that someone might start a fire up there by kindling a light. But some of the community leaders knew the real reason:

No one was ever to know that Joseph the Golem is lying up there.

The Third Day

The Conversation of Two Ghosts

This happened to a pious Jew, who once, on the Eve of Rosh Hashanah [New Year's] gave a ducat to a poor man for the year had been one of great dearth. His wife was so angry at what he had done that he was simply frightened of going home again. So he went to spend the night in the graveyard.

In the middle of the night, he heard the ghosts of two girls talking to one another:

"Come on, let's float over the worlds and eavesdrop on God to find out what kind of a year it will be."

The other replied: "I can't go with you, I've been buried in a shroud of reeds. Why don't you go and then tell me everything you've heard."

The ghost flew off alone, and after a while she came back and said to her friend:

"I heard that the man who sows his grain in the first half of Heshvan [late October] will have his entire crop destroyed by hail."

When the pious man heard this, he sowed his grain in the second half of Heshvan (early November). A hailstorm ruined all the crops that had been planted in the first half of Heshvan. But the pious man's grain, which had been sown in the second half of Heshvan, was saved.

The next year, the pious man went back to spend the night in the graveyard and hear what the ghosts said to one another.

All at once, he heard one ghost say to the other:

"Come on, let's go and hear what will be happening in the world this year."

The second dead girl replied: "I've already told you, I can't move because I'm all bound up in a shroud of reeds. Why don't you go and then tell me everything you've heard."

So she left and then after a while she came back and told the other:

"I heard that the man who sows his grain in the second half of Heshvan will have his crop devastated by a hailstorm."

The pious man went home and sowed all his grains in the first half of Heshvan. A hailstorm destroyed all the crops that had been sown in the second half of Heshvan, but it didn't hurt the pious man, for he had sown earlier.

His wife was amazed, and she asked him:

"Dear husband. How can it be that all the crops were ruined, but not yours? There is more here than meets the eye."

So he told her the whole story, about eavesdropping on the two ghosts and hearing what they said, and how one of them couldn't move because she had been buried in a shroud of reeds.

Not long after that, the pious man's wife had a fight with the mother of the dead girl who had been buried in a shroud of reeds. Now women often get into fights. And the pious man's wife yelled at the mother: "Just go and see your poor daughter, who was buried in a shroud of reeds."

Two days later, the pious man once again went to the graveyard to hear the two ghosts conversing. Once again, one dead girl said to the other: "Come on. Let's go and hear what will be happening this year."

"Forget about it. The secret is out, people have been eavesdropping on our conversations."

A Good Laugh

Frankly, I just don't feel like telling you any more stories. And do you know why? Because when you hear my stories, you get too excited.

At the close of the Sabbath, I told you how the holy rabbi, the Baal Shem-Tov, speaking the words "Liberator of prisoners," in the Eighteen Benedictions, broke down the iron gates of a prison and liberated Jews who had been arrested for a Blood Libel. Your eyes shone, you smacked your lips, you cried: "What a miracle!"

But for me, it was as if you had said that when Jews are imprisoned and tortured because of a libel, that's natural, but when they're set free, that's a miracle! You concluded from my story that the Good Lord introduced injustice as a natural thing, but luckily there are wonder-rabbis who prevent His injustice with miracles.

Just look at the slough one can get stuck down in from too much fervor and excitement!

Well, you will ask me, where does the power of wonder-rabbis lie if not in miracles? And I'll say to that: Their power isn't as great as you may think. No greater than the strength of an angel. Now angels are no more than messengers, and wonder-rabbis merely carry the messages of the Good Lord, Blessed Be His Name. A greater one does something important, a lesser one something less

important. And that's all. None of them work miracles! There are
no wonders! Everything is quite natural.

However, if I tell you that you have to listen to a Hassidic tale
without ardor or excitement, that doesn't mean that you can take it
lightly—like a fairytale about how once upon a time there was a
rabbi and a rebbetsin, and all that. No! On the contrary. If you restrain your ardor and excitement, then you have to listen very attentively, you have to get into it fully. A Hassidic tale has to be
studied almost religiously, the way you pore over the Talmud, and
perhaps even more profoundly . . . .

But now, listen to a story about the Baal Shem-Tov.

1.

One wintery day, the Baal Shem-Tov and his followers were
relaxing from their religious studies. They were sitting together,
having drinks, smoking pipes, singing, and talking a bit. They
talked about this and that, but their words were filled with a
strange force. No matter what they talked about, even the deepest
mysteries of the Cabbalah—everyone understood. Each word of
theirs had windows to all levels of understanding.

And that was the secret of why their voices could be heard from
one end of the world to the other.

When Hassids drink and croon, they are sure to be merry. And
when they are merry—they laugh.

Whereupon Dovid Leykes said:

"Laughter is a fine thing. One can serve the Creator better with
laughter and joy than with bitter tears."

The Baal Shem-Tov heard him and said, almost to himself:

"There is an even greater level of humor, when, instead of laughing, you are laughed *at* . . . ."

Having spoken, he said no more.

His followers crooned to his words and meditated on them as
though unrolling a scroll of the Torah.

Wolf Kitses responded:

"When I laugh for joy, I feel a widening of my soul. But when
someone else laughs at me, I become like a stool under his feet, a
footstool on which the man who's laughing can stand and put
himself higher. And that puts me on a higher level."

But Dovid Firkes protested:

"No! There's something else behind it! If someone laughs at me, it means that what I've said or done is a surprise to the man who's laughing. And the instant I've done something surprising in the world, I've raised myself to a higher level."

But then, Ber Mezeritsher explained in his faint voice:

"If you add up the numerical values of the Hebrew letters in the word *tskhok* [laughter] and in *nitsokhn* [victory], they work out to equal sums. Now since victory can only come at the end of a war and is based on things that have happened, it belongs to the category of the past. And since the laughter of victory is a cruel thing, it is material in nature. And thus, the opponent, the one that's laughed at, is of the future and spiritual in nature."

The Baal Shem-Tov smiled and said:

"You know what? Why don't we go for a drive. Perhaps on the way, someone, somewhere, will laugh at us, and you'll understand what it's all about."

The Hassids were delighted. Going for a drive with the Baal Shem-Tov was always a holiday, and there was sure to be a surprise in store for them.

So they told Alexei, the Baal Shem-Tov's manservant, to harness the horse.

2.

Some people think there was something sublime about Alexei. But they're mistaken. He was a simple peasant, like any peasant, and a drunkard to boot. Still, he had the good quality of obeying without talking or questioning. If the Baal Shem-Tov told him to sit with his back to the horse, he did so. If he had told Alexei to harness the horse with its tail in front and its head to the wagon, he would have gone and done it naïvely, and never even dreamt of asking why. And not because you don't ask the Baal Shem-Tov any questions, but simply because he was incapable of asking questions. And he was incapable because he hadn't reached the level of will. Some people even speculated that Alexei was in the image of the golem of Rabbi Levi of Prague. Be that as it may, the Baal Shem-Tov was very fond of Alexei for obeying without questions, and at times the master would even tell his disciples to learn that fine quality from the servant. Once, when he was pondering the phenomenon of two existences that meet and do not meet, he said:

"The highest level of spirituality must bring you to the same denial of your own will and of all existence, which Alexei has attained on the lowest level of materiality."

Alexei harnessed the horse to a sleigh and—where were they driving to? That was up to the horse. Alexei was nestled up in fur, with his back to the horse, and sleeping. The frost burned and singed, the snow crackled, screamed, and ground under the sleigh. The wind blasted, and the trees in the forest popped like gunfire. But the Hassids couldn't care less. Even Ber Mezeritsher, an invalid, forgot to wrap his scarf around his neck. They were absorbed in their debate. About what? Reward and punishment.

The Baal Shem-Tov listened, smiled, as was his wont, and said, almost in passing:

"If punishment atones for a sin, then a reward atones for a good deed . . . ."

The Hassids promptly fell silent.

Dovid Firkes cried out:

"If a reward nullifies a good deed, then the pleasure of doing a good deed requires no reward!"

Wolf Kitses countered:

"Isn't pleasure a reward?"

To which Ber Mezeritsher softly replied:

"Then let's forget about pleasure! Let's put an end to good deeds and rewards! Let there be fulfillment of the Will of the Lord God Blessed Be He, as the only place of the life-spirit, that is to say: 'We must live with these laws.' "

Dovid Leykes asked:

"Well, then how are we to understand the question of sin?"

There was a silence, No one knew what to answer. The Baal Shem-Tov put in a helping hand.

"If you can have a person without good deeds," he said, "then you can have a sin without a person."

And he quoted Exodus:

" 'He looked and he looked, and he saw that no one was there.' For the looking and looking are the shape of the sin. And as soon as a sin is committed, we can see that the man is no one. For he loses his life-spirit and becomes as dead."

Jacob-Joseph grumbled:

"What about repentance?"
The master replied:
"Repentance is the resurrection of the dead."

3.

Their talk was done, and they drove on. All at once, the horse
stopped. And when a horse stops, it stops. It may have been necessary, even though they were in the middle of the woods.
So they climbed out of the sleigh. And since it was time for
evening prayers, they prayed. Suddenly, they saw someone in the
distance driving their way. They peered closer. There were two
people. From far away, they looked like children. When the sleigh
came nearer, they turned out to be a boy and a girl, snuggling together, nearly frozen. And their horse was on its last legs, it could
barely drag itself along.
The Hassids stopped the horse, took the young people out of the
sleigh, shook them awake, revived them a bit. They gave them a
few drops of brandy, and the youngsters came to their senses.
When the Hassids asked them where they were driving, they burst
into tears. Upon calming down, the boy told them the story.
He and the girl had been working for a tavern-keeper as his servant and maid. Since both were orphans and all alone in the world,
they decided to marry, and so they got engaged. But then one day,
the tavern-keeper's wife lost her temper at the girl and began
hitting and beating her. And even though the boy was just a servant, he stood up for his bride. Their boss got so angry that he beat
them and threw them out. Now since they had saved up enough
rubles, they bought a horse and a little sleigh, and drove into the
world. They kept driving, week after week, from place to place,
without finding a haven. Meanwhile, they spent their last kopek and
for two days now they hadn't had a bite to eat—and it got colder
and colder outside, and they were at the end of their rope . . . .
The Hassids gave them food. And when they were full, Jacob-
Joseph asked them gruffly:
"How come a boy and a girl are traveling alone—without a
chaperon?"
The girl was embarrassed, and the boy started explaining.
But the Baal Shem-Tov smiled and said:
"Then we'll drive to an inn and have a wedding."

So they piled into the sleighs, with Wolf Kitses joining the youngsters to chaperon them, and off they went. After a short drive, they halted at an inn. Upon seeing it, the boy and girl realized that this was the tavern where they had worked. They shivered and were amazed at returning here so fast.

Meanwhile, out came the tavern-keeper and his wife. Laying eyes upon their former servants, they screamed:

"So you've come back, you scoundrels! Get your sleigh out of here!"

The Baal Shem-Tov began calming them:

"There's no reason to get angry. We've taken them along with us."

The woman laughed:

"You've got yourself a real bargain."

But the Baal Shem-Tov went on:

"Since the boy and girl are engaged to marry, we would like to hold their wedding here."

The tavern-keeper guffawed. The very idea of having a wedding for the two scoundrels he had thrown out! He told the Baal Shem-Tov to keep driving.

To which the Baal Shem-Tov quietly said:

"No, we really want to have the wedding in your inn. And you will be so kind as to prepare a fine supper."

The tavern-keeper and his wife roared with laughter. A fine supper indeed!

"Yes," repeated the Baal Shem-Tov. "You will prepare a fine supper, with the loveliest dishes, the choicest wines, and I will pay whatever it costs."

The tavern-keeper, his curiosity aroused, asked:

"And about how much will you pay?"

"Whatever you charge."

And the Baal Shem-Tov showed him a pile of ducats.

When they saw the money, they stopped laughing. The tavern-keeper looked at his wife, and she at him. Both of them were wondering whether the money was stolen. And both of them answered the question themselves: "It's none of our business!" And the tavern-keeper said:

"If you really pay us well, we'll prepare a supper as you want us to."

So they entered the tavern and prepared for the wedding. And, when everything was ready, they began the ceremony, which the

Baal Shem-Tov himself performed. When it was over, they all sat down at the table with the bride and groom at the head. And the company ate and drank and made merry.

4.

When the seven nuptial blessings were spoken and the feast was over, the Baal Shem-Tov stood up and said to his Hassids:

"We have to give our newlyweds presents." And he called out: "I'll give them this tavern and all its furnishings, and the surrounding buildings, the horses, cattle, sheep, and other livestock."

The innkeeper and his wife, upon hearing him, broke into loud guffaws, and they sent for the peasants living nearby to come and watch the fine comedy.

And the Baal Shem-Tov and his Hassids did what they had to do.

After the Baal Shem-Tov, Jacob-Joseph stood up:

"And I," he said, "I'll give the newlyweds the forest around the inn."

"And I'll give them the stone mill down by the river," cried Ber Mezeritsher.

"And I'll give them the brewery," cried Wolf Kitses.

And Dovid Leykes gave them the barn with all its grain, which stood in the duke's courtyard. And Dovid Firkes gave them a hundred barrels of wine from the duke's wine cellar.

And thus each Hassid gave them his gift. And each time, the tavern-keeper, his wife, and the peasants laughed louder and louder. At last, the tavern-keeper himself went over to the table, and choking with mirth, he shouted:

"And I'll give the fine couple the ten thousand rubles that the duke just got from his tavern-keepers today!"

His wife didn't want to be any less generous than her husband, and she shouted mirthfully:

"And I'll give the lovely young bride the precious brooch and the earrings that the duchess has on!"

The Baal Shem-Tov said to them:

"Why don't you give them something of your own. After all, they did work for you for so many years."

The tavern-keeper screamed with laughter.

But his wife cried out sarcastically:

"Give them the old ruin behind the village!"

Everyone laughed. The ruin had no doors or windows, and the roof had caved in.

"Is that all you're giving them?" asked the Baal Shem-Tov.

"That's all."

The Baal Shem-Tov sighed, stood up, and paid hard cash for the supper. He added a ruble for the tablecloth.

Then he told the young man:

"Take all the food and drink left over from the supper and wrap them up in the cloth. Put it all in your sleigh, and then get in with your wife, and go in peace."

The young man asked:

"Where should we go?"

And the Baal Shem-Tov replied:

"To the right. The Good Lord will take care of everything else."

And he wouldn't speak another word. He and his Hassids piled into the sleigh—and off they drove. And before they could even think, they were back in Bedjibuzh.

5.

The young man did what the Baal Shem-Tov had told him to do. He put all the leftovers in the tablecloth, got into the sleigh with his wife, and drove off. And the tavern-keeper and his wife and the peasants accompanied them with mockery and abuse. And they drove without knowing what was happening. Everything seemed like a dream. But they did remember the people laughing at them, and they felt miserable, and wept.

Meanwhile, dawn was coming. And when it was daylight, the horse stopped all at once and refused to go any farther. The young man climbed out of the sleigh and looked for a twig to whip the horse. Suddenly, in the distance, he saw someone lying in the snow. He hurried over and realized it was a young nobleman, almost frozen, but still alive. The young groom called to his bride, and they started reviving the stranger, rubbing him with snow. The young nobleman opened his eyes. The bride remembered that they had some wine from the supper in the tablecloth. She ran back to the sleigh, got the wine, and poured a few drops into his mouth to refresh him. He came to his senses, and faintly asked for food. The bride remembered that they had a lot of food from the supper in the tablecloth and she gave him some. And he ate ravenously and drank up a whole bottle of wine. And, when he was full, he told them what had happened to him.

It turned out that he was the only son of the duke. The day before, he had gone out hunting, and the horse had run wild and thrown him, and then galloped off. He remained alone in the woods—and the farther he walked, the more he went astray in the depths of the forest. He had called out, but no one heard him. He wandered about for a day and a night, until his strength was gone, and he was so worn out, cold, and hungry that he collapsed and almost froze to death.

As he spoke, there was a sudden blare of trumpets, shouting, and the galloping of hooves. And then a troop of horsemen rode up with a carriage. When the horsemen sighted the young duke, they broke into a wild joy. They dashed over and kissed his hands, and then they picked him up and took him to the carriage and put him inside. And with a great commotion and a blaring of trumpets, they quickly drove away.

The young bride and groom remained alone in the middle of the forest. They still didn't know what had happened. Again, it all seemed like a dream.

6.

When they brought the young duke back to the court, the old duke and duchess ran up and kissed and hugged him, and they ordered a huge meal. And the rejoicing had no end.

When everyone had calmed down a bit, the young duke remembered the young couple who had rescued him from death, and he asked for them. But no one knew where they were. So the duke sent out a great number of horsemen to look for them. When they found the young couple, they brought them back to the court in triumph and led them into the largest hall. And the duke and duchess thanked them over and over again for saving their only son from death. The old duke asked them who they were. The young man told him that he and his wife had worked for the tavern-keeper, but that he had gotten angry at them and thrown them out into the cold. Upon hearing this, the duke became furious and shouted:

"Since the tavern-keeper threw you out, I'll turn over his tavern

to you for all time, with all the furnishings, the surrounding buildings, the horses, cattle, sheep, and other livestock."

And the duchess cried out:

"And I'll give them the forest around the tavern."

And the young duke said:

"And I'll give them the stone mill down by the river, and the
brewery, and the barn with all the grain and a hundred barrels of
wine from our wine cellar."

And then the old duke went on:

"They have to have some cash for the start of their marriage. I'll
give them the ten thousand rubles that I got yesterday from my
tavern-keepers."

And the duchess added:

"Since the young wife has only just married, she has to have jewelry."

And she unpinned her diamond brooch and diamond earrings and
gave them to the young bride.

And the young couple stood there, dazed by their great fortune,
it all seemed like a dream. And when they came to their senses,
they started thanking their patrons for the wonderful presents, and
the old duke asked the young man what he wanted. The young
man remembered the tavern-keeper and his wife, and, feeling sorry
for them, he said:

"What's going to happen to the tavern-keeper and his wife?"

The duke laughed:

"Why should you worry about them?"

And the duchess, laughing, cried out to the duke:

"Give them the ruin behind the village!"

And everyone burst out laughing.

Upon hearing the laughter, the young couple thought it was still
the tavern-keeper and his wife and the peasants, and they felt miserable and they wept . . . .

A short time later, when the Hassids were talking about the
whole thing at the Baal Shem-Tov's table, the master said:

" 'Even when they were laughing at me, my heart took pity on
those who were laughing. The poor things were doubly pitiful.' "

And he heaved a heavy sigh . . . .

The Possession

Once, an evil spirit entered a young man. The wise men tried to get the spirit to tell them his name or his wife's name. And whenever they reminded him of his wife, he began shrieking and said that she was an *agunah*, a woman whose husband has vanished. This meant that she couldn't remarry, even though he had drowned at sea. And the wise men could not allow her to take another husband.

The spirit wanted the wise men to allow the woman to marry again. And he gave them many signs to prove he had drowned at sea. But they didn't know where he had been at home, and so they said: "We cannot permit it."

And now he shrieked because she had become a whore, since they didn't allow her to take another husband.

The wise men asked him why he had no rest and what sins he had committed.

He said he had committed adultery.

The wise men asked who the woman had been.

But he wouldn't tell them, because she had been dead for a long time. "It wouldn't help you if I did tell you." And he added: "I am the kind of man who our sages said ought to be punished with all four capital punishments, for committing adultery. But I was not punished."

And as they were talking, the young man got to his feet. The wise men asked him:

"Why are you standing now?"

And the young man said:

"Because a scholar is about to come in."

They looked around. And just then, a scholar came in, exactly as the young man had foretold. And after him came a group of young men. They also wanted to hear what was going on.

Whereupon the evil spirit said:

"Why did you come here? To see me? There are some among you who have done what I did, and you shall be as I am now."

The young men were terror-stricken.

Then the evil spirit said:

"Why are you so surprised? That's the one, standing there in white clothes. He lay with a man. That's as bad as lying with a married woman.

The young men were terror-stricken and peered at one another. Meanwhile, the young man in white clothes began shouting:

"It's true, by God! I did it, and so did he!"

And they owned up to their bad deeds.

One of the wise men now asked: "How did you know what they did?"

The spirit laughed and said:

"It is written that whatever a man does is inscribed in his hand."

They said to him:

"How could you have seen their hands? They were under their cloaks."

The spirit laughed again and said:

"Can't I see everywhere?"

Then they asked him how he had come into the young man.

The spirit said he had had no rest in the water, the fish had eaten his body. His soul went out and passed into a cow. The cow had gone wild, and her owner, a Gentile, had sold her to a Jew. The Jew slaughtered her, and the young man was present and the spirit flew into him.

The wise men finally managed to exorcise the spirit from the young man, and the spirit flew away.

DOVID BERGELSON

At Night

At night once, I awoke in the dark, crowded, loudly snoring railroad car; instantly I saw him on the seat across from me and instantly I recognized him. There he sat, the old, familiar night-Jew, who, whenever he travels on a train, can never sleep at night; and when he can't sleep at night, he bores you, and when he bores you, he looks for something in your eyes, and exacts something from your soul, exacts mutely, but naggingly, and unceasingly.

"Young man," he glanced at me with his watery, ever mournful eyes, "where are you off to, young man?"

And his voice echoed in my ears, so acrid and ancient, older than time out of mind.

And because that was all he said, it seemed as though the voice were coming not from him but from somewhere far away, calling me to account.

"Young man, just where are you off to, young man?"

And when I opened my eyes a second time in the dark, heavily snoring railroad car, the train was still rolling across black swamps and desolate watery fields, and the night was still whining and lashing raindrops against the windows, and far off in the corner of the car, the light was still flickering, it kept flickering and vanishing. Beyond the thin wall, in the second train compartment, a swaddled baby was squalling endlessly, and there, next to the waking night-

Jew, across from me on the seat, someone else was already sitting, a
red-cheeked youth in a jacket and boots, and I felt as though I had
known this youth, too, for a long time. Some sort of misfortune has
always just come upon him and driven him from his home town,
and people are always listening to his story; looking pitifully into
his face and listening in silence. But, looking pitifully into his face
and listening in silence, they realize that he's a decent sort, and they
say:

"Young man, why don't you get up and fix us a pot of tea?"

By now, the youth had already told the waking night-Jew all
about the misfortunes that had come upon him.

"To top it all off, I can't sleep," he quietly lamented, "and what
can you do, what can you do, in such a long night?"

The bored night-Jew did not understand.

"What do you mean . . . ?"

He had been looking and looking for something in the eyes of
the red-cheeked youth and kept exacting something from his soul.
"What should you do?" he repeated, and again his voice became
low and monotonous, it sounded acrid and ancient, older than time
out of mind.

"Open up a sacred book," he said, "study the holy writings."

"But I don't know how," the youth lamented.

"You don't know how?"

The Jew meditated.

"If you don't know how, then just repeat after me, word for
word.

"In the beginning," the youth repeated, "the earth was waste and
wild, and the chasm was darkness, and the spirit of God hovered
over the waters."

All the way through, the heavily rolling, darkened car was still
full of the snoring and wheezing of the passengers who, in the flickering light, were asleep in three layers, atop one another. Sweaty
faces were ruddy and puffy as though swollen, cheeks bulged out,
noses were whistling, and each in its own way. There was a sedate
and respectable whistle that sounded like the very soul of innocence
and seemed to be saying:

"Well yes, I'm sleeping . . . . Of course I'm sleeping."

There was also a despairing whistle of helplessness.

"I'm sleeping because the world is waste and wild, the world is
waste and wild."

There was also a cantorial coloratura, spiraling up like a chant and inquiring: "So what . . . ? If the whole world is asleep, so what?"

And a stronger whistle that didn't care about anything, and warned:

"Do not disturb, it won't help."

And amid the snoring and whistling, the red-cheeked youth repeated what the bored night-Jew said, word for word, about how God created the heavens and the earth, the sun and the stars, day and night, reptiles and beasts, birds, plants, and humans; how the serpent was cunning, and the evil that men did increased, and God regretted that he had created mankind and he spoke:

"I wish to wipe from the face of the earth everything, everything that I have created, every last reptile, every last bird that flies through the air. For I must regret that I did create them."

And suddenly, suddenly, next to the bored night-Jew, there emerged some sort of man named Noah:

"Repeat word for word," he said to the red-checked youth, "repeat . . . : 'And Noah found grace in the eyes of God.' "

"And Noah," the youth repeated, "found grace in the eyes of God."

All around, there was still the hearty and heavy snoring. The train was still running across black swamps and desolate watery fields, and the night was still whining and lashing raindrops against the window. The only passengers not asleep were myself, the bored night-Jew, and the red-cheeked youth in the jacket and boots. The old Jew and the youth were sitting petrified, looking at one another, and I was lying and thinking:

"A good word: 'And Noah found *grace*.' It saved the world."

DER NISTER

In The Wine Cellar

And whenever the carrier who carries our earth-and-world upon
his back grows weary of carrying, he hands it over to someone else,
a friend of his with nothing to do, and the carrier goes off drinking . . . .

One evening, when it was dark and eerie, he came to a large and
respectable town. There, just off a bustling street, lay a deserted alley. And there, in a brick building you can find a storage cellar.
You can enter the cellar by going down a few narrow steps. People
gather there in several old rooms with low ceilings, and the walls of
these rooms are covered with enamel, a shiny black, and on these
walls, on the blackness, there are old pictures painted red. Inside
these rooms you'll find old tables, leftovers from the past, plain
wood, and scoured white, and next to the tables old benches, likewise plain, and long, so that several people can sit on them, and the
ceilings are low, and from the walls the old portraits of old-time
drunkards, great men and visitors, are gazing down.

When the world-carrier arrived in the evening, the little rooms
were already filled, couples were sitting at every table, but in one
room there were only men to be found, and here he found a place
at a table, sat himself down, and asked the waiter to serve him wine.
So he served him, and the clientele was already drunk, the faces
were red from wine and drinking, and their eyes couldn't see

straight, they were blurred and bewildered. And every so often one drinker or another would jump up from his seat to clink glasses with the man across from him, or simply, in his drunkenness, let out a yell.

At one table, there was a bunch of young men, young scholars who hadn't left their school benches yet, and among them rich children, and people who hang around the rich: Cheap dreamers and chintzy drinkers, who think they can make the world over and talk away its present condition. And they yell and they rage as they drink, and they shout and carry on, no one listening to anyone else, and one of them, the hottest head, sticks out from the crowd and carries on more than anyone else, and hollers and shrieks at the world:

"The world is up to its ears in debts, and even its hair is not its own."

"Send it to prison—it's bankrupt!" others shouted, banging their fists on the table.

"Pawn it," one of them threw in, "sell it to the owner of The Blind Man." (That was the name of the tavern!)

"Put a hole in it, stick in some powder, blow it up!" someone else hollered.

"Hey cousin!" a souser turned to the world-carrier, who, at his table, was sitting aloof. "Who are you and what are you doing here?"

"I'm the carrier of the world!" was the answer.

"Who?!" The souser didn't quite get it, and didn't quite believe what he got.

"The carrier of the world!"

"Hahahaha!" He burst out laughing and, turning to his boon companions, he cried:

"Gang, get a load of who's sitting here with us! The carrier of the world!"

And the gang dashed over to the world-carrier, surrounding his table in drunken mockery, they thought he was crazy and they advised him to carry the world gingerly, and warned him not to drop it, or else it might break, God forbid! . . . .

"Okay!" the carrier agreed.

"What a waste of effort, no one's gonna pay him for his trouble," said one of them.

"There are certainly better lines of work around," said another.

And the drinkers eventually gave up and left him there to sit and be crazy, they went back to their places and their drinking, on and on, into the night, until they had all gone to sleep where they were, some with their heads and arms on the table, some on a neighbor's shoulder, and some just sitting up straight. They fell asleep, and no one awoke them, because no one ever throws you out of The Blind Man, it's open day and night, and people can carry on as long as they like. At midnight, the rooms are actually cleared out, but whoever is staying simply stays, whoever is drinking drinks, and whoever isn't—can just sit .... So the carrier sat on, and there was no one left in his little room except for those who were fast asleep, and the other rooms were also empty, and the night waiters, idle at the table corners, were napping, and the bustle in town had faded out, and the alley outside The Blind Man was deserted, only the occasional feet of someone going home late and passing the low windows could be heard ....

At this point, into the carrier's room walked the night-wanderer, unnoticed by anyone and passing the napping waiters. And there he halted at the threshold. He was wearing a sort of tigerskin, like a sleeveless jacket, and the tiger's tail came after him, lifeless and dangling. And he himself looked red and puffy and bloated from constant drinking, and was still in his cups, which he had drained somewhere else and not just one. He stood there at the threshold barely holding himself up, but he knew what he was after and his face showed someone here was of interest to him. The moment he saw the world-carrier sitting at his table, he went over to him as though they were old friends, came to his table, and sat down opposite him, shaking his hand.

"How are things?" he asked the world-carrier.

"Fine, going uphill."

"And what are you so happy about? The fact that you're carrying these drunkards without pay?"

And the wanderer pointed to the nightbirds sleeping all around them.

"No," the carrier answered him, "what about you?"

"Bad!"

"How?"

"The pious are dead and gone, and the people still left are being grabbed up by, how do you say, the devil."

"And who are you left with?"

"I live with a distant relative?"

"Who is he?"

"He's small and slight, skinny and bony, and his face is yellow and wrinkled, and there's earth in the wrinkles. His eyes are messy, the whites have flooded the blacks, the sockets are filled with a gray liquid, and if he ever gets dreamy-eyed he looks other-worldly. He has nothing to do in *this* world, whatever he's had he's spent, whatever energy he had he devoted to wine and women, and that's how he is, and every evening he's afflicted by hallucinations . . . .

"Whenever he comes home at night to his bachelor's quarters, he closes the door behind him, switches off the light, and stays all alone in his room, and soon the opposite wall starts to move, a pale shadow appears to him, at first feeble and faint, but then a man emerges before him—tall and neat, his hair smooth and carefully parted, his manners impeccable, and with a monocle in his eye. He appears to my relative, sits down at the table, opposite him, crosses his legs, remains informal and relaxed, and my relative has gotten used to him, he's never frightened by him or his unbidden arrival, he just waves . . . .

"Recently though, he visitated my relative with his visit. He sat down, and kept silent for a spell, and my relative noticed he was holding a peculiar book: black covers and black pages, with a bizarre format.

" 'What's that?' he asked him.

" 'I brought it for you, I wanted to show you.'

" 'What is it?'

" 'What they wrote about us.'

" 'Who about whom?'

" 'A few millenia from now about our millenium.'

"And the man handed him the book, and my relative took it and peered inside. And the book wasn't anything like our books, it wasn't printed with black ink on white paper, but the other way around—white on black. And my relative couldn't read the writing and he couldn't make out the book at all. So he gave it back for the man to read to him. And the man read: It was all one to him—a writing from thousands of years ago, a writing from thousands of years from now, and he said that the book came from a black human race that took over the present world, without a single trace remaining of the whites, and only the history of the whites somehow or other flickers about in their memories and sometime or other someone remembers them.

"And the book says: 'After great battles and wars between the whites, when a great despair came over them because they saw that they would never achieve the peace they had been longing for, and that they would never become any better than they were, and that they had already given away anything good they had had, and that their time was drawing to a close, and that their blood and their mission were coming to an end, and that others, stronger ones, were to inherit them, and that these others might not be any better—then they brought their best and most carefully chosen minds together for a conference, and then, for the survivors, for their big and little nations, they passed a resolution: THE END! Let it be, there was no way of doing better, and there was no one left to bother about, let everyone end his life however he wished, it was senseless to worry about another group or another individual.'

"And the historian adds, and goes on to say:

" 'And it became a normal and regular occurrence, the magazines wrote it up, and you could read about it in the daily newspapers: Sometimes here and sometimes there, one after another, those sages who had passed the resolution were being found, every morning, in their homes, in their bathrooms, in their tubs, undressed and sitting in the water, quite dead, with the water full of blood. They had opened their arteries, thereby settling their accounts with the world . . . .'

"The man finished reading to my relative, closed the book, and exchanged glances with him.

" 'What about it?' my relative asked him. 'Are we supposed to follow their example?'

" 'Uhhh . . .' the man stammered, 'I mean, it's time . . . there's no hope for our world . . .' "

And the night-wanderer added:

"My relative and his man are already won over, and I've joined them myself."

"So what do you want?" the world-carrier asked the night-wanderer.

"We don't think you're any more foolish than we are, and so I've come to propose the same thing to you."

"For preventing cruelty to animals?"

"Call it whatever you like, it doesn't matter."

"No!" answered the world-carrier.

"And what about your joy, and your 'things are going uphill'?"

The carrier didn't answer. He merely clutched his winecup in his hands and turned his wistful face toward his hands, and The Blind Man was filled with a great nocturnal silence, and the young men sleeping at the carrier's table were sleeping now in truth, and the waiters as well, the ones who had stayed for the night, were drowsing and dozing, and sitting down on the corners of tables, for just a while, they remained seated, and the night-wanderer sat facing the carrier, sat there and waited for him . . . .

"Ha!—" the carrier awoke from his quiet mulling, and more to himself than to his opposite he exclaimed:

"My joy? Yes . . . . Not long ago, from the farthest corners of the universe, at night, I heard something like a quiet shot. Was it a world going under, was it a world encountering, colliding with, another world, I couldn't see . . . . However, I did see a window on earth, in a little house, respond to that shot with a light shiver. And a man woke up there and got out of bed, and washed his hands and looked at God's universe, and said: 'Something has happened out in the world, we've got to pray, and we've got to think.'

"And he stood there and said:

" 'What's happened up there? I can't tell whether a heavenly body has exploded or a new sphere has been born, it's not clear; but whatever it is, it's happened, and it's linked with eternal life and divine death, and perhaps it doesn't have any mouth, and someone has to be its mouthpiece, and I've been found worthy, and I heard it in my sleep, and I am already standing before God, outside his mansion and window, and the waking world-carrier is occupied, bearing his burden and labor, and who shall speak for what has happened?'

"And I was the carrier at the time, on the world's beaten path, and I heard the singing of rare spheres, and I was carrying my weighty burden, my holy and heavy load, when I caught the words of that man, and I bent my shoulders more and took the yoke more deeply upon myself, my yoke and my labor, my love and my joy . . . ."

"We've heard the like from you before," the night-wanderer broke in, "have you nothing new, world-carrier?"

"Doesn't the old mean anything to you?" the carrier asked angrily.

"No, I'm sick of it... and your man is a fool and he spouts foolish things."

"And what would you have said?"

"I would have spit and gone to bed ...."

And both remained silent for a while. The carrier again dropped his eyes to his cup, and the night-wanderer looked at him as though pitying his foolish innocence. At this point, the night watchman came over the threshold, and he also entered unnoticed, from the quiet street into The Blind Man, all bundled up in fur, roly-poly in his clothes, with a watchman's whistle dangling on his chest, in case anything were ever to happen, were ever to stir up the street—to whistle and inform the other watchmen. And in he came, a man of few words, an old friend of the carrier and the wander. He sat down at their table and filled out a place with his bundled-up-in-fur-ness—and the wanderer and the carrier were happy to see him, and the two of them turned their eyes and their attention to him.

"What do you say, watchman?" the wanderer turned to him in a joking mood.

"Say, say," replied the watchman, "say what you like, people hear you a lot, they sleep as a matter of course."

And the watchman fell silent, and earnest and watchful in his silence, and the wanderer turned away from him, and addressed the carrier:

"Talk to us, carrier, it's still too early to go home, the night is still enormous, and you've had experiences, the carrier mulled for a moment, and remembered something, and said: 'Listen, wanderer, and understand.' "

And the carrier began to talk.

Just the other night, he said, he had run into Aquarius, the water-bearer, with his pole and his pails across his shoulders, and the pole stretched across the breadth of his back, and the pails were bobbing about, and idly water-bearing he came walking toward him.

"And so I peered into the pails, and I saw they were parched and thirsty. So I looked at him and asked what was going on, it appeared as though the pails had run dry, and how long hadn't they seen a well? Whereupon he replied: 'Virgo the Virgin is getting married, and I want to pass her by with empty buckets.... I was the one who got her to heaven, I got her a place among the constellations, and she's marrying someone else.'

" 'What do you mean?' "

Aquarius' Tale

Her father was a fallen angel, he lived with an earthwoman, they had a child, and he coveted and was satiated, and thought of the heavens and earth as his own. But then, upon such angels, the punishment fell, and heaven had to close to them, and they were condemned not to return—they were given a tiny moment of time, and whoever wanted to use it could. Many of the angels, however, were busy with their earthliness and their wives, and thus they missed their moment, and wailing, and akin to men, they were left behind, and only a few of them perceived, and bethought themselves of the time, and up and back, in that moment, they went. Among these few was the virgin's father, and he didn't want to go back up alone, he wanted to take his wife and the fruit of her womb, so quickly and first he handed up his child, and I happened to be standing in the sky, watching him doing the handing, and I grabbed from his hands and took it over, and he wanted to boost up his wife, and then himself, but that very moment the heavens closed up, and the angel with his wife in his hands in the air found himself standing before a sky that was shut and bolted up.

And now the child was in my hands, and at first I didn't know what to do, but gradually it got used to me, and I was its father and mother. And I brought it up, and I got to like it, and it was always around me when I worked, and when I drew water from the well and showered the world with rain and plenty, and I always kept it at my side, and I never left it as a waif.

And when she was growing up and the other constellations saw her with me, they watched her and praised her to the skies, and some were even envious of her, and then of me for having her so close all the time.

Now in those days the heavenly spheres and constellations were still unsettled, and every now and then a star would slide away and would fall from the zodiac and be gone, it really happened every so often, and a constellation would stray from its path and wander off, perhaps into some gulf, and in the zodiac a tenant was gone, a place stood vacant, so the other signs got together and resolved to give that spot to the child I had raised and—fine, there was nothing to be ashamed of, she shone no less than the others, and she was lovelier than the others, and the child took the place, and she became an equal among equals.

And I grew so fond of the child, and I felt closer to the child than anyone else, and she never did a thing without me, and she came to me for the least little thing, because, as I've said, she barely knew her parents, and I had taken the place of her parents.

And I would teach her how to look down, and how to hold herself in the zodiac and not to get dizzy, and sometimes she would ask me, the waterman, to show her what to douse, and I never said no, I gave her the bucket, the child already knew the earth, and she knew the summer and winter, and what to do in summer and winter, and often, as she held the bucket, she would lose herself in daydreams, and douse too little or douse too much, like a child, and I would smile and forgive her for what she had "done to me."

And the child kept growing, and I grew to love her, and she took on forms as a *certain* kind of those children do, and she began attracting me, and frequently and secretly I would watch from the side, and she didn't know, and she didn't guard against me, but I did guard against others, and guarded *her* against anyone else: How did they act toward her, how did they look at her, who glanced at her, and to whom did she pay the most attention . . . .

I didn't notice anything except her loyalty and devotion to me, and I was glad and I was cheerful, and deep down I looked forward to the time when she would grow some more, and I would grow close to her, and I would explain to her what was impossible then, and in the meantime I guarded her, and allowed no one else to look at her. And the years wore on, and I kept looking after her, and she kept looking down at the earth, and she didn't really like the

earth, and often she would call to me and show me in back
and below.

"Uncle Aquarius, what doesn't grow of yours?"

"What doesn't?"

"Something you water and keep watering: Those grasses
and those trees of yours."

"But the trees are tall."

"You call that tall? How come they never reach the sky?"

"That's as high as they're fated to grow."

And she would turn away from the earth, and walk away
from me, hurt and disappointed, and she would go to the
other constellations, to pursue another interest with others
and not with me .... And they would tell her things and
spend a lot of time with her, and all of them told her what
they knew and brought out the loveliest things they had, and
told about bygones and made up never-was's, and she heard
and hung on their every word, and she believed anything, especially the unbelievable, and they thought up things that
she had never even seen any traces of on the earth or found
any signs of among the constellations; she fell in love with
the tales of higher-stars, and they provided her with such,
and they never spared their fantasies.

Now she became a stranger and hardly ever came to me,
and no longer took any part in my earth work, and she
would sit in seclusion, and it was hard to get her out of her
seclusion. And in the evenings, after sundown, she would sit
down on her star bed and for hours on end before falling
asleep she would stare at the sky and the faraway stars ....

At this point I felt it was the right time, and I wanted to
let her know how I felt, because I could see why the constellations were so occupied with her and why the constellations
were so attentive to her, because she brought them all such
joy, and everyone was so happy to be around her; so, one
evening, when they had all gone to bed, I whispered in her
ear—that when all were asleep and all in the zodiac was still,
she was to come out to me, I would wait for her, I wanted
to talk to her at the well ....

She didn't understand, she looked at me, and stared at me
in amazement, unwontedly, and yet, unsuspectingly, she
promised to come and she kept her promise .... I waited at

the well, and a moon went up, and summer night drew over
the earth, and from there a lot of good things and earthliness
came wafting up, and secret fragrances from secret woods
and rivers; and then she came and asked me something:

"What is it, Uncle Aquarius? What did you have to say to
me?"

"Nothing," I could feel her estranged question, I answered
it and looked at her in the moonlight. "Sit down."

And she sat next to me on the edge of the well, and I
reached out my arm and wanted to put it around her—

"You're all wet, and you smell of water, Uncle."

And she pushed away my arm and gave it back to me.
And I couldn't say a thing to her, but then I did say that I
couldn't sleep nowadays, and that I was very fond of her,
and that she ought to spend some of the evening with me . . .
and she spent it as best she could, and she sat with me until
she felt sleepy, and I told her to go to bed, and I looked after
her long after she left, and thus, remaining with nothing at
all, I mulled that evening for a long, long time.

And the constellations kept telling her stories, and they
looked at her from all around, and she didn't notice, and in
her unawareness of herself was more than happy; and she
herself was happy, and her beauty rejoiced in her, and her
beauty was prepared for others, and not for me and not for
any of the constellations: her prince was a *higher* constellation.

Once, looking up at the sky, one evening when I couldn't
sleep, I caught sight of a woman in veils. With a thin web
across her face, and fully wrapped and fully covered, she
was standing and staring at other constellations. I could see
that her hidden gaze was fixed on Virgo, guarding her sleep,
watching her bed, and coming into her dreams I
couldn't understand it because what I saw was so out of the
ordinary, it seldom occurs even in the heavens, so I stared
and I never turned my gaze, until she went away from
where she was . . . . The next morning, she whom I yearned
for came to my well, and because I was lost in thought when
she arrived, she called to me and called my name:

"Uncle, hey, Uncle!"

"What's up?" I started and caught sight of her.

"I had a dream last night."

"What kind of dream?"

"My mother came to me, all dressed up and in veils, and I couldn't see her face, but she stood over my bed, and talked to me, and said to me:

" 'Daughter, your father wanted to raise me to the skies, and that was why he had to stay on earth, and you were privileged, you were set among the constellations, now see if you can do something and raise us too.'

" 'And what should I do, Mother?' I asked.

" 'Love the lofty,' she answered. —"What did she mean, Uncle?"

"I don't know," I replied, and I became earnest.

And she walked away and she went to ask the other constellations, and they explained it all to her, the way they felt they ought to explain it, and they all set her thinking that her time was coming, that her time for love was coming soon, and all eyes were rejoicing with her, everyone loved the way she looked, and her mother had come to tell her it was time, and that she had said she ought to seek her love among the lofty.

And she thought to herself, and looked up at the welkin, and looked around among the stars, to find some explanation for the question of her youth . . . .

And after a certain time had gone by, I saw him one night, next to that star, her father standing, a man like any man, but with the face of a former angel, and he had no wings, as angels have, but instead of wings he had a bag—he looked like an earthly penitent, and he was standing there, and staring at his daughter, and in the morning she came to me again and with a new dream:

"Uncle, my father appeared to me!"

"And what did he say?"

" 'Love is aloft and love is below; there's no need to *fall* into great love.'—I don't understand, Uncle!"

"Neither do I."

Then she went to ask others again, and they told her what they had to tell. And she was starting to understand, and to reach the very beginning of that awareness . . . . She started casting glances about and in that time and in great youth she saw herself, and she had already heard of such things, and had understood more than she had heard; and I found that time was the very last, and if not now then all was lost. In the first case, whatever came her way, she would go and leave me, and let herself be led away at the first call of a stranger, anyone .... And I saw that the stars knew what I meant, and that they were laughing at me below. And having despaired of attaining her love, they were bursting with envy, and wanted to destroy my chances too ....

So I found a time, and once, when walking with brimming buckets, I caught sight of her and I asked her to halt with my buckets, and I stood before her, and standing there I revealed to her all the things that were in my heart. And so on, and so forth, and ever since she had come to the sky my gaze had always been turned to her, and ever since she'd been growing up I had never let her out of my care, and guarded her against all other eyes, and longed, and yearned for the time to come, and now my well was for her, and the welfare of the world was hanging on her given word. And if she became the mistress of my well, it would pour all its goodness upon the earth and turn the world back into a Garden of Eden, and she was the world to my well, and my well loved her more than the world ....

She stood there and heard what I had to say, and she seemed to be lost in her thoughts, and then, when I took her pensiveness for approval, for fondness, and I remembered the things I had done for her, I wanted to put the buckets down, and set them aside and go up to her, I knocked the buckets over, and the water poured out, and she burst out laughing and sobered me up from my haste:

"Ha ha ha, Uncle, you've spilled your water .... Hahaha, Uncle, what did you say?"

I couldn't go up to her and I couldn't move, and she went away and vanished from sight, and from then on we didn't meet, and each of us avoided the other, and our paths would never cross, and we never spoke of it again ....

And the constellations found out, they managed to guess, she never told them anything, they shouldn't be told, and whenever I happened to be walking past, they would point their fingers at me, and smile, and their eyes would wink at one another . . . .

And she remained free for a while, and didn't belong to anyone, until one day she laid eyes upon *him*, saw him and rose in love with him, saw him, and with all her heart and soul, the way a young girl, and a girl like her, can fall in love . . . .

He was the star, the one near whom her father and mother appeared to her, and it happened at nightfall again, when after a day of work, I was wandering around our constellation garden, around the fence, and I kept looking inside, but I wouldn't go inside, because she was inside, and spending her time by herself, rather than going to bed as usual. And the garden was filled with a peculiar evening-tree-hush, and even more than in the trees the hush was resting on the white, sandy paths, and the garden was fragrant with constellations, and with earthly goodness that the earth had brought up from its depth. I saw that next to that star a child had appeared, an infant, a little messenger, and the child was holding a lantern, and the lantern was burning, and the child was holding it as though preparing to start on a journey. And the star became bigger than a star, and grew, and grew out in his roundness, and yet he was covered and darkened up, but on one of his sides, and right on the edge, a thin round blade of light was sharpened and honed, and it looked like the roundness of the sickle of a moon during the early days of its being. —The brightness illuminated the star, and a face in the star began to appear, and that very moment, I, on my side of the garden, and she, on her side of the garden, we noticed the face, and she lifted her hands up to her head, and brushed back her hair, and felt slightly embarrassed and shifted her eyes from looking there, and the star was looking at her, and he saw me too, and he felt a little embarrassed then, and the child with the tiny lantern separated from its place, and then down, and to us, and straight to the garden, and to her, in her embarrassment, it came. And the child was coming, and lighting the way, and every so often she stole a glance, and noticed the child and its coming. And she was nervous and couldn't stay put, and the child kept coming from aloft, and it came directly to her in the garden. And the child then called her aside, and hid somewhere in the trees, and she hesitated, and at first she walked unsteadily, and you could see her follow the child, and not so much the child as him who was standing above and peering below—the star. And then she came into the trees, and I don't know what she did with the child, there was something it told her, and there was something it gave her, but what it was I couldn't tell. Then, when the child rose back up in the air and started back with its tiny lantern, I saw her emerge from the trees, and swiftly and quickly abandon the garden, stealing through the gate and closing it behind her, and silently, as she closed the gate, she raised her head one last time, and had another upward look, a single look and then away, and then she raced back to her home and her bed....

And she became a different person, and I knew what had happened. And other constellations that didn't know could also tell, and she kept smoothing her hair with her hands and she would suddenly blush, as though embarrassed about herself, and from then on and often I would notice her coming to the well when I wasn't there, and bending over the well, and silently and hastily catching her image in the well and its depth.... And in the garden too she became a frequent guest, and in that place among the trees, as though forgetting something, she would come and seek: She would conceal herself there with the picture of the star, with what the child had brought to her, and what she had concealed from everyone else, and I was the only one who knew, because I had peered after her and noticed it....

I was saddened, and I neglected my work, and my buckets would wait and wait for me, and I would forget them for a while. And huge droughts came upon the earth, and the trees and the grass were pleading for drink, and the fields were parched, and forests were smoking, and rivers dried up, and the beds of creeks lay empty, and I didn't notice, and the constellations kept reminding me, and even then I would work so lazily, and I did my job so listlessly.

And she was always in good spirits, and a great joy shone from her eyes, and the constellations beamed with pride, and their spirits became as good as hers, and they didn't know the why and how, but they did know that her time was upon her....

And fairly soon, on another evening, the star's messenger-boy came bearing gifts: necklaces and adornments of pearls, earrings and rings for her fingers. And these were things that she couldn't conceal, and everyone saw the gifts she was wearing, and they all surrounded her and estimated the value of the jewels, and she didn't know what to do, what should she say, what should she answer, and they all began to interrogate, and to encircle her with questions, and she ran from the well and she ran to the garden, and then from the garden to the well, and back and forth, and her young legs carried her....

And I lost my head, and I envied the star, and I didn't speak a word to her, and she always evaded me. And she didn't want to show her joy before me, and I was unable to look at her joy, and so I kept to myself, and I also avoided the constellations. And then, on an evening, the sky-beggar came, and he came and called the constellations together, called them together and said to them:

"Prepare yourselves, you constellations, Virgo the Virgin will be taken from you!"

"What's happening?"

"She's ascending, she's being given to a great star. Prepare yourselves, you'll all be asked to the wedding."

The constellations began to prepare, and they've been preparing themselves ever since, and they surrounded the bride with love, and they all provided her with the loveliest things, and she remained quiet and gave herself over to their devotion, and they're teaching her, and advising her, how to behave, and conduct herself. And all their hands are busy at work, to prepare themselves and prepare the bride, and they're looking forward with great expectations, they're unable to part, and they're giving her the best they can, the best of all good things and whatever constellations possess.... I'm the only one who can't go to the wedding, I'm the only one who can't lose his envy, and (this is only for *you*) I've secretly made up my mind to pass her by with empty buckets....

And the present state of the earth—it's all been caused by

my neglect. My abundance is closed off, and that's why your world is as it is—and the earth has to drink—though it drink blood for water, and people have to eat, though they eat people for bread, and spirit enters the houses and eats the garbage and dry pieces, and human seers are struck with eye diseases, and certain world-providers get drunk in the taverns, and poets mock, and certain writers, when they hear the constellations blowing their noses, they think it's thunder and portentous events—ugh!—and now I've been told that worst of all, the night-wanderer is hanging around in taverns, and among people like him, among the senile and infirm, he's recruiting members for a society, for preventing cruelty to animals.

" 'And there you have the story, wanderer,' And that's what Aquarius said to me .... That was quite a stone in my garden," said the night-wanderer.

"Yes, not bad," smiled the world-carrier.

"Well, and what about you and the wedding?"

"I've been invited, and I'll go."

"And what about the empty buckets?"

"I'm not afraid."

"What's going to happen?"

"The sky-beggar showed us a way. This is what happened:"

Recently, as I was walking along with the weight of the world on my shoulders, with my head in the clouds and lost in thought, and providing purposes for my things, and my heart was heavy and filled with rue, thinking about the times, and I felt so desolate, and a mountain of questions hovered above me, and I recalled the questions that people keep asking me, and all the mockers and laughers came to my eyes, and there was one question I couldn't get rid of: It's all in your hands .... One wrong move, and the ball will fall, and—that will be all, and the past will be past, and the future won't come, and so why bother holding it, where will you bring it, if the road is marked out, and the path is revealed, and there's no way of going out of your way ... ?

"There's a way!" something suddenly said in my ears. I turned my head to see where the sudden voice was coming from, and I saw the sky-beggar, in a cheerful mood, with a merry face, and he quickly spoke to me:

"World-carrier, you're invited to heaven, to attend the marriage of Star and Virgo, and don't wait to be coaxed."

"How can I go," I said to him, "and how can I think of marriages now that Aquarius has done away with our abundance? Aquarius has made his well run dry, and he's abandoned his job, his buckets are full of holes, and soon we won't have anything left."

To which the beggar replied: "Don't be afraid, something is going to happen at the ceremony .... The Seven Wayfarers and the Seven Beggars will attend .... And that will be a propitious time, and everyone in need will be asked to come, and in regard to you and your burden, you'll both no longer depend on your star; and what you've yearned for all these years, you'll get; you're going to be raised and you'll stand higher than the constellations . . . ."

"What do you mean?"

"It's possible, just be sure to come .... And here's the road, it's all uphill, and if you'll follow it you'll avoid the waterman with his buckets . . . ."

And so I started out on the road, and made my way upward, and soon I heard the winds of the spheres, whirling remote and strange, the likes of which I had never heard, and I heard the singing of alien suns, and their wheels of fire were dazzling, and I also sang out, and on the way I kept meeting people like myself, and all of them were invited too, walking along in sublimity, and in front the Elephant, shaking his heavy head, and with mountains of wealth, and with wedding gifts, to make the bride and groom rejoice . . . .

"And that," said the world-carrier, "is my joy and my uphill," and now, wanderer, I'm leaving . . . ."

And the world-carrier arose from sitting at the table, from sitting and from telling so long, and the night watchman in his furriness also got up, and nothing was written on his face, he had come that way, before the story, and even now, even after the telling, he still looked the same, and watchmanlike he straightened his fur, and the watchman's whistle was on his chest, and he turned around to the window there, and he saw it was true, it was dawning soon. He gave the wanderer a nasty glance, and the wanderer vanished from his sight, and the world-carrier left the room, and just before he left for good, he looked at the drunkards asleep at the table, and he left them in silence, and the watchman after him; and the day was already blossoming, and one by one, from the courtyards, with their brooms in their hands, the janitors started coming out, to sweep the yards and clean the streets, and the carrier said good morning to the watchman and took his leave, and the watchman went off, to his house, to his home, to spend the day resting for the night . . . .

And that morning, when the day was broad and bright, when the sun was high in the heavens, and a huge bustle in the streets, and the streets had been cleaned again to be dirtied again by the day and the din; and the carrier and the world had gone far, with his heavy weight to carry uphill, and to strain with it—it was only then that the drinkers awoke, the ones who had spent the night, in the tavern, in The Blind Man, they awoke and rubbed their eyes, and they were nocturnally pale, and had pale smiles on their lips, and they left the room in The Blind Man and came out on the street, and first they went to an unclean place, they went there and stood there facing the wall, stood there and yielded their nightly drinking . . . .

A Tale of a King
and a Wise Man

Once there was a king. And the king had a wise man.

Now one day the king said to the wise man:

"Listen, there is a king who claims to be powerful, truthful, and unassuming, that is to say, strong, honest, and meek. He seems to be very powerful, because his country is surrounded by the ocean, and he has a whole fleet of ships with cannon, and his men won't let anyone approach. And between the ocean and the shore, there's a huge swamp all around the country, with only one tiny path leading through it, and wide enough for just one person. And cannon are standing there also. And if anyone tries to wage war against the country, they shoot these cannon at him. So there's no way of getting inland. But what I don't understand is why he claims to be truthful and unassuming. Which is why I want you to bring me a portrait of the king."

Now the king had portraits of all other kings, but he had no portrait of the king he had just been talking about. For this king, who made such claims, was hidden from the world. He always sat behind a curtain and was far removed from his subjects.

And the wise man came to that country.

He realized he had to know the character of that country, the way the people behaved.

And how could he know the character of the country? By find-ing out the sense of humor of the country. For if you want to un-derstand a thing, you have to understand its sense of humor.

For there are all kinds of senses of humor.

One person, for instance, uses words to get at another person, and when the other person gets annoyed, the first one says: "I'm only joking." Just as the Talmud says: Like someone who shoots arrows into a man's heart and then says, "I'm only joking."

There are people who think they are only joking, but whose words actually injure someone else.

Thus, there are all kinds of senses of humor.

And among all the countries in the world, there is one country that embodies all countries.

And among all the cities in that country, there is one city that embodies all the others.

And among all the houses in that city, there is one house that em-bodies all the houses of that city that embodies all the cities of that country that embodies all the countries in the world.

And in that house, there is a man that embodies that house.

And he imitates the wit and humor of the whole country.

The wise man took along a great deal of money and went to that house. There he saw that the people were joking and mocking in every way. And seeing these things, he understood that the whole country was full of lies from one end to the other. He saw the way they played tricks on one another, the way they cheated one an-other in business. The victims of fraud would go to court, but the court was full of lies and bribery. They would appeal to a higher court, but this one too was full of lies.

The people made fun of everything, they joked about every-thing, they mocked everything.

And the wise man realized, from all this joking, that the whole country was full of lies and deceit, and that there was no truth in it anywhere.

He went out and did business in the country, and let someone de-ceive him in a deal.

Thereupon, he went to court.

He saw that the judges were full of lies and took bribery. He would bribe them on one day, and the next day they wouldn't recognize him.

So he went to a higher court—and there too he found nothing but lies and graft. Until he came to the senate. But the senate too was full of lies and graft.

So he went to the king himself.

And appearing before the king, he said:

"What sort of people do you rule? Your country is full of lies. From one end to the other, There is no truth in it anywhere."

And he began to tell about the fraudulence of the country.

When the king heard him speak, he bent his ears to the curtain in order to listen closely. For the king was amazed that someone actually knew about the fraudulence of his country.

And the dignitaries of the realm, upon hearing his words, became very angry.

The wise man stood there, counting up all the lies in the country. Then he said:

"People could say that the king is the same way, that he likes falsehood, just as his country does. But in fact, that's how I can tell that you're a truthful man, you're far away from your subjects because you can't bear the lies of your country."

And the wise man grew very fond of the king.

The king, being a very unpretentious man, belittled himself as much as he could because of the great praise that the wise man had bestowed upon him. For such are the ways of a modest man: The more you praise him, the smaller and more modest he becomes.

Unable to control himself, he pulled aside the curtain in order to see the wise man and find out who this person was who knew and understood all these things.

And thus the king's face was revealed.

The wise man saw his face and painted his portrait, and then he brought the portrait back to the king.

MOYSHE KULBAK

The Messiah of the House of Ephraim

Opening

All those who have set their souls on the word YAHWE, the Lamed-vovniks, the thirty-six secret saints, go about at the edge of the world, alone and isolated.

In the darkness, they suddenly come to a halt, they sense each other from afar, but no one sees anyone else. They walk about at midnight, at the edge of the earth, tall Jews with long staffs, hunched over against the blueness of the sky.

And on the Day of Doom, they come with their disheveled beards, in their fur coats and boots, clutching their birch staffs. And they ask nothing. They come and sit at the foot of the Throne of Glory.

They put one sleeve in the other and warm themselves in the holiness of the Almighty.

And they smoke their pipes.

The Almighty sits on the Throne of Glory and smiles. He likes his simple saints.

The Miller

Once there was a miller in the land of White Russia.

His wife died and his son was taken off into the army.

The mill was overgrown with mosses and weeds.

The roof crept down like a fur over the mill until it touched the ground.

The countryside was deserted.

Only magpies were flying around, just poor magpies.

The miller didn't know what to do.

He went into his stable and saw that of all his livestock only his cow was left.

He felt so lonely and miserable that he sat down on the threshold of his house and wept bitter tears.

His name was Benye.

What Happens When a Man Lives Alone

I once read in an ancient volume that a man should be careful not to remain alone. At first he thinks it doesn't matter. But then his mind turns to dismal thoughts. His voice changes and he walks about in a daze.

If Benye had known, he might not have stayed all by himself in the mill, he might have moved to a nearby town or else married again.

Life in the country is too hard for an elderly person.

Every day, Benye would cook his bit of food alone, milk the cow alone, and then stroll around the mill with his hands behind his back, or else recite the psalms, as lonely people tend to do.

One day, he came to wash at the well, and in the water he saw that his lower lip was hanging down.

Never before had Benye's lower lip hung down.

He realized then and there that it came from living alone. He went back into the house, took down the mirror from the wall, and lo and behold, his lip was really hanging down. Furthermore, his eyebrows were growing denser, and all in all, he was hairy, shabby, and shaggy, like a polecat. Benye clutched his lip, and it was as dry as clay.

And even though the evening was warm, he climbed up on the oven, snuggled under the old clothes, and fell asleep.

Benye Feeds the Cow

A forest of firs stood behind the mill.

It was the season of foggy days in White Russia, and the rains were drenching the entire countryside.

In the gray dawn, Benye took the cow to pasture.

They walked along the loamy paths, over the foul-smelling fields, and into the old forest.

Benye led the way with the rope in his hands and the cow at his heels.

They climbed through the thicket and among the trees, and the wet branches soaked them with water, but Benye was so lost in thought that he paid no heed.

Thus they went from one thicket to the next.

From time to time, the cow would nibble a few wet blades of grass by a root, and that was her refreshment.

The tree stumps were huddling and rotting in the ferns.

The moss covered everything, it touched the earth and the trees all over. And in the petrified stillness, the cold noises of the woods were mingling and fading out.

Benye led the cow along the road, through the rainy spaces.

They trudged along, worn and weary, their heads hanging down, loaded and heavy from not thinking.

Benye was used to having thoughts without the effort of thinking.

It was silent, his bare feet were red with cold and caked with mud. The cotton was spilling out of the dirty coat. Benye stopped, looked over his clothes and the clothes of the forest.

Benye, the fir trees have lovely garments!

Levi the Moneylender

Levi the moneylender, a brother of Benye's, had moved from Zamkevitz to Vilna, the capital of Lithuania. He quickly acquired power by doing business with generals and wealthy men.

He had a daughter and she was so beautiful, the most beautiful girl in Vilna.

He hung a sign in front of his house: Here I live, Levi Patashnik.

Levi dealt in lumber and grain.

At night, in his study, he would sometimes have his servant open his business books.

His beautiful daughter would read the figures to him.

His grain was being freighted along all highways.

His lumber was floating down all rivers.

Gold was being sown in his garden.

Gold was being laid by his chickens.

Levi Patashnik smiled.

"That's enough for now," he told his daughter, "you can go to bed!"

And all night long in his study, he walked up and down his soft carpets, thinking:

"Gold is, evidently, gold! Gold is, evidently, gold!"

The Three Guests

Benye was sitting out in front, looking at the road. It was a white evening in White Russia. Opening his eyes, he saw three men coming along the road.

He stood up and began walking toward the three men.

Three hairy Jews in furs, with bags over their shoulders, were trudging along from the forest.

Benye reached the travelers on the road and said hello to them, and the Jews returned his greeting, they stared at him and mumbled something in a hoarse tone but didn't say a word.

(There are people who are destined to keep silent.)

Benye led the guests to his house and opened the doors up wide.

The three Jews bowed as they entered, for they were large and tall.

Indoors, it was already night.

The guests slowly put down their bags and staffs. Their clothing smelled of pitch and the fragrance of the woods.

Benye stared at his guest curiously.

They sat down on the broad benches around the table, and their large bodies hulked in the darkness like the stumps of old trees.

Benye asked them: "Where do you come from?"

The eldest of the guests raised his brows, took out the clay pipe from his pocket, and said:

"White Russia."

Benye had nothing else to ask because his thoughts had grown into his flesh.

And in the gloomy darkness, the blue windows were shining, and the Jews spread their furs on the benches.

Benye kindled a pine splinter. The visitors turned around in the darkness, casting strange shadows on the walls. The cow in the stable sensed something, she left her warm stable and stuck her head through the window of the house. She was listening.

Benye quietly sat down at the table with his visitors, staring and making a great effort at framing a thought, but he was fully unable to do so.

All at once he turned to the guests:

"Friends, what should I do?"

The visitors looked at him stupidly, and a bit later the eldest of the three asked him:

"Do you have any food?"

"I do!"

"Don't do anything."

"Really? But what's the sense?"

"There's no sense."

And the eldest guest, who had answered him, now stretched out on the hard bench with his back to Benye and covered himself up in his fur from his feet to his head, just like the other two guests. They wanted to go to sleep.

Benye was standing over him.

He stood over him for a long time. Then he put his hand behind his back and quietly paced up and down the room, and the cow watched him from the window.

Suddenly a thought came into his mind and gave him a sharp jolt. He dashed over to the guest and started yanking his leg.

"What happens after this? Do I die?"

The visitor tried with all his strength to pull his foot back out of Benye's hand, but Benye wouldn't let go, he merely shouted even louder:

"What?! Do I die?!"

And he burst into tears:

"Die?"

The visitors sat up on their benches, and Benye wailed, grabbed at the walls, ran across the room, threw his clothes off breathlessly, and roared in pain.

At midnight, the guests got up, washed their hands, and took out their psalters.

All four Jews sat down upon the ground.

The clay floor was cold in the cool dawn. The cow was still standing at the same window and freezing. The air was icy.

The men recited the psalms in their hoarse voices with a gloomy enthusiasm.

They closed their eyes and gazed out of this world.

They didn't hear the voice that was squeaking, only the dark stillness that remained within and couldn't leave.

The prayer of a poor man who was hidden.

And he pours out his heart to God . . . .

And in the night, the first flames were already darting out of the dawn.

Toward morning, Benye was somewhat purified, his long arms were dangling about his body like alien things, pointing into the psalter, bony and cold. He stared at the guests and slowly leaned over to the man sitting next to him.

"What kind of work do you do, sir?"

"I'm a water-carrier."

"And you?"

"I'm a musician."

"And you?"

"A chimneysweep."

Benye liked these fine trades.

Meanwhile, the guests had already gotten up from the ground and were preparing to get underway again.

Benye was stumbling around them, not knowing what to do next.

Each guest silently kissed the mezuzah and went out into the red darkness.

A stork came flying past with its red legs tucked in, soaring from one meadow to the next. Its flapping wings nearly grazed the heads of the Jews.

The third guest, a grumbler, who had kept silent all night long, suddenly started talking a blue streak. He was furious at Benye, babbling that Benye would not resist. He touched the confused miller's sleeve and pointed at the scraggy bird in the sky:

"That bird is a bird." He peered straight into Benye's nose. "And you—are a jackass."

The third guest was a nasty man, he spit angrily, didn't look around, and wrathfully took off. Benye stood there dazed, not understanding a thing.

Now the eldest visitor came over to him and, saying farewell, he murmured:

"You will have temptations to resist, Benye."

And the three guests followed the road back to the woods.

The Prayer

The prayer of a poor man who was hidden.
And he pours out his heart to God.
Why are we so tormented, Lord!
Wherever I stand I am too much present, and wherever I go
    I carry
The smell of darkness.
I envy the bird who is better off than we are,
And the clay which is better off than all.
What shall I do with my hand, which is useless,
And with my heart, which is useless?

Knowledge

The miller spent the whole next day lying on the loamy hill that stood behind his home. He gradually understood the clay of his body, his face was buried in the sand, and his crooked fingers were clutching the roots.

He felt terrible.

He lay there with the hill and it was as though he had been poured into it; and if a blade of grass were to spring up anywhere, it would grow out through him, out of his back.

And it was as if the clay were breathing and shaping up in hands, feet, head, chest, and there were no difference in the world between Benye and the clay of the earth.

He spent whole weeks lying on the hill.

The cow wandered alone over the fields, hungry, and feeding on grass and indolence.

Benye had forgotten everything, he was nearly lifeless.

Sometimes, at dawn, a magpie would come flying out of the mists, it alighted on his back as on a hog, and he didn't care, for he was almost asleep and unable to tell reality from the dreams passing through his mind.

Nor did he know whether he was a human being or a stone lying on the road and overgrown with lichen.

One evening, he was sitting there, faint, at the edge of the hill. His feet were hanging down and dangling against the clay, and he himself was gazing, not thinking, just sitting quietly, and gazing.

He didn't know why something inside him was urging him to see everything, but it did give him a great pleasure. Slowly a feeling of amazement passed through Benye, his eyes bulged and gaped, big and round. For a while, he forgot how to think.

The world stretched out before him, vast and cold, and God was in it. The world echoed like a blue cavern of ice, and he crawled around in it like a muddy bear.

He stood with his front paws on the cold clods, gazing and gazing. He was looking for Him, for God, who was hiding from him.

The sparkling ice in the cavern shone a bright blue.

And here . . . .

Here he saw Him, God, but then God was gone again.

But he *had* seen God!

And a great joy poured through his body, a fine, bright joy. He smiled; a yoke had fallen from his heart.

Benye stood up, beaming with joy and goodness, and suddenly a shriek tore from his heart, a dull bellow, like the bellow of his cow. He stood with his arms akimbo, and the setting sun was gilding him red.

Benye the miller was transfigured.

Off to the west, under the sunset, there were flayed red oxen as at the Covenant of the Pieces, God's covenant with Abraham.

Now he understood the world in the very marrow of his bones, in the burning skin of his body. He smirked at the clothes he was wearing. Single strips of cloth were hanging on him, single strips of cloth.

Benye came down the hill. The old mill had become shaggier and older, and a sapling was growing from one wall.

He came to the door and was about to go in, but all at once he stopped. He could hear a voice full of tears and joy.

Levi Patashnik

One gloomy evening, Levi Patashnik was standing at his open iron cabinet as though at an open Holy Ark, where the Torah scrolls are kept in the synagogue. The fading light of day was spread over the shadowy wallpaper, shimmering, and spotting bright areas on the dark floors. Inside the cabinet, a heap of hot coins, imperials, was glowing, bleeding, stabbing his heart. Breathlessly Levi thrust both hands into the coins.

He slowly sifted the gold in his hands as though letting a white sand pour through his fingers, and he listened keenly to the clatter, the true clatter of gold.

His pudgy hand was rosy from the waning daylight, it softly caressed the coins, grazed them tenderly, the way a boy touches a girl's hair.

A deep, secret crooning emerged from the cabinet. Gold!

Wellsprings of gold are throbbing in the earth, and the eyes of man sparkle golden.

High up, above the golden stars, God sits on His royal throne of gold.

Levi Patashnik gently closed the heavy door of the cabinet, clutched the upper molding so as not to fall, and his heavy head dropped upon his chest.

The huge evening settled hauntingly in the room.

Levi stood there with his hot head lowered, leaning against the cold iron of the cabinet. His knees were buckling with fatigue, his eyes were shut, and deep in his breast, a thick drop was oozing out, heavy and glowing. It fell down his inner darkness and scorched his bowels with a sharp pain.

At the door, the eldest guest was standing in the shadows.

Simkhe Plakhte

Not far from the mill, just a few miles away, there was a Jew living in the forest. His name was Simkhe Plakhte.

Simkhe's work had been very hard. He thought to himself: It's hard enough living as it is, so I'll simply live in the woods.

He built himself a shack of branches and weeds and plastered it with clay inside and out.

Now Simkhe Plakhte was a cheerful man, he ate all sorts of vegetables, drank water, and smoked an herb that he himself prepared.

Simkhe raised chickens and doves. The chickens because they lay eggs that are good to eat, and doves because they lay eggs that are not good to eat.

He never met anyone, and was cheerful just the same.

He was always smiling: smoking his pipe, drowsing with half-closed eyes, and smiling—who knows at whom. He would talk aloud though he was always alone.

In wintertime, he would sit in his hut and crack jokes to himself. In the summer, he would look for fresh meadows in the forest and dance all kinds of dances.

He was a great dancer!

In the springtime, he was completely intoxicated. Even though he was sixty years old, he would scramble up a tree with the strength of a boy.

He didn't act rational at all.

Simkhe liked to eat the blossoms and the buds in the trees, climb through the dense branches, and sing like a canary.

That was how he lived in the woods.

Yes, Simkhe looked like a Christian peasant, he wore a straw hat on his head and, on his feet, shoes of birch bark; but he did have a beard, an enormous Jewish beard, that was bright gray.

His beard was beautiful!

As a boy husband, Simkhe had been a water-carrier. Later on, in his old age, he became a Hassidic rabbi, as everyone knows, kept a pious table and lived grandly, very grandly. But living among people was too difficult for him, so he ran away and settled in the woods as a hermit.

And, when the wind blasted the treetops and broke the branches, what did Simkhe Plakhte do?

He perched on an uprooted tree inside the thicket, with his pipe in his mouth, listening and listening:

The nests were tumbling from the trees.

The female birds soared maternally to the ground, but the fledglings were already lying there dead.

A rare featherless wing trembled here and there.

Simkhe would perch in the thicket, listening and listening. His hair bristled and fluttered on his body. His teeth shone in the thicket, and his eyes burnt from the storm.

And when a long, blue crackle of lightning sprang through the woods and tore through the trees, like a hot whip, what did Simkhe Platkhe do?

He would stand up, stretch his arms to heaven, and try to grab the lightning in its course. His beard was tousled, and a vapor arose from his hairy chest.

Simkhe Platkhe was alone in the woods!

But when it grew still:

The wet responsive woods echoed the whooping of the cuckoos.

The strawberries, like drops of blood, were splattered over the grass.

Then, oh then!

Simkhe Plakhte walked through the echoing woods, with his hands behind his back.

His head held high.

And he hummed and crooned.

And he clacked his tongue.

And he swung his feet.

Humming and crooning!

The man had no sense of modesty.

And that was his life in the woods.

It was a lovely day in summer.

Simkhe Platkhe walked out of the woods toward the town on the main road, and then along a side road.

On the way, he came to a low ground and saw a cow browsing on the grass. What was she doing here? He went farther and came upon a Jew lying in the mud, right in the mud, and the Jew had a big, swollen head and long arms down to his ankles, he was holding a psalter, and reciting, and rocking, and he was as gloomy as a cinder.

What was the matter?

Simkhe stopped and asked a question.

"Why sit here of all places?"

And the Jew snuffled, but then he replied:

"Where else should I sit?"

"Where else should you sit? In heaven, my friend!"

The Jew in the mud told him all the whys and wherefores: He was Benye the miller.

And Benye stood up, gazed at him with pleading eyes, and said:

"Help me, my friend!"

But Simkhe was already asking something else, he was asking Benye about the cow:

"Does she give milk?"

"Of course she gives milk."

"Could I taste a little of her milk?"

Benye replied that he didn't have a milk pail along.

Why did he need a milk pail? Who needs a milk pail?

And Simkhe Plakhte stepped over to the cow, went down on all fours beneath her, like a calf, and began to hungrily suck the milk from her udders.

He turned red and the sweat came gushing from him.

The Ten Sefirot or Emanations of God

There are thousands of worlds in the mystery of the ten emanations.

A human soul wanders through the crystal of the worlds and echoes the tone of each emanation that it traverses.

And know, the thousands of worlds reside in the glow of every emanation alone and all the emanations together. That is the mystery of the ten that are one and the mystery of the one that is ten.

The Infinite, which comes in the raiment of the ten emanations, includes the numbers and it inspires with the holiness of eternity, and the holiness of eternity does not enter the level of measure and quality.

And know that just as we cannot distinguish between the numbers of the ten emanations by the inspiration of holiness, we likewise cannot know or distinguish the area of the emanations.

The saying "The mystery of the ten that are one and the mystery of the one that is ten" refers not only to life that moves in succession, but also to life that moves hand in hand, that is to say, the numbers of thought are like the numbers of substance. That is why we do not say like the ancients: Our world is the world of action, which lies on the lowest level of the effluence of holiness.

The "mystery of the ten that are one" requires that our world contain the Emanation of the Crown, which is the crown of the Revelation of Holiness.

There are people in our world who find themselves under the power of the Emanation of Beauty. Their gait is different, their voices are different!

I have seen people whose souls were radiant with the light from the Emanation of the Crown.

The soul bursts asunder, it wants to absorb the light of eternity, it wanders through the crystal of the worlds and echoes the tone of every emanation that it traverses.

And know that the soul of a child that was born today, is as old as the soul of a dying man, and if you ever come to a festivity for the birth of a child, and you see the people rejoicing, say to them:

"Fools, what are you rejoicing about?"

And if you come into a house where a cleaned corpse is lying, and you see the mourners sitting on the ground, inconsolable, say to them:

"Fools, what are you mourning about?"

Man does not know the mystery glowing in Creation.

If you come to a city, do not look at the buildings and high towers. They are all smoke that will waft away.

Do not look at the people running around the streets, scurrying about as though they were busy. They are nothing but vanity and delusion.

If you come to a city, stretch out on the ground, place your ear to the earth, and listen to what the city is saying in utter secrecy.

And know: Benye, in his simplicity, saw the hidden things, he understood the millions upon millions of worlds and the Name:

YAHWE

It was a vast, a cold night, aglow with stars around and around.

Benye left his house, it was too dark and stuffy. He walked out into the deserted field and sat down beneath a tree.

The branches hung overhead in long rods, and the darkness came trickling down.

A hidden hush emanated from the earth, and Benye sat there, tattered, under the tree, his arms folded on his chest.

The heavens overflowed into one another, like rivers, and they were enveloped in a great coldness. And then Benye saw something.

The moon floated out, white and big, as in a wheel on the sky, a silent wheel.

The moon came floating from one side of the sky, and a shrouded figure was sitting on it:

The Archangel Raphael.

And the figure sat there, leaning over the moon, and peering through the darkness at the other side of the world.

And from the other side of the world, a star came floating out. It was Mars, dark and red, and blood was oozing from it, and a dark, shrouded figure was sitting on Mars:

The Archangel Metatron.

And the figure sat there, leaning over the star and peering into the great brightness at the other side of the world.

It was clear and cold in the abyss of the heavens, there wasn't a wisp of a cloud, and the space beneath was astir with echoes, like a house that has been untenanted for a long time.

And now the two stars came together and they poured patches of light and clumps of fire over the entire countryside.

The world was boiling with hatred!

And the landscape could hear a bitter weeping and a deep joy.

Benye fell upon his face and felt the universe crumbling overhead.

A keening sounded above him.

And suddenly he felt a wrench, he lifted his head and was amazed to see a tall, pure man emerging far, far away from the darkness on the earth.

He was approaching with soft steps, faint steps, his gait was light and without weariness. And the man approached Benye, who was so frightened that he dropped his head back upon the ground.

Benye could feel the palpable light from the man's clothing, he could hear the soft steps of the tall, thin man overhead.

The man walked softly over him.

Benye wanted to peer after him, he wanted to kiss the hem of his coat, but he couldn't lift his head, it was too heavy, and with his face to the ground he laughed joyously inside himself even though a dim longing enveloped his soul like a warm breath.

Benye lay there in the cold all through the night, never lifting his head.

At daybreak, he was all white and shrouded in frost, like a morning branch in autumn.

Levi Patashnik and His Visitors

It was late in the evening when Lord Vrublevsky, a Polish squire, left Patashnik's home. He had just sold him a forest of timber, the forest in which Simkhe had built his hut.

On the porch, Vrublevsky ran into Leah, Levi's daughter. Leah was startled because the man had such long eyes, and they lashed out like black rods. She curtsied and then breathlessly dashed into the hallway and slammed the door.

Levi was sitting in the leather armchair, his fingers dangling over the soft arms. He had one more matter to settle after Vrublevsky.

Today, one of Patashnik's men had fallen under one of the saws, the poor fellow had gotten all sawed up, and now he was coming to present his grievance.

Levi Patashnik was sitting heavily in the chair, his head buried in his hands, and the man was lamenting: "It was horrible!"

It had hurt terribly: After all, if you tumble under a saw, it hurts.

Hahahaha!

Levi Patashnik was sitting in the dark parlor with the chandelier sparkling in its rainbow glass throughout the gloomy space.

Levi Patashnik didn't care for light!

Wide highways opened in the darkness, long distances. Walking from road to road, you would run into people, an old brother, long forgotten, or Lord Vrublevsky, or a man who was all sawed up.

The door opened slowly, and in walked three elderly Jews, with sacks on their shoulders and staffs in their hands.

The newcomers stopped at the door, Levi was too busy to notice them. The three guests could barely be seen in the darkness.

Levi just sat there, thinking about his problems and arguing. Suddenly he started up, there seemed to be someone here, and he looked around toward the door:

"Who's there? What do you want?"

The three men stood there, wordless, like wooden beams, not answering. Then the eldest of the three blurted out quietly:

"Nothing."

And Levi got up from the easy chair, barely standing on his feet because of his heavy belly. He peered deeper into the darkness, and asked:

"What did you say? I can't hear you."

The eldest visitor replied a bit louder:

"We were passing by, and we thought we should come in."

Levi turned crimson with rage, clenching his soft, effeminate hands into fists. He strode over to the Jews and stuck his head in their faces.

"Are you going to talk to me or not?"

And his yelling left the visitors speechless.

Leah, blanching, hurried in from the other room. Pausing at the door, she could barely make out the shapes at the wall, and, with her white hands at her throat, she crept into a corner of the room, peering terror-stricken through the darkness.

However, the eldest guest finally answered:

"Why bother with words, Mr. Patashnik, there are no words to express it."

Levi screamed, he ran across the room and screamed: "I can't hear you, damn it, I can't hear you! What are there no words for?"

The eldest guest said to him, quiet and gloomy:

"There are no words for the grief, Levi, for the grief that passes to *Him*, to the long, pale face . . . ."

But Levi did not understand.

"What face? Whose face?"

The eldest guest refused to answer, he hesitated, and then he slowly leaned over toward Levi, gazed at him, and, dreadfully quiet, he said:

"The Messiah! The Messiah's face!"

Levi was stunned, he felt a sharp jab through his body, deep inside, and he stood there for a while, staring at the visitor's face, staring, because he understood nothing.

Gradually, he turned away, clutched at his own short, yellow brown beard, bit his lip, and started pacing the large room.

And the visitors stood hunched over at the door.

The only sound was the soft clapping of Levi Patashnik's slippers across the floorboards.

He was pacing to and fro with broad steps, pausing for an instant in the middle of the room, and then starting off again, angry and hasty. All at once, he turned around and stood face to face with the guests, and then he took the eldest visitor's sleeve:

"Come!"

And he took them into the other room. The door remained open. Leah leaned over to the open door, peering in and watching as her father led the visitors into a corner of the room.

The darkness was broken by a grating noise when Levi opened a lock. He was opening the door of the cabinet for the visitors. A heap of gold sparkled and shone, burning like a deep fire, glowing in the darkness of the cabinet like an eternal light in a synagogue.

Levi stood up straight and boldly pointed at the gold:

"This is the Messiah!"

One of the visitors, dark, hairy, and angry, let out a roar. The eldest turned and murmured something to him.

But Levi was exultant with victory, he stood there, short of stature and with his big belly jutting out, his arms akimbo, and his eyes sparkling.

His innards were swelling, and he thought he had put an end to things, but then the eldest of the guests said to him:

"Levi, gold is sin, gold is the fire of hell!"

"What is gold?" retorted Levi.

And he strode toward them with his mouth foaming:

"You beggars! Have you ever had a penny in your pockets?! Daydreamers!

"Tramps!

"Fools!"

"Gold is sin?—Then why do you want alms?"

And he slammed the door to the cabinet:

"There are no alms here!"

The angry guest, Ber Ben-Tsippe, raised his brown paw. He wanted to bring it down on the short, fat man, but the eldest guest pushed him away harshly, and said to Levi in a cold tone:

"Remember, Levi, gold is soaked in blood!"

And the third guest, tall and foolish, and as skinny as a beanpole, waved his hand, and stammered:

"It really did hurt him!"

Levi jumped at him:

"You impudent fool! Who got hurt?!"

"The man who fell under your saw!"

Levi's eyes bulged glassy:

"What saw? Huh?! That saw? How do you know? Tell me!"

He grabbed his own head, turned pale, and dashed into the other room.

The visitors remained by the cabinet.

Leah, trembling, ran over to her father in the darkness, trembling. She fell upon his neck, embraced him:

"Papa, what is it, papa?!"

And she began to cry softly.

Levi looked around, greatly upset, not knowing what was happening. He gradually got his daughter away from him, took a deep, hard breath, and peered through the open door into the other room.

"What's wrong, Leah? Don't you know?"

He calmly buttoned his robe, and suddenly he was taller. Standing up straight, he remained there for a while, and then he strode back into the other room.

The guests were standing by the cabinet, gazing at him coldly, apparently waiting for him to return. He muttered calmly:

"It hurt him, gentlemen, because it had to hurt him. Now, leave!"

They didn't answer. He told them to go, and they followed him, but they were boiling with rage. Levi stopped at the door and let the visitors pass.

"Leave," he said, "and tell them that I, Levi Patashnik, say: Who cares!

"Did you hear? Who cares!"

And he slammed the door. He walked back and forth across the room several times, lost in thought, and then he sat down again in his easy chair as though nothing had happened.

And sitting there, facing the window, he called out to Leah who was standing somewhere behind him. He told her, the grown daughter, to sit down on his lap:

"Did you play the piano?"

"Yes."

"Did you take a walk in the garden?"

"Yes."

"And do you want a new dress, darling?"

But Leah, greatly distracted, didn't answer. She said:

"Papa, their Messiah is better!"

And she was frightened by her own words. Levi stared at her with terror in his eyes. She moved away and hurried into the next room.

Gimpel the Philosopher

"You know, Benye, in late summer, when the fruit is fragrant through the world, it's not so bad to live on the earth." These words were spoken by Simkhe Plakhte.

Benye didn't answer. He was standing on a log by the oven, boiling potatoes. Simkhe was sitting behind him at the closed window, with a pipe in his mouth, staring out at the road.

The road was glowing in the sun. The gravel was twinkling in the sand.

Simkhe Platkhe was sitting and gazing into the distance because a man had emerged on the road. A thin man was walking in the distance with a staff in his hand.

Whereupon Simkhe said:

"Looks like a man coming along the road."

But Benye didn't answer, he was cooking the potatoes.

Simkhe opened the window and looked out. The man waved at him.

He was a very merry wanderer, jigging along, and the lovely songs he was singing could be heard from far away.

Gimpel Zamkevitser was his name, a clown, a "flossafer."

Walking toward the mill, he sang a cheerful ditty.

Then he entered the house as if it were his own. He leaned his staff in a corner, put down his sack, and said:

"Good morning, fellow Jews!"

"Good morning to you."

He spun around on his high heels, tied the red cloth around his throat, and asked with a smile:

"Do you have anything to nibble on, friends?"

"To nibble on? You'll get something soon enough, but just who are you, my fine feathered friend.

Gimpel had no steady trade and so he devoted himself to idleness, but no matter, he knew what to say:

"I'm a philosopher, a great philosopher!

"And pay no attention," he went on, "to the fact that my knees are worn. My suit was once dotted with dots and striped with stripes, yes indeed!

"And girls love me because I'm so handsome. It's too bad that Mr. Simkhe is old, he doesn't know about girls anymore." And he sang a verse of his ditty!

Simkhe was confused and was so embarrassed by the song that he began rubbing his hands. Gimpel was on his high horse now. Overjoyed with his victory, he began to chatter:

"I, Gimpel, discovered a new star in the sky."

All at once, Benye turned around to him and yelled as though his breath had been cut off:

"Two stars!"

"No, just one, and it's going to be called Gimpelinus."

"Two stars," yelled Benye, there was a white man sitting on one and a black man sitting on the other."

"No, there were no people." He had discovered one star and without men.

Benye spat and angrily went back to the stove, where he bustled around the fire. In a little while he said aloud to himself:

"The guy's a liar!"

Gimpel was stunned, he had been caught. He was so abashed that he rubbed his eyes and began changing his story:

"It could be that there's another star somewhere that still remains to be discovered. I, Gimpel, am certainly not a stargazer, I'm a philosopher. I've got my entire philosophy written out, right here in my breast pocket.

"Later on, when I've had a bite to eat, my thoughts will be clearer, and I'll be able to explain even the most difficult parts of my philosophy."

And while sitting at the table and devouring the hot potatoes, Gimpel said:

"There is no human being in the world. Everything exists, but there is no human being here, and that is the difference between me and a man named Schopenhauer. Man is a dream of matter."

And from his breast pocket, he took out a pack of papers, leafed through them, and gave Simkhe a note written in tiny letters.

"Here, read it."

Benye came over, and the two men sat down at the window and began toiling.

The Note

The mind is now against nature, which has no mind.

Behold, how small is the notion that man has of himself, in contrast to the mountain that has no notion. Man, renounce your mind.

We should curse God, for the sea is more beautiful than God.

Behold, God was invented to beautify nature, but in so doing, they merely annoyed him.

There is no soul and no matter, both things are inventions of man's mind.

Oh, just occupy your area, because the area outside yourself is stronger and more wondrous than you.

It is not the fire emanating from the soul that knows the world; it is the body that knows the world while we restrain it.

If we keep from thinking, we can find out the ultimate truth.

The world has to go through me, just as I go through the world.

Oh, the proper notion is: not to know that I understand.

Dr. Lionson

And Gimpel laughed, it made him feel good, but Simkhe and Benye didn't laugh, evidently because they hadn't understood.

The sun was about to set.

The house became hot and dark, and as Gimpel came over to them with a new note, he looked like a long, narrow stick. Grinding his black teeth in pleasure, he looked even skinnier, like a Frenchman in Russia.

"Just read this."

They didn't feel like reading anymore.

"This is about the fact that we're all a dream. It stands to reason that we don't exist."

But they didn't feel like reading anymore.

He stood before them furiously, the way a man stands before a huge audience, and he began to speak aloud, in a lovely voice, like a Germanized Jew:

"Gentlemen!"

There was a hush, the spectators sat there, all ears, their hands in their laps.

"Please be so good as to listen quietly to my lecture. You have asked me to explain the system of irrational thinking . . . ."

And he burst out laughing, and laughed so hard that Benye began to smirk, but Gimpel kept talking:

"When we reject reason, we also do away with the categories of rational thinking: space and time. We acquire an understanding of the world only when we refuse to give in to the traditional conception of pluralism and individual entities. The body does not comprehend pluralism, everything is *one* for it, inalterably and unchangeably.

"Gentlemen, just one moment!

"Knowledge occurs the moment the body realizes that there is no void between itself and the world. It is the object without a subject, like the world itself. When man becomes the subject, he stops knowing."

Simkhe stood up laughing, not because he liked what he heard, but simply because he felt like laughing, and he wiped his hand across Gimpel's face:

"Philosopher!"

But Gimpel shook him off, the thoughts kept pouring from his brain, leaping like fleas, running off to all sides—he wanted to gather them in one bundle.

"Gentlemen, may I ask you to maintain silence! You fail to comprehend me, gentlemen, now that you're involved in living, and your heads are working, but you *shall* understand me at night when you are asleep, you shall understand when you are dead or asleep.

"Dear friends, the world itself is the subject of its own object, space presupposes pluralism and individual entities, and just as the body cannot comprehend any pluralism, there is thus, according to correct knowledge, no such thing as space. Time is abstracted spatiality, gentlemen, and there is no such thing as motion, because there is no such thing as pluralism or individual entities. If motion does not exist, then neither does time, because we cannot imagine time without motion. Ergo, ladies and gentlemen, the world exists, but man does not exist! Hooray!"

Gimpel stationed himself before them with his hands at his sides, earnest and haughty, and all three men started gazing at one another like roosters, gazing and gazing, until they exploded.

Simkhe laughed himself under the table, gasping choking, panting with tears in his eyes, and Gimpel moved down to him, tickling his armpits. Simkhe couldn't stand it anymore and from under the table he yelled:

"You monster!"

Benye smiled too.

And at night they were stretched out on Benye's wide benches, fast asleep.

Simkhe Plakhte was lying in his furs with his face up and his hands under his head, and he was snoring away, but every so often he would suddenly burst out laughing like a thin bolt of thunder.

Benye was huddled up under the rags in his bed, facing the wall and softly sobbing, but every so often he would suddenly yell that someone was killing him. Gimpel was the only one lying there peacefully.

His skinny legs were sticking out from under the cover. Then, softly and sleepily, he got up from his bench.

Gimpel was a sleepwalker. He stood up on the bench with his pale hands stretched out before him. Softly, with quiet steps, he moved from bench to bench.

Benye was weeping hard.

The simple philosopher strained his entire body listening to the muffled weeping. Then he slowly climbed on the table which was lit up by the moon.

His short blouse reached down only to his belly.

He stood there with parted lips, pale in the moonlight, like an outsider, and he was murmuring something, whispering softly, speaking voicelessly to Simkhe Plakhte and Benye.

In their sleep, they were listening, catching every word, and answering with their terrified bodies:

"We understand, Gimpel, we understand . . . you . . . and the moon . . . and the field . . . ."

Benye was crying, and his tears blended with the moonlight, which Gimpel and Simkhe Plakhte were absorbing.

And the dreaminess that came wafting from behind the moon was spun about the shadowy men, and they were all living the same secret life.

The Cow

The cow came out of the stable and trotted off.

The cow was so overcome with loneliness that she started out to wander through the world, into her diaspora.

She wandered from one place to the next, and wherever she came she saw that life was a *tohubohu*, waste and wild.

In the daytime, she would sleep in the shade of a willow tree or in a birch grove, and at night in a ditch by the side of the road.

But the cow spent most of her nights wandering about.

Benye once awoke from his sleep, and in the darkness he crept over to the window and saw, far, far away, at the edge of the earth, looming against the sky, the cow, trotting along.

All alone, holding her head up, her ears taut, and her tail tucked between her legs.

She wandered along, a pious cow, a *tsaddik*, listening to the sorrows of the world.

And then, one moonlit night, she suddenly trembled, her eyelids opened, and in a far land, on a riverbank, she saw seven lean cows, her ancestral mothers!

They were lit up by the moon, haughty and helpless, and the strength of the earth was coursing through their bones with a hot, stormy darkness.

Their big bones stuck out like chunks of wood, and their rigid bovine eyes took in the entire world, for even cows yearn for the silent earth, they envy the mountains that stand quietly, and even cows curse the day they were born.

The cow's legs collapsed beneath her, and in the middle of the night she lay down, bellowing and lamenting that she had ever been created . . . .

Lilith

And in the night, Benye was lying on his bed at home, as in a deep grave. He was barely breathing, and he was drenched with sweat, he lay among the foul rags, disheveled and stretched out like a carcass.

He held out his hands in the darkness, trying to grab on to something, to keep from falling, a stench arose from him and the drool was running from his mouth.

Benye, the saint of his generation, was drooling.

He untangled his hands from the darkness, and he stretched his hands into the darkness, but then he quickly pulled them back.

Benye seemed to have touched someone next to his bed.

He peered deep into the room. Someone was really standing not far from him, a stiff shape, a tall, warm shape.

Benye sat up in terror.

It was obviously a female, her hips and breasts were curving out of the stiff, black cloth.

He asked her softly:

"What are you doing here?"

She didn't answer. Slowly, unhurriedly, she walked over to the door, where she turned around to face him and remained standing in that position.

A yellow radiance poured through the room like a fine dust.

"Benye," she said, "once you summoned me."

Her voice was burning hot, it was lulling and it drew his body to her.

"I?"

"Yes, once, when you were still a little boy."

Benye stuck out his tangled beard.

"I? I was a little boy?"

"Yes, yes, Benye, you were wandering around the cows in pasture, you had a big swollen belly and calflike eyes. Do you remember? Whenever a bull would lust for a cow, you would wring your hands, and weep in pain, and start counting on your fingers to see how many years it was till you could marry."

Benye began recollecting, but he didn't want to answer.

"Benye, you summoned me then . . . . But I don't come to little children," and she added with a smile: "Now you're a solid adult, a man . . . . A strong, handsome man . . . . Handsome and dear! I want to put my head on your young chest . . . . I want your hot hands embracing me, darling! I want to feel the fresh breath of your body . . . ."

Benye's calflike eyes bulged in the dark. He stammered:

"Woman, you must be mistaken."

"Look," she cried ecstatically, "you're the only man for me! Look at my fresh young body . . . ."

And wordlessly she began tearing off her clothes.

"Benye, my hips are still chaste, virginal, solid, and my thighs are supple and straight . . . . The nipples of my breasts are stiff, and my breasts have never suckled a child . . . . never suckled . . . . never suckled . . . ."

And she wept with passion, wept, glowed, and her naked body sparkled in the yellow darkness, like the scales of a serpent.

Benye heard the benumbing voice, and in the yellow twilight he saw her, Lilith, standing at the door, bending slightly, her hands over her head, framed in the doorposts.

Benye grabbed the sides of the bed and clenched his teeth. He felt drawn to her. He was choking, and suddenly he screamed, and an alien voice yelled out of him:

"Get out! Get out of my house!"

He started throwing the rags and the pillows at her.

"Go away, you monster!"

He spat, tore his shirt, all at once he sprang from the bed and, in confusion, began beating his head and his chest.

Lilith stood at the door in silence, staring gravely with a grave smile on her lips. She was waiting until Benye calmed down.

"You whore! Get away!"

Benye realized he was practically naked in front of this woman, so he jumped back into bed, pulling the covers over him, closing his eyes, and turning his face to the wall.

He groaned softly.

Lilith stood there quietly for a while, then she slowly tiptoed over to him, and gently tickled his armpit.

Benye bit his lips, the pleasure ran through his entire body, every nook and cranny. He wouldn't turn around, but he gradually stopped groaning.

Lilith sat down on his bed, smiled, and began tickling the soles of his feet.

It was so delicious that it dazed him.

Benye knew that Lilith was sitting next to him, so he held back his deep laughter, and lay there as mute as a wooden beam.

She began stroking his hair, and her slender fingers curled up the disheveled strands. He couldn't bear it anymore, he turned around to her, and his thick yellow teeth were grinding with his sweet sufferings.

He tittered like an old goat: "Darling, sweetest . . . !"

Lilith said: "Your beautiful face drives me crazy, Benye, darling! Don't smile at me like that!"

Suddenly Benye realized it was Lilith, and he started laughing and grinding his teeth all the harder, to drive her away.

She moved away from the bed.

"You slut!"

He leaped after her, dropping his rags in his excitement, but she managed to elude him.

"I'm going get you, Lilith," he shouted, "I'm going get you."

Benye dashed after her through the yellow light, storming like a wind, panting, screaming, until he caught her with his right hand, in a corner.

He dug his brown, dirty fingers into her white body and thrust his tangled beard into her face. Lilith curved away from him, but he pressed her closer and yelled with foaming lips:

"Deborah, you Deborah, you!"

For his dead wife's name was Deborah.

Lilith tried to fight back. She was delighted, but she fought back. Suddenly she grabbed his dirty beard and kissed him so hard on the thick parched lips that Benye nearly fell over, then she lifted him up on her hot shoulders and carried him off to his bed . . . .

"Oh God! Oh God! And the rooster hasn't crowed!"

It grew dark in the room, their breath merged, sparks were flashing in the darkness, and slippery limbs were wrapped around the body with green eyes, and with a faint flickering . . . . There is no salvation, oh God!

And Benye was struggling, he didn't know with whom, he fell down and reached out in the darkness to take hold of something, he dashed off the bed, but it was quiet in the room, and no one was there.

And his blood stopped in his veins, it curdled, froze.

Lilith, fresh, young Lilith, the wife of Satan, had killed him.

Adam's first wife.

Benye dragged himself across the room, climbed up on the oven, and then climbed down again. He sat naked, as he was, on the floor, sat and sat, and then stood up again with his head drooping, crept over to the pail of water, thrust in his hands, and then kept dragging around the room . . . .

He stumbled over to the door and opened it. The cold air refreshed him. He opened the door to the porch and stepped out. A cold, silvery blueness enveloped his face and naked body.

At first he didn't notice that a Jew was standing there with a sack and a staff in his hand—it was one of the three guests that had once visited him, and now the man touched his hand.

"Benye, you didn't resist!"

Benye remained cold, he didn't care, but then all at once he turned to the guest, and his eyes filled with blood:

"Thieves! Damn you all!"

And he burst into moans:

"Why don't you leave me alone?! You monsters!"

And he dashed back into the house, grabbed a stick of wood, and ran out again to the porch. But the guest was gone.

Benye hurried down the road after him.

Leah

Grandmother was sitting at the window, and the girl sat opposite her, pale, with a book in her lap. Bending over to the old ear, she asked:

"Is he handsome?"

"A delight, Leah, he's out of this world."

"And where is he, Grandmother?"

"He lives alone in his home, secluded and remote, where there are no people."

"Alone, all alone?"

"Yes, he walks around, all alone, in the ancient woods."

The cool blue fires of evening drew around the world, frozen and fine, making reality look like a dream.

And Leah, Levi's daughter, longed for the Messiah. The long pale face that the guests had spoken about floated like a radiance through the vast house.

She felt it in the rustle of the empty rooms.

She avoided the large mirrors on the walls, she was frightened of the dim reflections of the furnishings.

"Maybe he's resting somewhere with that hidden face of his."

Levi remained in the dim room, more somber every day. He kept silent, stopped in his tracks, not knowning why.

Leah would avoid him, and if they met she would lower her eyes. She wanted to tell him something, but she couldn't find the words. She wanted to tell her father, Levi Patashnik:

"Father, I have to go to him . . . ."

And her father would reply:

"Silly! Respectable girls aren't pious, girls shouldn't be pious at all."

But she would retort:

"No, Papa, I'm not pious at all."

He would then leap up and shout:

"Well, then what do you want?"

"I want to go to him. I have to go to him."

"But he doesn't exist, silly!"

"I know he *does* exist, he *has* to."

And her father came closer and stroked her hair:

"But Leah, I'm old. What will I do all by myself?"

She didn't answer, she had nothing to say.

"Don't go away, Leah darling, don't go . . ."

But at lunch they would sit like mutes, never uttering a word. Levi would mumble something in his beard; he was afraid to express what he was thinking. He threw the dishes . . . . Got up in the middle of the meal and angrily hurried to his room.

At the table, they could sense someone, a third person, who drove them apart.

And haunting days and nights wore by, without rest or sleep.

It was past midnight. Leah was wandering through the rooms, dressed only in a nightshirt.

The place where the visitors had spoken his name, that was where He must be . . . .

The rooms were filled with a silent darkness. *He* couldn't be heard. The place where the visitors had stood was empty.

She slowly opened a door into the next room . . . . Half-naked, holding a candle, Levi was standing there, bending into the open cabinet . . . counting, counting . . . .

Leah quietly hurried to bed and began weeping, whispering incomprehensible words to Him . . . to Him . . . .

And one evening she put on her coat, took her umbrella. Silently she crept out of the house, never to come back again . . . . Outside it was raining . . . .

At the corner, a squire was standing, with a feather in his hat, a rifle over his shoulder, and a drenched hound on a leash.

In the Forest

Simkhe Plakhte and Gimpel Zaskevitser were lying by the hut in the woods, which were blue deep into the thickets.

The fir trees were stretching out their strong branches, hung with cobwebs, and the redness of evening was dripping from them.

The sun was just going down.

Dark Jews were passing between the trees, they were soaked in the redness and dipped in the shadows.

No foot had ever trodden through the forest. What were these Jews in furs doing here, with their lambskin hats and their staffs, walking in single file, foolish, hidden? If they met anyone, they would slip behind the trees.

"Maybe they're Cabbalists," said Gimpel.

"Hey! Out of my woods!" yelled Simkhe into the thickets. "Out!"

The Jews vanished for a short spell into the bushes.

"They're giving him a hard time, they're making fun of Benye!"

"Is Benye one of them?" asked Gimpel.

"Yes."

"A Lamed-vovnik?"

"A Lamed-vovnik."

"Do the Lamed-vovniks want to turn the world upside-down?"

"Leave me alone, you monster!"

They were lying on the earth, chewing straws, wallowing and talking.

Where had they driven Benye?

"They drove him to the devil, Gimpel. They tortured him, damn their eyes!"

"A peasant saw him at night, riding a cow."

"Really?"

"Is that Cabbalah, too, Simkhe?"

Simkhe Plakhte didn't answer, he sat down, hugging his knees, and just gazed into the woods.

"Gimpel, you're a fool. Why don't you go back to town? We and those people in the trees, we've all got old blood!"

"So what?"

"So old blood stinks."

Gimpel propped himself up on his elbows and cocked his ears.

"If only you didn't talk so much, you monster. All those men among the trees bear the yoke in silence, like an old forest. But you talk too much, Gimpel, much too much."

"My mind has worn me out, Simkhe."

"Too much mind, you're right."

After a silence, Simkhe Plakhte began talking again.

"Now once I was a Hassidic rabbi, I had a large, pious following, I delved into the secrets of the Torah. But then I couldn't stand it anymore, I fled here, to this hut."

"Why couldn't you stand it?"

"There was no one I could really talk to, Gimpel. Too much intellect!"

And Simkhe turned red with anger, leaped up, and yelled at the Jews in the thickets:

"Hey! Get out of my forest! Out!"

And then he said to Gimpel:

"That's *my* forest. It's grown up around *me*. *My* forest. If you want to come to me, you have to pass through the thickets, walk between the trees, on tiny paths, and you'll find me at home in my hut. Gimpel!" He took hold of Gimpel's jaw. "Don't come to me in a storm. I, Simkhe Plakhte, would be struggling along with the forest, and every dead bird would be lying dead here, right here, in my heart."

"You must be important, Mr. Simkhe."

"Important?" cried Simkhe Plakhte. "Some day, they'll be coming to me in carriages!"

Gimpel broke in excitedly:

"Really? When?"

"When our friends in the woods are no longer in the world."

"Oh really? And who'll come?"

"Not snotnoses like you. There'll be others coming. Lusty men."

Meanwhile, a Lamed-vovnik came up behind them, a tiny little Jew, a famished creature. He asked for water.

"What do you need water for?"

The Lamed-vovnik in his meekness answered:

"To drink."

"So go, you little creep, to the right, you'll find a little spring, drink, and praise God, but don't come to me."

The little man walked off wordlessly into the darkness of the forest.

It was very late now. The dew was settling on the grass. Gimpel was stretched out, with his head in his hands, staring at a beetle crawling through the haulms.

Simkhe went over to the hut, he sat down on a log and sprinkled seeds for the pigeons. The Lamed-vovniks, somewhere deep among the trees, were finishing their evening prayers, they began scattering again one by one, each with his winter hat and his secret.

Each one chose a tree in some corner, sat down all by himself beneath the branches, slipped one sleeve into the other, and waited. What does a Lamed-vovnik wait for?

Perhaps for Him, the man sitting at the gates of Rome.

His footsteps are burnt out by fire in the high mountains.

He's taking His time, the man born in torment, but He has to come any day now, He *has to come.*

A dry darkness was burning in the woods. The leaves were softly veiling the trees. Here and there, glowworms were glowing. Gimpel was all rolled up in the grass, sound asleep.

Simkhe was sitting at the threshold of his hut, his burning blue eyes flashing into the forest.

A dull heaviness hung over the trees.

A cry rang out deep in the forest. A Lamed-vovnik was singing tearfully with an old, hoarse voice, lamenting, wailing from the forest darkness, and it was mirrored in his voice, the way he lay there, with his face to the earth, bowing to the old sacred city, which had been destroyed:

Jerusalem, Jerusalem,
We hung our hearts on your walls,
We built you with our tears,
Your stones are our bodies
And our eyes—your caves.

Jerusalem, Jerusalem,
City of priests, of kings and prophets,
You lament over us like a storm,
And tear the blood from our burnt hearts.

We bear the yoke upon our bony shoulders
Of your towers and your bridges,
And with the foxes of your ruins we grieve:
Jerusalem, Jerusalem, Jerusalem!

With his burning blue eyes, Simkhe Plakhte peered sharply into the darkness. The voice choked, it was throttled in the thickets.

Suddenly Simkhe leaped up as though something had bitten him. He turned his broad shoulders, stretched out his arms, clenched his fists, and let out a scream that was cast in copper:

"Crows, hey crows!"

And he dashed up a tree, like a cat, soft, and with sharp nails, grabbed hold of the branches, and then leaped from tree to tree, from one treetop to the next . . . .

In the stillness, he glided over the heights of the forest, screaming through the night, waking the birds and storming, as before the start of day.

Lord Vrublevsky

Lord Vrublevsky had a palace near the town of Lebereve.

In the evening, people could see him walking around in the vast blue fields, a tall, thin man, with his rifle over his shoulder, and a long hound running ahead of him on a leash. Gloomy and lonesome, he would wander over his ruined estates.

Benye's mill was his property.

The woods, his ancient woods, were standing ready to be

chopped down, and his villages, all ruins, lay in the valleys with protruding beams, like petrified birds.

Lord Vrublevsky, at night, would take his dog and poke around the Jewish villages, looking round in the farms, peering into windows, eavesdropping.

He fancied Jewish girls!

He had a marble palace, it was empty, the beds were untouched, the heavy curtains drawn across the windows, and he, the lonesome master, wandered through the blue fields, poking around, eavesdropping.... The palace stood empty. But at times, once a year, the windows would light up, the flames of large lamps would flash through it, and the palace would resound haughtily in the night. Lord Vrublevsky was celebrating.

And now, what was he after?

Walking through the darkness almost every night, looming firmly against the blue sky, the Gentile was seeking a salvation for his Gentile soul.

And once, in early winter, during his nightly wanderings, he came to the edge of the sky and met the angry guest, Ber Ben-Tsippe, walking out of the world.

Ber, the dark, angry vagabond. They faced one another, stone-still, like two gray wolves.

Vrublevsky's dog, about to pounce upon the vagabond, remained in midleap, with his front paws raised and his body stretching through the air.

And Jewish hatred clashed with Gentile hatred.

Towns .... Towns ....

Rainy days had come. The little Jewish towns were shaking, house against house. The muddy streets were rocking, the ancient roofs, one atop the other, were dancing with the thick rains, swaying back and forth, gray and soaked.

Shoemakers were banging their hammers. Bathhouses were heated up, chimneysweeps were standing on the roofs.

From White Russia to Zhamut, from Zhamut to Lithuania, the little towns banged and yelled to one another, like huge clocks scattered across the plains ....

Draymen traveling through the countryside heaved their shoulders against their wagons, which were heavily loaded down.

Psalms were recited in all homes—a sea of psalms.

Kyril, the Gentile who took care of the bath, was preparing the rubbing brooms for the pre-Sabbath cleansings on Friday. He sat, sickly, on the ground, staring at his big toes. He was tormented by the mystery of creation.

Velve the water-carrier, a Lamed-vovnik, was walking with his shoulder board on his back, drudging with his body to understand the world. He caught sight of Motte up on a roof, with his smoky beard in a chimney. Velve set his full pails on the ground.

"Motte, hey Motte!"

And he raised the long tangles of his beard up to the sky:

"Velve, is that you, Velve?"

And the two drudging saints conversed from roof to ground, comforting one another in the midst of their toil, looking at one another, but their thoughts were somewhere else.

"Motte, hey Motte!"

The tall, thin cap-makers were measuring the peasants for enormous caps, Gittel, the beadle's wife, was standing at the window, casting down food to the magpies. Hammers were clanging in smithies.

Big, silent blacksmiths in leather aprons were standing and dreaming, in the tiny smithies, they were so tall they looked as if they might surge through the roof at any moment.

Seven silent blacksmiths in Zhamut, Lamed-vovniks.

But unexpectedly, and gradually, there came a hush—tick-tock, tick-tock, and then nothing.

Velve stood there with his beard raised to the roof.

The magpie was unable to fly down from the pig.

The draymen on the roads stood up straight, rubbed their eyes, and gaped all around. A peculiar hush.

And from the foggy fields, into the little town, Benye came riding on his cow.

A shred of clothing was hanging from his naked body, his miry feet were dragging along the ground, one hand was holding on to the back of the cow, the other was clutching—a piece of clay.

The rain ran down his body in muddy drops.

And Benye's eyes? Like the eyes of a pike when it's hauled in from the water.

The cow with her craning neck, with her stiff tail between her legs, was carrying a man more dead than alive, heavy and worn out—an atonement for a cow, for grave sins, for a wretched life.

And Benye was babbling, rattling to her from his parched throat . . . .

Benye was riding through the little Jewish towns with the tiding on his lips.

Velve, moaning, heaved the pails up on his shoulders. The narrow streets began shaking inside, from house to house.

The hammers were clanging in the smithies.

Kyril sat there, staring at his big toes, and all at once his calflike eyes opened wide and he saw:

Somewhere on a main road, there was an ancient crucifix soaked by the rains.

And from it, Jesus came climbing down, God's son, he looked around at the autumn fields, sighed, and started off through the world.

On the Way

Leah traveled by train, by wagon, on foot, and everywhere she met shrunken Jews, who spoke to her compassionately. They were standing along the main roads, but Leah didn't need the signposts, she knew the way instinctively.

The fine autumn drizzles splashed through the ragged mists, and the clay squeaked underfoot.

Once, at a crossroads, she ran into a village tailor, huddled under an ancient crucifix.

The wooden cross was leaning over him, like a weeping willow branch, the kind used in the Sukkoth ceremony. A tin garland was attached to the wood, and inside it, nailed to the cross, hung Jesus.

The painted deity had faded in the rains, his loincloth was rotting, and it fluttered in the wind.

Leah stopped suddenly. Jesus and He, both had been thrown down from heaven. Who knows, perhaps He too would be hung up on crossroads for the sins of mankind?!

The wind blew apart the ends of the black shawl that stiffly enveloped her white face. Her widened eyes gaped at the worn-out deity, at the tin crown suspended over him.

"Is that God?"

Leah trembled, with tears in her eyes she stared at him and absorbed the solitude of the crucified Jesus.

The tailor, half-dazed replied:

"Daughter, the cross goes throughout the world, from land to land, like a shadow of God, it is the gospel of Him who has to come, He will pass through gallows and crosses . . . through dead forests . . . to us . . . ."

The tailor broke off, dissolving in tears. He huddled more into himself under the cross, frozen and soaked through; shuddered with muffled sobs and wiped the tears on his sleeve.

"My daughter, I have been sitting right here under this cross for twenty years now, waiting. It keeps rotting and bending more and more from year to year . . . . But He . . . He doesn't come."

The tailor drew up his knees, buried his head in his lap, and fell silent.

Leah, willy-nilly, and with a heavy heart, bent down before the cross and murmured something, praying quietly, whispering wordlessly, and the wind toyed with Jesus' loincloth.

A man came walking down the road, Vrublevsky. In his green hunting outfit, he looked like spring dew on the autumn field. His black eyes sparkled like pitch, he stopped before Leah, stood there mute, and began undressing her with his eyes.

Leah, terrified, began to back away. She thought the man had suddenly leaped down to her from the cross.

The tailor was huddled up, he didn't turn around, he seemed unaware of the aristocrat's arrival.

Leah, blanching, ran out into the field, she tried to scream but couldn't, and she felt the aristocrat behind her, following her, coming closer . . . .

The eldest guest appeared on the road. Calm, and with great strides, he went over to Leah, took her hand, and gently led her to another road.

Simkhe Plakhte Says That Gimpel Is Right

Indeed, why should Simkhe Plakhte care?—The Hassids yearn for their spiritual leader the rebbe, and come to him like calves to their mother's nipples.

There were two old Hassids sitting at the reader's desk in the synagogue, talking about the rebbe's deserting them and going off to the woods.

But why should Simkhe Plakhte care?

He was lying on his fur in a treetop like a stork in its nest, and the wreaths of smoke from his pipe were curling up to the sky.

The lush countryside faded far away into a foggy blueness.

The streams gurgled along, through the fields, up and down the hills, the way people go to God over mountainous roads, uphill and downhill, to God.

You, oh you, who are so overcome by the world that God yells out of you, you, the terror of the fields echoes in your bones, it echoes in your voice, why should you really care, after all?

Isn't Man a vanished forest, an upheaved stone? Doesn't Man wash by, like a wave over God, like water over the shores?

Gimpel, oh Gimpel. We have to curse God, because the sea is more beautiful than God!

Yes, Hassidism is a heroic cloak, but I, Simkhe Plakhte, go about naked!

No one opened up for me, and I stepped in all alone and did not find soul, only a steamy field and laughing earth in my body . . . .

And as long as I, this clod of world, have a loaf of bread in my shack and a sheepskin, why should I care?

And singing proudly, he climbed down from the tree, danced off into his shack and flung open the window.

"Holiday! Holiday!"

He kicked off his bast shoes and sprang like a goat, intoxicated with the summer.

Look! The body is a motherly earth! Does the earth breathe? Doesn't the misty earth live, doesn't she think?

> No one opened up for me, and I stepped in.
> Raw, irritated branches,
> Soaked moss,
> fragrances, like faraway violins,
> blood,
> sleepy stones.

That is a strong, radiant weeping from me, Simkhe Plakhte, through dampnesses, wails, roots, veins, sucking out the fragrances,

benumbing, crushing marrow, and passing, passing, like light in all
things.

Gimpel, oh Gimpel, we have to curse God, because a bird is
more beautiful than God!

And then a peasant girl trudged past with a bundle of wood on
her back. She didn't see Simkhe although she sensed a man nearby,
and he beamed proudly, with his rosy eyes shining, delighted at
what he saw.

The tawny breasts were fresher than the forest, her bare feet,
with their springtime gait in the high grass, hurried to the window.

Simkhe laughed, a laugh like thunder, and he yelled out:

"Hey, Marilia! Haven't you seen, haven't you looked at God?"

And the strapping, radiant peasant girl answered: "What haven't
I seen, what haven't I looked at!"

He leaped through the window, took her in his arms, danced
with her, and spun her around.

The peasant girl laughed, struggled, tickled him saucily, and they
tumbled down into the grass, heady with the wet earth like trees in
springtime, and their hot faces drank up the cold dew of the grass
haulms . . . .

Gimpel, oh Gimpel, the mountain has no power of conception!

Yes, Simkhe had been a saint among the Hassids, he was the piety
of the world, and perhaps, who can say, he might have been the
Messiah of the House of David.

> He committed no *sins*,
> He knew no *hatred*,
> He knew no *love*,
> He never desired or needed justice,
> No war,
> No peace.

While the earth was raging in his blood, and his limbs were scattered by God among the trees in the forest, the waters, the cattle at
pasture, the fields and the plains.

Gimpel, perhaps you're right, the world exists and man does not
exist!

And he came with heavy strides, Simkhe Plakhte, into the thicket,
and stopped by a dark meadow in the forest.

The earth shook dull beneath him, something was working dully on the dark, isolated meadow, a writhing of clods of earth, tree stumps, a silent joining of unmolded limbs.

And now, a heavy piece of coarse cloth stirred, and then crept grossly, crept from the earth, a cruel, gray, earthen head was creeping, the earthen man.

The gray eyelashes—nettles; the eyes—waters; the nose—earth; tangled hair—like branches; teeth—stony; and the lolling tongue—clay.

Not grieving, not smiling.

And now, slowly, the head was creeping forth, stuck without a neck on the wooded shoulders, his chest matronly, and his arms, twisted into the trees of the forest, intertwined with the roots and herbs, it spread out to Simkhe.

And then out from the earth all the way to the knees, but still interkneaded with the motherly field, and the clay tongue snuffled something to Simkhe in the eternal language, and he, understanding the blossoming voice, fell into the crooked lap and nestled in the bosom, disheveled and stirred up, like a bird in a storm . . . .

And suddenly Simkhe felt a radiant presence overhead, he was so intoxicated he could barely open his eyes: The Prophet of Tashbe was standing next to him, looking like the eldest guest. The venerable old man was not grieving, not smiling. He barely grazed Simkhe's shoulder:

"Simkhe, son of Stetye, what is the matter?"

And Simkhe burst into tears and tumbled upon the earth's lap:

"Oh, God! I want to live, why did you make me a human being? I want to live, live . . . ."

The Great Assembly

In the middle of the night, the Lamed-vovniks gathered at Benye's home. Simkhe came too. A scant fire stick was burning by the oven.

The Lamed-vovniks trudged into the room, the water-carriers with their yokes on their shoulders, the chimneysweeps with their brooms, the draymen holding their whips.

Gimpel, a heretic, was not permitted to attend. But he began hollering, and so the Lamed-vovniks had to give in.

The eldest guest put his bag on the table, and then sat down gravely and rested his head in his hands.

The Lamed-vovniks sat down on the benches and the beds, others climbed up on the oven.

The seven silent men sat down on one bench in a corner, big, strong, tan Jews in large fur coats—the seven from Zhamut.

Kyril, the Gentile in charge of the bathhouse (Abraham son of Isaac), stretched out at the threshold. He too was a Lamed-vovnik.

And all that was visible in the darkness were the tangled beards, the ragged knees, and eyes filled with a turbid fire.

Simkhe was sitting somewhere, hidden, with his pipe in his mouth.

The hot leaden air weighed down on the heads, it smelled of the sweat on furs and bodies, and a sorrow was gnawing deep inside the hairy chests.

The eldest guest, Wolf the son of Bird, quietly asked for politeness' sake:

"Where is the host?"

Gimpel, who had been waiting for this, blurted out:

"The host is away, he's ridden off on a cow."

No one replied.

Wolf raised his head and looked at the others. They were sitting crowded together, around the room. The silent ones were silent, the oven-sitters stuck out their heads. Wolf cleared his throat, apparently about to speak:

"Masters and friends!"

But the air suddenly turned foul, the Jews looked every which way, Wolf held his nose and peered around. A tiny Lamed-vovnik, upon whom suspicion fell, defended himself:

"I swear, as sure as I'm a Jew, it wasn't me!"

It was the same one who had asked Simkhe for a drink of water in the forest.

Wolf began speaking. His voice was barely audible, and the Jews craned their necks, amazed, hanging on his every word.

"Oh, the sadness that comes to Him, with the long pale face from eternity to eternity!

"He wanders about in the ten sefirot,
"Seeks to join the body,
"But,

"But the body is mere clay, the members unmolded,
"No arms or legs.
"And the long pale face wanders from eternity to eternity."

Wolf was breathing heavily, he buried his face in his hairy hands, and in a trembling voice, he spoke deeply, as though to himself:
"Who lacks the Divine Image?
"The seas have the shape of eternity.
"The earth and the heavens have the shape of eternity.
"The stars drift from eternity to eternity.
"Only Man does not have the Divine Image."
And Wolf rocked and began weeping and spoke:
"Man on earth is seeking his face!
"He thought that Adam was his image, but Adam did not know the torment of being born.
"He thought that Moses was his image, but Moses did not know the torment of being killed.
"He thought that Jesus was his image, Jesus of Nazareth . . . ."
Tears were pouring from the seventy-two gaping eyes, the listeners sat with bated breath, with open mouths, drawn irresistibly to him. Wolf sighed and then spoke faintly:
"And here, Man stumbled."
Kyril, the son of Fedot, was sitting at the threshold with his head drooping, his fists rubbing away the tears. His heart was heavy. Someone, a drayman, jabbed him to make him stop, they couldn't hear. Kyril kissed the hand that had jabbed him, and stretched out his arms beseechingly.
All at once, Wolf began talking in a loud angry voice, pounding the table, rocking to and fro:
"Crosses stand on all roads, and on them hangs Jesus!
"Woe to us, men have sinned, they have gone to him so that he would be tormented in their stead.
"And he, the fool, he took the gallows and went up to Golgotha.
"Men say: We have sinned, now someone must come to be tormented.
"Crosses stand on all roads, and on them hangs the Messiah, and the Messiah is nailed to them.
"And so they call him *Messiah*.
"Woe, the world has become clean, and the world has been purified, because he, the Messiah, hangs on all roads."

Gimpel shot up like a spring, propped his hands on the table, and screamed with all his might:

"I protest!"

The Lamed-vovniks stood up, terrified, no one knew what was going on. Clambering down from the oven, one of them knocked over the burning fire stick. In the darkness, they all bumped into one another. There was a stampede, and Gimpel's shrieks drowned out everything else.

"This isn't scientific! This is fanaticism!"

The Lamed-vovniks were furious, Ber Ben-Tsippe, managed to grab hold of the "flossafer," and Gimpel's poor bones cracked in the darkness:

"Shut your mouth, you shrimp, or I'll smash you!"

And the seven silent men of Zhamut dashed over, the way powerful rocks plummet in a storm. They roared and pushed. Someone kindled the fire stick.

Simkhe was still sitting in a corner. He looked at the silent men, and when he saw that things were going badly for Gimpel, he slowly got up. The little Lamed-vovnik was standing in his way, he grabbed his scrawny neck and twisted the creature around, and then he quietly went over to Gimpel, took his arm and led him back to the corner.

The silent ones glared at him fiercely. Ber grumbled into his beard, but they still felt reverence for Simkhe——though they weren't sure why.

The Lamed-vovniks sat down again in their places, Wolf didn't even turn, he had propped his head on his elbows the whole time as though not noticing anything.

It was already late at night, the exhausted men were dying to go to sleep, but Wolf wouldn't begin. A tall, skinny beanpole of a man, the one who had spoken to Levi Patashnik about the saw, gave the eldest guest a pleading look, leaned toward him, and said:

"Wolf, can you hear? Your listeners are waiting."

Wolf didn't answer, and the beanpole was so overcome with despair that he shrugged his shoulders and sat down again.

The men lost all hope that Wolf would ever speak. They sat there, wordless and waiting. Simkhe, however, smiled faintly. All at once, the eldest guest turned, straightened, and looked about for Ber. It was evidently because of him that he wouldn't speak.

Ber was holding both hands on the table, he sat there like a log, his hat slouching over his eyes.

Wolf smiled, his face turned radiant, his eyes moist, as though from a faraway joy. He began rocking with enthusiasm, his voice became purer and more joyful. The listeners became more relaxed, they breathed more easily.

"Listen, but we say: The Messiah of the House of David does not atone.

"But we say: Each man must take his gallows and go to Golgotha by himself, and every beam must be taken from the wall, and every tree from the forest, for *we* shall hang ourselves on all roads.

"We!"

Wolf pointed his finger, he had broken into a strong chant of deep joy and enthusiasm.

"Gallows stand on all roads, and *we* are the ones hanging on them.

"The blood running down the wood of the crosses burns like an impure sunset.

"*Our* blood, our blood, is running down the wood of the crosses.

"And from this blood, *He* shall arise—the Messiah of the House of David!"

But now it happened, the thing that Wolf was afraid of. Ber lumbered off his bench like an ox, red, with bloodshot eyes. His mouth was foaming, he couldn't speak.

The Lamed-vovniks retreated into the corners, and he began scurrying around the room. Suddenly, he stopped, dashed over to the table, and pointed at his own chest:

"*We*?! *We*?!"

And he wrung his hands at the ceiling, clenched his fingers, and let out a dark roar that sounded as if it came from under the earth.

"Scoundrels! For whom?! Scoundrels!"

And he ran amuck around the table, pounding the benches with the full strength of his fists:

"Revenge! That's what! Revenge for little children. Revenge for blood."

A dreadful hush fell upon the room. Gimpel was so terrified he slipped behind Simkhe. The quiet Lamed-vovniks wept, whining into their beards, and Ber tore himself bloody, tore the hair from his head, and yelled:

"We want blood!"

He grabbed the little Lamed-vovnik on whom suspicion had fallen earlier. The Lamed-Vovnik writhed and struggled in his hands. Ber clutched his mouth:

"You rebel, did you draw blood? Why didn't you draw blood?"

And Ber spat in his face. The little Lamed-vovnik twisted out of his hands, barely alive; he quietly crept into a corner and wiped his face on his sleeve, on his coattails, on a cloth, there was so much spit on it. Ber didn't quiet down. The others were terrified, they hugged the walls, Kyril crawled under the bed, frightened that Ber would take vengeance on him for the Gentiles.

Suddenly, Simkhe got up, totally pale, his eyes gaping.

"Look!"

He pointed at the windows. A strong, turbid white light was glaring through the panes. Blood was running down the doorposts. The terrified Lamed-vovniks peered outside, they could hear the heavy tolling of a thousand bells.

Ber was the first to run to the window.

Benye Rides His Cow

And that night, Benye, riding his cow, reached the edge of the world.

The cow dug in her hooves, poked her tormented head and stiff ears into the darkness, and her tail curled upward.

Benye sat up straight, stopped breathing, the life in his heart came to a halt; he peered with dark, empty eyes—gaping holes; his mouth opened, he gazed and stared into the dark void of the dreadful beginning . . . .

The cow stood with her legs wide apart, the disheveled rider and the cow looked like one single creature.

The stony landscape, with its huge crags, loomed into the cloudy emptiness. Far, far off, among the stones, a small silver calf was standing all by itself, radiating a thin blueness upon the edges of the towering rocks.

Benye gingerly leaned over and peered into the chasm.

This was the chasm where Samael was falling head-first, heavy as a stone. Samael, the Angel of Evil; he plunged with outstretched arms, on and on, deeper and deeper, and his long, thin legs thrashed about, trying to land on something.

And all at once, his one hand grabbed a crooked thorn just at the side of the chasm and he twisted his head up to Benye.

His crooked skull was covered with wooly, pitchy hair.

Samael saw Benye, he gave him an evil smirk, and ground his long, narrow teeth.

Benye was astonished, he gaped at him, gaped, and craned his neck, but suddenly the face looked like that of his brother.

"Levi? Levi the moneylender?"

Samael gazed straight up at Benye. He pressed his thin black lips together and spat at him—a torrent of gold came pouring out of his mouth up to the highest edge of the chasm and stopped, he kept falling headfirst, the Angel of Evil, heavy as a rock, deeper and deeper, his arms outstretched, his long thin legs trying to catch hold of something.

The cow stood with her legs wide apart, her body alive with the terror of the world that has come to naught . . . .

And Benye gaped, gaped with bulging eyes.

The Spectacle

These things happened in a night without stars or moon. A bit of light flickered in the fields. No one knew where it came from.

The tombstones and the thick fresh woods of our graveyards turned over, and out of the depths came the bones—old men to old men, with wormy beards, women to women, foolish creatures, tiny children, toddlers.

Hosts of the dead went out on the dimly lit fields, and they walked along the highways toward the city of Rome.

All in step, all in step.

Old men to old men, and the wind sighed out of their bones, the lovely girls nestled together, and they were so modest that they covered their nakedness with their hands.

And the little children walked along, like flocks, in order, lamb by lamb.

Suddenly, an old man halted, a maze of patches, like an old Sabbath pot, he waited for the children on the roads, the old man liked death in the world:

"The Holy Flock of the Jewish People!"

And the passing herds of children replied:

"Baah, baah!"

And the old man laughed and laughed, he danced a jig, and slapped their empty behinds.

"You little rascals!"

At midnight, they arrived in Rome from all parts of the world, and the corpses groped the walls of the city—damp walls, they knocked on the gates, but no one would open.

"What should we do?"

The old men put their heads together, and the children put their little shoulders together, and they clambered up the walls, and if a corpse, a good-for-nothing, lost an arm on the way, the hand would stand up, climb on its own strength, and then, clever creature that it was, go through the city by itself. And one executed cadaver removed the noose from his neck, and tied on his boot so that it wouldn't drop . . . .

And thus they all silently lay down on the rooftops, in the soft attics, on the warm porches, and these heaps of the dead beleaguered the high towers of the city.

The church bells slowly began swaying, and then tolling heavily of their own accord. Vast peals, heavy as stones, fell into the city. And a red turbid stream ran down from the bells, looking like blood, oozing down to the earth in heavy drops, drip, drip, drip . . . .

Rome!

A corpse was lying under every window, a cadaver under every bed. The old men, exhausted, sat down in the cradles and covered themselves with the quilts: Goodnight, Father. And there were two occupants in every bed—one living and one lifeless, for brotherhood. The girls modestly crept in with the young boys, for love, and secretly, silently, they scraped their bony voices and snored into the night:

"Vengeance . . . Vengeance . . . Vengeance . . . ."

And far, far away, in the windows of Benye's house, the Lamedvovniks were piled atop one another, breathlessly watching the spectacle.

Ber was pressing his head against the window, forcing back his tears, and cursing the Christians. The others were choking and gasping, they were squeezed into the windows like herrings, with their eyes bulging, and Gimpel stood higher than anyone, peering through his fist, as though through a telescope.

A piece of night tore open for the city of Rome, revealing the spectacle of the bones. Gimpel observed every last detail.

"Look at that virgin!" he cried. "What passion!"

The little Lamed-vovnik ran over to Gimpel and nagged him: "Show me, show me! What is it?!"

Gimpel showed him, the Lamed-vovnik clutched at his own beard, screwed up his tiny face, and felt such delight that he scratched himself.

"Why are you so excited, friend?"

The Lamed-vovnik pretended not to hear. Meanwhile, the distance grew darker, the scenes in that depth began fading, all that was visible now was a white emptiness, far beyond the darkness.

Some of the Lamed-vovniks at the windows were dozing off. The elder ones, the Cabbalists, were sitting barely conscious, staring at the white void and saddened by the long night.

All at once, in the silent brightness, a shape appeared, it was Benye, he was leading the cow.

Benye was walking ahead, with the rope in his hand, and the cow trudged after him. They only reached the mill at dawn.

The cow was carrying a mangled wolf on its horns.

The Town Blesses the New Moon

It was a cloudy night in winter. The snow warmly covered the roofs, and icicles hung from the thin looming trees.

The whole little town was doubly illuminated by the snow and by the moon.

The Jews came out of their homes, sheathed in furs and wrapped in scarves. Silently, they moved toward the courtyards of the synagogues and the white marketplaces to bless the new moon.

Through the dazzling whiteness they trudged like bundles of rags, past the houses and street corners.

The god of the town was sitting on a low rooftop, an old scrawny nag with dried-up hooves and a ragged tail behind.

The Jews clustered in the marketplaces, rocking to and fro, and their long shadows stretched across the clean, twinkling spaces of the streets.

The houses curved their roofs, stretching aloft with their crooked edges, like fearful humps.

The praying Jews raised their hands to God. The white bony fingers stretched out, across the moon, and their shadows moved over the vast, white bluenesses.

The dark shapes of the Jews grew high, they were as thin as sticks of wood, with their skinny knuckles stretching in the snow, and with their flat heads looming in the sky, and the scrawny, narrow bodies swayed across the entire landscape.

A yearning was blended in the snow, in the squinting eyes, and in the narrow little houses, whose bright crevices stretched out longer and longer to the sky.

The god of the town stretched out on his low rooftop, trying to put his front hooves around the moon, which was lying ready above the town, like a large, cold sickle.

A group of tall Jews emerged from a side street, hunched over, gloomy, a wordless flock, they made for a corner of the marketplace, and hollered greetings at one another.

These were the old Hassids of the town, the ones whose spiritual leader, the rebbe, had recently disappeared.

The Jews stretched their hands across the sky, beseeching help for themselves and salvation for the man who had forsaken other men and gone to end his life in the fields and woods.

The heavy snow echoed out of its blueness, and a hushed yearning passed through it from the other side of the world.

A man who was not celebrating peered out along the houses, it was Lord Vrublevsky coming into town, with a lantern in his hand even though the brightness of the night was dazzling, and the snow and the new moon were shining with a fresh radiance.

In the Palace

The windows of Lord Vrublevsky's palace were aglow. The Jews came from the corners of the town, staring in amazement at the sudden light in the distance and not saying a word to one another.

Terrified, they went back to their homes, still silent, and locked their doors and shutters.

On the roads, buggies, coaches, and carriages were streaking through the night, cracking whips, and racing with a solemn laughter to Vrublevsky's family celebration.

The huge lamps of the palace were blinding. Footmen were hurrying up and down the snow-covered steps, carrying the fur coats of the guests, whispering busily, bowing and scraping.

Then Prince Lubomirsky arrived with his daughters, and Lord Vrublevsky welcomed them personally, smiling so politely, bowing, kissing the fingertips of the lovely girls.

The trains of their French crinolines rustled along the stained checkered floors, the thick moustaches of noblemen were rocking in the air.

And the wide doors stood open, the servants were bringing long platters with spiced geese, cakes, wines in silver buckets.

The impoverished squires were sitting in readiness, holding their forks, telling jokes, greedily eying the food.

And a Jewish orchestra was playing. Wolf, the eldest guest, who was standing in front with closed eyes, began playing a fiddle. His soft, tired hand guided the bow, stroking, weeping secretly.

> The prayer of a poor man who was hidden,
> And he poured out his heart to God . . . .

The officers strutted in, fresh and stiff, like roosters, their spurs sparkling on the floor, and their smiles going out to everyone. They called to Lubomirsky's beautiful daughters in the distance.

A priest with a dry face was walking through the crowd.

The couples presented themselves for the dance. White and pink ladies in a long row, against the black jackets of the men, their fingertips met over the heads of the women, the dancers turned slowly in a circle, bowing ceremoniously and sometimes whispering amorous words to one another.

The bottles popped open.

The fat wives of landowners, with big bosoms, were dancing with young boys, the little gentlemen led them about with both hands, pressing hard against the bosoms, forgetting everything, and not abating.

The priest halted at the orchestra, listened for a while, and then came closer to Wolf:

"I don't really care for your music, sir!"

And before Wolf could even get a look at him, the priest hurried away, apparently frightened by his own words. He caught sight of Vrublevsky at the corner of a table, the man was sitting all alone, a bit sad, by an open bottle.

The priest sat down next to him.

An old aristocrat at the table ignored etiquette, he quickly tucked in a napkin at his throat, grabbed a knife and fork, and, fiercely mumbling, he started carving the goose.

A few of the guests came from the ballroom.

The women were dazzling, they swished their white plumes with nimble hands, and smiled saucily as they listened to the tender words of their escorts.

Lord Vrublevsky leaned over to the priest:

"What can I do, Father, I feel sick at heart."

"Repent, my son, confess your sins!"

Lord Vrublevsky scowled into the priest's face:

"But I don't believe in God, Father!"

The old aristocrat with his mouth full of goose felt obligated to join in:

"One must believe, Lord Ignats, one must believe."

But Lord Vrublevsky ignored him. He moved closer to the priest, took hold of his hands, and, even gloomier than before, he shouted into his face:

"But I don't believe in God, Father!"

His nostrils were flaring. He grabbed the bottle from the table and smashed it on the floor. The laughter in the room broke off.

The entire crowd was transfixed.

From another corner, Prince Lubomirsky hurried over with quick steps. He began soothing Vrublevsky, stroking his head, and he turned to the company with a smile on his lips:

"It's nothing, a bottle fell down."

And the orchestra played and played without stopping. The musicians were on a platform, crouching, bending over their instruments, with their coats, their beards, like a swarm of spiders. They ignored the sparkling all around them, the joyousness of the young bodies. They were absorbed in the instruments and reciting psalms through the trumpets, flutes, and drums.

The company began to drink. Officers were quietly downing bottles of wine like water. Ladies were telling one another marvelous things about their sons in Paris. The old aristocrat was getting drunk. With one hand on the back of his head, he guzzled down glass after glass, arrogantly shouting:

"What do you young pups know about drinking?"

And he would grab his long thick mustache and pull it down to his shoulder while refilling his glass with the other hand.

Young girls were falling in love. One lordling was performing black magic, with gold coins vanishing from his hands. And Vrublevsky ordered more wine, the oldest wine they had. Standing up to talk to his footmen, he suddenly caught sight of Wolf in the orchestra. Something jogged his memory. Vrublevsky slipped away from his guests and, with a pale face, he went over to Wolf in the corner:

"Haven't I seen you somewhere before, sir?"

Wolf looked coldly into his eyes:

"I can't say."

"Wasn't it over on the crossroads, by the old crucifix?"

"I can't say."

The orchestra played on. Wolf joined in again with his fiddle. Vrublevsky remained before him, transfixed. The melody had struck him to the quick, it drew tears from his heart, and he suddenly felt as if he were standing in front of the orchestra in a coma, with his heart in his hands.

The old aristocrat joined the dancing. He banged the high heels of his red boots, squatted down, stood up, bowed his head, flung out his hands like a cross, whirled in a wide circle, jigged about, quickly, quickly, banged his boots again, while boastfully clapping his hands and panting like an ox.

The guests were gathering around him, egging him on, admiring his dexterity, making fun of him, the impoverished landowner, who had to feast at other tables.

Lubomirsky was standing in the circle, holding his loveliest daughter, the youngest. She had a full figure, and a birthmark on her lips. Lubomirsky's daughter, a decent person, realized she ought to smile at the old nobleman, but she didn't feel well at all:

"Unbelievers!"

The nobleman was dancing more wildly, he was so drunk he didn't know what he was doing, he dropped his head and flung his arms about like a scarecrow. The guests moved away in annoyance, they glanced around; the room became too quiet, the guests stopped talking . . . . Someone was standing at the door, a disheveled, barefoot Christian: Kyril.

He was gawking at the landowners, he couldn't understand what this celebration was all about. Diamonds from shapely female ears were glittering at him, gold on hands was scorching him, his breath was cut off, his eyes were dazzled, he was so exhausted he could barely regain consciousness. Scratching himself with his long hands, he began to speak in a husky voice:

"Brothers, Jesus has climbed down from the cross, oh my brothers!"

The guests stood there mute. The old aristocrat was already lying on the floor with his head flung back, but no one even bothered to glance at him. They stood at a distance, head by head, with round eyes, and there was no air to breathe.

Kyril was talking as though out of a darkened room:

"I swear by my life, I saw him on a rainy day, he climbed down from the crucifix at the crossroads, and went out into the world . . . I swear by my life, brothers . . . ."

And he crossed himself. The guests remained mute. A heavy, cold-blooded lady stared at the barefoot intruder. She had been the first to recognize him, and suddenly she burst out laughing:

"Why are you all gaping? That's Kyril, the bathhouse attendant!"

Now the priest, the Protector of God, came to his senses. With a pale face and tight blue lips, he emerged from the crowd and stomped over to Kyril, and his dry face began showing red spots:

"You, stop profaning God!"

The guests bent toward them. Kyril gave him a sheepish stare, failing to understand what the priest meant:

"Who, me?"

And the priest hollered out:

"You're profaning God, you bathhouse attendant!"

"Who, me?"

And Kyril suddenly flared up, the breath poured out of his nostrils like smoke from a chimney. He came to his senses and pointed his finger at the priest:

"You, Father, you're the one who profanes God, you, do you understand!"

The guests burst into a roar and threw themselves at Kyril. Bitterly, he pushed them away with his bony shoulders. The guests rolled on the ground, they were stunned, they choked one another, and spat in the old aristocrat's face.

Lubomirsky's young daughter quietly took Kyril aside:

"Kyril, please, go back to your people, they'll kill you here . . . . I'll come too, I'll come to you and your people . . . ."

Kyril stared at her in fright, and she smiled at him excitedly, instead of weeping. She led him out to the door, and then all at once she clutched him:

"Come, Kyril, come . . . ."

And the orchestra gave a fearful crash. The musicians ran into the crowd. Wolf tore his bow across the strings, as he stepped over the heads of the prostrated guests. A shofar blasted darkly. A small musician with a stiff hat over his ears exerted his last ounce of strength pulling and pushing the long slide of his trumpet, puffing out his cheeks, and marching with military steps over the guests.

The company dashed out to the carriages.

The whips cracked, the furious horses charged away with their light buggies, over the foggy fields, flew through the night. The confused guests threw off their clothes, moaned, tore their hair, screamed for help.

That night, Lubomirsky's daughter disappeared.

An Incantation

And he, who came from the House of David, goes from land to land, from city to city, and wherever he meets people, he says to them:

"Sons of man, why do you love one another?

"The mountain knows nothing of love.

"The field knows nothing of love."

What Lord Vrublevsky Did to Gimpel

And the dawn broke through, red. The worms got up. The soaked forest was smoking, and patches of fog were hanging from the branches.

Gimpel climbed out of the bushes, shaking from the cold, rubbing his drowsy eyes with his fists, and yawning.

The grass was astir and arustle with creatures. Far, far away, the fresh morning air resounded with the thudding of axes. They were chopping away at the forest.

Gimpel felt sick at heart. He put his finger to his lips and listened carefully. They were chopping away at the forest! He took off on a path towards Simkhe, not knowing why he felt so awful.

Breathlessly he ran from path to path, and suddenly, in the denseness of the forest, he saw Lord Vrublevsky coming toward him with a feather in his hat, and with his dog trailing him.

Gimpel quickly struck off to the side, but Vrublevsky stopped him:

"What are you doing in the woods?"

"Nothing my lord!"

"What do you mean *nothing*?"

"Just that, absolutely nothing, my lord."

"Who mangled a wolf in the forest? Was it you?"

"Not me, my lord."

"Who?"

"A cow."

"What?!"

"A cow, my lord!"

Vrublevsky slapped him several times. With his cheeks burning from the blows, Gimpel thought to himself that the man must be an anti-Semite. He touched his cheeks, lamenting:

"Why did you hit me, my lord? Why should I mangle your wolves! Don't I have better things to do?!"

But the lord was already creeping off into the bushes. Gimpel dashed down the road. He thought the man was chasing him, and he ran into an enclosure. Plopping down on a tree stump, he wiped the sweat off on his sleeve, breathed a sigh of relief, and then a keen thought jabbed through his mind. He took out his pencil stub and a scrap of paper and started jotting down the thought.

A rabbit came leaping wildly out of the bushes, jumped over Gimpel's head, and then the hound came shooting out of the thickets, and there was Lord Vrublevsky again. Gimpel sprang up as white as a sheet:

"What are you doing in these woods?"

"Nothing, my lord!"

"What do you mean *nothing*?"

"Just that, absolutely nothing, my lord!"

And Gimpel got two more burning slaps. Not looking around, he sensed that he ought to vanish on the spot, and he dashed off into the thickets. The hound forgot about the hare and took off after Gimpel.

Gimpel ran helter-skelter. He wouldn't stop, but the hound ground his teeth into Gimpel's calves and tore off the legs of his trousers, which had once been dotted with dots and striped with stripes. But he didn't stop, he ran straight to Simkhe.

He could already make out the hut from far away.

Gimpel reached the door with his last bit of strength and began pounding with his fists:

"Simkhe, help!"

Simkhe Plakhte was sitting inside, very calm. With no loss of composure, he asked:

"What's the matter?"

"Simkhe, the carriages are here!"

The door whipped open, Simkhe dashed out, pale, disheveled, horrified.

"What?! Where are they?!"

He saw the philosopher with his calves naked, his trousers gone, and his birdlike face full of terror. Simkhe calmed down again.

"Listen, Simkhe, do you hear?"

From far away, they could hear the dull thudding of the axes. Birds were flying from that direction, their nests had been destroyed. Simkhe glared toward that area, listened hard, and then exclaimed furiously:

"Levi the moneylender! May he rot in hell!"

And he trudged back into his shack, locking and bolting the door behind him. Gimpel stood there, dazed, not knowing where to turn. He cautiously knocked at Simkhe's door:

"Simkhe, can you spare some trousers?"

"Can't you go without pants, you dandy?"

Gimpel stared a while at the door which had been slammed in his face. Then he lost heart, thrust his hands in his pockets, and started off into the woods. The road was asparkle with dew, and Gimpel burst into song:

The road merged into the highway. Each blade of grass awoke in the moistness of dawn. Never had a daybreak moved him so deeply.

He strode proudly along the road, danced a bit, and sang the song of the idler.

At the edge of the woods he ran into the little Lamed-vovnik. The kind little Jew was shouting at the bushes:

"Come on out, miss, this is the road."

And a young, black-haired girl, with a pack on her shoulders, leaped over the ditch. The Lamed-vovnik stared at her with a bit of drool on his lips, admiring her agility. It was Leah.

Gimpel's passions were aroused. Leah slowly glanced at him and then modestly lowered her eyes again. He clutched at his pants, felt as if the earth were opening under him, and then he cautiously walked over to her, from the side, as red as a glowing ember, and introduced himself:

"Dr. Gimpel Abramovich Lionson!"

Leah shook his hand. The jealous Lamed-vovnik ran around to Leah's other side and his eyes bored into the handshake.

"I must apologize for meeting you in my work clothes, mademoiselle . . . ."

Leah put her arm into the Lamed-vovnik's. The little saint didn't resist, he actually kept time with the music of her gait. Leah felt terribly good between these two men, she walked calmly, thinking about *Him* and smiling. Gimpel was talking:

"But actually, my area of specialization is speculative science. With my philosophical system I have succeeded in refuting the greatest thinkers in the world. Socrates was a bourgeois, he was unable to rise beyond social life. Kant, you see, is a learned man—"

"Did you ever talk to him?"

"Who? Kant?"

"No, the man who lives in the mill."

"You mean Benye? He's quite backward, even though he does possess a certain intuition in regard to universal understanding."

Gimpel looked around at the sides of the forest, he had to run off into a corner for a while, it was vital and crucial. He apologized and dashed into the thickets. It was already noon . . . . Returning into the depths of the forest, he felt a terror, and wanted to run back out, but it was too late. Behind a tree, he caught sight of Vrublevsky with a feather in his hat and a rifle over his shoulder, and cold as ice. Gimpel lost his voice:

"What are you doing in these woods?"

Gimpel was speechless.

"Why don't you answer?"
Gimpel was speechless.
"Who mangled a wolf in these woods?"
Gimpel was speechless.
"Was it you, you wanderer?"
Gimpel was speechless.
"Who?"
Gimpel was speechless.
"Speak up!"
In the darkness of the thicket, sparks of phosphorus came flaring from hand to cheek. Gimpel realized there was no way of dealing with Vrublevsky, and another fear caught hold of him, an unknown fear, interwoven with the earth and the stars. The tip of his skull and the point of his nose began freezing. Suddenly he burst into a run, screamed in terror, and leaped from bush to bush. He ran around the squire in a circle and stretched out his hands to him.

The Ten Sefirot

Now, know that the myriad crystal worlds in the mystery of the ten sefirot overflow into one another, an orbit into an orbit, like waters.

And the light that overflows from one world to the other echoes for trillions upon trillions of leagues.

Now, know that no human being ever born knows his road or the worlds through which he shall go in and through which he shall go out.

Trillions upon trillions of radiant leagues in length and in height, and a black, thin man is crawling along them.

He climbs up the dazzling walls from one world to the next, strains his big ears, opens up his eyes, and scans the various resounding waters to find out who is listening. No one, no one is listening to him, *no one is listening*.

Now, know that there is no one in the great world, no God, and no devil, no kith, no kin, no redeemer.

The crystal worlds are shining, sparkling for millions of leagues upon leagues, and the thin black man knocks on a dazzling wall, puts his ear against it, and listens: And the loud enormous distances respond with an emptiness, a splendid void.

And know that this is the secret of Infinity.

Leah Comes to Him, and He Also Claims that Gimpel is Right

The little Lamed-vovnik was standing by Benye's house, showing Leah the work she was supposed to do. The daylight was waning.

Leah was pale, more pale than ever. She listened to the sounds of the countryside, looked about in amazement, her heart racing. The Lamed-vovnik was comforting her, but Leah paid no attention, she wanted to wait and see: Should she enter the house tomorrow, or should she keep out of it altogether? The Lamed-vovnik explained that Benye was one of our people, Benye would welcome her with open arms, she could count on it, and he pinched her arm, the old lecher!

"You sly thing!"

The Lamed-vovnik had been accepted by the saints only because of his great meekness, although he had committed a good many sins with women. He scurried around Leah like a rooster. Leah finally got up enough courage to enter the house. She walked over to the door with her pack on her shoulders, carefully raised the bolt, and then turned her face once again to the Lamed-vovnik. He waved his hand:

"Go on in, silly, c'mon!"

Leah entered the porch. It smelled of rotten sacks and tatters. In the darkness, she could make out old, unnailed wheels up on the rafters, and a bagpipe on the wall. She saw the door leading into the house and went over to it with soft, gentle steps, not daring to raise the bolt. She remained standing at the entrance.

All at once, she opened the door wide. The house was pitch dark. The oven had gotten larger in the course of time, it filled half the room. She looked for *Him* in the darkness . . . .

Benye was sitting on a log in the corner, he had been wringing his hands and now they were clenched together in his lap, his heavy head and tangled beard were drooping on his open, dirty chest. He was in mourning. His thick lips kept closing, parting, closing, like the mouth of a fish, and single words came rolling out, clumsy, mossy, like stones:

"I'm going to the earth ... Gimpel is right .... There is no God ...."

Leah clutched at the wall. Her knees began shaking, and the whole room turned upside-down. Burning dots flashed before her eyes, her head became heavy and fell to one side, she could barely sit down on the bench against the wall.

Patches of darkness were weaving before her eyes, intertwined with bright spots, and her heart was gnawed by bitterness and despair. She wanted to say something, but couldn't:

"Give me some water!"

Benye heard a voice asking for water, he got on his feet, trudged over to the wooden bucket standing by the oven, barely heaved it up, and lugged it over to Leah.

He stood in front of her for a while, holding the bucket. She raised her hand lifelessly and stuck it into the water, opened her eyes, but they closed again, her head fell even deeper on her breast.

Benye stood and waited, he saw she wasn't drinking, so he carefully took her hand out of the pail, and brought the water to her face.

He whistled heartily as though giving water to a horse, he wanted to talk her into drinking. Leah turned her face to the water, drank, and felt a sense of relief ....

The Lamed-vovnik was moving past the windows, surprised that the welcome was taking so long. He was already suspecting Benye of a sinful act. He raised himself up to the window and peeked through the glass, but it was dark inside. He slowly clambered up on the mound of earth surrounding the house, pressed his face against the window, covered himself with his hand—he couldn't see a thing. His heart hammering, he climbed back down with the intention of going in, but then he heard a running from far away. It was Gimpel whizzing through the night, his naked calves shining in the dark, he ran up to the Lamed-vovnik, panting:

"Where is she?"

But the Lamed-vovnik played the fool:

"Who?"

"You oaf! I'm asking you: Where is the young lady?"

"Oh, the girl. She's inside, with Benye."

Gimpel wiped his sweat off on his sleeve. He didn't want to have

anything to do with the Lamed-vovnik. He halted at the corner of
the house, crossed one leg over the other, and whistled a tune. The
Lamed-vovnik looked at him suspiciously. Gimpel suddenly remembered something, he pulled out a pouch of tobacco, poured some
into a slip of paper, rolled it up, and smoked a cigarette. He held
one hand in his pocket, and smoked with the other, smoothed back
his hair, and serenely blew the smoke into the air.

The Lamed-vovnik held his beard, and stood there silently
looking at Gimpel, and looking. All at once he got up on his tiptoes
and blurted right into Gimpel's face:

"That is pride, nothing more!"

Gimpel put the cigarette in his mouth, turned his back to the
Lamed-vovnik with his hands behind him, and casually strolled past
the house.

But then the door opened, Leah stepped out as white as snow,
holding on to the doorposts, and Benye came after her with the pail
in his hand. Gimpel's heart froze at the sight of the wan girl. He
stared at her, and sudden tears poured out of his eyes, he couldn't
hold them back. He ran over to her and threw himself on the
ground:

"Darling, I love you!"

And he hugged her feet and kissed her black shoes, he wept and
twisted on the grass like a long, thin worm. Leah mechanically
stepped back to the wall and burst out crying, her whole small
body was trembling, and suddenly everything turned radiant before
her eyes.

An Incantation

And he, the Son of David, comes to a city that is being built. He
sees the masons on the scaffolds, the bricklayers at work, the car-
penters in the windows, and he is overcome with a deep joy, and he
says:

"Look, work comes out of men as a web comes out of a spider.

"Look, the water is working in the mountains for the sake of
work."

Perhaps Simkhe Is Also a Saint

Simkhe was spread out like a piece of cloth in the autumn field, he was silent and bitter. Somewhere people were eating the harvested rye, and here the pieces of straw were withering. The earth was lying there deceived and forsaken, like a woman who had been promised things and then cast aside.

The brown gold of autumn was grieving, and the trees that were barely surviving, and the wet bony rocks in the ditches.

Simkhe threw himself upon the earth like a mourner, he clenched his hand into the soil, pressed his face and body into the ground, and wept bitterly for the vanished life of the earth.

The foggy countryside was grieving, and so were the rows of storks flying overhead through the bluish wetness of the rains.

He could hear one branch after another dying, the millions of grass haulms languishing, and once they had so silently been woven into the large brown body of the earth.

Simkhe was lying on a corpse—the earth was exhaling her final motherly pang, and she came out to Simkhe in her warm grief.

Simkhe slowly got to his feet. A melancholy was gnawing at his bones. With his large body bowing, he walked around, raking up the fallen yellow leaves.

He gathered together a heap of leaves in the middle of the field, like a huge hill, the fog embraced, crushed, and extinguished the melting glow of the living body.

Simkhe sat down on the heap of leaves, took out his clay pipe, and blew out curls of smoke that enveloped him like a cloud.

The thudding of axes echoed through the smokey blue forest.

Fresh logs were visible through the thin fog at the edge of the forest, fresh wood, with its bark stripped off. A few enormous boughs with clumps of needles on them had been flung around the wood, like limbs that have not been buried with the rest of the body.

Simkhe was sitting in his fur, which was wet with dew, he was squinting through the smoke into the distances which had faded in the fog.

A shout came from nearby in the forest. Leah ran out of the

trees, exhausted, with her hair flying, she was screaming for help, and Lord Vrublevsky and his hound were raging after her.

Leah dashed over to Simkhe in the field and collapsed, the squire managed to grab her hair with a shriek of lust, clutched her in his arms and showered her breasts with kisses.

Simkhe quietly climbed down from the heap of leaves, his eyes filled with blood, he slowly moved towards Vrublevsky.

He lifted one foot heavily and then put it down again heavily. The field bent beneath his tread.

Vrublevsky didn't notice him, he was bending over Leah, crushing her against his body, swaying, with his lips on her throat.

Simkhe trudged over, grabbed Vrublevsky and lifted him high in the air while his foot pressed the dog's head to the ground. Leah was lying on the earth, stretching her hands out to protect herself. Terror-stricken, she looked at Simkhe, who was growing broader, bigger, with his solid, bony chest swelling, and she looked at the green nobleman whom Simkhe was hoisting aloft.

"God, pour out Thy wrath on the Gentiles! . . ."

And then he flung him across the autumnal fields, hurled him with all his strength across the meadows and woods up into the sky. His thin legs struggling to catch hold of something, he swam like a fish through the fog, not knowing where, perhaps to the jagged and gloomy Mountains of Darkness. The dog shot off, whining, after his master, who was plunging and whizzing like an arrow, and the poor animal clutched his tail between his legs.

Levi Patashnik Looks for His Daughter

And in the middle of the night, Levi Patashnik began smashing the objects in his home, he knocked out the windowpanes, splintered the mirrors, tore down the drapes and the pictures.

He scurried around the rooms, half-naked, calling for Leah, peering under the beds and in the closets. But no one answered.

The tufts of yellow brown hair were bristling around his bald pate like prickly straw, and his eyes were shaking madly in their sockets.

From under a bed, he took out a sack which, as it turned out, had been prepared long ago. He slung it around his neck and ran over to the open cabinet, and his hot hands raked all the gold into the bag. But he couldn't rest, he rubbed his head, his short beard, and ran from corner to corner.

Suddenly, beneath a bed, he saw one of Leah's shoes, grabbed it, and then dropped it, as though it were a piece of white-hot iron, into the bag. Whimpering like a beaten dog, he stood up and made for the door.

Outside, there was a terrible darkness, a few scant windows were shining yellow under a roof somewhere . . . .

Levi passed through the streets, weeping, screaming, flailing his arms, clenching his fists at heaven . . . .

But no one heard him. Clouds lay on the sky, like lichen in old forests.

Levi rambled through the autumnal fields, shaking, his bare feet treading in clay, he wandered from the roads to the isolated meadows.

The silent villages were sprawling over the dewy plains, they were so quiet, as if covered with moss.

They were indifferent to the wanderer.

He came into the villages, poked around the courtyards, looked into the stables, and tearfully knocked on the walls of the peasant huts.

"Have you seen, have you heard, anything of my daughter Leah?"

No one had seen, no one had heard, anything of Levi Patashnik's daughter Leah.

Frightened sheep bleated in the folds.

The ignorant peasants sleepily crawled back into bed with their wives.

A pointed moon slipped out from the clouds, it had eyes, and beams of light rained down on the sides of the roads.

Levi trudged across the fields, munching and gnawing the silvery silence of the night . . . . Somewhere far, far away, in a dale, a dog was howling long and sorrowfully.

No other soul was awake. Levi climbed down into the valley to find this one living creature.

A long female dog was standing there, weeping her yearning for her master, who had been hurled away, she didn't care about Levi although she knew the secret of his wanderings.

Somewhere in the moonlit night, her green master was plunging headfirst, plunging like an arrow, and no one could help him.

Levi stood crouching near her, with the bag of gold around his neck, staring at the bony ribs of the dog, while tears came gushing into his eyes.

And all at once—Levi turned to the moon with bulging eyes and began whining in the night, even louder than the grimy dog.

A Light World, Nearly Like a Dream

or

Gimpel Talks in Rhymes but Means Something Else

It was snowing, a dense, warm snow, at the end of autumn, reviving the countryside. Simkhe's shack once again received a thick white cover, which gave it a festive air, and the white forest all around it bore the bright, noble yoke joyously.

Simkhe, Leah, and Gimpel the philosopher were sitting inside the shack.

The snow had a healing effect on their lives, it opened many new eyes inside them, and they watched as the world became transfigured, transparent, and its clear, quiet heart was open and would tremble at the slightest rustle of a branch . . . white joy . . . white, sad joy . . . .

Simkhe lay on the broad bench by the window, leaning on his elbows and staring into the festive room, not thinking, but dreaming with his body, and warmly inhaling the breath of the cool golden air seeping in through the windows. Leah was sitting next to him on the same bench, her bright clear eyes staring into the woods, as she talked to Simkhe. He comforted her, assured her that the Messiah shouldn't be handsome, and that Benye might well light up in his last hour, his hide would slough off and he would appear to her fresh and young again.

Gimpel shook the pouch of tobacco over the table, snorted, and rolled a cigarette. He spoke wordlessly, joyously, warm thoughts came from deep inside him, drifted through him like mists, talked silently in his limbs, as light with light. He fixed his moist eyes on Leah, and a white joy lamented within him:

"I, Gimpel, need no language; I, Gimpel, can get along without language."

And Simkhe lay comfortably on the oaken bench with his beard spread out on his chest, he was gazing at the philosopher, who was sad because of the sweet dazzlement beyond the windows.

He sat opposite Simkhe, transparent, looking as if he might shatter into pieces at a single touch, tinkling gently and blending into the airy world around him.

Gimpel smoked the cigarette, put his hand in his pocket, stretched out his legs, and, staring at Leah, he began speaking in rhymes:

"Smoking this cigarette of mine,
"I quietly sit here and I feel so fine, so fine . . . ."
Simkhe said to him comfortably:
"If you feel fine, then I feel dandy."

And Leah, peering through the window, folded her arms and cupped her elbows in her hands. She didn't turn toward Gimpel though she did listen and clearly understood his dismal intention. Gimpel had never been so pale and radiant, even if he cracked jokes and kept up the pretense of speaking in rhymes:

> The above necessity
> To wit, that accumulation brings noninfinity
> Will someday be decorated by a man like me
> With a bald pate for all to see,
> With eyes—bags
> And legs like crags,
> And will bring me to the Almighty
> —A person like me, who's very flighty."

"Fine, Gimpel, fine. You're a very flighty person."

But Gimpel didn't answer, he didn't feel like scolding him. He wasn't dealing with Simkhe. He was sitting and, in his way, longing for Leah. He explained to the mistress of his soul that the two of behind his back, he lifted his whiskers up to the tall guest and the world:

> God is God!—A twofold substance,
> In infinity,
> A female possibility,

> Dynamic and static,
> An inference,
> A birth pang and a song and dance.

He twirled the cigarette. His long fingers dangled on the table. He looked at the soft profile of the mistress of his soul, who was even paler and more quiet because of the snow outside. Suddenly, he felt a slow twinge under his heart a tearful twinge. Very nobly, and with utmost devotion, he asked her, using her Russian name:

"Liza Leonovna, why are you silent?"

She turned to him with a doleful smile:

"I'm not silent at all."

And Simkhe stretched out on the bed and replied:

"Because you do enough talking for everyone else, Gimpel."

"What a day," said Gimpel, "it's a transcendental day, it is."

And Leah was silent.

"A snow, a springtime snow?"

"Yes."

And the thing he had wanted to convey was uttered past the words. Actually, he had already expressed it, and now he fell into a sudden gloom. He stood up from the bench and started walking around, he felt as if he were a little too big, a little too present in this world. He stopped at the wall, touched the plaster (Simkhe's work), meditated, and then began talking to himself in rhymes again:

> A person like me who's very flighty.
> A voice in the chasms began to call:
> What is his name?
> What is his name?
> I don't recall.
> A lazy fellow, oh God, an indolent . . . .

Poor Gimpel felt hemmed in by the world, even though this day was lighter than crystal. He was permeated with the yearning snow. His mind turned white, and tender as if prepared for the softest sorrows around him. Then all at once, he couldn't bear it anymore, tears came gushing out of his eyes, he burst into a bitter weeping, on and on. With bated breath, he shrieked:

"Will the Messiah come, or not?

"The Messiah!!"

He ran over to Simkhe, fell on top of him, and started hitting him with his skinny little hands, writhed against his chest, lamented, and tore the poor man's clothes:

"Make the Messiah come! Make Him come!"

Gimpel wept, Leah trembled and buried her face in her hands, she held her breath and froze. She could see Benye before her eyes and smell his putrid smell, and now she remembered his chest which looked like the mangy hide of a carcass. Simkhe sat on the bed, took Gimpel in his arms, and began speaking softly, as though not to him:

"Why are you bawling, you poor devil?"

Simkhe was somewhat affected by what had happened, gingerly she started, turned to him, and fell wordlessly upon his breast. Simkhe softly caressed her hair, he was still holding Gimpel, and he said to them:

"My goodness, you're still children, little children!"

He gazed through the white window, far, far away . . . . Among the soft, snowy trees in the woods, Lubomirsky's daughter was wandering about, looking for the road. She clasped herself, shivering with cold, in her summer clothing, which she had been wearing at the family celebration in Vrublevsky's palace.

They Work Upon Benye

The Lamed-vovniks assembled by Benye's home in the morning cold. The mill, already looking like a mountain of garbage, was covered with frost. The Lamed-vovniks were sitting with frozen beards on the logs by the roadside, some of them clustered in groups, mournfully talking to one another.

he touched Leah, who was sitting with her back to him. Suddenly Princess Lubomirksy was standing on the road, not far from the mill, trembling with cold; she was peering at the windows. The Lamed-vovniks had often seen her around the mill, wondering what she was doing there. None of them spoke about her, though all of them had noticed her.

It was late autumn, the cold crept under the fur coats, noses were freezing, and red, swollen hands cracked and dangled like alien things.

The village tailor was sitting on the seat of earth around the house, he had a sack of potatoes on his shoulder. Jews were standing around him, trying to get him to say something, but he merely gazed at them, sick and feeble, and kept silent. Wolf and the angry guest had gone into Benye's home at dawn, they had argued with him, trying to tell him about redemption. The Lamed-vovniks kept waiting outside, but no one asked them in, no understanding was reached.

Simkhe and Leah appeared on the road, silently walking towards Benye's home. Leah was afraid of Benye. She hated him, but she had to obey Simkhe and come along. The Lamed-vovniks were becoming uneasy, they paced around the house warmed their hands under their armpits, there was no end to the waiting. The silent ones were annoyed, but the talkative ones were hoping: If only it would end!

The tall guest, who looked like a beanpole, was standing in front of Kyril, counting off on his fingers the delicacies in store for them on the table of the Messiah:

"Winey apples, pears, paprika, white bread, smoked herring, sausages . . . ."

And the little Lamed-vovnik was standing there with his hands behind his back, he lifted his whiskers up to the tall guest and beamed with ease and joy:

"And we'll drink, won't we, raisin wine or even cyprus wine."

Meanwhile, the tall guest, lost in thought, wandered off somewhere else, meditating, walking about among the silent Lamed-vovniks. One had been a great Cabbalist, knowing the secret of the seven shepherds, but in his old age he had become senile. People would think he wanted to tell them something and they lent him an ear, but all he did was to fill it up with nasal ramblings, and nothing more. The silent ones were sitting on a log, like oxen, with broad necks, big, sheeplike eyes, not uttering a word.

The eldest guest came out on the threshold and stood there for a while, thinking, wavering. He finally motioned them to enter the house. The Lamed-vovniks streamed over to the door, each one trying to get in first, a pushing, shoving mob. The tall guest remembered something, he peered around, looking for Kyril in the stampede. He could just barely make him out, and with all his strength he elbowed his way over to him and said:

"Yes, and ice cream too!"

The crowd burst into the room and climbed up on the benches, and windowsills, blocking out the little light that came in through the panes. Benye sat on a log in the corner, wringing his hands on his knees and not even looking about. The Lamed-vovniks thronged around him with bulging eyes, the shorter men standing on tiptoe, and everyone shoving noisily.

Wolf waited until they quieted down.

The seven silent ones went out first, the men who had understood the world, like mossy stones in ditches, who had not tasted of death or life, and knew the secret of creation with their oxlike shoulders.

Wolf distributed them around the room, he and the angry guest slowly walked over to Benye, placing themselves on either side of him like the men who lead a groom to a wedding canopy.

A hush fell, and it was so quiet you could hear the woodwork creak.

Benye was sitting with his head drooping, he was staring at his dirty toes and didn't see anyone, as though he were already dead. Wolf began talking in a loud voice:

"Benye, son of Blume!"

Benye didn't answer.

"Benye, son of Shloyme. Because of the great torment of our life on earth, we hereby declare you to be the Messiah of the House of Ephraim!"

Benye didn't answer.

"Benye son of Blume, tell us what you want."

With difficulty, Benye lifted his head, his open mouth was charred, he could barely reply:

"I want to die!"

The Lamed-vovniks turned around with a sigh, a few began crying, for all of them suddenly felt that death was better than life, and that there was nothing left to lose anyway. But Wolf raised himself over everyone else and kindled like a flame, his face radiated, lighting up the others:

"Benye, listen, I want us to be redeemed, I want us to rip off the hide of the living world! Benye, listen, I want us to break through to God! Do you hear!"

But Benye didn't answer.

Gimpel Gives a Sermon on the Mount and Then Goes to Sleep

It was a hot, blood-red evening, crimson mountains floated out from the other side of the world and loomed on the fields, and the sky burnt over them like blazing copper. The gory sunset stormily flooded the countryside, the old forest was flaming in its blueness, spurting fire and darkness.

Gimpel Zaskevitser, dunked in the evening redness, was climbing the loamy mountain behind the mill, he lifted his arms to the blazing landscape and spoke to the four corners of the world:

"Why shouldn't I use reason? If it were a bird, I would prepare it for dinner; if it were a necktie, I would wear it to attract girls.

"My body works day and night to comprehend the world—reason interferes with me and my work.

"Oh God! Irrationality can understand irrationality.

"Just look, the earth is alive, the earth thinks and works, and there is no divinity in it—and no rationality.

"What is life, God?—I want to comprehend my own area in the world.

"Here am I, Gimpel, all alone in the field. My power of conception soars over the plains and valleys, but—it never lets my body know the secret of the world.

"Oh God! I want to throw my reason out the window!"

And he came down the mountain with his head flung back, the way a general gets down from a horse after a war.

He walked down to the road, looking for a soft ditch to lie in and sleep. He felt around in the holes, hoping that Leah would come to him in his sleep.

Somewhere, in a mossy hole, he snuggled up with his head on his hand, and went to sleep. The moon shone on his back, warming him, the green light soaked through his clothes and lapped at his body like a sweet water.

He smiled in his sleep.

Someone softly touched his shoulder, telling him to stand up. He got to his feet, holding out his arms, and walked off across the silvery misty fields.

The moon was driving him.

He walked lightly, almost on tiptoe, whispering soft words, with his eyes closed, yet he saw the white landscape clearly before him, the splotches of the trees and villages in the valleys.

Leah didn't come to him, so he went off in his sleep to scour the world. The drops of light fell heavily upon him, like drops of rain, and coursed over his body, and he felt as if he were walking across a riverbed.

Suddenly he halted, there was a shoe lying in the road.

Gimpel bent over, keeping his head toward the moon, he took hold of the shoe and pressed it to his heart. It was clear to him that the shoe belonged to Leah, she had worn it once, he could feel the breath of Leah's body in it.

The road stretched on between shiny poplars.

Gimpel walked along with the shoe at his heart, his eyes were closed, and he was smiling at the moon, he felt as if he were walking over the heads of people. No one knew about him, but he didn't need anyone. He went out on the highest lunar fields, eyeless, and the earth bent out beneath him, writhing, like a big river in the moonlight.

In the stillness, he could make out voices from the trees, the earth, the singing of heaven and the ultimate secret of the world.

He raised his head; over him, someone was standing among the clouds, a long, green shape:

"What are you doing here?"

"Nothing."

"What do you mean nothing?"

"Absolutely nothing, Gimpel, just that."

Lord Vrublevsky was still floating over the world, and now—the roads were swaying, there was no earth underfoot—a dream, a dream.

And the world was transformed for him into moonlight, the field was white smoke, Leah a foggy sound emerging from him, from infinity, and Gimpel didn't exist at all.

The Trek of the Lamed-Vovniks

And then came the night of the annual Jewish Day of Judgment. Clouds from the farthest ends of the world gathered overhead, brown and blazing. A thick, crooked rain lashed into the faces; and it was so dark they couldn't see their own hands.

At the mill, the Lamed-vovniks got into line, with Benye in front, he had no hat on, his hair was soaked and snarled, and behind him stood the seven silent men of Zhamut. The Lamed-vovniks were holding one another. Gimpel, half-naked, was also wandering among them.

The wind bent the trees over, tearing their boughs aloft, it ripped the furs and swept the coats up over the men's heads, and the air was so thin they could hardly breathe.

Simkhe Plakhte and Leah went to the end of the row, with the cow behind them. But no one noticed that Princess Lubomirsky had slipped in among the Lamed-vovniks. She walked through the crowd, wringing her hands, crossing herself, and praying to God in her language.

The road led across loamy fields. Dense fogs emerged from the darkness and drifted over the landscape like enormous rags. The travelers would put down a foot, not knowing where. Water came pouring down the mountains, and the jutting ridges were freezing. The winds tore into the clouds, scattering dark shreds over the fields and pouring torrentially on the Lamed-vovniks. The cow, who didn't have a hair left on her skin, kept lying down, she could barely keep up with the trekers. The land became deeper and darker, each Lamed-vovnik was absorbed in himself, staring mutely into his own darkness, praying to God for mercy:

> God, God, have mercy on the boot tree,
> On the tiny hammer,
> On the needle and on the scissors.
> Have mercy on our tiny little souls,
> A patchwork of torment and tatters,
> On our children, who want cake.
> On our wives, who do not lust but have too many babies.

On our daughters whose blood has dried.
Have mercy on those who lie behind the ovens,
On the putrid,
On those with ruptures,
On those who go begging.
Have mercy on the broken-down horses,
On the traveling draymen,
On the hatters and the tailors . . .
God, God!

And the air was so thin they could scarcely breathe. They sighed in their misery, only the silent ones held out their gravel faces and peered into the darkness with their calflike eyes. The little Lamed-vovnik trudged along, with his coat folded up on his head, he was wringing his hands and weeping.

They came into the forest. The trees were tearing at their roots, a suffocating steam came up from the ground and weighed on backs like a yoke. Simkhe's shack was lying on its side, the furnishings were smashed and scattered. Simkhe didn't halt, he hollered into the weeping of the wind:

"I'll build it again!"

No one heard him. The wind was whining overhead, through the treetops, it struck against the chests of the men and tugged on their beards. Its lament sounded like a human voice. The Lamed-vovniks opened their mouths; somewhere, deep in a ditch, a man was screaming, wailing from the earth, like an old branch. Wolf trudged over to the roadside and screamed into the darkness with all his strength:

"You, who are you, you accursed man, come with us!"

A man came crawling out of the ditch on all fours, with a bag around his neck. Leah shuddered, nestled against Simkhe. In the darkness, no one could discern what the man looked like. The wind flung him among the Lamed-vovniks, he merged into the crowd and remained silent.

And in the town, the Jews came trudging out of the houses, whole families, tattered men, women wrapped in shawls, disheveled children. Out came the lame, the blind, the consumptive with swollen bellies, the ruptured with empty eyesockets, asthmatic men in rags, men in sacks.

They gathered in the crooked marketplaces, along the sides of the streets, head to head, nestled together, and the clammy rain lashed into the faces and poured over the bodies. The houses, ramshackle with age, were about to collapse, they cracked and leaned on one another, and on the low rooftop sat the god . . . .

An Incantation

And the Jews came out to him from the synagogues, the priests from the churches, the yeshivah students, the women. They gathered around him, they kissed the tails of his coat.

"Messiah, what have you come to add to the Torah?"

And he replied:

"I have not come to you to add anything to the Torah, I have come to take back the Torah."

"Gimpel, do human beings exist?"

"No, human beings do not exist."

"What *does* exist?"

"There exists a body without eyes, a mouth that does not speak, and a heart that does not beat."

"But Gimpel, we believe that the body sees, the mouth speaks, and the heart beats."

"Because, Leah, our shapes are reflected in streams, because waters speak and trees bloom."

"Tell me, Gimpel, what does a tree dream about?"

"Leah, *I* am a tree and I dream about you."

Help, Lord of Heaven, Help

And the Lamed-vovniks arrived in the town. The wind banged them along like hammers, it wouldn't let them go back. The seven silent men trudged and trudged, bowed over as though they were carrying the world on their backs.

The houses moved closer to the marketplace.

Benye trudged at the head of his crowd, trembling, his hands dragging over the mud. The mouths were full of rushing wind, the eyes sealed with cloudiness, and the tongues parched.

The marketplace stirred with the clatter of crutches—the cripples were trying to walk without them, the blind men were yelling to their wives that they could see. Women were holding their bellies, perhaps they had become pregnant. Dying men were being carried out on their beds, and the barren women came dancing out, waving mannish hands toward the Messiah, jigging with long, dry bodies like withered trees, lowering their heads in shame, and the wind accompanied them on the roof shingles. The Lamed-vovniks entered the marketplace. Benye thumped his broad, bare feet over the miry pavement, he saw the courage in the eyes, and he crooned his last prayer to God:

> The prayer of a poor man, who was hidden,
> And he poured out his heart to God . . .

There was someone walking next to him, the dark man who had sat on Mars. He looked at him cold and taciturn. From time to time, Benye turned to the man, waiting for him to say something, but the man showed him that he had no tongue and he continued to follow him. The women saw Benye from afar; screaming, they flung themselves toward him with flying hair; the men stretched out in the mud before him; the cripples and the asthmatic came leaping toward him, the dying held out their arms to him; and the blind, in tears, broke into a run toward the other side of the marketplace, not knowing where he, the Messiah, could be, they stopped at the pump, dropped to the ground, and began weeping to it and holding out their blind hands to it. And Benye was trudging somewhere else, there were men lying at his feet, kissing the ground he stepped upon:

"Messiah, step on us!"

"Messiah, touch *my* womb, I have no children!"

"Messiah, take the hump off my back!"

"Messiah, I have no erotic desires!"

And he, the Messiah, walked over the heads of the men, over the drooping breasts of the women, letting them kiss his feet. The Lamed-vovniks, mute and bitter, followed him, scanning the marketplace with their calflike eyes, choking, and suddenly they screamed:

"Help, Lord of heaven, help!"

Benye was struck deaf, he turned around to the Lamed-vovniks, saw them lifting their hands to the sky, their faces looking up toward God. Benye heard the weeping and shouting in the market-place, he was terrified. And suddenly he felt the torment of all these people, tears poured out of his eyes. He lifted up the first woman lying at his feet and kissed her bare breasts, he healed the lame, he stroked the heads of the scabby, he comforted the despairing:

"Die, my poor things, die!"

And the blind came running, with holes under their eyebrows, a foam gushing from their mouths, they fell upon him, threw him down, gouged the eyes out of his face:

"Messiah, we were praying to the pump!"

Benye lay on the ground with bloody eyes, he no longer felt the people. He saw the great beginning, which was nothing, like the time he and the cow had come to the edge of the world, and a great joy overtook him, his soul was leaving him, it was being redeemed. The cripples attacked him with their crutches, tore his legs from their joints, the hunchbacks jabbed him in the back, felt him to see whether he had at least a tiny hump.

And the Lamed-vovniks prayed to God. Simkhe and Leah stood over Benye; in the darkness, they couldn't see what was happening to him, but both of them sensed that he was nearing his end. Leah tore out of Simkhe's arms. She felt all her hatred for Benye, he had deceived her. With her hands outstretched, she dashed across the marketplace, weeping; she wrung her hands and yelled at the Jews:

"Kill him! Kill him!"

And mobs of men and women ran over to where Benye was ly-ing. The old crones threw rags at him, they kicked him into the mud, the men beat him with sticks, they threw stones at him, struck him with hearth brooms, rollingpins, paving stones.

"He deceived us, oh God, he deceived us!"

And Benye lay there, tattered in the mud. His soul left him, and all at once he became as big and as strong as the earth, his limbs joined together with his body, they grew out for miles, permeated with the icy soul of the world. He was lying in the town, in the fields, seeing with other eyes, lying, hearing differently, amazed at the greatness of God. The Jews were crawling about on the earth, kicking him, pouring out the anger of their despairing lives upon him. The rain was plunging in torrents, the houses were cracking, collapsing in the storm, and the men, women, and children were lying in the mud, weeping, cursing their lives. Suddenly, Simkhe Plakhte rose up above the Jews, he struggled over them, like a bright flame from a living sun, and a choking scream boomed across the town:

"Worms!"

Simke trod over the Jews with gigantic paces; in the darkness, his huge body shone with a quiet light. He trod away over the houses, huge, fearful, and solid, and returned to his shack. Now, the poor cow was standing by Benye, hanging her head, with Kyril sitting next to her, his arms around his knees, rocking back and forth, lamenting the death of the Messiah. Out of the night came Lubomirsky's daughter, white and terrified. She fell upon Benye, kissed his bloody face, held him in her arms, and wept over him, wept over him . . . .

The Prayer

The prayer of a poor man who was hidden,
And he poured out his heart to God,
Why are we so tortured, God!
Wherever I am, I am too much present,
And wherever I go, I take along the smell of the darkness.
I envy the bird, who is better than we are,
And the clay, which is better off than anything else.
What shall I do with my useless hand,
And with my useless heart?

The Fourth Day

A Tale of a Prince

Once upon a time there was a king. The king had no children. He consulted doctors so that his kingdom would not pass into strange hands.

But the doctors didn't help him.

He thereupon decreed that the Jews should pray for him to have children. The Jews sought a *tsaddik* whose prayer would move God to let the king have children. And they came upon a hidden *tsaddik*.

They asked him to pray for the king to have children. But the *tsaddik* replied that he didn't know anything.

The Jews reported to the king that they had found a hidden *tsaddik* who said he didn't know anything.

The king sent for him. And he was brought before the king.

The king began to talk to him in a kind way: "You know that the Jews are in my hands. I can do whatever I want to with them. So I ask you kindly: Pray for me to have children."

The *tsaddik* assured him that he would have a child that very year—and he went home.

That year the queen bore a daughter. And this princess was a great person. At the age of four, she knew all wisdoms and all languages, and she could play all musical instruments. Kings would come from all countries to see her.

The king was overjoyed.

Now the king greatly desired a son so that the kingdom wouldn't go to a stranger. And again he decreed that the Jews should pray for him to have a son.

The Jews looked for the *tsaddik*. But they couldn't find him because he had passed away long since. So they kept looking. And then they found another hidden *tsaddik*.

They told him to give the king a son. But the *tsaddik* said he didn't know anything. So again they reported this to the king. And the king told the *tsaddik*: "You know the Jews are in my hands."

And so the wise man, this *tsaddik*, said: "Will you be able to do what I tell you to do?"

The king answered: "Yes."

So the wise man said:

"I want you to bring me all kinds of diamonds. For every diamond contains a virtue of its own. The angels have a book describing all the precious stones."

The king said: "I'll squander half my kingdom, as long as I can get a son."

And he went and brought the *tsaddik* all the different kinds of precious stones. The wise man took them and pounded them down. Then he took a beaker of wine and poured them into the wine. And he gave half the beaker to the king, and the other half to the queen. And he told them they would have a son who would be made of diamonds, and he would have all the virtues of all diamonds.

Then the *tsaddik* went home.

Now the queen had a son. And the king was overjoyed. But the son was not made of diamonds.

When the son reached the age of four, he was a great person, a great wise man in all wisdoms, and he knew all languages.

Kings would come just to see him.

Now the princess saw that she was not getting as much attention as before. So she became envious.

However, she did have one consolation: The *tsaddik* had said that the son would be made of precious stones, and so it was good that he wasn't made of precious stones.

One day, when the prince was chopping wood, he got a cut in

his finger. The princess hurried over to bandage it. And there she saw a diamond. She was very jealous. So she made herself ill.

All sorts of doctors came to treat her. But none of them could help. So they summoned wizards. And she told one wizard the truth, that she had made herself ill because of her brother. And she asked the wizard whether it was possible to put a spell on a person and make him leprous.

The wizard replied: "Yes."

She said: "But suppose he finds another wizard to reverse the spell and cure him?"

The wizard, however, said that the spell would be thrown into water, so that no one could reverse it.

The princess worked the spell and then threw it in water.

The king frantically consulted doctors and wizards. But they couldn't help him.

So he decreed that the Jews in his land should pray for him.

The Jews went to the *tsaddik* who had prayed for the king to have a son and they brought him before the king.

The *tsaddik* always prayed to God: He had promised that the king's son would be made of precious stones, but the boy wasn't. The *tsaddik* told the Almighty: "Did I do this for *my* sake? I only did it for *Your* sake. Why didn't it come true as I foretold?"

The son became very leprous. He had leprosy on his nose, on his face, and on the rest of his body.

The *tsaddik* came to the king. He prayed that the prince would be cured of his leprosy, but it didn't help.

Then he learned from above that the illness had been worked by magic.

Now the *tsaddik* was higher than any wizards.

And the *tsaddik* came and reported to the king that his son was under a spell, and that the spell had been thrown into the water. The prince could be cured only if the wizard who had cast the spell were thrown into the water.

The king said:

"I'll give you all the wizards to throw into water, as long as my son is cured."

The princess was frightened and ran over to the water to take the spell back out. For she knew where it was.

And she fell in.

There was a great uproar, for the princess had fallen into the water.

The *tsaddik* came and said that now the prince would be cured.

And the prince *was* cured.

The leprosy hardened and fell off.

And then his skin peeled off.

And he was made purely of precious stones and contained all the virtues of precious stones.

For when the skin peeled off, people could see that the prince was made entirely of precious stones just as the the *tsaddik* had foretold.

The Dybbuk

This is a wondrous moral tale about a wicked woman who later became a penitent, and her son, a wicked man, from whom the holy Baal Shem-Tov exorcised a false and unclean spirit and replaced it with the pure, the true soul, which had been wretchedly wandering in the World of Chaos.

1.

What Jew doesn't know the proverb: The apple falls close to the tree. Who else is meant by the tree if not the mother? It is a great and well-known rule that a woman who is chaste in thought and deed can be married to an evil man and still be privileged to bring forth from her loins gabais and Hassids and pious Jews, whereas an evil woman, albeit married to a saint, will always have wicked and dreadful children. Long ago, our sages said that the most important influence on a child is its mother. She is the first to guide the young uncertain steps of her infants and teach them good manners, to plant in them a desire to become good and pious so that God and men shall be pleased with them.

2.

Now once in a small Jewish town near Cracow, there lived a clever and capable woman called Toybe (Dove), not a very fitting

name. Toybe was the only child of a very wealthy man, an innkeeper, who found a fine young scholar of a good background to
marry his daughter. Joseph, the noble young man, was the light, the
prodigy of the yeshivah of Bohorodgin. The innkeeper gave the
wedding for the happy couple and, as is customary, took the son-
in-law to board with him so that he would be free of all material
concerns and could fully devote himself to religious studies. The father-in-law was delighted with this arrangement and was very
boastful about his wonderful son-in-law.

However, it was not granted that he enjoy his children for long.
He passed away before his time, and in a short while the mother,
unable to survive her good husband, closed her eyes.

And thus, Toybe received her inheritance, took over the large
household, and became the sole provider and breadwinner.

And now, all at once, and no one could clearly see why, the Evil
Spirit, which had been hidden and held back in her for so long, finally awoke.

The rooms were filled with the yells and screams of the lady of
the house as she hollered at the maids, and sometimes with the
wailing of the maids because, as it turned out, Toybe was not very
cautious and did not always prevent her pure little hand from going
astray to another person's face with far from pious intentions.

Her husband's gentle warnings and kindly requests to behave
more decently were of no avail. She merely turned a cold shoulder
and a deaf ear to him.

And moreover, losing all sense of shame, she gradually began insulting her husband. First, little by little, she began shouting at him
and then raised her voice higher and higher. You can be sure that
she never used any affectionate names for him such as "darling,"
"sweetie pie," "dearest."

3 .

Once, after a raucous argument with her maids, when her husband tried to soothe her with kind words, her face turned red and
she unexpectedly pounced upon him, grabbed his round velvet cap
and yanked it down over his eyes, with jeers and abuse: "So that's
how it is! My delight! My sweet comfort! Light of my soul! If you
had your way, anyone could clean the floor with me! That's how
he defends his wife, the monster!"

His mother's blood froze in our Joseph's veins. He simply didn't know what to do with his wife, and in addition, he was very embarrassed about what people might say. So he held his tongue and swallowed everything. With all his sorrows, he still loved her, his darling young wife, and tried to rectify her harsh curses with blessings. The more she cursed him, the more he blessed her.

4.

Toybe's wineshop was frequented by nearly all the burghers and squires from miles around, and she did a particularly thriving business during county fairs. Landowners, young and old, liked to joke with Toybe and exchange idle and even waggish words, which didn't bother her in the least.

Among the men who liked her almost as much as the alcohol and wine that they drank in her shop, there was a rich hog dealer named Maxim. A young, bold man with an enormous mustache, which Toybe was not coy about staring at. And thus whenever she handed him his drink, he would try to touch her fingers, as Gentiles are wont to do, and she would demand his respect and tell him in Polish: "Keep your hands to yourself!" And these words would kindle an infernal fire in the hog dealer with the huge mustache, a fire he tried to douse with wine and mead, in vain. Toybe curiously played with the fire, the way idle women do. She enjoyed the man's helpless mortification, and she warmed herself a bit at the fire. But this alone was a great sin, merciful goodness! Now her ideas didn't go so far, heaven forbid, as to make her forget herself and inflict shame on her husband—she *was* a Jewish woman after all! From a rabbinical family. And she wasn't so totally wanton as to break her marriage vows. However, in the telling of this story you will see that a sinful thought is accounted the same as a sinful deed. It's enough to bring the Company of Satan, who will cause goodness-knows-how-many bitter and dreadful calamities.

5.

Until now, Toybe had not had any children. After a few years went by, she began to feel uneasy and long for children, and as barren wives usually do, she started visiting wonder-working rabbis, charmers, and even consulting witches and fortunetellers. The latter, of course, in great secrecy, without her husband's knowledge.

But then one night her father came to her in a dream and gave her a remedy of herbs. He blessed her, comforted her, and said:

"Look, my dear daughter, I have brought you a holy remedy, which I got in paradise from our grandmother Rachel. It will open your sealed womb. Cleave unto your husband with love, faith, and joy, and you will be blessed with a saintly son, the envy of God and men, and I, your father, will have a name upon the earth. But you will have to do penance for going to witches, I tell you, without fail . . . ."

Having spoken these words, he vanished, leaving his daughter bewildered and overjoyed.

6.

What does a foolish woman do? Instead of keeping the dream to herself and ardently and chastely doing what her father told her to do, she blabbered out everything to her husband. The dissenters, demons, and cronies of that wanton woman Lilith, needed nothing else. They simply danced for joy and boasted: "Just wait, gang, we'll gather our strength and play a nice trick on them, we'll bring down the roof!"

And thus it was.

At night, when Joseph approached his beloved wife with a blessing on his lips and fear of God in his heart, the devils led Toybe into unclean ideas and made her think evil thoughts that she was lying, God forbid, in the arms of the burly, lusty hog dealer with the huge mustache, Maxim. And the devils went to Maxim and inveigled him into thinking he was lying with Toybe. And the demons took the soul from the Christian seed and fast as lightning they brought it over and put it into Joseph's seed, robbing the little Jewish soul from the drop, an offspring of Joseph's pure soul.

The Gentile's soul attached itself to the drop of Joseph's seed.

The demons and devils were bursting with pride and gasping with laughter as they told Lilith, the wife of Satan, what they had done. "We're very curious to see what the upshot will be," they giggled and gaggled.

And the little Jewish soul floated in the air, buffeted and driven, wandering about, hoping for salvation, miserably crashing against the white walls of space.

7.

And when her time came, Toybe went into labor and gave birth to a boy, whom they circumcised in a happy hour and named Moses, after his grandfather.

Little Moses, in the luxury of his home, shot up like a weed, turning into a wild and sassy child. Unlike other children, he didn't allow himself to be led quietly off to school. When the attendants tried to bring him to class, he caused them no end of trials and tribulations. He showed no respect to anyone, not even his own father, whom he did not take after in any way—as you can well imagine. Nor did he feel any particular love for his mother. He was concerned only with himself, stubborn and refractory. Pity the poor housemaid who tried to oppose him in anything!

Joseph, the father, kept repeating: "How did such a changeling ever find its way to me?" He had very little joy from his only son.

On the other hand, Toybe forgave all the pranks and tricks that her spoiled little darling played, and by now she really could no longer live in peace with her husband. Since his son and heir did not bring the domestic happiness they had expected, Joseph turned more and more to his religious books and his brandy. And then one fine sunny day in winter, after a brief illness caused by a chill, he gave up his afflicted soul.

Toybe, a widow, remained with her little Moses, who was about to have his bar mitzvah.

8.

It wasn't long before the rich young widow got over her grief and remarried. But her second husband was no Joseph. Once, when she lost her temper and threw a cup at him, he threw a plate back at her. They had a knock-down, drag-out fight. And shortly thereafter they went to the rabbi and got a divorce.

She tried her luck once more and repeated the dangerous game. But her third husband was even worse. He didn't have a penny's worth of patience. He not only yelled, he also used his fists, like a

Gentile, whenever things got that far, and he had no respect for
Toybe or her son. So again they went to the rabbi, were granted a
divorce, and said: "Blessed is He who has freed me from the responsibility. Good riddance!"

After that, she refused to listen to any of the offers that scores of
matchmakers brought to her, and she remained a lone divorcee.
Now she suddenly began living with Joseph in her thoughts. "Oh,
that Joseph, what a pure soul, I'll never find the like of him again,"
she would say, gushing tears of repentance. And from now on, she
devoted all her heart and strength to her precious darling, her little
Moses.

9.

Moses, with God's help, had his bar mitzvah and began to put on
phylacteries like any adult male. His rabbi had a wretched time
drumming the speech into the boy's head. But the speech turned
out fairly well.

"He's got a sly head on his shoulders, that Moses, but he only
uses it for pranks," people would say.

Actually, no one could cheat and bully his friends as well as
Moses. He had a mass of buttons, mirrors, knives, and similar objects which he had gotten from his friends in various cunning ways.
His mother beamed with pride: "Ah, my little Moses will be a great
merchant some day!"

And Moses did become a merchant. His mother put him in the
care of the distinguished Jewish burghers and merchants of the
town, who borrowed money from her at interest. They were to
take him to Leipzig, Cracow, and other large fairs so that he might
come around in the world and gain some experience in commerce.

Moses reached the age of seventeen, and marriage-brokers began
proposing matches for him. They stormed his home. Each brought
an even better offer, until one broker succeeded in winning over
Toybe, the wealthy divorcee, for a beautiful girl named Sheve, the
daughter of Borukh, a distinguished elder in the city of Tarne.

The engagement contract was drawn up in a happy hour, and the
young couple were married. Toybe, who didn't want to part from
her one-and-only child, took the newlyweds into her home, where
they were treated lavishly.

Moses became a young man, and he would go to synagogue in his prayer shawl, sprawling in his father's pew among the elderly burghers.

10 .

How wonderful it would be if I could finish the story with the last section. But as it happened, Maxim the hog dealer's soul, which the demons had nearly forgotten about, woke up and stirred in Moses.

The demons were reminded of it by Maxim's terrible death, which occurred as follows: Maxim, while drinking more and more and attaining higher and higher levels of swilling, at the same time hit lower and lower economic levels. He no longer twirled up his mustache, it drooped like an old broom. Late one night, returning home from some kind of carousing, he slipped and fell. A devil had tripped him. He was sleepy, and so the demons lulled him until he dozed off—forever, on the hard, frosty ground.

The next day, the town was racked by a great tempest. "The drunkard's making a row!" whispered the Jews fearfully. The wind shattered panes, ripped shingles from the roofs, and created a sudden change in Moses, who began playing tricks and pranks that were very ugly and very un-Jewish. He shamelessly ran after Christian girls, taunted young Jewish wives with his impudent, sinful lusts. He ate and drank like a pig, and gave in to every lust and need of his body. He gave up praying and going to synagogue. Instead, he sang wanton Polish ditties which he learned from the drunkards in his mother's wineshop. Naturally, he paid no attention to his young wife anymore. Sheve, who was pregnant, went about in deep, endless sorrow, her heart was broken.

It was only now, too late, that she remembered: During the engagement ceremony, at the wedding, and while they were saying "God is merciful" to the bridegroom, when they spoke the bridegroom's name, there was something like a moaning and a soft weeping in the air. She had scarcely paid it any heed, thinking it was just her imagination and refusing to believe her own ears in those days of joy. But now she realized it had been a warning, a sign of something, a bad omen.

Neither she nor anyone else knew what the moaning and the soft weeping signified. It was the real and wretched soul of Moses, the offspring of Joseph's soul, lamenting and seeking a purification.

11.

Now, Toybe took fright. Her son's behavior was the talk of the town, and everyone hated him. What do women do in such a predicament? They start consulting healers and charmers. They try various remedies. But it was all useless. Our Moses got worse than ever, he stayed out all night, and no one knew what became of him. He would come home drunk, turn the house topsy-turvy, and make such a row that the whole neighborhood came running.

People kept saying he had joined that accursed Jacob Frank and his sect, who were doing such awful things in the towns and villages of southeastern Poland. Around that time, Frank—may his name be blotted out!—had undertaken a disputation with rabbis in Lvov, among them Rabbi Israel Baal Shem-Tov, the Master of the Good Name, whose renown was spreading with a sweet resonance throughout the country. As it turned out, the rabbi of the town was one of his devoted followers and disciples, and when Sheve came to him, lamenting and weeping bitterly, he advised her and her mother-in-law to go to Lvov with Moses and consult the holy Baal Shem-Tov. If he could not help them, then no one on earth could possibly help them, and they would have no choice but to dissolve the union and save at least one partner from perdition, the pure Jewish wife Sheve.

Toybe shuddered at the thought of this. She knew her son very well, and was afraid to lose a treasure like her young daughter-in-law.

They decided to go to the Baal Shem-Tov.

A great fair was taking place in Lvov, and Moses for quite a while had been preparing to attend it. Toybe and Sheve succeeded in convincing him to take them along. Toybe was taking Sheve to the Baal Shem-Tov, whom Moses had already heard about. They wanted the master to bless Sheve so that she would have an easy time giving birth, she was terribly afraid of a hard labor. Moses couldn't be so cruel as to refuse, even though he didn't like the idea at all, they might interfere with his carryings-on in Lvov. But he agreed.

They hired a large covered wagon, which they filled with comfortable cushions, and in a happy hour they started out for Lvov.

12.

The Baal Shem-Tov, instilled with the Holy Spirit, could foresee who was about to consult him. When the guests opened the door to his room at the inn, he welcomed them with a joyous face and greeted them by name. He asked them to be seated. The visitors were stricken with a peculiar panic. Cold drops of sweat emerged on Moses' forehead.

The Baal Shem-Tov fixed his blue eyes on him and stared sharply into his face.

Suddenly he turned, put on his praying shawl, took three paces toward the writhing sinner, and in a raised voice he ordered:

"Impure soul of Maxim, I command thee in the name of the God of Israel, depart hence, from this Jewish body, in which the company of Satan did plant thee, and yield thy place to the real heir, Moses the son of Joseph, who is floating about in space and wishes to cleave unto his body, from whence thou hast driven him."

All at once, a wailing voice came forth from Moses' body, uttering in Polish:

"Oh, God, my God, where will I go? I felt so good here."

Toybe and Sheve fainted dead away. A disciple of the master came over to revive them.

The Baal Shem-Tov raised his voice once again:

"Thy fate is to go to the fields of waste and wild because thou comest from a Gentile's spilling of seed . . . ."

In his heart, the spirit groaned: "Oh God! My God! I'm going, I'm going, holy man!"

No sooner were these words spoken than Moses slipped from his chair and fell upon the floor. He was lifeless. His body was without a soul.

The women sprang up weeping. The Baal Shem-Tov put them at ease: "Be quiet, women, be quiet, he shall live, you shall soon be happy with him."

And the master turned to the eastern wall and cried out in a loud voice:

"Soul of Moses son of Joseph, thy body is free!"

Moses opened his eyes. Now they looked so gentle, so soft. A happy smile appeared on his lips. He stood up from the ground, cheerfully walked over to the Baal Shem-Tov, took the master's hands, and bowed over them with these words: "Holy and saintly man, I thank you!"

The master replied: "It's all right! It's all right!" He embraced him and kissed him on the forehead.

And then Moses, weeping happy tears, threw his arms around Sheve and begged her forgiveness. He did the same with his mother.

The Baal Shem-Tov watched, smiling gently from under his blond mustache. Then he asked everyone but Toybe to leave the room.

"Holy and saintly master, what does this mean?" she asked humbly.

The Baal Shem-Tov explained everything to her, everything, and then said: "And you, Toybe, gather all your strength and do penance. You committed a grave sin against your husband."

Greatly excited, and full of pious oaths, Toybe left the master's room.

13 .

They remained in Lvov for a few more days.

Moses, whose true soul had always absorbed the religious lessons that could not reach the false soul, visited the Baal Shem-Tov every day, sitting among his intimates and disciples and devouring his sacred words.

This time, Toybe did all the business at the fair herself. And when at last it was time for them to say farewell, the master blessed them all and said: "Remember, my dear children, always serve the Lord with joy, with joy."

And they came back safely to their town.

14 .

At home, people simply didn't recognize the young couple at all. Such a great change had come over them. Their faces were aglow with tranquility and love. The townsfolk just couldn't stop gaping. And the entire family praised the Baal Shem-Tov to the skies.

Toybe's house became a refuge for the homeless and needy.

And nowhere was a guest welcomed with so much honor and hospitality as at Moses' table.

And nowhere was a beggar sent away with such rich alms as at Moses' door.

Sheve's womb was blessed. She had sons and daughters, and the parents and the grandmother brought up the children, and they lived happily ever after. May the same happen to all of us. Amen. His will be done.

A Passion for Clothes

In Shebershin, below Zamosc, there once lived a woman named
Bashe Gitel, who came from a very fine family and was married to
a Hassid. Now the Hassid, Elimelech, was seldom at home. First of
all, being a merchant, he had to go to Leipzig a great deal, and in
those times, a journey to Leipzig took longer than a voyage to
America nowadays. Secondly, Elimelech would visit the saintly
rebbe of Lublin at least once a year. And so it occurred to Satan to
take advantage of the husband's absences and talk Bashe Gitel into
sinning.

Satan realized, however, that he could never persuade her to
commit a *gross* sin, for she was truly a pure soul, well-versed in the
holy books, which she read in Yiddish translation. And she meticu-
lously observed all the duties required of a woman. He thought
about it and then decided to kindle within her a lust for clothes and
jewelry. For the Hassid Elimelech was very rich and gave her generous sums for housekeeping.

Now Satan didn't just come to her bluntly. He knew she would
simply laugh and jeer at him. Didn't she know you have to clothe
and adorn the sacred soul and not the sinful body, which is nothing
but meaningless clay, rosy one minute, dead the next!

So Satan disguised himself as the Good Spirit and inveigled Bashe
Gitel with fine, sweet, pious words. He murmured something about

good deeds, heaven, and, as is customary, he presented his cunning as fear of God.

"There's a sacred holiday coming," he said. "Passover.... Jews are commemorating the exodus from Egypt, and the Good Lord has blessed you with so many wonderful things, Bashe Gitel. Wouldn't it be right and fitting to wear a new frock in honor of the holy festival? Not just right, but positively a religious duty and a good deed? The tailor will earn something for Passover and you will be doing a fine thing."

Bashe Gitel was hesitant. So he reminded her that before leaving Egypt, the children of Israel had borrowed precious utensils, clothing, and jewelry. "And why?" he whispered in her ear. "For the holiday."

It made sense to her. So she baked fewer matzohs, prepared less food, donated a smaller sum to the Passover fund for the poor—and got herself a new dress with a silver decoration.

Shavuoth, the Feast of Weeks, he told her, is an even greater holiday, Jews celebrate the giving of the Torah. So she bought a new necklace.

Along came Sukkoth, the Feast of Tabernacles. She had new jewels set in her headdress, retailored her bodice, and bought new diamonds for her earrings.

Next, he told her she wasn't doing full justice to the Holy Sabbath, which is greater than any holiday. She obeyed, and on every Sabbath she went out of her way to wear something new, even if it was small—a silk kerchief, a fichu.

And at New Year's and on the Great Hosanah—the seventh day of the Feast of Tabernacles—how could she pass up buying some new ribbons, white and pale blue!

And Purim was also a holiday, and Hanukkah of course. A joy, a miracle! Whatever happened! Then came the Fifteenth of Shebat, which is New Year's Day for trees, and then came Lag b'Omer, a spring festival. The Jews, though in exile, have no lack of holidays!

And when her husband was expected home, it was certainly a good deed dressing to beat the band. A decent woman, a daughter of Israel, has to find grace in her husband's eyes....

And as for jewelry the Evil Spirit had special arguments. Bashe Gitel had once had a difficult pregnancy. Why not buy a ruby necklace? Everyone knows it's an excellent talisman for an easy childbearing.

Plus—a few emeralds. A fine touchstone for the soul. If you wear one and (God forbid!) you commit adultery, then the emerald bursts. And if you have just a sinful thought, then it clouds up. If Bashe Gitel were to stumble and have a bad thought, she would instantly be aware of it and do penance.

Her husband was away for months at a time and she occasionally had to settle accounts with merchants herself. Why shouldn't she wear a few little sapphires, to aid her wisdom. Bashe Gitel certainly had a good deal of wisdom—but the more, the better!

And so on, more stones with more virtues. Especially a fine gem to wear when her husband was at home, to make herself more attractive in his eyes, and he would love her all the more, and so she put it on.

In a word, Satan led her down a garden path—may God protect and save her! And with every passing day, she sank deeper and deeper into her craze for clothing. Satan saw he had gotten the best of her, she was like a well-hurled stone plunging downhill with the force of the initial throw, he simply stayed aloof now, and she went on of her own accord. She was stingy with alms, chary with food for herself and the children, sent the boys to inferior teachers, did everything she could to pinch pennies, and spent all she had on clothes and jewelry.

Even that wasn't enough. She fired the maid and docked her for all the damages in the house, whether or not they were the poor girl's fault. And then, feigning charity, she took in a poor young orphan, a starving child, who was a close relative, and she told her she wouldn't pay her any wages, but when her time came and she found her destined bridegroom, Bashe Gitel would give her a dowry and presents, and some of her own dresses, and she would lead her to the wedding canopy and dance toward her with a braided challah .... And instead of giving her a salary, she spent it on her passion.

Her husband, the Hassid Elimelech, had no idea what was going on of course, and so year after year wore on, until Bashe Gitel fell ill and couldn't move her legs.

When they tried to help her, it looked as if the sickness were heaven's doing, no healer in the world could tell what was wrong. She was generally fresh and sound, she could sleep and eat. And there wasn't a single wound on her legs, not a spot, not a speck, but they couldn't move at all!

It would appear to have been the best time for her to recover from her lust. When a woman is bedridden and can't go anywhere, not even synagogue, then what good are clothes and jewelry? What use are they within four walls?

But her passion was too deep. She expected to get up any day now, and so she kept making herself more and more clothes and buying anything brought into the house, and several times a week she would have the clothes and jewels displayed on chairs and benches at her bedside, and she lay there and looked, and feasted her eyes on them. And the poor orphan worked her fingers to the bone.

Once, when the clothes were being laid out, Bashe Gitel saw that some of her best silk and velvet finery was spotted and stained with food and liquor and full of rips and tears. She made such an uproar that the neighbors came running, they saw what had happened and everyone agreed, only the orphan could have done it, a "still water," with a God-fearing face, who hardly ever said a word and only went out on errands, but "still waters run deep." She must have put on her employer's clothes at night and gone to festive houses where people ate and drank and did all sorts of dreadful things. What was the world coming to?! Jews wondered that even then, so obviously the world must be getting worse all the time!

The orphan wouldn't own up to the crime, so they took her and yelled such indescribable things at her, words that should never even be spoken, much less written, and they struck her and beat her.

Then they took her to the rabbi, and testified against her, it could only have been her and the proof was: she looked so scrawny and skinny, though she lived with such a good woman, a wealthy relative.... It was obvious she never slept at night but drank and swilled and committed all kinds of sins and vices....

And they took the orphan and shaved her head to make her ugly so that no one else would be fooled, and they drove her out of town, running and hooting after her, as was the custom in those days.

The Hassid Elimelech wasn't at home all that time. He was with the saintly rebbe of Lublin and flatly refused to leave. He wanted the rebbe to obtain a full recovery for his wife Bashe Gitel.

The saintly man told him: "Go home and come back with your

spouse." The meaning of his words was this: The saint had already prayed for the woman several times, but to no avail, and he wasn't accustomed to such a failure. What was worse, he felt at times as if the prayer had been taken and flung back into his head. He realized there had to be some great obstacle, a strong accusation of great sinning.

He had asked several times: "What is it?" But heaven sent no answer! It must be an intricate matter, a hideous thing that could not be spoken aloud. And the Hassid Elimelech knew nothing about it. Since the saint of Lublin was an expert in human physiognomy, he wanted to meet the woman face to face and see what was written on her brow.

The Hassid Elimelech went home, rented a large wagon, and rigged it up like a bed, straw everywhere, with pillows and cushions, and drawn by two pairs of horses abreast. And then they took off for Lublin.

In Izhbitse, in Krasnatov, and in some other town, fresh horses were waiting since they couldn't spend the night with the invalid, and they wanted to arrive auspiciously in Lublin.

On they drove. But during the final leg of their journey, it suddenly began to snow. They lost their way and wandered through a forest, unable to get out. Night fell, but no matter how hard they peered and scanned, they couldn't sight a road—no moon, no stars .... They decided to stop and wait for daybreak, but were terrified of robbers and wild beasts. In those days the forest was like a jungle, reaching to the sky with interlocking branches, the day was dark, concealing robbers and wild beasts, and the night was mortally dangerous.

All at once, they were thrilled to see a sudden fire in the distance, the fire was growing, and then there was a second and a third fire—they couldn't be far from an inn. Off they went toward the fire. Driving along, they could hear musicians playing, and loud mirth. Coming closer, they heard a stamping and stomping, people were singing, playing, dancing.

Then the inn loomed up. The windows were ablaze. What was all the celebrating? Perhaps some Polish squires had gotten together, carrying on the way Polish squires do. You take your life in your hands when you encounter them during their revels, but they're preferable to robbers and beasts in the forest.

They fetched up at the inn and now they could hear better.

These weren't Polish squires, the bandsmen were playing Jewish ditties, all kinds. And a jester was entertaining the guests with rhymes and calling them to a wedding dance! The Hassid and the drayman nearly fainted, their mother's milk curdled in their veins! They instantly realized that the carousers were *those* people, the demons, who back then, before the woods were cleared, celebrated weddings in deserted inns.

Elimelech said to his wife: "Listen, Bashe Gitel, we've fallen into terrible hands. Just remember, for God's sake, we mustn't answer them at all, not return any greetings or accept any invitations, and not taste anything, God forbid, or we'll be done for!"

Bashe Gitel lay there half out of her mind with terror, and nodding her head to show she knew; and indeed she did know— from the holy books in Yiddish,

Meanwhile, the relatives of the bride and groom came pouring out of the inn, along with the jester, the musicians, all carrying torches, milling around the wagon, lifting the canvas, telling the travelers to wish them good luck, and invited them to the wedding. The men begged, the women begged, and the bride and groom also came over and asked them in honeyed tones, told them not to hurt their feelings, and the jester recited rhymes and jokes, and the band played, and the forest boomed with all the commotion.

Waiters carried out silver trays with all sorts of beverages in crystal and golden goblets and all sorts of delicacies and cakes, and they pushed the food and drink in the faces of the travelers: "C'mon, have some, say a blessing, join the fun!"

But the travelers didn't answer.

Suddenly, Bashe Gitel looked out and saw that the womenfolk, the relatives, bride, and guests, were wearing her best silk and velvet finery, and spilling liquor and food on her dresses, and catching them on the wagon.... Her heart sank, she lost all control, and screamed:

"Murderers, bandits! My hard work! My dresses!"

That was all they needed!

She was barely breathing as they took her to Lublin. All along the way, she kept fainting, and her mouth was all twisted up.... She was more dead than alive.

When they brought her to the rebbe, he instantly realized what had happened. He told his disciples to look upon her as an example. If a Jewish woman has new clothes made, then she has to distribute her old dresses to the poor and needy. She should never make any clothes she can't wear. For if there are dresses hanging unused in the closet, *those* people would come at night and take them out and put them on and dance in them at their feasts and weddings . . . .

Upon hearing these words, Bashe Gitel accepted the judgment as righteous and death as her due, and asked only that they forgive her, and the rebbe assured she was forgiven!

Just before dying, she called for her husband, the Hassid Elimelech, and told him what she had done to the orphan, and made him swear to find her and have her be a mother to their children, to make good the sin that Bashe Gitel had committed against the poor girl.

The Hassid Elimelech did as she asked. After the seven days of mourning, he sought out the orphan and married her, and she became a mother of his bereft children.

The couple were blessed with more children, they brought them up with learning and good deeds and married them off happily.

May the same be said of all Jews!

King Solomon and Ashmedai

This is a true story.

When King Solomon was building the temple, he was not permitted, as we all know, to use any iron. As a result, he didn't know how to cut the stones. So he sent for his wise men and asked them for advice on what to do.

The wise men answered: "We shall tell you. During the Six Days of Creation, God created a stone named Shamir. This stone was also used by Moses (may he rest in peace), when he hewed the stones for the breastplate of the high priest. There is nothing in the world so hard that the stone cannot cut it in two.".

Solomon asked them: "How can I find this Shamir?"

The wise men answered: "We will tell you how to find it. Go and catch a demon and a demoness and torture them until they reveal the secret of how to get the Shamir."

Well, they caught a demon and a demoness and brought them to Solomon, who asked them where to find Shamir. They replied: "We don't know, but Ashmedai, the king of the demons (may God protect us), *he* knows where."

Solomon went on: "I won't let you go until you tell where I can find Ashmedai."

They replied: "We'll tell you. Over there, on that mountain, he has dug a pit that is always full of water. However, the pit is covered with a slab of flint and sealed with Ashmedai's very own seal. Every day, he goes up to heaven to study the Torah at the celestial yeshivah, and when he's finished, he comes back down from the sky, and since he's very hot, he drinks water from the pit. But he never touches wine. Before he even tastes the water, he makes sure that the seal is whole and that no one has stolen over and poured wine into the pit. When he sees that no one has been near the pit, he drinks his fill, seals up the rock again with his seal, and then goes on his way."

Upon hearing this, Solomon sent for his adviser, Benaiah, and gave him a chain bearing the Name of God, a skein of wool to stop up a hole, and a jug of wine.

The adviser then started out, and he walked until he reached the pit from which Ashmedai drank. There he dug a hole under the pit, so that the water would flow out while the seal on the rock remained whole. Then he stopped up the hole with the wool he had brought along. Next, he dug a hole above the pit and poured in the wine from the jug, so that the pit filled up with wine, Naturally, he wanted Ashmedai to drink the wine and fall asleep, so that he could tie him up and bring him back to King Solomon. When he had finished his work, the royal adviser concealed himself. He climbed a lofty tree and waited for Ashmedai to come back from studying in heaven.

As soon as Ashmedai came back down upon the earth, he went over to the pit to make sure the seal was whole. He opened the pit and was about to have a drink of fresh water, when he smelled the bouquet of wine. He thought to himself: It's an old rule that when you drink wine, it blurs your mind. So I'd better not drink. But in the end, he was so tormented by his thirst that he could no longer hold back, and he had a swallow of the wine. As soon as he had drunk a good bit of it, he grew drowsy, and he lay down to sleep. This was the moment the royal adviser was waiting for. Just as Ashmedai fell asleep, the adviser climbed down from the tree and threw the chain with the Name of God around Ashmedai's neck.

When Ashmedai awoke from his sleep, he tried to tear off the chain with all his strength. The adviser said to him: "You won't be able to tear it off because the Name of the Lord God is engraved upon it."

Ashmedai saw that he had no choice, so he went along with the adviser. They walked for a spell, until they came to a tree. Ashmedai began scratching himself on the tree, and the tree toppled over.

From here, they went on and came to a house belonging to a widow. Ashmedai felt like scratching himself on the house. The widow rushed out and with cajoling words she begged him not to do it. Ashmedai tried to turn around, and wrenched his foot out of joint. He thereupon recited the biblical verse: "He who letteth himself be cajoled with fine words, will wrench his foot out of joint."

And so they walked on. They met a blind man, who was straying, and Ashmedai led him to the right path. The adviser then asked him:

"My dear Ashmedai, what was that all about? Why did you lead the blind man to the right path?"

Ashmedai replied: "That blind man is a great saint, and heaven has proclaimed that the man who does good to him will go to heaven. That was why I led him to the right path."

Walking farther, they came to a place where a wedding was being celebrated, and the crowd was very merry and cheerful. But Ashmedai began to cry. So the adviser asked him:

"Goodness, why are you crying?"

Ashmedai answered: "I am crying because the bridegroom is going to die tomorrow, and the bride will have to wait for thirteen years before she is released from the obligation to marry his brother."

From there, they came to the house of a shoemaker. And they heard someone say to him:

"Make me a pair of shoes that will last seven years."

The shoemaker replied: "Fine, I'll make you such a pair."

Ashmedai laughed out loud and said: "He's ordering a pair of shoes to last him seven years, and I don't even know whether he'll live for seven days, much less seven years."

They went on, and Ashmedai saw a drunkard wandering astray. Ashmedai walked over to him and led him to the right path.

The adviser was astonished and asked him once again: "Why did you show him the right way?"

Ashmedai replied: "Heaven has declared that he is bad, so I showed him the right way so that he may get his reward in this world."

They kept on walking. But then Ashmedai saw someone digging

for a buried treasure and using magic to find where it was hidden. Again Ashmedai laughed, and the adviser asked him why he was laughing. Ashmedai replied:

"Why shouldn't I laugh? That man is drudging and using magic to try and find where the treasure is hidden, whereas the treasure, with which King Solomon will build the temple, is right under his feet and he doesn't even know about it. So how does he expect to find another treasure?"

When they arrived in the royal palace, King Solomon made Ashmedai wait for three days without receiving him.

Ashmedai asked: "Why won't the king let me in?"

He was told: "The king is sick, he drank too much."

To which Ashmedai said: "Give him less to drink."

On the second day, he again wanted to go in and see the king. But he was told: "You can't see him. He is still sick: he ate and drank too much."

Ashmedai said: "Give him something for his easement."

On the third day, Ashmedai was admitted to the king. He took along a cubit and measured out four cubits in front of the king. The king asked him what his measuring meant. Ashmedai said:

"I will tell you. When you die you won't have more than four cubits of earth, yet you dare to conquer the entire world and it's still not enough for you. In the end, you even had to subjugate me."

The king replied: "Be quiet. All I want you to do is to get me the Shamir, because I wish to build the temple and cannot use any iron for splitting the stones. But with the Shamir, I would be able to split them. That is why I had you brought to me, so that you might give me the Shamir."

Ashmedai replied: "Your Majesty, I must tell that it is not in my possession, but in the possession of the Guardian of the Ocean. He will not entrust it to anyone else, only to the woodcock, but she has to promise to bring it back."

Well, when Solomon had heard this, he took a glass, gave it to Benaiah and told him to go and look for the nest of the woodcock's young.

Benaiah started out, and kept searching and searching until he came to a mountain where there were no people living, and there he found a nest. He took the glass vessel and threw it over the infant fledglings. All at once, the woodcock arrived and wanted to go to her young, but she saw that they were closed off from the outside. So she quickly flew off to the Guardian of the Ocean, got the Shamir, and put it against the glass. The glass split in two. She was about to fly off again, but Benaiah frightened her and she dropped the Shamir. Without delay, Benaiah grabbed the Shamir and dashed off with it. When the woodcock saw that she had lost the Shamir, she strangled herself, for she could not keep her promise and return the Shamir to the Guardian of the Ocean.

Now that King Solomon had the Shamir, he began building the temple. One day, after the temple was built, Solomon happened to be alone in a room with Ashmedai. Solomon said to him boastfully:

"What can you demons do better than any human beings?"

Ashmedai answered: "Take off the chain you bound me with, and give me the signet ring on your finger, and I will show you something marvelous."

Solomon took the chain off Ashmedai and gave him his signet ring. Ashmedai put one foot squarely on the earth and the other up to the sky and swallowed the king. He spewed him out four hundred leagues away. Then, Ashmedai sat down on the royal throne as though he were the real king.

Solomon spoke his famous proverb: "What profit hath a man of all his labor which he taketh under the sun?" And thus he wandered about the face of the earth, begging for a crust of bread from door to door and always saying: "I, the Preacher, was king over Israel in Jerusalem."

He roamed and rambled about the world until at last he came back to Jerusalem, where he went to the Sanhedrin, the supreme court of Israel. Wherever he went, he kept repeating: "I am the Preacher, a king over Israel in Jerusalem."

When the seventy-one scholars of the Sanhedrin heard him repeating the same words over and over again, they said: "A madman doesn't repeat the same words over and over again. There is more here than meets the mind. Let us see whether he is not the real king."

They asked Benaiah if he had been to see the king lately. He answered that he hadn't. They sent for the queen and asked whether the king had visited her lately. She said:

"Yes, he lay with me only last night."

The sages asked her: "Did you look at his feet?"

The queen answered: "He came to me with socks on his feet and he wanted to lie with me during my time of month. Why, he even wanted to lie with his mother Bathsheba."

When the sages heard this, they saw the truth. They gave Solomon the chain on which the Name of God was engraved, and the signet ring which bore the Name, and put Solomon back on the throne.

As soon as Ashmedai saw what had happened, he dashed off to the ends of the earth.

Solomon now sat on his royal throne, but he was still afraid of Ashmedai. So he wrote down charms and hung them over his bed. And at night, he had guards stationed around him, as described in the Song of Songs, threescore valiant men, for he was afraid of Ashmedai.

May God be with us and shield us against all evil.

A Tale of a Rabbi and His Only Son

Once there was a rabbi. The rabbi had no children. But then he finally had a son.

The rabbi brought up his only son and got him a wife.

And he, the son, would always sit upstairs and study the holy writings, as is customary among the wealthy.

He did nothing but study and pray.

Yet he sensed that something was missing. But he didn't know what it was.

And he felt no interest in his studies and prayers.

He finally spoke about it to two young men.

They gave him some advice, they told him to consult a certain *tsaddik*.

The son did a certain good deed which helped him attain the level of the Lesser Light.

Thereupon the son went to his father and told him that he felt no interest in his studies and prayers, something was missing, but he didn't know what it was, and he therefore wanted to go and consult the *tsaddik*.

The father answered: "Why should you go to him? Your learning is greater and your family finer. It would not do for you to go to him. It would be better if you changed your mind."

And with these words, the father prevented the son from going to the *tsaddik*.

So the son went back to his studies.

And once again he sensed that something was missing. So again he consulted with the two young men. And again they advised him to go and see the *tsaddik*.

So the young man went to his father again. But again his father dissuaded him and prevented him from going.

And the same thing happened over and over.

The son kept feeling something was lacking. And he longed and longed to do away with this lack, but he didn't know what it was.

Once again he went to his father, and pled and pled with him.

The father finally gave in and agreed to go with him on the journey since the boy was his only child. The father said:

"I'll go with you and I'll show you that the *tsaddik* has no authority."

They harnessed the wagon and drove off. And the father said to the son: "This will be a good test. If everything is in order then the journey will be the will of heaven. If not, then the journey will not be the will of heaven, and we shall turn back."

Off they went.

Driving along, they came to a small bridge. One horse collapsed, and the wagon turned over. The father and the son barely escaped drowning.

The father said:

"You can see that things aren't working properly. Our journey is not the will of heaven."

And they turned back.

The son returned to his former tasks, his studying. And again he saw that something was lacking, but he couldn't tell what it was. Again he pled with his father, and again the father had to start off on the journey with him.

As they were driving along, the father again made a sign so that everything would work properly.

On the way, however, both axles broke. Whereupon the father said:

"You can see, it's not right for us to travel. For it's not in the nature of things for both axles to break. We've driven so often in this wagon, and nothing like this has ever happened before."

And they turned back.

The son returned to his former tasks, his studies.

And again he felt that something was lacking.

The two young men once more advised him to go and see the *tsaddik*.

So the son went to his father once again and pled with him as before. And once again the father had to undertake the journey with him.

The son said to the father: "We should not make such signs again. For it is in the nature of things that a horse should collapse or that axles should break: unless something really terrible happens."

They drove on and then fetched up for the night in a hostel. There they met a merchant. And they began talking with him the way merchants talk. But they didn't tell him they were traveling to a rebbe. For the rabbi was ashamed to admit that he was going to a Hassid. They talked about worldly things and finally the conversation turned to the subject of Hassidic rabbis, and where they can be found. The merchant told them that a rebbe could be found there, and also there, and also there.

They began talking about the *tsaddik* whom they were traveling to see. To which the merchant replied in a tone of amazement: "But he's not a decent person! I'm just coming from him. I saw him committing a sin."

The father exclaimed: "See, my child, what the merchant is saying. He just came from the rebbe."

And they turned back.

Now the son died and returned to the father in a dream. The father realized that the son was very angry, and he asked him:

"Why are you so angry?"

And he answered him. The son, who had died, answered the father in his dream, telling him to go to the *tsaddik* whom they had once planned to see. "He will tell you why I'm angry."

The father awoke and thought to himself: "It's a dream, it's not real."

But then he had the same dream once again. And again he thought it was a false dream.

And the dream occurred three times in all.

He now realized it was not a meaningless thing, there was something to it. And so he set out on the journey. The rabbi went to see the *tsaddik*, to whom he had once started out with his son.

On the way he met the same merchant whom he had met before when traveling with his son. The rabbi recognized the merchant and asked him: "You're the man whom I saw in that hostel, aren't you?"

"Indeed you did." And he opened his mouth and said: "If you like, I'll devour you."

Whereupon the rabbi said to the merchant: "What are you saying?"

The merchant replied:

"Do you recall that you were traveling with your son, and that the first time a horse collapsed on the bridge. The next time the axles broke. And then the third time you met me, and I told you that the rebbe wasn't a decent fellow. Now that I've gotten rid of your son, you can go to the *tsaddik*.

"For your son had reached the level of the Lesser Light. The *tsaddik* to whom he wanted to travel is on the level of the Greater Light. If the two of them had come together, the Messiah would have come. But now that I've gotten rid of your son, you can go to the *tsaddik*."

And having spoken, the merchant suddenly vanished, and the rabbi was left all alone.

Thereupon he drove to the *tsaddik*, and shouted: "Help! Help! Woe to him who is lost and cannot be found again!"

And the merchant was the devil, who had disguised
himself as a merchant and deceived them. When
he met the rabbi the second time, he teased
him for having listened to him the
first time; for such is the way
of the Evil Spirit, as we
all know. May the Al-
mighty save us from
him and lead us
to the Truth.

The Conjuror

Once, a conjuror showed up in a small Jewish town in eastern Poland.

And even though he came just before Passover, during the anxious and costly days when a Jew has more worries than hairs on his head, the man's arrival caused a great sensation: What an enigmatic fellow! In shreds and patches, but with a top hat (though crumpled) on his head. A Jewish face—with God's image on his nose, but—clean-shaven. And no identity card, and no one ever saw him eating—not kosher, not Christian. What a mystery! If you asked him: "Where ya from?" he'd say: "Paris." "Where ya goin'?" "London." "Whatcha doin' here?" "Lost my way." He seemed to be traveling on foot. And he never went to synagogue, not even on the Sabbath preceding Passover. And if people started getting pushy and crowded around him, he would melt away as though the earth had gulped him down, and then pop up on the other side of the marketplace.

Meanwhile, he hired an auditorium and began performing his tricks.

And what tricks! In full view of the spectators, he would swallow live coals as though they were noodles, and pull a whole medly of ribbons out of his mouth, red ones, green ones, in all the colors of the rainbow and as long as the Jewish exile. He reached into a

381

boot-leg, and out came sixteen pairs of turkeys, and what turkeys! As big as bears, and alive, and they scurried all over the stage; next, he lifted one foot and scraped golden ducats off the sole, an entire bowlful of golden ducats! The audience cheered; he whistled, and the air was filled with loaves of straight and braided challah flying around like birds, doing a circle dance or a wedding dance beneath the cciling; and when he whistled again, everything vanished into thin air as though it had never been! Gone were the ribbons, gone were the turkeys—*poof!*

Now we know that black magic can do a thing or two! The wizards of ancient Egypt very likely performed even greater feats. And so the townsfolk wondered: Why was he so poor? A man scrapes ducats off the sole of his boot, and he can't even afford a room at the inn; he merely whistles to bake up more loaves of challah than the biggest baker, he pulls turkeys out of his boot—and yet his face looks like he just stepped out of a coffin, and his eyes are ablaze with hunger. People joked about a fifth Passover question: "Why is this man different . . . ?"

But before we get to Passover questions, let's leave the conjuror and turn to Jonah and his wife Rebecca. Jonah used to deal in timber; he bought a forest at a good price, but then the government declared it a natural preserve; he lost his shirt. So he got a job as a manager in a lumberyard; but then they laid him off; that was months ago, and he had been out of work ever since. The winter was so awful you wouldn't wish it on your worst enemy; then, on top of everything, came Passover. And they had already pawned all they had, from the ceiling lamp to the very last pillow. So Rebecca said: "Go to the Community Passover Fund and get some money." But Jonah said he had faith, God would help, he didn't want any handouts. Rebecca once again started hunting through every nook and cranny, and up she came with a worn silver spoon—a downright miracle, the spoon had been mislaid for years. Jonah pawned it, and donated the tiny sum to the Passover Fund. The poor, he said, come first. Meanwhile, time went on. Passover was just a few weeks away—he had faith! God, he said, doesn't abandon you! So be it, Rebecca held her tongue; a woman has to obey her husband. But another day wore on, and then another, Rebecca couldn't sleep a wink, she buried her face in the hay mattress and wept silently so that Jonah wouldn't hear; not a thing for Passover. And the days were worse than the nights—at night, you can cry your heart out, but in the daytime you have to put up a front. The neighbors gawked and gaped and goggled, needling her with glances of pity .... Others asked her: "So when are you gonna bake matzohs? How ya doin' with beets?" Those closer to her asked: "What's goin' on with you, Rebecca? If you need anything, we'll lend it to you," and so on.

But Jonah wouldn't accept gifts from anyone, and Rebecca couldn't act against her husband—so she made up all sorts of excuses, and her face grew redder and redder ....

The neighbors, realizing things weren't quite in order, hurried over to the rabbi to get him to do something. The rabbi, poor man, heard them out, sighed, pondered, and finally answered that Jonah was a learned and God-fearing man, and if he had faith, then that was that!

Rebecca didn't even have any holiday candles.

And all at once—Passover.

Jonah, coming home from synagogue, saw that all the windows around the marketplace were bright and festive, only *his* window stuck out like a mourner at a wedding, like a blind man among the seeing. But he refused to despair: "God willing, we'll still celebrate Passover!" he thought to himself. Entering his home, he cheerfully said: "Happy holiday," and then, more emphatically: "A happy holiday to you, Rebecca!" And Rebecca's tear-soaked voice answered from a dark corner: "A happy holiday to *you*, my husband!" And her eyes glowed out of the dark corner like two live coals. He went over to her and said: "Rebecca, today's a holiday, to commemorate the Exodus, don't you see? We mustn't be mournful! And what's there to be mournful about anyway? If God doesn't want us to have our own seder, we'll simply have to make the best of it and go to someone else's. We'll celebrate in some other place. People will take us in all over .... Tonight all doors are open. The Haggadah says: 'Let anyone who is hungry come in and dine.' C'mon, get your shawl, and we'll go to the first house we find."

And Rebecca, who always did her husband's bidding, fought with all her strength to hold back the sobs that were struggling out of her throat; she wrapped herself up in a tattered shawl and was about to set out—but at that very moment, the door opened, and someone walked in and said:

"Happy holiday!"

To which they replied: "The same to you," without seeing who had entered.

And the man who had entered said: "I want to be your seder guest."

Jonah answered: "We're not having a seder."

The guest replied that he had brought the seder along!

"In the dark?" Rebecca let a sob escape.

"God forbid!" answered the holiday guest, "there'll be light." And he waved his hand: Abracadabra. And two pairs of silver candlesticks with burning stearin candles appeared and hovered in the middle of the room. The house became bright. Jonah and Rebecca saw that it was the conjuror, and they gawked and were so amazed and frightened they couldn't utter a single word. They grabbed each other's hands, wide-eyed and gaping. Meanwhile, the conjuror turned to the table, which was standing all neglected in a corner, and said: "Okay, chum, set yourself, and come over here!" And no sooner had he spoken, than a snow white tablecloth dropped from the ceiling and covered the table, and the covered table began to move and slid over to the middle of the room and stopped right beneath the candles, and the silver candlesticks descended and came to rest on the table. "And now," said the conjuror, "all we need is Passover seats—so let there be Passover seats!" And three chairs, from three corners of the room, marched over to the table and stationed themselves on three sides. The conjuror ordered them to grow wider, and so they widened out and turned into easy chairs. He called out: "Softer!"—And they covered themselves with red velvet, and, presto, white, snow white cushions came down from the ceiling, and, at the conjuror's command, plopped upon the easy chairs—which turned into Passover seats. At his bidding, a Passover plate with the seder paraphernalia also emerged and came to rest on the table, followed by red goblets with bottles of wine, and matzohs, and everything you need for a proper and merry seder, including gilt-edged Haggadahs.

"Do you have water to wash with?" asked the conjuror. "I can bring water, too!"

It was only now that they recovered from their astonishment. And Rebecca whispered to Jonah: "Is it all right? What do you think?" But Jonah didn't know what to say. So she advised him: "Go, husband, and ask the rabbi." But he replied that he couldn't leave her alone with the conjuror. He wanted her to go instead. But she said that the rabbi wouldn't believe a mere woman, he'd think she was out of her mind. So the two of them went to the rabbi, leaving the conjuror behind with the seder.

The rabbi said that anything fabricated by sorcery has no substance, because sorcery is merely an optical illusion. He told them to go home, and if they could break the matzohs and pour the wine into the goblets and feel the cushions on the seats, etc., then fine . . . it was all from God, and they could enjoy it.

That was the rabbi's verdict. And so, their hearts pounding, they went home. When they came in, the conjuror was gone, and the seder was just as they had left it. They could feel the cushions, pour the wine, and break the matzohs . . . . And only now did they realize that their visitor was the Prophet Elijah, and so they had a merry holiday.

A. B. GOTLOBER

The Gilgul
or The Transmigration

For many years now I've been a member of the Jewish Burial Society. In accordance with custom, I started out as an apprentice, my job being to attend patients, many of whom were about to breathe their last. I thus became an expert in dying. When I put a feather to the patient's nose and it doesn't stir (the feather, not the nose), then I can be sure that the patient is dead and I see to it that he gets a decent Jewish burial.

Now, today's enlightened Jews have lit upon the notion that lots of people are buried before their time. Stuff and nonsense! No Jew is ever buried too soon! Believe me, the feather is the best proof in the world. If the feather doesn't move, why not go ahead with the funeral? Naturally, if the feather *did* move, we wouldn't be in such a hurry. Now you can bet your life that our forefathers knew what they were doing. It would sometimes happen that they gave a corpse a good smack (first begging his pardon, of course) if he stirred after death. Make up your mind already, they would tell him. If you're dead then why are you moving? Go to your eternal rest!

And if he wasn't dead?—In a pig's eye!—How could that be? They had put a feather to his nose. So what was it? A demon, a fiend, an unclean spirit? Merciful God, save us! Take a smack and go already! ...

But that's neither here nor there.

I want to tell you a story about something that happened to me when I was still a burial apprentice.

Before I start, though, I want to make it clear that I'm not just some infantile Jew who thinks a cow has jumped over the moon. You can see I'm just a simple man and I don't believe in superstitious nonsense. I'm never afraid to go out alone at night. Now, granted, things *do* happen—but still and all, I'm not afraid. I've been known to sleep in a house without a mezuzah, and I managed to sleep peacefully and fearlessly—of course, I put my *tsitsis* under my head!

Another time, I was in a mill—just imagine, I wasn't alone, and the miller was a conjuror. But I wasn't scared. Naturally, I wouldn't have spent the night there for a million rubles. Only a wild and abandoned person would sleep in a mill.

Now, I'm telling you all this so you won't think I'm making anything up. What I'm about to tell you is a true story, you can take my word for it.

This is what happened.

One day, after burying a corpse, I was still lingering in the cemetery. I was supposed to put another body to rest and set up a gravestone. Inside the mortuary, as usual, I had a few sips of liquor and a bit of cake, said some prayers, and then, as customary, made my way home in high spirits.

Walking along, I passed the house where that man had died—the one I had just buried a couple of hours ago. In accordance with religious custom, a candle was burning in the window, and next to it stood a glass of water with a piece of linen for a towel. I peered over—the man's ghost was standing there, washing and wiping himself.

I'm no coward, mind you, I strode right over to that window and said to the ghost:

"That was quick! You got here faster than I did. But that's not surprising—a dead body can be spirited away. Praise the Lord that we meet again. It shows you've gotten over your trouble, the Angel of the Dead has let you go. I certainly consider it a great honor, seeing a dead man is always a great honor. I've heard that in ancient days, great saints saw dead men who were coming to them for a *tikun*, a drink on the anniversary of their death. But nowadays, when the Hassids have started drinking their *tikuns* in the house of study and all the little synagogues, every corpse has had his drink and needn't bother coming to the rebbe. That's why modern rebbes only see spirits, but no corpses. A simple man like myself should really consider it an honor to see a dead man. And since the Good Lord has granted me the privilege of seeing a dead man, let me ask you something, my dear corpse. Tell me honestly. Is there any truth to what the enlightened Jews say that because Jews bury their dead so quickly they sometimes—God forbid—lay a living man in the ground? I buried you so quickly, you were still warm. Could I possibly have buried you alive?"

"Bah!" said the phantom. "If the dead could speak out of school, the living would learn a lot of things they don't know. But don't you know that dead men tell no tales? Whether you buried me dead or alive, you can be sure it will be a dead secret, I won't breathe a word of it to anyone. Not every man is privileged, as you are, to speak with the dead. It would be better if you didn't ask. I've also buried corpses in my time, and I've never had any complaints. Believe me, I've filled bigger cemeteries than the one you bury your customers in, for a doctor puts more people underground than a gravedigger."

"A doctor!" I exclaimed in amazement, almost jumping out of my skin. "What are you talking about?! *You* a doctor?—But you were a contractor. That means you've wound up in the wrong winding sheet. Please don't be offended, I'm only reminding you because I'm worried that you may be wandering around in the World of Chaos."

"You've got nothing to worry about," replied the ghost. "I'm in the Other World, the True World, and not in the World of Chaos. And as for my winding sheet, I've got nothing to be ashamed of in our graveyard. If you knew what I know, you'd know that a lot of people whose headstones say 'Here lies the wealthy and prominent, etc.' and similar titles, and who have left thousands to their wives and children, have wound up in the wrong winding sheet. When I tell you I was a physician, you needn't find that so hard to believe. I'm not just talking through my skullcap. I really was a doctor, though not in the body you just interred! It was a long, long time ago. There's not a speck of dust left of that body. And I haven't only been a doctor, I've gone through lots of reincarnations, a different one each time."

My doctoral question was answered, but nevertheless I asked the corpse: "Well, if you were a doctor, no wonder you never got any complaints from your corpses. I don't think any doctor has ever buried anyone alive!"

"In reply to that," said the ghost, "I have two things to say. First of all, who says they had any complaints about being buried alive? On the contrary, they complained that I had dispatched them before their time. Secondly, you ought to know that if anyone is buried alive, the doctor has his share in it. Without his certificate, no one gets put to rest."

"Dear me!" I cried out. "Is the rabbi responsible too? He also makes out a certificate!"

"Now why," replied the ghost, "do you think that a rabbi is known as a physician of the soul? Rabbis and doctors do the exact same thing. However, I've said too much, you've already pried more than enough out of me. You've just about discovered the things I didn't want you to know. Let's not talk about it anymore, my dear burial man, and stop asking so many questions. Don't forget, you're talking to a *gilgul!*"

The ghost gave me a ghastly look, and I was a bit scared. Now I certainly wouldn't be afraid of an ordinary phantom, but a gilgul is a wraith of a different color! A gilgul is no laughing matter, it's something to watch out for. Why, merciful goodness! A gilgul is practically a dybbuk, it's a soul wandering from one body to another, trying to atone for the sins it committed in a previous life.

But then I realized it was God's will for me to talk to a gilgul. Most likely, I could find out things to tell the saintly men about obtaining redemption for him. I gathered my courage and asked:

"My dear ghost, perhaps you feel like telling me about the things that have happened to you since you first began existing in this world. I might be able to do you a favor and study the Talmud for you. I don't know it all that well, but certainly as well as anyone studying for a corpse. And I'll communicate all your words in synagogue so that we'll drink to your salvation every day instead of just once a year!"

"Thank you kindly, but it's not necessary," replied the ghost. "Reeling off your Talmud and not understanding hide nor hair of it is useless—like flogging a dead horse! And your drinking will do more harm than good. I don't need any favors, thank goodness. I've already done my atonement, the body that you buried was my final incarnation. My wanderings are over. But still, I'll oblige you and describe everything that happened to me in all my different lives so that you can write it down for people to read. Perhaps someone will take an example from my experiences, and it will do him some good.

"But before I start my story, I have to remind you that I'll be telling you about things that happened a long time ago. Don't forget that I spent close to seventy years in the body you buried. So if my stories contain anything that might happen today, please remember that any references to persons living is purely coincidental. It may be that certain people are exactly the way I was in a former lifetime, for is there anything that I was not? But I certainly don't mean anyone else, for my previous incarnations were a long time ago.

"And now, listen, I'm about to begin my story . . . ."

The first time that I was to be born as a human being, my parents had been childless for many, many years. People started telling them: "Why don't you do something about it. Go to a rebbe! Who else can help you? A rebbe holds the key to childbirth!"

My father, however, didn't think much of rebbes. He felt that the key was held by God alone, and that if ever a rebbe happened to help a woman get a child, he did so with a passkey. That was why he didn't want to go to a rebbe. But a woman is a woman! My mother listened to what people told her, and she began to visit rebbes without telling my father! She went from one rebbe to another, until it finally worked.

This rebbe prayed and prayed and made a great deal of progress, until at last he brought my soul from the music of the spheres into a body inside my mother's womb. My mother was no longer childless, she was in a family way. My father thought that God had blessed him in his old age without their having to resort to a rebbe. But my mother knew the truth. She had been helped through the merits of saints.

A Hassidic Singer

Since I was such a precious baby, for whom saintly men had had to intercede just to get me to be born at all, my mother, who had such strong faith in the rebbe, did everything in her power to spoil me. My father never interfered, and so she could raise me however she wished. By the age of ten, I already knew what liquor tasted like, and I was stuffed to the hilt with tales about wonder-rabbis. My mother hired a tutor for me, a young man—not to teach me anything (he didn't really know very much), but to tell me stories—at which he was a past master. He also instructed me in religious duties. I never went anywhere without him. We even slept together. He revealed so many secrets to me that by the age of fifteen I was a complete Hassid in every way. I could drink like a fish, pray for all I was worth, take hot and cold ablutions, grab the leftovers from the rebbe's plate, and perform my share of youthful peccadilloes. The latter stood me in good stead, they left me as skinny as a rail and made my eyes water.

I looked like a wrung-out herring because I spent so much time in the bathhouse. Furthermore, no one could bear standing too near me—the more I splashed around in the bath, the worse I smelled. My hair was always freshly shorn, my throat bare, with a huge Adam's apple, my coat unbuttoned, my chest exposed—and for all these reasons I was known as a silken young man, highly esteemed by the rebbe, the apple of his eye!

In addition to all my golden virtues, I was also a fine Hassidic singer; after all, the rebbe had brought my soul down from the music of the spheres. My greatest talent was my ability to scream. I could outscream any other Hassid. Yet no one but myself realized what this constant screaming cost me. I soon had to buy myself a truss. But does a Hassid ever listen to anyone? I couldn't care less. I screamed in a falsetto, in a bass, in a head voice. For the prayers ushering in the new moon, I boomed like a kettle drum. The rebbe was so enamored of my singing, that I became chief singer at his table. Without my crooning, his soul could not ascend to the higher spheres. In short, as luck would have it, I became a maker of Hassidic melodies, I devised them to the rebbe's fancy, full of religious ecstasy and enthusiasm. Whenever I composed such a tune, I first had to drink a lot in order to work up the proper ecstasy and enthusiasm and meet the rebbe's taste. Whenever I was to sing my melodies for the rebbe, I first had to drink like a fish to remain at that high level and show the rebbe the great ardor infusing my song.

But I sang not only for the rebbe, I sang at all tables and carouses, the new-moon banquets of our people, and we had meals for religious festivities every single day, sometimes even twice a day, and for every performance I drank more than I ate. I started drinking alcohol as though it were water, and pure spirits—firewater!

Once I created a new melody for the prayer "He will proclaim liberty," and it caused a turmoil! The rebbe was so enflamed, so excited, so exhilarated, so ecstatic, that everyone thought his soul was about to expire. Needless to say, the chant, the excitement, the exhilaration, the expiration of the soul caught on like wildfire. Hassidic Jews sang only my composition, working themselves to an ardor and ecstasy that very nearly did make their souls expire. Each Hassid wanted to flaunt his emulation of the rebbe. And I most of all, I, the author of the new chant, who started the whole thing in the first place. I most of all wanted to show my masterful ability to bring the rebbe to such a pitch that I worked myself up to more ecstasy than anyone else, practically more than the rebbe himself. Such matters urgently require a good stiff drink, and since drinking was an everyday affair with me, I needed a double portion, and of much stronger spirits. In short, I started drinking large glasses of wood alcohol.

Saturday night, at the meal ushering out the Sabbath, I again sang my chant for the rebbe, just as I had sung it a dozen times before, at all the other Sabbath repasts, and for guests that very afternoon. I had already drunk several glasses of wine, brandy, mead, kirsch, and then plain brandy again, in the little Hassidic synagogue before evening prayers. And each time, I drank and ecstacized. At the final Sabbath meal, you're supposed to have a drop of liquor, and the rebbe himself poured it for me with his own two hands. The rebbe didn't drink an ordinary alcohol. He drank to my health and took my hand, holding on to it for a long time, longer than usual.

Then, with great enthusiasm, he once again shouted: "*L'haim! L'haim*! I can assure you that with God's help you will live to a ripe old age! It is written of the Holy Torah: 'The Torah is the life of the Jew and it lengthens his days.' You, my child, truly make the Torah come true! The true Torah of the saints! The Light of the Torah! That is why I say unto you: You will surely live a long life! *L'haim. L'haim!*"

Having pronounced these words, he drained his cup and then replenished it and handed it to me. No sooner had I emptied it than a flame darted out of my mouth and my nose! The alcohol, which filled me like a barrel, had grown so hot that it kindled and began to burn quite cheerily.

An ordinary blaze can be put out with plain water, and every town has its firemen. But the only remedy for that kind of conflagration is saltwater, and the rebbe's firefighters are his disciples. The rebbe issued a command and a whole sea of saltwater poured into my mouth. But it didn't help, the bitter decree had been spoken, and I was charred to a crisp.

There were two schools of thought on the matter.

Some people said that the rebbe had already seen that my death was ordained because with my ecstasy I had obstinately been trying to make the Messiah come before his time, and the rebbe had taken away the Angel of Death's knife so that he couldn't do anything to me. That was why the rebbe had so ardently drunk to my health. However, the Angel of Death had gotten a spark of inspiration and simply burnt me up.

Others said that I merely wanted to bring down the Angel of the Torah (because the rebbe had testified that I had truly made the Torah come true), but that I had made a mistake and brought down Gabriel, the Angel of Fire, instead. The same thing had happened to one of the original Hassidic rebbes.... It was written about in one of our holy tomes.

Well, they could talk until they were blue in the face! The precious passkey child, the silken young man with all the virtues, was dead—incinerated. The Messiah hadn't come, the Angel of the Torah had not been brought to earth. All that was left of me was a heap of cinders and so—ashes to ashes.

The following Friday night, the rebbe preached on the verse: "He sought the sin offering, and behold, it was already consumed." And he said mysterious and unintelligible things.

On Saturday morning, he announced that I had come to him in a dream with the interpretation of that verse, which had been given to me by the ministering angels, but he would not reveal it. Now, however, after so many generations, let me reveal what I told him:

"Offering! Shmoffering! You burn me up! You're consumed with your own stupidity!"

A Horse

But now let's get back to me.

As soon as I was put underground, the Angel of the Dead came and asked me in Hebrew:

"What's your name, my boy?"

"It shouldn't happen to my worst enemies—I don't know my own name!"

Dead drunk, burnt to a crisp—how was I supposed to remember? I didn't answer. He even wanted to get to work and whip me a bit, which is what he normally does to a corpse that can't tell him its name. But what can you whip if everything's burnt up? How could he whip a heap of cinders? The hell with it! He didn't fool around with me for long, he promptly told me my judgment:

"Because you did wicked things that your tutor taught you and then soaked yourself afterward in the bath; because you poured a whole Gehenna of fire into you and thought that taking cold baths and rolling in the snow would douse the fire; because you yelled your guts out and screamed with a clumsy voice at the rebbe's table, God alone knows what!—things that you could have spoken in a softer tone—you would have done better to study something that could have helped you and your nation and the world; because you stuffed your head with foolish things and your heart with sanctimonious piety—for all these things, it has been decreed that you are to return to earth as a *horse*, which trots about in water, and cold water to boot, which rolls in snow and neighs in a clumsy voice, which has no mind and no wit—just like you! But this is the difference between you and a horse: A horse is a teetotaler, he only drinks water."

The Angel of the Dead had no sooner spoken these words than I looked about and—*poof!* I was a horse!!

Becoming a horse, I really did trot about in cold water again, in the winter I rolled in the snow, I neighed like the biggest Hassidic fool; I never looked at a female; I always walked with my head down—but all the same, I started trembling the moment I heard a female voice or even smelled her from afar. And no liquid except for water ever passed my jaws.

There are four kinds of horses. There are thoroughbreds with pedigree documents testifying that they descend from such-and-such a horse, and have been horses for generations. Experts say you can judge a horse by its member; the bigger the member, the greater the pedigree.

Then there are horses that dance, horses that perform tricks. These are all valuable horses and very well trained and pastured.

And then there's a difference in the color. Some people prefer white horses, some black horses, gray horses, chestnuts, and so forth. Among all these colors, there are valuable horses, less valuable ones, and horses of no value whatsoever. All of them labor, but not equally, and not all are maintained in the same way, there's a great difference in the fodder. If I had been reincarnated as the right kind of horse, I could have eaten like a pig, and I wouldn't have been beaten. But as my bad luck would have it, I became a common horse belonging to a poverty-stricken driver, whose sole income derived from carrying Hassidic Jews to the rebbe on Sabbaths and holidays, and if there were no passengers, he would haul clay.

Lugging clay isn't exactly my idea of fun, but taking Hassids to the rebbe is a thousand times worse. Ten or fifteen Hassids squeeze into a tiny wagon, on top of one another, all of them dead drunk, and all of them egging on the poor horse, who can barely move with that load. They all scream, beat, jostle, one Hassid with a stick, another with a tobacco pipe, still another with his feet, his skullcap, or his arms! Not one feels any compassion. And how could people who care so little for themselves, who spend their lives guzzling and loafing—how could they feel any compassion for a horse?!

Now one day, I was hauling some fifteen Hassids to the rebbe for the Sabbath preceding Purim. It was already Friday. We had started out on Thursday morning, right after prayers, and the rebbe was thirty-five miles away. My master calculated that I would make it by Friday afternoon, so that the passengers could get to the bathhouse in time. But he didn't foresee that it would rain on Thursday night, and the downpour left a terrible mud. He didn't ask my opinion, and he forgot that he had only fed me a scrap of stale hay on the previous day. I never exactly ate myself sick on oats, but he did give me a handful to nibble every afternoon. However, on the day before leaving, my owner apparently wanted to teach me my p's and q's, and dropped his h's to give me some 'ay. And that was all. Now I knew my alphabet from *A* to *Z*, and I wanted to show him that the road to *L* is paved with good intentions. But ignoring my horse sense, he told me to gee-up! How could I feel my oats if I didn't get any?

Friday morning my dear little Hassids said their prayers and had a very merry time of it. They had a good round of drink plus some pot roast and fresh rolls, and they stuffed themselves because meat is so cheap in taverns. The upshot of it was that the weight of my load doubled. They drank a lot of liquor, before the pot roast, after the pot roast, and just for fun. And when they boarded the wagon, they lay there like rocks. The rain began pouring again, so they decided to cover the wagon. Two of the Hassids who were sitting in the back corners of the wagon held up a mat of rushes, and my master, who was driving, held the other two corners in his teeth, so that the entire wagon was virtually covered. I dragged my cargo with all the strength I could muster. Seven miles short of the rebbe's house, my strength gave out, I couldn't even stagger, and I halted in the mud.

And now a commotion began, an uproar, with everyone shouting at once: "Giddyap! Giddyap! For God's sake! Move your goddamn ass! It's almost nightfall!"

Let them yell their guts out! I couldn't budge a hoof!

And now they all pounced upon me and started beating my scraggy bones. They undid the poles and began pounding me with them or with their shoes, the way Hassids beat up a rationalist preacher! Well, they kept banging and bashing me until I finally gave up my soul!

Now, my dear burial man, you are going to ask: How can a horse have a soul? Let me tell you that an ordinary horse has no soul, but a gilgul horse does have one, and let me point out that if ever you meet a "horse with spirit," then you'll know that's really a reincarnation.

My poor master mourned me with tearful eyes. I was his business after all, his only source of income: "Oy! What a horse he was. He never ate more than a teensy bird. Soon, he wouldn't have cost me any fodder at all. I was teaching him how to fast, and the very moment he learned his lesson, he had to bite the dust on me!"

A Cantor

Since I had been privileged to die in sacrosanctity, en route to the rebbe, and was beaten with shoes, like a rationalist preacher, and since a decent and pious Jew, a drayman of Hassids and clay, had delivered a eulogy over my body, my soul was raised to a higher level and I was once again incarnated as a human being.

To reward me for having spent my entire horse life in sorrow, never eating my fill, never drinking anything but water, and drudging day and night, the Celestial Council of Justice decided I should become a cantor and eat like a horse. A cantor eats like a horse, but not like a horse that lugs Hassids; and he drinks like a Hassid, but not like a Hassid that burns to death on alcohol.

This exchange was certainly no loss to me. A cantor for a horse isn't a bad exchange. A horse drinks water and eats, at best, hay and oats; a cantor drinks well and eats big fish and roasts at weddings and circumcisions. A horse neighs for nothing; a cantor won't even breathe until he's paid. When a horse sounds off in the street, it's awful, people dash in all directions; when a cantor sounds off at the top of his lungs, people are simply carried away. When a horse starts rolling, people shout: "Watch it! He'll get you with his hind legs!" When a cantor starts rolling, people smack their lips: "Ahhh! What a voice! A miracle!" When a horse drops, the owner beats him until he stands up again; when a cantor drops to his knees, the beadle is already there to help him up even though the cantor is perfectly capable of standing on his own two feet. Indeed, he makes sure that no one kicks him. When a horse gets stubborn, my dear burial man, you know very well what happens to him, you've already heard what they did to me when I got stubborn while hauling those Hassids. But you should have seen how overjoyed those people were when, in my cantorial life, I was passing through a little town, and I pretended I didn't want to sing at the Sabbath ceremony for so little money, but the supervisor whispered to me that I ought to stay, because, just between you, me, and the lamppost, it's no loss to a supervisor having a cantor lead the prayers; when he gathers in the money, he always skims off a bit for himself. How does the saying go? If you're counting money, you certainly don't add anything, especially if you're counting by yourself. Many a supervisor has built a house and married his children into fine families because of the cantors who sang in his synagogue. Well anyway, you should have seen the rejoicing when I balked at remaining for the Sabbath for thirty rubles! (If you have an instinct for business, my dear burial man, you'll understand that with prayers one may achieve part of one's wish!) Nevertheless, when a horse *canters*, at least he's getting somewhere; but when a cantor is *hoarse*, then he's stuck.

Still, throughout my cantorial lifetime, I never got hoarse (having already done my time as a horse), and I was famous for this throughout the world. I was cantor in a large town, but I could never stay at home, I traveled the length and breadth of the land in order to become famous everywhere. I would only come home for Passover, and even then not always, for I became cantor of a different town almost every other year—first in Kamienetz, then two years later in Mohiliv, next in Dubno, after that in Kishnev, then in Jassy—in short, at the ends of the earth.

In the beginning, I would perform with only two choirists. To my right stood a little boy, squeaking like a fife, and to my left stood a bass, bellowing like a cow. I would hold one hand or both under my chin, squeezing my thumb against my Adam's apple, and, with my two-man choir, I neatly executed a prayer to the melody of a polanaise that was making the rounds of all the taverns. At the proper point, my fife would start repeating over and over again: "Ta-ta-ri-ti-ti-ti-ti-ti!" Then I would join in: "Tu! Tu! To! Ti-li-li! Tlo-tlo! Tno-tno!" It would take me half an hour to soar down to the next word, and then I would twist off.

I was an expert in Turkish modes. How many people had heard Turks singing and swore they had never heard a Turk singing Turkish like me. And I would sing some prayers in an Italian style, so that merchants who traveled to Germany, Brody, Lvov would say that it was a miracle, I simply sang Italian like a true German!

My greatest triumph was the "Great Love" mode. I could whine so well with all my heart and soul: "Oh God, oh me, oh my!" All the women burst into tears. And that was all the renown a cantor needed. If the women bawled—then fame was his! For the eighteen blessings, I didn't hesitate for an instant. I crooned in a Turkish manner and then switched to a cheerful Russian tune. The bass boomed away like a drum, my fife squealed, and I launched into a falsetto like a bird.

The synagogue was bursting at the seams. When it was time to read the Torah, the crowd thinned out a bit. I rested for a spell. When the reading was done, a new commotion began, more services, and still more services, and a lively beggar's tune that pierced all listeners to the very quick. They devoured every word, blessings flew in from every side: "Oh, damn his soul, can he ever sing—it's a miracle!" Or: "Why, he draws your soul right out of your body!" Or: "Oh, make him stop! I just can't stand it anymore!"

Don't take it lightly. Such curses are the greatest compliments a cantor can hope for. I saw that the crowd was ready to take the synagogue apart, so I curtailed my singing in the additional Sabbath service. And that was what I did every Sabbath.

Later on, when I was doing very well, I had several singers, and I netted even more money from the public. In short, things weren't going at all badly. And women in particular thought the world of me. People murmured against me, but I didn't even spend two years in a town. They didn't think much of me. But I couldn't care less, I was already in another place. Now you can't hang a lock on a person's mouth, no one put a spell on me, and no evil eye brought me harm. Wherever I was cantor, the whole town prospered, there were so many circumcisions, girls were quickly married so that the circumcisions wouldn't take place too early, and circumcisions or weddings were no loss for me, I was extremely hard-working. Mine was no easy lot.

But there's no rose without a thorn. And being a cantor also has a thorn. When you grow old you lose your voice, and all you've got left is your throat. In synagogue, they hear the cantor less and less, and at weddings and circumcisions they can see his throat-craft very well. In synagogues, they say: "He already neighs like a horse." And at weddings and circumcisions, they say: "He still eats like a horse!"

My throat was my misfortune too. It ultimately caused my demise. I was no longer a cantor and I had stopped eating roasts, although I continued eating fish—as you shall presently see, my dear burial man. But I was very sorry about the meat.

One day, while attending nuptials in the mansion of the richest Jew in town, I ate so much that I came home with a terrible cramp. My wife wasn't particularly fond of me, she didn't much care for my "Great Love" rendition, and my overeating didn't fill her stomach, on the contrary, she was always famished. So she acted as if she didn't notice and pretended to be fast asleep. I groaned all night, but there was no response. The next morning, I sent for a healer. A day passed, and the healer said I needed a doctor. The doctor came, wrote a prescription, collected his fee, and left. On the way out, he whispered to the healer that there was nothing they could do, I had a misery—my bowels were all tangled up and he couldn't untangle them.

Well, to make a long story short—that very same day, I was given a decent Jewish burial.

A Fish

The Celestial Council didn't waste any time. It appeared as if my judgment was already signed, sealed—and delivered; for I scarcely managed to turn over in my grave when I realized I was in a river, I was a fish—dumb, voiceless.

I recollect that when I was a cantor the people who didn't like me said I sang like a catfish. But I didn't become a catfish, I came back to life as a pike, a water wolf. I devoured the smaller fish like dumplings, even my own kin, little pikes, I would wolf them down mercilessly.

One day, I swallowed a tiny worm. Suddenly I felt a sharp pang, a hook was caught in my gills, and it hurt terribly. The pain was so great that I plunged into the deep. But it did no good! I pushed down, and I was pulled back up. I peered around. Aha! Someone was dragging me out with a fishing rod! I was carried off somewhere. Lying on a kitchen block, where they were going to slice me apart for the Sabbath, I looked and recognized the home of my synagogue supervisor. The supervisor had bought me in honor of the Sabbath because he was having a guest: A new cantor had arrived!

I felt a jab in my heart. But that wasn't all. The cook came over to the block with a huge knife, I looked up and—oh my God! My wife! She was working for the supervisor, and now she was about to cut me in two.

And who was standing next to her and dillydallying with her? It was the new cantor! For you see, my wife was still a young woman when I died; it had been my sixth marriage, I had divorced my five previous spouses. Now just imagine how miserable I felt to watch what was happening. And when she thrust the knife into my belly, I let out a shriek. It shouldn't surprise you. A fish that was once a cantor might find his voice again in such dire misery. The cook was terror-stricken. She had never heard a fish's voice before. The poor fool didn't realize that the sounds she had heard from me as a cantor had also come from fish. How many fish had screamed from my belly? And if a fish can scream from a cantor's belly, then a cantor can certainly scream from a fish's belly. But try reasoning with a woman!

She merely said: "The fish has a gilgul! May I hear the Messiah's trumpet as clearly as my ears heard that pike scream: 'Help!'"

And the rabbi's verdict was the same as hers: A gilgul! The fish was to be interred like a Jewish corpse. I was put in a shroud, they asked my forgiveness, and then they buried me in the graveyard.

A Tax Collector

As soon as the fish had been decently buried, my soul was elevated again, and once more I was reincarnated as a human being, if you could call him human—a man who devours his own poor brethren the way a pike devours the little fish. I was now a tax collector, a Jew who leases the concession for collecting the tax on kosher meat, and he makes sure that poor Jews don't upset their stomachs and accustom themselves to eating flesh like carnivorous beasts. But he himself eats like a pig. He holds on to both the meat and the money!

It's great to be a tax collector, besides the fact that he eats his fill of the best meat and gets all the udders, all the sweetbreads—the best pieces that his heart desires. Furthermore, he is the most powerful man in town because everyone has to deal with him. The rabbis and ritual slaughterers are in his clutches—after all, their livelihood depends on him. The slaughterers go to synagogue every day—after all, a kosher slaughterer is a pious Jew and he has to visit the rabbi. And if the slaughterers belong to the tax collector, then all the synagogues, big and little, are also his. The butchers are his—after all their livelihood depends on him. The butchers are in all the taverns and in those houses where there are people whose favors you often need when you want to play a trick on someone. And if the butchers belong to the tax collector, then all the useful people belong to him. The rich men are his, since, though he may be a tax collector, nearly all the rich men, and especially the wealthiest, have a share in what he does. No one else in town can speak a word to him, ordinary burghers, artisans, and the like; with them, he can do anything he wants to.

As for the meat standards, he treats them like a joke. He slaughters carrion, carcasses, sells putrid, unclean meat, gives nothing but bones to the poor—and false weight to boot. And who is going to speak up for the poor? Thus, when the richest man in town is selling oxen, and some of the beasts already have three hooves in the grave and are about to stick in their fourth, they are quickly dispatched to the slaughterhouse and declared kosher. And poverty-stricken Jews snatch up the "meat" like hotcakes. For the rich, of course, there is a different meat.

The tax collector charges whatever he thinks right, he gives up just enough so that the poor can never complain of overeating— God forbid! Furthermore, they don't sell the poor any real meat. What are paupers going to do with flesh? They can gnaw on bones, can't they?

Now in every town there are people that get meat not just tax-free, but free period! I know, my dear burial man, that you're thinking of those who have a right to it, for instance teachers at Jewish public schools, who are tax-exempt and yet lower-class, living on their salaries and of use to the town—they educate the children. If you think they get meat tax-free, then you're sadly mistaken. First of all, you heard me say not just tax-free, but free period. And why should teachers get meat gratis? They don't even ask for it, all they request is their legal tax-exemption, and that's one thing to which the tax collector turns a deaf ear. What can they do to him? Who can they complain to? The rich men in town? The rich don't need the teachers. They don't send their children to public school. Wherever the teachers may turn, the tax collector will get there faster; and if a ruble will help, he can give one more readily.

So then who, you will ask, gets meat for free?

Well, thank the Lord, every town has its share of agents, tale bearers, and informers. You have to stuff their mouths with food. The town lives in constant dread that they might let a few cats out of the bag. And the number of cats isn't exactly tiny. So enjoy the free meat, my friends, and shush!

I was a tax collector in a large town. Raking in the taxes year after year, pursuing other businesses, mostly the kind where you put in very little and get back a great deal, being very stingy and never giving a beggar even a crust for free, paying my employees less than nothing, and reducing even that less-than-nothing on false pretenses—all this and similar things eventually made me an extremely wealthy man. And I lived in a grand style. I had a beautiful home with beautiful furnishings, a large collection of silverware, and all sorts of valuable silver articles, such as a menorah, a spice holder, a Book of Esther mounted in silver, a silver box for the citrons on Sukkoth, and similar precious objects. But none of these items cost me anything to speak of. Some of them came from paupers, rich men who had come down in the world, and who left them with me as collateral for a trifling loan. The interest had increased so greatly that the property wasn't worth redeeming. These men, impoverished and embarrassed, were too ashamed to lodge a complaint. And if anyone did happen to weep and wail, it was usually a widow with fatherless children. So the case was taken to the rabbinical court, and the verdict was generally in my favor. The rabbi twisted and turned, consulted one tome after another, chewed on his beard, twirled his sidelock—you could slice it any way you liked, I was rich, thank the Lord, the rabbi, bless his soul, adored me, and I had a special dispensation permitting me to charge interest (with all due safeguards). What could the rabbi say? The widow had a good cry, and the silver remained with me!

There was only one thing that cost me money. I treated the rebbe with kid gloves and I never bargained with him. Please don't think me a fool, my dear burial man. The money was well-spent. The rebbe was worth ten times what I paid him. You see, I was a tax collector for many years, and I held all sorts of other concessions as well, in both towns and villages—for a song. No one dared to bargain with me—the rebbe would have made mincemeat out of him. No Jew would have eaten that man's meat or drunk his brandy, and the man would have gone the way of all flesh! So you can see how valuable the rebbe was!

But, while the rebbe may have cost me a pretty kopek, I tried to make up for it as far as possible. I never gave alms to any Jew, even the greatest pauper, though he might have been starving to death. I bargained down any craftsman who worked for me, and he even sustained a loss. No one ever got a sip of anything in my home for nothing, and I took the bread right out of the mouths of my own wife and children. What could I do? You have to cover your overhead, after all. What do you think? Wasn't I right?

At this point, I, the burial man, said to the gilgul: "No, my dear gilgul, you weren't. And it seems to me that was why your transmigration continued. Your future lives were no beds of roses either. Why, according to what you've told me, you were a robber, a murderer, a ruthless barbarian, a blood-sucker! I can't understand what kind of a rebbe he was to hold you in such esteem. That was no rebbe, that was a Tartar!"

The gilgul put his hand across my mouth: "Shush! What are you saying!" he exclaimed. "If you knew who we were talking about you would beat your breast a hundred times for that word you've just uttered. My rebbe was—Rabbi Yokeniu—may his memory be blessed!"

"Rabbi Yokeniu!?" I cried out. "May his merits help me and all Israel! Why, he was a great saint! I don't understand how he could have held a gilgul like you in such high esteem!"

"What do you mean?" said the ghost. "Do you think he knew all there was to know? Who could have told him? His gabai was in cahoots with me. I was a very pious Jew, I went to the bath for my ablutions every day. I put on two sets of phylacteries, and on the Sabbath I wore a fur-lined cap and a satin gabardine. My sidelocks were curled over my ears, my throat was bare, I had slippers on my feet. So what could the rebbe have against me? And furthermore, you ought to know that the rebbe knew the value of money. One good turn deserves another! If the rebbe hadn't had such respect for me, I wouldn't have had such respect for him. What would he have lived on if not on people like me? The enlightened rich men and free-thinkers? They wouldn't have given him a plugged kopek! And the rebbe, bless him, needs a lot, you know. He has to have a carriage with fine decorations, and with braided manes on the horses, an expensive place to live and expensive furniture, silver and gold as well—he *is* a *tsaddik* after all, a noble, saintly soul! And not only he, but his children, his sons, his daughters, daughters-in-law, sons-in-law, grandchildren, long may they live, they all keep maids, servants, nurses. Imagine the yearly expense! He doesn't do business, he doesn't run a store or own any properties, factories, offices, enterprises—so where is he going to get money from? From the Hassids, those barefoot paupers? He needs them for business. Without Hassids you can't be a rebbe, but you can't make a living off them either. So you can understand that if the rebbe was dependent on me for his livelihood, how could he open his mouth?"

"You're right," I said. "It's true. There are no two ways about it. I'm no heretic, God forbid! If that's what Rabbi Yokeniu did, then it must be all right! But tell me how everything came out, how did it end?"

"End?" replied the ghost with a deep sigh. "If only it hadn't ended! I've never had such a good lifetime as when I was a tax collector. But what can you do? Nothing lasts forever!"

One day, a rumor started that the tax was being abolished, and kosher meat would be the same as nonkosher meat, no matter who slaughtered it. I was thunderstruck. Not only did I earn a fortune through the tax, but it also made me a big shot, the most important Jew in town, I was held in esteem by the rebbe, who got his share of the tax, and by all the people who got meat for free. Without the tax, I was lost! No more slaughterers with their big and little synagogues, no more butchers with their ale houses and other houses, where I got help in an emergency, when I had it for someone. No more a big shot, no more the most important Jew in town, no more esteem from the rebbe and all the other important men.... I was simply marooned! *Mine enemies shall be restored!* I felt as if people were already saying behind my back: "Just wait till the tax is abolished! We'll show him a thing or two—that scoundrel, that blood-sucker. He wants to be a big shot on our money? He wants to bury us and then charge us a funeral fee? Just wait till the tax is lifted, just wait till he's knocked off his pedestal, then we'll settle our accounts and find out where our money's gone."

These words kept echoing in my ears. Wherever I went, wherever I stood, wherever I sat, I kept thinking that people were talking about the tax, about me, about settling my hash. Well, to make a long story short, I fell ill. I called the doctor, he wrote a prescription, I took the medicine, but it didn't help at all. The doctor knew nothing about my sickness, I was suffering from a melancholy. I sent money to the rebbe for his blessing, he said I would recover (God willing), but that I should change my name anyway to fool the Angel of Death. So that's what we did, and the very same day that I got my new name, I died. I was promptly buried. I can't complain. I had a grand funeral, my children distributed money to the poor in front of my bier. They had every right to it. I had robbed enough from them and taken good care of it.

When I arrived in the Great Beyond, I found that I had died for nothing, the tax was never abolished! I was very sorry that I had been in such a hurry to die. But what good did it do! It was too late! You never come back from the dead!

A Dog

Because I had eaten the finest meat but given poor people the bones, because I had extorted taxes from those who were legally exempt, the Celestial Council decided that I should come back to life as a dog, who only gnaws on bones.

Goodbye tax collector! I was already a dog! A stray cur hanging around the meat market, hoping to grab a bone, ruthlessly beaten by everyone. My trials and tribulations as a dog are beyond description. Had I been reincarnated as a hunting hound, my life wouldn't have been so awful. I would certainly have had to work harder than a tax collector who eats gratis, I would have had to go hunting, chasing, tracking, running, dashing, tearing, biting, grabbing, fetching. But, on the other hand, I would have had my livelihood, I would have eaten regularly, and my master would have hung a tag on my neck so that I needn't fear the dogcatcher. And just think, if I had returned to earth as a lady's lapdog, I would really have been living in style! I wouldn't even have envied a tax collector! Not everyone can boast, as a lapdog can, that ladies spoil him, handle him with kid gloves and feed him bonbons instead of bones.

But as it happened, I was an ordinary mongrel, a homeless alley mutt. I never spent the night where I had spent the day. No one would give me a crust of bread, and I only had what I could rob and steal—just like a tax collector! But unlike him, I had no meat, nor did I enjoy the rebbe's esteem.

At first, things weren't too bad. For all my troubles, I did have a bit of bread. I belonged to a farmer, I guarded his house as well as his horses and cattle. In return, he gave me food—but what food! It shouldn't happen to my mortal enemies! The things they call food! But at least I didn't starve to death! The worst thing about it was that he kept me on a rope, I couldn't stand it! I was so angry, why couldn't I be free, and I hated my owner's guts because he didn't let me run around. I didn't realize it wasn't his fault. You can't let a dog run around free, especially a surly dog, the reincarnation of a tax collector. If such a dog weren't leashed or chained up, he would take huge bites out of every passer-by. But what dog doesn't feel he's in the right? All I could think of was running away from my master.

One day, a town dog came by our farm and we got to know one another. We asked each other what strangers like to ask:

"How are things in the country?"

"How are things in town?"

I poured out my heart to him and showed him how the rope had chafed my neck.

He replied: "I can't see why you bother to stay here in the country. Run away to the city, your life will be a thousand times better. For one thing, you'll have a meat market. All you have to do is stroll through it and you'll get a chunk of meat. You won't get a smidgen of meat on this farm here! And then, there are weddings, circumcisions, especially in rich houses. There's even a proverb now that if a dog goes to a rich man's wedding, he'll carry off a whole head. And that's how easy it is to get a piece of meat. There's only one thing wrong with town life, you have to watch out for the dogcatcher. As long as you keep out of his way, you'll be a lot better off than here in the country." That sounded really good, and so I made up my mind to turn my back on country living and run off to the city.

"Listen," I said to my guest, the town dog. "How do you watch out for that terrible dogcatcher? How can you recognize him among all those people."

"Recognizing him is no big thing!" said my town dog. "He's the man carrying the huge stick with the knob at the end! That's what he uses to kill our fellow dogs. The whole trick is to keep out of his hands. It takes a bit of skill to elude him. Once he's caught sight of you, it's hard to hide. A dog with a good fur coat is in the worst danger. Dogs wearing expensive furs have to be extra careful."

"Well, that's one problem I don't have," I said to my guest. "You can see for yourself, my coat isn't worth a scrap of hay. I've got long legs, I'm light and lean, which means I can run fast. As long as I can recognize the dogcatcher easily, I won't have to be scared of him."

Well, to make a long story short, I decided to say farewell to the country and seek my fortune in town. No sooner said than done! The next day, my friend the town dog and I arrived in the next town, not far from my farm. We went for a stroll in the meat market. Some meat had just spoiled. The doctor had gotten into an argument, and so he had declared the meat bad, and they had thrown it out for the dogs. We had a royal feast. And I thought we would have one every day. But the feast didn't turn out so well for me. As I was stuffing myself, who should I see but a man carrying a big stick with a fat knob at the end. The moment I laid eyes on him, I knew who he was. Head over heels—I was off! I ran a blue streak, and I didn't look around at my friend, the town dog, who was dashing after me with all his might, yelling at me at the top of his lungs. I didn't hear him and kept running. When I was convinced that the man with the stick wouldn't be able to get me, I stopped for a breather. My friend caught up with me and asked: "Why did you run off like that? Who was after you?"

"Who was after me?" I said. "Why, the dogcatcher!"

"What dogcatcher? You're crazy! For God's sake!"

"What do you mean!" I said. "That man carrying the big stick with the large knob!"

My friend cracked up. "You idiot, you! You're really nothing but a country dog! How could you take him for the dogcatcher? That man with the round belly? That man with the red jowls, in the satin gabardine? The one carrying that official-looking stick with the silver ball on top? That's our town moneybags, the tax collector! He's the one we owe our banquet to! If he hadn't had a fight with the doctor, we wouldn't have had our feast. What a moron! How can you make such a mistake!"

"How was I supposed to know?" I asked. "You were the one who told me that the dogcatcher has a stick with a big knob."

"That's true," said my friend. "I did tell you that, but I forgot to say that the dogcatcher carries his stick with the knob down, and

the knob isn't made of silver either. Next time, take a good look at
the stick and you won't make the same mistake twice."

After that, I became a bit more experienced, but I never got over
my terror. The moment I glimpsed a stick, my heart began hammering and I was off! In short, I got tired of living like that, wandering around homeless. I regretted having left the country, but it
was too late to return, I was afraid my master would hit me, or even
beat me to death. I decided I would try my best to find someone in
town to attach myself to. I started looking up into everyone's face,
no matter who it was, and tried to judge by the face whether the
person was decent and merciful. One day, I met a man whom I
liked. I began following him. I saw him look around at me in
silence, he didn't drive me away. I followed him all the way home.
He went indoors, I kept by the entrance. He stayed inside for a
long time. After a few hours, he came back out and saw me stationed in the same place. I noticed his great surprise. He had someone give me food. I heard him say: "I can see that this dog will be
loyal to me. Let him hang around, don't bother him."

From then on, I had a home of sorts. That is to say, an outside
home, they never allowed me into the house, for I wasn't a very attractive dog. I fully realized that everything depended on my loyalty. As long as I proved loyal, I would be fed; if not, I would be
driven away sooner or later.

But how does a dog show his loyalty? I would bark and howl all
night long, and if any passing stranger came too close, especially a
man who wasn't so well-dressed, and in the middle of the night at
that, I would simply pounce upon him.

I acquired a reputation as a vicious dog, so that people were nervous about using the street where my master lived. Whether or not
he liked it, I can't say. But they never bothered me, and they fed
me every day.

But one day—what an awful break! One day, who should come
but one of my owner's brothers! He lived in another town, and he
hadn't seen my master for a long time. Well, whether he was poor
or whether he wore such ugly clothes only for the trip, I mistook
him for a beggar going from house to house. To make matters
worse, it was nighttime. I leaped upon him and took a good bite of
flesh! The out-of-town brother fainted dead away. I jumped upon
his face and began mauling. The people inside the house saw it and
came running with sticks, they could barely tear me away from

him. It was only now that my master realized this was his brother. He was dumbstruck! I couldn't possibly reckon up the number of strokes I got, but even though they broke one of my legs and bashed my head, I still managed to stay alive. I thought to myself: Sooner or later, they'll have to stop beating me—you don't throw away a good job like this. But when I heard my master say: "Get the dogcatcher, kill him!" I got on my three whole legs, dragging the fourth behind me, and dashed off to wherever they carried me. After running and running, and whining in a lamentable voice, I just barely made it to a garbage heap. I lay there without food or drink for several days, nearly starving to death.

Suddenly, I heard some Hassids singing not too far away. I was well acquainted with their crooning from my own Hassidic lifetime, and as a tax collector I had also danced with them, and they often used to sing in my home. Since it was twilight now, I realized there must be a rebbe presiding at a Sabbath dinner. It was already getting dark, so I stole over. The Hassids were singing my old chant, but I could barely recognize it, they were murdering the tune. And the rebbe wasn't as ecstatic as my rebbe had been when I was crooning. Anyway, no one noticed me, I crouched down under the table near the rebbe's feet. He was an old friend. As a tax collector, I had given him enough money; he was the one who had changed my name when I had died. But if he had seen me lying under the table, he wouldn't have recognized me, for, whenever I went to him in my tax collector's lifetime, even though I had the heart of a dog, the rebbe couldn't see inside me, he had only looked at my face and my hands.

Well, I lay there, a dog under the table, sniffing and smelling for a piece of meat, or even a bone. Suddenly I caught a whiff of meat on the rebbe's plate, one of the leftovers that the Hassids hadn't managed to snatch. I realized what it was, and looked upon it as a miracle that the Hassids had left anything at all. But as things turned out, I was sadly mistaken. Hassids don't leave anything for anyone.

Anyway, I was pining away for it, since I hadn't had a crumb of food for days, I couldn't stand it any longer, I leaped upon the table and grabbed at the plate—a dry bone! But for a starving dog, a bone is a find! I seized it and jumped off the table. But do Hassids allow a dog to lick a bone? That very instant, they all pounced upon me with chairs, sticks, whatever they could lay their hands on.

What?! Permit a dog to run his tongue over the holy bone in the rebbe's leftovers? They absolutely wanted to bash it out of me, wrench it out of my jaws.

Some of them screamed: "Let him! Let him! He's a gilgul!"

Other said: "No! If the dog were a gilgul, he wouldn't have jumped on the rebbe's table! He would have lain at the rebbe's feet!"

Those blind fools hadn't seen me lying at his feet earlier until I had gotten a whiff of his bone. Anyhow, I wouldn't allow them anywhere near the bone. But since they were banging away at me from all sides, I decided to swallow the bone and get rid of them. Once they saw the bone was gone, they would stop hitting me. But when I tried to swallow it, it went topsy-turvy in my throat, and I choked.

I stretched out on the floor with bulging eyes, a lolling tongue, and glaring teeth, as if to say: "Rebbe, help."

But what good does it do to stick out your tongue if you don't have any money for the rebbe's blessing!

The rebbe didn't give me a second glance. I died again. And with no regrets for such an awful life. Naturally, I had had more troubles when dying as a tax collector. But my death on account of a holy bone did stand me in good stead. I had died in a holy way, and so my soul once again entered a human body. But since I had been a dog and barked at everyone, attacked everyone, bitten, and mauled, it was agreed that I come back to life as a critic! . . .

A Critic

"A critic?" I said to the ghost. "What's that? I've never heard of it!"

"A critic," said the gilgul, "is a kind of writer. The fact of the matter is, that there are really good and fair critics, just as there are true saints among the Hassids, honest cantors, and there may even be honest tax collectors in the world, but they are not reincarnations. A gilgul-Hassid, a gilgul-cantor, a gilgul-tax-collector, and a gilgul-critic take after the beings from which they have been reincarnated. The gilgul-cantor has something of the horse left in him; a gilgul-critic—something of the dog, he attacks, he barks, he bites, and everyone beats him, they strike him with pens, and sometimes even with swords."

"My dear gilgul," I said to the ghost. "You've got to make things perfectly clear to me, if you want me to write them down. Just what is a critic? What does he do? What's his occupation? Why does he attack and bite?"

"That's just it," replied the ghost. "He's a critic because he doesn't do anything, he doesn't have any occupation. Why does he attack people? Why does he bite? He himself doesn't know why. Since time began, people have been applying their brains, their minds to all sorts of wisdom and useful matters, which the world needs to become wiser and better. The things that the sages and scholars have thought, they have written down, so that others might know what they know and make use of their wisdom, their ideas, their experience. Now, the things that learned men have written for humanity's benefit are known as books. Some great sage hit upon a way of spreading books around the world with little effort to save the trouble of endless copying. This invention is known as *printing*. The mass printing of books has been of enormous benefit to the world, because anyone can obtain them for little money, can study them, and master all the good things.

"However, there's nothing on earth, no matter how good, that doesn't have some failing, just as there is no bad thing without some kind of virtue in it. And thus, book printing did have one defect. Earlier, when men wrote out every single book, it was taken for granted that they only copied manuscripts that were useful and necessary. Only a fool would waste his time and get writer's cramp, copying a lot of rubbish that isn't worth the parchment it's scribbled on. He needs it like a hole in the head! And so, the only books in circulation were good and useful books that everyone needed.

"But when printing was invented and book production cost no great effort, when ten thousand copies could be spirited out of one book, then, along with the spread of good and useful books, they also distributed a lot of useless and even stupid and harmful books, and the men who wrote them did good business, they had them printed and sold cheap. Ordinary people couldn't tell the difference between good books and bad, useful and destructive ones. They buy them and read them and are led astray by them, taught vice and superstition, and made to believe in every sort of trivia and nonsense. So what did God do? God doesn't let the world get corrupted. God runs the world in such a way that every generation has good, wise, and honest men who strive to write and to show which books are truly useful and worth studying so that people can get something solid and practical out of them, and which books are empty twaddle and a complete waste of time, especially those which are destructive, which lead people astray from the right path, and make them miserable, because the bad, foolish, and corrupt books turn their brains upside down, so that they begin thinking that good is bad, and bad good, that truth is falsehood, and falsehood truth. Now, these good, wise, and honest men who aspire to open people's eyes, so that they can tell the good and useful books from the bad, foolish, and harmful ones—these men are known as *critics*. Naturally, they don't just talk off the top of their heads, they reason, they submit evidence, and they prove that what they say is true.

"Those are true critics, not gilguls. But what does a gilgul-critic do? The very opposite. He only attacks the good and useful books, and exerts his bad faith to demonstrate falsely that they are no good, he makes fun of them, insults great and respectable men, whose books have rightly earned them a name. For example, such a gilgul-critic will insist that such-and-such a great man, who is generally regarded as highly intelligent and whose books are considered highly useful, is merely babbling stupidities and that his books are absolute garbage."

"But listen," I said to the ghost, "I don't understand. According to what you say, a critic ought to be able to learn how to pass judgment on books. So how can a Jew, who is able to learn, say such awful things?"

"It goes without saying," replied the ghost, "that a real critic ought to be able to learn. But not a gilgul-critic. He's a fool, a jackdaw in peacock's feathers. He picks up a smattering here, a smidgen there, as long as he can stick his nose in anywhere and put in his two kopeks. But in reality, he knows nothing. All he can do is bark, attack, maul, and that's it!

"So do you understand, my dear fellow, what a gilgul-critic is? That's the kind of critic I was. Can you imagine? A fine person indeed! I really gave it to those authors! I kept them in constant fear—that is to say, I thought I did until someone banged me over the head with a pole, I began to scream at the top of my lungs the way I had howled in my former existence when they bashed my head and broke my leg for biting my master's brother.

"If my earlier life hadn't been so awful, I can assure you, my dear friend, I wouldn't have had much pleasure from my life as a critic. Is it really such fun to criticize a book if you hardly know what it's about? To demonstrate to someone that he's a bad writer, that you can't see why he ever bothered, and you yourself can't even write half as well?—But a dog like me was delighted to be anything, as long as he was something.

"As soon as I became a critic, I began thinking about what class of authors I ought to attack. Should I provoke scholars? I would have to study, I would have to be well-versed in the Talmud, the Bible, the Responsa, and a lot of tomes. No, that wasn't my cup of borscht. Should I concentrate on the Hassids? That would certainly have been a lot easier. All you have to do is catch the spirit of a few books by Hassidic rabbis and know how to blabber—mumbo jumbo, harum-scarum, abracadabra. Just twist your tongue. But the question is, first of all, how can you criticize a lot of double talk when the writer himself has a forked tongue and doesn't even know what he's after? And secondly: Would the Hassids even bother listening? Who would give my criticism a second glance?

"No. The best victims are the enlightened Jews. They started criticism in the first place, you know. After all, any real critic is an enlightened person. Real critics are decent, honest people, intelligent, educated, and only interested in the truth. And why did I bite and maim? Because I was reincarnated from a dog!

"Nevertheless, I knew that even among enlightened Jews there would be small-minded, flat-headed men who would latch on to me and regard me as a great critic, for in what class of people won't you find a few idiots with shrunken brains?! Meanwhile, I would gain influence and prestige as a critic.

"I began by writing for newspapers. At first, no one took notice of me. Here and there, I gave one person a scratch, a nibble. A little later, I started barking somewhat louder, took bigger bites at people, until they began feeling my fangs and noticing that a dog had joined the pack.

"But I really attracted attention when I published a little book in which I poured all my bile, running roughshod over famous writers and ridiculing the sacred Jewish books.

"Can you understand, my friend, how far I went? I took wide aim!"

At these words, I started up and yelled (I was so excited I even stopped being afraid of the gilgul): "What?! So that book was your work? I burnt it with my own two hands! And you were the author?! Let me tell you frankly. That was nothing worth getting reincarnated for. You could have written that as a dog."

"Come on!" exclaimed the ghost. "I *had* to be reincarnated. What else could I do? Should I have remained a dog for all time?"

"Well, if you stopped being a dog, then I think you should have stopped barking, don't you think?"

"Now, really, my dear fellow," said the ghost. "Have you ever seen a dog turn into a diamond? Things have to go gradually, not by leaps and bounds. That's the trouble, you human beings go around with blind eyes; you think you can see, but in the end you're as blind as bats. Do you really believe that I was the only one in the world? Just listen and you'll see how many people are barking. You can tell who they are by their voices. You won't be so astonished at me and you'll stop asking all those questions. On the contrary, let me ask you. What should I have done as a critic? What else should I have written? I just had to look for flaws and give authors my views."

"You should have been interested in truth!" I said. "You should have praised books that deserved praise. And when you came upon a book that didn't deserve praise, you should have pointed out its failings, but without getting nasty about it!"

"Oh my!" said the gilgul. "It's easy for you to talk. You've never been reincarnated! Of course you're right! Of course I've come to my senses! But at the time, in that existence, I was a very defective person. That was why I had to be reincarnated again, and you'll hear all about it if you'll stop interrupting and let me talk."

I promised the ghost that I would keep quiet, and he continued.

When I put out my book, where I wrote all those delightful things which I just told you about, there was a great commotion among the enlightened Jews—scholars and Hassids didn't want to have anything to do with me, and if any of them happened to know me, he thought I was lower than a dog, and ignored my book. However, the enlightened Jews and the true scholars were scandalized that I counted myself as one of them, and they gradually began attacking me in the newspapers, sometimes more, sometimes less. But I got it on all sides. If I had sat peacefully for a while and waited it out, it wouldn't have hurt me at all; people aren't bad by nature. But I wasn't content with what I had written in that book, and so I wrote another piece, which infuriated people even more, because I took a poke at one person, a tweak at that one, a bite at another. I ruffled some sharp plumes, people who could write, and they whipped their pens at me in all the newspapers. I threatened to give a sound drubbing to anyone who provoked me. But who listened? I was the culprit after all, I was the one who provoked everyone else. I as fully aware of this, and I didn't give a damn. Meanwhile, I was getting it on all sides, and it was so bad that even I didn't have the strength to endure it. In short, things were so awful that I got sick, I suffered briefly, and I died.

"Bury the dead!" people say. But I was buried before I ever died. "Bury the living!" would have been more accurate.

When a man like me dies, there's a great uproar. Pens are wielded, one man writes a venomous tag, another delivers an epitaph which is more like an epigram. The newspapers ran obituaries and proposed texts for my headstone, and whoever read them just had to laugh. I can recite all of them from memory, they're still fixed in my mind. The Angel of the Dead, out of spite, presented them to me in my grave. But most of the jokes and witticisms were pointed at my renown and the renown of my book, and since I'm telling you the entire story, so that you can write it down and publish it, I'm well aware that all this happened over a century ago— and what man, today, has even heard of me? I've long since been forgotten. And my book—if you could call it that—was already forgotten in my lifetime. Who ever bothered to look at it?

Now, there was one epitaph that someone suggested for my gravestone, and I'll repeat it to you, because I was so surprised when the Angel of the Dead showed it to me. It was a kind of prophecy:

HIS BARK WAS WORSE THAN HIS BITE!

Upon seeing it, I broke into a cold sweat. I remembered what the Talmudic sages, whom I had had such a low opinion of, had once said: "A sage knows more than a prophet." One might almost think that the author of this epitaph must have known that I had been reincarnated from a dog.

The Angel of the Dead did the worst thing he could do. He let me go for a long spell without a new existence, and he would report to me every day, telling me what was happening, and showing me the newspapers and what they wrote about me, how they poked fun at me, made a laughingstock of me, and thanked the Lord to be rid of such a pest!

I was furious. I almost killed myself; there I was, lying in the earth, unable to reply! Once, when the Angel of the Dead saw that I couldn't stand it anymore, he said: "You see, you scoundrel, how angry you are that you're six feet under and can't get back at the people writing about you? Just remember, you're furious because you're a nobody, and everything they say about you is true. Just think how you must have incensed those truly great people whom you laughed at and made fun of after they died. Here is your judgment. The epitaphs won't bother you anymore, you've already been forgotten, and now you'll come back to life as—guess what!"

I was aghast. "Oh my God!" I screamed. "I repent my bad ways! I've done wrong! I was such an ass!"

"You guessed it!" said the Angel of the Dead. "You will now come back to life as a donkey, because, while human, you made an ass of yourself, you shot off your mouth, not knowing what you were talking about, and then you criticized and accused others. Yes indeed, you must be an ass. In your earlier life, you were a burden on everyone's back, no one could stand your insolence, and now you shall bend your back under heavy burdens. You once made everyone eat your prickly words, which burnt like nettles, and now you will only eat prickly thorns, nettles, and thistles. You never rested, you were always hitting out, striking everyone in turn, and now you shall be beaten from morning to nightfall, and you shall be the biggest fool among all animals, and everyone will laugh at you."

The Angel of the Dead finished, went away, and I instantly turned into a donkey.

A Donkey

I must tell you, my dear friend, that in this reincarnation, almost the only thing I really changed was my outer appearance. Otherwise, I was still the same conceited fool I had been as a critic, and I really thought I was the finest thing alive. I regarded myself as having the purest pedigree of all animals because Father Abraham had ridden on an ass when taking Isaac to be sacrificed. I actually boasted that that famous ass was my own grandsire, and that the famous she-ass who spoke Hebrew with Balaam and saw an angel was my granddam, and that the donkey who was a great saint, I mean the one belonging to Pinkhas, and who never ate hay or straw without first offering a tithe to the priests, was also a member of my dynasty. In other words, no one could hold a candle to my family tree.

Imagine how the animals laughed at me whenever a bunch of them got together, or even just two of them with me! They poked fun at my long ears and my braying. My worst misfortune was my great desire to sing hymns. I foolishly supposed that I knew Hebrew because it had come down to me from my granddam whom Balaam had ridden (may she intercede for us!).

Now, human beings assume that donkeys cannot speak, but that is a mistake. There are donkeys among us who know several languages. I personally distinguished myself in the Sacred Tongue as well as in donkey language, which donkeys also regard as a holy language. I composed a great number of hymns in that language and I went around among the animals, singing them in my donkey voice. By acting so foolish everywhere I went, I gained even more prominence as a fool. I thought the animals were all beaming at my braying, but in the end they were all laughing their heads off. Conceited as I was, I felt that I deserved the right to rule over all the other beasts. I simply couldn't understand why the lion was king and not I.

One day, I was walking through the woods, when I found a lion's skin. I was overjoyed! Now, I said, I'll really be king! Along with all my other virtues, I would put on the lion's skin, and who could then hold a candle to me? I pulled on the skin though it was too short and tight, and I stretched it on all sides so that it would cover me totally, but when all was said and done, my donkey head was still sticking out. I examined myself thoroughly and I saw that I looked like a lion, but all I could view was my body, for who can see his own head?

Next, I dashed into the forest to where the animals were holding an assembly. The king had died and they had to choose a new ruler. When the animals caught sight of my lion's skin in the distance, they all stood up and began walking toward me respectfully. When I saw this, my head began swelling even more, I was practically bursting with pride. Then I recalled my hymns, and I began singing. The animals heard my voice, and at first they said: "Look, our new king is a merry fellow. Long may he live! He's nobody's fool. Just listen to him making fun of the donkey, it's a perfect imitation."

It might have worked, they might have thought I was a lion mimicking a donkey. But when I came nearer and they saw my head, my famous ears, there was a general alarm and commotion, the animals were in a rage:

"What?! The donkey wants to make asses of us? A donkey in lion's skin? He wants to rule over us?"

They all pounced upon me, biting, mauling, and tearing me on all sides, until they ripped away the false skin. I can scarcely make you realize my shame, my disgrace, my humiliation. Have you ever seen a wealthy ignoramus who puts on airs because of his money and regards himself as intelligent and butts into everyone's affairs, and has the biggest say about everything? Have you seen what happens when his fortune fizzles out, when he goes bankrupt and becomes a pauper, a beggar? Do you know what he looks like? That was what I looked like when they tore the skin off my back. They were all screaming: "Look, look! He's a donkey! We thought he was a lion! Beat him! Beat him! Serves him right! He wanted to be big and rule over us!"

"I've told you a fable," said the gilgul, "about a rich human being. Don't hold it against me! You know that human beings tell fables about animals. Well, animals tell fables about human beings. For instance, when people want to say that somebody is very vicious, they say he's as vicious as a dog. But animals say that another animal is as vicious as a teacher, or a rabbi's wife. When people talk about falseness, they say that someone is as false as a cat. But animals say: As false as a young wife with an old husband, or as two friends hugging and kissing. Humans beings say: As proud as a peacock. But animals say: As proud as a man who's made a fortune. People tell the story of a fox who tricked a raven into giving him a piece of meat. But animals tell a story about a man who cheated another man out of a goodly number of rubles and his wife in the bargain.

"And since in between my human reincarnations I came back to earth as animals, I'm familiar with their speech, and I told you a fable about a human being. But that's neither here nor there. Let me continue my story.

"When the animals were laughing their heads off at my head, and I was smarting from the cudgeling I had gotten, I fell ill from my embarrassment and pain. Nevertheless, I might have survived. But my owner saw that I was sick, I had a game leg. So he sold me to an undertaker. As my bad luck would have it, a cholera epidemic was raging at the time, and there were a lot of corpses in town. It made life miserable for me, until I couldn't stand it anymore, and I died.

"Since I died while doing good deeds and thus had a sacrosanct demise, the Celestial Council resolved that I should once again be reincarnated as a human being.

"A human being? Yes! A human being. But then they began reflecting as to what kind of human being a donkey could become. Well, they mulled and they mused, and they finally reached a unanimous verdict. A donkey that hauled corpses can only become one thing—a quack, a mountebank, a doctor. The Angel of the Dead seized my ears, gave me a good shake, and said: 'Go!' "

"How can the Angel of the Dead," I, the burial man, asked, "get to an animal, a donkey?"

"Come on," said the gilgul. "You're so innocent! The Angel of the Dead shakes all donkeys by their ears. You can take my word for it. I'm better informed than you are. Now, keep quiet and listen!"

A Doctor

I held my tongue, and the gilgul continued his story.

There are all kinds of doctors in the world. And like the physicians in any nation, there are good Jewish doctors and bad ones. It's obvious why. Not every man who becomes a doctor was destined by nature. Man proposes, and God disposes of him: "Plan what you like, but you'll do what *I* like." For instance, God creates one man to be a cooper, but he decides to become a cantor. And doesn't everyone who hears him say: "He really ought to be cooper." Another man becomes a watchmaker, whereas God meant him to be a blacksmith, and doesn't everyone say he ought to be a blacksmith? And what does God do when the man he destined to be.a coachman actually becomes a physician? The whole world knows that he's really a drayman even though he styles himself a doctor. And that's a true transmigration—from cooper to cantor, from blacksmith to watchmaker, from drayman to doctor, and so on. And that was the kind of transmigration that happened to me.

I was an oaf beyond your wildest dreams, a Jewish ignoramus. But I *was* cunning, and my doctoring was nothing but slyness. Gilgul-doctors of the world! Come one, come all! Learn how to be a gilgul-doctor!

All the world knows that a doctor enjoys greater freedom than any other Jew. He can certainly be a Jew at heart, but not always in deed. He may have to travel or write a prescription on the Sabbath. After all: "The saving of a life annuls the Sabbath." (Or, as I used to say as a doctor: "Annulling a life saves the Sabbath!") And since a doctor's first duty is toward his own life, he can do anything he likes on the Sabbath.

A doctor doesn't care much for praying either, and for similar ceremonies, which are hard for him to observe punctiliously. But I behaved otherwise. On the Sabbath, I would walk two or three miles to visit a patient, and if a Jewish doctor goes by foot to a remote patient, Jews won't summon him unless it's absolute necessary and there is no closer doctor. So, more likely than not, the sick man died or became dangerously worse by the time I arrived. But why should I care? All the Jews knew that I never traveled on the Sabbath, except on foot. I did charge for the visit, I put the money in my pocket, and no one was the wiser. Everyone saw me walking, for I deliberately went by way of the marketplace and pretended to be tired, and everyone I met asked me: "Have you walked far, Doctor? You look so tired."

"Oh, my friend!" I replied. "It's hard being a doctor, especially if you want to remain a Jew! I'm just coming from a patient who lives three miles away from here. What can you do! I'm not interested in the money; after all, I don't charge on the Sabbath. But how can I let a sick man down? And now I have to go to the apothecary myself, I can't very well write on the Sabbath the way other doctors do."

If ever I happened to be in a patient's home at twilight, I would pull out my handkerchief, tie it around me, and say evening prayers, although I didn't know them by heart—or for that matter: *at* heart, for I had scarcely ever prayed in my life, it was all an act! Anyone present would point at me: "Just look at the doctor pray. A Jewish soul is priceless! May he live to a ripe old age! Now that's what I call a doctor!"

For certain cases, say, a woman having a difficult labor, a man in the throes of cholera, a sick child, smallpox, measles, and the like, I wasn't ashamed to advise going to the rebbe for his blessing. I thus enjoyed the rebbe's esteem, and he would send me all the patients. You scratch my back and I'll scratch yours! Or, as the Russians say: Share and share alike!

As for my piety, there's a great deal I needn't tell you; you can guess it on your own! I never ate anything questionable, because no questions were asked in my home. There were several rabbinical assistants in town, charged with settling questions of ritual cleanliness. And each assistant thought that since no questions ever came from the doctor's house, I must be submitting them to some other assistant. But nevertheless, I felt I had to do something to make my neighbors know how kosher my household was. I lived on the third floor facing the street; from time to time I threw a plate out the window, and it smashed with a loud bang. The neighbors would usually ask what had dropped from the doctor's window? A plate had become ritually unclean, no doubt, so he had broken it. If a plate could become unclean in the doctor's home, then he must be a very observant Jew! Such things gained me prestige throughout the town and netted me a lot of money. I wrote expensive prescriptions and got a cut from the apothecary. In short, I became very wealthy very soon!

I'm sure you can guess that I wasn't such a pious soul at home as out in the world. Now, my home appeared to be kosher, I had a Jewish cook, and she always prepared a Sabbath pudding because the healers would visit me on the Sabbath. But while they were eating the pudding, I sat in my cabinet, and my Christian servant brought me my favorite dish from a restaurant—a portion of crabs. The healers thought the world of me because I still treated patients with leeches and cupping-glasses. And I owed the healers almost my entire practice. As is customary when a Jew gets sick, they would first call the healer, but the healer, upon coming to the patient, would have a look and then shake his head:

"This is a perfectum," (he meant effectum) "you see, an inflammation of the nervous fluid under the bowels. You've got to call the Jewish doctor. I certainly know what I'm doing, but what good is it if I have a pen in my hand and can't write—a bull has a long tongue but it can't blow a ram's horn. The Jewish doctor doesn't charge very much—just half a rubble."

They would send for me, I would examine the patient from all sides, clap his chest, auscultate him with my right ear, write a prescription, and order sixty leeches, with leeches costing thirty kopeks each. I didn't know what became of the patient until they came for a death certificate. And I split my fee with the healer.

Nothing in the world is so bad that it doesn't have something good. Thus, at first, my hypocrisy had some benefit for others, though in the end I ruined even that. I wasn't destined to be of true benefit to anyone. People regarded me as a highly devout doctor, who never traveled or wrote on the Sabbath and said evening prayers with a handkerchief tied around him, and even Hassids would say of me: "He's a decent fellow." (A doctor can't aspire to the title "decent Jew" even when he bites the dust.) And so the young men in town started saying it wasn't so wrong and it was probably all right to read the scholarly books and study a little German, Russian, and other languages. Just look at the doctor: He studied, and he's still a good Jew, he prays, and he doesn't travel on the Sabbath, and if a plate becomes unclean, he throws it out (they always repeated this, because there weren't that many virtues of mine to praise). In other words, young men gradually began studying something solid, and some good might eventually have come of it—but then my bad moment came, and it all turned out differently. Just listen to my dreadful misfortune!

One Sabbath, the Hassidic rebbe in town, half of whose income came from the blessings he sold to patients I sent him (which netted me a good portion of my income)—one Sabbath, after prayers, this saint felt a desire to visit the doctor, the pious physician who never traveled on the Sabbath, who prayed with a handkerchief bound around him, "and who sent patients for the rebbe's blessing." The rebbe wanted to honor the doctor with his presence. I didn't know about it, he wanted to surprise me. Oh, if only he hadn't!

It was Sabbath, twelve noon, I was in my cabinet, sucking and slurping on my beloved crabs, the healers were in the dining room, eating pudding. All at once: A tragedy! The door flew open, and there stood the rebbe in white Sabbath garments, the fur hat with the white top on his head. He walked in and a bunch of Hassids crowded in after him:

"Good Shabbs, Doctor!"

"Good Shabbs to you—"

I was in serious trouble. A crab was in my mouth, and the rest were sprawling on my plate, I couldn't conceal them, I was caught dead to rights! I was so confused and panicky that I tried to swallow the crab in my mouth, and it stuck in my throat. I began choking. My eyes practically fell out of my head. There was a great uproar. Scads of people came dashing in to see that amazing sight—the pious doctor choking on a crab.

The rebbe promptly realized I wouldn't be sending him any more patients to bless. He saw that I was about to die, and that soon I wouldn't be saying any more evening prayers or eating any more crabs. So he quickly made up his mind and turned things around. He said he already knew I was a heretic, an irreligious man, and he had long since wanted to reveal my evil doings to other Jews, but it had been hard to catch me in the act, because Satan and his fellows—may God have mercy!—had put it into my head to send him, the rebbe, patients to bless, and that force had defended me from being detected in a sin and exposed to the world! But on that Sabbath, as he had been saying the eighteen blessings during prayers, heaven had shown him the verse in Psalms:

"The young lions roar after their prey and seek their meat from God."

Well, to make a long story short! I died and they buried me—not in great honor!

A clamor arose in town: See! That's what comes of studying science and languages! (My enemies should only know as much science and languages as I did!) You obviously can't be a Jew if you study anything but the sacred Jewish writings. No, no! Jews dare not peep into the profane books! Every father turned his home inside out to see whether his son had any such books. If he found any, he would rip them up and burn them! All the modern books were cleared out! That year, the rebbe penned a tome containing all sorts of earth-shattering wisdom. Every single Jew bought his book and began studying it zealously. I was soon forgotten, but in Elul, the last month of the Jewish year, when all Jews visit the cemetery, my grave was flooded with saliva, because everyone would spit on my resting place.

The moment I was put underground, the Angel of the Dead appeared to me. I was terrified that he might see the crab still sticking in my craw. He asked me: "What is your name, oh man of science?" Unable to reply, I was forced to point at my throat as if to say: I'm choking. I can't talk. He thrust his fist in my craw, pulled out the crab, and roared with laughter. I felt better, and I was now able to speak. I was so delighted and overjoyed that I was impudent enough to ask the Angel of the Dead why he was laughing.

"I'm laughing," he said, "because your Defending Angel wanted to save you, and that was the reason you died before your time. This is what happened. While you were eating crabs on the Sabbath, the Accusing Angel came to the Celestial Council in a great uproar. Our present Accusing Angel is a terrible fanatic. He began clamoring: 'For God's sake! Has anyone ever seen the like! A Jew eating crabs, and on the holy Sabbath to boot!'

"The Defending Angel, who is a lot more enlightened, began arguing: 'Why make such an issue out of it? What's all this uproar for? There are much greater sins, and no one mentions them! All the tables are covered with lawsuits for robbers, deceivers, hypocrites, who cheat the entire world with false piety, and similar sins. And we've got nothing better to do than try a doctor for eating crabs? Aren't there loads of people who aren't doctors and who aren't supposed to eat unclean things for their role in the world, and yet they do eat them and don't even pretend otherwise? So what do we want from this doctor? He likes crabs! A fine thing! He can choke on them for all I care!'

"The Defending Angel wanted to save you and was only thinking of your good. Unfortunately, those last few words were spoken at the wrong time. They passed into God's ear, and you immediately choked to death!"

When the Angel of the Dead had spoken, I thought to myself: "Well, it's too late. I'm dead. But I see they won't chop my head off for those crabs. The Defending Angel seems to be such a decent sort, I needn't be afraid."

The Angel of the Dead rested for a while, and then he asked me:

"Brother, were your dealings in the world honest?"

"Dealings?" I said. "I didn't deal in anything. I was a doctor."

"Indeed you were," said the Angel of the Dead. "But nevertheless you had dealings. You dealt with the apothecary and you wrote expensive prescriptions, and the apothecary paid you a monthly retainer. You dealt with the healers, you prescribed no end of leeches and you raked in a share of the money. You dealt with the rebbe, you sent patients for him to bless, and he sent patients to you for prescriptions. You dealt in evening prayers, in breaking plates, in traveling by foot on the Sabbath. And your dealings were dishonest, highly dishonest. That was even worse than eating crabs. It won't help the Defending Angel find anything in your favor. And choking to death is no great shakes. Look around the cemetery. A number of these corpses, big and little, young and old, just about died from your prescriptions. Some of them would have been very useful to the world. You were their Angel of Death, and in addition, you were a hypocrite, a wolf in sheep's clothing, an ass in a lion's skin. The verdict is as follows. After I've given you a good whipping, you will return to life as a leech, because you treated patients with leeches and drew their blood for nothing, just to enrich yourself and your healers."

Having pronounced judgment, he began thrashing me on all sides. When he had broken all my bones, he grabbed my feet and flung me into the river and that very same instant I turned into a leech.

A Leech

But it didn't last long. That very same day, my healer came to catch leeches, and I soon fell into his clutches. He threw me into a jar of water with other leeches and put it on a shelf.

I hadn't even been there a quarter of an hour when the healer was summoned to put leeches to the rebbe's hemorrhoids. In honor of the rebbe, the healer took the jar of fresh leeches, which he had only just caught, and went to his patient. I was still furious at the rebbe, it was his fault that the crab had stuck in my throat. And so I really dug into him and ardently sucked his blood until I fell off dead.

Since I had perished in sacrosanctity, from the rebbe's hemorrhoids, I was once again elevated and permitted to come back to life as a human being. But just guess what kind of a human being a leech becomes!

"Why, the leader of the Burial Society," I, the burial man, spoke up. "He's a blood-sucker if ever there was one!"

"No," said the gilgul, "you're not even warm."

"Well," said I, "then it must be a government tax collector, a messenger of the Jewish assembly, an army kidnapper, they prey on the living and on the dead, and are ruthless to everyone!"

"Guess again!"

"A schoolteacher, who skins the children alive. Yes. That's it. You became a teacher!"

"Nope!" said the gilgul. "They're all paupers! The only creature who can be reincarnated as one of them is a sinner who wasn't privileged to die in sacrosanctity and become elevated. I, however, who was privileged to suck blood from the rebbe's hemorrhoids, I returned to earth as a rich man, a usurer, who lends money on interest!"

A Moneylender

A money-lender is one of those necessary people without whom the world could not survive. People cannot possibly always have ready cash at hand, no one can get along without borrowing or lending. And there's nothing wrong if the moneylender takes interest, because the loan benefits the borrower. His money is no worse than the house he rents. No one would claim that another man should let him live in his house for free. Then why shouldn't he charge him for letting him have cash to do business with? It's perfectly fair to take interest. But how? In accordance with justice and nature, so that neither the borrower nor the lender should have any cause for complaint. There are a number of men who act in this way. They help someone out with a loan, and charge a small percentage, whatever one can normally earn on such an amount. Both parties are satisfied: The borrower is satisfied with the good turn, and the lender—with the small interest.

If I had been that kind of a lender, my wanderings would have been over, and the contractor whom you buried today would never have existed. A lot of oxen, turkeys, geese, ducks, and capons would have stayed alive, a lot of bottles of wine and porter would never have been uncorked, a lot of bribe-takers would have had no money to get drunk on and gamble away, and the scribe of the Celestial Council would have had a lot fewer sins to register.

But that's not the kind of moneylender I was. I behaved otherwise. Pity the poor man who came to me for a loan. Five or six per cent interest a month was practically a gift in my terms. And naturally, I never lent a kopek without a formal note. And to make doubly sure, I took collateral worth three times as much as the loan itself. And the note also had to be for a triple amount. And if my debtor didn't pay the entire sum by the exact date, right on the button, then I would have the collateral valued, and I would make sure that it was valued for a third of what I was owed. As for the rest of the loan, I would foreclose, confiscate my debtor's property, and have him put in prison until the entire amount, minus the collateral, was paid off. Yelling, weeping, pleading, cursing—nothing bothered me. I was never afraid to perjure myself, I had no respect for anyone. I demanded respect from others, but gave none myself—let them call me all the names they like!

I took my highest interest from Gentile landowners, not because I sympathized with Jews—perish the thought! Sympathy wasn't high on my priority list. It was only because a Jew borrowing money from a paragon like myself must be a pauper, a beggar, and just how much could I extort from him anyway? Once I foreclosed on his estate and squeezed the marrow from his bones, what more could I hope for?

But a Gentile landowner is a horse of a different color. He's got a village, a mill, a distillery, houses, farms. Now that was a bonanza! I could pluck him bare and feather my nest! I would lend money to a lordling with great pleasure, and I was in no hurry to get it back, on the contrary, I kept advancing him a few more rubles, as long as it was added to the IOU. Naturally, the note had to be made out for three times the amount. Later on, when he was so heavily immersed in debt that he couldn't possibly repay me, I would demand an enormous percentage and, to make doubly sure, I would make out a note for five times, and occasionally, if I could manage it, for ten times the amount of the loan. I would usually allow the debt to run for a spell without dunning him, particularly if the land-owner was an old man. But the moment he stopped breathing, there I was with my IOU and for every single ruble I took back ten, fifteen, twenty—as many as I could get away with. But if the old man was a diehard and wouldn't kick the bucket, and I got tired of waiting—well, I would have my revenge, I made his old age miserable. He had to watch with his own eyes as I auctioned off his village, he had to leave his manor in his old age, abandon his father's legacy, and wander off abroad. Served him right! He shouldn't have borrowed from me! Did he think I was working for the afterlife—you can't take it with you! If the interest had been decent, he would have been able to redeem the note, and there would have been no problem. The village had to be sold only because my account added up to ten or fifteen times as much as he owed me. But why should I care? It was no skin off my nose. Too bad for him! Why should he have the right to own a village? If I wasn't allowed to own a village, I could at least have money.

Let me tell you even better things! I got fed up with the bother of having to wait and wait for months or even years, with my little bit of cash in other people's hands. And so one day I made up my mind. When a man summoned me to borrow a thousand rubles, and he had an estate but not a ruble in cash, and he needed money to play cards, and because a beautiful actress happened to be in town—what do you do in such an emergency? He smothered me with affection: "My dear fellow, do give me some money!"

"I'll give you money all right, honored sir. But the note will be for five times the amount. You know my rule, sir."

"Fine! Here's my IOU. Give me the money!"

"Very good!" I took the note, read it, everything was in order. I reached into my pocket. "Oh dear! Excuse me, my lord. I've forgotten the money. I'll have to go home. I'll be right back." Without waiting for an answer, I left—with the note. Do you think I ever came back with the money? Not on your life! What was the use of his losing the money at cards or giving it to an actress? He was better off without it! A few months later, he gave me my money, the entire note plus interest.

Do you think that with all my robbing and cheating I had any pleasure from my money, that I permitted myself any joys, that I lived in high style? Well, I have to tell you that my nickname in town was "Hog," because I really lived like a plain, simple hog. I begrudged myself every crust of bread, I was scrawny and scraggy and emaciated. I only lived when I was counting my rubles.

I had a pious wife, she may have been a gilgul too, for she was as stingy as I, and she took high interest as well. She would recite psalms, but all that her psalter contained was: "Oh, Lord. Rubles! Rubles. And more rubles!" Her blessing for the Sabbath candles was: "Oh, Lord. Rubles. Rubles!" Her entreaty in synagogue was: "Oh, Lord. Rubles!" Her prayer day and night, weekdays and holidays, was: "Oh, Lord. Rubles." That was her Haggadah at Passover, her lamentation on the Day of Atonement, her weal and woe, her blessings and curses. "May God favor you with a lot of rubles!" was her good wish to anyone who did her a service. "May you never get a ruble in your life!" was her curse to anyone she had a fight with.

All in all, we hungered amid wealth and honor. For we did bask in honor. People would invite us to all their weddings—because they owed us money. And that was when we stuffed ourselves. If it hadn't been for weddings, we would have starved to death.

My wife, curse her soul, was the death of me. Loving money more than her own husband, she would give it to anyone who promised to pay a high percentage—no matter how bad the risk. What could we do with debtors who had nothing we could take from them? Imprison them? We would have to pay for their food. Good money after bad! In short, my wife was my misfortune. My money was beyond recall! The interest had devoured the principle. What could we do?

Realizing that things were going downhill and that my money was out the window, I traveled to the rebbe since I thought the world of Hassidic masters. My wife always consulted witches, sorceresses, and fortunetellers, but I didn't believe in them, I had more faith in the rebbe. He *was* a saint, after all. Well, I gave the rebbe some money for his blessing—not thousands of rubles, mind you, giving money was always a big problem for me, my hand was only capable of taking. But you do have to give the rebbe *something*, after all. The rebbe blessed me with the verse: "Thou shalt lend to many Gentiles though thou shalt lend to no one." But he translated it as *borrow* rather than *lend*.

Now, being somewhat versed in Jewish lore, I exclaimed: "Why, Rebbe, what are you saying. The Hebrew word means: *Lend*."

"You idiot!" snapped the rebbe. "What do you think you are? An expert in Hebrew? God forbid! The word means: *Borrow!* 'Thou shalt not borrow!' Go home, and don't worry!"

On the way home, his words buzzed in my ears, and I hit upon the plan of forging IOUs from wealthy lords. My brainstorm worked. I found an expert who knew his craft, he manufactured notes from lords who had died long since, and I went and dunned their children. The children, who didn't want to bring dishonor on their parents' names, paid through the nose.

At first, business was excellent. The young lords redeemed the notes I had forged in their deceased parents' names, and they didn't say a word. I was so confident that I even forged the name of a lord who was still alive, and I went to dun him. The aristocrat looked at me as if I were crazy. "When did I ever borrow money from you?"

"What do you mean when?" said I. "This is your receipt. You can read the date yourself. Isn't this your signature?"

The aristocrat lost his temper and began beating me. I fell on the floor. He kicked me, and beat me for such a long time that I was carried home in a sheet. After a week of agony, I died.

The Angel of the Dead didn't beat about the bush. "You acted like a hog," he said. "People called you a hog. And because of your sins, you shall come back to life as a hog!"

A Hog

It's not so bad being a hog. First of all, I had a fine livelihood, more than enough to eat, and it didn't cost me a cent. I had an excellent place to sleep and I wallowed in every mire. The only thing that really bothered me was that as a moneylender I had to work so hard, deal with people, profit from them, forge signatures, so that someone had broken every bone in my body—all that effort just to make money, and more money. Rubles! Rubles! My wife used to say that only a hog could do without money. What good did it all do? The money stayed with my wife, and I was a hog and remained a hog.

There was only one thing that preyed on my mind. I was worried and fearful that there would be no salvation for me now, I would have to remain a swine forever. When I was a horse, a fish, a donkey, a leech, even a dog, I always ended up with Jews, I could hear an occasional hymn or blessing, until my soul ascended and I was reincarnated as a human being, a Jew, an awful Jew, yet still and all a Jew! But now that I had become a swine, how dreadful was my life! What suffering! No Jew would lay eyes upon me! I could only associate with Gentiles, I was miserable, I never crossed a Jewish threshold—how was my soul to be elevated? I did everything I possibly could to get into a Jewish home, just to knock over a slop trough or carry off a piece of salted kosher meat. More than once I got beaten with a stick or a poker, and I put up with it unprotestingly just for the privilege of hearing a holy word from a Jew—but all my trouble was for nothing. The moment the Jew caught sight of my unkosher snout, he was thunderstruck. He stopped praying, he refused to go on.

"There's a pig in the house! Drive him out! I can't pray!"

In short, I wandered and wandered, unable to achieve an elevation for my soul, until I grew big and fat, whereupon I was slaughtered, singed, and chopped to pieces. My flesh and my fat were used for different things, and a good part of me was made into sausages, which turned out to be lucky for me, as you shall hear.

As soon as my sausages were brought to a Gentile tavern, a crazy Jew walked in and ordered a sausage. He doffed his hat, said grace very earnestly, and then ate with gusto.

Upon hearing this, I, the burial man, said to the gilgul:

"Why are you telling me a story about a mad Jew? Do you think I'm a simpleton? I know perfectly well that there are Jews who are fully sane and will eat a sausage in secret!"

"Yes," said the gilgul, "you're quite right. There are Jews who are perfectly sane and who will eat even several sausages. But when a sane Jew eats sausages he won't say grace, and my stroke of luck was the fact that he said grace. For as soon as he said it, I was elevated and reincarnated as a devout and decent Jew, a contractor, who goes to auctions, not to close a deal, but to take money from people, and that was why the swine came back to life in that form."

A Contractor

Reincarnated as a contractor, I began to lead a dreadful life again, but a different one this time. Imagine a man who slaves day and night, not for himself, not for his family, but to give bribes and pay for lodgings. I can't even say I really ate and drank. The wine flowed like water, but it tasted stale because I was always getting gloomy letters from my wife, saying she had no money for bread. I never had enough cash to send home because I had to dole it out to minor bribe-takers. And whatever was left went to landladies for food or tavern-keepers for drink. There was never anything to mail back.

I ran around from one provincial capital to the next, looking for auctions, for deals, for contracts to negotiate. My expenses were always higher than my earnings, I was always up to my ears in debt. If I had approached a deal cautiously, calculating how much it would cost me and how much I would get, and fixing the expenses accordingly, I would have always been able to make an honest living and support my wife and children. But I never bothered calculating. What should I calculate? Did I have any business? Did I think about what I accepted? I had contracting parties, and I needed their business. Naturally, I gave them a larger price than I took myself. How was I to pay? I had to hustle and bustle. Find a new deal! I had to shell out a fortune on my outer appearance, my toilet, my wardrobe: combs, brushes, pomades. I had to throw ruble after ruble for buggies, wagons, coaches. Cigars and cigarettes, pills and powders. I needed these things for my life. But I could never meet my deadlines. I could scarcely fulfill my contracts. The rat race was terrible!

Finally, I hit upon the idea of only pretending to bid at auctions so that someone would pay me hush money to withdraw. A fine business! No overhead. Only profit.

But how profitable was it? Rooming houses, card games, travel, and the like, consumed my income.

After wandering around as a contractor for so many years, I finally contracted the real thing: consumption.

So I went back to my wife and starved to death. At last, the community gave her alms—for my winding sheet.

"Well, my dear burial man, you know the rest yourself. After all, you buried me.

"I think I've paid my penance in full, and I won't be reincarnated anymore. My life as a contractor was so hideous that the Angel of the Dead didn't even punish me in my grave. You can see for yourself that before you even managed to have a drink, I had already escaped his clutches, and here I am! I've probably been forgiven everything, and soon I'll be in paradise. I'm dying to get there, because I was absolutely starving when I passed away, and in heaven, I'll be able to eat and drink.

"But maybe I'm wrong. Maybe it's just a trick. Maybe the Angel of the Dead just wants to pretend to let me go home so that he can grab me and make me come back to earth in a new incarnation. If this happens, than I can promise you, I'll appear to your grand-children years from now and bring them up to date on everything that's happened to me. For now, however, the story is ended. Go home and write down everything just as I've told it to you, so that all Jews can read it and perhaps draw a lesson from it. A Hassid who devises melodies for the rebbe might recognize himself. Or a cantor who turns a house of worship into a tavern. Or a tax collector who fleeces the poor. A critic, a physician, a moneylender, a contractor. Perhaps they'll realize they're on the wrong path, and turn over a new leaf. Thus, both you and me will have done a good deed, and both of us will profit—I in the next world, and you in this world. And there'll be fewer transmigrations and fewer gilguls on the earth. Amen."

The Fifth Day

Haninah and the Frog

A true story.

Once there lived a rich Jew in Palestine. He walked in the ways of God and he was good and pious. He was very learned and could foresee the future. He knew what was going to happen. So the king made him his prime minister.

The rich man had a son, and his name was Haninah. He was very learned and thoroughly versed in the Torah. When his father was old and about to die, he called in his son and told him his will: He was to sit day and night and study the holy Torah, and observe the religious commandments and do good deeds.

"Don't forget the poor," said his father, "for I and your mother will die on the same day."

He also told his son that the last of the seven days of mourning would be the eve of Passover, and that he therefore shouldn't grieve for long. When the seven days were over, he was to go out to the marketplace and buy the very first thing he saw, even if it cost a great deal of money. If he bought a living thing that had to be raised, he was to keep it and care for it, for something good would come of it. But he didn't tell his son what this would be.

When the father had thus spoken his will to his son, he and the mother passed away just as he had foretold. The son, Haninah, did everything his father had told him to do. When Passover Eve came and the seven days of mourning were over, he stood up and went to the market. There he met an old man hawking a beautiful silver vessel. Haninah asked him:

"Tell me, how much is that vessel?"

The old man replied: "It costs eighty ducats."

Haninah offered him sixty ducats.

The old man replied: "I can't give it to you for so little."

In the end, Haninah did buy it even though the price was exorbitant. After all, he was carrying out his father's last wishes.

On the first night of Passover, he put the vessel on his table. Upon opening it, he found a second vessel inside, and within it there was a frog, merrily dancing and springing about. Haninah gave the frog food and drink, and by the end of Passover week, the frog was so big that the vessel was too small for him. So Haninah made a small cabinet and put the frog inside. He didn't stint on food or drink for the frog, and soon the cabinet became too small for him. Haninah built a room for the frog so that he would feel comfortable. He fattened him up with the best and finest foods until he had spent all he possessed. He did this in order to carry out his father's dying wishes. At last, Haninah was so poor that he couldn't even take care of his wife.

One day, Haninah and his wife went into the frog's room and said to him:

"Dear friend, to our great sorrow we can no longer keep you for we have nothing left. Everything we possessed we have spent on you."

The frog opened his mouth and began to speak.

"Dear Haninah, don't grieve. Since you've been taking care of me and feeding me all this time, you can now ask something of me. Just tell me what your heart desires, and you shall get it."

Haninah said: "There is only one thing I desire. Teach me the entire Law."

The frog answered: "Fine, I promise I shall."

And that very moment, he taught him the entire Law and, in addition, all the seventy languages. And this is how he did it:

The frog took a piece of paper, wrote down several charms, and then told Haninah to swallow it. In this way, he promptly knew the entire Torah and the seventy languages. He could even understand the speech of the beasts and the birds.

Next, the frog turned to Haninah's wife and said:

"You treated me very well, and I still haven't rewarded you. I will give you your reward too. But now the time has come for me to say goodbye. And before I leave, I would like you to accompany me as far as the Forest of Trees, and there you will see what I want to give you."

And so they went to the woods with him and, upon arriving, the frog emitted a loud croak, calling together all the beasts in the forest. No sooner did his croaking resound through the woods than an endless number of beasts and birds started running from all sides. The frog ordered each of them to bring as many jewels and pearls as he could carry. In addition, they were to bring all kinds of herbs and roots to cure the ill. Meanwhile, he taught Haninah and his wife the virtues of each specific, and then ordered the animals to bring everything back to Haninah's house.

When the frog was about to leave, he said to the couple:

"May the Good Lord bless you and be good to you for all the work and trouble you had with me. After all, you didn't even ask who I am. But I will tell you the secret. I am the son of Adam, and he had me with Lilith during the hundred and thirty years that he was separated from Eve. The Lord God gave me the power to change shape at will."

And with these words, he bade them farewell and went on his way.

Haninah and his wife went home, and from then on they lived in wealth and honor. And he also found grace in the eyes of the king, like his father before him.

In those days. the nation of Israel was ruled by a wicked king who didn't have a wife. The elders of Israel came and asked him to take a woman to be his queen, for it wasn't proper for a king to be unmarried. In reality, they hoped that if he took a wife, he would mend his ways and become decent and pious.

The king told them to come back in a week and he would give them an answer.

Around this time, Haninah was teaching his pupils the Talmudic laws about birds and telling them many new and surprising things. Suddenly a raven flew up and spoke a prayer to God, begging Him to protect Haninah from the great troubles he was about to face. Haninah, who understood the speech of the birds, was surprised at what the raven said. Soon, another bird flew up, and, just like the first, it screamed loud and begged the Good Lord to take pity on

Haninah and save him from the awful troubles. We know, of course, that Haninah understood all this, for the frog had taught him the speech of the beasts and birds just as we have read above.

That very day, the elders of Israel had again come to the king, as he had bidden them, to hear his promised answer. While they were talking to the king, a huge bird flew up with a gold hair in his bill, and he dropped the hair on the king's shoulder. The king took the hair in his hand and saw that it was as long as he was tall. He thereupon said to the elders of Israel that he would take no other woman as his wife but the one whose hair this was. And he ordered them to go out and bring back without fail the woman whose hair this was. If they refused, then he would kill all Israel (God forbid!).

Upon hearing these words, the elders were greatly frightened and didn't know what to do. Among them, however, there were several men who hated Haninah with all their might because they envied him for being so highly respected by the king. And they hit upon a plan for getting even with him. They told the king:

"Your Majesty, in your entire kingdom there is no better man to carry out your will than Haninah, whose wisdom and learning are great. He will surely be capable of finding the whereabouts of the woman with the gold hair."

To tell the truth, their praise and sound advice were not meant for Haninah's good. On the contrary, they wanted to thwart him and bring about his downfall. For if he didn't find the queen, the king would despise him and his doom would be sealed.

When the king heard what his lords said, he sent for Haninah and ordered him to go through the world and look for the queen. Naturally, Haninah could not oppose the king's will for he was deathly afraid of his anger. He had no choice but to accept the mission. The king wanted to send someone with him on his journey, but Haninah refused, saying he would rather go alone.

And so, Haninah went home and said goodbye to his wife and children. He took twelve ducats and three loaves of bread for provisions, and then he started out. His students went along with him until outside the town, and there he told them to go back.

And thus he went off, alone, down roads and over fields, often in a deep snow, until he was so worn out that he dropped down beneath a tree to rest.

All at once, he heard a raven lamenting that she hadn't had a bite to eat for three days. Upon hearing this, Haninah went over and gave her a piece of bread just to keep her alive.

On the second day, Haninah heard a dog howling and lamenting in its doggish whine that it hadn't eaten for six days. Again, Haninah went over to the dog, and gave it a piece of his bread to keep it alive. By now, Haninah had no bread left for himself.

On the third day, when he came out of the woods, a hot sun was blazing, and Haninah came to a lovely green meadow where all kinds of delicious herbs were growing. He ate and refreshed himself.

Walking farther, he came to a huge river. He caught sight of some fishermen who were fishing in the water and who had caught a fish that was so big they couldn't pull it out. So he went over and helped them bring the fish ashore. It was a large, fine fish, and Haninah bought it from them for twelve ducats. Then he took the fish and threw it back into the water. The fish was overjoyed at being released from the hands of its captors.

Haninah walked on until he saw a town lying before him. He went into the town, where the queen with the golden hair was living. Haninah kept making inquiries until he found out where she was: When he came to her house, she happened to glance out the window and saw him standing in front. She promptly realized how wise and accomplished he was, and she told her advisers:

"There is a man standing downstairs who is very wise. Go and bring him up to me."

They did what she asked.

When Haninah stood before the queen, he spoke to her with great respect and reverence, as one should speak to a queen. He told her about his mission and informed her that if she didn't agree to marry the king, then there was a great danger that all the Jews would be killed—God forbid!

The queen replied:

"I have heard what you said and I am ready to go along with you and save the Jews from destruction. And since you are such a wise man, I would like to ask you two things. If you do them, then I will go with you, and if not, then I won't. That is my condition.

"My first wish is that you bring me two jugs of water: one jug of water from heaven and one jug of water from hell. When you've done that, then I'll tell you what else you have to do for me."

But to herself she thought that he would not succeed in carrying out this task, for it was simply impossible, as indeed it was.

When Haninah heard what she said, he became very sad. But the queen said to him:

"The hair certainly comes from me. And I know exactly how it happened. Once I was washing my hair in the garden. Suddenly a bird flew up and pulled out one of my hairs. Now go ahead and fulfill my request, and I will go along with you as you have asked."

What could the poor man do? He went back out through the door and prayed with a heavy heart to the Good Lord to take pity on him and help him obtain the water, so that he could save the Jews from the great peril. God alone knew that he had gone on this far journey full of danger and suffering. How could he return empty-handed? And as he poured out his sorrow to the Lord God, a raven came flying up. It was the same raven who hadn't eaten for three whole days until Haninah took pity and fed her his own bread. The raven called Haninah by his name and said to him:

"Dear Rabbi, don't you recognize me? I'm the bird you gave bread to in the forest. I heard your cries about the water, and I want to help you. Tie two jugs to my wings, and I'll fly off and bring you the water you have to have so that you can save the Jews from the evil decree."

When Haninah heard this, he was overjoyed. He tied a jug to each of the bird's wings, as the bird had asked. The bird flew off to hell and filled one jug with boiling water, but the terrible heat singed her feathers. However, she speedily flew to the river that flows out of heaven and plunged in. Her feathers were restored and she was cured. Then she filled the other jug with water from heaven and, in great joy, she flew back to Haninah to give him the two jugs of water.

Haninah went back to the queen in high spirits and brought her the two jugs of water. The queen said:

"Let me first make sure that the water is genuine and not false."

The queen took the jug of water from hell and splashed some on her hand—it burnt her badly. Quickly she took the water from heaven and rubbed it into her hand—and it cured her. In this way, she made sure that Haninah hadn't fooled her, and that the waters were genuine.

Now she turned to Haninah again and said:

"Now I will ask you to perform a second task for me. Once when I was sailing on the sea, a gold ring with a jewel in it fell off my hand and dropped into the sea. If you can find that ring for me, I'll go with you wherever you like."

But to herself, she thought that he would never be able to find it anyway. But again, the Good Lord in his great mercy did not abandon him and helped once more.

With a deep sorrow in his heart, Haninah walked out of the town, stopped by a river, and offered ardent prayers to the Lord God. All at once, along came the big fish that Haninah had bought from the fishermen. The fish said to him:

"My dear Rabbi, don't you recognize me? I'm the fish you once redeemed from the hands of the fishermen. Tell me what you desire and I'll do it for you."

Haninah said to him: "I have to have the ring that the queen once lost in the sea."

Quickly the fish sped away to Leviathan and told him the whole story, and how the man had once saved his life when the fisherman had caught him. Now the man was in great trouble and had come to him with a wish. The queen had lost a precious ring in the sea, and the man wanted to find it and return it to her. "And so, Your Majesty, my wish is that you help Rabbi Haninah."

Leviathan promptly called together all the fish of the Great Sea and told them to reveal, under pain of excommunication, who had swallowed the ring and to return it right away. Well, a fish appeared and coughed up the ring. The big fish then took the ring and brought it to Haninah, spewing it out on the shore.

Suddenly, up dashed a wild boar, pounced upon the ring, and swallowed it. Haninah again began to weep in great sorrow, and to cry out to God for His help. All at once, along came the dog he had given his bread to in the forest. The dog said to him:

"Dear Rabbi, don't you remember me?"

Haninah said: "No."

The dog went on: "I am the dog you fed your piece of bread to in the forest. I've come to help you in any way you need me."

Haninah said:

"You've really come in the nick of time. I lost a ring, and the wild boar swallowed it."

Without further ado, the dog took off after the wild boar, seized him, and tore him to bits. Haninah thus found the ring and took it back to the queen.

When the queen saw the ring again, she was deeply frightened, for she had never dreamt that he would bring it back to her. She said to him:

"I promised you that if you would perform my two tasks, I would come along with you. You have done your part, and so I shall keep my word and come back with you." And so, together with her advisers, she started out on the journey to the king of Israel.

When the king laid eyes upon the queen, he was deeply smitten. He sent Rabbi Haninah to invite one and all to the wedding. When the nobles of the king saw how well Haninah had succeeded in his mission and that he was still a favorite of the king's, they devised a way of getting rid of him. They were so envious that they lay in wait for him in a quiet street and murdered him.

When the queen heard what had happened, she was terror-stricken. Quickly, she hurried to the place where the corpse was lying and announced that he wasn't dead. She took the water of heaven and splashed it on him, and Haninah came back to life as never before.

The king and his nobles were amazed that the queen could have raised him from the dead. And the king said:

"I will marry the queen only on condition that she murder me and then raise me from the dead."

The queen said to him:

"My dear king, I beg you, don't do it, the danger is great. If I was able to bring someone back from the dead, it was only because he is saintly and God-fearing in every way."

But for all her reasoning and arguing, the king insisted on having his way, and he ordered one of his servants to kill him.

What did the queen do now? She took the water of hell and poured it upon him. And the king fell into ashes and dust.

The queen turned to the lords and said:

"Just look for yourselves, my dear nobles! If the king had been truly pious, he would have come back to life again. But as I see, he was evil in every way."

When the king's wise men saw how wise and pious Rabbi Haninah was, they held counsel among themselves and resolved, one and all, to make him king of Israel. Since his own wife had died in the meantime, they gave him the queen for a wife and he ruled over Israel for many years.

The moral of the story is that because he performed his tasks so well, he deserved to have the queen with the golden hair as his wife.

A Tale of a Menorah

A young man left his father's home and spent a long time traveling in other countries and visiting foreign nations.

After a while, he came back to his father and boasted that while abroad he had learned a great craft: How to make a highly artistic menorah.

And he told his father to gather all the men who practiced the craft of menorah-making, and he would show them his great ability.

The father did his son's bidding. He gathered all the men who practiced this craft so that they might see his son's ability and see what he had accomplished while living among foreign nations.

When they had all gathered together, the son took out a menorah that he had made.

It looked very ugly to all the people who were present.

His father went around and asked all of them to tell him what they thought.

They were obliged to tell him the truth, namely that it was very ugly.

But the son kept boasting: "Just look at my great craftsmanship."

So his father told him that the menorah was not considered attractive by anyone.

To which the son replied: "That's the proof of my craftsmanship. For I showed each man his own failings. This menorah contains the failing of each one of those craftsmen. You can see that this part is ugly in this man's menorah, whereas another part is very beautiful. But with another man, the exact opposite is true: The part that's so ugly in his friend's menorah looks marvelously beautiful in his eyes. But how is it really? That part is ugly. And the same holds for all of them. What one of them finds so beautiful, another finds ugly. And the other way around. My menorah consists only of failings so that everyone will see that they do not command perfection. Everyone has a failing, for whatever he considers beautiful is ugly in the eyes of others. In reality, however, I can make the menorah as it should be."

If a man knew all the failings and imperfections of a thing, he would know the very essence of that thing even though he had never laid eyes upon it.

No two people are alike.

All miseries were contained in Adam, His very name contains all miseries. All lights were included in the word *light*.

And thus, too, all things of creation, even the leaves of a tree, for one leaf is like the next leaf.

The Legend of the Madonna

1.

Poor women freeze and go barefoot. And the Dolorosa, who led a life of bitter suffering and in the end wailed over the cold, blue limbs of her cruelly murdered son, is now decorated with jewelry in all churches, long after her death: gold, pearls, and precious diamonds. The poor woman was a carpenter's wife, who never wore anything but coarse cloth throughout her life. And now her images are bedizened in the most expensive laces and in glittering brocades embroidered with pearls.

The poor and devout of the Christian nation tell one another endless legends about things that happened to those who were in great need and prayed to the Dolorosa, and whose prayers were wondrously heard and answered.

Nowadays, we never hear about miracles, even though the faithful wait for them and their faith has not diminished in the least. How often, how often does a miserable Christian mother lie at the Madonna's feet, begging and praying for salvation for her only child, who is lying ill on straw and planks, and the mother is so poor that she doesn't even have a drop of milk or a crumb of food to give to her poor darling.

"Maria," she cries, "men have forgotten us. Take pity and help us, help us! . . ."

And Maria Dolorosa feels the silk and brocades burn her, and the sparkling precious stones scorch and char like fire, and she, the poor and merciful mother, is doomed to silence and wordlessness . . . . A bitter fate. For the present age is not a time of miracles . . . .

But now I want to tell you a story about when miracles were natural and normal, and the story is even more amazing and meritous, because it happened to a Jewish woman. I found the story in an ancient manuscript, a dusty and moldy chronicle that was lying about, unnoticed, among the old books in our family home. In this chronicle, I came upon a detailed account in Hebrew of the events which I will now relate to you in simple Yiddish.

2.

Long, long ago, it happened that a poor Jewish woman named Haya-Dina, the widow of a judge, was about to marry off her beautiful daughter Miriam to a fine yeshivah student named Aaron, an orphan, whose father had been a dear friend of Haya-Dina's husband (may he rest in peace). But how can a Jewish mother fulfill the most sacred duty if she lacks the necessary money? The poor woman had made up her mind to go begging and experience the commiseration of her fellow Jews, who are glad to buy themselves the benevolence of contributing to a poor bride's dowry. The mother prayed to the Good Lord to help her when she went out begging hopefully . . . .

In those days, begging was not so shameful as today, for throughout that country, all the Jews had been through a grim ordeal. They had only recently come back from a cruel expulsion and bloody and murderous rebellions . . . .

As was to be expected, Haya-Dina, after a few weeks of wandering, still hadn't brought back the necessary amount. Disappointed, and with a heavy heart, she was making her way back along the road to her town: "Oh, God, God, what can I do?" she thought desperately. "The wedding is taking place this week. What can I settle upon my children? How can I help them lay a foundation for their new household?"

3.

As she was walking along, the sky darkened over with storm clouds, and suddenly a wild wind began driving masses of dust across the highway .... The swallows flew low, speeding back to their clay nests under the roofs of the village houses, deep in the valley, far from the highway .... Bright cracks of lightning split open the heavens, and then thunder began roaring, like a booming from hell. Thick, heavy hailstones began sprinkling down, a violent cloudburst was brewing ....

The tired widow felt her heart tighten within her. All around her, the fields stretched on and on; and along the highway, the tall, slender poplars rocking in the wind were too weak to protect her. There was no shelter anywhere, anywhere, except in the large, beautiful chapel, erected by the roadside as a memorial, in the place where the devoted and courageous pageboy had saved the prince's life in the last, victorious battle when the Christians drove the Turks from the fortified capital.

Terrified by the lightning, whipped and soaked by the rain, the widow had no choice, and with her last strength she ran over to the chapel and dropped upon a stone bench in the portico.

In her heart, she thought to herself: "Our good Father in heaven will forgive me for my sin. He himself is a witness that I couldn't do anything else. Where else could I have taken refuge, a cowed and beaten dove, trying to save my life in this bad, wild storm? And if I did do it, it was for the sake of my children."

And a heavy sigh tore out of her breast: "Oh, my Miriam, my darling Miriam!"

4.

As she sighed, the chapel door flew open, and out came a woman, wrapped in a dark blue shawl, a Jewish woman, extremely beautiful and radiant like a home on a holiday. She gazed so mildly, so kindly with her deep, black eyes .... Our old widow, cheerful now, and amazed, lifted her tired head and before greeting the woman, she wondered: "How did this rabbi's daughter get here? Or perhaps she's even a rabbi's wife?"

"Good afternoon!" replied the younger woman.

"At least I'm not alone!" the old woman thought cheerfully. "Another Jew is caught in the same situation. May God not punish either of us!"

"For goodness' sake, don't be afraid, it was a matter of saving our lives.... God will forgive a sin like this," the younger woman said with a smile.

And the older woman thought to herself:

"She must be a rabbi's wife, she can give such wonderful comfort." And her heart felt so light. She felt livelier and bolder, and casually asked:

"And what are you doing on the road all by yourself, Rebbetsin?"

The woman's eyes filled with shiny tears and she replied: "I? I'm looking for my son, he died in the last expulsion.... He was praying for his brothers, and they clapped him in chains, and I don't even know where he died.... And why did you sigh so hard?"

And the old woman poured out her suffering heart. The "rebbetsin" felt sorry for her and her daughter Miriam, and after deliberating for a while, she said:

"Your daughter's name is Miriam. What a nice coincidence, my name is Miriam too. I'm very rich, and I own lots of jewelry. I'm going to help you. Perhaps God will reward me and grant me the joy of finding my son alive." With these words, she took a rich gold necklace from her throat, added a precious string of pearls, and ducats—and gave all these things to the widow, who could scarcely believe her eyes and was weeping for joy.

"How did I come to deserve this from God, how?" she exclaimed with tears in her eyes.

Meanwhile, the storm was dying down. The clouds drifted away. The sun shone out, victorious and cheerful. The soft, wet earth was fragrant, and the drops of water glittered on the grass like diamonds.... The world was pure and beautiful, like the heart of the widow, who had received a great boon from heaven. The splendid rainbow that stretched across the sky from east to west was also a sign that fortune had made a covenant with the widow and her family.

And the rebbetsin called out: "Now, we have to say goodbye, Haya-Dina!"

They embraced, blessed one another, and kissed, and then they went their separate ways, each toward a different arm of the rainbow....

5.

Our old widow came home safe and sound. Her Miriam's happiness was indescribable. Good cheer entered the squalid, dark walls of the widow's home. First of all, she changed the ducats and bought the things they needed most. Now their poor table was blessed with a fine golden soup with dumplings, with tasty beans, white bread, carrot stew, a Sabbath cauldron, cookies, Sabbath fruits, and other good things, and those whom God blesses say grace over them . . . .

Miriam and her fiancé received new clothes. And they wore them for the first time in honor of the Sabbath. And when they went to synagogue on Friday evening, with Aaron leading the way, and the mother and the bride in back, the men and women in the Jewish district paused at their homes, amazed and wondering: "Where did the widow suddenly come into such wealth? The bride absolutely looks like an aristocrat, and just look at the groom! The son of a rich man, a rabbi! . . . What a miracle! What a miracle!"

And shaking their heads, they entered the old, large synagogue to welcome Queen Sabbath . . . .

6.

But it was not given to our happy family to enjoy their sudden wealth for long. On the contrary, they became the dismal messengers of a dreadful calamity that befell the sorely tried community.

In synagogue, the Jews were welcoming the Sabbath with their hymn, when the heavy forged-steel doors burst open and armed thugs trudged in under the command of an officer. There was a panic, a turmoil, until the excited crowd fell silent under the threats of the thugs, and by the time they discovered the reason for this sudden, insolent assault, the elders of the community, the rabbi, the judges—in other words, the entire Eastern Wall of the Synagogue, were all in chains . . . .

Next, the officer, with a halberdier, went up to the pulpit, unrolled a parchment with a large red princely seal flapping down from it, and in his loud, clumsy voice he boomed out the following words over the heads of the deathly frightened flock:

We, by the Grace of God, the Prince and Ruler of this pious land, have received the sorry tiding that criminal and Godless hands have robbed Our cherished chapel, which was built as a monument and gift for Mary, the Holy Mother of God, on the place where She saved Our life and helped Us to expel the infidel and heathen Turk. In the most blasphemous manner, thieves have dared to rob the Madonna. From Her throat, they have taken the precious string of pearls and the golden necklace that the Princess, with divine grace, My dear, pious wife forever, promised the Madonna for the miraculous saving of My life. In addition, ducats were also removed. However, since in Our opinion and in the most sacred judgment of our Church Synod, no Christian soul would be able to commit such an infernal deed, We suspect, and rightly so, the infidel and ungrateful Jews, eternal enemies of the Christian Church, who can be said to be guilty of all foul deeds, such as the accursed Blood Accusation, and, what is even worse, the theft and defilement of consecrated wafers. It is obvious that in this case, too, they have committed a crime. We therefore decree that the elders of the Jewish community be clapped in chains and thrown into prison, and if the jewels and money are not returned within three days, then the elders shall be decapitated. And their bodies shall be thrown away like dogs to be consumed by the birds of prey. The rest of the Jews shall be expelled from Our land for all time.

Issued in Our castle.

Prince N.

It would be hard to describe the pall that seized the Jewish community. A terrible weeping and wailing broke out, and all voices joined in. And the loudest lament, of course, came from the women's balcony.

Our widow was petrified. "All the signs fit," the thought sped through her mind. "The string of pearls, the gold necklace and the ducats, all the things the blessed rebbetsin gave me. The chapel is the one where we took shelter from the rain. There's something uncanny about the whole thing, something eerie is going on . . . . Perhaps Satan, may his name be blotted out! Or perhaps there's some other intention, perhaps God is once again testing the poor nation of Israel, who has suffered too little, and I may be the sad messenger. Oh God! And perhaps I've committed a terrible sin and

You merely want to punish me. But then, punish me alone, and not the poor innocents!"

A decision quickly formed in her mind. Her old, trembling hand pushed aside the curtain of the balcony window, through which the women could see down into the men's section, and with all her strength, outshouting the laments, she hollered:

"Hear, oh Israel! Listen, Jews! Do not be afraid! God is with you. I know where the precious objects are. Put your hearts at ease. I know . . . ."

It took a while for everyone to understand what she meant. They all raised their heads: Could God have sent us help so quickly, and the solution to the mystery? Will we able to observe the Holy Sabbath in peace?

The congregation could breathe easier now. The weeping stopped.

"The objects are here!" The crowd turned to the officer. "A woman knows where they are!"

"Get her over here!" he shouted.

Two soldiers ran up to the balcony, and after a while they brought her down. The officer ordered her up to the pulpit.

"The judge's widow! The judge's widow!" a murmur of incredulity and amazement passed through the crowd. They gaped and gawked. Then the synagogue become so hushed that they could hear the beating of the hundreds of excited and terrified hearts. Countless thoughts flew overhead.

"Just what do you know about the stolen treasure?" the officer asked sternly.

"I know those valuables weren't robbed. They are here. I have them," she sighed, pale and resolute.

The frightened astonishment of the Jews was boundless. Even the soldiers opened their grim, murderous faces and stared in surprise at the small, old Jewess.

"How did you get them?" the officer interrogated her in a truculent voice, and deep in his heart he was overjoyed at so easily distinguishing himself in front of his lord.

The widow began to tell what had happened to her, and she spoke to the Jews and to the officer in a soft, trembling voice, which was lucid and intelligible. And when she came to the end, and told about the beautiful and radiant rebbetsin in the dark blue shawl, and what she had said about her son, and how she had given

the widow the treasure and how they had fondly embraced one another—the officer and the soldiers burst into guffaws, and the officer
threatened:

"Just wait, you insolent infidel. We'll teach you to try and fool
loyal sons of the church. So you want to turn our Madonna into a
rabbi's wife, and tell us a pack of lies and make fools of us! Maybe
our Madonna will work some miracles for you, you old witch!"
And he guffawed again. And his men joined his mirth in a derisive
chorus.

The Jews didn't know what to think. They couldn't grasp the
wondrous confession for all its simplicity. And they couldn't accept
her tale, even though they knew her to be a righteous woman.
They couldn't believe it and they didn't dare believe it.

Neither the Jews nor the Christian soldiers.

"The story isn't so simple. We can find out more if we drag it
out of them," the officer thought. "I'm destined to become a captain
in a very short time, thanks to you, Mary."

And he ordered his men to take the widow, Miriam, the bridegroom, and the community elders, clap them in chains, and lead
them off to prison. Together with two soldiers, he went to search
the widow's home, which wasn't far from the synagogue.

He hurried, for on the one hand he was still skeptical, but on the
other hand he wanted to bring the precious objects back to the
prince as rapidly as possible.

7.

The synod deliberated all morning on the Sabbath, interrogating
the Jewish prisoners, and even though it applied all the methods of
the inquisition, it did not obtain the desired goal. Like the Jews, the
Christians were absolutely unable to believe the story about the
"rebbetsin" Miriam. Instead, they sensed a much greater and more
dangerous conspiracy, and when they saw they weren't getting
anywhere, despite all the juridical tactics and all the terrible
tortures and torments, such as scalding with hot irons, crushing
fingers, steaming in hot air, the synod finally decided with great enthusiasm to deal with the prisoners in a different manner, that is, to
pay tribute to the offended Madonna and have a lovely auto-da-fé,

a burnt offering, opposite the defiled chapel, to appease Maria for the defilement.

They agreed to have their fireworks on Sunday, with a ceremonious procession, crucifixes, flags, and icons, with the prince and his family and the synod leading the way to the chapel, and the princess would take the allegedly stolen jewelry and put it back on the Madonna with great pomp. They would say prayers, recite psalms, and finally get to the closing portion of the festivities, the living fireworks.

8.

But for the Jews, the Sabbath was one of grief. The women wept and wailed and said prayers, children held their frightened faces in their mothers' aprons and bawled. Men recited psalms in the synagogue and pleaded with the God of Israel to take pity on his congregation and work a miracle. They sat in synagogue all through the night, waking, praying, beseeching, and determined to fast on Sunday.

And Sunday morning, they heard the bells of all the churches and the celebrating voices of the priests and the pious singing of the Christians which grew heavier and heavier.

This meant that the procession had already left the town and was on the way to the chapel, out in the open fields.

The blood of the Jews froze in their veins, and their hearts turned to ice.

9.

It had been a long time since the country last saw such a procession. The summer morning was beautiful, the air was filled with the fragrance of ripening fields and the singing of birds. It was no surprise that the whole town poured out through the walls, old and young, entire families. Beggars dragged themselves in the rear, and cripples hobbled along. Even the dogs wouldn't let themselves be driven away and they ran after their masters, merrily wagging their tails. The procession was led by a host of priests, followed by dignitaries and noblemen surrounding the prince, who, together with his consort and his children, was riding in a silver coach. Behind them, escorted by two large, tall mounted soldiers, the condemned Jews were packed into wagons. At the rear, behind the soldiers, in a long, wide row, trudged the mob with crosses and banners, the guilds with icons of their patron saints, women, men, children, all in holiday clothes, singing the pious hymns, which the priests kept intoning over and over again.

From time to time, they glanced at the wagons with the Jews, mimicking them and making nasty faces. But the condemned prisoners had other things on their minds.

Wrapped in prayer shawls, they sat on the narrow planks, their eyes raised to the heavens, despairing and confessing. In the first wagon, the widow was sitting with Miriam and Aaron. The young couple had never dreamt they would be taking leave of the world so early, in the dawn of their lives, which they had barely tasted, without fulfilling their human missions. The old woman was weeping softly, broken-hearted at the sight of the children sitting opposite her, mutely and stubbornly gazing at one another through their tears. They didn't dare touch one another or hold hands. Jews don't do that sort of thing in public . . . . And their hushed gazes brought them solace: "We'll be married in the other world, the better world." And Miriam's eyes said: "Since I'm dying for the greater glory of our God, I, too, shall be privileged to enter paradise, even though I'm a woman, and we'll be together, Aaron, forever."

And Aaron's eyes responded: "Yes, darling, yes!"

10 .

Trudging along for another hour or two, the procession finally reached the chapel. The priests and dignitaries went inside. There wasn't enough room in the small building for everyone else. So the crowd gathered around in a large circle. They violently dragged the Jews inside to show the offenders to the Holy Madonna before they punished them.

The archbishop began to say prayers. All the Christians fell to their knees. The weak, sickly Jews, who refused to emulate them, were beaten with fists until they finally knelt.

After prayers, one of the dignitaries handed the princess the jewelry on a red velvet cushion, so that she might have the honor of adorning the Holy Madonna again.

Escorted by ladies-in-waiting, who carried the train of her dress, she walked over to the statue at the altar with rapid steps and was about to hang the string of pearls around Mary's neck. But then, all at once, to the amazement of the Jews and to the dread of the Christians, a miracle occurred: Mary raised her right hand and pushed away the terror-stricken princess. The stillness was broken by a sweet, tormented female voice, like the echo of distant flutes: "Christian, I do not need your jewelry. Return it to the woman to whom I gave it as a wedding present for her daughter, who is my namesake. Why did you refuse to believe this woman and why did you destroy the work of my mercy?"

It is impossible to describe the turmoil that broke out when the Jews got such an unexpected advocate who proved their innocence in such an unprecedented manner.

The Christians crossed themselves in terror and fell to their knees, not knowing how to shake off the wrath of the offended Madonna. First they dashed over to the innocent Jews, who were dismayed and frightened, and they took off their chains.

With tears in their eyes, the released Jews fell into one another's arms, crying: "God has worked a great miracle with us, may His Name be praised! Thank and praise the Lord God!"

The bride and groom could no longer control themselves. Joy, intoxicated joy, roared and stormed in their young hearts, and they hugged one another, long and hard. But soon, Miriam felt embarrassed, she extricated herself from Aaron's arms, and, weeping sweet tears, she ran to her mother, who was so astonished that she still hadn't recovered, and was gaping at the statue in the dark blue mantle, which now stood mute at the altar. Her paralyzed face was clouded with endless grief . . . .

"So this is my 'rebbetsin' Miriam. Was it she who took pity on me and my child?" she thought to herself, unable to grasp it.

11.

And the Jews, who had been cast down and humiliated, were raised. The prince, the princess, and the priests begged their forgiveness. The Jews joyously forgave them all. With great honor they were put on the same wagons, which had previously been carrying them to their deaths, and they were brought back to their lives and to their ecstatic families.

Sadly, the procession returned home. This time swiftly, because the sky was darkening. Nasty flashes of lightning crackled in the melancholy heavens, accompanied by louder and louder peals of thunder.

Finally, the rain began falling, and it continued until the soaked procession reached the town.

The people of that country spoke about the miracle for a long, long time.

12 .

And now let us go back to the ghetto, which was filled with joy and gladness. For three days and three nights, they danced in the synagogue, and intoxicated themselves on wine, mead, and other good beverages, and ate delicious foods at the wedding of Aaron and Miriam, which took place that Sunday evening amid great rejoicing. At the ceremony, the rabbi wept and the crowd wept— these were happy, mirthful tears.

But when she heard the prayer for the dead, the old mother was heart-stricken at the thought that her poor husband was not alive to join in the merrymaking.

The young couple received wedding presents galore. The most expensive were sent to them by the princess: the gold necklace, the string of pearls, the gold, the ducats, the things that the "rebbetsin" Miriam had given the widow, and more.

In addition, the bridegroom received an edict from the prince, written on parchment and sealed with the seal of the country and the prince's signature. This document made Aaron a Court Jew. He now frequented the castle and became a good spokesman for the Jews and a fine executor of the court's business dealings.

13 .

And now bright days came to the ghetto.

In the evening, when the Jews went to pray in the synagogue, and the air was atremble with Ava Marias and vesper tollings from the churches and the monasteries, the Jews no longer were as frightened as they once had been. And they thought to themselves: "Now the Christians are praying—to Mary." And it was easier for them to understand.

But they didn't keep this thought for long. On the contrary, they considered it evil and dispelled it with a pious and fervent Jewish prayer.

A Tale of Kings

1.

Once there was a king. A king like any king, with a crown on his head and a throne to sit on, and all the qualities and everything that pertains to a king.

One day the king fell ill. And this is what was wrong with him: He trembled for his crown and his throne, he no longer believed in his kingdom and his people, nor did he trust his lords and near-and-dear. Every night, he would dream of poisons and swords, plots and uprisings, revolts and upheavals. Always, every time he slept, he would see wild and terrifying visions, that made him go cold and go hot. He would wake up in the midst of them and never sleep a full night or full sleep.

All the doctors from his kingdom were summoned, and then all the doctors from other kingdoms, and they inspected and examined him, listened and looked, and each one prescribed a different remedy. The king followed each doctor's orders and listened to each physician's advice, and did everything they told him to do, he took every medicine, yet nothing changed, he obeyed and listened, but his illness remained.

Finally, the king despaired of the healers and the healing, and he stopped taking the medicines. Now he turned to conjurors and holy men, to the most pious and best-known in his generation and kingdom and in others as well, he invited all of them to his palace and opened his heart to all of them, begging them to intercede for his health. They promised to help, the conjurors and the holy men, and each in his language addressed his god and prayed for the king, and spoke all kinds of spells over him, familiar spells of their own, and also spells that they got from others—and they did their best to intercede, and spoke midnight prayers at midnight for him, and tried to help him in every way—but they couldn't help.

And so a stretch of time went by, and the king grew older, and was losing his strength. The hair on his head began to go gray, and the head itself was becoming weak. And thus the king turned very gloomy, very mournful and very sad, and heard no advice and took no comfort, and in his neglect and despair he no longer believed in his health or recovery—and thus, unbelieving and broken-hearted, he spent whole days and whole nights, grieving and brooding, alone with his worries and despondency.

But then once, it was evening, the king was sitting in his solitude, in his palace, in his room. Suddenly, at the gates of the palace, a poor beggar appeared, a homeless ragamuffin, dusty from long trampings and wanderings, with no shoes on his feet, and only a long staff in his hand. He banged at the gate and he told the watchman he wanted to see the king, he had to talk to the king.... When the watchman hesitated and looked the beggar over from top to toe and saw his poverty and homelessness and wondered whether to let him through, the beggar saw the watchman mulling, and looked at him and said to him:

"Watchman, don't look at me, and don't be bothered by my clothing. Just announce that a beggar wants to see the king, the beggar has something to say about the king's health...."

The watchman obeyed, he reported to the proper person, and one servant transmitted it to the next, and a lower one to a higher one, and then higher and higher, until it came to the highest one, and the highest conveyed it to the king, and the king commanded: "Bring him in!"

So they brought the beggar into the palace and he came into the royal chamber. There he found the king upon his throne, mournful, and dusky, and melancholy. He stopped at the entrance and bowed at the threshold, he silently knelt and paid respects, and then back on his feet, he spoke these words:

"Great king! I heard about you and your illness, and the way

you've been treated, and the treatment didn't help, and so I've come
to you with a remedy."

"And just what is your remedy?"

"A story, Sire, a very long one, and the ending is meant for *you*."

"I'm listening."

The king motioned to his side, to a chair, and told the beggar to
have a seat. The beggar obeyed and sat down respectfully, and
sitting silent for a while, he finally started the story and told it:

2.

In a certain country, under a certain king, in an enormous field,
right in the middle, there lived an old man, eighty years old; in a
shack that could barely stand with age, with crooked walls, and a
tiny roof that was full of holes. The shack lay low, close to the
earth, with a tiny window, and only one, and a tiny door that was
bent and bowed, leading in, right into the ruin. This was where the
old man lived, this was his home and his alone, and day and night
he talked to his walls, he never saw a living creature, ever, except
for them, and he never needed anyone, ever, except for them. And
time wore on, a good long time.

Then, one evening, when the old man was sitting at the threshold
of his ruin, looking at the remote and silently setting sun, he noticed that, from afar and opposite him, from the horizon and from
where the sun was drooping, a little person had appeared—appeared
and was walking toward him and his ruin. He waited and waited,
and looked and looked. And finally the person arrived, and silently,
and from the road, and to the seated old man, and to his face, he
presented himself . . . .

It was a youngster, very young, not yet ten, and all alone, and
poor and ragged, and forsaken, and no one to rely on in the world,
but young and with youthful confidence, and trustingly hopeful for
reliance.

"Old man, I've come to you," said the boy.

"What have you come for?"

"To serve you."

"I'm old and lonesome."

"I'm young and I'll remain with you."

"And what do they call you, boy?"

"They call me Bovve."

And his face lit up in a smile, and he looked devotedly and warmly at the old man, and his eyes were trustworthy and loyal, and showed that he was ready to serve him.

The old man was agreeable, and silent, and not answering and concurring, he looked at the child, gazed wordlessly, as if accepting his remaining and serving him.

The boy moved in with the old man that very evening, spending his days with him and his nights with him, and doing what had to be done in the hovel, and never leaving him at all, and around the shack and out in the field, never taking a step from his side, and always, wherever, accompanying him.

This was how they lived: The old man kept getting older, and the child stronger, and growing and growing he rose up to a height and a stature. The old man would weakly do his old-age work, and the child took everything upon himself and for both of them—for himself and for the old man. He did all the work around the house and outside the house, and prepared the meals and got food in the field, cooking whatever was needed, serving the dishes he fixed. The old man thanked God in heaven for not forsaking him in his old age, and prayed for himself and for the child, always thinking about what would become of the child in this life and the next; and whenever the child was free of his work, the old man would always call him over, sit with him, and, elderly and loyal, converse with him and his intimacy.

Then, on quiet country evenings, when the sun was setting at the edge of heaven, shining upon the field and the shack, the old man and the child would sit at the entrance, facing the sunset, in shine and stillness and radiance. The old man would muse in silence, elderly, and sinking his head, worrying and not sensing the child next to him. After musing on and on, the old man would finally notice the child, he would turn to him and look at him, and take his hand in his own, and rest his other hand, in a long stillness, on the boy's shoulder, rest it so long, so still, as though worried about the sun and the child . . . . sometimes, and from time to time.

And time was wearing on, the sun in the sky went up and went down from day to day, and the days went by, and the weeks and the months, and even whole years. The old man was broken now, and never left his bed anymore. The youngster had become a youth, and the youth moved about the shack by himself, doing everything, just about in charge, silently serving the old man, doing whatever the old man said, always devoted, fulfilling his smallest wishes, anticipating his needs and wants. Now the old man was feebly and barely alive, always in bed, and never stirring, spending whole days on one side only, never turning over on the other, constantly silent, constantly wordless, never sharing his old thoughts with the youth; he lay there, growing feebler from day to day, losing strength as time wore on.

And at last he came to his last days, and one day he felt his final day. With his last strength, he called the boy over and told him what was happening. He asked the boy to prepare him for death, to change the bed linen and change his clothes, to wash him well and properly. The boy heard these things and they bewildered him, but nevertheless he set about doing the old man's last will: He washed him well and changed his clothes, and changed the bed linen, and prepared him for his death; he did no other work that day, and only worked for the old man and his departure; he listened to him and his feeble words, and leaned over him and stood over his head and his lips; and whatever came from the old man's lips, the boy fulfilled and carried out. And thus, standing over his bed, and fulfilling all his wishes, he served the old man in every way, and never stopped serving him.

Stillness—and the old man was ready. Silence—and the old man was washed and dressed and lying there. His feet stretched out, his body straight and on its back, his head raised upon the pillow, and quilts and covers blanketing his little length and short lying. The old man lapsed into silence, and wordlessly gazed at the ceiling, which was lying low above his head and all lit up with the light of day; and the day was dawning and shining, glowing and lingering, and then glowing with a steady brightness. The glowing waned, and the day slowly wore down to evening and wore away from the shack and what was happening inside, and the light slowly faded. The day moved on and left the shack in quiet darkness, in a gloomy field, in a silent evening field.

Now the shack began to grieve, with the one tiny window, and the tiny door of the ruin, and the walls inside, and the small bed standing there, with the old man lying on it. The old man was all stretched out, lying there for his departure, gazing up at the ceiling and seeing nothing, and the boy was standing over him and gazing at his gazing. That moment, from the far end of the field, the sun, with a final beam, flickered through the window, into the shack, sending in its final glow, reflecting on the old man's face, and thus quietly reflecting, the sun took its leave forever from the day and from the field, from the shack, and from the life in the shack.

That moment, just before the end, the old man's eyes became clear, he shifted them from the ceiling and from his long gazing to the boy who was standing next to him, he looked at him and stared at him, and then, having stared his fill, he said:

"My child . . . . You've served me in your loyalty, you honored and you respected me, and you comforted and supported my old age. And I wish for you and desire for you: a life of loving, a youth of comfort, and you shall stand before kings, and comfort kings.

"And listen: The last hour of my living has come, and soon my last bit of strength and my last touch of life are being taken. I'll stay on this bed, and I'll lie here dead. Leave me in this room, and close the door behind you, and go away from here, and as soon as you leave here, the first event will happen and the first call of life will call to you . . . ."

And it came to pass! Soon the old man turned away from the youth and grew silent from speaking, he raised his eyes to the ceiling and stared aloft and never removed them again. He stared in stillness, until they started closing, he closed them and remained outside, he lay there in tranquility and, still and tranquil, gave his soul to God and his breath to the room . . . .

The boy stood at his bed for a while, lingering, waiting, gazing at the dead man, and convinced himself that he was dead. Then he walked away from him, saying farewell to the old man, and left the shack and stepped outside, closing the door behind him in silence, and then, after leaving the shack, he set out in the field, from where he once had come, from where he once had appeared to the old man.

3.

And behold: quiet after the sunset and after the boy had left the shack, the field lay empty and orderly. Only a dimness was left of the sun, and the shack itself—a dismal memory. The boy thought of the shack and then walked through the field, recalling the old man in his death and yielding, softly recollecting as he walked through the evening.

He gazed and gazed upon the ground, never looking at himself or his path, never looking around at all, and he didn't notice that far away, upon the horizon opposite him, a rider loomed into view, on a large mount, finely saddled and true to the rider. He loomed up, scanned around and across the field, and found it empty and after sunset. His eyes searched long and hard till at last they alit on the walking boy. He spurred his horse and charged toward the boy, and silently and unnoticed by him he drew nearer to him in the evening. As the rider came close, the boy lifted up his eyes from despair and mulling, and felt the rider and saw him astride, and the rider was coming closer and closer, and the two were coming toward one another. Then the horseman reined in his horse and pulled it back. It halted and didn't budge, and the boy and the rider stood face to face . . . .

"Good evening, boy."

"Good evening, rider."

"You're coming from the field and the old man?"

"Yes," replied Bovve.

"And the old man is dead and you're free of your service?"

"Free," said the boy in sadness.

"Get up on the horse and ride with me."

"Where to?"

"To the king."

"And what will I do there?"

"Give me your hand, and I'll tell you as we ride."

And the horseman reached out his hand to the boy who stood before and below him, the boy stretched out *his* hand to the horseman, and the rider took him, and lightly and nimbly lifted him onto the horse and the saddle.

And there, and as the rider reined his horse toward the horizon from which he had ridden, and as the horse obeyed and quietly turned, and obediently galloped to where he was bidden, the rider looked at the boy who was sitting on his saddle with him, and said:

"Don't be surprised, my boy, and don't be amazed that I knew about you and where you were. Our stargazer told me and showed me the way."

"And who am I?"

"A servant to the king."

"And why was I sent for?"

"Let me tell you. Our king has a little daughter, young, and lovely, and lively, and the same age as you. The king dotes upon her. And recently she turned to him and said: 'Daddy, darling, I want a friend, a boy the same age as I, I want him to be a brother to me, and make my heart feel glad.' For the king has no sons, our king has no boys, his daughter is his only child, his girl is the apple of his eye, and the king can never say no to her, and everything that her lips pronounce has to be done as soon as it's said.

"And the king gave his word, and discussed her wish with his ministers, he gathered together the Council of Peers and told them what his daughter desired, and that her desire would have to be done, but *how* and *who*, he didn't know and what did *they* think?

"They listened to what he said, the peers, and understood the king's request, and that some person had to be chosen, with virtues and qualities hard to find. They brooded and thought and racked their brains, and each man looked among his children and wanted to find the fortunate boy among his own. Each one quietly offered his own. The king listened to their proposals, and then respectfully turned them down, he offended no one, said nothing against their children, nothing against the boys that they proposed, but accepted none, and agreed to none, and then he turned to the stargazer, relying on him and his advice: The stargazer knows, the stargazer sees, so he banked on him and what he would say, and what he would offer.

"So the stargazer mulled and the stargazer mused, and then, turning to the peers, he said:

"'The matter, my lords, is rather grave, the situation, honored sirs, is exceptional, the princess is precious to us, and her wish is our command. Thus, you must know: We don't need just a friend for her, to pass the time, not just a playmate to act as a brother, but a friend, a real one, devoted and loyal, a brother by birth as it were. He has to help the princess in all her troubles, and all the time, and be prepared to risk his life for her at any time. Because . . . we will need his life, the princess will require his life, for crises, great ones, are lurking ahead of her. That's what I've seen in the stars, and the stars say: Do not seek the boy among the lords, nor among the royal next-of-kin, nor among his friends or his family, nor in our royal capital, nor in other cities, nor in any town or village of any country, but far away from any men, remote and distant from human settlement—there you shall find such a quality, there you shall find such a boy. And my lords, with all due respect to yourselves

and your children, you know me and you know my disinterested-
ness, and no one will suspect my motives, but the truth, as given
from heaven, is *my* truth, and tongue cannot deny it. Thus, I propose: Let the king give me three nights, I will prepare myself in
that time, and stay awake, and whatever the stars will say to me, I
shall transmit to the king and his servants.'

"And that's what happened. They gave the gazer two or three
nights, and he didn't sleep a wink all the while, he stayed awake on
his high tower outside the city, holding his head up toward the sky,
his eyes toward the stars, scanning and peering and seeking in the
heavenly heights, and at last, after the third night, he appeared again
in the royal palace, in the morning after the king's levee. He entered, and had himself announced, and they announced him to the
king, and he came before him, and bowed in respect, and softly, after bowing, he said:

" 'I saw, Your Majesty, I saw and was shown: In a field, far away,
in your land, there stands a shack, tiny and old, an abandoned ruin,
about to collapse . . . . And an old man lives in it, and a boy lives
with him, a servant, and the old man is about to pass away, and
the boy will remain alone, and go off into the world when the old
man leaves it, and you'll have to send someone out after him to
overtake him on his road . . . . And—the boy will go out because he
loves the old man, and he'll do the old man's final bidding, for the
old man told him to put himself in the hands of the first person he
meets on the way and follow him to wherever he summons.
I say to you, Your Majesty, command one of your devoted horsemen to saddle his horse immediately and ride out and ride to the
field, and this is the way . . .'

"The king promptly sent for me, and ordered me to prepare for
the journey immediately, so I saddled the horse and the king transmitted the stargazer's words and directions to me. I rode and rode,
and I left the capital and came to other cities, and I left those cities,
and avoided others, and ignored the towns and settlements, and
rode through the countryside, on and on, and farther and farther,
until I saw you leaving the shack and crossing the field. And that
was it . . . ."

And now the rider stopped his telling, and paused a while, riding
wordlessly, slowly, and holding the boy next to himself, gazing at
him, and then, after gazing briefly, he added:

"And now we'll ride and ride, a day and two, across our wide land, and then we'll arrive in the capital, and then I'll bring you to the king and his daughter. All right?"

"Yes," said the boy, boyishly, not musingly, not boastfully.

And thus it came to pass. The rider rode upon his horse, drawing nearer and nearer to the settlement, and the field was farther and farther back, and the shack was farther and farther away, and he rode quietly with the boy, and at last, after several days, he arrived one evening in the capital, on the king's street, at the king's palace.

Upon their arrival, they took the boy into the palace and presented him to the king. The ruler scanned him from head to foot, and he liked the boy. With his quiet standing and his holding himself well, with his appearance and his modesty, he was bidden by the king to approach, and the king stroked the boy's head and stared into his eyes, and then had him taken to a separate room to change his clothes and rest from his long riding.

He was led away and his clothes were changed, and he was dressed in the stateliest garments and given everything he needed, and prepared, and then when everything was done, he was left alone for the night, to spend the night in the room.

The next day, when the boy got up from his sleep, relaxed and rested from the previous day, refreshed and restored from riding, he was brought to the king, to the royal levee, and presented in his newness to the morning eyes of the king. The king cast his eyes upon him and received him with a cheerful face, blessed him with a "good morning" and inquired about his needs and wishes: Might he need anything, might he lack anything, he need merely ask, and the king would have his wishes fulfilled. The boy bowed from the waist, thanking the king for his concern and his bounty, but everything was fine, he had all that he needed, nothing was lacking, and may the king be exalted, and as soon as the boy needed anything, he would apply to the king . . . .

The king listened to the boy's words, and his face broke into a smile, the king was cheerful and happy, and then, before dismissing the boy, he had them summon his beloved daughter into the reception chamber before him. They brought her in, the daughter, in front of her father for the morning blessing. She, too, bowed and curtsied to the king, bending her young body and her knees to him, presenting herself lovingly and daughterly to his fatherly highness.

"Good morning, daughter."

"Good morning, father."

"And this is your friend."

And now the daughter took her eyes from her father on his throne and lifted them upon the boy, who was standing aside next to the royal throne, gazed at him in curious surprise.

"Yes, daughter, this is your friend, make friends with him and accept his love, and he'll be together with you, and stay with you in the palace."

The daughter blushed childishly, the daughter removed her eyes from the boy, and, lowering her head and youthfully blushing, she dropped her eyes to the ground, and she stood there before her father and his gazing . . . .

"And now, children, for you," the king addressed them both as "children."

"Get back to your rooms and your conversation and yourselves." And the king motioned, and commanded the servants, and the children went off to their chambers, led away from the reception.

4.

And so, from that morning on, the boy remained in the palace, with the king, to be with his daughter, together with her, and be reckoned as a child of the king, a friend of his child, a companion, devoted forever . . . .

The years elapsed. The boy was brought up in the palace and grew up with the princess, and he was liked by everyone, and more than anyone by the king's daughter. And without the boy, the girl would never take a step or play a game or enjoy a children's pastime, and they were always together, eating and drinking and playing and studying together. And time went on, and the two of them were of the same age and grew at the same pace, and were endowed with the same youth.

The princess flowered and bloomed in youth, and the boy did not remain behind, he kept up with her and flourished with her.

And after a time, they reached an age of youth, young and yet ripe, growing and awakening. And they awoke from their innocence and their ignorance, and saw one another in ripeness and the same age, and both of them seventeen . . . .

Others noticed as well: the king with his fatherly eye on the daughter, and the peers with a begrudging eye on the boy, the stranger. The lords discussed it among themselves, each one telling another one, and the king saw it too, but kept it to himself. Now he held close watch on the children, and sometimes his royal eye would alight on them and follow them and observe what they did: The way they came before him with lowered eyes; how close they were and one together, and yet, when standing before him, how remote and shamefaced with one another . . . .

He saw it and he pondered it, and after a spell of convincing himself and making sure and mulling it over, he summoned the stargazer, his beloved adviser, to give him advice.

And the stargazer came at the king's beck and call, and the king ordered the attendants to close the door behind him and admit no one else as long as he was there, and none of the footmen were to disturb the king: He had business of utmost importance and had to remain alone with the stargazer.

Now the king told the stargazer the things he had noticed about the children, and his lengthy watching and observing, his keeping an eye on them and a watch on them, and the things he had seen and the things he had noticed, and he told all these things at length and at breadth to the stargazer, and he called upon his advice and his wisdom and his common sense.

And the stargazer had to understand: The king was just one and the peers were many, and his daughter was the apple of his eye, and her love was his healing. But the peers and the courtiers would fight and oppose. For in truth: As all did know and as all could bear witness—it had never happened, it had never occurred, not in his family, and not with other kings, that a princess should get her beloved from the street and from the fields. And such was the case: The boy was poor, and had no father or mother, no pedigree and no lineage, and there were so many children around, courtly and close to the king—and what was he to do? . . .

The stargazer listened to what the king said, and he reflected, he understood the king and his predicament, sympathized and uttered his sympathy, and then he mulled the matter some more. And then, after having thought it out, he spoke to the waiting sovereign:

He told him not to fret or worry for now, the children were still young, and their hour of union was far away. It was better to wait, and time would bring counsel.

Again the gazer mulled and mused, standing in silence for a while, turning his thoughts around in his head, and then he added further advice:

The king must know, as it seemed and appeared to his friend, that the bridegroom was marked by the heavens and set by the stars, and no power and no impediment could ever prevent the children's love. But for the moment, let it wait.

The king thanked the stargazer for his advice, and said goodbye, and the stargazer returned to his home, and the king remained on his throne in his palace. He thought about the stargazer's advice, and agreed with it, and he felt relieved, and, quietly as hitherto, he let the children be.

And meanwhile time went along on its way, and the children became closer and closer, and they kept on growing, and the courtiers whispered about their growing, they clustered in private groups and talked about them, and about the boy and his role at court, and their envy of him increased, and some of the courtiers, the highest, no longer bothered to hide their envy. They hated him and looked down at him, and scorned his being here in the royal palace, for himself and as their equal. They bore a deep grudge and treated him poorly, and whenever they met him they would glare and scowl.

The boy perceived it, and the princess noticed and knew of their hatred, but both of them avoided it, and never talked about it together, nor even mentioned it, and they merely looked with silent eyes at the king, at him and his wisdom, at what he witnessed and overlooked. They waited—but the king never spoke to the lords, and the children never to the king, and time wore on, and things were slowly coming to a head, and all at court could feel it coming, but nobody said a word.

But then one day in the palace something happened:

5 .

The king set a day for his annual hunt and told the lords and the courtiers to perpare for that day. And they began to make themselves ready. The lords took out their coursing-clothes and told their servants to clean them up, and the courtiers whetted their spears and swords and took apart their guns and cleaned each part, and all were absorbed in their preparations, and throughout the royal palace, the readyings and arrangings were great, and the servants and footmen scurried about, and they labored like madmen in the stables. The horses and wagons were led from the stables, and carriages and harnesses were rigorously scoured, and the royal firearms removed from their cases and inspected and cleaned, and also for Bovve and for the daughter of the king, everything was prepared so that they might take part in the hunt. For ... this time the princess begged her father and pleaded with him to take her along, and not refuse her or leave her at home, she wanted to watch the coursing and everything that happened. The king did not say no. He agreed to her request, and told his servants to include his daughter and her playmate in his cortege, the two of them would ride with him, along with him at either side.

The day came closer, and the morning dawned, and all the lords and all the huntsmen gathered at the royal palace, and all were adorned in their hunting best, and all were equipped for the hunt, and the horses were harnessed, and the hounds by the steeds, all set to start, out in front, and some would start first and some start last.

Then the hunting horn blared out, and the king appeared as the first, on his mount, at his side his daughter, with her escort, riding on a lovely horse, and next came the lords arranged in a line, in the usual order of long tradition.

The trumpet pealed a second time, and then it blasted once again. The king rode out of the court and the palace, and next came his daughter with Bovve, and after them came all the lords. They galloped across the first street, and then the second, and then the third, and thus advancing from street to street, they rode through the city and into the fields. And onto the road, and into the forest where they were heading.

The king and his hunters came to the middle of the forest, and the horsemen reined in their steeds, and waited for the hunting master to give the signal for the hunt to begin.

They stood for a spell, and the morning hung over the woods, sunny and quiet, peaceful and radiant, and the woods and the trees stood perfectly still, and the horsemen among them sat still on their mounts. But then the hunting master gave the sign, the hunters dismounted and untied the hounds, and the hounds sprang off in all directions, and after them the huntsmen with rifles and guns, and they all wandered among the trees, each man following his tracker and his forerunner. The woods became hushed, and the riding host scattered and vanished, and only the rarest of rustles came back from the thickets, a hunter leaping or a dog prying, and no voice and no bark disrupted the peace, and the men got farther and farther apart, and the place where the riders had left their horses grew stiller and stiller, and only the servants who stayed with the horses stood and held their reins, and kept themselves and the horses still. And even the king, the hunter, escorted by Bovve and by the princess, moved off to a side, deep in the woods, like everyone else, in a silence of woods, like everyone else, intent on the hunt, deeply intent.

And then, when the king with his daughter and Bovve, had vanished deep inside the woods, and all around them, except for their tracking, no human could be sensed, nor a human sign, and not a dog and not a bark of other dogs, and only their own hounds and forerunners, from bush to bush, tore onward, seeking with long noses and sharp noses, and sniffed and pried and all in vain, and then dashed on, and, with the king and the king's children, reached the heart of the forest, and the woods grew denser, and overgrown with undergrowth, and interbranched and intertreed, and silent, and unusually silent, and undisturbed by any noise—when all at once, from a bush, an animal, a terrified beast, aroused from its rest, from its lair and its wooded life, streaked past the king and past his escorts, bumping past them and startled and not counting on being saved, it suddenly halted in front of them, not knowing where to turn, not having anywhere to flee—and all at once, with a cunning animal-leap, it sprang upon the princess's breast, and with its hurling leap and its bewilderment, it flung the princess upon the ground.

And they flung themselves and aimed their guns, the king and Bovve, at the beast, and fired, and shot the beast, and killed it, and then turned to the princess, who had been thrown to the ground, and they quietly bent over her, seeking the place where the beast had wounded her.

But then it turned out that the king's daughter hadn't been touched and hadn't been hurt, and had no wound nor injury, but she lay there, pallid, on the ground, stretched out, and not stirring a limb. And her eyes were staring but not seeing, and fixed on one point, and she didn't speak or move her lips, or moan or emit any sound.

The king gave Bovve an order. He told him to blow his horn, to announce to the entire forest that all the huntsmen dispersed in the woods were to gather together and hear that a misfortune had occurred . . . .

And Bovve did as he was bidden, Bovve blew his horn, once it was a sign of sadness, and the second time a dreadful tiding. And from all sides the horns responded, and tidings answered from everywhere, and all the horns appealed to one another, and all the huntsmen came stampeding, and—and after the huge trumpeting, from all the corners and all the lairs, the hunters all came hurrying out, and all at once, and all of them arriving at once, they found the king standing by his fallen daughter, and Bovve with both of them, trumpeting the great misfortune.

And the lords surrounded and observed the princess, and they looked at her and the king bending over her. Then some of them bent over and lifted her from the earth, and quietly and carefully they took her, and silently they carried her away from the place and quietly, accompanied by all, they brought her to the place where the servants and horses and carriages were waiting, and brought her there in a hush. They put her in the king's carriage, carefully put her down, and secured her there, and then all of them mounted their horses, and dolefully and wordlessly, they let the carriage roll out first, and all of them, hushed, accompanied her.

Arriving, the princess was brought into the palace, after the forest and the dismal yearly hunt. They took her to her chamber and to her bed. The king then gave a command:

"Let all the healers and all who can cure listen, from the capital and from around the capital, and whoever loves the king and his daughter, and no precious thing will be too precious for the king, and let them come, and let them cure."

And soon, all the healers of the capital collected in the palace, and they were brought into the daughter's chamber, and they inspected and examined her, and palpated and auscultated. Thus they saw: Something unwonted had happened to the princess, no blow and no injury, her entire body was untouched, and not a sign of animal teeth, and not the slightest trace of a wound, and yet the princess lay as though dead, but still her pulse, a feeble flutter, hinted at a hidden life.

The doctors consulted among themselves, quietly speaking in medical parlance, and all of them were earnest, and the distinguished and the serious men were quiet and lugubrious, and their eyes and their hushed gazes uttered an earnest situation and their helplessness: "The situation is earnest, and the accident is unwonted, and He in heaven is a healer and only He can help . . . ."

And the doctors did and tried what they thought was needed, they stayed and stayed in the princess's chamber, never leaving and always busy, and always consulting, and always attempting a new medicine, and everything within their knowledge and what they had learned in their medical school, and did it all with all their might and all their strength—to lessen the king's sorrow and to bring his daughter back to life. They did and tried everything, that day and evening—and when the king came over to their elders and asked about his child and her illness, they turned their earnest faces to the king's face and said:

"The matter is serious, the illness is unwonted, and we have done whatever we could, and proceeded by all the laws of medicine, and the rest is not in the hands of doctors, the rest is the will of heaven."

They had their say, and they went their way.

And the princess remained lying, with no improvement and no relief as of that day, after the yearly hunt, and the capital's doctors could offer no good and no relief, and not the doctors who came from elsewhere at the king's bidding.

The princess, as when she had fallen, lay there, unstirring, as though paralyzed, with open and with staring eyes, unswerving and unmoving, and not seeing anything. And exorcists tried to dis-spell her sickness, but none of their spells had any effect. And the princess lay there, not living, not dead, and the king sat at her bedside, guarding her and her soul. Long nights and hushed days, and he never removed his gaze from her, and he stared at her and never stopped staring, and stared in hope and faith. Perhaps a limb of hers might stir; an eye, perhaps, might flicker . . . . And so he sat there. And Bovve, the beloved of the princess, would come to her chamber from time to time, come and observe her, and also the king, sitting beside her, in his lostness and great oblivion. Bovve felt sorry for the king and wanted to comfort his misery and his fatherly grief, but he couldn't and he had nothing. He would walk away, leaving him alone with his daughter, sitting over her misfortune, at her bedside, and again for days and nights in a row, sometimes visited by the stargazer too, his best friend and his dearest.

"Well?!" the king would exclaim every time the stargazer came to visit him. "What have you to say to my misfortune?"

"Indeed, royal friend," replied the stargazer, "your sorrow is great and cannot be comforted, but ... God is in heaven, and your child is not doomed."

"What are you saying, dear friend?"

"Remember my words and never lose faith, for the stars say: All is not lost. Recovery will come, and your child shall be restored—she restored, and you comforted, with fatherly pride and joy galore."

And the king believed, and every time he looked forward to the stargazer's visit, to his coming and his bringing solace. And perhaps he would have a tiding, a forecast and a star-word of encouragement, and perhaps the help would arrive for his child, and an end to his sorrow, and a true resolution.

And meanwhile time wore on, and the princess still lay upon her bed, and the king still sat at her side, and Bovve was quietly nearby, and the lords took care of the kingdom alone, and the king took no part in their governing. And the princess still did not recover, and no remedy and no medicine could be found, and the king looked forward to the stargazer alone, and the stargazer to the stars—until one day:

6.

He came and had himself announced, the stargazer, after a lengthy night of sky-scanning he had made his way at dawn to the royal palace and had them announce him to the king, and the king told his footmen to let him in, and in he walked and bowed low to the king at dawn, to the weary and worn-out king, who had thus been spending his nights, and he bowed to him and wished him a good morning, and his face was aglow with something new, his eyes with a tiding:

"Good morning, friend, and why so early, and why are you up at the crack of dawn?"

"For something new, for a tiding, Sire."

"A tiding?"

"Yes, friend king."

"What is it?"

"The time of your help is drawing near, the end of your sorrow is under way."

"Tell me."

"Listen:"

And the stargazer's eyes, with all their loyalty, and devotion, and mildness, rose to the king's face and his eyes of sorrow, and he said:

"King, issue a command today, this very day, by midday, that all the lords and all the sons should gather together in the palace, all the children and all the sons who looked forward to your daughter and desired her heart's desire; let them all come together, and let your daughter in her illness be prepared for her marriage, for her wedding, dressed as befits a bride, and adorned, with nothing lacking, and let Bovve also be invited, and I will also attend—for the event is earnest, for this hour will be major and mighty in the life of your daughter."

The king listened, and that very morning he made an announcement to all his lords:

They were to hear and to know and all to be ready, to come at the hour that the gazer had set, and they all were to bring along their sons, and not a one was not to come, for the king had need of them all today.

The lords listened, and the lords were amazed, and unable to grasp the king's intention and his command. They talked about it among themselves, and asked one another about it all, but no one knew what to say, for the king had told no one in advance. They wondered and they wanted to guess, and they were amazed but they couldn't guess, and then, at the appointed hour, all of them, as one, came, as ordered, to the palace, and gathered there, and all the lords were brought in to the grand reception room of the king, and all of them, even the highest lords, were here in private, and they kept talking and talking about the event, speaking and murmuring, each advancing a different idea—and thus discussing and conjecturing, they waited together and failed to hit upon a clear idea.

Now, after all the lords had gathered, suddenly a door flew open, a door into the reception room, and the king's footmen appeared with a bed they were bearing, and in it lay the princess, ill and leaden and unstirring, and despaired of by all the lords, and the footmen carried her in on her bed, to where the royal throne was standing. They put her down, and the lords saw this:

The princess was all dressed up and all adorned for her marriage and her wedding day, in cleanliness and in white and in purest silk, as fitting and proper for a royal bride. And on her face, her bridal veil; and on her brow, a royal diadem, and adorned and covered with jewels, and only her right hand had been taken from her under the blanket and uncovered and left exposed.

Soft and silent, amazed and confused, the lords peered at the scene and at the princess, gazed in amazement, confused and finding no solution.

Next, a second door opened, between the royal chambers and the reception room, and the king appeared, wearing a daytime robe and his crown and his scepter, as for a major event, a royal act.

He appeared and entered among the lords and walked over to his righteous throne, and he bowed to the lords who were gathered there, and then quietly stepped up to his throne and to his kingliness.

And then, through the same door wherein the king had come, the stargazer entered in his learned robe, his long robe, that reached down to the floor, his black and narrow robe that encased his noble body, and he entered the reception room, and behind him, in great meekness, behind his back, came Bovve, following him.

And the stargazer walked over to the king's throne and the princess's bed, and he stopped and cast a glance at the princess, and deep pity welled up in his eyes, and then he looked at the lords who were gathered there. And they all looked grim and grave. And then, looking at the king on his throne, the stargazer took the floor and began to speak:

"With the permission of the king and the permission of all the lords gathered here, I take the floor and I announce: Know, lords, that the stars have sent me to the king, the stars have told me to tell him, in his grace: This: His daughter cannot recover, his daughter will not be cured, until she comes to her beloved, until she comes to her one-and-only. And now we all have gathered here, and all the sons of the lords are here and all who have sought her hand. And here is the hand of the king's daughter, and here is the nuptial ring. And now, any of you who wishes to try, can go and take the nuptial ring and put it on the princess's finger, and he shall be her husband and master, and inherit the crown and take over the kingdom.... But he must know, he who assumes this love, that the princess will not recover so soon, that she will lie on her bed for long, and he will have to wander through the world and endure much hardship and overcome many obstacles and impediments, and at last, and when he has overcome all, only then will he come to his beloved, only then to his desire. And here is the ring for you!"

And now the stargazer held aloft for all to see a wedding ring, great and golden, and showed it to the lords and their sons, and showing it, called out to them:

"Lords and sons of lords, the nuptial ring and the princess are waiting, and the king upon his throne—for the fortune and healing of his daughter .... Hence, come and see, and take the ring and try to slip it on her finger, and if he does, then his will be the princess."

But none came forward and none drew near, of all the sons and the eligible youths, at the stargazer's call and the show of the ring. They all shrank back, terror-stricken, staring at the bed and the princess, half-dead, stretched out, and her hand, pallid, reclining. And no one responded and no one reacted to the stargazer's words, or drew near to the bed. The stargazer held the ring aloft for a long spell—and the king gazed at the crowd, and waited in silence. And the daughter's eyes were fixed on the crowd as if waiting for whoever would step forward and come over.

But their waiting was useless, and at last the stargazer let down his hand, and the king his eyes, embarrassed, to the floor, and the daughter, the bride, was abandoned and unpitied and unloved.

Now the stargazer turned to the crowd for a final word and repeated for a final time:

"For the last time, sons of lords, for the last time, I call upon you: Who wants to take the royal princess? Who wants to be privileged with her hand?"

No one!

From the crowd no one responded.

"I!"

From a side, unnoticed, unseen until now, from behind the stargazer's back, came a voice.

"I!"

Said the voice quietly, and, from behind the stargazer, out came Bovve.

And cheered and heartened, the stargazer turned to Bovve with a happy face. And gladdened and excited, the king raised his eyes from dejection and sadness, and even the princess's eyes had something in their gaping, a kind of quickening and joyfulness ....

And Bovve went over and held out his hand for the ring that lay in the stargazer's palm, he held out his hand and took the ring, and leaned over the princess and took her hand, which lay uncovered upon the blanket, and he slipped the ring over her finger:

"For me, to belong to me, to be bound and never sundered, for all things and for all time, and whatever may happen to you and to me throughout our lives."

And Bovve lowered his head and face to the princess who was now wearing the ring and belonged to him, and he lowered his head and face and lips and he left a long kiss.

And the king, too, stepped down from his throne and his sitting and his height, and walked over to his bridal daughter and placed a kiss upon her forehead, and then stood up straight and gave Bovve a joyous look and a joyous hug, and then he went over to the stargazer, to his best and only friend:

"All the luck in the world, my friend!"

"All the best and all the luck in the world," replied the stargazer in gladness and joy.

And the king motioned and issued an order to his servants, who had brought his daughter into the room and to his throne. And now the servants took the bed back out of the room and back to the daughter's room. And they left and were gone.

The king remained alone with his lords, with the silent lords, the witnesses of what had happened, who stood ashamed before the king, and stood there for a while in silence and shame. And then the king sent them all away, and they all dispersed, and only the king and the stargazer and Bovve remained in the room, and then, sitting in private, the stargazer turned to Bovve and said to him:

"And now, Bovve, dress yourself down ... as a wanderer and a beggar .... And that's how you'll wander into the world and that's how you'll leave the palace soon. And you won't see your bride before you depart, and you won't look at your beloved until she recovers. Now go: And let the blessing of your old guardian help you, and let his blessing shield your head, and you shall stand before kings and comfort kings. And know: Each king for your comfort will give you something, from every king you shall receive a present, and in the end, and when you are at your third and last arrival—remember: Your help is near .... And here you have a present from me."

And the stargazer put his hand in the pocket of his robe and took out something like a whetstone and gave it to Bovve, and softly giving it to him, he said:

"Carry it with you and take care of it, bear it in mind and think of it, and for the first time of your need you will use it, and you will rid yourself of your need . . . ."

And now the stargazer said farewell to Bovve, he shook his hand and he wished him luck, and having said his hearty goodbye, he led him before the king, and put Bovve's hand in the king's hand, and thus, putting their hands together, he joined them forevermore, to cherish one another for always, in allegiance and in devotion for all time.

And Bovve left the reception room and threw off his clothes, his palace garments, and put on other clothes, beggar's garments, poor and mean, and thus dressed down in beggar's weeds, he left the palace and all he loved, and set out through the city and beyond the city on his way and on his wandering.

7 .

And Bovve went away and walked far, and left the palace and the youth he had spent there. And he roved and ranged for a long time of walking and wandering. And he never stayed anywhere, and never spent the day where he spent the night, and nothing ever happened to him, and he never encountered anyone. And so he wandered on and on, and all he carried was the food in his knapsack and the present that the stargazer had given him. And thus, just carrying his knapsack and the present, one day, after much walking and weariness, late in the soft and sunny day, Bovve came into a country and reached a city, its capital.

It was toward evening, the sun, behind the capital and its houses, was setting, and vanishing, and shining with a final shine on the city and the rooftops. The city was cramped into a far corner, with houses blurred together and radiant with sunset glimmers.

Bovve went around to the other side and saw the city in its illumination and its remoteness. He approached the walls and the gates, planning and thinking of spending the night. But as soon as he came up to the entrance, he encountered a guard with a rifle in hand. And as soon as the guard saw Bovve come up, he stood in his way and made him stop, and peering into his face, he asked:

"Who are you and what do you want?"

"I'm a beggar, and I want to spend the night in the city."

"You can't. You won't be allowed to enter."

"Why not?"

"This is the capital, and it's closed to all wanderers and way-farers."

"And who closed it?"

"The king himself."

"And why?"

"Because of something that happened."

"What?"

"Something."

And the guard cast a glance at Bovve and his appearance, first his face, and the rest, inspecting him from head to foot. He liked the stranger, he found him appealing, and he did have time, the guard, and he was sad and bored with guarding and standing on and on at the gates and hardly ever seeing others. Now he saw Bovve, and slowly took his rifle from its shoulder position and put it down upon the earth, and leaned against it, and thus, holding himself on it, he turned to Bovve, who was standing before him, and agreed and was willing to tell him the story.

And this is what the guard related:

8.
The Guard's Story

Our king has a vineyard, a large and wondrous garden, a rarity and a marvel for visitors. Once, the king built a palace in the vineyard, a lovely and summerly palace, bright and airy. He would come there in summer with the queen and their children, the princes, to enjoy themselves among trees and grape vines, all wondrous, and he walked along the paths in the morning and evening, past brooks and past fountains, resting by their waters and by their splashing, and the peace and stillness would enter his limbs, and the king would be rested and strengthened for the summer, and gather his forces and renew his vigor for the future and his royal labors. Year after year, and summer after summer, on and on, ever since the king became king, it always was and that was how it was, ever since the king had taken the throne.

But then, one day . . . .

It was a year ago, it was summer too, the king was in his vineyard, strolling as always, every morning and every evening. And it came to pass, at twilight, when the sun was setting, the garden was half-sunken in shadow, and only the tree-tips were

aglimmer with sunshine, and the garden was filled with an unwonted hush, a strange evening silence, a shadowy stillness, and no
haulms and no leaves were stirring . . . .

The king was walking along a path, strolling slowly, step by step,
and he looked at everything attentively and earnestly and in solitude. And walking along, he came at last to a little creek, to a calm
and still water, cooling off from a torrid day, in coolness and evening, and a whitish mist arose from the water, silent and hovering,
foggily swaying upon the surface. The king paused and stood
there, looking there, at the calm, and, as he gazed in silence, something loomed up to the king in the midst of the creek.

From the middle and from the mist, a head stuck out, a beggar's
head, all gray, with tangled hair, but dry, as though it hadn't come
from water, and it fixed its oldish and watery eyes upon the king,
calm and silent eyes, as though from elsewhere and from a water
nation. And the eyes stared at the king, and stayed on his face for a
long while, and at last, when the eyes had held him and beheld him,
on and on, the beggar said to him:

"King, the water has sent me to you, the water creatures have
told me to tell you: King, beware of water."

Having spoken and waited and tarried a while, he finally went to
where he had come from, went back, and where he had surfaced he
now submerged.

And it was evening. The sundown-and-garden brightness was
gone from the green and the trees. The shadows that had snuggled
below, by the ground, were creeping out of their lairs and spreading over the entire garden. The fountains and jets of water were
pouring over their wet stones and cool furrows, refreshing the
garden and its shadowiness with night and coolness.

The king stood there, before the creek and after the looming of
the head, stood and stared at the place where the head had loomed
and where it had vanished in the water. The creek now looked as it
always looked whenever the king would come to it, and steamy
with mist and calmer after the event and the waning of sunlight. It
lay there blurred and dusk-like in its banks, its verdant edges, that
were mirrored in water and deepness. There the king stood, and
still, and after his standing and his stillness, he turned around and,
hushed and thoughtful, he returned to his palace for the night.

And the king felt fear of the watery head, and its shape never left
the eyes of the king. That night, the king spent a sleepless night, he

couldn't close his eyes all night, and in the morning—when the king was still disturbed and disheartened, he sent for all the old men and wise advisers to come and gather in the palace, and all of them came, his counselors, and he told them all that had happened to him, his strolling at twilight, and his coming to the creek, and the vision on the creek and the warning of the vision.

They listened closely, and when the king had finished telling, and asked them for some kind of solution, the old men waited a while, pensive and pondering, and after reflecting a bit, they addressed the king and advised him:

"You must not take it lightly, king, you really must beware of water, and not so much you as your children, be watchful of them and wary of water . . . ."

The king took the words to heart and to mind, and from then on he was wary of water, and he kept clear of creeks and pools on his walks, and avoided them all. He himself, and also his children, and he told his children's nannies and tutors: "Beware, beware!" They were not to take the children near the waters in the garden. And they obeyed him, they never took the little ones to the creeks, and avoided them and evaded them, and the older ones, too, were forbidden ever to set foot near the waters, and the older ones, too, followed the order.

Only the king's eldest son, the prince and heir to the kingdom, did not listen and did not hear the shalt-not, and paid no heed and paid no mind to the forbidding and the foreboding.

And this is what happened to him:

It was an evening again. The prince was strolling through the vineyard with his tutor, among dense trees and thick vines, intertwined and cool with twilight. Hushed and wordless, the two of them walked, from path to path, and from lane to lane, and at times they stopped at the sides and peered into the thicket, the twilight denseness, that was making ready for dusk and darkness. And thus they were lost in their pondering, and the tutor, peering, forgot about the prince, and the prince, in his musing, didn't think about his teacher.

And then, the prince saw something white and vague coming from somewhere, and who could say where? And it lured him on, that unclear thing, without his fully realizing it, and he turned from where he was, from the sandy path, and entered that thicket, and left the road and what lay behind him, and went deeper and deeper, and all at once, and farther and farther, at a peaceful pool, isolated and twilit, something happened.

Hushed and overgrown, the pool lay there with its surface mirror and its reflection, and all that lay and grew around it could be seen in the pool and within its water, and the pool was green and reflected greenness, and from the surface, the water mirror, a quiet mist hovered white and low.

The prince walked up and looked. And he stared at the isolation and the solitude, and he pondered it, and suddenly, as he was staring ... a voice, a desperate voice, let out a terrible shriek of shock....

And suddenly, from the middle of the pool, from the stillness and the mistiness—up loomed the beggar's head, old and disheveled, with tousled hair, and melancholy, and just as it once appeared to his father the king. And silent and face to face with the prince, and more silent and eye to eye with the boy, the beggar made wordless signs and signals, meaning the pool and what was within:

"Come in, prince, come here, come into this place ..."

The prince let out a terrible cry, and started back and turned around to flee this place and make his escape. But he couldn't move, his knees buckled, his strength dwindled, he had no power or potency, and so he flung himself back from the water, and half-dead and struck down he sprawled among the blades of grass.

From afar, the tutor heard the prince's voice and his despair, and he realized he was gone and had gone astray. He looked high and low and got lost and was terrified at being lost, and in his great terror and bewildered hurry, he began to cry out and to call for help....

And once, and twice, and then over and over, he shouted—and no one replied to his shouts, and no one was frightened by his shouts of fright. And he went even farther astray, and he looked all around for help, but he saw no one coming to help.

But suddenly, from where he was, he saw from where the prince had seen: a mist among the trees, and it was white and it rose from the trees, and thick as though rising from a creek. And now he realized and now he knew the reason for the prince's cries. He rushed and dashed blindly to the misfortune, and arrived, and upon his arrival and looking around, he saw upon one of the banks of the pool:

Dead, and like all the dead, with glassy eyes, with open and with bulging eyes, the prince lay there as though already belonging to the earth, not stirring and not moving a limb, and still and staring, but not seeing . . . .

The tutor bent over the prince, and began to shake him and tried to revive him and attempted to lift him, but he felt the prince's heaviness and his body's sluggishness, its laxness, and its helplessness, its pulling to the ground and its falling back. He hauled it up and he heaved it up, and with all his strength and his final strength, from the creek and the nightly stillness of the creek, he let out a final shout:

"An accident has happened to the prince, the prince has been struck dead, help, come here and help!"

And far away, in the garden and in the evening hush, they heard him, and they told the king and all the servants in the palace, they dashed through the park, from pool to pool, and helter-skelter, and from pond to pond, and hugger-mugger, looking for the prince and his tutor, and at last, when they came to the creek, where the prince was lying and his tutor standing over him, they surrounded them both and quietly stared at them both, and stood where they were, a minute or two, astounded and stony . . . .

And then they leaned over and looked at the prince, and picked him up and carried him into the garden, and then into the palace. And then, in the capital, and then outside the capital, to all the physicians, to all the the greatest and most famous doctors, they announced:

"Let them all come and let them hurry. The king's son has had an accident. No one knows what and no one knows how. But the prince is dead, and the prince has shown no sign of life . . . ."

And promptly, that very evening, the doctors came together, and they surrounded the prince and his bed, and they examined him and inspected him. And tried to arouse him and tried to revive him, and made every effort and every attempt with all the means at their disposal, and rubbed him and rubbed and gave him drops and things to smell.

And at last they had some success. The prince stirred, and his eyes cleared and he seemed to be coming to his senses, but then he saw the people standing around him, and he was even more terrified, and after his shock he closed his eyes, and, burying his face in the pillow, as though afraid of something, and trembling all over, in every limb, he kept stammering and stuttering, and his lips kept repeating the same words over and over:

"The beggar, the old beggar . . . the beggar, the water-beggar . . . ."

The prince lay all night, raving and ranting, and writhing about, and terrified and with words of fright, and shudders ran over his entire body. And then he was quiet and confused, and the doctors never left him for an instant, and held watch over him all through the night.

And at last, when the night was going, and day was dawning in the prince's room, and the king came to the doctors at the end of night, and besought them with wordless eyes. And the doctors looked at one another, and they understood one another's eyes, and then for all of them the eldest addressed the king who was waiting for his words of comfort and his answer of hope:

"The prince has had a dreadful shock, and he has lost his senses and his power of speech, and the physicians have done whatever they could, and the rest is not in the hands of doctors."

And then the eldest doctor listed all the remedies and what was needed, and what to do with them, and how to use them. He explained it all and reckoned it all. And on that day and in that dawn, the doctors took leave of the king and wished him well and tried to calm him, as doctors do, and then, upon leaving the prince and his bed, they walked out of the palace and its garden, and went back to the city, and returned to the capital.

And since that day and since that time, so much time has worn away, and after that summer, a winter, and after the winter, another summer, with the prince still lying in his bed, and he still hasn't risen from his bed, and the shock has not worn away from him, and his speech and senses have not come back, and the doctors have stopped treating him, the doctors have given up on him, and the king has no faith that his child will recover, and the king only sits by his bed, sorrowing for his legacy and succession . . . .

And right after the accident with the prince, the king gave an order, an angry command:

No beggar and no vagabond . . . not from his realm and not from another . . . and not in the capital and not in its suburbs, as of then and forever more—was ever to cross the threshold of the city gate, not a single one, and no beggar should ever be found here! . . .

9.

"And that's the story, and that's why you can't come in."

And the town guard finished his tale and motioned to Bovve to keep on going, away from the city, to leave and get on his way.

"And outside the city?" Bovve asked the guard.

"That's allowed," replied the guard. "That's perfectly legal, but keep your distance from the gate." And the guard motioned again, into the distance. "That far. That's legal. That's where a beggar can spend the night. That far, at that distance, the king's edict does not apply."

So Bovve obeyed the sentry, and went to where his hand had motioned, and he found a level and grassy place, overgrown with green, and from where he could see the city. It was evening and late already, and the sun had set behind the city, and the buildings and their rooftops were shrouded in the darkness.

Bovve lay down in that place, with his beggar's bag under his head, and he stretched out upon the earth, and quiet and lying there, he raised his eyes to the evening sky, and even more quiet, and weary from his wandering, he waited there for the very first star to come out in the heavens over his head.

And then the first star came out, the one that Bovve had been waiting for, and he gazed up at it from his lying on the earth, and his gazes reached it, and they reached its pallor and its loftiness, its skyliness and its twinkliness. And thus, staring up and fixing his gazes upon the star, he finally closed his eyes for sleep and closed his eyelids in weariness, and drowsed away and drifted into sleep. And he finally fell into a deep slumber.

And that night Bovve had a dream:

Softly and unexpectedly, his friend the stargazer and the old man, who had brought him up, appeared to him, and they were holding hands, coming to him along some road. Stillness and two old men, two bizarre old men, holding hands, emerging before his eyes. They came and told him not to go on. They looked at him, and then, first the old man and then the stargazer, they spoke to him.

"Bovve," said the old man, "are you already forgetting my blessing?"

"Your blessing?"

"You shall stand before kings, and you shall comfort kings."

"I haven't forgotten," Bovve replied.

"Why did you turn away from the king, the king who needs your comfort now, when his royal heir has fallen ill, and all the doctors have given him up for lost, and even his father has lost all faith in his recovery?"

"How could I help?"

"How?" the stargazer turned to Bovve, interrupting the old man. "Have you already forgotten my present? Didn't I tell you to use it when you had to? Didn't I bless it with a healing force? Doesn't it have the power to cure?"

"Then what should I do with your gift?"

"Take it and ask to see the king."

"And how should I use it?"

"This is how." And the stargazer held in his hand the star-stone that he had given Bovve to take on his journey. And he held it up, and showed it first to the old man and then to Bovve, and thus he held it for a while, and then a nursery appeared to Bovve's eyes, a nursery in a royal palace, and it was still and hung with drapes, and a glow came in through the windows, a quiet evening-glow, as if for a quiet patient. It was evening now indeed, and a bed appeared by a wall, with bedding white and clean and tidy, and on the bed, lay, covered with a blanket, a young boy, tender and frail, a prince, with open eyes staring into the room, bulging and big and senseless. And the boy lay there, and his father sat on a chair by the head of the bed, gazing at the child and never shifting his eyes, and he sat there sadly and pondering, and lost in grief and kingly despair.

And as the king sat there in stillness, the stargazer took the stone in his hands and approached the foot of the bed and stood before the prince's open eyes and put the star-stone before his motionless stare and held it for a spell.

And the prince stared on and on at the stone, as before, and never stirred, as though unaffected by the stone and unaware of it, and as though it weren't before his very eyes, and as though there were *nothing* before his eyes—and all at once, in the midst of his senseless staring, his eyes began to clear and become sane and sensible again and notice everything around him and see everything that was happening. And all at once he caught sight of the star-stone. And overjoyed, he reached out for it, and raised his arms and half his body from the bed, and raised himself and went for the stone, and from his lips, which had long been silent, there came a voice, a shout, a voice—a shout of joy:

"Father! King! ..."

And the king bolted up from his chair and his grief, and the king sprang up from his sitting when he saw the prince in his sudden surge, and he dashed to him as though to help, and a shout burst forth from his lips too, and joy and help from his throat:

"My son!"

And Bovve, too, was overjoyed, and Bovve wanted to dash to the stargazer and thank him, and he surged and he rose, and he—opened his eyes ... and .... He found himself in the morning, on the field, and far from the city gate, and lying down.

And the night was gone, and the field lay in broad daylight. So Bovve stood up from his resting place and picked up his bag from the earth, and in it he felt the "star-stone," the stargazer's gift, and he recalled the dream he had had, the nighttime vision, and he grasped its meaning, and he turned back to the gate, from which he had walked so far that night, and he found the sentry in his place. He went over to him and right up to him, and, arriving, he said to him:

"Pass the word, sentry, that a beggar wishes to see the king."

"The king won't allow it."

"Tell him that I have help for him."

"For whom?"

"For the prince in his illness."

"And what if you're fooling?"

"I'll wager myself and my life, and let them do what they always do in such cases."

"Death?"

"So be it."

And the sentry looked at Bovve and his seriousness, and the way he stood there self-assured and gazed at the sentry and took on such a responsibility with such self-assurance. And the sentry regarded him for a while, and thought about it for a minute or two, and after briefly pondering, he turned and strode up to the gate, and he knocked on it, and after knocking and knocking, he told the officer on the other side what had happened on his side:

"And a beggar came here last night, and he slept in the field, and wasn't permitted to enter the city, and now he's back, and he asks if he might see the king."

"What does he want?" a voice rang out on the other side.

"He knows about the king's misfortune, and he says he has help for him."

"And what if he deceives the king?"

"He knows what he'll get."

"Open!"

The sentry opened the gate for Bovve, and Bovve was admitted into the city. He stepped across the threshold of the gate and presented himself to the officer, who was standing on the other side. And Bovve waited, and the officer relayed the matter to *his* superior, and he to his, and so on and so forth, from rank to rank, and at last, a few hours later, the matter was taken to the king, and the king commanded that Bovve be brought before him.

A courier hurried to the city gate and to Bovve who had been waiting so long, and they took him to the royal palace and brought him in and presented him to the king. Now the king gazed upon him gravely, and looked him over from head to toe, and having eyed him, he turned to his servants and told them to lead Bovve to the prince's room and to his bed and his lying there.

So they led him there, and the king came after his servants and Bovve to see and to witness what Bovve would do. And all of them came to the prince, and he, as always and ever since the shock had felled him, lay on his bed, dazed and deranged, and it was very still in the room, as for someone ailing, dangerously ill, and everyone silent and walking on tiptoe. A stillness and darkness prevailed, with windows draped by day and the curtains drawn, heavy and letting nothing through. And the prince lay there in the stillness and darkness, and his eyes stared and stared unseeingly.

Bovve walked over to the foot of the bed and stood opposite the prince, and then he took down the bag from his shoulder, and untied it, and drew out the star-stone, and then—taking the stone in his hand, he held it up before the prince's eyes and placed it before the prince's eyes . . . .

And then in the prince's room by day, it all happened—what Bovve had seen at night in his dream while asleep.

And this is what happened:

Bovve held the star-stone up for only a few minutes, and the prince stared at it for only a few minutes, as though not noticing it—then the others noticed how brightly the star-stone lit up in Bovve's hand, and a glow came forth, starlike and unwonted, streaming and bluish white, and turning the darkness of the room even darker, and the stillness of the room even stiller.

The others in the room behaved as one behaves during a miracle. And a hush prevailed in the room, as during a great event, and only the glow, the wondrous glow, shone upon the prince's face. He lay there for a few minutes in brightness and illumination, and after his lying there in silence, his eyes began to clear, and sense and senses and comprehension seemed to come back to them. And he began to look all around, as though trying to seek and trying to find someone among the servants and those assembled at his bedside. And as he hunted, his eyes alighted upon the king. And all at once—he raised himself, and a voice, a shout of joy, tore out from his lips and into the room and into the hush:

"Father! My father!"

"My child!" And the king dashed from where he was standing, and he made for the prince, who was rising from his bed. "My child, my treasure!" And the king clutched him and hugged him and kissed him and held him, and couldn't stop kissing him . . . .

And the king held tight to his prince for a spell, and they didn't let go, and they hugged and they kissed, and they kissed again, and clutched again, and at last, when the king and the prince had come back to their senses, from their joy and their delight, the king left the prince and walked over to Bovve, and with one hand on his hand and one hand on his shoulder, he hastily took him and said to him:

"Thank you, beggar, for your comfort and for your miracle, for the great wonder you worked, and may God bless you, as you deserve to be blessed, and may God comfort you as you comforted me."

And the king held Bovve's head and his shoulder to his own breast, long and still, and with gratitude and hearty tears, he kissed his head:

"Thank you, beggar!"

And the king turned away and he told his servants:

"Tell the courtiers and the lords who are close to the king, and tell the entire city, and let everyone know, and let everyone hear: The prince is a prince again, the son of the king has regained his health and his life, and all who are loyal to the king and all who love the king shall come and rejoice with him, and whoever wishes and whoever wants to, he shall give presents to the healer, and he shall present gifts to the beggar."

And so the servants went away, and spread the news throughout the city, and soon the people gathered in the crooked streets, and the courtiers came to the court, and intimates came to the palace, and all the rest, the large population, and the king's people assembled before the palace and below the windows.

And the prince was taken from his bed and put on his feet, and barely managed to stand and walk, and his knees buckled, and he stood there and he faintly smiled and he still looked ill. But his servants, nevertheless, dressed him in his weakness and put his clothes on him and held him as they dressed him, and then, when he stood there, dressed and ready, the king motioned to him, first to him, and then to Bovve, to follow behind him, the king. So they followed him, and Bovve walked by himself, and the prince was supported on either side, and thus, with the king leading the way, and the prince and Bovve following his lead, they strode from the prince's room to another room, and then to a third, and from there out onto a balcony, and they stood before the populace and showed themselves to the assembled people.

And the populace welcomed them with a shout and a roar and a huge and loving enthusiasm, and having shouted, and shouting again and again, and huzzahing and hurrahing and waving their hands and surging up, and flailing their arms, and waving their hats and their caps, the people reached a wild exultation, and to their beloved king and prince on the balcony, and on and on, they shouted and cheered, and didn't stop yelling.

The king thanked his people and bowed to them in gratitude, and Bovve and the prince at his side, they also bowed in contentment and delight and smiled at the people, and the people cheered them once again and deafened them with their shouts and joy, and thus their yelling and cheering escorted them into the palace and even after they turned and entered, and for a long time through the palace.

And the king commanded that a feast be prepared. And the servants did his bidding, and the king took his place, with the prince to his right and Bovve to his left, and then all the lords and the friends of the king took their seats, and the servants served and passed the food, and the diners dined and enjoyed themselves, and they drank and felt good cheer as they drank, and then, when all had caroused and feasted, the king made a sign to the company and the crowd at the table began presenting the gifts they had brought and giving the presents they had prepared.

The lords and the intimates brought gold and jewels: the closest servants to the king took the loveliest things they had upon them, and took them off, the golden rings and chains and thimbles and earrings set with gems, and it was all placed before Bovve. And the king for *his* part put down *his* present, and it was the loveliest and the rarest and most precious of his secret treasures, and it surpassed everything else and its value mesmerized all eyes, its preciousness and ancientness, like nothing that's ever seen nowadays.

And everything collected in front of Bovve, and the prince for *his* part took what he had, and all the gifts he had gathered throughout his youth, and he brought them over. And it was a mountain of wondrous things, and unwonted things, and matchless things; and all these things were piled up for Bovve.

Then all the doors of the palace opened, on all sides, and to all rooms, and the people, the populace, also brought presents, some of them big and some of them little, but all of them loving and well-wishing. And the people came in and the people went out, and the doors never closed in the palace. And an hour passed, and another hour, and half a day, and then it was dusk, and late in the evening, and the gifts kept growing, and the table in front of Bovve grew higher and higher with presents. And in the evening, when the crowd was gone, and it was getting late, and only the king and his closest friends were still at the table and at the feast, the door flew open all at once and for one last time, and in the stillness after the turmoil of day, there appeared an old woman, shrunken and bowed with age, and she entered the palace and entered the hall, and trudged to the table, where Bovve and the last few diners were left, and she trudged up to Bovve and halted before him, and stared at him for a spell, and, having stared, she said to him:

"I'm a fortuneteller, I'm old and practiced and I've come to you to give you a gift, but first I want to tell your fortune."

And the crone took hold of Bovve's hand, and peered at it and examined his palm, in the hush of the hall and the quiet company, and she looked at the intertwining lines and the furrows in his palm, and one line, and then the next, and her aging eyes moved from one to another, and then, after peering and pondering, she raised her head and she fixed her eyes upon his eyes, and gazing at him, quietly, and long, and divining, she said to him and then to all who were there:

"No beggar, no vagabond by birth, but a prince and perhaps a king. Yet misfortune struck you, prince, and your life, and something happened to you and your love, something, but I don't know what, something, but it's not clear to me. But there's one thing I do know, there's one thing I'm sure of—a misfortune . . . ."

And there the fortuneteller stopped for a while, and kept still, and gazed at Bovve, and soon, and after staring a while, she added:

"And your misfortune, prince, is great, and your misfortune, prince, will come to an end, but before it ends you will have to render three kings happy, and—you've already made the first king happy . . . . And when you first went out, you received a gift to help you in a time of trouble. And for the second lap of your journey, I'll give you an even *better* present . . . ."

And the fortuneteller reached into her hollow and shrunken bosom and she took a tiny mirror, old and cheap and tawdry and common, and she pulled it out and gave it to Bovve, and then, casting a glance at the gift-heaped table, she added:

"And all these things are superfluous, prince, all you've been given and offered will just be a load while you wander, so leave it here and wander without it. But take the mirror along . . . . And there's a power and a virtue in the mirror, you must know, *whatever* you wish and *whomever* you wish to see you can see reflected here, and any time and whenever you desire, and you can perceive what your beloved is doing far away, and what will happen to you some day . . . . And so, prince, farewell, and may your wanderings be happy, and my mirror will come to your aid and my mirror will stand you in good stead . . . ."

And the fortuneteller took leave of Bovve, and of the people gathered there, and bowed and curtsied in homage, and quietly returned to where she had come from, through the door, which she closed behind her.

Bovve got up from where he was sitting and turned to the king, and he bowed to the king and he thanked him for his hospitality and his kindheartedness, and for the gifts and for the presents all, and gently peering about for his bag, he said to the king:

"I thank you, Your Majesty, for the day and for the rejoicing this day, and for letting me spend the day under your roof, and for your royal satisfaction. And now, I have to say farewell, and now I have to get underway."

The king tried to talk him into staying a while, but Bovve begged off and turned down his request, and he looked about for his beggar's bag, and he found it, and he put the mirror inside. And then he took his leave of all, first the king, and then the prince, and then all the courtiers and intimates who had remained. And then he slung his bag over his shoulder and took his staff in hand, and then he bowed to all, and quietly, and striding toward the door, he opened it to leave the palace.

"What about the presents?" the king recalled and asked Bovve.

"For others, Your Majesty, for the needy."

"Farewell."

"Farewell to you, Your Majesty."

And Bovve went on his way.

10.

Bovve left that land and crossed the border into another land. And Bovve went from village to village, and from place to place, but mostly he wandered through the fields and stayed out under the open sky. And he sometimes spent his days and also his nights under the heavens, for the land was huge and full of empty fields, and from one village to the next the distance was great and the emptiness huge. And he wandered through the country wastes.

And time stretched by, and on and on—and Bovve was far away from his home, and Bovve had wandered far from his loved ones and could only faintly imagine them; and he couldn't evoke the way they looked, and he couldn't recall their faces and shapes. But whenever he craved to see them, he would come to a halt and sit down on the ground in the midst of the fields, and untie his bag and take out the mirror that the fortuneteller had given him, and he would peer into it, and sometimes he'd see one and sometimes another one of his loved ones in the royal palace: Sometimes the stargazer and sometimes the king, and very, very seldom, also her, the princess, his beloved.

And Bovve would meet her in the mirror and in the reflection— just as he'd left her when leaving the palace, upon her bed in her terrible condition, stretched out and straight, petrified, deathly, and fixing her eyes straight in the air: and thus she lay, and when Bovve saw her, she kept her eyes on him all the while. He would look at her, sometimes for a minute and sometimes more—but he never spent too much time with the mirror, and always and after looking a bit, he would put it back into the bag and turn it over.

And Bovve felt, and his heart always assured him, after he saw her when he peered in the mirror:

"The princess looks ill and helpless, and abandoned and beyond all possible remedies, and nothing can help her, and no remedy can ease her condition, but there's one thing left, and there's one thing possible . . . love . . . ."

And thus, Bovve, lying in the field and on the ground and thinking about the princess and his love for her, pondered and pictured her as a lover, with his coming to her and her meeting him, and her throwing her arms around him and falling upon his breast, and her eyes blazing with feeling for him, and her body filled with devotion for him, and great gratitude and unwonted loyalty, and ready to be with him and be true to him with all she had. And with these concatenations of thoughts, he would bolt up from the ground, and wake up from his musing and lying there, and picking up the bag from the earth, he would get underway across the big fields and never come to any real settlement.

And he trudged and trudged, and on for a while, and on for a spell, and kept wandering through the land, and through its empty fields, and he never spent the night where he spent the day, and he roamed and ranged between the hamlets, all of them scattered and far apart, and nothing happened to Bovve ever, and nothing occurred on the way. And after a space and after a time of meeting no one, he finally, stopping in a field, took out the mirror from the bag again and looked at it and questioned it:

"Mirror, mirror, where am I going, and what will happen to me in the near future?"

For a while the mirror looked normal, and Bovve peered, but saw nothing. But soon, when he had stared for a while, its appearance changed, its glossy smoothness—and something like smoke and clouds wafted across, and it darkened and withdrew, and it kept to its nonreflecting for a while, and then when it had darkened over fully, it finally showed a dusty path, a long road across the length of the mirror, straight and running to the horizon—and far, far, and only faintly visible, something appeared on the skyline, and low, something like a tower, and lofty, and on top of the tower, and upon its peak, a flag was waving, and flagging and fluttering.

And Bovve's eyes alighted on the tower, and Bovve was wise enough to see and grasp what the mirror meant and guess the mirror's reply to his question:

A capital was near, and his road led there, and that was where he had to go, and all that would have to happen to him would happen there.

And the mirror's appearance changed back to normal, and the cloudiness lifted, and the mirror looked as it usually looked, and Bovve put it back into his bag, and Bovve started out again, and this time on his certain road.

And Bovve kept walking and never paused anywhere, and Bovve hurried and he halted in no village. He trudged all day and trod all night, and only rarely halted in a hamlet, and only for food and when he had to stock up. And having his food and all he needed, he kept away from the other hamlets along the way and never paused in any of them, and passed through them all, and some of them he avoided altogether and walked around them instead of through them, and kept rushing and hurrying, as though heading for a certain place, a specific place. And then one morning, one country day, Bovve arrived at the capital, at the city with the tower.

In the distance he saw a high-built tower, a spiraling and ancient tower with smooth walls and a slanting roof, and a brick molding around the roof, and even spaces between the bricks; and on top of the roof a stick was stuck, smooth and lofty, and a flag was waving from the tip, and fluttering thus for travelers from afar and wanderers afoot, it showed, at an enormous distance, the capital city and its crowning.

And Bovve came to the capital, and he met no guards at the gates, and the gates were standing ajar, and no one guarded the entrance or *his* entrance. Bovve was astounded, he couldn't understand the guards, and he wondered about their negligence and their unwatchfulness, for he wasn't used to finding a royal city unguarded thus; but he did find it thus, and he saw no one to talk to about it, so he didn't ask, and he stepped across the threshold and through the gates, and thus, and undisturbed and not stopped by anyone, he came into the capital and into its streets.

And that was in the morning: the sun had just arisen from under the sky, and it shone on the city and on the buildings, and the first inhabitants were up and about, the early risers, the early birds, lone workers going to work, and along the sides of the streets, and each was busy with his walking and going. And thus they went, and none of them even noticed Bovve. And Bovve stared at the streets and the houses, and he gazed at the courtyards and buildings, and he saw: On every building and every porch, and in front of all yards and all doors, a flag was hanging, black and mournful, a sign of grief in front of all houses, and Bovve wondered in surprise: What is this, and what does it mean, what can it be and what could have happened in the city?

And in his surprise he wanted to ask someone, but there was no one at hand, so he halted and waited: Perhaps somebody would hurry this way, perhaps somebody would come along, and that person would explain. But no one hurried his way, and no one came along, and he stood there and stood there, and stared at the city, its streets and its early-morning appearance, and the courtyards and the emptiness and desertedness. And every so often in the courtyards, the doors opened up, and there were more and more people waking up, and the doors were letting them out, from houses into yards, and from yards into streets—and the city came more and more to its dailiness and its dayfulness. And people were already coming along toward Bovve, and he turned to one of them, the first and the nearest, and stopped him and asked him:

Could he be so kind as to explain: What were those flags, and what was the grief in the city?

And the passer-by looked at Bovve and his appearance, observed him and scrutinized him from top to toe, and having inspected him and convinced himself of his unimportance, he retorted tersely:

The king was in grief, and this was the capital, and the capital was expressing its sympathy by hanging flags on its streets and houses.

And why the grief?

No time to explain, and would he be so kind as to ask someone else.

And the passer-by went on by and hurried away, and left Bovve alone and in his earlier ignorance. So he asked another passer-by, but he didn't find out any more. And he asked a third—and the same thing again; for Bovve had forgotten all about cities and their ways, and their great needs, and that the people are busy in the morning and all of them are hurrying to their work.

And so Bovve walked on, from one street to the next, and from the back streets to the grand avenues, and things were the same there, and the city was clad in black, and black flags were hanging on the houses and on the front doors. Bovve saw the flags, and he tried to stop the passers-by, and he received the same answer here: And the people were busy in the city, and everyone had to rush in the morning.

He hung around there for a long time, and at last he left, and then at last, after roaming for a long time, past noon, and when the sun was perched on the head of the city, he came to a street, a quiet street, off to the side, an old street, where poor and common people lived—and it was empty and deserted, and then he came to a courtyard, old and with a ramshackle fence, and completely vacant, no hide nor hair of man or beast. But soon a dog began to bark, and then an old man, no longer able to work and not going to work, appeared at the threshold of the entrance, appeared and asked Bovve what he wanted, and, at the threshold, what he was after.

Bovve replied to his question, saying he was a wanderer and a beggar, asking for a place to rest and spend the night, for he had been away so long from human settlements, and hadn't rested so long under a roof. The old man asked him in through the gate and into the house, and Bovve stepped in. The old man showed him a place to put down his bag and a place to be seated. And Bovve didn't wait to be asked a second time. He put down his bag in the place he'd been shown and sat down on a bedstead he'd been shown. And sitting, he looked around at the room, at the lowly house, the poor house in which the old man lived alone, the house which was left untended and to which no housewife's hands attended.

Now the old man gave him some food, something to eat—and Bovve didn't turn it down. The old man put something on the table, and Bovve sat down and ate what was there. And he talked to him while eating, the old man talked, and asked him about his roaming and roving, and how a wanderer lives along the way, and about the things he saw and did. And Bovve replied, and told him things, and spoke for a long time, about the things he saw and did, in this country and in other countries. And the conversation was friendly and restful, and he passed from topic to topic, and subject to matter, and at last, having told him everything, and clarified everything that was unclear, he asked *him*, the old man, a question, thus:

"And what's happening in the city, old man, and what is the grief in the city?"

"It's a kingly grief," the old man answered.

"And what is it about, and what happened in the kingdom?"

"Something happened to our king."

"And could you tell me?"

He could, it was possible, the old man agreed.

And the old man began to tell the tale:

11 .
The Old Man's Story

Our king, for a long time, after his marriage with the queen, didn't have any children. This caused him great sorrow and made his life empty, and he renounced all the pleasures of the world, and left his kingdom and his throne derelict: let come what may, let happen what will, for the matter wasn't his concern, the kingdom wasn't his business, and its affairs didn't interest him.

Thus the king; and even more so the queen. The queen isolated herself in her chambers with her body maid, and she remained locked up in her apartments, and never appeared in court among the courtiers, never on holidays and never on ordinary days, never for celebrations and never for state banquets, for courtly events. She kept to herself and lived like that, and never appeared in brightness and light, and merely sat in her room, and silently, and sitting there, she brooded and mulled, and spent her time with her grieving and her childlessness.

And thus she sat there, on and on, but at times a rumor spread to the royal court: and thus, and thus, and it was said that there was talk throughout the land that a wonder worker had appeared in a place, and he had been performing miracles, and bringing people back from the dead, and making sick people healthy, and giving children to the childless. The queen would hear this, and all her body and all her senses would tense, and her eyes would grow big, and her ears would strain, and she was fully prepared to hear about anything and about the wonder worker. She would ask and ask about the wonder worker, and his town and where he was, and where he lived, and in what land, and then, and finding out everything, she would send her servant to the king, and invite the king to visit her, and softly and sternly like a queen, she would order the king:

"King, that wonder worker, bring him to me."

The king would follow her command, he would promptly send a man to where the wonder worker lived, a horseman, the best of his riders, and give him a letter with his seal—and with no explanation of any sort, and as fast as possible, tell him to bring the wonderman to court. And he would ride away, the horseman, and gallop along at lightning speed, and with documents from the king, so that no one would stop him along the way, and with other documents, so that all the subjects of the king would help him along the way. And they helped him, and as quickly as ever possible, he dashed to that place, and he came to the wonder worker, and to his town, to the place where he lived, and to his home, and when he came, he would knock at the door:

"A messenger from the king!"

And the wonder worker would come out of his home, and the messenger would give him the letter from the king, and the man would not answer anything, he would merely prepare to get underway, and right away and without a word he would ride with the horseman off to the capital.

And after the road and after the ride, they would welcome the wonder worker and lead him to the queen and her chambers, and bring him and present him to the queen, and she would receive the wonderman with great honor, the way you receive a wonderman, and thus, and welcoming him, and holding him in great honor, she would take him into her private chamber, and show him a seat and ask him to be seated, and he would sit down, and the queen would stand before him, and thus and standing several minutes in front of his chair and his honor, she would softly pour out her heart and her trouble and her sorrow.

And she would talk and talk, the queen, and total up all the nostrums and potions she had gotten from physicians, and things that had *not* come from physicians, and what old crones had counseled her, and what she had done with the elixirs, and how she had used them and how they all hadn't helped at all, and how she remained without any help, and—could he (and she hoped he could), and was it possible (and she hoped it was possible for the wonder worker), could he possibly see her misery and sorrow, and might he be her good messenger, and she would give him anything: the crown and the kingdom, and anything his lips uttered.

He would listen to all she said, and look at her heartache and sorrow, and he would feel great pity, and he would promise her— and everything he could, he would do, and assure her—and everything in his power. Then he would go about his work, and give her various potions of various herbs, and instruct her when to drink, and teach her spells to recite while drinking the potions. And for a while she would rely on his remedies, and everything he had taught her she would carry out, and everything he told her to do she would do. And then she would show her gratitude for his instruction, and after her gratitude she would keep him at court for a time, and then, for the future, when he had taught her to do without him, he would take his leave of the queen, and then to his home, and back to his house, he would go.

And the wonder worker would ride away, and the queen would remain alone, and for a while she would be certain of his remedies and would take them, and exactly as he had taught her, and once, and once again, and yet another time, and over and over, and then, when they, too, hadn't helped, she would put them aside and give up on them, and settle back into her despair, and retreat once more into her chambers, and again, as before the wonder worker, she would not appear in the radiant shine and in the radiant world.

And thus a while, and thus a time, and the queen grew older, and she was changed beyond belief, and the king himself was greatly altered, and he looked unkempt and ill-kept. And the lords and the courtiers saw all these things, and they felt great pity for the royal couple, and felt sorrow for them, and wanted to help them for all the world. But there was nothing in the world they could do, and they asked one another and took counsel together: Perhaps they could hit upon something for them?

And they pondered, and they looked for different devices, and all of them asked their friends for remedies. But no one in this country knew, and so they sent to other countries, and inquired of great men and wise men; and these men sent them back various counsels and all kinds of advice. And the king and the queen listened to them all, and obediently did what they were told to do, and thus, following and never arguing, they took all the remedies and all the elixirs, and they remained as they were before, with their earlier unfruitfulness . . . .

And one day, in an ordinary morning, something happened in the queen's chamber:

The queen had only just awoken from sleep, and hadn't yet left her bedchamber and hadn't yet been dressed by her body servant, and wasn't prepared for going out, when all once there was a knock at the door, and a servant-girl, from the court, from the king, announced herself and asked to be admitted.

"What do you want?" asked the queen's servant.

"To see the queen," said the other one, standing on the other side.

"Why?"

"It's very important, really."

"Open!" said the queen to her body servant.

The servant left the queen in the midst of dressing her and before she was done, and she strode over to the door and opened it, and then, opening it, she admitted the servant who had asked to be admitted.

"What is it?"

"Not me, but the woman, the old one."

"Who?"

"The royal midwife, who tended the king's mother at every childbirth, and who attended the king's birth and the births of all the princes."

"And what did she want?"

"She wants to see you, Your Majesty."

"Let her in."

And the servant-girl left the queen's chamber, and the queen's servant meanwhile started to finish dresing her mistress, so that the queen was ready, and she left her bedroom and stepped into the next chamber, and at this time, the woman, the old one, led by the court servants, was brought into the same chamber. And she presented herself, shrunken and shriveled, and clean and neat, and dressed like a grandmother, she trudged over to the queen and bowed before her, and having bowed, she said to the queen:

"Your Majesty, my precious gem, I have seen your sorrow and known of your misery, and your desire, your strong yearning, your great wish to be a mother, and I have watched you for a while, and known about all that you did and tried, and all the things that didn't work. And I, too, wanted to help you, with all my heart and with all my devotion to the court, but there was no way that I could help you, and so I never appeared before you, and never came before you. But I couldn't rest, and all the time I kept inquiring of the old and the elders in our land and also in other lands, and I sent to all the practiced midwives, and asked them all for help for you. So they sent me various remedies, and I inspected them and tried them out on other women, but they didn't help anyone, and they didn't make any woman fertile. And so I didn't bring them to you, and I held them to be useless, and I kept from appearing before you and coming before you . . . .

"But I still didn't rest, and I pondered and probed, and I cudgeled my brain and didn't stop thinking, and then I recalled: There was one thing left, one last and untried remedy, and in an ultimate case, one uses the ultimate—and that is: Magic . . . .

"And so I went out into the fields—in a dewy dawn, a summer morning, and before the sun had even risen, and while the night was still resting on the vastness of the fields. And I came to the middle of the meadow, among the grasses and herbs, and I trod among them, and peeped and peered at them as I trod, and I looked for the magic herb. But I couldn't recognize it, and I couldn't distinguish it among all the others. And then I began reciting the spell, the one my mother once had taught me to whisper over herbs, and just as I had learned it in my youth . . . . And thus speaking, and thus walking among the herbs in the field, I at last noticed one, a different one, and it loomed up before my eyes, so different from all the others, and it showed up before my eyes, and as though it were saying: 'Take me!'

"So I bent over and tore it out, and I brought it home and dried it out, and did what one does with a magic herb, I made a potion out of it, and started coming to you with it, and had myself announced to you, and now, and I stand before you now, and the potion is ready for you."

And the old crone took out from under her robe, from under her early-morning wrap: a vial, a tiny one, a greenish one, containing a liquid, and then, showing it to the queen, to her eyes, she held it and she added:

"And behold, Your Majesty, inside this is your remedy and this will help you . . . . However . . . you must know: Magic remains magic. Magic can summon to life, magic can perform a trick, but to keep alive, and to live indeed—That is not in the power of magic . . . . And now, as you like, my precious."

"I want to drink it!" cried the queen after several minutes of reflection and after coming to her thoughts from the old crone's long talking. "I want to drink it!" Let come what may! Let happen what will! A mother is a mother—even if to a piece of flesh!"

And the queen reached out her hand to the old crone's hand and to the vial, and took the vial and looked at it, and peered at it in curiosity, and then, and asking about all the rest, and how to take the remedy, she thanked the old midwife, and showing the old crone out with thanks, and then after having shown her out, and ever since that day, and after the old crone went away, the queen, believing in that remedy, and devoting herself with all her devotion, and with loyalty and with total yielding, she applied herself to the matter.

And the queen did not reject magic, and she took the magic potion, and the queen said the word, and agreed to everything: and in a time, the remedy had its effect on the queen, and in a time, and in a propitious hour, the queen became pregnant.

And quickly the secret news spread, first through the court and among the courtiers, then outside the court and throughout the capital, it was passed quietly from person to person and tongue to tongue and ear to ear, and the secret wrapped and wrapped the queen up, and all who met her stepped aside quietly and with quiet gazes; and the queen kept apart and to herself, from everything and everyone, and sat in her chambers all by herself, yet not as before, in despair and desolation, but in unwonted tenderness and wistfulness, and pensively, and preparing herself for quiet motherhood. And thus she sat in the morning and at midday and in the afternoon and at twilight—in her chamber, which was quiet, and which no noise and no voice reached from the court: thus she would sit between the impenetrable walls and at the heavily draped windows. And sometimes, at twilight, during a sunset, the king would come by, also quiet and also pensive, from the court, leaving the entire court behind and leaving it behind the door; he would come in, and the queen would receive him in silence, and he likewise, and looking at her, didn't speak or say a word—and thus, in silence, and thus in wordlessness, they would sit through that time and through the sunset, and then, and before retiring for the night, they would take leave of one another in silence, and having taken leave, they would part for the night . . . .

Thus a month, and thus two months, and so on, and so forth for a time, and the queen saw that her time was coming. And the king would visit her from time to time, and the queen never spoke a word with the king, and the queen never told a thing to the king, about the herb, or where it came from, or about magic, or about taking the magic upon her—she concealed it in silence, and the king only knew about the old crone and her remedy, and that heaven had taken pity on them, and that heaven had seen *his* sorrow and *the queen's* suffering. He was overjoyed, and every moment, and every minute, he thanked heaven and Him Who dwells in heaven. And thus, thanking, and thus, in his heart, praising Him Who dwells above, he waited for the good day and for the longed-for day, and looked forward to the happy hour and the fortunate hour and the wished-for hour.

And the good day came, and the good hour, and the midwives who had been ordered earlier were summoned to the queen, and their helpers and the helpers of their helpers, and all the old women, well-known and renowned in the courtly household. And the queen felt her first pangs, and the midwives got to work, and they did what they had to do, and they eased her pain as far as they could ease it, but the pangs got stronger, the queen grew weak and worn with suffering, with no strength, and with a belated first birth.

The doctors were worried and they saw the queen would be having a difficult labor, and the king could see it on the doctors' faces, and the king understood the difficult situation. So the king turned to all the houses of worship, sending them both candles and money, the candles to be lit for the saints and the money to be doled out to the poor and needy. So the candles were lit and the money doled out, and prayers were prayed in all the houses of worship for the queen's health and for her safe delivery, and all the city and all the inhabitants of the city found out about the queen's labor, and they all gathered in clusters and crowds in front of the court and in front of the palace, and all of them spoke in whispers, and seized on any news that came every so often from the court and from those coming from the court, about the queen and her difficult labor. And they stood and whispered thus, and every so often they lifted their eyes to the court: And perhaps someone would come and bring some news, some happy tidings. But no one did. And the people came out and came from the court, and their faces were gloomy and worried—and silence as in a terrible danger, and absorption as during a grave event and a bad occurrence, lay on their faces. And they kept coming out from the court—sometimes a doctor, and sometimes a helper, and sometimes a servant, and sometimes a messenger sent to go somewhere.... They had to run somewhere, after something, and the crowd would surround them and ask them what was happening; but they wouldn't halt and they had no time to answer, and with their hands and eyes they would give a sign, sometimes "bad" and sometimes "very," and thread their way out of the crowd and hurry off to where they had to hurry and for what they had been sent for.

And thus the first day wore away, and the second day came, and the situation became more serious, and the labor pains didn't ease, and the queen had no strength left, and she lay on her bed more dead than alive, and the medicines didn't help and the remedies brought no relief, and there was no sign of a delivery, and not a trace of a child to be born. The king kept sending servants into the queen's chambers to inquire and to bring him news, and the reply was always the same—the same and what he already knew: the situation was bad, and the queen was doing very poorly, and the queen had no strength left, and the labor would have to be hard. The king would listen, and his face each time became sadder and sadder, and the king would stay in the place where he heard the news, sometimes sitting and sometimes standing, and each time, after hearing the news, the king couldn't move from the place where he was—and thus, and not moving, and thus remaining in that place, he would keep silent and wait for a while, and then again, and then once more, he would send for news.

And thus the second day, and thus the second night. And no one at court could close an eye, and no one at court could possibly rest ever since the labor began: and servants were on their feet, and the midwives and nurses gave orders to the servants, and every so often a doctor would think of something new. And he would consult with the other physicians and then quickly order: "Have the servants go and bring thus and thus, have them hurry and bring this and that." And the servants ran and brought what the doctor commanded, and they used it as the doctor ordered, and obeyed him, and this, too, didn't help; and so for a while they remained without remedies, and they stood there and did nothing, and no one could think of anything new or anything that had not been tried, and so they stood there and stared at one another, and all at once, someone did think of something new and someone else hit on something else . . . .

And the second night wore away, and the third day came, and everyone was worn to the ground, and all the remedies had been tried, and all that could be done had been done, and all the advice had been followed to the letter, and all the midwives stood there idle, and the doctors sent no servants for anything, and even the king stopped sending for news, and in front of the palace, in the palace square, the people were still crowded and clustered, and talking about the queen and her hard labor. Whispering and glancing toward the court, talking and lifting their eyes to the palace windows. They stood there and softly conversed—and all that time, no one came out of the court, and no head and no body appeared at any window, and it was silent in the palace, and no noise and no voice came from there, and everything was closed and draped, and no one was let out to the crowd, and no news was released.

And the people stood there and patiently waited, and clusters with clusters, and crowds with crowds—and the gathering became stiller and stiller, and the eyes and the ears became more and more curious and more and more eager; and they talked and listened to one another, and every cluster had its man, and every cluster listened to its man. And thus they were busy and whispering, and thus, murmuring and nearly forgetting about the palace—when all at once, on the upper story of the palace, a door opened up, a door that led to a balcony, a balcony where usually the king himself appeared only at certain times, but now only a servant appeared, and his face was slightly cheerful and slightly glad, and his eyes shone and were joyful about something, but it was only the servant, and his coming out all by himself, and his not hurrying when coming out, did not attest to any joy, or at least not to a total joy. He appeared, and came out through the door and on to the balcony and over to the railing, and he bent over the railing, and thus, and bending over, and waiting until the entire gathering was gathered, he addressed the crowd and called out and said:

"Hear ye, the palace announces: "The queen has survived her delivery and has born a child, but the child is stillborn, the child did not come into the world alive."

Having spoken, he turned away, and went back through the door and back to where he had come from.

And thus it was: The queen brought the child into the world with her last strength, and after bearing the child, she lay unconscious and close to death, and the doctors crowded around her, and tried to revive her with all that is used in such cases, and they revived her and brought her to her senses, and she opened her eyes and looked around, and then, after opening her eyes, she addressed those surrounding her and asked about the baby:

"The . . . baby . . . ?"

"The baby is with the midwives," they replied.

And the baby really *was* with the midwives, and it was passed from hand to hand because the child was stillborn, and the midwives started to slap it and wake it, and the first one failed, so she passed it on to the second, and a younger one handed it over to an older one, and the older one tried to slap it and wake it, and at times the baby moved a tiny limb, but then the movement was quickly gone, and then at times it opened an eye, but then the eye was quickly closed, and so they passed it from hand to hand, and pricked it with pins and burnt it with candles, and every so often it came awake and then it fell back into deathly sleep; and now the midwives didn't know what to do, and so they called the physicians, and the physicians looked at it, and gravely, and inspected it and examined it: And it was still like all stillborn babies, and yet it wasn't like other still babies—and they didn't know, and they all came to the same conclusion, that the child wasn't alive, and they all wanted to wash their hands of it: But the old crone, the midwife who had given the queen the magic herb, stuck to her very own opinion:

"No, and no, the baby is alive, the baby has life inside itself, and the doctors don't know because the doctors have never had such cases . . . ."

And the baby was put aside, and no one talked to the queen about the child, and the queen understood by herself, and the king himself, looking at the midwives and at the doctors, sensed what had happened. So they fell silent and did not speak, the king and the queen, and the king merely came to the queen and stood at her bedside, and gazed at her, and grieved over her and mourned with her; and thus keeping silent and waiting in silence, and thus, and as they stayed there and looked at one another and watched one an-

other, the midwife, too, came to the queen, the old crone who had
given her the herb came over, and standing quietly before the king
and the queen, she addressed the king and she said to him:

"And I, Your Majesty, still insist: The child has life within itself,
and its little limbs do stir at times, and from time to time its hands
come awake, and the child is not to be given up for lost, and the
child is not doomed, and Your Majesty should not despair, and
Your Majesty should heed my advice."

And the king listened to the midwife, and the queen believed
what she said, and the queen gave the midwife the power to do
what she felt she had to do. And the midwife turned to the king
again, and exclaimed to the king:

"Your Majesty, I will inform the city, that the city may pray for
you, and proclaim a state of mourning, and have the people hang
black flags on the gates and the doors, and let all see the flags, and
whoever has any remedy for you, let him bring that remedy—and
hope for the best, and I shall go to the child."

And the midwife turned away from the king, and the midwife
went off to the child, and she took care of it, and all by herself and
with no one's help, for all the midwives had given up and all the
helpers could no longer help, and she took care of the baby with
what she knew and with the remedies she had from others and with
the remedies handed down to her, and she tended to the baby for a
long, long time; and the king did as she had told him to do, and
ordered a state of mourning in the city, and black flags to be hung
on all gates and doors; and the people obeyed, and the flags appeared in front of all houses and buildings, and all the streets and all
the alleys were draped in black, and all the people and all the inhabitants in town found out about it, and began to pray for the
royal sorrow.

And that is the grief, and that is what happened to our king, and
that is why the flags are hung out, and that is what you saw in the
town.

And thus the old man ended his story.

12.

"And how long ago did this happen to the queen?" asked Bovve.
"Just yesterday."

"And the baby?"

"The baby is just as it was yesterday, the baby's in the same condition still, and the old midwife won't leave it: She still hopes."

"For what?"

"For help and for a helper. The helper, she says, may still come."

"By when?"

"By the third day."

"And what if he comes later?"

"Too late. And tomorrow is the third day."

Bovve lapsed into thought and asked the old man no more questions. He thought about the story and remained quiet and where he was. And now, in the old man's house, the twilight and the darkness of twilight gathered, and the house became silent and dismal. The old man got up from his seat and began to prepare for the night and for bed. First for himself, and then also for Bovve, he prepared a bed, and then he called Bovve to his nightly meal, and Bovve went with him and sat down at the table, and quietly, and they ate their nightly meal. And then, and after eating, they went to their beds, and undressed by their beds, and each in his bed and each lay down for the night.

Softly then, in the house, came the evening and midnight, softly and undisturbed by anything, and unbroken by any noise or voice, only the windows peered into the darkness and quietly watched Bovve and the old man on their beds and asleep. And thus, and quietly and watching them sleeping, one of the windows, a quiet and nightly one, a dark-glassed and small-paned one, let someone in, a careful and an unnoticed someone, a cautious and a weightless someone, the dream-dreamer with his pack on his back.

And then Bovve had a dream, and he saw, far away and on a wayfarers' road, in a faraway field: the old fortuneteller, the crone who had given him the wonder mirror, and she presented her person to him, with the same appearance and her same agedness, and as he had seen her that night in that royal palace; she appeared to him and she stood before him and stared at him in silence and watched him, and then, and after staring and silence, she spoke to him and she said to him:

"I forgot something, Bovve, I didn't tell you this: Besides the power I told you the mirror contains, there is another power it possesses: Put it to the face of a person, a sick man, and whose fate the physicians cannot tell, and the mirror knows, and the mirror will say: If he's fated to live then he'll soon be healthy and restored to life; but if not, then soon he no longer will live. One way or another, and listen: And soon you will need it, the mirror, and soon it will be of use to you in such a case, and have no fear, and use it well, and the mirror will bring life, and the mirror will lead to health, and when you are called upon, do not hold back."

And the old crone vanished, and Bovve kept sleeping, and the dream-dreamer turned away from Bovve and from his bed, and went on to the old man, the owner of the house . . . .

And the old man, the owner, could see and watch: himself sitting quietly, as always, in his home: it was evening and dark and inside the walls of his house, and a peace and a twilight stillness hovered on the ceiling above. And he sat there at his little window, and sat staring out into his courtyard, quiet, deserted, into which hardly anyone ever came—but then he saw: suddenly and unexpectedly, from the street and from the other side, someone had taken hold of the knob on his gate, taken hold and opened up, and crossed the threshold and entered the courtyard. It was a person—someone close and yet a stranger, and besides it was evening in the courtyard, and the old man couldn't see so well. The stranger for a while looked about in the courtyard, walked about everywhere and then paused at the old man's house and walked over to it and opened the door and entered the house and halted at the threshold, and all at once . . . . And what did the old man see?

The king, and crowned with his crown, and standing at his threshold, and in the evening stillness. The old man hurried and ran to the king and stopped before him and stood there wordless, but he looked at the king and found him in great sorrow and great dread, and not like a king, but like someone who comes to plead for something, and not as to a subject, but as to a peer, and thus, and bowing, and thus in loyalty and deep devotion, he spoke to him and he asked:

"Your Majesty, my precious king, why have you come here, how can I serve you?"

"Not by serving," the king replied sadly. "But I have come to you with a plea. And this is my plea: You have a guest here for the night, a beggar has come to you, but he is *not* like others, and you know my misfortune, and you've heard what happened to the queen, and *he* can help us, and he can bring gladness to our hearts. I am here to ask you: Send me the beggar."

"Whom, great king?" the old man looked around in amazement, and searched through his room and did not find and did not understand. "Whom?"

"Him, the one who is sleeping there," the king pointed at Bovve and at his bed standing opposite them.

And.... When the old man opened his eyes from sleep and from dreaming and arose from his pillow and his bed, he saw: The room was filled with gray dawn and no more night, and the grayness peered in through the windows and was already paling on the walls and the ceiling. The old man got up from his bed and found Bovve, opposite him, up and awake already. And he stared at him, and Bovve at the old man too, and their eyes met and stared strangely, and then after gazing in the dawn, the old man spoke to Bovve and he said:

"Strange, beggar, really very strange .... I dreamt about you and about our king, and the king appeared to me in my dream, and the king told me to tell you: He summons you, and he invites you to come to him."

"Why?"

"To help him out of his misfortune, the misfortune I told you about."

And the old man stared at Bovve, and Bovve understood and asked him no more, and Bovve got up from his bed, and he put on his clothes, and began to prepare himself to go. Having dressed, he took his staff in his hand and his pack on his back, and having dressed and prepared himself, he turned to the old man, who had been watching him the whole time with surprise and respect and reverence, and Bovve said goodbye to the old man, and thanked him for his hospitality and for his bed for the night, and he started for the door of the house, to open the door and go through the door ....

And Bovve stepped out of the house and stepped into the courtyard, and then from the courtyard into the dawn street, and the street was still, and still deserted, and all the gates and all the doors were closed and locked, and shutters were shut, and the people were still asleep behind the shutters; he walked from that street to the next, and from the second to a third, and the first people, the early birds, were already coming out, and there was stirring in the courtyards, and now and then a passer-by would pass in the streets.

Bovve walked along the streets, and thus, and striding from one to the next, he at last came out on the main thoroughfare, the last street, the avenue where the royal palace stood, there, where he had to go.

And Bovve strode over to the palace and Bovve asked the guard to announce him: and thus, and thus, a beggar had to see the king, and there was no time to tarry, and could they announce him *right away*, and could they take him to the king as quickly as possible.

But it was still very early in the palace, and they didn't hurry and they didn't tell the king so quickly, for the king hadn't had any rest for so long, not before the birth and not after the birth, and only this night, and for the first time, he had fallen asleep while sitting on his throne; and thus, they didn't want to awake him, and they kept Bovve before the gates for a time, and he stood there and waited and looked forward anxiously to the king's awakening.

And at last the king awoke, from his sleep and from sitting in the silence, from his uncomfortable sleep and not sleeping in a bed. He caught sight of a servant waiting in front of him, and he addressed the servant:

What was it, and what had happened, and why was he standing there, and what did he have to say to him?

So the servant announced:

And thus and thus—and a beggar was standing at the gates . . . and he had been standing there for so long, since daybreak, and he wanted to see the king, and he wanted to come before the king; and, he said it was very important, and he said there was no time to tarry.

So the king commanded the servant:

Let him go and get him, and let him bring him into the palace, and no longer keep him at the gates, and the king would now have a look at the baby, and the king would soon come and receive the beggar.

And the king got up from his throne, and into the room where the baby was lying he went, and the servant went from where he was, and took off with the king's command to Bovve and to the gates.

And Bovve was brought into the royal hall, and was left there alone: and the king stayed with the child for a while, and stared at it as yesterday and the day before, and it was no better and was no worse, and it was in the same state and the same condition; and he stared at it and stood there a while, and merely sighed softly, and then before he went away, he cast a glance at the old midwife, who sat next to the baby; he stared at her as she sat there, and then, and no longer tarrying, he went back to the room where he had been before.

And there he found Bovve waiting for him, and standing the way you stand in front of a king, and the king gazed and stared at him, and at his humbleness and his foreignness here and his outlandishness here in this land, and then, and after looking at length, the king addressed him and asked him what he wanted:

What was he after and why had he come?

To the king, and with help for the king.

"Help?" the king was taken aback.

"Yes, great king: I heard about your fortune and your misfortune, about the birth of a long-awaited child, but it is ill and its life is doubtful, and so I have come to you now, and with help and with healing for your baby."

"And what is your healing?"

And Bovve started telling him about the mirror and its power, and about putting it in front of a sick person's face, and the mirror would bring death to someone who's doomed—and to someone who's fated to live, the mirror would bring life, and in this case, and he was sure, and the mirror would *heal* the child, and the mirror would bring it life and health.

"And how can you be so sure?" asked the king.

And Bovve told the king about his dream, and also the end and the promise of the dream: that he was to go and when he was called, and that he was to act and to use the mirror; so he obeyed and he acted and followed the call.

And who had called him?

The dream-dreamer, and through another man's dream.

And Bovve told him the story of the old man and *his* dream, and how the old man had told him how the king had come to him in his dream and asked him to send his guest, the beggar, into the palace, and so he heard him and heeded him, and he did it and went to where the old man sent him.

The king listened to Bovve's stories and his dreams, and they struck his mind and struck his heart, and he listened to them, and asked and asked, again and again, and Bovve told him all over again and with clarity and simplicity, and the king believed in Bovve, and he ordered that all the lords and doctors be told: and all the doctors

and all the lords were to come and stay; and the servants quickly
carried the message, and from one to another, and dashed and
rushed and hurried about with the king's command, and all were to
gather in the nursery: and thus and thus—and the king believed in
the beggar—and all were to come the faster the better, because the
king was relying on him.

And that's how it was: And all the courtiers and all the doctors
soon collected in the baby's room, and they surrounded the baby's
crib, and Bovve stood at the baby's feet, and the king was there too,
and the old midwife: and then, Bovve undid the bag containing the
mirror, and he took it out, and he held it and bent over the baby
and held it up to the baby's face, and he held it quietly, and soon,
and as he held it, and after a while and after a time, and all of them
saw and noticed, and all observed:

The baby's face began to color and to redden, and acquired a
living appearance and fresh and as though newly born: and its little
hands and little feet began to stir and pull, and stretch and reach,
and every so often another part of it began to show life, and more
and more, and its entire body was stirring and moving: and after
moving and stirring its limbs for a long, long time, and it opened its
eyes, which had been closed, and opened them and stared into the
mirror, and gazed and gazed for a long, long time, and after lying
quietly for a while, it suddenly twisted its face and its mouth, and
suddenly—with a yell, a babyish and childlike yell, out, out,
and—it broke into a wail . . . .

"To the breast and to the queen!" the midwife cried, and bent
over the child, and took it in her hands, and took it out of the
cradle, and took it to the queen, to the queen's chamber, and
brought it to her.

And the baby was brought to the queen, and the baby grabbed
the breast of the queen, and thirsty and starving as if for long, and
greedy and hungry, very, very, it grabbed it, and then lost it, and
hunted it eagerly, and found the nipple, and thus losing it and seeking it and finding it quickly, it at last began to suck, and with all its
breath and all its might it began to suck . . . .

And now the queen became a mother, and the king a father, and
the kingdom had an heir, and the entire palace looked different: lively and alive, happy and merry. The joy and the news soon went
beyond the palace and into the streets and through the capital, and
the people promptly took down the flags of mourning, the black

flags, and they hung out flags of rejoicing and colorful flags, and the people crowded in front of the palace, and milled and roared, and cheered and hailed and saluted the king: and they yelled for him to come out of the palace, and out he came, at his one side the midwife, the crone, and at his other side Bovve, the beggar. They escorted him on either side, and behind them the courtiers and the intimates all, the friends of the king and also the doctors. And he presented himself, the king, and he thanked the crowd for its best wishes and cheers, thanked them and bowed and waved joyously to the crowd, and then, and first Bovve and then the old woman, he pointed to them, and brought the crowd's attention to them, pointed to them and said:

"Know, people, that my truest friends, those who brought us joy and delighted our hearts, are the ones who are standing here, right here: and first of all He in heaven above, and then these friends—to them all we owe our joy and happiness."

And the people shouted their thanks to the old midwife and to Bovve, and yelled to them, and waved their hands and their hats, and waved and praised them to the skies the way people do: and they kept them there for a long time, on the balcony, and wouldn't let them go back in. "And let them remain out here, and let the people keep looking at them."

And then, and when the people had looked, and had looked their fill, the king, and then the midwife, and then Bovve, turned away from the crowd, and through the way that was made by the courtiers and relatives, they passed, and then passed on to the door, the one from which they had come, and went back into the palace, and back into the rooms of the palace.

The king then brought Bovve to a dining hall, to a table that was spread with wonderful things, and he had him sit down at the table there, and the king sat down in his usual place, and Bovve sat down at his right. There was a banquet there, and a huge one, and all the lords, and all the prominent men were invited to the banquet, and food and drink were brought and served, and such as were seldom even for the king, and the diners delighted and they pleasured themselves, and they ate and drank and made merry. And the king conversed with Bovve all the while, and kept remembering him, and kept asking him how he felt, and kept turning to him to ask his pleasure, and the best, and the finest, and let him enjoy, and the king wouldn't have it otherwise. And at last, and when the banquet was done, and at last, and when the banquet was over, the king turned to Bovve, and loud, and in front of the company, he said, addressing him:

"And now, beggar, whatever your lips shall speak. And know: And nothing will be too dear for me, and nothing will be too precious for me, whatever you and your tongue shall speak."

"Nothing, Your Majesty, I don't need a thing," Bovve replied to the king's proposal, to his good cheer, and to his readiness to do anything.

"What do you mean?" the king was amazed, and he turned astonished eyes to Bovve and then to all who were sitting about the table.

"Just that, great king: I don't need any presents, and I don't require anything. For what does a beggar want after all?"

"And gold and silver and costly things, and other precious objects?"

"No, dear king: The dearest thing is to sit at your table now, my greatest happiness is that I made you happy, and I need nothing else, and I lack nothing more."

And then Bovve briefly told the king his story, and all that had happened to him, and that he had to bring joy to three kings, and he had already brought joy to two, and now he had to get underway, because the way was crucial to him, and he could not remain in one place.

And now the king comprehended Bovve, and he refrained from gifts and presents, and only asked him to rest a while, here in the palace. And Bovve explained that he couldn't rest, but he thanked the king. And now, with the banquet finished, it was evening, and the dining hall was dark. Bovve stood up from his seat, and he peered around for his pouch (which he had left in the nursery that morning). He peered around, but he couldn't find it, and he was about to ask the king for permission to go to the nursery: He had left his pouch there. But at that moment a door opened, from another room and into the dining hall, and at the threshold of the door stood the old midwife with something in her hand and wrapped in something, and she entered and stood by the threshold, and she looked around the dining hall, the evening-darkened hall, and she looked for something in the company and among the guests who were sitting along the table, and her eyes darted from seat to seat and chair to chair. But what she sought she didn't find among the guests. And then she turned to the king who was sitting at the head, and she fixed her eyes upon him, and she saw Bovve standing up, and looking around and looking for something and not finding it. So the old woman turned to Bovve, and spoke to him, and said to him:

"Wait, beggar, tarry and do not hurry!"

And the old woman, from the threshold of the room, where she had been standing and waiting, walked away and over to Bovve, and then she held out what she held in her hand, and she handed it to him, and she said as she handed it:

"This is a wolf's tooth, beggar, take it and it will be useful to you . . . . I received it from my parents, and *my* parents from *their* parents, and thus from generation to generation, and it has been handed down from hand to hand, and now let me present it to you . . . . And you should know that it has a virtue and a power, this wolf's tooth, to hearten all hearts, and to dishearten all fears and terrors, and anyone, no matter what his terror or dread, and no matter what disquiets him, need merely wear it a while on his throat—and the disquiet shall be undone, and the fear and the terror shall be done away with. Take it . . . ."

Bovve thanked the old woman, and he took the wolf's tooth and he thanked her again. And then he turned to the king, and asked his permission to go to the nursery, for he wanted to get his pouch. And the king gave him leave, and Bovve went there for a while, and stayed in the nursery for a time, and then put the tooth inside his pouch, and put his pouch upon his back, and then, also taking his stick in hand, he returned to the hall, where the king and all the guests were sitting. And Bovve halted before the king, and he said farewell, and wished him well, and all the very best. And then Bovve said farewell to all the guests and also the old midwife, and all the guests and the old midwife gave him their blessings and wished him well and the very best. And he took the blessings from all the well-wishers and turned away from all of them, and then, after turning away, and from that room and from the palace he went out and found himself in silence and nightfall and lateness on the street and in the capital . . . .

13.

And Bovve left the capital, and he also left this second land, and
Bovve kept on walking, and started wandering again, and he went
from place to place and from one under-heavenliness to the next . . .
and he chanced into fields and tiny villages. And there he would
stop, and sometimes just a night, and sometimes he spent a night and
a day. He would spend whatever time he spent, and then he went
on, sometimes at twilight for an evening in the fields, and sometimes
at dawn before the eruption of the radiance of morning. He thus
would leave the villages and go off into the wide and open fields,
the treeless and the woodless fields, and horizons stretched out vast
before him, and heaven and earth, uncovered, loomed and lay before him. And thus, and roaming for a while, and thus, and ranging
for a time, he would stop in a field every now and then, right in the
middle of a field, and let himself down upon the earth and undo his
pouch with all his things, and take out his mirror, his magic thing,
and wordlessly look into his looking-glass, and have a look at his
past, and also at times inquire about his future and what was waiting for him.

And thus one time, and thus several times, and thus many times,
and ever since Bovve had left the latest land. And Bovve was weary
of wandering, and nothing happened to him all the while, and nothing occurred, he met no man coming his way, and no one driving
and no one walking to catch up with him from behind. And
lonesome, he wandered, and like one forgotten, Bovve, and he
found no villages or settlements. And his sorrow was great, and he
was afflicted with worries and cares.

And then one day, in the middle of the day, he halted in the
middle of a field, and walked no farther and stood in silence, and in
the radiant day, in the open field, under the sun and its burning
brightness. And he paused and halted for a while, and he mulled
about himself and about things beyond his situation, and he wandered and pondered, and then he seemed to remember something,
and he came to his senses and said to himself:

"The mirror, Bovve, ought to know, it ought to say what lies in
wait and what to await."

And Bovve sank down upon the ground, and he took apart his
pouch, and took out the mirror, and began to look into the

looking-glass, and the mirror tarried and waited a while, and for a while it wouldn't change, and it didn't alter its appearance. It was, as always, small and shiny and light, and it only reflected the sunniness and the dayfulness, and it only showed a piece of the sky, a bare, pure stretch, a clear, bright stretch, and with a tiny sun in the sky, and in a corner far away. So Bovve looked at the tiny sun, at its roundness and smallness and paleness, and at its fiery sparks in its paleness, and as he watched, he noticed that softly and under the tiny sun, from the lowest and farthest part of the sky, a tiny cloud, all white, appeared, tiny, and like a wisp of smoke, a tiny tuft, the kind of thing you see in a sky. The tuft emerged, and having emerged, it paused and didn't move for a while and didn't budge from its place—and then, having come and shown itself, it began so slowly to dissolve, and a horseman, a rider from far away, appeared to Bovve.

And Bovve saw the horse, and on the horse the horseman sitting, so quietly in an afternoon, on a border somewhere, on a horizon, and as at the start of a country, the horseman upon his horse. Softly, and on the border, and at midday, and in broad radiance, the horse was not visited by anyone or anything, not a man and not a bird flying past. And green was the grass there and covering and occupying everything—and no one came and no one showed up, and no foot trod upon the grass, and no wing beshadowed the calm of day. Only the horseman and alone on his horse, his silent horse, guarded the border of that land, and watched the day and the stillness by the border, by the beginning of the border.

And Bovve looked and looked at him, the rider, remote, and calm, and upon his horse, and it seemed as if the rider, too, were looking back at him, at his being in the middle of the field. They kept their peace and paused for several minutes, and all at once, and for a second—and Bovve recognized his *first* rider, the one who appeared to him in his childhood, in the field, and when he had left the old man's shack, after his death. And Bovve was terribly glad to see him, and all at once he wanted to rush to him, and he started toward him, and he forgot that ... the rider was only in the mirror—and at that very moment, the image in the mirror changed, and wiped the cloud away, and it was gone, as though it had never been, and the horseman was gone from under the cloud, and the looking-glass looked as it had before, glossy and glassy, and the sun shone into it from its corner, and the small stretch of sky was filled

with blueness. And Bovve peered into the pure blue and—even
though the horseman was gone, and not a trace was left of his
horse, but a hope that was pure and light and heavenly was left
with Bovve and even after the disappearance.

And Bovve stood up, and Bovve put the mirror in his pouch, and
he tied up the pouch again, and started off again with the pouch—
and he walked and walked, from that day into the night and from
that night into the next morning, and strode and never stopped anywhere, and sought no villages nor towns, and had no need for them
and no use for them—and thus, and walking on and on, and thus,
and roaming and rambling, until one day—

It was a sunny day, an afternoon, bright and radiant, clear and
pure, and Bovve found himself in a field, a vast and a horizoned
field, rolling and open on all sides. He came into it and he stopped
in the middle, and the field lay bright and radiant, and the green
grass was greening on it, and sunbeams coming from the sun played
and flashed upon the green. And a hush prevailed, a calm and fieldy
silence, an afternoon stillness, undisturbed, only the grasshoppers,
the soaring springers and grass-sawyers, kept leaping from blade to
blade and from hiding-place to hiding-place, always hiding in a
different place, stopping there and sawing and sawing.

And Bovve found himself in this field, in the middle, and he
found himself stopping there, and he kept turning to another side
and resting his eyes upon that side. And at last, and after seeing and
scanning, he spotted—silently, on the horizon, the most silent skyline, the farthest and least visible—a horseman, mounted upon a
horse.

And Bovve stared at the rider a space, and watched him sitting
on the horse; and having wordlessly watched and silently stared,
Bovve left his place in the field, and walking along the middle line,
he started out toward the skyline, where the rider was sitting.

Upon arriving, he found the rider languishing in a day of languishing, sitting slack with slackened reins, silent and staring, as if
accustomed to staring thus. Bovve walked up to him and addressed
his silence, and thus, and addressing him, he blessed him with the
day and with blessings:

"Good afternoon and God be with you, horseman."

"The very same to you, beggar."

"And why is the horseman standing here, and what is he waiting
for?"

"For beggars coming from abroad."

"And why does he need the beggars?"

"The king has commanded, and he observes the king's command."

"And why does the king need the beggars?"

"Because of something that happened."

"And what?"

"It would take so long to tell the story." But he *had* to tell and he *ought* to tell, and if the beggar so wished and desired, he should listen to him and give him some time.

And Bovve agreed, and Bovve silently stood before the horseman and the horse, and the horseman remained above, not changing his place and not changing his seat, and silently and with a fieldlike voice, dull and as though unaccustomed to speaking, he began to tell his story, and this is what he told:

14.
The Horseman's Story

Our king was strong and powerful, his might and his voice made generals and armies tremble, his pride and appearance made the people kneel before him, his word and command made mouths and ears harken, and his will and wishes had no bounds and no borders....

Now one day, the king desired: Wherever there were strong men and athletes in his land, let them be brought to his capital, he wanted to wrestle with them, and show everyone his strength. And it was announced throughout the country and throughout the kingdom, and riders rode out from the capital and announced the news in the nearby cities, and the nearby cities spread the news to the farther cities, and the farther ones to even farther ones, and thus on and on, and until the news had reached all the corners of the kingdom, and until the will of the king had reached all the borders.

And thus it was, and from every far-flung nook and cranny, they gathered the strongest and the most powerful; and whoever had a name in his town, and whoever had renown in his village, was selected and given enough for all his expenses and needs: And they were to go and they were to travel, and they were to test themselves and show the king their strength. And so they went, and rode, and traveled, as far as it was and as far as it went, to the capital.

And at last, and arriving, they gathered at the court and at the gates of the king, and each announced where he was from and each announced that he had come. And each was admitted and registered, and shown where to be and where to stay, until his turn would come in turn, and his time would come to wrestle. And until that time, they were left to their own devices, and they could do whatever they wished.

And so they went their separate ways, and each one went to where he had been assigned, to his definite place he went, and there he stayed and spent his time as he wished to spend it, and ate and drank and pleasured himself, and thus, and free, and unoccupied, and thus, and idle and indolent, he would wander all day through the capital, and thus roaming and roving, whole days and whole nights, they filled the houses of joy, the places of drink and love . . . .

And from time to time, another one, and when his time had come, would be called to court and to the king.

And he would arrive. And when he was there, he was dressed in something light, and flesh-colored and snug and skintight, to wrestle in and encounter the king. The strong man would don it and get soaps and things to smoothen his hands that were like shovels, and then to dry his smoothened hands. And they would give the wrestler these things, and then, and when the strong man was ready, and then, and when he had done everything, and the fixed time had come, they would take him into the court, to a fixed place. And there a circus building and a theater auditorium were built, a circular structure like half an apple, and closed on three sides, and only the third side, the one facing the seats, was open. And before the open side, there were rows of benches, whitewashed, and there the spectators would assemble, the guests invited by the king. And then the athlete would be brought in, into the open building, before the gathering, and he would stand before the spectators, and the servant would call out the athlete's name and the name of his town, and the crowd would silently stare at the strong man, and experts would stare at his limbs and parts, and now and again, the experts would point out his limbs to their neighbors and those who were sitting nearby. And sitting there, and staring at him, they would sometimes stand up from their seats, and stare at his *entire* physique, his form and shape. And the crowd would gaze at the athlete, and the athlete at the crowd, and he would see their refinement and their composure, their dress and their comportment, their courtly background and their familiarity with the king and closeness to the king, and he would contemplate them, and then, and the first sound (from a gong, and one not seen by the crowd) would resound for the king's appearance and the king's arrival. A sound .... A while, and then two, and the second sound .... And the athlete would turn around on all sides, and the athlete would look every which way—and then, and the third sound .... And the king would come, and to that place, and appear and step out to meet the athlete ....

And this is what happened: The moment the strong man caught sight of the king in his dress, his royal attire, in his wealthy attire aglow with golden tinsel; and the moment the king stood before him with his height and pride, with his body and bodily solidarity, with his assurance and certainty, and as the king approached the strong man with his bold tread, and with his confidence, and came before him—and the strong man lost his courage and strength, he felt like a common man before the king, an obedient subject of the king, and then, and when the king motioned for him to begin, to grapple with him and wrestle with him, the strong man could extend no hands, no strong hands, and no confident and self-assured hands, but as with a couple of slaves and a couple of weaklings, with yielding and with great abatement, and with a face that stared at the king and with crestfallen eyes with no courage or boldness. And then the king would take him, and one and two, and however he wished, and however was best for himself, and hold him and behold him for a spell, and generously, and giving him time, to think about himself and come to his senses, and the strong man would think about himself and about his situation and his vocation, but by now it was late: The king had already taken his first advantage, he had profited from the strong man's confusion and from the first few minutes. The king was the commencer by now and in control, he had the first move and the better position, he took him and he took him about, and held him for a while and a time before the crowd—and when the king gripped and clutched the strong man and held on to him with all his power, and the crowd could see him twist the man's backbone every which way, and contort him to one side, and bend him to the other side, and the strong man had no choice and the strong man had no will—and then, and after a few such minutes, and now, and after the strong man's helplessness and powerlessness, and the strong man was bent back, and weak, and over his back, and the king over him, and the king was smirking at his powerlessness . . . .

And the king was the winner, and the crowd applauded, and the strong man was abashed. And the strong man was ashamed to stand up again, and the audience turned away from the strong man, to avert their eyes from his shame and let him stand up by himself.

And that was how it always was, and thus from time to time, and every time with a different strong man, and the king outwrestled them all, and the king was always the victor, and the strong men were all abashed, and the strong men were ashamed in front of one another. Until one day . . . .

And this was the very last time, and all the strong men were still in the city, for none of them had been given leave to leave the capital, and so none of them had gone his way, and the king did it deliberately, to plume himself in front of them and everyone with his final victory, and he wanted to show them his greatness and strength, and so he gave an order, and it was proclaimed throughout the city: The king was to wrestle one last time, but this time not just in front of his courtiers, but in front of his people all. Whoever wanted to could come, and young and old could come if they wished, and all would be admitted to the wrestling ring, and the strong men too, who had all been beaten and hadn't left.

And thus it was, and the final strong man was soaped up and salved up, his hands smoothened, and then dried after being smoothened, and he was dressed like all the earlier ones, in a light-weight and light-colored garment for wrestling, and in this attire he was taken out to the wrestling place, where the king was to come. And the strong man went out, and the crowd gazed at him and gaped at his strength, for—he was unusually strong and solidly built, and his body was extraordinary, and he stood tall like the bole of a tree, straight and proud, as motionless as the trunk of a tree. He looked around the place he stood in, and at the crowd, the huge throng, that had gathered before his eyes and was gazing and gaping at him. He smiled and was proud, and then slowly rubbed his hands and waited for the moment of the king's arrival. And the strong men winked to him from their places and instructed him and counseled him with their blinks. And he obeyed them and followed their advice. And then, as always, a few minutes later, the sound of the gong resounded, and after the first minute, the second peal, and after the second minute, the third peal also came. And then, and when the third peal resounded, the king, from a place, from an unexpected point, emerged, and even statelier and more beautiful, and even wealthier and more embellished than usual. And the king halted opposite the strong man, and the king stood before his opponent.

And the king, this time, could see, face to face with the strong man, that this strong man did not look like all the others and did not look like the earlier strong men. Calmer and more self-assured, somehow, and more composed and more cheerful, the strong man now encountered the king's arrival, and although paying his respect to royalty, but nevertheless mindful of his duty and his business, which he had taken upon himself and which was not the issue, and the king himself, after all, had called him out, and the king himself had allowed him to wrestle with him on an equal footing. And the strong man thus had to be mindful, and he had to prove to the king that his subjects obey and do his bidding, and even opposing the king himself, if the king commanded and ordered thus. And he thought those things to himself, and the king could see it in the strong man's face and his eyes could read it in *his* eyes. And he was content, the king was, and a smile crossed his face, a royal smile, an all-forgiving smile. And yet, and soon, recalling his role and his place, after all, he removed the smile from his lips, he turned to the strong man with severity and gravity, and thus, and addressing him, he fixed his eyes, severely commanding, and his gazes, exacting obedience, upon him.

But the strong man had noticed the earlier smile, the royal smile, and he understood it, and he construed it in his own favor, and he gave himself his word: And he would fulfill his task with perfection, come what may, and be what will. And then, and when the smile was gone from the royal lips, and to his eyes and to his motions, the royal gravity and severity returned, it didn't really bother the strong man, he really didn't care, and the strong man himself burst into a smile, and then, and when the king strode over to him, stretching out his arms and reaching out to grab him, the strong man also stretched out *his* arms, solid and assured and confident, and obedient only to the strong man, and he stretched them out and took hold of the king, and the king began, and the strong man didn't back down, and the king got a good grip on the strong man's arms, and he on the king's—no less fast and no less tight. And the king tried the first assault on the strong man, and the strong man didn't let him try it, and kept the king away. And they gazed and stared at one another for a while. And then the king became graver, and the strong man smiled, and then the king made another try, and the strong man held him off once again, and the king, after the second time, looked at the strong man again and stared at him with severity: at his calm and confident stance, careful and cautious, and all aloof, and with a self-assured respect, not approaching the king and not attempting anything on *his* part, and merely watchful and merely alert, and evading danger. And the spectators got up from their seats and regarded the strong man, and he became close to all of them, and all were on his side and favored his fortune, and the audience was even more interested, and they stared and they wouldn't stop staring at the strong man, and all of them hailed him and heartened him with their hails. And the king could feel it from above, and for an instant he lifted his eyes from his opponent toward the audience, the crowded throng of fascinated spectators, and he noticed: All eyes were turned from him and all eyes were fixed on his opponent. The king was rankled, it struck him to the quick, and he looked once again at his opponent and glared at him as at a servant who had to do his bidding, a disobedient underling, unruly, and the king kept glaring. And the strong man facing the king didn't even notice the king's glare for he was absorbed in himself and his actions, so as not to lose sight of what he was doing, and indeed he never lost sight for an instant, and he was sure of himself and his goal—and then, and for a third time, and . . . . When the king made a sudden and unexpected lunge to catch him unawares and wrest him from his calm, and the king grabbed the strong man around his back, to seize him in a stranglehold as was his wont—the strong man was waiting, and expected the unexpected, and when the king tried his stranglehold, the strong man got the better of him, and surging his body and firming his foothold against the ground and lifting the king and moving him from his place and his stance, and—before the king could defend himself and catch his balance, and—before the audience could move from their seats and from the terrible crowding, to watch what was about to happen—and the king was already in the hands of the strong man, caught and helpless and in his power and totally at his mercy. And the strong man—once, and then twisted, and once again .... And he twisted him to one side and then to the other, and after the king's first twist, and upon his back and facing the strong man, and bending over, and upon the ground and stretching out—and yet not dropped—and stretching out—and yet not felled.

"Ha! What is it . . . ?" and the spectators blurted out a sigh and a surprise and a puzzled terror and enormous shock.

And the strong man straightened out the king, and the strong man put the king in his place, and the spectators hurried to disband, and to get away as fast as they could. And they left the court, and left the place where the king and the strong man had had their bout, and they left the scene a vacant place, only the king was left in his place, alone and forsaken, alone and forlorn—by the audience, by the spectators all, and by the strong man who had bettered him.

And then the king went back into the palace, and the king locked himself in his private cabinet, and he wouldn't let anyone in, and he wouldn't listen to anyone, and he wouldn't receive any lord, and he wouldn't open to any servant. Shut in, locked in, and a day went by, and another day, and he saw no one, and received no one. He took no food during these days and couldn't sleep during these nights, and all the while he kept picturing the scene: his being in the hands of the strong man, and a weakling and broken in his power and his strength, and the strong man doing with him what he would, and bending down and making him bow, and being *able* to twist him over, and refraining only out of respect for the king.

The king was fully dejected, and he never stopped thinking about the thing, and ever kept musing about what had happened, and what it had looked like to the people, and what it had seemed like to the onlookers. His grief was great, and he fell into a deep melancholy and dejection, and didn't want to see anyone and didn't want to hear any comfort, the words of friends and the talk of near-and-dear.

At last, they turned away from him, his near-and-dear, they saw they were having no effect, and they sent him his court doctor, his personal physician, and then other doctors, not from the court. But he wouldn't listen to his doctor, and he wouldn't hear the others or what they said, nor would he heed their important advice, or the things they tried to talk him into, or the foolish things they counseled him. He paid no attention to all their talk, it went into one ear and out the other, let them say what they had to and talk what they could, and let them go away as soon as possible.

And then, and when the physicians left him alone and left his chambers, he would stay alone with his thoughts and what he had been thinking, and free and freed of everyone, with all his devotion and all his absorption.

And the king, as it were, rejected his crown, and the king, as it were, abandoned everything pertaining to the crown, and he never inquired about anything, and he wasn't interested in anything, and thus, and in his solitude, he spent day and night with his thoughts and his own melancholy.

And sleep deserted the king, and the king couldn't find any rest, and if ever the king did fall asleep, dreams and fancies and fantasies, and terrors would come to terrify him. He would wake up, he would leap from his bed, and scurry around in his chambers at night, and with gaping eyes and a frightened heart, and an even more terrified mind, and with memories and remembrances of the things he had dreamt. Then his fear would be even greater, and he would be afraid for a time to lean on the bed and lie down on the bed and put his head upon the pillows, and thus, and running around, he was afraid of himself and of sitting, and at times for an hour and at times for two, and even at times for all the night, and until the day, and until the paleness of day peered in.

And thus a while, and thus a time, and those near and dear to the king grew worried, and the entire household of the king took his sorrow to heart, and all of them, they got together, and took counsel with one another, and wondered how they could ease the king's sorrow and his situation, and they listened to one another's words and advice, and with a number of counsels and solutions were suggested, such as inviting healers and spellers. And this was done, and they were summoned, and they spoke their spells and rolled their eggs, and their spells didn't ease, and their eggs didn't help.

So someone proposed they summon a saint, and so they followed this advice, and they sent oil and ointment to the houses of worship, and money for alms to the cemeteries of the capital city. And various holy men sent the king various amulets and remedies, and also herbs, and all kinds of talismans, and the king's bed was surrounded with all these things, but none of them helped, and the king remained with his fears as before, with his terrors so huge, with his nights without sleep, and his fear of dreams at night.

And now, and one last adviser offered advice and made a suggestion:

In the name of the king and at the king's command, let them send out riders and send out servants to all the borders and all the frontiers of the country. Let them be stationed along the borders, and let them be posted there, and let them wait for the beggars and the wanderers. And let them tell any wayfarer and every wanderer the story of what happened to the king, and ask them and inquire of them whether they might know and whether they might have some sort of remedy for the king. Because, the last adviser added, the wanderers wander everywhere, the beggars come from every land, and the wayfarers meet all kinds of people, and they witness all kinds of things and events, and only beggars know, and only beggars *can* know . . . .

15 .

And now the horseman finished his story, and Bovve was standing before him and his horse, and the horseman asked him the question in the king's name, the question for which he had been stationed here:

Might the beggar know, or might he have heard, of such a case, and might he have a remedy for the king?

"For the king?" said the king, to whom the beggar was telling the story, the long tale, all this time. "For the king, you say? But *I* am the king. *I* am the king that the story's about, I am the king who's deprived of sleep, and who's been afflicted with dread and terror, and my friends have been seeking advice for me, and I've done everything, and nothing has helped, nothing, and in the end I sent out my riders and told them to station themselves along the borders of my land. Why, that is *me*! That's I, the king!" the king then cried in the end.

"And this is *me*!" the beggar replied. "And this is I, whose name is Bovve, it's I and me, who's visited various countries and who's stood in front of different kings, and this is I who cheered the hearts of two kings, and now I have come to *you*, to gladden *you* and *your* heart. And know, Your Majesty: I have a remedy for you, and I have a healing for your dread, and you know my solution, and you know my method from my tale."

And now Bovve undid his pouch, and from there he took out the wolf's tooth to be hung on a string to be hung around the neck, and he reached out and handed it to the king, and with it he addressed the king:

"Put it on, Your Majesty, and let it hang on you and on your neck, and I am certain and I am confident that this is your healing, that this is your sure remedy, and let your servants, Your Majesty, give me a place in one of your rooms, for me to spend the night and spend some time with you, because I want to pass the time until you regain your health, until you recover with my remedy. And today, and this very night, your sleep will return to you, and the fears and terrors will vanish from your slumber . . . . Put it on . . . ."

The king obeyed Bovve and his words, he took the wolf's tooth from his hand, and hung it on the string, and hung the string around his neck, and then he smiled, a faithful and believing smile, a good and confident smile: And let him only recover, and Bovve would see his kindness and reward, and meanwhile, and he thanked him kindly, and meanwhile, and he believed in the remedy.

And now the king clapped and summoned a servant, and a servant appeared in the room, and the king told the servant to take Bovve to a room for the night, and to prepare everything and take care of everything, and provide him with everything he needed and all comforts, and in the morning, and the servant was to be ready in the morning, and ready to attend upon Bovve's needs.

And Bovve was taken to a room, and Bovve was shown everything, his bed for the night, his bed linen, and he was provided with everything, royally and regally, and then, and after preparing everything and providing everything for Bovve, the servant stole out of the chamber, leaving Bovve to his own devices. And Bovve undressed, and for a while and a length of time, he lay in a soft bed, and tired and drained, he forgot himself, and not even turning and not even tossing, but lying as he lay, and forgetting himself, he dozed off into the night and into his fatigue.

And in the morning, and when Bovve opened his eyes, and he saw the broad daylight through the window, his limbs still felt the fatigue and the long wandering, and he didn't feel like getting up, but then he remembered the place where he was and what he had promised the king and assured him, and that he had told him he would be sure to fall asleep, and that with that night, which had just passed, he would have his restfulness and his healing. Bovve remembered, and Bovve arose from his bed, and got off his bed, and he put on his clothes, and then he clapped his hands and summoned a servant. And the servant quickly came. And the servant asked him his wishes and desires, and then he hurried to fulfill them. And Bovve washed and cleaned himself, and Bovve made himself ready, and in case the king were to summon him, and when he had eaten up and had drunk up what the servant had served him, he really did receive an order, through another servant, that the king indeed had called for him, and that he was to come to the king immediately.

And Bovve didn't hesitate, and he came in to the king, and Bovve halted at the threshold, and scarcely recognized the king, for the king looked rested and relaxed this morning and from the night that preceded it, and his eyes sparkled and smiled and brightened, and he felt glad and he felt cheery, and his body and his bearing radiated gladness and cheer. And smiling, he turned to Bovve and said, wishing him a good morning and blessing him:

"Good morning, Bovve, you beggar!"

"Good morning to you, Your Majesty!"

And the king told Bovve about his night and how he had spent it, and how he had rested and slept in its restfulness, and never dreaming a single dream and never seeing a single nightmare. And thus he spoke, and full of good cheer, and he gazed at Bovve in love and gratitude, and felt closer to him and nearer to him, and thus, and whiling the morning away, and chatting with Bovve for a while, he gave him leave to leave his chambers: and he could go and do as he wished, and he could be free and spend his time as he wanted to, and only return during the day, at noon, and only come back absolutely at lunchtime.

And Bovve obeyed, and Bovve then took his leave of the king, and Bovve strolled around the court, and Bovve had a look at the palace and the palace environs, and thus an hour, and thus another, and more and more, and longer and longer, and then, and when it was time and it was noon, Bovve returned to the palace and to his room, and waited for the king's order and waited for the king to summon him to lunch.

And then the king sent for Bovve, and he called for him through a servant, and Bovve was brought to the dining room, and Bovve was offered a place of honor, and the dining table was already set, and covered with all the best and finest foods, and the repast was waiting for guests, and wines were sparkling their bottles. So Bovve sat down, and next to him and all around, courtiers and friends of the king were sitting. The others began to talk to him, and before the king could appear at the threshold, and they inquired about Bovve's country and Bovve's home, and what life was like there, and how things were, and about the customs and traditions. And Bovve told them about his country, about his land and other lands that he had seen and he had passed through, and he made a good impression on the guests, and they liked him and they felt warmly toward him, especially when they heard why he was here and why he had come, and that he had brought a remedy for the king, as of that night, the very first, and the king felt fine and dandy, and to-day, and this was the very first time since his illness began, that he had invited his friends and was having a banquet with them, and so they loved Bovve even more, and they surrounded him with even more respect and attention, and they asked him about everything and about his entire life, and Bovve answered and replied to their questions.

And then, a door leading from another room into the dining hall opened, and the king himself appeared, he who had been isolated and not seen for so long, but now he looked fine and kingly, just as he had looked before his illness, slightly under the weather and slightly estranged, but he was back, and back as ever, and slowly recovering his health. He appeared, and the lords and the friends of the king at their places and at their chairs stood up and remained standing, and encountered the king, and Bovve too, he too, was among the standing lords. And the king looked at the company and at the guests who were gathered here, and first he wanted to see one man, one special guest, and he saw him then—Bovve. And the king strode over from the threshold, and the king strode over to Bovve, and his face shone upon Bovve, and he greeted him, and he smiled at him, and he led him from his place to another place, and then, and telling him to sit down in this new place, the king turned to the lords and to his friends, and greeting all of them and then each in turn, he hailed them and expressed his friendship to all:

"Greetings, lords," the king then said, "greetings, and for such a long time, of not seeing one another and my not appearing in your company—but you know the reason, and the fault is not the king's. And know, lords, that the king would not be with you now, and I would not be seeing your faces or you mine, if it hadn't been for this man, if it hadn't been for this best friend of the king."

And the king told the lords what they already knew, what they had found out from the servants when summoned to the king, when they had asked the reason why they were summoned, and the servants had told them the reason. The king told them a second time, and the lords listened with respect, and they were glad and they were cheerful, and they kept looking at Bovve, the benefactor to the king. When the king had finished telling the story, he turned to Bovve and found him where he had shown him his place. And then the king signaled to the lords, and the lords sat down wherever they sat whenever sitting at a feast. And sitting down, and quietly, and respectfully, but amicably, as ever, they began the banquet, the beautifully prepared and quietly readied feast.

And the company ate, and the company chatted, and the company drank and exchanged all the news, all the new things that had happened in the capital, and all the events that had occurred throughout the land, and not only their country, but other countries, nearby and far away, and all the things that people, passing through, had told. And the king was interested in all the news, and kept asking the tellers and inquiring about everything, and letting nothing slip by, and hearing all that was vital and crucial. And thus, and hearing the news, and thus, and feeling of good cheer, the king kept remembering Bovve, and turned to him as well, and thus, and addressing him, he chatted with him every time, and kept drawing him into the general conversation.

And thus they chatted through the banquet, and the feasting lasted well into the night, and didn't end until day was past and darkness was come. And then they got up from their lengthy sitting, and they took their leave of the king, wishing him a speedy recovery and a total recuperation. And then, and after nodding his head and bowing his head to everyone, the king left the dining hall and went to his chambers, and Bovve went to *his* room to spend another night in the palace, and the lords went home, and each to his family and to his household.

And the king slept that second night too, and he spent that second night, too, in sleep, and the king was becoming better and better, and every day made him healthier and healthier. And a week went by, and two weeks wore by, and the king returned to his earlier condition, and his interest returned in the kingdom and in everything pertaining to the kingdom, and his interest kept growing, and nothing slipped by, no details and no trivia, that didn't spark his interest. And then one day, Bovve told the servants he wanted to see the king, and the king ordered that Bovve be admitted, and Bovve came before him, and halted before him, and bowed in deep respect—and then, and after properly bowing, Bovve addressed him and said to him:

"Your Majesty, your health and well-being have returned to you, and your dread and your terror have left your thoughts, and I am certain and confident that your healing is complete, and solid and sure, and the cure is for the rest of your life, and therefore, and I have come to you to tell you that my being here is no longer needed."

Having spoken, he waited for the king's answer and for the king's response. And the king took a while to answer and then the king said to Bovve and suggested that he stay a while, here in his home, his palace. But Bovve once again addressed the king, and he said to the king:

"Do not detain me, Your Majesty, for you do know, and I did tell you, and indeed I told you for what and for whom I went out in the world, and that they are waiting for me in the royal palace, and that they're looking out for my return to the royal palace, and therefore my request to you, Your Majesty, and therefore, please do not keep me here any longer."

"All right," said the king after holding his tongue and quietly thinking about Bovve's plea, and then agreeing to it, and staring at his standing and staying before him, with love and devotion: "All right, Bovve, go and prepare for tomorrow, prepare yourself for going away."

And the king for tomorrow ordered that another feast be prepared, and let the lords all come together, and again the courtiers were to gather, for the king was saying farewell to his friend, and the king's will and wish was that all should say farewell to him.

And that was what happened: The banquet was prepared for the next day, and the banquet was huge, and such as was rarely given in the palace, and the lords came, and they were dressed and adorned in a lordly fashion. And the lords sat down, and all around, and all as always, and all of them in their usual places, and the king addressed the company, and all who were sitting around the table. He pointed to Bovve who was sitting at his right, and he drew the company's attention and their eyes toward Bovve, and then he turned to the company, and he said to the guests:

"Lords and my friends, my friend will be leaving us shortly, our friend can no longer stay with us, and so we say farewell to him today, and we wish him all the best for his journey. But how can we reward him well?"

"With gold and silver, with precious things, and all the wealth that we own," was the response of the lords.

The king, after the response of the lords, turned to Bovve, and fixed his gaze on him, and thus, gazing, he waited for his word, he waited for him to speak:

"No, dear lords," Bovve cried out. "I don't need any gold or silver, and I have no need of precious things or valuables, for a wanderer doesn't require unnecessary objects, for all those things would be heavy for a wanderer: And so I thank you, and so I renounce any valuables."

"If such is the case, dear lords," the king then cried out, "if he doesn't need any gold or silver, and if riches and wealth are heavy for him, then I have something else for him, I have something that will *lighten* his travels. And that is my wolf-horse, and that, as you know, lords, was brought to me by a gypsy at my coronation, and the gypsy told me and he taught me when he gave it to me: The wolf is lacking a front tooth, the wolf has lost a tooth. If a man mounts him, and the man has a wolf's tooth, and he ties it to a long stick and sticks out the stick before the wolf's eyes, the wolf will whirl and whiz away, and he will chase the tooth in front of him, and he'll run for a day, and then another day, and streak across an entire country, and thus in a short while he will cross not just one land but several lands.... And now I will give this wolf-horse to my friend and my healer, and also the tooth with which I was healed by my friend, and I hope and I pray that my friend will accept, and I have faith and confidence that my friend will thus be spared a great deal of travail and trouble."

And now the king told the company to eat and drink and enjoy themselves: Eat and drink and honor his friend, and wish him a happy journey and a joyous homecoming, and might he be healthy and travel in health, and as all the lords and as the king himself wished him.

And they ate and they drank and they obeyed the king, and they honored Bovve and wished him well, and Bovve returned their wishes all. And the king himself ate and drank and was unusually merry and unusually cheery, and he rejoiced in Bovve and his friendship, and he shook his hand and thanked him and embraced him. And when he had thanked him and rejoiced in him, and when all had eaten and drunk, the king then turned to Bovve and told him to make ready for his journey.

And Bovve obeyed, and he left the table, and went back to his room, and there he put his pouch upon his back and took his stick into his hand, and having thus dressed himself and reassumed his beggarly look, he went back into the dining hall, where the king and the lords were waiting for him. And all of them turned toward the door, and all of them went out through the door—first the king, and Bovve after him, and after Bovve, all the lords, and all the servants of the king.

They came from the palace into the courtyard, and then to a corner of the courtyard, to a stable, a huge one, closed and secluded from all the other buildings, a stable with many horses and chariots. And they opened the stable, and all of them entered, and they went past many stalls and pens, avoiding them and ignoring them, and they came to a corner, and the king told the riding master to open a little room that was barred. And the riding master opened it and led out a wolf—a gray wolf, that was acting wild, and that looked like a dog. And he led it out, and the king told him to muzzle it, and he muzzled it. And then the king took the wolf's tooth from his neck and ordered a servant to tie it to a stick for Bovve. And the servant tied the tooth to a stick, and then they led the wolf out of the stable, and through the courtyard, and in full sight of everyone, and they came to the gates, and they opened the gates for him. And now the king turned to Bovve, and made his farewells, and he bade him farewell, and he hugged him and kissed him, and then he told all the lords to bid him farewell, and that was what they did. And then the king motioned to Bovve to mount the wolf—and Bovve got astride the wolf. And then, and when Bovve took hold of the stick with the wolf's tooth and stretched it out in front of the wolf and in front of his eyes, the wolf surged forward from his place and from before the gates, and quickly and swiftly, from in front of the king and in front of the lords of the king, he bore Bovve out into the street and bore him on his back out of the city.

"Be well, stay well!" were his words to the king and the entire company with the king, as the rider rode out into the street, and turning his head.

"Fare thee well, and have a happy journey!" they shouted after him, the entire company, with the king at its head, by the gates.

And Bovve rode away, and he galloped away on the wolf, and Bovve sped out of the capital, and then he came into the country, and the wolf carried him, and the wolf never swerved from carrying him, and Bovve always held out the stick, and he never removed it from the eyes of the wolf, and the wolf sped on and the wolf dashed on, and he charged and streaked, like a wind through the fields, and he flew, and even faster than a wind, and never halted anywhere, and never rested in any place, and at last, and he left that country, and he entered a second country, and thus, coming from the second into the third, and at last to the land where he had to come, and into the capital, where the king and his daughter lived, to the very palace, and to the very gates, and Bovve arrived . . . .

16.

And the news came out, and the rumor spread, and the tidings soon reached the royal palace—and Bovve was back. The first to hear were the servants themselves, and they hurried from room to room, and tried to outrun and to outdistance one another. And rushing and scurrying, and breathlessly, they dashed from wing to wing in the palace, and thus, and rushing, and thus, and dashing, they ran together, and barely could shout the message, and barely could yell out the news:

"Bovve! Bovve is back!!!"

And turmoil and tumult, and clamor and cries filled the palace, and soon the king strode out of the palace, and Bovve came hurrying toward him, and fell upon his heart and his throat, and the king fell into a faint, and Bovve brought him back to his senses, and the two of them went into the princess's chamber, and Bovve knelt down before the princess, and his beloved lay as earlier, and as he had left her—with gaping eyes, and her body stretched out and covered, and with eyes staring straight at one point, and her limbs and her parts unstirring from their long lying.

Bovve stood up from his kneeling, and he picked up his pouch and his belongings, and he pulled out the mirror, the present from the fortuneteller, and he put it in front of his beloved, and she stared into it and didn't stop staring, and her eyes were fixed upon the mirror and they didn't swerve from it at all, and soon her face began to change, and her eyes began to come alive and leave their glassiness and their fixed staring. And then she saw Bovve in front of her, and a joy, an enormous joy, possessed her, and she stirred from her place, from her earlier lying, and she sat up and she lifted her body, and all at once, and with a cry, a terrible shout, that tore from her heart, she flung herself upon Bovve, upon her beloved:

"Bovve! My Bovve!"

And her voice returned to the king's daughter, and her youth returned to the king's daughter, her youth and her liveliness, her youthful life, and for a time she couldn't stop hugging Bovve—and then, and when they let one another go, and then, and when they came apart for a while, they only grabbed each other again, and thus, and falling upon one another, and thus, and holding one another, and not letting go, they remained in one another's arms and couldn't tear themselves loose for a time . . . .

And the king watched the two of them, and his tears rolled freely, and the king stared at the children, and his tears came in torrents, and when the children had quieted down, the king sent for his friend, his old and beloved friend, the stargazer, and he had him come right away, and after the stargazer, all the lords—and all were to gather this very day, at court. And all of them came and were overjoyed with the king, and the king turned to the stargazer and asked him for his counsel: Should the marriage be celebrated soon, or should they wait with the wedding? And the stargazer said: "Now!" And so they brought out the wedding canopy, and all the court was overjoyed with a rare joy, and all caroused with a rare delight, and the two children loved one another and couldn't stop loving one another, and the king wept and couldn't stop weeping, and—and I, too, was there at that wedding and ate gingerbread, and . . . whoever doesn't want to remember this tale, he can forget it.

The Sixth Day

The Mare

Introduction by Mendele the Book Dealer

I, Mendele the Book Dealer, say unto you: Glory be to the Creator, Who, after making the great universe, took counsel with the angelic hosts and finally fashioned a small world, namely man, who is known as the microcosm for combining within himself—if you take a close look—all manner of creatures and animals. You will find in him all species of wild beasts and all breeds of cattle. You will find a lizard, a leech, a Spanish fly, a Japanese beetle, and similar creeping and crawling pests. You will even find a demon, a devil, a satan, a fiend, an imp, a Jew-baiter, and similar hellhounds, hellcats, and freaks. You can also view wonderful sights in him: a cat toying with a mouse; a fox sneaking into a chicken coop and twisting the necks of the poor fowls; monkeys aping everything and everybody; a dog prancing and wagging its tail for anyone who throws it a crust of bread; a spider inveigling a fly, entangling, enmeshing it, and then sucking it dry; gadflies hounding you and buzzing your ears off; and similar wondrous things. But that's neither here nor there. Praised be the Good Lord, Who silently contemplates everything taking place in this microcosm and yet never makes mincemeat out of him; Who keeps His temper, endures the transgressions, and shows great benevolence to sinful man. In short, what I am leading up to is to tell you about the vast grace that God bestowed upon me, a poor sinner, after punishing me a bit.

Dear Reader, my equine hauler had trotted on to greener pastures! My horse kicked the bucket! My loyal nag, who had been in service since time immemorial, laboring with devotion and knowing nothing more than our books; who had been a renowned expert in all roads, with an unfailing memory for all taverns; who had traveled about with me to nearly every corner of the Jewish globe and was well known in all our Jewish communities. This equine being, this horse, had met with a dreadful demise in Dumbsville, during spring, on the Jewish holiday of Lag b'Omer! It wrenches my heart to talk about it, but poverty is no disgrace—the poor thing died of hunger! Its usual fodder was chaff, with occasional crusts of dry bread that I purchased from beggars. Ah, woe betide the poor dobbin that winds up with a Jewish book-peddler! It hauls and hauls, laboring perhaps even harder than the beasts dragging heavier goods. But all that the poor thing gets to eat is garbage, and all that a Jewish book-peddler gets to eat is garbage, so that he and his wife and children starve to death a dozen times a day!

But that's neither here nor there.

God punished me and I was left without a horse. I didn't even have the wherewithal to buy another, and yet I had to get to the county fairs. I felt awful!

And as I sat there, down in the mouth, along came a friend of mine. He walked straight up and said:

"Mr. Mendele, would you like to buy a mare?"

"Of course I would," I moaned, "but what am I going to do for money?"

"Bah!" he said. "Don't worry! You won't have to lay out a kopek! Maybe they'll even advance you something. Why, everyone knows how honest you are."

"If that's the case," I said, "I'd be delighted to buy the mare. Right now! C'mon, let's go and have a look at it!"

"You can save yourself the trouble of going anywhere," he replied. "I have the mare right here, on me!"

"What do you mean, right here?" I asked him in surprise.

"Right here, under my coat," he smiled.

"You're pulling my leg!" I said, exasperated. "Get yourself another victim. I'm in no mood for jokes."

"Me pull your leg? God forbid!" he said and pulled out a huge

*bundle of paper from inside his coat. Look, Mr. Mendele, the whole
thing belongs to a friend of mine. You'll find his name right here on
the manuscripts. And one of these pieces, you see, is entitled* The
Mare. *The author himself is . . . (may you be spared) sort of,
well . . . confused . . . not quite all there. And his friends are very
anxious to have his stories printed and distributed. Now who else
could we have chosen for the task if not you, Mr. Mendele, who
are so famed among Jews. We would like you to look over these
papers and put each story in the right shape—we'll trust to your
judgment. And the first story we want you to print is* The Mare.
*We'll discuss the terms later. I'm sure you'll be satisfied. If you
need any money now, we can give you some on account. Well,
what do you say, Mr. Mendele?"*

*"What do I say?! With all my heart and soul!" I exclaimed, prac-
tically jigging for joy.*

*After attending to all my business matters, I eagerly tackled the
mare—put her into shape, divided her into chapters, and gave each
chapter a fitting title—a drudgery for which some people would affix
their names to a manuscript and call themselves authors . . . . In
short, I spared no pains, I did my duty faithfully.*

And now, my friends, a few words about the mare.

The Mare *is written in a lofty manner, the style of the ancients.
Each reader will comprehend it in accordance with his intelligence
and on his own level. For people on a surface level, it will simply
be a lovely tale, and they will enjoy the plot. But those on a
deeper level will also find an allusion, an application, to us sinful human creatures. I, for example, on my level, found in it nearly all
Jewish souls, all our beings, and the secret of what we are doing in
this world. I am convinced that during your perusal, a number of
you, each according to his nature, will be unable to help himself
and will ardently call out: "Why, that's an allusion to Mr. Yossel!"
Or: "Oh! That's a reference to Mr. Nathan! Mr. Zalman-Jacob!
Mr. Hershke!" Or else: "Hey! I've discovered the secret behind
our kosher-meat tax, our philanthropists, and all our behavior!"
And so on.*

*I submitted a question to the rabbinical judiciary in Dumbsville,
and the local bigwigs. Since I had promised my readers that I
would put out a sequel to my play* The Kosher-Meat Tax, *I was
virtually under oath and as good as committed.*

"Now what does the law say, gentlemen?" I asked them. If I put out my 'Mare' now, would that count as fulfilling my promise?"

They mulled and mulled, the poor men, scratching and scratching their heads, and at last they pronounced their verdict.

"Yes, indeed, Mr. Mendele, having had a sniff, a whiff, of the essence of your Meat Tax, *we would be most willing to release you from your oath. May your equine surrogate be reckoned in all due value as an equivalent of your having fulfilled your promise in all good faith and published an additional section to* The Meat Tax, *with all the particulars. By all means:* The Mare, *according to all opinions, will be an excellent way of keeping your word!"*

How grateful am I to God! If I had gotten the mare without any advance, just to buy myself a horse, that would have sufficed. If I had gotten her with an advance and she had not had something of the essence of the Meat Tax, *that would have sufficed. If she had had something of the* Meat Tax *and the rabbinical judiciary had not released me from my vow, that would have sufficed. If the rabbinical judiciary had released me from my vow and not scratched their heads so much, that would have sufficed. If they had scratched their heads so much and I would not have known the reason, that would have sufficed. If I had known the reason and not comprehended that the mare was something to scratch one's head about, that would have sufficed.*

How much more then am I grateful to the Lord that I found the mare, and with an advance to buy a horse, and that she had something of the essence of the Meat Tax, *and the rabbinical judiciary released me from my vow, and scratched their heads so much, and I know the reason, and comprehend that the mare is evidently something to scratch one's head about, an atonement for our sins.*

That, my dear readers, is what I was after in my brief introduction. Out of the abundance of the heart, the mouth runneth over!

On the 29th day of Elul, on the bookwagon, between Dumbsville and Yawnstown.

Yours truly,

Mendele Moykher-Sforim
(Mendele the Book Dealer)

CHAPTER ONE
Izzy Wants to Become a Human Being

Just as Noah, in his ark, was the only survivor of all the creatures in the world, who were drowned in the Deluge, so I too, Israel the son of Tsippe, was the only survivor in my little town, the only bachelor among all my friends, who, because of that pestilential nuisance known as marriage-brokers, had become boy-husbands before their time and were up to their ears in poverty and squalor. That scourge of God—the marriage-brokers—beat a path to my mother's door, proposing matches for me. My mother, a simple woman, but with a good head on her shoulders, was a widow, not what you would call wealthy, but then not quite poor either. She made a living off her haberdashery, wore a few strings of pearls, and did rather well. I was her only child, her pride and joy. She indulged me in everything. I put my foot down about not marrying young and I got my way. At first, she did try to make me change my mind:

"Izzy! How often have I prayed to God to let me live long enough to see you getting offers from matchmakers! You're the apple of my eye, I'm only thinking of you, please do what I say and get married! It's high time, Izzy, just look at yourself! You're a grown man (may no evil befall you!)—you've got a beard! All your friends married by the time they were bar-mitzvahed. Listen to your mother. Do what God has ordained so that you can still bring me some joy!"

But when she saw that she was wasting her breath, that no matter how much she talked I stuck to my guns—No! No! And no!—she finally relented and dropped the subject. I simply told her the plain truth. I was resolved to bone up on everything taught in the Russian schools, take the examinations, and enter the university to study medicine so that later on I might be of use to myself and the world.

"Mama," I said to her. "The world's different today. It's time we opened our eyes to that great happiness of early marriage, the grandeur and glory of our young householders! Parents used to marry off their children in the faith that 'God sent us enough to live on, He'll probably send them enough to live on too, they certainly won't starve.'

"Back then, that sort of faith may have been useful, but today it can only cause suffering. In our time, it's hard, very hard, to live by the sweat of your brow. You can't turn dross into gold. A man should make every effort as early as possible to make sure all his major needs are covered, for always, for all his life. Particularly we Jews, who live in such awful conditions, hemmed in and stifled on all sides. There's no other way for us to heave ourselves out of our misery than by means of some scholarly or scientific pursuit, say, medicine, or a similar profession. If I don't plan my future now, while I'm still young, then what's going to become of me, for heaven's sake! The same thing that's happened to so many young men from our background. Supposedly, they made good matches and landed in a goldmine. But the gold turned out to be fool's gold, and they were shafted! Some of them are scattered now, some are Hebrew teachers, and some can't even do that! But if I become a doctor, the world will open up for me, I'll make something of myself, become a human being, and have no trouble earning my living."

My mother had no choice, she had to let me have my way again. I could study, but I had to promise her I would remain a good Jew.

I had a sharp mind. Nothing in the Talmud had been too difficult for me, and people used to say that some day I would become a great rabbi. Leaving such aspirations to others, I locked myself in my room and sat up day and night, eagerly studying all the subjects required for the university entrance examinations. Mathematics, plus physics, Russian grammar, as well as languages—all easy as pie. The only thing I had any problems with was history, and what the Russians call "literature." I had to cram it all, word for word—inane stories and battles, descriptions of how people have been killing, murdering, and slaughtering one another since time began, inflicting heartache and mayhem on each other, and in every case I had to memorize the exact year and place! This and similar stuff was known as history . . . . In addition, I had to learn all kinds of wild fables, fairytales about transmigrations, about witches and warlocks; stories of living waters and dead waters, golden apples and golden horses.

Furthermore, I had to be able to chatter like a parrot about some writer's fancy words and phrases, and find all kinds of subtleties, niceties, and hidden meanings that neither I, nor the author himself, nor my tutor ever saw. You were supposed to be all excited, ablaze, shouting, flailing your arms and legs, talking full blast, as if these things were occult mysteries or cabbalistic formulas. You had to clear the way, so to speak, with long preambles, in order to make the whole affair more complicated, more confused, so that others would understand it in a different way and not just straight-forwardly. All this rigamarole, all this mumbo-jumbo, all this twisting and turning, was known as "literature."

You can say what you like. Once you're past boyhood, it's very hard to store up things like that in your head, especially if you've got a good mind and a passion for learning more useful things. Yes indeed. I found all that stuff very difficult.

The constant grind numbed my brain. It robbed me of my health, my vital strength, it turned me into a zombie. At times, I felt dazed, I reeled about more dead than alive. My head buzzed, it whirled like a windmill, driving me crazy. I would start doubting whether my plan of going to the university would ever work. Who could tell what might happen? At the examination, I might forget some stupid tale or trip over some author's gibberish and fall flat on my face. And so much for all my efforts, my studies, my medical ambitions, which I was so anxious to realize. My hopes would be a shambles, and so would I! What would I do, and what would I look like? I would be left a downtrodden little Jew. I would completely lose face and, like all other Jews, have to put up with insults and injuries from the rest of the world. I would remain a *luftmentsh*; up in the air for the rest of my life, force without fuel. I would feel the energy to do something, but have no way of activating my energy, applying it to something useful. I would be like so many pitiful failures among us Jews.... I would be a Jew and not a human being.... An enigma! A hobgoblin who sweeps up, cleans out, but lives in dirt, off in a corner somewhere. A hobgoblin who is up and about and yet doesn't exist in this world. Flesh and blood and yet nothing to anyone!... I knew one of the three hobgoblins from my studies—a broom—and the other two.... But what difference does it make! Who cares if I knew or didn't know! I was what I was but I wouldn't be a human being!

Cooped up all the time, cramming and reviewing, constantly fearing it was all a wild-goose chase—perish forbid!—I finally broke down. I lost weight, became as skinny as a beanpole, feeble, high-strung, and so anxious and depressed that people almost didn't recognize me. At times, I walked around dazed and bewildered, my

actions, my behavior, were very peculiar. When a depression overtook me, I would curse all the witches, Baba Yaha, that old shrew,
and that wizard Kashtsey. To hell with them all!

When I felt better, I made up with them. Back to Baba Yaha,
back to Kashtsey, and the whole pack of them. My mother would
cry when she saw me and started calling in doctors and healers.
They gave me vials, poured serums down my throat, and strongly
urged me to take long walks in the summertime, for goodness' sake
and for heaven's sake—to get some fresh air outside of town, and
don't think so much.

Ah, if the doctors had only been more understanding and freed
me of the nonsense that made me so sick and confused!

CHAPTER TWO
Izzy Explodes When He Sees What's Happening

One lovely summer morning, in Tamuz [early July], when the heat
was unbearable, I walked out of town and into the open fields. I
was very gloomy that day, my head was spinning, my temples were
pounding, my heart was boiling like a kettle. I was very bewildered,
worse than ever. For a long while, I rambled about, not quite
knowing where my feet were taking me. I trudged and trudged,
until I collapsed under a tree by some ditch and stretched out full
length.

When I plopped down the whole world seemed to collapse with
me. Everything turned black. My ears were banging and bursting as
if rockets were zooming through them. I felt as if I were sinking in
a bottomless pit, deeper and deeper, through an awful din. I wanted
to clutch at something, grab hold of something. But I didn't seem to
have any arms or legs. I was beside myself, out of my skin, a mere
Izzy, or Izne, an airy thing, with no body, no limbs, nothing left of
me, only my bare, naked soul.

Suddenly, I rose upward, I was swept higher and higher until I
touched the ground and lay there with the sun roasting my back. I
felt like a new man, completely reborn, completely transformed.
Everything around me, the earth, the sky, the trees, and the grass,
looked newly hatched. They sprang and rocked and greeted one
another, unable to stay put, motioning to me: "C'mon and join the
hop, cousin, grab a dance!" Two crickets leaped and jigged out of

the grass, peered at me with big, foolish eyes, waving their feelers. And now they seemed to be climbing into me. And then they really jumped, one, two—oh, my head! My head! . . .

I waved them away and turned my head, and as I lay there, I looked around, gazing, musing, mulling.

In the field, I saw some animals pasturing, aristocratic rams, donkeys, whole troops of horses, not coarsened by any labor, pedigree horses with patents of nobility attesting to the pure blood of their parents. One steed's grandsire was an English stallion who, anciently, while passing through the land of Canaan, had wed an Arab mare. Another horse's granddam came from a renowned dynasty, which had smelled its share of gunpowder. And still another horse's great-grandmother had enjoyed a fine upbringing, an education, on a famous breeding farm. She had been very learned and, in her time, together with many other educated and well-trained horses, she had given recitals of dancing and cantering.

For you must know that pedigree is very important in horses. Blue blood is greatly in demand, and scions from a good stud farm are known as blood horses or thoroughbreds. This nobility was dining unmolested, working mischief, destroying the grain that poor peasants had sown in the sweat of their brows. And the onlookers turned the other way and said nothing disrespectful to them. The horses capered, neighed, and stamped their hooves. Their strength, their power, their fierceness were extraordinary.

And lying there so angry, I suddenly heard a dreadful scream in the distance, men were yelling and dogs barking. At first I thought it was the peasants running together with a shout, to drive out the noble rams and horses from their grain. But I was wrong. The hubbub kept receding and shifting. What was going on? I stood up and followed the turmoil, until I came to a large grassy meadow, where I witnessed a terrible scene. Young, wild bullies were harassing a skinny, haggard mare on all sides, pelting her with stones, sicking whole packs of dogs on her. Some of the dogs were doing no more than barking, grinding their teeth, some of them were pouncing on her and biting as much as they were able.

I couldn't simply stand there as a silent observer to such misdeeds. For one thing, compassion and decency won't put up with such barbarism. And besides, disregarding compassion, the mare actually had a right to my assistance, what with my being a member in good standing of the Society for the Prevention of Cruelty to Animals, which prohibits tormenting or hurting any living creatures, for they are flesh and blood and have the same right to live in God's world as we do. I don't want to launch into that venerable and profound discussion about human beings vs. beasts. Let us grant, as some maintain, that I, Homo sapiens, am the crown, the ornament, the apex of creation; that all other creatures live on this earth only for my sake, for my needs and my pleasure, for me the acme. Let us even grant that I, the acme, am the king, the overlord, of all animals, and that they are meant to serve me, wear the yoke, and sacrifice their lives for me. Nevertheless, I felt that the mare, such an ordinary drudge, had a right to my assistance. I would have to fulfill my duty toward her, if not by law than at least out of humanity . . . .

"Savages!" I said, making straight for this pepper of the earth. "What do you have against that poor horse?"

Some of the bullies didn't ever hear me, others did catch something and guffawed arrogantly. A few of the dogs looked at me in surprise, several of them barked at a distance, others glared, ready to leap at me from behind and tear me to shreds.

"Savages!" I repeated. "Why are you harassing and tormenting a poor creature of God?"

"Poor, my eye!" they sneered. "Why is she pasturing here? Why is this fine mare pasturing over here?"

"Why not!?" I exclaimed. "This *is* a meadow, the town's livestock have been pasturing here for ages!"

"The town's livestock," they replied, "are different. They can but she can't!"

"Why can't she?" I said. "Doesn't she have a soul like the town's livestock?"

"Maybe she doesn't!" they said.

"Bullies!" I said. "But she must have an owner who pays taxes in town and all the other duties. She's a town animal too!"

"Says who!" they answered derisively. "We'll have to find out whether she really is!"

"Be that as it may," I said, "the mare is hungry now, the poor thing wants to feed!"

"Let her eat worms, garbage, dirt," they replied. "What are we supposed to do?! Why should a brute like her eat our own cattle out of house and home!"

"Cutthroats!" I couldn't contain myself any longer, I screamed in anger. "Why don't you look over there at the aristocratic rams, the herds of horses in the grain, gobbling up the sweat and blood of poor peasants! You begrudge a broken-down mare a heap of grass and yet you don't mind those horses wreaking immense havoc and bringing unhappiness to a lot of people. The grain that they're trampling and destroying without a second thought would be enough to feed generations of mares until her children's children's children. Bullies, you haven't a shred of justice in you, no loyalty to anyone but yourselves. And yet you have the colossal nerve to defend the town's animals!"

"Hahaha!:" replied the bullies. "My-oh-my! Isn't he angry! And isn't he asking questions! C'mon guys! Why argue! Let's go!"

One of them whistled and the whole gang and their dogs chased after the mare and fell upon her again. They hounded her and harassed her, ripping and biting, until they finally drove her into a deep mudhole.

CHAPTER THREE
Blessed Is He Who Transforms His Creatures

The evening was silent and beautiful. The sky was pure, starry, and very near. At its lowest point, the moon, blood red, arose as if from the earth. The town cows, well milked as usual and having eaten their normal supper from the troughs, were sleeping peacefully in the byres. I procured a bundle of fresh hay to bring to the unfortunate mare in her ditch, just as a decent member of the Society for the Prevention of Cruelty to Animals ought to do. The poor creature was lying in the mud, exhausted. If she hadn't been panting and writhing in pain, you would surely have taken her for a carcass—she was so haggard, all skin and bones.

"Neighhhh, neighhhh!" I said in horse language, going over to her. I stroked her neck and put down the sheaf of hay.

The mare lifted her head and gazed at me in surprise. To think that a man like me was paying my respects to a common horse, visiting her mudhole in the middle of the night.

"Neighhhh, neighhhh!" I said in horse language. It meant: "Good evening, mare! .... Neighhhh, neighhhh! Here's some supper for you, some hay, if you've got a tooth left in your mouth. Neighhhh!

Neighhhhh! May God pity your soul, you poor creature. Neighhhh!" I caressed her and put the hay right against her nose.

"Welcome!" came a muffled voice.

I froze at that "Welcome!" Where could it be coming from, I wondered. Who was talking? There wasn't a trace of a human being for miles around.

"Don't be afraid, young man!" the voice reassured me. "Don't be afraid. It's me, the mare, talking to you."

"The mare!" I screamed in a horrified voice. A hot stream of ants scurried over my limbs, making my blood seethe. I could make out a cricket chirping in my head. That does sound like the good mare, I thought to myself. And then I realized it was Wednesday night, the time when the demons come out.

"Don't mull over it," the voice continued. "It's really quite simple. I, the mare, am talking to you."

"What?! How can a mare be talking?!" I said in astonishment.

"There's nothing extraordinary about it," she replied. "Such things have happened before. The chronicles mention any number of speeches by jackasses and sermons by horses, from Balaam's ass till the present."

"Ha! Maybe it's really so!" I said to her, scratching my head. I remembered the stories I was studying for my examinations. "Yes indeed, I do know of talking horses—but a mare?"

"Why not a mare? On the contrary, if anyone talks, it's usually the female. Balaam's ass was a mare. But calm down, it's not really a mare talking to you."

"What do you mean? First you're a mare, then you're not a mare!" I said, amazed, and then bent over to have a closer look at the matter. "Why, you must be—"

"A demon?" she broke in. "No, no, my friend, you're wrong. I'm no demon, I tell you, and no mare either. My shape and appearance are those of a mare, but I'm really something entirely different. If you knew what's happened to me in the world, you would understand and you wouldn't be surprised any longer."

And suddenly, two eyes were gazing at me, expressing sorrow and weariness, as well as an entreaty and an infinite kindness, the eyes of a sick, downtrodden, browbeaten person, who gazes at everyone in utter silence, and whose every gaze reveals his innermost sufferings; every gaze talks, cries fury, pleads for mercy, and tears out a piece of your heart.

I stared and stared. Was this a horse? I saw a human face before me. How did a human being get here so suddenly, where did he come from? This freak! ... And as I stared, transfixed, at this creature, it held out a hand from somewhere below, and, taking it courteously, I felt: A hoof!

"Blessed be He Who transforms creatures!" The familiar blessing came to my lips willy-nilly. And a noise hit my ears, something like a bitter wailing, like a mother weeping for her child, like the hustle and bustle of servants around a sick man. I felt as if something had yanked me and thrown me around and dashed icy water over me. It was so cold that my arms and legs were trembling—I huddled against the mare to warm up on her body.

"How long have you been in such a peculiar shape?"

"As long as the Jewish Exile!" she replied with a sigh.

"How did it happen?" I asked, moving a bit closer. The creature rested her eyes on me and stared as though I were mad. Then her expression became earnest and she began to talk in a dismal voice:

"The man who has peered into tomes or listened to the words of his elders knows that people have been said to take on the shapes of all kinds of creatures and cattle, things that creep and crawl, either turning into them while still alive or else as a reincarnation after death. It happens all the time. In the past, such things occurred frequently, and they still keep recurring in our time. Great scholars, including clergymen, have given us oral and written confirmation. The history books tell us that Semiramis, the Queen of Babylon, became a dove in her old age. Daniel, in a prophetic vision, saw the four empires in the guise of lions, leopards, and bears. And he relates that Nebuchadnezzar, King of Babylon, turned into a bear at the end of his days. As for the Greeks—they experienced such things all the time. Their god Zeus, if you'll pardon me for saying so, was quite a ladies' man, and once he changed himself into a bull, and Princess Io, the daughter of King Inachus, into a heifer. The poor girl wandered around in that guise for a good long time. The Greeks also had a species, half-animal, half-human, known as centaurs. One centaur, whose name was Chiron, and who had a beard and sidelocks, and a fur hat, was the teacher of Prince Theseus. Well naturally: Like nation, like teacher: If the people are wild then so are the teachers.... And how many old women and maidens, too many to count, were seen by European scholars and God-fearing men, changing into frogs, dragons, and other venomous reptiles, and riding shovels and brooms through the air. These things were confirmed in black and white, beyond the shadow of a doubt. Conjurors, black-magicians, and illusionists had the time of their lives! They played mischief and did the ghastliest things! A lot of princes and princesses were turned by them into wild beasts.... Just read the lore and the written tales of each nation, and you'll see that so many princes, so many kings, were transformed by them into rams, horses, bulls, or the like. And so many princesses and queens were changed into cows, calves, or nanny goats. So many lords, so many earls, were conjured into dogs, wolves, bears. They maimed and mangled people, sucked out their blood, drew the marrow from their bones. Yes indeed, whole villages, whole towns, were bewitched into herds of sheep and suffered the worst troubles, torments, and tortures.... These things happened, caused by the powers of illusion, sorcery, and necromancy. Those poor, unhappy people!"

The words boomed out as if from an empty barrel. It wasn't like the speech of lips, it wasn't as if the mare were speaking, but as if some spirit were talking out of her. It tore my brain, roaring and humming, as if a stream of cold water had crashed down on it from the eaves of a house. The mare gazed at me and continued her story.

"In those days, there lived a king's son, a fine, handsome, intelligent prince with all the virtues—a splendid man. In his youth, the prince had wandered a great deal, undertaking many voyages to see the world. And wherever he went, people would sing his praises. A king of Egypt (that famous land of gypsies and conjurors) was very angry at the prince, who had come to visit him. Terrified that the prince might go after him later on and drive him from his country, the king summoned his great sorcerers and said to them: 'Let us deal cunningly with the prince!' Which meant; in plain Yiddish: 'Give it to him, boys!'

"The magicians applied their sorcery and turned the prince into a mare. And then they made the poor creature work like a horse.

"The unfortunate mare had to lug whole mountains of bricks and clay, and she built treasure cities for Pharaoh—Pithom and Raamses. The Egyptians tormented her for years, making her life wretched, until God took pity. There came a great, a renowned man, a Miracle worker, who made fools of all the Egyptians with their sorcery, and performed greater feats with the Holy Name of God. He pronounced an incantation and transformed the mare back into a prince!

"As long as that great Miracle worker and his disciples were alive, the prince retained a human appearance and lived in wealth and honor in his own land. But then, when those friends of his all died out, the prince's enemies turned him into a mare again, and in this form he has been driven around from one place to another, year after year. The unhappy prince really deserves the name of The Wandering Mare or The Eternal Mare. For the mare wanders about eternally to all corners of the world. Anyone with a merciful heart climbs up on her back. Anyone who believes in God, hits her and kicks her. Anyone who feels like it, dumps his pack and his bundle on her. She roams eternally, in her yoke, dragging about, lugging bricks and clay with great effort, and her blood and sweat have gone to build entire cities! ..."

At that time, when my head was full of marvelous tales about sorcerers and conjurors; at that time, when, besides perusing such storybooks as *The Arabian Nights*, or *The Book of Bovve*, which I had eagerly read in my childhood, I also devoured other tales like dumplings; at that time, when my blood was hot, my heart boiling, and my imagination aflame, when my feelings were gunpowder, kindling, blasting, at the slightest touch; when my eyes were well-springs, thermal baths, when anyone who suffered could find hot tears in them—it was at that time that the story of the unhappy prince so greatly moved me. I was seething!

"Please tell me," I said. "Tell me, where is he now? Where is the poor fellow, the unfortunate prince?"

"The prince, the unfortunate prince, is lying before your very eyes, in the likeness of a mare!"

I sighed, I wept, I poured scalding tears over my poor unhappy mare.

CHAPTER FOUR
Izzy Has a Heart-to-Heart Talk With the Mare

Coming to my senses somewhat and raising my head, I saw the moon shining and peering with her silvery beams into the ditch. My mare was chewing hay, calm, nonchalant, without a care in the world, like a real horse, to the stable born. Contradictory feelings were grinding in my heart. One moment, I felt as if my life were about to end out of pity for the poor, broken-down mare. The next moment, I was furious. How could she just lie in the mud, calmly, nonchalantly, as if she didn't sense or grasp her awful situation! How could she open her mouth to champ hay after such a terrible experience, after the awful beating she had gotten! Perhaps the whole story was just a dream. Perhaps she was just an ordinary nag without a drop of blue blood in her veins, with no sense of honor or self-respect, unable to feel her desperate situation, the boundless insults and injuries. For if she had had even a shred of sensitivity, even a trace of horse sense, she could never possibly have lain there so coolly. Every drop of her blood ought to have been boiling furiously. Every last part of her, every last vein ought to have been shuddering. She ought to have realized it was no good remaining the Wandering Mare, suffering at the hands of any bully, the teeth of any dog. She ought to have made every effort, put her whole heart and soul into turning human again.

I was simply ashamed, I must have been crazy! What had I been doing? For whom had I sighed and wept? For whom had I shed scalding tears? For whom had I been ready to sacrifice myself, offer up my days, my years, my entire life? For whom! For a mare! For a worn-out, asthmatic, old gray mare! . . . I looked all around me and then moved off a bit, with a broken heart.

The mare let out a sudden sigh. And her sigh thundered in my heart. I shuddered. Ardent feelings of compassion kindled my blood again. That one sigh of hers caused a whole upheaval within me, pulled me toward her like a magnet.

That's fine, I thought. Sigh, sigh, my mare! That's good. Your sighs reveal the unhappy prince struggling with all his might to achieve a human shape. Your sighs contain his voice shouting: I'm still alive! I still feel everything like any human being! We can hear him shouting and pleading: Help, people, have mercy! Let me take on my shape again!—

Sigh, my mare, sigh! A sigh can do something, it can move and rend hearts, it can pierce the ears of men, making them tremble, feel pity, and spur them to help you. Keep it up, my mare. Sighing is good!

I glanced at her. There wasn't a wisp of hay left next to my mare. She had eaten it all up, not overlooking the tiniest shred. Aha! So that's what her sighs meant. Her tummy wasn't stuffed, because she didn't have a second bundle of hay, a second heap of grass. If she could get a whole bale of hay and grass, plus a few measures of oats, she'd be blissfully content. She didn't care what happened—as long as she had a mass of oats and a full belly. A pure, inveterate mare, by God! ... I was so upset, so angry and jittery, that I could barely restrain myself.

"Why are you trembling?" her words tumbled out to me. "Maybe you don't have enough room. You don't look very comfortable."

"You may like it here, but for an intelligent and sensitive human being who knows what's good, a place like this is bad, very bad!" I said, a bit angrily, trying to jab her with my sharp tongue.

"It's so good of you to say so!" she exclaimed, shaking her head. "If anyone else had been transformed into a mare for such a long time, if anyone else had been through so much, wandering around, getting beaten and massacred, suffering so much trouble and sorrow from everybody, I'm sure he would have lost his intelligence and sensitivity long ago. He wouldn't even be able to speak anymore. He'd be a complete brute."

"Now, now!" I interrupted her. "Do you like the dirt, do you feel good down there?"

Said she: "I seem to. At least, better than before. There were times when I was constantly harassed and not even allowed a breathing spell. My enemies drove and drove me, robbing me of my last ounce of strength. Now, at least I can rest a bit. The mud is soft to lie in and I can straighten out my old, sick bones."

Said I: "But what about the beating you got from those bullies today, and the dogs that attacked you just a short while ago? Have you forgotten them already? Do you feel good about that too?"

Said she: "At least, better than before. Do you call those curs *dogs*? You should have seen the dogs that those devils the Germans sicked on me. Those were big, trained, obedient hounds. They stood on their hind legs, wagged their tails, and did everything they were told. They were simply professors among dogs. They practically had the intelligence of human beings—but the hearts and teeth of dogs! Their fangs were terrible. I still bear the marks.

"The dogs you saw today are puppies, mindless lambs. They don't even know how to attack properly, how to bite. You call that barking? They can't even bark up the wrong tree! All you have to do is stick a crust of bread into their mouths and then you can rob, steal, and pilfer right in front of them, to your heart's content!

"And do you call those yokels *bullies?* There were real bullies back in the old days! They acted innocent, drove everyone crazy, and thought up all kinds of mischief. They used to disguise themselves as bears, waylay people, and scare them to death. Today's bullies won't stop at much either, that's true. But they can't hold a candle to bullies of the past. When *they* started in on me, I felt I had nothing left to live for. And those horses you saw in the grain. Can you imagine how *they* tormented me?"

"What?!" I exclaimed, horrified. "What are you talking about? Horses tormented you too? What do horses, today's horses, have to do with you?"

"If people could see inside all things, a lot of riddles would be solved. Don't worry, I'm answering your question. Those horses are reincarnations of wild, savage, ugly bullies who lived long ago, extorting and tormenting people, wreaking damage and havoc. Not one of them had a soul himself, and yet a thousand souls had to work for him, eating nothing but a dry crust in the sweat of their brow, and enjoying nothing else, not even the things they raised and produced with so much drudgery. And he, their master, lived off the fat of the land, devouring their labor, frittering and squandering. They worked their bodies to the bone, their blood and sweat brought him vast estates, villages, towns. Their toil earned him a huge fortune; and the few crumbs they occasionally got from him, scarcely enough to keep body and soul together, were known as alms. They were called poor beggars, and he was called—merciful, generous, charitable, philanthropic. When they were slaving away for him, it was perfectly normal, the way things ought to be. But if he ever gave anything to the sick and the starving, from their own labor, people would talk of nothing else, it was praised and admired in the gazettes and discussed in detail—let the world know about this benevolent, kind-hearted, pious, noble humanitarian! ...

"Once these horses were indolent aristocratic humans. Today they're indolent aristocratic horses. Why? Let's not fool ourselves: What good are trained thoroughbreds? For work? But it's the little horses, the common horses that do all the drudgery. They plow the soil, haul water and wood, pull, carry loads, and do all the farmwork. Whereas the blue-bloods lead happy lives in the stable, amid hay and oats. They go out driving occasionally with their lords, prance, swagger, and strut around with their bulging bellies, their fine harnesses. Or else dance and do tricks in the circus, mulcting the audience of its money. What good is it if a horse capers and does hocus-pocus? Why should a horse like that be wearing gold and why should they cover its enormous body with money? Wouldn't it be better if they were made to carry rather than carry on!?"

"Shush! Not so loud!" I said. "Do you always talk this much?"

"Ahhh!" the mare answered with a sigh. "Normally I'm silent and I can't even speak a word. People don't want me to talk. Very often, I can't even let out a squeak, and I become a mare to the last detail. You could blabber away at me for a year, and I wouldn't bat an eyelash. You could yell: Turn right! And I'd go left, unless you grabbed my mane and dragged me by force. At such times, anyone can ride me, a kid, a fool, a scamp, a scoundrel, a good-for-nothing, a ne'er-do-well.

"But then there are times when my mouth opens up, and at the drop of a hat, I start talking a blue streak, I'll chew your ear off. The words come pouring out like fire and lava from a volcano. Everything that's been bottled up in my heart, whole floods of anger, chagrin, frustration, sorrow. My blood boils like a river in spring, it roars up to my head in horrible waves, tears my brain apart, and gushes out through my eyes. My gall explodes, my bitter heart and my aching spirit cry out!"

"Tell me, my friend," I said. "Now that you've brought the matter up, why do you cause harm? That was why they attacked you before. That was why they were yelling: 'You're causing damage!' "

"Think about it," she replied, "and you won't be so quick to condemn me. If you talk about the evil I cause, you also ought to mention the good I do. You can't pronounce a verdict, for good or for bad, unless you balance both sides and see which is heavier. Otherwise, you could say that almost everyone does damage. No one is faultless, not even the man crying bloody murder about it. The way things are today, anywhere in the world, doing harm is a fault, a sin that can't be blotted out and that can be defended only with the same kind of misdeed. Why, they say, does that man do damage?—That is a sin that endures, no matter how much you may shout. All you can do is cover it up, conceal it, with alms or something useful.

"Simon, the victim, shouts: 'Oh! Reuben is causing damage!'—
'Yes,' they reply, 'Reuben *is* being a bit destructive. But what can
he do, what choice does he have? On the other hand, just look how
useful he is somewhere else! . . .'—Am I not useful? Haven't I done,
and don't I still do, useful things for the world? No one, I think,
would ever deny it. People have been riding me for ages and ages.
Everyone has made hay with me. Is there anyone I haven't carried
on my back? Is there any destruction I haven't endured? I think my
labor is worth a lot more than a heap of grass! . . . That's my first
point. And secondly, don't forget: I'm a victim of circumstances
and misery. If I don't go out and look for food on my own, no
one's going to serve it to me in a silver trough. I might as well just
live on air and bite the dust. I can't wait for respect. No one can
live without eating. What more do I want than to eat? And just
what sort of damage do I cause anyway? A shred of hay, a bit of
grass! But those fine horses over there, they have the best of everything, they get whatever they need, they have the right to pasture
freely on any grass, anywhere. Then why do they damage the
crops? And what damage! They trample the grain, ravage entire
fields, cause total havoc."

"What was the relationship," I asked her, "between you and
those horses, or, as you phrase it: bullies?"

"Those bullies, or as you phrase it, horses," she replied,"used to
torment me outrageously. They tortured me to death. Once, when
a company of them set out to war against the Turks, they kicked
me and trod on me, they crushed the marrow from my bones.
They flayed me, slashed my veins, branded and scorched me with
glowing coals. My hide bears the printed history of the cruelty,
barbarism, and stupidity that ruled those grim, harsh times. My
worn, bruised skin, my shredded, wounded back, are the written
chronicles of those old generations. Look at my hide and read!"

CHAPTER FIVE
The Mare Rises Like a Storm Out of the Ditch

My mind was spinning like a windmill from all the things I had
heard, and the world and its creatures were spinning along with it,
everything mixing and mingling together. I felt as if nothing and no
one were what they seemed. No one on the inside was what he ap-

peared to be on the outside. The Hindus, who believe that human souls pass into all sorts of creatures, and the Cabbalists (if you'll excuse my mentioning them in the same breath) are right, so it seems. The entire world is nothing but transmigrations. The Daily Prayer Book says it's a good deed to eat fish on the Sabbath in order to reclaim the souls reincarnated in them—and this is perfectly true.

And if such is the case, the world seems altogether different, you have to look at it with different eyes and regard everything in a completely different way. That may really be a man in the doghouse, and a dog in the man's house. A pound of fresh fish may really be a pound of palpitating souls, a fine carp may contain a chatterbox, an orator, with pepper and onions, on the platter right in front of me.

If these stories are true, then they explain a lot of the riddles of Providence and human behavior. They explain where all those people come from—the fools, idiots, hypocrites, idlers, climbers, military kidnappers, tax collectors, rabbinical managers, civic leaders, advocates, philanthropists, politicians, aristocrats, noble gentlemen, moral preachers, toadies, bootlickers, and big butt-ins. We can now understand who they are, where they come from, whose character they have, and what their goals and purposes are in this world, among us unfortunate, sinful human beings . . . .

It often happens that a man spends his whole life studying and remains a fool. While another man quickly becomes a sage without much effort.

That night I became a sage. And as soon as I became a sage, I naturally became skeptical of everything, not only of other people, being perplexed as to who and what they are—but skeptical even of yours truly, my own true self. Perhaps I was not truly I. Perhaps I was in the hand of another power living within me and I was not the master of my body, doing everything according to my will and mind. Perhaps that other force controlled me and compelled me to do what he wants, to do his business and live his life as he once lived it. Perhaps I am the substance and he the spirit; I, the matter, and he, the mind. Perhaps I am merely the mule who doesn't matter and who has to mind the master, whereas he, the master, is all that matters, and it is he who does the minding. But no matter. And never mind.

Who could that be inside myself? And whose ghost spoke through my mouth? Perhaps one of the sublime souls was residing

in me—King Solomon, for instance. And it *is* conceivable! He became a sage in just one night, like a bolt from the blue, wiser than
all men in his time. And I, a mere youth, now had as much horse
sense as—a nightmare. He obviously wanted his wisdom to continue
through me so that I would be wiser than all men in my time.

Or perhaps some other great soul was residing in me. If the mare,
a female, was a prince, then I, a male, might easily be a princess,
and it was highly possible for souls to be exchanged in transmigration so that a male became a female, and a female a male. I
remembered reading the very same thing in a romance by a French
astronomer. And if it were true, then it was possible that I was hers
truly the Queen of Sheba in person. And it was no coincidence that
the mare and I had come together here.

Well, and if I were mistaken, and neither of those two souls were
in me, it didn't matter, I didn't mind. As long as it was a grand and
lofty soul. And aren't there many grand and lofty souls among us?
Judging by my hot, turbulent blood, my wild enthusiasm, perhaps
the spirit of Judah Maccabee had entered my body. My strength
was in my mouth, my power in my tongue. A deep urge overtook
me to let out a scream as dreadful as the feelings of my heart, a
scream that would make the world shudder.

And the moment I opened my mouth and screamed, there was
thunder and lightning, and a terrible maelstrom, a wheel like a
column was spinning high in the air, there was a surging, a crowding—all kinds of shapes, dancing, leaping, flying insanely like devils,
pulling all and sundry into their circle. It swirled and whirled, roaring violently, accompanied by a mad orchestra: cawing, croaking,
crunking, cackling, cricking, squeaking, yawling, yapping, yelling,
grating. The trees in the forest echoed the chaos, swaying on all
sides, soughing, lashing, cracking, crashing. The terror-stricken
moon took refuge behind a bank of clouds. I was petrified. Could
that bedlam, that tempest, really be coming from my shriek, from
the breath of my lips? Perhaps the pan-demonics were celebrating a
marriage, with a witch and her bridegroom being led to the altar.
Lively and merry witches, old and young, were dancing, leaping,
spinning in a round with demons.

I glanced over at the mare but I didn't recognize her. She was
changing, fluctuating into a new shape every minute. Now she
seemed to take on a human guise: a skinny, scrawny throat with a
craggy Adam's apple, tangled earlocks full of elflocks, a gaping

mouth, a drooping lip, letting out sigh after heartfelt sigh. And then a second later, she assumed a bizarre form, some incomprehensible monstrosity. And suddenly she cocked her ears, listening, sensing something. Trembling, she struggled to her hooves as if a snake had taken a bite at her, and she stretched out full-length, waving her tail like a genuine horse. Then a creature jumped up from nowhere, mounted the mare, struck her, whistled—giddyap, giddyap! The mare leaped out of the ditch and vanished.

"Oh, oh! My mare! Oh, oh! My mare!" I yelled with all my strength.

The tempest raged on, the thunder boomed louder and louder. The cyclone grabbed me, and I was spinning inside it with other wild creatures. I could make out a murmuring of words in an unfamiliar language. My head was swirling, my eyes were closed, I was bathed in sweat. Then I felt a hand touching my head, touching my feet. I screamed as I fell. And opened my eyes.

I was aware of pillows under my head. I couldn't tell where I was. I heard strange words, like the mutterings during my whirl in the round, but I couldn't see who was talking. In a little while, gradually regaining my consciousness, I could make out in succession: a disheveled beard, long sidelocks, and the weird face of some creature, a man. This freak was rummaging in a corner, gaping, making the strangest grimaces, stamping as though arguing with someone, and irately emitting such words: "I conjure you in the name of Luciferial and in the name of Plutonial, Cerebrial, Proserpinial, in the name of, the name of . . . and in the name of . . . of . . . so that you may have no power over Israel the son of Tsippe. Be gone, flee and fly, into the wild fields, the wild forests. There, a rock rocks on a rock, and on that rock another rock, mounted by a mountain which is mounted by another mountain, and on it sits Shmendrik tending his cats and bats! Catch a cat and drag a dragon! Grab all the flies in the world, all the roaches, crickets, fleas, bedbugs, and go dance with them, dance through all the fields and forests, dance and prance and never cease, and leave the world in peace!"

And an old Christian peasant woman was standing there, softly whispering to herself in a corner. She spit and broke into a loud, cavernous yawn.

"Porhe zike limrike, bikh, bikh!" murmured the creature, bending over me and grabbing the tip of my nose.

"Hassikh a passikh a passikh,!" replied my nose, wheezing and sneezing loudly.

"God bless you!" the creature wished me joyfully and dashed over to the door with the cheery news.

"Tsippe, come here, your son is safe and sound!"

"Where am I?" I asked, astonished.

"You're at home, Izzy! May you live a long life!" replied my mother, in the doorway, and a moment later, she was at my bedside, hugging me and weeping bitterly.

"Shabriri, briri, riri, ri," whispered the creature, huffing and puffing as though driving someone away. Then he turned to my mother and said:

"Tsippe, I've been fighting demons for thirty years already—yes, Tsippe, that long. Soon after the first panic—may God preserve us—I became a miracle worker. A couple of years before the great fire, around the time when Tevye-Kalman found a buried treasure in town, approximately a year before they dredged the river and cleaned the bathhouse—yes, Tsippe, that was thirty years ago, if not more. I've had my share of dealings with them. I really let them have it today, by God! This was their doing, it was!"

"Hoooooooaaaaaaa!" the old peasant woman yawned loudly, said something, spit, and yawned again: "Goddamn their mothers!"

The miracle worker cut seven splinters from the table and chairs, scooped up seven heaps of dust from under the threshold, wrapped seven silver coins in one of my woolen things, which my mother had given him, and then he said to her:

"I need all this to pronounce an incantation at night, in the moonlight, over at the crossroads outside town. I'll also need seven hairs from an old dog's beard, as it is written. But if worse comes to worst, and I can't find a dog, then a cat will do. Tsippe, your cat must be in the kitchen. I'm going to go in and get seven handfuls of ashes from the stove, and while I'm there I'm going to pull seven hairs from the end of the cat's tail."

Having said these words, the miracle worker kissed the mezuzah on the doorjamb and promised to come tomorrow, God willing, and finish his work. He motioned to the peasant woman, and the two of them left our house.

"Mama, what's going on?" I asked sympathetically, for my mother, I saw, was weeping. "Why are you crying, Mama?"

"Oh, I feel so awful, I feel so miserable, Izzy!"

"What happened?"

"Oh, may it never happen again!"

"For pity's sake, Mama, tell me. I won't calm down until you put my mind at ease. Stop crying, and tell me, Mama dear. I've got to know!"

"Just wait a bit, darling, till I've had my cry."

It was quiet. My mother was leaning her head on my chest, sobbing quietly, her body trembling all over. After a while, she looked at me, pulled herself together, and, with a sigh, she told me the following:

"When you went out walking in the fields and didn't come home even though it was getting late, we all went looking for you outside town, in every direction. We hunted high and low, until we found you asleep under a tree by some ditch. When we brought you back, we realized you were very confused. You couldn't fall asleep and you were very excited. The next morning you didn't eat at all, you were still a bundle of nerves, and you were lost in thought, talking to yourself, and nothing you said made any sense. None of us could understand what it meant. But then, it came out, God forbid, may we never see anything like it again, not we and not all Israel!—

"No," said my mother tearfully, breaking off. "No, I can't talk anymore. Every single word pricks me like a needle. Please, Izzy, let me rest, and it's time for you to get some rest too. You'll feel better after you've slept. Sleep, my child, sleep, it'll be good for you, Izzy!"

"Only on condition, Mama, that you promise to tell me everything tomorrow."

"Whatever you like," said my mother. "Sleep, sleep, my child, sleep, Israel! . . ."

CHAPTER SIX
The Servant Continues Where Mother Left Off

The next morning, my mother came in to ask how I felt, and when I pleaded with her to keep her word and tell me the rest, she wiped her eyes with her apron and said with a bitter sigh:

"I simply can't tell you exactly. Everything you said and did was so peculiar. That day (God preserve us!) you raved on and on about animals, cattle, and, in the same breath, about human beings, and you were all broken up about some poor, miserable mare, who was sick, and mauled, and very unhappy. May God waft your words away like smoke over waste fields and wild forests! And meanwhile, people are talking about you in town, they say that you're .... Oh God! May *they* go crazy, our enemies who wish such evil on me and all Israel! You were tossing in fever for a few days and you were totally confused. Thank God you're all right this morning. Oh, if only you stay sound and healthy!"

"Tsippe!" said the miracle worker. He and the peasant woman had tiptoed in so as not to disturb the patient, and they had been standing behind my mother while she was talking. "It wasn't him doing the talking, those were *their* words, the demon was talking out of him."

"Pravda! That's right!" the old peasant woman butted in, for she understood a little Yiddish. "That's *their* doing. Goddamn their mothers!"

They all spit three times.

In walked Braindel, the prayer prompter in the female section of the synagogue. Mother had sent her to the cemetery to leave no stone unturned and plead with our ancestors, and to measure the graveyard with cotton threads in order to make candle wicks. Braindel, upon entering, kissed the mezuzah three times and ran over to my mother, tearfully sobbing and telling her in the threnody of Lamentations:

"I prayed to Grandmother Yente, Aunt Zelde—may they rest in paradise—they were pious souls—and I prayed to his father, his grandfather Shepsel, and the whole family. I also prayed to the old rabbi's wife—a devout woman—may her virtues help!—to make them intercede for us. The Lord God will hear their prayers—He *is* a father, after all, merciful and just. Izzy will recover—God willing. You should try rolling eggs over him again and pouring wax. He's suffering from shock. The same thing happened last year to the son of that teacher from Brody. Kroyne rolled her eggs skillfully and just whisked his illness away. How is he now, Tsippe?"

"Not bad!" broke in the miracle worker. "Out of danger. You say he got it from a sudden shock, Braindel? Wrong! I'm an expert in such matters. That was their work, Braindel, their doing! You can ask our Christian friend here, she understands Yiddish. We've gone through all sorts of things together."

"Pravda, Braindel," said the old Christian woman, nodding her head. "What's true is true. This is their doing, Goddamn their mothers!"

"I really don't know," said my mother in surprise, almost at random, "where he gets his peculiar notions. Probably from his books, I think, he's so completely absorbed in them. How often have I said to him: 'Izzy, the devil take your books, and the devil take that whole examination. Don't stuff your head with such stupid books and such crazy stories.' Can you imagine, he spends months memorizing a story about some giant who cleaned out thirty-six stables, a story about a nightingale who was a highwayman, a famous knight who guzzled down a whole sea of liquor and tore out entire oak trees as though they were hairs. And stories about a sorcerer named Kashtsey and some old woman named Yaha who made a big commotion and had horses that talked like human beings. And stories about a lady who turned her stepson into a goat. And stories about fights and brawls and battles and misery and unhappiness, and goodness knows what else! Now can any good come of all that, I ask you?"

"But, Mama dear!" "Aren't there similar stories in our own Jewish books? Haven't you told me a lot of them yourself? And haven't I heard a lot from other Jews, and stories about werewolves and reincarnations? And dead people roaming through the World of Chaos, and tales about demons, ghosts, little children, brides and grooms who fell into the hands of devils. How many roasted chickens have Jews heard clucking, right on the platters in front of them? And how many calves, how many cows, how many bulls, how many oxen, horses, and donkeys have suddenly started weeping and begging to be saved? How many of them have the miracle workers saved and given a decent Jewish burial? *Me mune afar Yankev?*" I added in Hebrew.

"What's he saying?" my mother exclaimed in dismay, thinking I was delirious again. "What's all this *moony* business?"

"May you live one hundred and twenty years, Tsippe," Braindel spoke up, beaming with delight at this opportunity to show her learning. "There's no problem, darling, it's really quite simple: *Me mune*—who can count; *afar*—the dust, which means the graves; *Yankev*—Jacob—the graves made for Jacob, which means the Jews, who are called Jacob. That's a verse in the *Tsenerene*, and Bekhaye says—"

"What he says about transmigration," broke in the miracle worker, "I can swear on a stack of Bibles that in my lifetime I've exorcised a lot of lost spirits. I personally heard them shrieking, and may I hear the trumpet of the Messiah that clearly."

"Oh, spirits! Spirits! That's nothing to sneeze at!" said Braindel, her face pious. "Why, it says so in the Torah! It's perfectly normal. What more do you want? What about that possessed man in Poorsville? The whole world was talking about him. Hey wait!— 'Blessed be He Who bringeth to remembrance things forgotten!' Didn't we have that affair of the black tomcat? That was three years after my second marriage, may he rest in peace, right at the time when I was carrying my little Hatske, may he stay healthy. Why, I remember it as though it were yesterday, there was a proclamation in all the synagogues that we should go and watch the exorcism, but pregnant women mustn't go—"

"Do you hear, Mama dear?" I asked her. "Do you hear what the miracle worker and Braindel are saying?"

"Why, honestly, Izzy!" she answered, at a loss for words. "Why, that's different. Uh, what are you talking about? Uhhh, uhhh, how can you compare the two? One comes from the unclean and the other from the holy, don't you see?"

"That's so true, Tsippe. I'll swear to that on a stack of Bibles!" the miracle worker agreed. "A good refutal! It really is, Tsippe. That's the truth, I'll swear to it!"

"Well, and what do you say?" I asked the old peasant woman, seeing that it was no use my talking, no one was listening.

"He's right!" she answered, nodding her head. "It's *their* doing! Goddamn their mothers!"

It sometimes happens that a person has a dream, and when he awakes, there's not a trace left of it. Later, however, he feels a flap in his brain, an echo of that dream, and it keeps haunting him until he remembers the dream in full. And the same thing happened with me.

My mother's few words, ambiguous as they were, kept preying on my mind, nagging me to ferret out the rest, which was hovering dimly before me, unwilling to lodge in my brain. Before long, everything became clear to me.

In my mother's store, there was a clerk who had been working there since boyhood. Now he was a bearded old man, a

thoroughgoing Jew and a thorough-paced servant. His name was
Sender Sholonu, which is Hebrew for "Our Sender." Sender was
very disturbed that I had left the straight and narrow path to fool
around with poppycock. Furthermore, my peculiar carryings-on
were no credit to such a superior family (pure nobility) as mine.
To make matters worse, he took it as a personal offense, like any
employee who plumes himself on his boss's honor. He would give
me a jab whenever he could, though he kept within bounds. But
this last incident had made his blood boil.

"How could he do it!" he said. "How could he bring such shame
upon us!"

Once, when we were having words, and he wanted to show me
how far my heresy had taken me, he finally let the cat out of the
bag, giving me a long lecture on what I had done:

"You were coming out in the yard and our big turkey cock
strutted over to you. You addressed him as 'Your Lordship!' and
doffed your hat: 'You're a guardsman, Your Lordship, you wear
spurs and fine plumes. The world regards you as educated and
highly intelligent. But, forgive me for speaking frankly. Your behavior really isn't topnotch. Ever since you've been with us, all
we've heard you do is scream, carry on, and fight—one argument
after another, fuss and feathers, and always over a woman, over
nonsense. You have enough romances every day as it is, why do
you have to take away someone else's one-and-only! What did you
have to go and pounce upon that poor fellow for? What did you
have to fight a duel and wound him for? Is that why you people
have spurs, so you can gouge out one another's eyes? Is that what
you call honor? Self-respect? Common folk simply call it murder!
It's your wife I feel sorry for. The poor woman runs around like a
chicken without a head, worrying about your children. And you
won't even look at them, you chase after other women, and that's
all you think about. Mr. Gander and Mr. Drake are much more to
my taste! People think they're nothing but birdbrains. But they really behave very decently, they're devoted fathers and fine bread-
winners, as God has commanded. Compared with them, Your Lordship, you really have nothing to crow about!'

"When you were going away from the turkey cock, you saw our
cow and her calf next to the tub of chaff. You greeted her very politely:

"'Ah, Madam Cow!' you said. 'How are you? How is your dear

husband, Mr. Bull? Your toilet, Madam, is most appealing. It is dur-
able and attractive at once. And that tail you have dragging along
in back is *so* fashionable, simply the last word, it suits the ladies perfectly.... A fine thing! I hear you've bestowed a pair of horns
upon your husband! What a lovely present! He must be terribly
pleased.... But why is he always so busy? A husband has to go out
strolling with his wife occasionally, they ought to visit people together. What else does a lady have to do? ... You, Madam Cow, apparently go along with those who believe the weaker sex were not
created for serious work, as men were. A fine sight when a female
drives the horses! And have you gotten to know our Dutchwoman?
Ah, such a fine, plump lady. There's really nothing quite like a foreign woman! Mr. Bull seems to have gotten rather... close to her.
Oh, do have a bonbon, Madam....' And you pointed at the
feeding tub. 'Help yourself and give some to your lovely daughter!
Don't be bashful, Miss Calf!—It's certainly sensible of you, Madam
Cow, to keep your daughter at home. What good does it do to send
young girls away for their education? A waste of time and money,
I tell you! You would be better off summoning the matchmaker.
Don't be shy, Miss Calf, why that's the way of the world. I see that
Miss Calf is as decent and pious as her mother. I'm not flattering
you, Madam, perish the thought—I'm merely telling you the plain
truth...'

"At this point, who should drop by but Mr. Tsempel with his
wife and daughters. May God preserve us! You grabbed the tub,
carried it into the parlor, plopped it down in front of our guests,
and asked them, in cow language, to have some chaff. 'It's about
time we milked the cows,' you said, 'and sent them home. How
long can they stroll around like that! Our farm is really a
shambles!'

"Now you can imagine how everyone sat there dumbstruck and
thinking God knows what! You were taken away on the spot. Suddenly we heard a shriek, we ran out, looked—and we nearly fainted! Mr. Isaac-Wolf, a pillar of our community—the rabbi's manager no less—he runs all the charitable organizations, and his word is
law.... Well, he was standing in our home, and you were standing opposite him and—God preserve us!—you were yelling at him:

" 'It's scandalous the way our community is run! The minute we
get a community goat, we let him loose, and no one bothers about
him anymore! But what does the goat do? He usually goes to

synagogue, that's his place of relaxation. He kisses hindquarters, if you'll excuse my saying so, rummages around in the stray leaves, leaps about in the gardens with the whole bunch of nanny goats, and sneaks into everyone's home. The moment you turn your back, he sticks his nose in a trough, a chest, a box, and works mischief. Community! Beard your billy goat in his den, and make sure he never jumps into your gardens or steals anything from your troughs again! But no! None of you will do it. Everyone is too scared to even touch him. Sometimes, when a group of Jews are standing around, talking about important things, they catch sight of him far in the distance, the community billy goat—their skins crawl, and they scatter in all directions.'

"Izzy, you've brought shame and sorrow upon us with your carryings-on. You've treated such fine, decent people like cattle! Oh me, oh me!" exclaimed Sender, grabbing at his head. "If only the earth had opened and swallowed us alive!"

CHAPTER SEVEN
Izzy Still Wants to Become a Human Being

I was infamous in my town because of three sins: 1: I was over twenty and still unmarried; 2: I had abandoned the study of our sacred Jewish lore and completely forsaken the Talmud; 3: I had given myself over fully to the secular books. The townspeople regarded me as a heretic, glaring at me and keeping out of my way, unwilling to come anywhere near me.

It's hard enough to be solitary abroad, but pity the poor man who is solitary at home. In a foreign country, the miserable stranger doesn't know anyone, and no one knows him. That's certainly a heartache, and there's no shame in it. But to be a stranger in your own hometown, among your own people—that means both heartache and shame together. Such bitter feelings are known only to a poor man invited to a meeting or a feast but left to sit alone, ignored by everyone, whether purposely or not. He's something like an invisible man, able to see everyone, but with no one able to see him. If he says anything, no one hears him, and his words just come back to his own ears. If someone does occasionally answer him, in a half-hearted mumble, it's as though the man were doing him a favor while thinking to himself: "Take it and go to the devil!"

If I had still been locked up in my room, poring over my books night and day, I wouldn't have been so acutely aware that everyone hated me. But now that my precarious health (God preserve us!) forced me to study less and at times leave off altogether for a while, I could feel how grim and bitter it was to be isolated from both outsiders and my own people, belonging to neither one nor the other.

My mother was deeply hurt that I was acting the way I was, going off in a completely different direction from all the other Jews. But she took care not to say anything unkind, she didn't want to offend her only child. And so my love for her became even greater. And whenever I got despondent, I so strongly felt the need to pour out my bitter sorrows to her.

"Oh, mother, it's so awful!" I once lamented to her, in a dark moment. "It's so awful to be all alone!"

My mother was startled by my words, and then her face lit up:

"How wonderful, my child! We were just talking about it. Speak of the devil—I mean, the Messiah! That's obviously the best sign that what I'm about to tell you comes directly from God. I'm certain that today you'll want to hear everything I have to say. From now on, I hope that your fortune (may God grant it!) will shine like the radiant morning star. Listen, my son! Today, someone proposed a marriage for you, a really marvelous girl ... beautiful, and rich, too—"

"That's enough, Mama, that's enough!" But my mother didn't hear, she merely continued heaping praises.

"She's got a lot of money, and presents, and jewelry, gold and silver, diamonds, a lovely wardrobe, and you'll live with her father, in the finest style—"

"It's always the finest style among Jews!" I screamed, breaking in. "Always the same old story! You start out rich, in the finest style, and you always end up in the poorest style: children, a whole swarm of them, poverty, a grim life, teaching, sitting around and doing nothing, trying to pick up some money by acting as a broker, breaking your back, bowing and scraping and kneeling, 'Why thank you, sir!' and servility, and praising to the skies, praising Goddamnit! Praising, praising, praising, praising—"

"Stop it! That's enough!" screamed my mother, jumping back in terror. "Such a deluge of words! May God protect us! It's all right, I'll hold my tongue. If you hadn't started, I wouldn't have said a word. You were the one who said it with your own two lips, that Bible verse: 'It is not good for man to be alone.' That means it is not good for a man to be without a wife."

"Oh, Mama! I said that because I feel so alone and so estranged from people!"

"But Izzy, you're the one who's strange. You don't do the things that other people do. If you wanted to, you could make everything all right."

"Are you telling me to return to the fold, Mama? To become a *luftmentsh*, with all it entails, like any other Jewish *luftmentsh*? To go against my will and my better judgment, and remain a fool for the rest of my life just to please a bunch of fools? No, Mother! I'd only make things worse for myself! A man who acts against his own will and his better judgment—is a nullity, worse than a corpse. That's true of anyone, not just Jews."

My mother kept silent. She gave me a worried stare, shaking her head and sighing. My heart felt so bitter, and I lamented to her in great sorrow:

"Oh, Mother. I curse the day that I was born to be miserable and hated by all the world! My own people, the Jews, are so terrible to me, and so are the 'others,' the Christians! The Jews hate me for not being a Jew after their own hearts, and the Christians despise me for being a Jew—'Ah, that's the trouble! A Jew!' For this sin with which I and my ancestors were born, and which has been handed down to us from Father Abraham, we are punished with misery, oppression, expulsions, afflictions, sufferings, and every possible torture. I feel it's my foremost obligation to do anything in my power to fight this misfortune. A man who's been expelled from the rest of mankind, in whom God's gift of human dignity has been degraded, who's been crowded into a confining area like a bird in a cage, unable to budge—if that man doesn't give a damn, then it would be better for him not to have been born at all. I'm a human being, Mama! I'm alive and I want to live. I want to get out of this narrow confinement and live on an equal footing with other human beings in God's great world. I have to do my best to keep my being Jewish from harming me and to improve my condition."

"Oh, Izzy, what are you saying!" screamed my mother, turning chalk white as if about to faint.

"Don't worry, Mama!" I comforted her. "Your son Israel is still Israel, and he'll be Izzy forever and ever. I want to improve my condition by getting an education. With a university degree I can obtain special privileges, including the right to leave this narrow confinement, the Pale of Settlement, and move about freely anywhere in the world."

"Well, Izzy, so you want to go back to your fairytales, and sweat over your books day and night!" said my mother, anxious about my physical health and my peace of mind. "Oh, your books, your books! They won't bring us anything but sorrow and misery! I'm only a simple woman, and I don't understand what that outside world of yours is all about, the world you keep talking about all the time and find so attractive. Stay here with your mother, you've got everything you need right here at home—thank goodness! Who am I laboring for and working my fingers to the bone for? No one but you, my darling child!"

"The very thought of never doing anything and being a burden on my mother for the rest of my life makes me sick! A grown man like me, hanging on to his mother's apron strings, eating and not working! It would have been better for me and you and the whole world if I'd never been born! I don't want to be a daydreamer. There are enough Jewish daydreamers as it is!"

"Please, Izzy, do me a favor and put your books away, those books of yours.... Israel.... There's a way of getting the right to live in the forbidden areas. All you need is money and an artisan's license."

"What do you mean 'money'?"

"Well, you just buy a business license from whatever guild you like, and that gives a Jew a right to settle in the world, which you find so attractive."

"Ah, Mother, pity the poor man who depends on money and not on himself. A privilege that's gotten with money is a disgrace to both the man who sells it and the man who buys it. Damnit! I don't want it, and I hate commerce anyway. I hate it because of the businessmen! Most of them, from the ragpickers to the shopkeepers and bankers, are devoted followers of that great thief Laban.... And I hate them because of their competitiveness, and that enormous chaos in the business world, which rubs off on them, whether they like it or not. There are enough Jewish ragpickers and shopkeepers as it is! And that thing you talked about, Mama,—

the artisan's license! What connection do I have with a craft?! I haven't the foggiest notion about any craft whatsoever!"

"The craft isn't so important," murmured my mother. "The main thing is the license, don't you see?"

My reply was a grimace. Her words made my gorge rise. Actually a rabbinical permission may be obtained in a matter of life or death, to hit upon some stratagem, say, a wire strung on the circumference of a town to classify it as enclosed private property so that Jews can carry things on the Sabbath. A rabbi can also give a dispensation to charge interest, and so on. But a craft license?

I kept silent for quite a while, just curling my nose. And then I spoke again briefly, and to the point: "The only thing I'm interested in is a university degree, and I'll do anything I can to get it. I won't rest until it's mine. Once and for all, I want to study at the university!"

"Study? You call that studying?! Oh my goodness! Your studies are devouring all your strength, Israel."

"Loafing weakens your strength even more, and it wipes you out!"

What could my poor mother do? She let me have my way. But only on condition that I budget a time for studying, a time for going on walks, for sleeping, and the like, to safeguard my health. A sound mind in a sound body!

And so, in a happy moment, I went back to my books, studying hard and systematically, just as before, until the time came for my examinations.

CHAPTER EIGHT
Mother Knows Best

One lovely spring morning, a wagon stopped in front of our house to bring me to Dnieprovitz, where I was to take my examinations. My mother was very mournful, she couldn't hold back her tears. She kept crying and looking at me, looking at me and then crying again.

"Don't cry, Mama!" I begged her and burst into tears. My heart felt so heavy.

"Please don't cry, Mama dear! I'm not going to some God-forsaken place. I just have to get it over with. I've studied and

worked so hard. God will help me get my wish. I'll be able to earn
my living respectably, and I'll be a free man. And then you'll be so
proud of me, Mama. Oh, please don't cry, Mama, please don't cry!"

"Oh Izzy!" she replied. "That's easy for you to say. When a
mother's heart cries, you can't just calm it down like a child. It's
got its reasons for crying. It senses something. It knows something
that no mind can grasp. Please, Izzy, think it over and don't go!
Why should you work so hard at your age, you poor baby! How
can you tell whether it will be worth all the trouble and drudgery?
How many educated Jews are there among us, without even a pair
of boots to their name? How many scholars come to nothing and
suffer terribly all their lives? Israel, all the Gentile schools and education are just some new-fangled nonsense. Our ancestors didn't
even know there was such a thing. I hope to God it doesn't bring
trouble to us and the Jewish people, and tear children away from
their parents. Please, Izzy dear, stay home! It's so hard for me to
say goodbye to you, so hard!"

The driver came into the house and took my things, thereby ending the conversation. My mother and I tearfully kissed and said
goodbye. I climbed into the wagon, and away we drove.

Laugh all you like, you modern, enlightened Jews. Laugh at anything you like. But please don't deride the notion that a mother's
heart has its reasons for crying! As long as you remain silent and
fail to tell us what life is, how all our thoughts and feelings arise
and flourish inside our brains, how marvelous dreams are spun and
woven within us from a stuff, a thread, that, for now at least, doesn't
exist in the world and won't be developed till later on. As long
as you remain silent and without the least shimmer of understanding, I just won't let you guffaw at the notion that a mother's heart
feels and divines! You musn't laugh, you don't have the right to
laugh when I say that my mother's heart had its reasons for crying!

I flunked!

It doesn't hurt to know how and why. On the day of the examination, I felt plucky, and to bolster my courage I had a drink,
though I usually never touch the stuff. Don't worry, I thought to
myself, God will help! Why should I be scared? The examiners are
fine, educated people. They're sure to treat me gently, decently,
like gentlemen and scholars, and raise my spirits.

But oh God! When I stood before them, I quickly learned the er-
ror of my ways. The teachers sat there, dressed in uniforms with

brass buttons. They glared at me, as grim and severe as if I had robbed or killed someone. They scowled like a police official who welcomes you with: "Where you from! Why, I'll.... Show me your passport!"

Now why should teachers, whose job is to make us and our children sensible and sensitive, whose job requires them to be decent, straightforward, and accessible to everyone, so that all hearts will open to them and let them sow and plant the seeds of decency and virtue—why should teachers have brass buttons and glare like police officers? Say what you will, I just can't imagine Socrates, Plato, Aristotle, and the others with such brass buttons, sour faces, and grim looks....

Naturally, their welcome unmanned me. I no longer knew what was happening. If that was their goal, then they certainly achieved it—with a vengeance. My head began spinning. One teacher addressed me with a look that seemed to say: "Get a load of him! I'm the one with a great mind, an open mind. I'm asking the questions! Do you get me? I'm asking! Respect, do you hear!" He turned to me with that look and treated me to one question after another, a line from here, a verse from there, until we came to a fairytale, to Baba Yaha of all people! I was befuddled, lost my bearings, and went completely adrift. The teachers did me the honor of laughing their heads off, with cheerier expressions!

And thus ended my examination, thus ended my great efforts, thus ended all my hopes!

I felt so awful that I couldn't stay in my room. I wandered around the city, up and down the streets and the lovely surrounding hills. I only stopped at my hotel to have a bite and to sleep! But actually, sleeping became impossible, and I spent terrible nights, tossing and turning. The moment I closed my eyes, wild creatures would loom up, glare at me with sour expressions—and a spectacle began, a fine spectacle. There was a comedy, and I played the sacrificial rooster. But I had nothing to crow about! I felt myself soaring through the air, whirling around and around. My hands and feet were tied. I was being spun around as a sacrificial rooster on the Day of Atonement. Up against a stone wall.

Once, during such a spectacle, I crowed at the top of my lungs, so loudly that I was terror-stricken. I tumbled from my bed more dead than alive, and raced out in a dreadful turmoil. I thought some person was at my heels, yelling: "Where is he? Stop him!" Dashing helter-skelter, I cannoned into someone. I felt a clammy hand clutching me with an iron grip. An old hag stood in front of me, scrawny, scraggy, not an ounce of flesh on her frame, all skin and bones. Instead of eyes, she had two yawning holes lined with a dirty, wrinkled, leathery skin of a disgusting color. Her mouth gaped from ear to ear, toothless, hollow, empty, except for the tongue flicking around inside, writhing, twisting, like a worm in a pit. From her arm dangled a basket of huge live crabs, crawling, lumbering over one another, waving their nippers. She glared at me in silence, her mouth widening even more, as though laughing, if you could call it that—a mirth that casts a dark shadow of melancholy on the soul and freezes your guts. I thought of Baba Yaha, my nemesis of the past few years, obstructing my path, preventing me from getting ahead. A cold sweat covered my body. I felt so sick I nearly fainted. I pulled myself together, tore myself away from where I was standing, and ran like a madman.

Baba Yaha had kindled such a panic in me that as I ran I kept looking around every which way to make sure I wouldn't meet up with her again. I had heard long ago that she lived in Dnieprovitz, keeping people with long noses in constant terror. If one of them ever crossed her path, she would grab his nose and whistle—and then her gang came, the demons and devils. She would pull on his nose and the others would push him from behind—and the long-nosed would come to rest. From that time on, I kept touching my nose and hid it from danger as well as I could.

CHAPTER NINE
He Bumps Into Her Again

One day, when I was wandering along the street, I came upon some policemen dragging an animal and beating it murderously. Cognizant of my duty as a member of the Society for the Prevention of Cruelty to Animals, I promptly strode over to the policemen to ask them for mercy. As I drew near and looked, a cold sweat covered my body. It was she, in the flesh—with her tangled hair, her bony neck, and her crooked, flayed back! There she was—my old, scraggy, downtrodden mare!

"Why," I asked the policemen, "are you beating this poor, living creature?"

"Mind your own business! Get moving and don't bother us!"

"I'm a member of the Society for the Prevention of Cruelty to Animals!"

"We're taking her to the stationhouse," the policemen rapped out reluctantly.

"But why do you have to beat her?"

"It doesn't look right if we arrest someone without beating them. Sort of like a wedding without musicians," they replied sarcastically.

"But there's such a thing as love of animals. Aren't you hurting her when you beat her? Why, you're beating a living creature, a human creature!"

"Whaaaaah?" said the policemen, with angry faces, eying me like kosher-meat inspectors.

Their triple-peaked "Whaaaaah?" and their fulminating eyes set my entire body atremble, particularly my nose. And almost willy-nilly my hand slipped into my pocket and then from my pocket into their hands, and then they really did turn milder. Taking advantage of their cheerier mood, I asked them amicably:

"Now just what did this creature do?"

"This animal doesn't have the right to run around in town. The law says she has to remain in her stable."

"But others are running around the streets here!"

"Don't argue! That's the law and that's what we're doing. By the way, since you're so interested in her, could this perchance be your mare?"

I wanted to reply: "Yes, she's mine, the mare is mine!" But then I looked at her, and I was angry at seeing her stand there so calmly, without a trace of feeling, as though the entire conversation didn't concern her in the least, as though we were talking about someone else, as though she were thinking: "Well, fine, if they insult me and poke fun of me, so what, who cares?" Or as if she were thinking nothing, absolutely nothing. All she seemed to care about was finding something to stuff her belly. I was so annoyed that I felt like saying: "No, she's not mine, we have absolutely nothing to do with one another!" I wanted to wash my hands of her and go away.... But I felt a wrench in my heart and I exclaimed heatedly:

"Of course she's mine!"

There's no need to dwell on my conversation with the policemen.

I bargained, paid their price, and ransomed her from their hands. But only on condition that I take her out of town. If she ever crossed their path again, then I could be sure it would cost me a pretty penny.

I kept my word, and without giving it a second thought, I started off with the mare.

Imagine my situation! I, Izzy the bungler, on foot, and leading a mare along a road full of potholes, stones, and brambles! I strained and slaved beyond my strength, leading her on, and she barely slogged along, scarcely able to lift a hoof! If that wasn't enough, at times she stumbled, balked, and though I went at her tooth and nail, hammer and tongs, she wouldn't budge an inch! She even wanted to step off the road and bog down in the quagmire. What could I do? What could I resort to? I grabbed her mane and pulled her by brute force. But then I was overcome with fatigue and sweat. It made my heart bleed to drag her like that. The poor creature must have been in terrible pain. What a sorry business! I stopped dead, folding my arms. I cursed her furiously.

"Damn it!" I shouted angrily into the air. "I never expected such trials and tribulations for my loving kindness! I fight for her, wrangle for her, take her part, throw in a good word for her. I do what I can to keep people from treating her like dirt. For her sake, I walk on foot like a beggar, without a shred of self-respect, I sacrifice my health, torment myself—for what?! So that she can lead a better life, relax a bit, breathe free—and what does she do?—She drives me up the wall, she makes my life a hell, like my worst enemy. Now I ask you, is that fair of her, is that decent of her?—Goddamn it! I go to all the trouble of making plans for her. I think of nothing in the world but her, her, and only her—and she knocks all the thoughts out of my head with the way she's acting now.... I say to her: 'Move!' And she stands still behind me! I yell: 'Stay on the road!' And she climbs into the mud. I'm so good and kind and devoted to her, and she's so nasty and cantankerous and contrary! Now, is that fair, is that decent?! Damn it, it's ridiculous!"

After a brief pause, I thrust my finger in her face and said: "I know damn well that if I got on your back and stuck a bridle on you and gave you a good lash, you'd go wherever I'd force you to. You broken-down jade! You have so much respect for anyone who rides you, you tremble at his every motion, his every glance, and you consider yourself fortunate when you satisfy him, even when he rips the hide off your bones. But my heart won't let me ride you. May my tongue cleave to the roof of my mouth if ever I say to you: 'Carry me!' If ever I lash you, poor creature, may my right hand wither! Bear that in mind!"

I spoke to her in vehemence, argued with her, preached at her with all my soul. I wept like a heartbroken child. And she just stood there, coolly nibbling grass on the roadside. What could I do? What could I say? Arguing didn't help, sermons didn't help. There was nothing to do, by fair means or foul. I just didn't have the heart to cast her aside, I felt so sorry for her, and something drew me to her like a magnet.

So I grabbed her mane again and dragged her haphazardly, any which way. I prayed to God not to let any people come by, or at least not to let them laugh at me and my mare. "Please don't let strangers see what's happening, let it remain a secret, a dark horse!" But my prayers were ignored. As my bad luck would have it, people, both genteel and common, came in droves from all sides. Each passer-by pointed his finger at us, cracked a joke, and guffawed.

One person taunted: "Where did you ever get such a lively trotter? What a find!"

Another counseled: "What are you doing with such a broken-down nag, young man? Go your own way and let that carcass rot! Why ruin yourself? You'll never get anywhere with a creature like that! Can't you see she's already got three hooves in the grave! She's ready to say her prayers!"

A third: "Climb up on her and break her bones, and just watch—she'll lift her legs and fly off."

And yet another: "Why don't you sling that old nag over your shoulders—you'll have a much easier time of it, by God!"

And God alone knew what I felt like, hearing all these comments from every passer-by!

Meanwhile, night had gathered. The sky was overdrawn with black clouds. Lightning crackled here and there. But the mare kept pulling the same old tricks. I was in a hurry, I wanted to stop some place for the night, so I decided to drag my misfortune with all the strength I could muster. In a pig's eye! When I gave her a good tug, she reared and ramped and balked and kicked against the pricks.

"Ho ho!" I thought. "So you want to kick me, you want to bite

the hand that leads you. Well, then goodnight! Sleep alone! I'm
leaving. I'll be rid of all my troubles. I'll be spared any further embarrassment and indignity. I won't make a fool of myself with you
anymore."

But then I thought it over: "Haha! You're kicking, you're angry,
you want to hit me. That's great! You're starting to feel, you care
about something. And if you care and feel, then there's hope you'll
come to your senses—God willing! And then, things will be different! ..."

Full of love, I hugged and stroked my mare, and led her slowly,
gingerly, until we came to a large, dense wood, which we entered
to spend the night.

CHAPTER TEN
What Happened to Izzy that Night

We threw ourselves down under a large, tall tree, for we were both
tired and drained from the arduous journey (may you be spared!).
A flash of lightning split the sky, bathing the world in fire. A peal
of thunder crashed, and its terrifying echo boomed from all sides
like a thousand cannon. A tempest arose, whistling, wailing,
howling like a pack of famished wolves—as if a hundred warlocks
had strung themselves up that day. The sleeping forest bolted
awake in terror. Everything came to life, each blade of grass, each
twig, each leaf, rustling, soughing, swishing, chattering in a Babel of
noises and tongues. Magpies, ravens, owls, and all their cohorts
cawed and croaked a dirge. They moaned, and sighed, and yelled,
outshrilling one another until a sudden torrent drowned them out.

How dreadful such a night in the forest! How terrifying!

I crouched and hugged the tree. The rain soaked me. I trembled
all over, and in between the thunderbolts the divine and powerful
words of the psalm resounded in my ears.

> The earth shook and shuddered,
> and the footings of mountains
> quivered and quaked,
> for He was blazing.
> A smoke arose from His nostrils,
> from His mouth a devouring fire,

that kindled coals.
He bent the heavens, and came down,
with stormy darkness under His feet,
He rode the cherub, He flew,
He swept down on the wings of the storm.

There was God! Soaring through the tattered clouds!—A patch of thick black fog with radiant edges was racing along, in the shape of an enormous charger with a pure white mane on his dark-dappled neck. From his nostrils and mouth, crackles of fiery lightning came zigzagging out.... And there was—the cherub, and on him, a gigantic rider, heroic, in a purple cloak, with long gray locks and a long curly beard as pure and white as silver. At his heels came an entire host of giants, Og the king of Basan, and Gog and Magog, with all conceivable manner of beasts. All with earnest, thoughtful faces, hurrying, dashing, God knows where—and leaving a blue, clear trail behind them in the heavens. The moon poked a bit of her head out from behind the clouds and peeped after the host, full of reverence, like a nobleman when a higher-ranking lord is passing through his territory .... The trees lowered their heads and bowed in deep respect, looking as if they had just gotten a thorough lashing—to teach them manners! Shush! And drops of water came dripping from their green mantles, dripping, dripping on the earth, dripping, dripping on my head.

"Oh, holy God!" I yelled, and prostrated myself on the drenched grass.

A terrible din came from somewhere, like the howling of a dog, the meowing of a cat, the growling of a bear. I panicked, shuddered, sprang to my feet. Were there four different beasts, or a single beast screaming different noises?

After a while, I could make out footfalls in the distance, like someone treading through the forest over leaves and broken twigs. Before I even had time to arm myself with a stick that was lying on the ground, a pair of eyes flashed at me like lanterns in the darkness. A head appeared, an open mouth, a red tongue, sharp, pointed, snowy teeth. Then an entire body, and *pow!* A huge, fearsome wolf loomed up before me—a growl, a leap, and I was in his clutches, like a senseless mouse writhing in the claws of a cat.

But then my agony faded. I felt a heavenly euphoria such as a saint must feel when he goes to his glory. I saw myself resting in

peace, under a canopy of purple wool. My hands and feet were
bound with linen cords. A huge icebag perched on my head like a
crystal crown. And servants in white priestly robes were attending
to my every need. Then I was placed in a marble tub, and a cold
stream gushed over me. My mother was standing nearby, along
with the miracle worker and the old peasant woman. Their faces
beamed, their eyes shed tears of joy, as they witnessed the honors
bestowed on me.

I was delighted to see them, and they were delighted to see me.
But such unceasing elation, such continual joy, such indefatigably
beaming faces finally got on my nerves. Ugh! It was like honey
with sugar and licorice. I wanted to vomit. A man given to constant
ecstasy must be a towering idiot! And my head was already beginning to lie uneasily under the crown. I was so annoyed that I closed
my eyes so as not to keep looking at those radiant faces with their
continuous joy. Late at night, I finally dozed off.

I fell asleep above, and I awoke down below, in a thicket. I was
near a cave covered with large branches from old trees, red-fir
branches, like the ones we use to cover booths on the Feast of Tabernacles. Not knowing how I had gotten up there or down here,
I peered out through the foliage and saw a clearing. In the middle
of the clearing stood a tree stump, and in the middle of the tree
stump a knife was stuck, glittering in the moonlight. A wolf was
bounding back and forth, and I promptly recognized him. It was
the wolf that had caught me earlier. He loped over to the stump,
eyed it with a soft growl, and then retreated as if to practice
jumping. At last he halted, reckoned the distance between himself
and the stump, girded his loins, took a good fast start, and vaulted
clear across the knife. But then he crashed down on the other side
and stretched out full length on the ground.

"Praised be the Judge of Truth!" I exulted. "The wolf's dead!"

I stood up and went over to the carcass to do the decent thing—
i.e., skin him. Yet who should be sprawling on the earth but a
robust man with ruddy hair, a powerful neck, a huge beard, a thick
mane, a nose like a pumpkin wedged between the eyes, and a head
like a jug. Altogether, he looked like a drunkard sobering up. At
the sight of him I remembered what our sages have written about
werewolves. There are wizards and witches who turn themselves
into wolves and back into humans again—just as this one had done.
And they can change themselves not only into wolves, but also

dogs, and other wild beasts, and goblins, and all kinds of ugly slithering things that go bump in the night. I rubbed my hands in the grass, which is what you're supposed to do in such a case, pulled my hat down over my brow, and spoke an ardent blessing:

"Blessed be He Who gives of His wisdom unto a man!"

When that person saw me whispering with a twisted face and eyes bulging toward heaven, he gave me a murderous look. He thought I was trying to cast a spell on him. But as soon as I told him the facts of the matter, praising our scholars to the skies for understanding the art of transformations, knowing everything, writing on everything, talking about everything—his anger subsided. When I saw that he was no longer angry and that he was gazing at me in silence, I held out my hand and asked him his name.

"My name is Kashtsey," he mumbled between his teeth. He stood up, stretched his legs, and tossed his mane.

"Oh my God! Kashtsey!" I said, startled and chilled, and I bowed, trying to flatter and please him. "How lucky to meet a person as world-famous as yourself. Why, even the babes-in-arms know who you are."

Kashtsey waggled his head, a sign that he was pleased. And I put every effort into it. I reeled off all the praises listed in the books, I dragged Baba Yaha in the mud, along with all the sages and stargazers, who weren't even fit to tie his bootstraps, and he had more intelligence and knowledge in his little finger than they had in all their heads put together—why, he was a regular Jewish scholar of the old school.

Kashtsey was lapping it all up. He said genially:

"I'm delighted, good sir, that I didn't eat you while you were in my paws. When I'm a beast of prey, there's nothing I enjoy more than a nice scrumptious Jew. You can thank your lucky star that I was stuffed to the hilt. But I'm glad to have such a guest—why don't we drink to your health!"

When Kashtsey got slightly tipsy, he felt like showing me how great he was and what great things he could do. He whistled, and there was an instant uproar. Creatures came running from all sides; owls, magpies, ravens, bats, cats, monkeys, frogs, salamanders, lizards, serpents, vipers, basilisks—a formidable mob. The whole forest quaked with their pandemonium. I stood there, chilled and terrified.

But then Kashtsey puffed at them—there was a huge upheaval—

and lovely damsels, beauteous maidens, dazzling nymphs were standing before me. Through the brief, snug, cambric tunics shone clear, rosy complexions. Their limbs were shapely, their movements a sheer delight. Their eyes were ablaze and piercing, they scorched your soul and heated your blood, they filled your heart with such deep longing that it nearly burst. The human heart cannot endure so much splendor.

Kashtsey said something—and a singing welled up. Female voices poured out songs, chants that tugged at your soul, bore it, wafted it, from one billow to the next, in a sea of voices and passions. Throngs of maidens floated in dances, in tunics, in veils of gauze, dazzling your eyes with rainbow colors, blended into flowerbeds, roses, and all manner of beautiful blossoms.

Kashtsey's excitement grew. He leaned among the dancers, yanked me along, and the two of us joined the round. He danced like a Cossack, squatting, and I hopped and whirled about in one spot. He sang a Russian ditty, and I a Sabbath hymn, bowing and scraping. A singing, a dancing, a playing, a swirling and soaring of tunics, like silver tops, arms and legs shining like marble columns. The noise grew louder. The crowd danced and I shook, totally drunk, I toppled dizzily, not knowing where or what I was.

Waking up at daybreak, I found myself sprawling under a tree, in the very same place where I had dropped. My head was heavy, I felt sick at heart and bewildered.

CHAPTER ELEVEN
Izzy Ponders the World

A sweet, fresh breeze was blowing, and no trace was left of the storm or the clouds. The forest, washed and tidy, stood there, like a bridegroom, in a green mantle, newly tailored in the spring, and it shone and sparkled like the bright morning star, which came to announce the glad news that the sun was about to arrive, the dear mother of the bride, so that the wedding could begin!

Everything around me glittered and glistened. Everything seemed to be preparing for something. The earth, once barren and dirty, now looked like a bride, radiant in her finery, with beautiful bouquets and wreaths of fragrant blossoms. Everything was festive and scented, and the air was filled with the sweet, lovely perfumes of spices. How beautiful is the dawn of a spring morning in the forest!

That renowned musician, the nightingale, was perched somewhere in the forest, welcoming the holiday. And there was something mournful in his mellow tune, the heart poured out its deepest feelings in song and dirge, like the prayer for the dead that musicians play at a wedding of orphans.

My dear, sweet nightingale! What's wrong, why are you so downhearted? Why do your merry songs contain a bitter drop of melancholy. Why does the ocean of your sweet melodies surge and moan with waves of bitter tears. Just look! Life is stirring all about you, you're celebrating! Your wife has given your home a good spring cleaning. She's prepared a soft, fresh bed, and now she's about to give birth. The air is redolent with summer. The forest is wearing his festive green cloak. The earth in her wedding dress is looking forward to the bridegroom's passionate kisses. And now, of all times, you have to blend sadness and gaiety.

Oh, I can read your heart, my dear, sweet nightingale! A poet's heart feels the sorrow of the world. It can sense what is lacking—and he plays what he feels, he always remembers it at feasts and celebrations. You sing a fresh and lilting lovesong for your wife, and then, right in the middle of it—a sigh, an echo from a terrible winter when you were wanderers, strangers in a strange land! You serenade the forest, radiant in his new green cap, and yet in your friendly wishes there is a tearful strain, a dirge for last year's leaves, which are rotting at the foot of the trees. And then, for our earth in her bridal flowers, you utter funeral prayers in memory of her children, whom she bears and buries year after year. How I like you, my world-famous singer, my nightingale! That sad note in your sweet melody touches me more than all your songs. For my mother bore me in torment and anguish, and she cradled me in sorrow, and her lullaby of suffering has remained the song of my life! What does a hapless fellow like myself have in common with spring? What does a lonesome creature like myself have to do with this festive crowd, the beautiful forest, freshly blossoming Nature? The joy of the world is not for me. When others live in happiness, anguish is my fate. When they celebrate, I face violence, blood, fire, flames, and smoke. When the land turns green and the birds start chirping then my days are full of fasting, grieving, and lamenting.

Sing, nightingale, sing! Sing a sad and poignant song! Let it move me, touch me—to the quick!

The nightingale sang and lamented. His warble stirred chords deeply buried in my heart. They growled, yelled, spoke, and all kinds of scenes flashed through my mind, old thoughts and new, unhappy memories.

I heard the sighing of a desperate soul—and a dismal image, as though alive, passed before my eyes.

Wintertime. Clouds. Wind and snow. A dreary day.

Under the table, on the brace between the legs, sat Clucker, our hen. Perching there lonely, all by herself, her head tucked beneath her wing. At times she seemed asleep, motionless. And at times she trembled. She dreamt of the summer, those lovely days when life was wonderful. She had been loved and honored by Rooster, her husband, a tall, young, handsome hero, with spurs, and a comb like a shako. Rooster was madly in love with her. He billed and cooed all the time, he hovered around her day and night. Every morning, he would take her from the chicken coop and they would stroll through the farmyard and the gardens. He scratched the sand and played there with her. And he poked and pried and brought her whatever he found. All wives deserve the kind of life she enjoyed with him! She roosted and brooded and hatched forth chicks. Ten children at once. Tender, downy, yellow little things. The moment they crept out of the eggs, with pieces of shell on their little behinds, they stood on their tiny legs and squealed: "Hello everybody! *Sholem-aleykhem!*" Right into the world. They liked the world. It was good and radiant and delightful. And they laughed, bright and cheery, scurrying around to their heart's content, to wherever their eyes carried them. The mother was blissful. She held them under her wings, shielding and warming them. And they thanked her with friendly cheeps. She took them around all day, wherever there was a bit of space, a heap of dung. Pecking and poking, and as soon as she found anything, she would yell: "Hurry up, children! Come here! Hurry up!" Passers-by halted and gazed at her and her young, and they beamed.

Clucker was recalling the good old times, quietly perching, with her head tucked beneath her wing.

And all at once, Clucker trembled, her feathers swelled and stood on end. She remembered the end of her happiness, the start of her misery. One lovely morning, the hawk snatched up one of her chicks and carried it high into the air. The poor mother shrieked: "My baby! My little baby!"

But she could cry her heart out! The child was gone. Only one little feather, a soft little feather, bloodstained, tumbled down to the earth, drifting, rocking in the wind.

From then on, her dear little babies were doomed, and they left her, each in turn. One was eaten by a polecat. A second was strangled by a kitten. Others fell into human hands. One Friday, the miserable mother came into the kitchen, pecking about as usual— and she nearly fainted! Oh God! Oh me! Her daughter, a fine, decent girl, lay slaughtered, on the salting board! The cook split open her belly, took out the innards and threw them to the agonizing mother, and to the cat who was stretched out on the floor!

Of all of Clucker's children, only one was left, a young rooster, with his comb barely peeping out of his head. When he came into his feathers and got bar-mitzvahed, earning his spurs as a full-fledged rooster, a far cry from babyhood, he stood up on his own two legs and let out his first cock-a-doodle-doo, publicly, with great pomp. His mother simply melted and cried: "Amen! May Cockaloud, the God of chickens, Blessed be His Name, grant that you have something to crow about like that wise father of yours!"

All her comfort was now her darling son and her beloved husband. She hadn't lost all hope of a good life. But wide and deep is the beaker of tears. She had not yet drained it to the dregs.

It was autumn. The three of them, she, her husband, and her boy, were out for a walk. They were picking, pecking, poking, and chatting. When they came home in the evening, her mate and her son were seized and tied up before her very eyes. The people in the house grabbed them by the legs, and whirled them overhead. The miserable captives sighed and groaned, and the captors whirled and whirled them. Then, holding the prisoners by their heads, they flung them to the ground. The slaughterer slashed their throats and Clucker was left all alone in the world—no husband, no son!

My heart bleeds for you, unhappy Clucker! You're like a member of the family, after all. You grew up in our home. And of all the birds in the world, you're the only one I'm acquainted with. I've watched the way you live, I've always been interested in anything you do. And ever since I saw you sitting alone, your head tucked under your wing, I haven't been able to get you out of my mind. You're gloomy, care-worn, grief-stricken. You unhappy thing. Poor Clucker! Your sorrow, your suffering are the kind that have been inflicted on the world since God created it. The sorrows of the world come in all shapes and sizes, piling on top of one another, higher and higher. And I, alas, have endured them all. Oh me! I've gone through all of them!

Sing, little nightingale, sing! Pour out your melodies! And let me pour out my heart, my mournful heart.

The nightingale trilled—and another picture came to my eyes, a dark and dismal one.

Autumn. A small, squat hovel. Darkness, squalor, the beds unmade. Everything out of place. The oven unheated. No smoke has curled from the chimney for a long time now. Every corner is gloomy and messy. The walls are weeping. Hinde the widow is sitting on the dairy bench, cowering, mourning. Her legs tucked up beneath her. She's hushed, stock-still, motionless. Her head hanging. Her eyes bulge, stare. And now she trembles, clutches at her head, moans and wails. Not because she's poor. She's used to poverty. She's never asked for luxuries, never craved them. She was always content with what little she earned from her work. It's her son she's lamenting, her last child, gone forever.

Five sons were born to Hinde, and all of them came to grief. The eldest was drafted into the Czar's army. The world's not big enough for most people. So they quarrel, fight, try to conquer one another, devour their neighbors. This means they need men to protect them against the enemy with all kinds of weapons. Thus, Hinde's son went off to kill or be killed, and he hasn't been heard from since.

The second son was claimed by the Angel of Death. Oh, what agony until he gave up his pure soul!

The third son was martyred. Not by a wild beast, not by a wolf or a bear. He was killed by human beings, by his fellow-men. A spirit of evil and madness had come to the world. Men grew savage, their hearts turned to stone. They pounced like wild animals upon their brothers, smashing and maiming ruthlessly!

The fourth son, robbed, beaten, humiliated, was so miserable that he put a pack on his shoulders, took a staff, and wandered over oceans and deserts, to the ends of the earth, and not a word has come from him till this very day!

The fifth son, the last apple of her eye, became a soldier in the middle of the war. Just yesterday, he left his poor, miserable mother and went off over the hills to lay down his life far, far away . . . .

And now Hinde was sitting there, desolate, somber, brooding about her terrible misfortune, the dreadful things that had happened to her and her children. She had brought forth in sorrow, and brought forth in sorrow again. And there was only sorrow for her and for them!

Clucker! What pleasure your chicks had in the world the moment they saw it. One day they were only eggs. And the next day they were carrying on—like old-timers, picking and eating, lively, merry, hurrying, scurrying, as if they had known the world for years, known what they needed and what they had to do. Your chicks lived. They had a youth, a wonderful youth.

But as for Hinde's children—why were they ever born! With them came their troubles, scourges, diseases: bellyaches, toothaches, smallpox, measles, scarlet fever. They had their share of hardship, poor things, heaven afflicted them. Until they opened their eyes and saw the world. And when they saw the world, they wanted to play a little, treat themselves to life—and instantly, a fury descended upon them, a torment, a punishment by human hands.

Hinde raised her children with so much trouble and worry, they cost her so much effort, night and day. And no sooner had she brought them up, than they were spirited away from her. She was no mother, she had no right to them, she was only a maid—to the Angel of Death and to human society; a slave, a drudge, and neither she nor the children were hers. *She* had birthed them, *she* had reared them—in so much agony. And when everything was done, the children were snatched from her. The bondswoman might feel, love, yearn herself sick for her children—who cares?! She was just a servant!

But Hinde was still a mother, a human being. She beat her breast, ripped out her hair, wept, wailed—and her bitter lament rose to heaven!

Sing, little nightingale, sing. But gently, gently! My heart screams, its hidden strings quiver and twang so loudly as if they were about to explode.

The nightingale burst into a loud chant, and his stormy waves of trills buffeted my soul in turmoil and dismay. It swept away my mind, and a hurly-burly of images flooded past. A forest, green fields with grain and flowers. The morning star was gracefully reflected in the dewdrops. And then came the town with its noise and commotion. A pall, a gloom lay over it. The sun and the moon sneaked in their light. The buildings and the narrow little lanes blocked their path.

I could picture a day in the town, the way the people lived, the way they got up, and the way they went to sleep. I could picture a morning: Jews rising and groaning! Not knowing what to do, where to go, where their next meal was coming from. Their faces were pale, their foreheads furrowed, their eyes shooting to and fro, hunting something to grasp at, lean on, so as not to drown in the torrents of day. They sighed, they moaned, and kept knitting their brows.

I could picture a Jewish home in the daytime, the door never shut for even an instant, poor people coming in and out, young and old, women, girls, and little children. Among them, the gracious wives of synagogue managers. Then, fine Jewish burghers in silk coats, demanding money on the basis of their ancestral merits. Next, in walked a preacher, a man whose house had burnt down, a traveler from Jerusalem, a messenger soliciting for some charity, an abandoned wife with ancient, moldy documents. On their heels, a beadle from the synagogue, demanding the rent for the pew, money to read the Torah at service, kopeks for a blessing, for a prayer for the dead, for a pledge. When the beadle had been taken care of, along came a swarm of synagogue officials, one after another, some with alms boxes, some without. One wanted money for the Holy Land, another for a school, a third for the fund for poor brides, a fourth for the hospital, a fifth for the Talmud Study Fellowship, a sixth for the Eternal Light Society, and on and on for all sorts of funds, groups, and associations. In between, two respectable householders swaggered through, whispered something in the host's ear, sighed and said aloud: "Well, you know who I mean." And took some money. The community attendant showed up and collected for the register, the deputy wanted to quarter soldiers, the butcher announced via the maid that, begging their pardon, but meat would now be costing seven kopeks more a pound because the kosher tax had gone up . . . . In short, people were pulling and tugging on all sides, everyone gave a yank, a pinch, a tweak, tears came to the eyes, it was unbearable.

Sing, little nightingale, sing. I want to cry a little. I saw Jewish money and Jewish blood squandered, lavished like water, bringing no benefit whatsoever. Ah! What use was all our love, all our charity?

Here was the market with all its different creatures, big and little. The market with its merchants and commerce, with its swindlers and victims, its wild desires, its foolish sense of honor, its competitiveness. Now came a swarm of paupers, beggars, schnorrers, people who had come down in the world, had fallen from grace, needy, hungry, suffering, diseased, broken, haggard, emaciated, pale, with drawn faces. The place was acrawl with old-clothes dealers, shopkeepers, brokers, deep in thought, their hats pulled back, Jews with sacks, Jews with sticks, idlers, dreamers, all of them scurrying around like madmen, poking about, looking for work, anything, just to keep alive, to keep body and soul together for their wives and children, just a little bit longer. All of them tense and bustling, trying to hit on some way of making a kopek, drawing it out of someone else.

I could picture groups of people, fine Jews, waiting like dogs, ravens, next to corpses and carcasses—feeding on their flesh and blood. Men who weren't worth a kopek but enjoyed great prestige. Men who were known to be very low but stood very high in the community. Men who were a boil on the community, corrupting its blood, sucking it out. Men who, if you looked at them, seemed terribly occupied, involved in important business, their brows were always sweaty, they were always secretive, mysterious, ambiguous— but in reality they were loafers, good-for-nothings, ne'er-do-wells. Men who were always hovering around the community council, always trying to save money for the town and do well for it, always sacrificing themselves for the town—and living in honor, eating the choicest food and drinking a good glass of wine. Men who hovered about in the community offices, near the wealthy, at meetings, in the butcher stores and ale houses, pulling rank at elections, whispering secrets into each ear and then shouting "Aye!" or "Nay!" for all Jews. Men who bow and scrape and doff their hats to every little official, every little nobleman, and who always creep to introduce themselves to every new governor, every new police commissioner, and who mail in reports about the town. Men who prowl like dreadful wolves among the poor, unhappy sheep in the market! . . .

Oh, how awful the market is! How much trouble, anxiety, hardship, and suffering, how much humiliation, shame, disgrace, how much falsehood, swindling, deception, trickery—for a crust of sinful bread! How hard, how bitter it is to earn a living! My heart is breaking! A sad, dismal tune.

Softly, nightingale, softly. Not so loud, singer! A string is bursting, has already burst in my heart.

You are unfortunate, Man. You are cursed among all the creatures in the world. The Good Lord created you masterfully, with so many virtues, more than in any other creature, for your own benefit. And you've used your good qualities for your own misfortune. God gave you reason and you misused it. You started mulling too hard, thinking, meditating. You went astray, acting against yourself and against nature. Too much thinking leads to too many mistakes. Too many achievements and new inventions cause unhappiness, deficiency, compulsion, tribulations.

Your mind has brought forth so many new contrivances—to your own sorrow, taking the work out of your hands, the bread from your mouth, keeping you in a terrible predicament, shortening your years!

You make yourself miserable, man, with your reason, and with your power of speech, your language. This gift, bestowed on you in grace, has turned out badly for you. The dog, for instance, that dog barking at you right here—he barks just like his comrades anywhere else—in Spain, for instance. All dogs attack and all dogs bark in the same way. The donkey in our climes opens his maw and brays like all donkeys anywhere in the world. It doesn't matter which donkey—they're all alike. All the frogs in brooks and swamps croak the same way and have always done so, from ancient Egypt to the present.

But human beings are foreign to one another, and this is a terrible misfortune.

How unhappy you are, man with all your imagination. God created man in His image, giving him a human soul, the same for all people. But you had to act wise and add something to the human soul—artificial, collective national souls, opposing one another in so many ways. The national soul is allowed to do so many things that the individual soul cannot do. What is wrong for the individual soul is considered a great virtue for the national soul. What is a must for the individual soul, one of the Ten Commandments, does not apply to the national soul. And the result is agony and bloodshed! And, in

your piety, your decency, your goodness, there is often a worm—
your misfortune!

A divine spirit, the spirit of knowledge and devoutness, rushes
like a mighty torrent from the Throne of Glory, rushes to bring
life and happiness to all humanity. But the banks of this river are
lined with mills and factories. Each factory draws off water, stopping it, damming it, to turn the gears of its machines. The raw
material for all of them is the same. As soon as it comes into the
world, it is divided up. A bit of it goes to one factory, a bit to another. The material is shaped and formed into a finished object.
Then it leaves with the trademark of that factory, often obstructing
the product of another factory. The goods are varied, the rivalry is
great. Each factory wants to corner the market. The result is
hatred, hostility, fighting, theft, murder. Ah! How much sorrow,
torment, and suffering have passed through the world since its
creation. And now people come and add more!

Gently, gently, little nightingale. Another string has snapped in
my heart!

"Weep, Izzy, weep!" the forest musician urged me with every
note. I felt like a bridegroom. "A bridegroom is like a king!" said
the wedding jester, and he reminded me that I was fatherless, a
half-orphan. "Izzy!" And he launched into his jingles:

> An orphan goes through the world
> And suffers every day.
> So weep, Izzy, weep!
> And play, musician, play!

An orphan, Israel, and a bridegroom too! A bridegroom, like a
king—and an orphan, a mere worm, trod underfoot. Honey mixed
with gall. The orphan, always humiliated, and the brief glory of a
bridegroom. A bitter joke. A dreadful joke. Cutting to the quick. I
felt sick at heart, my head whirled, and everything around me was
spinning and dancing. Plants were leaping in the fields, the forest
was hopping, and the trees were keeping time with crashing
branches.

Figures gathered and joined the dance—rabbinical managers,
beadles, and holy officials, the shapes of rams, bulls, horses, and
greyhounds, all together, swirling, around and around, sidelocks flying, tails, arms, manes, horses' tails, donkeys' ears. I heard music,

gladness and joy, it was springtime, weddings upon weddings. All the rascals in town dashing ahead. Behind them, a large company, a mob of "recipients," paupers, beggars, schnorrers, good-for-nothings, cripples, teachers, husbands who had married ten years ago, one year ago, and were still boarding with their in-laws. Candles were burning. A wedding party was going to synagogue to wreck the lives of a boy and a girl, an innocent couple who knew nothing of the world.

Wedding canopies kept passing till late at night. Countless marriages took place. Old crones were clapping. Relatives dancing. The crowds had a grand time. Joy and gladness!

"Congratulations, your brand-new paupers! Congratulations for your whole pack of idlers! Your new candidates for teaching and receiving! For warming benches and getting hemorrhoids! Congratulations on your new list of dirty laundry! On your lazy, filthy, empty people! Congratulations on your fresh, writhing leeches! Hand over your blood, Jews. Hand over your money, money, money!"

Stop, nightingale! Stop singing! My heart was breaking. All the strings had burst!

CHAPTER TWELVE
The Mare as an Exegesis on Job

"Is that your voice, my dear old friend?"

"Yes, indeed, my unfortunate prince, my poor, unhappy mare," I replied, bursting into tears.

"Why are you crying?" she asked, vehemently heaving her neck, as though trying to shake off a mountainous load. She gave me a friendly stare, truly human. "Because of all you've gone through for my sake?"

"Ah!" I replied. "My troubles don't matter. You didn't cause them deliberately. It's not your fault, poor thing. But *your* sorrows are endless, like the ocean. I cry when I look at you, my fallen, wandering prince. How long can you endure it, dragging about the earth, suffering from everyone? How long will you be the Eternal Mare, the Wandering Mare?"

"Until," she said, "human beings become human—better and wiser. Until there is no more cruelty and pity, evil and good, spite and favoritism. Until truth and justice alone rule the world. Until no distinctions are made between human beings. The wolf will lie down with the sheep, the bear and the cow will feed together, and the lion will eat straw like a bull. Until evil vanishes, the dark powers lose their strength, and the tears are dried from every face! . . ."

"Alas!" I moaned. "That's too far away! By that time, I'm afraid, they'll wipe you out and tear the soul from your body!"

"For me," she went on, "life is just as it was for an old friend of mine, Job. When God put him in Satan's hands, He said: "Satan, do what you like to my Job. Hit him, torment him, beat him black and blue. But don't touch his spirit, his soul! . . .' "

"Job!" I shouted. "Was Job your friend? No! *You're* Job! His story was a parable about you! It shows your happy life in riches and glory. It shows your sorrows, your persecutions, the sneers of people when misfortune struck you. It faithfully shows every last detail. *You're* Job! You're Job with his Satan, his boils, his false friends, who attack him in his bad time and accuse him of not being good, and not being pious . . . . The Book of Job is *your* story. The beginning and the middle have already come true for you. And so will the end. I'm certain. The tempest in which God and justice will appear shall be greater and stronger than the storm we just had! . . ."

"People say," she said, "that the Book of Job was written by that great man who once changed me back into a human being. That was very far-seeing of him!"

I looked at my mare. She was prostrate, almost lifeless, panting hard.

"Ahh!" she groaned. "They tortured me ruthlessly. I feel as if my strength were still dwindling. When I open my mouth to talk, when I look around and start observing everything, I begin feeling my pains. They really weakened me, they made me sick. I don't think I have a whole bone left in my body. Some people were just recently tormenting me. I barely escaped with my life.

"Help me, please, just help me raise myself a bit so that I can lean on my side. It's not proper for me to lie like this. I can't move—may you be spared such things! Oh, my head! My head!"

"What is it?" I asked sympathetically. "Does your head hurt?"

"Oh!" she answered. "Every part of me hurts. Every limb. My whole body. My head. My front side! And also—if you'll pardon me—my backside!"

"Try and hold through!" I begged her. When we're in town to-morrow, I'll have a doctor examine you and prescribe something."

"Oh no!" she exclaimed terrified. "Don't! Please don't talk about doctors to me! Who knows them better than I do—those *horse doctors*! With their prescriptions, their medicines! The moment they lay eyes on you, they start bleeding you! Sticking leeches on you! I've had enough bruises on my skin from what they've prescribed! Do you see these fresh black-and-blue marks? They were made by a quack in Dnieprovitz with his tools and prescriptions. Nothing makes him feel better than to write a prescription! And there are so many doctors like him. At the drop of a hat, at the slightest excuse, they'll write anything, they'll write volumes!"

"Tell me," I asked "where were you the whole time you were gone from me? What sort of creature jumped on your back and rode you? Where did he come from?"

My mare pulled herself together and hoisted up half her body, leaning on her front legs. She gave me a friendly look, and started to tell me the story.

"That creature who rode me was a demon. Whenever the no-good bullies give me some peace, a fiend turns up from nowhere, mounts me, and drives me over hill and dale, fields and forests. As soon as he's started, a whole mob of other devils come springing out, in all shapes and sizes. They jeer and guffaw to the skies, chortle all kinds of strange prayers and psalms that make no sense, give me the finger, stick out their tongues. All of them, little and big, jump on top of me and pull me about. They get into fights over me. One says they have to treat me one way. Another says another way. One demon wants me to fly through the air. A second demon wants me to gallop on the ground. There's a clamor, a shrieking, a tumult, a pandemonium. It makes my head split. They play and scream to their heart's content. But the 'eternal question' about me never gets resolved. People say it's good fishing in troubled waters. They could say the same about me. In the middle of the awful chaos, one of the gang mounts me, rides me out into world, does business with me, and sells me to different people. I say 'different,' because in a short time I serve many masters. Before I can even get my bearings in one place, along comes the demon and takes me off to another. Is there anyone I haven't drudged for? Is there anyone who hasn't made hay with me? Is there anyone who hasn't cashed in on me? From a petty nobleman, to a rural police commissioner, a high official, and on and on, higher and higher. From preachers, extorters, moralists, pious men, up through divine policemen and similar heavenly functionaries. Flunkies, overseers, clerks, supervisors, up to directors of Jewish schools. Beadles, community scribes, military kidnappers, tax-officials, attorneys, deputies, counselors, philanthropists, collectors of the kosher-meat levy and the candle duty, and the whole administrative mob. School-helpers, teachers, marriage-brokers, wedding jesters, idlers, thousands of rabbinical managers, messengers, arbitrators, yeshivah students, recluses, scholars, fine burghers, silken gentlemen, sons of well-to-do fathers, psalm speakers, Talmud perusers, prayer leaders, shofar puffers, dreydel makers, Purim players, matzo bakers—up to judiciary assistants, ritual slaughterers, porgers, supervisors of dietary laws, bathhouse women, ritual-candle makers, grave-measurers, and all the sacred officials. All of them have mounted me. I had to toil for all of them and carry all of them. They've drained my health and vigor. They've caused me no end of agony. If only they had been satisfied with my labor! But God forbid! No matter how hard I drudge, it's always too little, never enough. It's no joke, I tell you, working for such a mob, such a hungry bunch of people! If only my labor were of some use! But God forbid! I toil and slave—for whom? What a waste! And what devilish luck! I always fall into the hands of such people. They squeeze out my life's blood, deaden my mind and my soul, lash me with their whips and tongues. These people have taught me a great deal. There's a lot to say and ask about them. But you can't talk about everything you know. You can't ask every question, and you can't get an answer to every question you do ask. What can you do? At times you have to make do with *one* answer to all questions: "For we were slaves to Pharaoh in Egypt." That means: "The king of Egypt turned me into a mare!"

"There's one question I do want to ask you," I said to her. "How come those noblemen you listed are willing to take on such a poor, broken-down mare like yourself?"

"The devil only knows!" she replied. "He blinds their eyes. He makes them think I'm anything but poor and miserable. He makes them think I'm hardworking and first-rate!"

"Unhappy prince! Miserable mare!" I moaned and fell to pondering.

CHAPTER THIRTEEN
*A Letter to the Board of Directors of the Society for
the Prevention of Cruelty to Animals*

"You're thinking too much today," the mare said. "You're so confused. Lie down and sleep. Have some rest."

"Go to sleep? Me?" I exclaimed in a fiery voice. "I should go to sleep while you suffer there, a bundle of aches and pains?! I should sleep when you need help? When you can't even budge from where you are, you poor thing! When you have to have someone help you up, put you back on your feet! I know I'm not the one you need in your misery. How can such a puny little fellow like me help you? What kind of strength do I have anyway? What a laugh! I can barely stand on my own two feet. All you have to do is puff on me and I fall over. You need a man who's strong and rugged and tough and experienced. But until he comes, and as long as you don't have anyone else, I can't just ignore you and go to sleep. I have to use all my strength to help you in some way. No, by God! How could I possibly sleep? You tell me to have some rest! But how in the world can I rest after all I've heard and seen? How can I rest when such things scream to high heaven? When the whole mob of idlers and blood-suckers daze my mind and whirl before my eyes like horrible swarms of locusts? I feel as though they were attacking me and tearing me to shreds. Each of them takes a nibble, and they eat me up without a scrap left over. No, I tell you. I won't go to sleep. I won't rest!"

My mare shook her head: "You talk like a fiery young man, if you'll forgive my saying so. Like students fresh out of school. They make friends promptly and cling together. The least little injustice makes them explode. They burn and blaze, they talk a blue streak, they fill up their minds with all sorts of stuff, they think they're going to set the world on fire .... I've seen a lot of them in my time. When they get a little older and come out into the world, when they have to worry about making a living, then they hang their heads, lose their voices, and all they care about is their own interests. It's not so bad as long as they remain honest, and don't sell truth for a song or join the people they used to attack. It's not so bad as long as they don't praise these people to the skies and heap coals on the heads of their former comrades.... The same thing will happen with you. Now you're young and ardent. A little later you'll cool off, you'll forget about me and sleep the sleep of the just. What will you care about a poor old mare? You'll see. In the end, you'll get cooler and quieter. That's the way of the world, for both men and beasts. Just look at a tiny calf, for instance. Watch it kicking out its little legs, thrashing its tail, and jumping around like a devil. And then, just look at the same calf when it grows up into a bull. Watch how quiet it is, how it plods about with its head in a yoke. What can you do? It's so. In the end, everyone becomes an ox...."

"Not on your life!" I shouted even more ardently. "You're wrong about me. I swear! Oh, if you only knew what I feel, if you only knew what I've already done for you and what I intend to do!"

"What you've done and what you intend to do?" exclaimed the mare in amazement. "Well, tell me. Let's have it!"

I fumbled around in my breast-pocket for a few minutes and finally pulled out some written pages.

"Here," I said with a solemn expression, taking one of the pages. "This will prove that I like to act and not just shoot my mouth off like other people. Listen, this is a letter about you to the directors of the Society for the Prevention of Cruelty to Animals. I wrote it as soon as I got to know your terrible situation."

My mare perked up her ears, and I read aloud to her:

" 'The quality of mercy has become so powerful in these days and so widely accepted that people are starting to feel compassion not just with other human beings, that is to say: No longer hate them, no longer torture them, embitter their lives as in olden times. Nowadays, we regard other men as our brethren, our comrades, our neighbors, and we make no distinctions as to nation or creed. And it is not just with other human beings, I say, that we feel mercy and compassion nowadays, but also, and even more so, with animals. We display our compassion to them and look upon them as God's creatures. And for this reason, our era rightly deserves the name of: The Age of Humanity—' "

"Rhetoric! Rhetoric!" the mare broke in jeeringly, "What fine humanity! You might have added that nowadays people take one another's lives so quickly and easily with the good firearms and cunning devices that the compassionate generation thought up for their brethren!"

"Just wait!" I shouted, even more fiery. "Just hear me out! What's the good of your talking?! Just listen to the rest of it and don't confuse me! Where was I? Oh yes, here:

" 'Our era rightly deserves the name of: The Age of Humanity. The glory of such fine qualities also redounds to you, gentlemen, to your precious, wonderful, and decent men, to you leaders of the world-renowned Society for the Prevention of Cruelty to Animals. Your efforts have kept alive so many living creatures, so many animals, so many birds. Because of you, people now treat them better, more humanely, and have turned away from the fashion of torturing, beating, and tormenting them! Everywhere, on all roads and highways, in all towns and villages, in every last out-of-the-way nook, one finds your merciful envoys, the fine, sympathetic members of your organization, ever on the alert and always ready to settle accounts with anyone for the least offense to any animal. Woe to him who offends animals today!—' "

"Rhetoric! Rhetoric!" the mare interrupted again, jeeringly. "Hail to you, living creatures, and hail to your children for living in such a generation in which these society members take care of you! Dance, little animals, dance! ... Sir! Why don't you go into the slaughterhouse! You'll hear a fine concert, you'll hear and see hens, geese, turkeys, and other fowl singing, jumping, writhing for joy! You'll see God's little darling, the king of all the creatures, a little slaughterer, a pious soul. He says a blessing, cuts a rooster's throat, and plucks out all the feathers. The rooster crows 'Amen!' and simply melts in delight. He struggles and writhes in his nakedness, sometimes for quite a while, until he finally gives up the ghost, and while giving it up, he's absolutely thrilled at the privilege of joining all the other chickens in town and bequeathing his feathers to the good, pious, merciful little slaughterer. In my time, I've hauled enough bulging sackloads of feathers for the slaughterers of Dumbsville. I've sweated and slaved, dragging that precious legacy—or as they call it, their feather-privilege. My bones ache at the very thought!"

"Now, now!" I said, all ablaze from reading. "What does that have to do with the price of eggs? Honestly, you don't know beans about writing. You don't have a feel for it. Just listen to the rest! Pipe down and pay attention while I read further:

" 'And as I have the great honor, and also the good fortune, of being a member of the Society, it is, therefore, incumbent on me to submit a report on a creature of God, which doesn't even have a name, so that I scarcely know what to call it. I could call it a mare, but—please don't laugh—it seems to be sort of human. Let me call it a human being, and it seems to be a mare! Again, gentlemen, please don't laugh at me! I am not making any of this up. The matter is quite simple. This creature lives in our world. It is a mare. But it has the same feelings as a human being, and all the paraphernalia. Now, philosophically speaking, we can submit, as King Solomon said in Ecclesiastes: "There is nothing new under the sun." That is to say, anything can happen. What, for example, were the Pariahs in India? Though most certainly human beings, they were treated like dogs. And what about the slaves in America? They were neither human nor animal—may God preserve us! What more do you want? Didn't a great Jesuit, Father Burgstaller in Feldkirch, recently lose his temper at Alexander von Humboldt, that famous scientist, and call him a beast? He simply turned him into an animal, a brute! It is indeed a miracle that people noticed in time and had a good laugh, so that nothing came of it. But I don't want to lose myself in philosophizing and in the higher spheres.

" 'Be that as it may, you must know that, lo and behold, in our province there is a poor creature that is suffering terribly. Anyone who needs it, exploits it for his own ends. It bears a yoke and hauls loads far beyond its strength. Nevertheless, people treat it wretchedly, that is to say, they keep it apart from the town herd as though it were in quarantine. If it manages to get a nibble here or a munch there, the people sic dogs on it, raise a hue and cry, accuse it of wreaking havoc—and blows rain down from all sides upon the ill-starred creature. Numerous members of our Society for the Prevention of Cruelty to Animals witness these scenes and yet—O wonder of wonders—refuse to intercede, as though the creature were an outlaw and no concern of our Society. Several times now, I have tried to stand up for it, and merely gotten my share of trouble. For God's sake, I shout. What is going on here? Even assuming that this creature, about which I am writing to you, is simply nothing more than a mare, and leaving other considerations aside, it is still a creature of God, no worse than any other mare. It, too, deserves our commiseration for animals!

" 'And so, gentlemen, you merciful directors of our splendid Society, you, whose commiseration is so vast for all animals, all beasts, please take pity on the poor, wretched mare! Stand beside it in its misery and protect it against tribulations. Spread your wings over it and help it to salvation. Let the ill-fortuned creature know that the world is no longer an abandoned place! Today, we have a Society for the Prevention of Cruelty to Animals!' "

CHAPTER FOURTEEN
What the Board of Directors Undertakes in This Matter

I boomed out these last words with such vehemence that the whole forest resounded, as though all the creatures were overjoyed at hearing such tidings and were hugging one another and saying "Mazel tov!" and shouting: "Long live the Society for the Prevention of Cruelty to Animals!" I could hear the name of the society echoing through the woods.

The mare, however, kept silent, shaking her head, and smirking as if to say: "Goodness, what a fool!"

I was slightly piqued, but thought to myself: "What does she know about writing! She's been a mare all these ages!"

I scratched the back of my head, unfolded another sheet of paper, and read aloud the answer from the directors of the society.

" 'In reply to your inquiry about the mare, or the creature about which we fail to comprehend what sort of wretched animal it is, we, the Board of Directors of the Society for the Prevention of Cruelty to Animals, hereby inform you, gracious sir, that prior to your missive, numerous petitions from many sides have come to us concerning the aforesaid mare. A portion of these petitions complain about the individuals tormenting her, describe her wretched situation, and plead with us to issue clear instructions to all our members everywhere, advising them, wherever the aforesaid mare may be, to treat her humanely, like all other creatures and animals deserving of our protection, with no distinction. These same individuals adjure us to announce, once and for all, that our commiseration applies to all animals, even the aforesaid mare, and that if any individual abuses or mistreats her in any way, our members ought to bring him to account at once with all due process. Among these individuals petitioning us there are some who make much ado about the mare, and carry on, if you'll pardon our saying so, as you do, worthy sir, about all manner of wonders concerning her.

" 'On the other hand, a portion of these petitioners take the very opposite view. "You cannot and you must not," they write, "engage in conflict with those who deal her an occasional blow. This blow is quite necessary. There is no other way of dealing with her." They allege that she behaves rather dreadfully, her comportment not being as it should be. If anyone tries to harness her as is customary, she simply balks and rears. If you happen to look the other way, she throws off her shafts and her load, she likes to kick people on the sly and bite little children. She requires a whip. Without a lash or two, there is no possibility of handling her. Furthermore, she is unclean. Her mane is a tangle of elflocks, her head is covered with oozing sores, and she herself is asthmatic. We simply cannot possibly allow her among our horses, she is sure to infect them. As for working, she is useless for any labor except certain unattractive tasks. Along with all these virtues, she is also very destructive. One can often catch her in the grain, devouring, trampling, causing dreadful damage to the poor peasants, whereas other horses, better and more attractive ones, feed quite genteelly and properly on the green grass. It is thus dangerous to allow creatures like herself in our villages. You need therefore in no wise concern yourselves or undertake anything against anyone treating her with an occasional blow. The Society cannot show commiseration to just anyone. The mare deserves what she gets. She is an affliction, a divine scourge!' "

The poor mare let out a sigh from deep within her heart. She cocked her ears and opened her mouth at hearing such calumny and libel. I paused to draw my breath, and then continued reading.

" 'We, the Board of Directors, having listened to both sides in this matter and having also gathered secret intelligence about the aforesaid mare through our agents, did turn over the entire matter, along with all documents pertaining thereto, to a special commission, whose task was to sift through the entire problem and determine a proper method of correcting it. The Commission worked very hard on this matter, investigating it thoroughly, until, God be praised, it did indeed achieve something—' "

"How much longer is all this gibberish going to last?" asked the mare. "I'm getting tired of listening!"

"Don't worry so much. You'll be enjoying it soon," I answered and kept reading.

" 'In its report, the Commission submitted its opinion as follows:

" ' "First of all, the mare ought to have her elflocks removed. Let her become more presentable. In order to avoid a great measure of conflict on this issue and to improve her condition in the future, it is, in our opinion, necessary to do something about her dreadful ignorance. She has to be led onto the right path, she has to be trained and educated, taught how to walk properly, etc., etc. Then, when she has learned all the tricks required of a trained horse, she will be worthy of our commiseration, and our society will stand by her and not permit any maltreatment of her. In the meantime, we should take care to keep her away from the crops, for her own good. That is to say, however the case may be, whether or not she causes damage, we must not let her be assaulted."

" 'This proposal submitted by the Commission has been passed and accepted, and we, for our part, have done everything in our power to put it into execution, God willing, in so short a time as possible.

" 'In informing you of these matters, we cannot refrain from expressing our gratitude to you, merciful sir, for your constant loyalty in serving the Society, and for your great commiseration toward the innocent and wretched creatures. The Board of Directors has its eye on you and knows how to appreciate such useful individuals as yourself. Etc., etc.' "

No sooner had I finished reading the Board of Directors' encomium than I heard a scream in the woods. It sounded like a wild beast or a highwayman—goodness only knows what can happen in a forest! I thrust the letter back into my breast-pocket, hid in the branches, and sat there frightened out of my wits. The screaming grew louder, and a few minutes later, a peasant drove out of the forest in a huge wagon filled with wood. He was yelling, cursing, scolding, and murderously lashing his small horse. The poor creature was having a wretched time dragging the load, and it kept halting. What a relief! Since there was no danger, I boldly stepped out of my hiding-place, strode over to the peasant, and said:

"Hey, listen! Why are you beating that poor horse? How awful! You shouldn't treat it like that!"

"Who says I shouldn't?!" he answered in surprise. And thrashed the horse even harder.

"Hands off!" I exclaimed angrily. "Don't you dare lay a finger on it!"

"What d'you care?! What gives you the right to butt in and stop me from beating my own property?" the peasant answered insolently.

"I, sir, am a member of the Society for the Prevention of Cruelty to Animals!" I replied proudly, thinking that the man would be awed and doff his cap.

"Go to hell! You and your society both! Get your ass outta here, you nut! Eat shit! I ain't got no time to argue with you. I gotta get this load of wood into town!"

"But the horse can't haul your wagon, it's too full."

"Well, so get your ass in the harness and help him if you're such a good Samaritan."

"Throw off a little wood!"

"Pay me, and I'll throw it off!"

"Pay you?! Are you out of your mind!? What should I pay you for?"

"You're either crazy or drunk—or are you a demon? Ughh! Get away, you pest! Go to hell!" shouted the Christian in a rage and lashed the horse.

"I'm a member of the Society for the Prevention of Cruelty to Animals, do you hear?"

"I'm gonna bash your head in, you nut! Go to hell with all your societies!" yelled the peasant, raising his lash against me!

More dead than alive with terror, I dashed back and sat down.

CHAPTER FIFTEEN
Learn How to Dance!

I sat in silence for quite a while, my tongue was incapable of speech. Finally, I coughed and cleared my throat, and then I asked the mare:

"Well, so what do you think of the society now? It's so good, so fine, and it's really thinking about you and your future! It wants to improve your lot so that people won't mistreat you anymore. But a good deal depends on you. Your future welfare is really up to you alone. If you obey, and take on the ways of trained horses, then, God willing, things will work out beautifully for you. Instead of crude drudgery, they'll use you for fine and easy work. Who knows what else may happen in time? You can make something of yourself, you can become a horse of distinction. Well, what do you say?"

I was sure the mare would be overjoyed. I just knew she would be beside herself at hearing these words. She would lean over backward, jump at the chance, grab the opportunity. She would be so delighted that she would thank and praise the Lord as well as myself, His envoy, who brought her these glad tidings.

I must admit I'm always delirious when someone thanks me for a benefit he's gotten from me or through me. I feel as though I were his master, and he my servant. I'm the noble benefactor, the merciful patron, the counselor, and he is just a . . . poor devil. I, of course, deserve everything, money and pleasure. And he? Well, he can thank his lucky stars that a man like me showed him mercy and gave him something. Why, I could simply have thrown him out on his ear. For instance, he might have come and asked for something that was a matter of life or death to him, but a mere trifle to me. I could have felt like glaring, not letting him talk, and making such a face that he would barely have managed to find the door. I could have crushed him like a fly with a single look and torn apart all his hopes like a cobweb. Everything hung on a thread.

When such a person thanks me, I feel how great I am. I feel as if he were showering me with blessings, giving me this world and the next, but regarding himself as a nullity. I, naturally, deserve an easy life, with no toil, no effort, no worry. After all, I'm a fine, noble person. Whereas he—well, that's a horse of a different color! Both of us are certainly human beings, flesh and blood. But there's red blood and then there's *blue* blood. And noble blood is simply in a class by itself.

And our characters are quite different too. I'm accustomed to the best things in life. If I don't get my tea or coffee on time, or I don't like a dish at lunch, or I have to bend over once too often, then I'm done for. But he's inured to drudgery, he's become coarse and unfeeling. A poor man's belly isn't picky. Bread or flint—who cares, as long as it's edible. How can he hold a candle to me.

When such a common little man, a wretched fellow, thanks me with a quaver in his voice, I stand there with a faint smile, almost a wry smirk that beggars descriptions. A smile containing both humility and pride, gravity and sarcasm, something intimate and something holding you at arm's length, and a bit of sympathy, why not, and a go-to-hell, why not, and permission to speak and a hint that you should nevertheless not overstep the boundaries of reverence.

And when I honor my beneficiary with a glance, he seems absolutely delighted. I add a few words, condescend to him, do him the kindness of preaching to him, for example:

"A man has to keep his nose to the grindstone. He has to earn his bread honestly, in the sweat of his brow. Don't twiddle your thumbs. Plan ahead."

Or else I simply put in my two kopeks at random, poke my nose in his business, throw out a few opinions off the top of my head, he ought to do such and such, write such and such, this is good, that is bad, etc., etc.

At such times, it seems to me, he is simply beside himself with joy, says amen to every word I speak, and thanks me for my edifying sermon and my intelligent advice.

In this way, I think, I'm no different from a lot of wealthy, charitable, important men. I can always recognize such an attitude in their faces, their smirks, their glowing eyes, their words, their counsels, their sermons.

But at times, it shows even more clearly in the way they shake hands. Now just what is there, offhand, about a handshake? With ordinary people, it's quite ordinary. You stick out your hand, a full hand, just as it is, artlessly. But a fine gentleman proffers his hand quite artfully and craftfully, and in so many different ways. Each way contains a whole code of laws, an entire language. When I became a fine gentleman, I spent a long time studying the fine art of shaking hands. If God grants me health and long life, then I plan to publish a thick tome in several volumes, entitled *The Art and Craft of the Hand*.

The first volume shall discuss "taking." Now, that may be an easy matter, a rule for all time and for all individuals alike, namely: Take with your entire hand, and, as is customary everywhere, with both hands at once.

The great difficulty, however, lies in "giving." This problem perplexes most commentators. It has occasioned a thousand exegeses. And that shall be the crux of my opus.

I am convinced that this book will be of enormous use to the world, especially to those people who suddenly come up in the world, who want to play a role in society and imitate the grand and the noble. It will also be of enormous help to those Jewish women

who, in later life, throw away their marriage wigs, bedizen themselves in the latest fashions, try to make themselves attractive, put on
all sorts of airs, and turn into *grandes dames* overnight!

This time, however, I was not accorded the pleasure of gratitude.
Not only didn't the mare thank me, she wouldn't even hear what I
had to say. She turned and chomped grass, acting as if she didn't
know I was right next to her. I was hurt, and I repeated what I had
said before. But she ignored me and kept munching, as though to
say:

"Let him ramble on. I'm not interested in his teachings."

I simply couldn't brook such an insult. What?! Was I blabbering
nonsense? I was talking about Enlightenment, Education! Exasperated at her indifference, I scrambled to my feet, faced the mare, and
launched into a sermon.

"Everyone knows," I said excitedly, "everyone, big and little,
knows that all our sages liken education and learning to light. It is
written that knowledge is light. Whereas they compare coarseness
and ignorance to darkness. A learned man glows in his eyes and all
his parts. Education, like light, gives a man fortune and long life.
An educated man lives happily, in wealth and honor. He enjoys the
world, and the world enjoys him. Everyone loves him passionately.
People give him the finest, the best things in life, the blue of the
sky, the choicest things in the world. He lives well, wonderfully
well. The rich, the wealthy, gush all over him, they simply can't get
enough of him, they lick their chops at every word he speaks. Everyone wants to get him into their home like a precious jewel. And
if they have a ball, a banquet, a celebration, then he's at the top of
their list, a paragon! Yes indeed, they realize that money makes the
world go flat. Here today, gone tomorrow. But he himself is
money, as it were. He's gold and silver, he's worth a king's ransom.
What good is money to him? What good are jewels? He himself is
a gold coin, a gem! If he asks for a loan or something of the sort,
they are delighted to fulfill his request. What wealthy man, what
important person has ever in his life refused anything to an educated Jew? Who, I ask you, who?! No one, I'm sure! Now if anyone complains that such a thing ever happened, then he's a liar. And
if he's not known to be a liar, then there must be some mistake, a
misunderstanding no doubt.

"The aristocrats, that is to say, the fine people, who turn up their
noses and put on airs, just like that, for no reason whatsoever, who

demand reverence from one and all, for their fashionable trousers and boots, and what not, and for being such connoisseurs in fine wares and tasteful things, and for their exquisite dinners which have a bit more meat and fat and a course or two more than the meals of simple folk—those refined creatures, I tell you, run toward an educated man with open arms and pay him the highest honors. And those ladies who turn on their charm so that when you're in their presence, you feel like nothing, you change color, you don't know where to put your feet, where to sit, where to keep your hands; you get so confused that you talk gibberish, choking on every word; your voice changes, your ears buzz so loudly that you can't even hear what you're saying. Those ladies, in whose presence even the most dashing men behave with a constrained lack of restraint, that is to say in plain speech: they strain themselves not to act strained, but to seem free. Those ladies, who think they make men blissful with a word, a glance. Who are bowed down with such weighty matters: a mountainous wig and a mass of ragged flowers. Even those ladies hang on to an educated man and dote on his every word.

"And shouldn't it be that way. Isn't it written in Proverbs? 'Happy the man who has found wisdom!' Why? 'For its profit is better than silver, and in its left hand there are riches and honor.'

"Well? Is there any better proof than a verse from Scriptures? ...

"Now I don't want to talk at too great a length, demonstrating how hard and bitter life is for the untutored, how weak and browbeaten the poor things are, how they are not even allowed to raise their heads, how terribly they suffer. Nay, nay! Now is not the time to speak of these things. I only want to prove what a wonderful thing Education is, and thus I want to speak about you, to make you realize how enthusiastically you must embrace the plan to have you—"

But all at once, my mare got to her legs and trotted off a short distance. She started eating grass, quite nonchalantly, without even glancing at me. But I refused to hold my tongue, I was determined to win my case, I was really exasperated. Just what was I anyway? A child or something? Was I jabbering nonsense? Although at a distance, and despite her refusal to listen, I continued my sermon, yelling a verse from Isaiah: " 'If ye will obey and listen, ye shall eat the goodness of the land!' "

CHAPTER SIXTEEN
Eat Now, Dance Later

Having had my say, I was tired and sweaty, my face was burning
and my heart aching, and I slumped under a tree.

After the way the mare had acted, I was through with her. She
was doomed, as far as I was concerned, doomed forever. She would
never make anything of herself. Her enemies were probably right.
The whole world can't be crazy after all. She was really a failure,
an affliction. Was I supposed to mother her or something?

I'll just wait a bit, I thought to myself, until daylight. And then
I'll get away, I'll run as far as my legs can carry me. I won't even
say goodbye. Just good riddance. She can do what she likes. I've
had it.

As I sat there, I could hear a voice calling me out of the distance:

"Why run away? Why in the world should a fellow like you run
away?"

"The mare's a witch. She can read minds. She sensed I want to
run away!" Such were my thoughts. I assumed that the voice came
from the mare, that she was talking to me. Putting on an innocent
air, I stammered:

"Run away? Who me? Run away from who?

"From the peasant!"

"Oh! The peasant! Why I ran away from the peasant!" I said,
somewhat calmer. "Well, a peasant's a peasant. A savage. He actually wanted to hit me!"

"What!? Hit you? Hit *you*?! And you didn't say anything?"

"What could I do?"

"Oho! So you couldn't do anything! You ran away! And he just
kept on beating his poor little horse. What?! Aren't your merciful
fellow-members out on the roads and the highways?"

I was flustered. I didn't know what to answer.

"Yes, indeed. The merciful are merciful and the innocent creatures, the unhappy horses, keep right on suffering. Yes, indeed.
Those miserable victims who were tormented earlier—they're still
tormented now! Is the world an abandoned place?"

I was crushed by her words.

"What did you mean? 'The world is no longer an abandoned

place. Today we have a Society for the Prevention of Cruelty to Animals!' "

I couldn't look into her eyes. I turned away.

"When you read these words aloud from the bottom of your heart, it really sounded as if the Messiah had come! All the beasts and animals have gotten together like brothers, wolves and sheep have become inseparable, leopards have made friends with goats, they all beg one another's pardon for the sins they once committed and for all the awful things they used to do. What's past is past. From now on everything's going to be fine and dandy. We'll no longer go at anything tooth and nail anymore. Shedding blood and eating one another are out of fashion. No more pedigrees, no more privileges. Everybody's equal. A shout rings through the air: 'Hurray! Hurray! Long live the Messiah!' And in the midst of all the joy and dancing, along comes a peasant thrashing a horse within an inch of its life—and he poops the party! Just tell me, please, what did that savage say to you?"

"She's making fun of me!" I thought angrily, and refused to answer.

"It's all a mistake. It's a Purim skit! It's a farce! By God! Here we have a Society for the Prevention of Cruelty to Animals. They worry, they chatter about compassion, humanity—and someone is tormenting a miserable creature. Anyone who feels like it, loads down the horses beyond their strength and plagues the living daylights out of them. The only help that's given them is a benevolent word, a sigh, a moan. It's pure theater! By God! Modern times really deserve the name: The Age of Moaning, Talking, and Blabbering!"

"Stop!" I shouted in a nasty mood, unable to endure any more mockery. "Stop it! Please! How can you scoff when I'm trying to speak seriously to you, when I'm trying to tell you about Enlightenment and Education!"

"Speak seriously?!" The reply was equally nasty. "Now, listen! Why are you stretched out on the ground like a carcass? Just listen! I'll give it to you straight! You say you're speaking seriously! Bullshit! Since you're forcing me to talk, I have to tell you that you're pretty bizarre. Your words and your letters are all very peculiar. You're out of your mind!

"You tell a poor creature: Get an education! I ask you, first of all, my little sage, just why? Aren't there already lots of untrained horses in the world, simple horses who weren't born with a silver bit in their mouths or raised at an exclusive stud farm, and yet I wouldn't mind trading lives with them!

"Secondly, even if I can't prance like a well-trained thorough-bred, I still can't be called a coarse beast! Who says every horse has to have a diploma from a breeding farm?

"Thirdly, even if I can't dance and caper and perform like those breeding-farm horses, people still get a lot more use out of me. The others are exempt from working, all they know is carriages and hunting. But I'm called upon for all sorts of drudgery. I have to carry all kinds of loads! Where is my flesh, my life? All gone in my labor! You can say what you like, but my efforts, my hard work, have done a lot of good!

"Fourthly, what do eating and basic needs have to do with edu-cation? What right do you have to prevent someone from eating, from breathing freely, until he masters some trick or other? Every creature that is born is a living thing. Nature has provided it with all the senses, all the organs, for its own use, to get everything it needs to live. It has a mouth to eat with, a nose to breathe with, legs to walk with, not for dancing and prancing and capering. All that fancy rubbish was invented afterward and given a name: *Education.* I don't want to start philosophizing now about whether education and all those tricks and feats are good or bad, and whether all the things that are taught, and the way they're put together, and where they're taken from—whether all that is really Education. After all, we see a lot of tricks that were once part of the program and highly thought of, and now they're forgotten. And then there are tricks that are included only because of one person's taste and opinion. And then again, there are a few supposedly earnest tricks that are included because of one man's wishes and whims, or an-cient, moldy customs. There are subjects that have no foundation whatsoever, they're just based on someone's fantasy and imagina-tion. And there are things that are founded on facts, that is to say, on things that have taken place. But the facts themselves are twisted, everyone tells them in a different way, everyone has a different outlook. Besides, they're only described from the out-side—who knows what's happening on the inside? And then, we mustn't forget that those supposedly serious matters are nothing but tricks, gimmicks, games, horseplay, monkey business. The basically good ideas, the fine and noble things of this world—they're simply swept under the rug.

"I tell you I don't want to get into a profound philosophical discussion about whether education and all its tricks have anything to them, whether they've done the world good or bad. Such philosophizing is neither here nor there. All I want to say is that those things aren't essential. When a creature is born, it knows nothing about them. It only wants to eat, breathe, and move freely before it has even the foggiest notion of those contrivances. What's the use of lovely harnesses, expensive decorations, and all those showy spangles, baubles, and trinkets—all these rewards for clever performance? Eating, breathing freely, and all the things necessary to life, the things required by the body and which the creature cannot do without—these are the things you have to give it, these are the things it has a right to! These are the things you absolutely cannot deprive it of! You can't keep the creature locked and hamstrung. It will wither away and die! You've robbed it of its right to live. You can't just torment it, beat it. All you're doing is hurting it. You might even cripple it for good, and you're robbing it of its right to be healthy and enjoy life!

"Since you're forcing me to talk, I'll tell you very plainly. I don't need your compassion. I don't want you to keep people from tormenting me, to make them give me enough to hold body and soul together—just for compassion! Just for the Prevention of Cruelty to Animals! I don't even want you to beg for the things I need to live—just because people use me or can get good things from me! That's an old story. I've heard it so many times through the ages. Whenever the world starts looking about and thinking, then people begin talking about Humanism, that is to say, about humanity, decency, compassion. A little later, the world gets a bit more practical, and it's fashionable to talk about Utilitarianism, about usefulness. But then, when the world acquires common sense and fairness and a better understanding of nature and all her creatures, then people start talking about Truth and Justice.

But I don't even want to hear the word *compassion*, I don't want to hear anything about usefulness. These are things that the world can't rely upon. 'I'm equal to everyone else,' says the creature, and rightly so. 'We're all flesh and blood. Our needs are the same. And we all have the same right to live. If someone takes pity on me, that means I live only by his grace. He has the right to live, and I don't! If I manage to stay alive and just barely breathe, I owe it to him, and him alone. Even though both of us are equals and have the same needs, he allows *me* to live because I'm of use to him. Which means that he's the goal, the crux. And I live only because I can be of service to him. There was no need for me to be created for my sake alone.'

"But I want to live like everyone else. I'm a being in my own right. Do you understand, my Advocate of Justice, my Compassionate Lord? I cannot rely on your compassion or on your finding me useful. Tomorrow your heart may harden, you might be in a bad mood, or I might not haul the proper quota of bricks—you'll lose your temper, pour out your wrath, and so much for me! If you can treat me with justice, the way you act toward others, then, perhaps, we can talk about prancing and capering. When conditions are good, when things are going smoothly, well then fine, we can start thinking about such stuff. You'll even be able to save me the trouble of sermonizing. So what do you say, my little man?"

"What do I say?" I replied. "I say that the devil's gotten into you. Yes indeed, the devil!"

CHAPTER SEVENTEEN
Speak of the Devil!

"Here I am!" exclaimed a stranger of a bizarre appearance. His hair was disheveled, and he sported a red cap adorned with all kinds of plumes. "Here I am!" he said, jumping out from the bushes. He stood before me, fixing his gray, feline eyes on me.

I was shocked and frightened at seeing such a person here in the woods. All the ghastly stories about robbers came dashing into my mind. A highwayman, I thought. His powerful neck, his vicious face, his terrible eyes were those of a robber who has already killed a lot of people in his time. I could picture him hurling me to the ground and drawing out his huge knife, while my heart hammered, my teeth chattered, and I tasted death with the knife at my throat. I closed my eyes and muttered last prayers.

"What are you mumbling, my fine young man?" he asked, and burst into such a wild laughter that my ears rang and a terrible echo crashed far into the woods, like a thousand witches guffawing at once.

"That's a good laugh!" I thought to myself. "It's over, I'm done for." And the world, as though out of spite, seemed so fine, so beautiful, that I would have given anything to live. No kingdom could possibly command the wealth I would have bartered for a few more minutes of life. Ah, how lovely the world is, how wonderful the people! How happy the man who lives in this beautiful world, among the living! If a lot of others were to feel what I felt then, they would say: To hell with pride, pedigree, and prestige! To hell with anger, slander, fighting, backbiting, rivalry! Vanities of vanities. Stuff and nonsense! All men are brothers, comrades, all of them have the same father, all were created by one God!

If someone, for instance, were leaving life and were still in his right mind as I was back then, he would say:

"Why didn't I realize it earlier? What a waste it was putting on airs, arguing: 'That man's a pest, a beggar, a pauper, a vagabond.' Or: 'That man's of a heretic, a fraud, a creep, a footpad!' Ugh! Phooey! I was grumpy and nasty, a chatterbox, a hypocrite, a slanderer, a gossip, I spread falsehood with my tongue and my pen! What did I have against others, those poor helpless people, humiliated, downtrodden, miserable? Didn't they have enough troubles of their own? Enough cares and torments from everywhere else? Enough wants, worries and frustrations, every minute of the day? Why did a nuisance like myself have to add to their misery? Why, Oh God, why?"

As I was lying there with the knife at my throat, I tried to make up with all those people. I felt how foolish it is to fight, argue, persecute one another. Had it been possible, I would have hugged and kissed them all and begged their forgiveness. I loved the world so much that, when I was about to leave it, I longed for another glimpse.

I half-opened my eyes and peered in confusion. Everything was topsy-turvy. There were flashes in my eyes, my ears boomed, thick beads of sweat covered my body. I felt hot and cold. Fiery wheels, dots, pinpoints of all hues and shapes whirled in front of me, eddied away the devil knows where! In their midst stood a huge, black dog, who kept changing every moment. He glowered, ground his teeth, made dreadful grimaces, took on different appearances, twisted, until at last he became a ferocious-looking person, in whom I recognized the stranger with the knife.

"Hahahahaha!" he jeered. "You're trembling. That's the way I like you fine people, when you tremble and keep silent!"

I glared at him wordlessly, the way a mouse peeps up at the cat that plays with it before strangling it and wolfing it down!

"Well, since you're quaking," he went on, "you should at least know who you're quaking at!

"I am he who opened the way into a new world so that the old world would always remain new. Through me, men always go away, somewhere, to make room here. I am he whose strength squarely opposes the strength of my adversary. We struggle, and each wants to devour the other, and this gives rise to new things in the world, and thus all things are born. I am he who existed before Nothingness sprang forth from me radiant. And Nothingness took shape and tried to cut a figure and wanted to drive his old father from the world. We follow in one another's footsteps, and time arises and grows from every step. I am the Prince of Darkness, the King of the Demons. I am Satan, Ashmedai!"

I nearly fainted when I heard this. Ashmedai put his finger upon me and I promptly felt strong enough to stand on my feet and even talk.

"Do excuse me," I spoke with great respect, "for asking. But I, a simple human being, took your words to mean the following: You and your adversary are working against one another in the things that exist in this world. He attracts, and you repulse. He holds together and you take apart. Whatever he builds, you destroy. And what you destroy, he builds back up again! He is the Maker, the Creator, and you, Ashmedai, are the Destroyer, the Annihilator. And that is the basis of the world and all its creatures. That is why we always see and feel new life in the world, hustle and bustle. And there is evening and there is morning—day and night, space and time. If I understand you correctly, and those things are true, then what you do isn't so evil at all."

"That's what I'm getting at! I, Ashmedai, do not ruin the world the way you little human beings do! What you down here call my evil doesn't cause as much trouble and pandemonium as your goodness. Naturally, I'm known among you as the Evil One, as Satan. If anything happens, everyone starts shouting and complaining about me. But you human beings, you slaughter whole masses, torture, wreak destruction—and call yourselves good and pious! You even get a pat on the back because you do all these things for such virtuous reasons! You consider yourselves so wise. You find fault with nature and the way of the world. You convince yourselves that you've created a paradise with your intelligence. But when you got your hands on a finished world, then, oh my goodness!, you really finished it off. You mangled it and wrecked it, and now it looks like an expensive watch that's fallen into the hands of a child.

"I am as I am. Nature has her laws, which apply to all alike. She knows nothing of pedigree, aristocracy, compassion. Everything acts and moves by just and eternal laws.

"But you good human beings, you can't stand it, you won't have any truck with order. You've sliced yourselves up into thousands of nations, religions, groups, classes, kinds, sorts, guilds, and what not! And these in turn are divided and subdivided even further. Each one has its own rules, all of them different, all of them varied."

"But just why," I asked him, "are you telling me this?"

"Hahaha! Why? I'm not talking the way you humans do—when two of you get together and jabber and gibber just to show how smart you are, how philosophical you are, and you can't even distinguish between chalk and cheese. I'm telling you these things because of what you were saying about compassion and about your Societies. I want to show you where all that stuff comes from! It's quite simple. You people keep talking about compassion, and your merciful societies keep multiplying, because there's so much cruelty among you, so much persecution, so much wrongdoing. If you were ruled by truth and justice, you could spare yourselves the trouble of feeling compassion, you wouldn't have so many merciful men, so many philanthropists and societies. I'm telling you all this because of your goodness and virtue! Do you understand?"

"Bu—, bu— . . . ." I stammered.

"You see?" he said. "When you humans baah rather than butt in, you're already a damn sight better off than when you're talking. For your own personal problems you sometimes manage to say something intelligent. For instance: 'Here's a kopek, give me a bagel.' Or: 'Take this money and do this work for me.' And so on and so on, things that concern you personally. And it's easy to get your drift.

"But when you have to talk or even write about things pertaining to the community, then your minds go to the devil! You sound crazy. Like animals! You avoid the issue. You tell a thousand lies, you quote a thousand verses, a thousand old saws. Nothing makes any sense! You deceive one another. You tilt at windmills! You twist, muddle, so that no one can make head or tail of it all. No one knows what you're talking about. One can only stand and gape in amazement that people can write, talk, and shout without managing to say anything. They can use their gift of language to make themselves totally unintelligible, like animals!"

"But why," I asked, "are you so vehement about it?"

"Why, why, why!" he exclaimed. "I'm obviously not just talking through my hat or to make fun of you! I'm talking about your correspondence with the society. I'm talking about your conversation with the mare. I'm saying that your earlier 'bu-bu-bu!' made you sound, if you'll forgive me, like a jackass. But it really sounded better and smarter than any of your speeches. You can decide for yourself whether or not you're off your rocker! You've got a broken-down starving mare before you, desperately needing a little rest, a bit of oats, a handful of hay. And all you can do is tell her to sing for her supper and how good and fine it is to master all sorts of tricks! And do you imagine you're the only one blabbing on like that? Not on your soul! Come along, I'll show you thousands of people prating the same sermons as yours to starving, brow-beaten human beings. My affairs often take me among human beings. You must know that a Satan, an Ashmedai is kept very busy. I make a lot of visits down here, I know a lot of important people. I watch what they do, I see them work, I eavesdrop on their conversations, their sermons . . . .

"Take the following, for instance. Imagine someone carrying on about the Jewish-school teachers! How much longer are we going to hand over our kids to such morons! All they do is turn their pupils into total good-for-nothings!

"Or what about this? How much longer are we going to marry off young kids? How much longer are marriage-brokers going to bring together two people who don't know each other and don't even meet till after the wedding?

"A third man screams about the idlers who sprout like weeds among you and lead people astray with their mindless nonsense and their crooked ways!

"A fourth man yells: How much longer will we have to put up

with all these philanthropists, kosher-tax collectors, do-gooders, and similar pests?

"Everyone roars and rages: 'It's time we got rid of all this and became wiser, more educated, more competent!'

"But does any of their blustering help? Everything stays the same. Nothing can come of all their hullabaloo. Why? Because there is a law in the world that is the same for all creatures and all human beings. A law that nobody, no matter who, can abolish. No amount of screaming can alter it, no talk, no sermons, nothing on earth! A law that is stronger than all strength, more stubborn than all stubbornness. And if you try to stave it off, it finds a thousand ways, a thousand devices, a thousand tricks to survive! I mean the well-known law that *everyone wants to eat.* Everyone wants to preserve his life, no matter how, no matter what.

"Just who are those teachers anyway? They're a huge mob of people who want to eat, who want to live. And the only way they can do it is by getting your children into their schools. Such needy people will do anything and everything to get their hands on your kids. You're fighting a force, a law of nature. A couple of men with edicts and speeches are not going to abolish it.

"The same is true of early marriages. You can yell all you like. What's the use! There's a whole mob of people among you who can live only by arranging marriages. And they move heaven and earth to keep up a bad custom and get your children into a state of holy matrimony. You've got to get your offspring hitched in their teens. That's why you've got all those troops of matchmakers. They *have* to be marriage-brokers. That's what they live on!

"And the same goes for all your nonsense and folly! You can laugh all you like, you speechifiers, you quick wits! It's no use. Just what are those idlers and drones? They're people, a huge mob, who can't live any other way. They couldn't exist without their follies. They work assiduously, do all sorts of tricks, use all kinds of artifices to keep folly alive among you. You've got to put up with all that nonsense. That's what those mobs of fools are for. They *have* to make fools of themselves, just to get a crust of bread and live.

"And the same goes for your philanthropists and your guardians of public welfare. You can scream your heads off, by God! It won't help! Just what are all your do-gooders and altruists? They're a bunch of people who wouldn't know where their next meal was coming from, they would starve to death, if they didn't strain with all their might to bring you all kinds of benefits. They keep up your kosher taxes and devise all sorts of new levies on flour, salt, fat, candles, and what not. They support your recipients in Palestine and they bury your poor right here. They raise your orphans and take care of your schools. And they prevent dreadful laws, so that the Jews, poor things, may enjoy some prestige, as in olden times, and remain what they are. Those poor fellows *have* to worry about you. They *have* to feel sorry for you. And you, for your part, you *have* to accept their good deeds.

"I tell you, there are forces working against you, there is a law of nature in all those people who want to eat and who'll do anything to make a living and stay alive. You earn your livelihoods off one another. You devour and destroy one another.

"But if you were allowed to exist like other people, free, as is your right, then such things wouldn't happen. If the world is opened up to you, then these evils will stop automatically and you'll be rid of all your troubles.

"But as long as I, Ashmedai, am around, I won't let it happen. I'll work my spells so that Jews will scream, and sermonize, and harangue—and accomplish nothing. Everyone will talk about you, but they'll never reach any agreement. There's no other way! There's no other possibility! Eat, eat! Devour one another! Gulp one another down like fish. Bite one another, tear one another apart! To the devil with all of you!"

"Ahh!" I moaned, clutching my head. "What do you have against us? What did we do to you?"

"What do I have against you?" he said, baring his fangs! "I hate your guts, all of you, because of the way you tormented me!"

"What are you saying?" I exclaimed. "When did we torment you?"

"That King Solomon of yours!" he retorted furiously. "Once, he captured me, Ashmedai, and kept me in chains. He tortured me dreadfully!"

"Oh my God!" I shouted. "But why is that *our* fault? Why should *we* have to pay for something that happened thousands of years ago? You have to hear both sides of the question! Why do you blame *us?* Why do *we* have to atone for it? Why is it *our* fault?"

"King Solomon is yours!" he raged, and punched the poor mare, who was standing there the whole time, bitterly trembling. "You're

guilty! All of you! My curse lies upon you! You will see everything, except what you need! You will listen to everyone, except
your true friends! You'll talk and talk about others, but as soon as
the conversation turns to you, then you'll go dumb. Try anything,
but not the road to happiness! Your do-gooders will be fruitful and
multiply like fleas in summer. They'll do so many favors for you
that you'll get sick, and you won't even have the strength to take
any more. Your societies and organizations will sprout like weeds,
and their ledgers will vanish without a trace. The taxes on your
kosher meat will never stop. You'll grow skinny and haggard, and
you'll pay through the nose and gnaw on bones! If someone ever
does stand up for you, then you'll attack him like madmen and
stone him. Your rich will spend money like water, but not where
it's needed. Wherever it *is* crucial, they won't spend a kopek. You'll
feel compassion whenever your compassion isn't worth shit! When
the poor victim's been reduced to begging or is about to kick the
bucket! But while he's still alive and kicking, and looking for an
honest livelihood, you'll persecute him, knock him down, kick him.
You'll don satin coats and trudge in muck and mire. Even a pauper
will prefer having rags of silk to a suit of whole cloth! In the matters of *this* world, everyone will only be concerned about himself.
But in matters of the next world, everyone will be responsible for
everyone else. And so Gentiles will introduce the law of collective
responsibility. If one Jew commits a crime, then all of you will be
guilty. If you ever produce any journalists to defend yourselves
against the nations, then you'll like and support the writers who
don't know what they're talking about. The greatest among you
will cringe before the lowest Gentile and consider it an honor to
enjoy the pleasure of his company. And among yourselves, the
lowest Jew will have no respect for the greatest. Every nobody will
think the world of himself. Every moron will consider himself a
genius. Every hooligan will regard himself as a polished gentleman.
Every ignoramus will have the nerve to jeer at scholars. Every boor
will look upon himself as more pious than a Talmudist. You'll bite
and tear one another apart. You'll devour one another. Damn you
all! It serves you right! It serves you right! Oh, how I enjoy it!
What ecstasy!"

He guffawed, filling the entire forest with his mirth, and then
vanished.

CHAPTER EIGHTEEN
Izzy Up in the Air

Demons laughed, devils jeered. They mocked, they jabbered, it was maddening. My head swam, my poor feet felt nothing solid underneath. I was up in the air.

"Barkhe!" a voice seemed to come from the sky. "Go and attend to him. Prepare him properly, and then bring him to me in that place..."

And now I saw a highly peculiar figure.

"Take that, Izzy!" he said, peering at me, and then giving me two hard slaps.

"Why'd you slap me?!" I exclaimed in surprise.

"Don't worry. Israel deserves a slap. That's one reason. And secondly, that's how we welcome people!"

"Oh," I pouted. "That's a devilish kind of welcome!"

"You've hit the nail on the head," he grimaced. "I'm of that company. That's how we devils behave. But why are you so surprised? Isn't that how people act too?"

I kept still, not knowing what to answer.

"I really like you, Israel. Just bend your head, and I'll put this cap on you."

"But that's a cap for lunatics!" I cried in dismay. "I don't want it! You can do what you like to me. Beat me, burn me. But I won't put on that cap! I'm not crazy!"

"Oh, Israel! You're such a fool! Can't you see my intentions are honorable. This cap will make you invisible, and remaining unseen is just the right thing for you. It's the best thing in the world. It'll help when you're earning your living, and it'll protect you against assault in bad times. When the roughnecks pounce upon you with their fists, you can put on the cap, pull it over your nose, and melt into thin air without leaving so much as a by-your-leave."

"How do I deserve such a grace?"

"You're a lucky stiff, Israel, knock on wood. That's what I was told to do, and that's what I'm doing."

A school attendant wakes up a child, washes it, dresses it, and carries it to school on his shoulders. And that was what Barkhe did with me. He thrust me under a flood of cold water, wrenched and straightened out my bones, put a strange shirt on me, a cap, a linen coat, and similar things necessary for my health.

Barkhe was a decent sort of demon, a talkative fellow. And he served me with great devotion. He fixed the cap on me, wiped my nose, and simply beamed at my gorgeous appearance. And he told me harrowing stories about the demons and their way of life.

The demons, he explained, are divided into different classes. And he, Barkhe, belongs to the hobgoblin class. The hobgoblins are terrible pranksters. They play all sorts of jokes on people, driving them crazy, and sometimes pulling a mean trick. Wednesday night and Saturday night after the Sabbath are the best times for them. In those nights, they can take on any shape they like, human or animal, to fool passers-by and lead them astray.

Barkhe told me he had once appeared to a wise man in the form of a beautiful woman, and they had played together until cockcrow. Then he whizzed off, thumbing his nose and laughing hilariously.

Another time, on a Wednesday night, he had appeared to a drayman as a trussed-up calf. The man had climbed down, heaved up the calf, and thrown it into the wagon. While he was puttering around, our friend flipped over, cocked his tail—and was gone!

Barkhe laughed his head off at our wonder workers and the Christian magicians and healers with their spells and amulets. He said they were big liars and fools, the devils didn't give a damn about them.

I felt Barkhe's head and said in amazement: "Why, where are your horns?"

He guffawed: "Horns? We don't have any, and we've never had any. It's simply a figure of speech. Like the horns that wives give their husbands among humankind."

And when I asked him if what our sages claimed was true about demons eating and drinking like human beings, and being fruitful and multiplying like us, he nodded his head and added: "Not just *like* people, but *with* people." And he cited the Torah and the Talmud. "The serpent in the Garden of Eden," he said, "who, as everyone knows, was Samael himself, seduced Eve, after all, and she conceived Cain. And Adam, as we all know, lived with demonesses for a hundred and thirty years, and they had fiends and spirits by him. On the other hand, the angels Shenkhasai and Azael lived with the daughters of men, and they bore giants in the earth. But it would be better if you didn't pry into these things. You're still single, after all, though you're over twenty! Oh me, oh my!" He got very angry, raised his hand, and the slaps flew fast and thick. And, hitting me, he said: "Don't brood about secret things, my boy! Take that, and that! I'll teach you to stick your nose in other people's affairs! Take that and that, to remember me by! And tell the other young men you're friendly with not to soil their lips and pens with amorous things!"

Oh, those slaps! They had a fine effect on me. I fell sound asleep, as after a bath. I don't know how long I slept, but when I awoke, I found myself lying in Ashmedai's hand, and he was flying through the air.

CHAPTER NINETEEN
Israel Flies

"Greetings!" said Asmedai with a smirk. "I'm delighted to see you flying through the air, Israel. Look! All the space in the universe is lying free before you!"

A roaring of whole armies thundered through the air. And then I saw troops of spirits, imps, fiends, demons. And there were magicians among them, prestidigitators, jugglers, charmers of all nations, together with mermaids, old witches, gypsies, fortunetellers of all creeds. Some of them were riding on vampire bats, some on dragons. Others were on owls or lizards. Young sorceresses were mounted on ladders, ladles, brooms, pokers, or shovels. It was terrifying to look at the pack of them, whirling and eddying like a tornado of dust in the wind. They whistled, droned, hissed, howled, danced, frolicked, never resting for an instant.

"Where are they zooming to?" I wondered, sticking out my nose, which I use to sniff things out, like a beetle with its feelers. And my jostling made Ashmedai, who had forgotten I was there, turn to me and say:

"How are you doing, dear boy? How do you feel down there, Israel? Please forgive my rudeness in not asking you at my very first welcome."

"How I feel down there? What can I tell you?" I asked, groping

for words. "Well . . . so-so . . . I'm . . . . Business isn't so great . . . .
There's nothing coming in . . ."

"Which means that everything else is all right," said Ashmedai,
eying me with a sly smirk. "Things aren't bad. Congratulations,
Israel! But why are you wandering around, my boy? Don't you
have enough space down there? Just bend your head and look
down at the earth!"

I didn't care for this. The earth, a stepmother to me, did not attract me at all. I decided to play a little trick on Ashmedai and in-
veigle him into a conversation on politics, in which, thank goodness,
I know a thing or two. Perhaps this way I could escape my doom.
And so I launched into a big discussion about the countries, decree-
ing where there should be war and where peace, and scrambling everything in one big jumble.

"Don't act so cunning, Israel! Do what you're told," Ashmedai
glared at me and bent my head toward the earth. "Look and see!"

"I'm looking, I'm looking," I said, terrified. "But it's hazy. It's
like wearing dirty glasses."

"Just wait a bit, and you can look through clean, rose-colored
glasses," he said, passing his hand over my eyes. And then I really
could see well, and a terrible fear took hold of me.

"Stop trembling, Izzy!" said Ashmedai with a smirk. "Don't
worry, I'm holding you tight. Just look and tell me what you see."

"I see . . . wide, wide fields covered with the sprawling corpses of
men and the carcasses of horses. Some of the bodies have lost their
arms, others their legs, and on some, the guts are crawling out.
Among them, something is twisting and writhing, human figures,
nearly dead. Blood is pouring from wounds, their mouths are
gaping. The eyes are glowing, the lips are burning, they're dying of
thirst. Far off, dogs are carrying away entire heads. Ravens and
other birds of prey are attacking the cadavers, pecking at their eyes
and tearing out pieces of flesh . . . . Rivers of blood are gushing,
flowing, they're giving off a hot vapor that's going up to the
clouds."

"Not bad, my poor boy!" Ashmedai broke in. "And from the
clouds it will drip down in thick drops and irrigate the fields and
the grain, and the lovely vineyards, and their wine will be bountiful
and gladden the hearts of men . . . . Not bad, my darling boy. Keep
looking! Go on!"

"I see dogs licking the blood—and people, ugh! People are

pouncing upon their dead brothers like dogs ransacking them, robbing them, fleecing them, without a drop of humanity or pity. I can see one man, he's wounded and barely gasping, and now he opens his mouth, stretches out his arms, begging for water, and the others are searching him, going through his clothes, and taking everything they can find. And they're so coldblooded about it. No! I can't look. It's awful, awful!"

"Bah!" said Ashmedai with a sarcastic twist of his lips. "Wars are perfectly normal affairs! I'd really be very bad off, if people, heaven forfend, hadn't been killing one another since the dawn of time. That's the only bit of pleasure and profit I can get from you fine and lovely creatures. That's what so wonderful about human beings. They destroy, annihilate, wreak enormous havoc, and then put the whole blame squarely on my shoulders. They kill, and it's put on my bill. Hypocrites! In the Bible, ah yes, there the wars and carnage are quite in order. He Whose Name I can't say is the Lord of Hosts, the generalissimo there, a field marshal in a crimson uniform and spurs. There all the killing's perfectly all right. But here, it's awful, awful! . . . Don't be coy, Izzy. Look!"

"I just can't! I swear on a stack of Bibles. It's against my nature! Ugh! As sure as I'm a Jew! . . . Take me away, you devil, take me away!"

The devil flew on in silence. I thought he had listened to my prayers, and I wouldn't be seeing such hideous scenes anymore. My mistake! In a while, he stopped in midair and told me to look down again.

Down below, there was a city. I saw mobs of people scurrying around like lunatics, attacking houses like locusts, hurling rocks through windows, breaking down doors, chopping, crushing, tearing, yanking, beating murderously, worse than any wild beasts, killing young and old, ruthlessly. And it all took place, alas, out in the open, in the middle of town!

"Oh my God!" I cried in a state of shock. "Where are we? Where are we now?"

"Well, well! Just look at our fine young intellectual!" laughed Ashmedai, winking at his swarm of fiends. "They spend the best years of their youth on geography. They travel all over the map of the world with their five fingers, pointing out every corner, every little stream. They think they've got the whole earth in their hands. Such minds, such walking encyclopedias, are not to be trifled with!

But when it comes to real life, then they're nothing but mindless ignoramuses. They can't tell a mountain from a molehill. They can't even see beyond the tips of their noses! ... Jackass! ... We're flying over Rumania now. Look, you moron! Just look!"

"Oh my God!" I screamed, like a child, when the school attendant is carrying him from his nice warm bed to a dark school. And I closed my eyes.

"Shush, my precious friend!" Ashmedai assuaged me, smacking his lips and stroking my cheek. And his caress simply opened my ears, the better to hear with them. "If you have trouble looking, my poor precious baby, then just listen for a while. Well, what do you hear?"

"I hear screams. I hear the pleading of unhappy, miserable people. I hear groans, death rattles...! Oh!" I begged him for mercy. "Not again! Oh, God! I can't stand all this warfare and barbarism and bloodshed!"

"Shush, my little baby, shush! Don't get your dander up, Israel. That's not war! It's all just good clean fun, a new-fangled game! People are just feeling their oats. It's a kind of hunt, poor baby. People strike, and then laugh."

"Who's striking whom?" I asked.

"Didn't you recognize the hands? Didn't you recognize the voices? 'The voice is Jacob's, but the hands...'"

"Jacob! Oh my God!" I cried, grabbing my head. "Oh, but why, why?!"

Ashmedai burst out laughing and his goatish beard waggled. "He asks why! What's the difference? Why not? As long as they can strike! That's what the sport is all about! Hahahaha! Sunshine and rain at once, tears and laughter at the same time. Just lend an ear, Izzy!"

"Oh please, Lord Ashmedai. Leave me alone! I swear, I can't listen anymore. I can't bear the sound of my brothers' blood, which screams from the earth."

"Coward!" His sarcasm cut me to the quick. "He can't endure it! He can't look and he can't listen! You're perfectly able to read those stories of yours, what do you call them? History, hysteria! Oh my! These human beings are quite capable of drawing up a list of torture, persecution, agony, hardship, and martyrdom. They can run off an account of people being driven out, uprooted, beaten, thrashed, tortured, murdered. They're experts at such lists! God forbid that anyone should forget. On the contrary! Let the children and children's children commemorate! It strengthens the soul of the nation, it's so fine, so beautiful, a sheer delight. If they dig up a long-lost victim in some ancient generation, they grab him like a precious gem! Another martyr! And *poof!* The list is one head longer! Just look! Let the world see and admire our strength! It's so honorable, so beautiful. Our pride and joy! We feel fresher, livelier, more human. But if anyone happens to suffer personally, no matter how minor it may be, or see brutality with his own eyes, or hear it with his own ears! Hoho! He flails his arms and legs. He just can't! Why Izzy! What a hero! What a scholar! What a lineage! Dreadful!" He guffawed nastily, squeezing me so hard that I shrieked.

Naturally, I didn't care for the whole business. Not the squeeze, not the sarcasm, and not the pointed innuendos about what he called "those stories." Ugh! It was really unpleasant! But what can you do if you're in someone else's hands, hanging in the air, literally dependent on his good will? If he felt like it, he could have waved his hand and thrown me out—and that would indeed have been my downfall.

No matter how furious I was, I had to hold my tongue and swallow my pride. No matter how annoying he got, I had to ignore it and put on a brave face, and swallow my pride. It was all meant for other people. You can use slyness and cunning, think anything you like, as long as you keep a pious expression and a sugary tongue. But the devil can't be fooled, he knows what you're thinking. Don't people say: "As sly as Satan!"

"You seem to be at sixes and at sevens, Izzy, and rather disgruntled. Maybe you feel cramped in my hand and would prefer to leave," said Ashmedai, eying me sharply. And he didn't stand on ceremony, he simply took me and put me on the tip of his pinky.

Now I was truly in suspense. The slightest puff of air, God forbid, could have hurled me into the distances and made me a martyr, and no one would ever find my remains. My body was quaking with fear! Oh, what a predicament! . . .

"Izzy, it's up to you," said Ashmedai, offended. "If you don't like it here, then by all means leave."

"Who says I don't like it?" I stammered with a cajoling smile, grabbing at the evil spirit with both my hands. "On the contrary, Mr. Ashmedai. It's delightful being here with you, a true pleasure. I'm getting a free ride, with no ticket, like a lord. Your hobgoblins do have their fun with me, but no matter, imps will be imps. I'm quite accustomed to them."

And thus, talking to him, I stole into his bosom like a flea and settled in a forbidden zone.

"Oooh! Are you cunning, Izzy!" said Ashmedai, laughing nastily and trying to catch hold of me.

I was like a terrified hare, running away from a hunter. My head was in a whirl, my eyes were darkened, my ears were bursting with the roar of a waterfall.

CHAPTER TWENTY
The Things that Ashmedai Can Do

Far, far off, in the highest worlds, toward the east, the skies split open, and out came the fiery heads of bright and lovely cherubs. Seraphs and wheeling angels, the entire heavenly host, stood there reverently, calling to one another: "Holy, holy, holy, God the Lord of Hosts!" And the angelic chorus cried: "Hallelujah!" And it poured through the world on a divine chord, in a sweet, soft melody, touching every soul, awaking all creatures. All were thanking and praising the Lord. The world was filled with His splendor!

The mobs of devils turned into a pandemonium. The hobgoblins trembled and quaked, the fiends were flustered, dazed, there was a turmoil, a panicky flight.

Ashmedai shook feverishly. He curled up into a ball and then, shrieking and whistling, he straightened out, hopping miles through space, and screeched to a halt with his head gawking out. He opened his mouth in a boiling rage, shook his fist at the heavens and shouted insolently.

"Damn you all, with all your chanting and praising! ... You can't fool me! You're all slaves, servants, with no will of your own. Morons! Idiots! ... And I know that boss of yours, the high aristocrat! He just loves flattery and compliments all the time, praises and gratitude for his goodness! The very things he can't stand in others! The things he counts as wicked sins. God forbid a human being should want a reward for a good deed or gratitude for a favor! But He has to be blessed and prayed to and worshiped and thanked and lauded incessantly for every trifle! And you're not chary! You heap full measures of paeans on him! Peons, flatterers, hypocrites, brown-nosers, leeches!"

I was about to recite my morning blessing, as I always do, but it stuck in my craw. Try and pray, try and do your Jewish duties when the devil's around, especially after that awful tirade!

In an ear-splitting turmoil, the demons whizzed over planets and stars, far, far off to the ends of the universe. Everything around me turned black. There was a roaring, a storming, a blasting, a crashing! It was the primal chaos, raging like a wild beast behind bars, trying to smash into the limits of space and time. It was Ashmedai, flapping his wings, banging on the gates of the everlasting primal darkness, scratching and searching for a crack, to allow the darkness to escape and eclipse the universe.

Oh, how awful this place was! How terrible! This was the frontier between light or reality and darkness or nothingness, a yawning gulf. It raged and stormed and struggled against its barriers. Black, mountainous clouds arose, as if to swallow the heavens and the earth. But fiery angels, on guard with naked, flaming swords, released thunder and lightning and cried: "Stop! Stop here, and go no farther!" There was a whizzing and a whooshing, and everything swept back into its borders.

The two worlds differed from one another in their cycle of night and day.

In one world, the day got brighter and brighter. The heavens sang the glory of God. The hosts of angels sang hymns. Each soul praised His Name: "Hallelujah!"

The opposite world was pitch black. Night! It was crawling with all kinds of vermin, swarming and oozing with all kinds of wild creatures. Evil spirits were screaming like leopards, trying to destroy, to murder—all hells had broken loose!

Jonah had a more pleasant time in the whale's belly than I in Ashmedai's bosom. Both of us were in a bad way, of course. What a predicament to be in! What a mess! What an awful place! But still there was a big difference between the prophet and myself. Jonah could at least scream and pray to the Good Lord to let him go home. But I had to hold my tongue. I didn't even dare emit a squeak. Shush! Otherwise the demons might hear me, God forbid, and the devil could remember me and throw me out, like a squashed bedbug, into the bottomless pit.

A roaring, a turmoil! Worlds were spinning and flying high in the heavens. Suns and moons were rising and setting, each on its own. Seasons changed, the stars took over one another's watches, some came, some went, each in its time, each in its place, not off by a hair! Ashmedai observed everything, he was bursting with rage, gritting his teeth, heaping insults on the entire universe. He had apparently made no headway in stirring up the heavenly hosts against God.

Drumming together his pack of demons, he descended with them to our earth, which whirled and whirled, looking, for all the world, like the head of a pin, far, far away. So he didn't want to leave it after all. No other planet was as useful for his work. He had more than his share of helpers and the means to show his strength. Down there, he had some hope of overcoming, some chance of winning the war against the Lord.

"What good are you all? . . . What use are all the heavens, all your Edens, when you're nothing but slaves and lackeys? You have no freedom, no will of your own. You're just puppets, acting, moving your lips, jabbering if someone instigates you! To hell with all of you!" And Ashmedai raised both his fists, spewed out pitch and sulphur. His eyes flashed and winked. He shot out a guffaw that cut like a knife, exchanged yells with the demons, emitted bizarre sounds to get them to fly faster.

He whizzed through space. Each flap of his wings brought him one world nearer. The closer he flew, the bigger the earth became, and Ashmedai grew calmer and calmer. All at once he halted in midspace, twisted, writhed, as though dumping a mass of mountains. He reached into his bosom—to scratch himself, no doubt—and unexpectedly felt: me.

"Why, Izzy! Just look where you've landed! The instant I let you out of sight, you creep and creep, and goodness knows where you'll end up. C'mon, Izzy, up and away! Just a little more, Izzy!" said Ashmedai courteously and yanked me out, squeezing me between two fingers.

It was really disgusting—you can't imagine how disgusting! But I didn't lose heart, I screwed up my courage by thinking of all the wondrous things that had already happened to me, and I said to myself: "It'll be all right. I've already come this far, and it was no joke, a trip like this, to the ends of the universe, among all these imps and fiends. I'm still hale and hearty, and, God willing, I'll get through it in one piece."

Filled with faith and hope, I writhed between Ashmedai's fingers, peering up at him strangely, my expression saying: "Well, a squeeze is a squeeze. I'm used to such things . . . . Bagatelles! But now what! Where do we go from here?"

"You're damn lucky I'm in such good spirits, Izzy, I forgive you everything. I won't put an end to you. On the contrary, I'll give you more space. You can sit on my hand!"

Having been graced with some kind words, I felt exulted . . . and, as though we were old friends, I ventured to ask Ashmedai out of curiosity:

"What are you feeling so good about, Mr. Ashmedai?"

"You'll find out soon enough, you jackass!" he replied with a weird smirk, tweaking my nose and bending my head. "Well, what do you see down on Earth?"

"Practically nothing," I said, rubbing my nose and my eyes. "There are columns of smoke, like from a thousand volcanoes. It's some kind of cataclysm, like Sodom and Gomorrah!"

"Don't be a fool!" retorted Ashmedai, blowing the smoke aside. "Look now and you'll see chimneys. Big, tall chimneys smoking from my thousands of factories. These factories make cannon, guns, all kinds of lethal weapons—more than enough factories to pervert vital things and produce bric-a-brac that's anything but vital; factories for tools and machines, to spare human hands, make their work cheaper, and take their jobs away; factories for devices that shorten space and time and thus often shorten lives; factories for speedily printing and distributing all kinds of nonsense—lies, falsehoods, slander, hatred, envy, and similar ugly stuff and evil things by everyone against everyone. In a word: That is the smoke of 'civilization,' as you call it down there. Wait a while, just wait. Here's a panorama. Look and enjoy yourself!"

A stretch of land opened up before my eyes, as beautiful as a painting. Fields in a velvety green mantle of young, fresh grain, the edges sprinkled with flowers. Sheep pasturing in the valleys, and snow-white goats cavorting through the mountains. The air resounding with a concert of many voices: a singing and trilling of birds in woods and groves; a hissing, buzzing, throbbing of gnats and bugs flying through the air above, and crickets and grasshoppers scampering through the grass below; and at times, a neighing of horses and the broad lowing of cows. All around, there were villages, crofts, big houses and farms, and beautiful gardens and vineyards.The grapes were blossoming, the fig tree was unfolding its leaves, roses and fragrant herbs made the air balmy. Children were gamboling about in the yards like goats, frolicking, laughing with all their hearts. And their elders were sitting under the trees, smoking, gaily chatting, eating, drinking, making merry.

"Ah!" I said. "How good, how lovely. That's life. That's paradise!"

Ashmedai gave me a sidelong glance and smirked, but didn't say a word. Then he grabbed my beard and yanked my head to make me look down.

"Oh!" I let out a bitter yell. "You can't even recognize the land. It's been wasted and ruined. The fields are bare, the wheat is gone, the rye is gone. Fire has burned and charred every last blade of grass. The trees are withered, the branches broken, the people no longer make merry. The cattle have stopped lowing—there's not a sound, the birds and beasts have died! ..."

"That's civilization for you!" chortled Ashmedai with his usual nasty laugh. "In her goodness, she came here, uninvited, with blood and fire and columns of smoke. She came from far away to introduce her benefits to the simple folks over here. And when the people said no thanks, preferring to live as before, without her favors, she taught them respect, she showed them who was boss! Now, what, you ask, am I feeling so good about? Jackass! It warms my heart to see civilization scorching and burning the world. If the forests don't satisfy her whims, she burrows deep into the earth like a mole tearing out the graves of plants that died before the Deluge and hardened into coal and she takes it all for her own needs. And soon, even this won't be enough. She'll burn and devour the insides of the earth, and then she'll grab for the sun. She'll steal the hot, burning seraphim from the old man's chariot up there in the sky and harness them to her machines and engines, and make them haul and turn wheels and gears, and lash them with electric lightning, and produce thunder and shooting and whizzing and quaking—Bang! Crash! Boom! ... You jackass!

"All those chimneys on endless, countless factories are altars—they're smoking in honor of me and in honor of the Golden Calf, the god of speculation, fraud, finance, and money. That incense dries out all hearts, smokes out all feelings, and turns all good things into goods, wares. Love, friendship, piety, faith, charity—all become merchandise. That incense, little by little, smokes out Him Whose

Name I dare not mention. He becomes more and more cramped here, He gets less and less space, He moves farther and farther away. And in time, there's hope that the earth will become all mine."

"Ah, you should only live so long! You scoundrel!" I thought to myself and put on a devout face. "You will be destroyed, and He shall abide in all eternity."

CHAPTER TWENTY-ONE
Israel Meets a General of King Solomon's

Ashmedai raised his head, snorting.

And then I heard a crashing and bashing.

"It's nothing, nothing at all. Some witches got cramps and fainted," said Ashmedai, laughing. "It's perfectly normal. I just don't know what the world's acoming to! Witches aren't what they used to be! In the good old days, when a witch went riding, she put everything she had into it. She never got tired, and to hell with everything else! But modern witches—what a laugh! The least little thing gives them spasms. They go into hysterics, and then they just love to have some gallant gentleman revive their drooping spirits. Oh, what an age we're living in! Just look at the people! And that's how the witches are. And the hobgoblins, and the demons. Hey! Rohirot!"

A demon, wrinkled and bowed with age, worn to a shadow, his body a bizarre color, with a huge hump and a long, thin, twisted nose, like an elephant's trunk, soared over to Ashmedai and halted before him, tucking his long, mangy tail between his chickenlike legs and lowering his narrow forehead, which had two stiff tufts of hair in the corners, like horns.

"Rohirot, my good, faithful servant!" said Ashmedai with a smirk. "How are the ladies getting along?"

"They're in a flirtatious mood, my lord. Just like a woman! What does a woman want? A bit of dancing. After such a long journey, they want to relax a little, freshen up, powder their noses, chat a bit, flirt a bit, even if it's with the devil himself . . . ."

"Very good, Rohirot! Go and do what you have to."

And in no time at all, an expensive silk carpet spread through the air, as far as the eye could see. It was embroidered with fine gold,

the loveliest blossoms, and the most artistic design in the world.
Emerald forests glittered and sparkled, ruby oranges peered through
the foliage, and lovely ripe peaches stuck out their full, rosy, fuzzy
cheeks, mutely asking for a hearty kiss. Black cherries flirted,
winked, twinkled, and tugged at your heart. My eyes burnt with
desire. Whatever I looked at was lovely and charming. Wherever I
turned, I was lured and drawn. It was maddening!

The devils came like locusts, big and little, old and young, scurried about freely and soon vanished. Ashmedai likewise set me free
and told me to take a stroll.

For a while after my release, I was like a rooster who, upon being
unbound, lies still for a bit, and then, catching his breath, he
scrambles up, stands ten feet tall, and blares out a proud cock-a-
doodle-doo like the best and biggest and cockiest rooster in the
world.

I forgot all my cares, strutted about, sauntered here and there.
And whatever I laid eyes upon, I desired. I wanted everything, my
heart ached for all those lovely things.

At one point, I halted by a bouquet of the most precious jewels:
diamonds, brilliants, sapphires, rubies, all kinds, mounted in gold.
Something flipped inside me. I could tell that the bouquet was
worth millions, maybe even a smidgen more, maybe hundreds of
millions, without exaggerating! I was all aflutter. Oh my goodness!
If I had it, I would sell it and have a nice nest egg, I could live like
Rothschild, I'd have enough for chicken soup and kasha, and live a
good life! My evil spirit seized hold of me:

"C'mon," he said, "why shouldn't you grab such a find, such a
wonderful treasure trove? What use is it here, what good does it do
anyone? No one's enjoying it, not God, not men! If the demons
lose it, they still won't go to the devil! They've got enough for
themselves. Take it! You can purchase your eternal salvation! Every
time you enjoy a bit, you'll say a blessing. Whenever you nibble a
cookie or sip a glass of wine, you'll speak a benediction and thank
the Lord! . . . 'Oh, He Who createth different kinds of food . . . .'
'Oh, He Who createth the fruit of the vine . . . .' God will enjoy it,
and so will you . . . . Take it, take it!"

I looked all around. No one in sight. I stood there, reflecting. I
screwed up my courage and—

Just as I reached out my hand, I felt something on my back, a lash, as if from a belt. Scared to death, I took a peek—and saw that old hunchbacked demon.

"Hello, hello! Peace be with you!" He smirked, and he flicked my hand, with his tail, as demons do in greeting.

"Peace be with *you*!" I mumbled in my beard, peering at him as though I didn't quite know who he was. "Haven't we ... met before ... ?"

"Why, I'm Rohirot! Have you forgotten me? I'm Rohirot, the governor of this carpet."

"Oh, yes! The governor!" I started, terrified, and thinking to myself: "Oh God! He must have sensed what I was about to do!"

"C'mon, Israel. Don't make such a fuss! I want to greet you here as a welcome guest. Oh, Izzy, Izzy! To think that I have the honor and privilege of receiving in my land the descendant of such a renowned ancestor!"

"Oh, go on! You're joking!"

"Heaven forfend! I'm quite serious. I knew your forebear very well. He was famous throughout the world for his wisdom—King Solomon, may he rest in peace! I served him a good, long time, the best years of my life. When I was young and before my tail went mangy. He was the one who made me governor here."

And this is what Rohirot told me:

"This carpet, which you see before you, and which is sixty leagues long and sixty leagues wide, once belonged to King Solomon. He could fly through the air on it so quickly that he used to have lunch in Damascus in the East, and dinner in Media in the West. He possessed countless armies, consisting of all the creatures in the world. His top adjutants, through whom he commanded and issued his orders, numbered four. The one in charge of human beings was Assaf ben Berakhya, the one in charge of demons was— yours truly Rohirot. The lion was in charge of the animals, and the eagle in charge of birds."

"But what about the woodcock?" I broke in. "People are always talking about the woodcock."

"Oh, poppycock! Please don't get things confused! The woodcock's a bird of a different feather, with that worm and everything. It's a whole other story!" said Rohirot with a sour expression. Then he continued:

"And King Solomon was proud. Not like a devil, but like a billion devils at once. He thought the world of himself. He believed there was no one else like him on the face of the earth. And so, with all due respect, he sometimes used to do terribly foolish things, making enemies and causing gossip. I myself once had a scene with him, and I refused to govern this carpet any longer, so that forty thousand people fell down upon the earth. There was a terrible scandal, and the king had to turn over a new leaf.

Another time, something else happened to him. Once, while whizzing through space, we flew over the valley of the mites and he heard one black mite saying to the others:

" 'Quick! Get into your houses! Before King Solomon's legions destroy you!'

" 'What!' said the king angrily. 'Rohirot! Go down to that mite!'

"I went down, investigated, and cried: 'What's your story!'

"She admitted her offense.

" 'Who are you?'

" 'I'm the queen!'

" 'What's your name?'

" 'Makhshama!'

"And so, after an interrogation, I arrested her and brought her to Solomon.

"He took her in his palm, held her up to his face, and said:

" 'Tell me, is there anyone in the world greater than I?'

" 'Yes!' she retorted.

" 'Who?'

" 'I.'

" 'In what way are you greater than I?'

" 'If I weren't greater than you, then the Good Lord wouldn't have sent you to take such tender care of me and hold me so lovingly in your hands.'

"Solomon blew up! He hurled her to the earth, crying:

" 'Mite, you don't know who I am! I am King Solomon, the son of King David . . . .'

" 'Don't let it go to your head,' she countered. 'You're just a human being like anyone else.'

"Solomon was dumbfounded and very embarrassed."

"I beg you a thousand pardons for asking," said I, Izzy, in surprise. "But it's hard for me to grasp. How can a mite say such things?"

"Hohum!" said Rohirot quite calmly. "If I show it to you in the Talmud, the way it's written there, will you believe me then?

"And I have another story to tell you, about the time Solomon was taking such an air trip and saw a wondrous palace. He was unable to enter it. And so he consulted with his seven-hundred-year-old eagle Alenar, the eagle's nine-hundred-year-old brother Aleuf, and his one-thousand-three-hundred-year-old brother Altamar. And they told him how to get into the palace, and so he entered it. And inside, he saw a golem and pulled a silver tablet from his throat. But he couldn't read the tablet. Then, however, a youth came from the desert and said:

" 'Your Majesty, the writing is Greek, and this is what it says: "I, Shadar ben Ad, ruled over thousands of lands, I rode on thousands of horses, I was sovereign over thousands of kings, and I killed thousands of heroes. And yet, when the Angel of Death came to me, there was nothing I could do." '

"Well, Izzy. I wanted to tell you all these things in detail. It's a very long story. But I see you're sort of—if you'll forgive my saying so—a bit of an unbeliever and that you have no faith or trust in an old, hoary demon. So it would be better and wiser if I kept silent. However, I can't just let you leave empty-handed. You're still a welcome visitor, Izzy, a very welcome visitor. A descendant of King Solomon, after all. Just tell me what you would like, Izzy!"

I wanted to ask for that bouquet of jewelry, I felt such a deep, deep hankering for it. But then I thought to myself: "No! I can't just ask for it straight out! The devil only knows what he meant! Maybe he was just pretending." So what should I do? I had to trick him, use cunning. And then I had a sly notion. I asked him:

"Tell me, Mr. Rohirot. You say that this carpet once belonged to my ancestor King Solomon—now those were your very own words. So the question is: How did it get to Ashmedai?"

That was a big, broad hint: I was leading up to the bouquet. If you give it to me willingly, then fine, I'll be satisfied with that. A man can live on a hundred million too, why not? Otherwise, I'll put in a claim as a legitimate heir, demand the entire carpet, and call upon you as a witness.

Rohirot, however, obviously took the hint. Perplexed, he made a face, stuttered, stammered:

"It's ... you see .... There's a whole story to it .... It happened between King Solomon and Ashmedai. He, that is, Ashmedai, you understand .... He hurled Solomon a distance of four hundred leagues .... Took over the kingdom, the wives, pardon me, and everything else . . . . It's a whole story . . . . Only . . . the trouble is you're sort of a . . . nonbeliever, you see . . . ." He finished, turned his tail, and disappeared . . . .

"Wait, wait. Goddamn you to hell!" I thought to myself in a fury. What an excuse! He took it! A fine story, by God! A fine story! Do you see? He *took* over King Solomon's realm, an "estate" of sixty leagues. And to hell with everybody else! . . .

May the enemies of the Jews feel as bad as I felt! At every step of the way, I had those wonderful and beautiful things before my very eyes, such wealth, such riches, all mine, mine, and oh God, not mine at all! . . .

CHAPTER TWENTY-TWO
Dancing for Ashmedai

All at once, out of the blue, or, more precisely, out of the earth, there loomed—a palace! And my heart jumped, my Jewish heart!

Inside, the palace was expensively appointed. Ebony furniture, silver tables set with golden services and crystal dishware. It was all shimmering, dazzling, blinding. Princesses were moving about, wearing ball attire, gauze, almost half-naked, with bare arms and open bosoms—dear me! Just like the fairytales.

In the middle of a high platform, someone was standing like a painted golem, bending his head, and with a bizarre expression on his face. It was Ashmedai himself. Young, beautiful witches were moving about him, touching him, stroking his goatee; and he grinned foolishly in deep pleasure. Old witches, green and yellow with envy, were watching from a distance, frightened of coming too close for he might kick them. And so they made do with mere hobgoblins, shabby old geezers. They pranced and frisked bizarrely in a round, and every time they passed him, they would pay their respects and show their awe: the devilish cavaliers would bow and the witchly ladies would simper and curtsy. They knelt, they scraped, they worshiped, they burnt incense to him. And Ashmedai inhaled the fragrance as if it were vital to his very existence.

All in all, Ashmedai, with his inhaling, his being caressed, and all his little airs, actually looked rather silly. It wasn't the old Ashmedai of before, but a poor schlemiel, who pleaded with women, hung on your every word, and needed other people.

"Dear, sweet Izzy!" he said to me in a soft, weak, wheedling voice. "Oh, please give me a little sniff!"

"Hell, no! That'll be the day!" I thought to myself, but I played the fool, pretending not to know what he meant.

"A sniff! A sniff! Of incense!" he explained with a woebegone look. "It'll give me strength!"

"What! How can that be?!"

"Stop acting like a jackass! Izzy! You know damn well that 'He,' that super-big-shot, He also gathers strength from his servants. Their service brings Him up in the world . . . . Hah! What do your holy books say to that?"

"And secondly," I went on as though I hadn't heard his babbling. "And secondly, why do you have to mooch a sniff off of me when you can have all the incense in the world? C'mon, you can sniff as much as you like!"

"Oh, for goodness' sake! He's philosophizing again! Izzy, these lofty things are way beyond you! . . . Just listen, an example: One man's tickle can make another man laugh. Do you get my drift?"

"Bah!" I said, making a face. "You've got enough people to tickle you."

"Oh, for—How can you argue with a Jew!" mumbled Ashmedai, turning away grumpily.

One of the princesses, a dark, beautiful sorceress, raised her eyes to me and eagerly said:

"Come dance."

"Phooey!" I spat, turning red with embarrassment, and my spit landed on one of the demons, the Spirit of Lust, right on his beard.

"Why, you oaf, you creep, you swine, you savage. You hemorrhoidal bookworm. You unfeeling, tactless, ill-mannered boor!" The Spirit of Lust hurled insult and injury at me and, as was his wont, he tickled me.

The sorceress kept motioning, her eyes never left me for an instant. Her gazes were like arrows striking my heart, tempting, tantalizing . . . . And suddenly, without knowing how, I was standing arm in arm with the beauty. We were smiling and excitedly dancing a quadrille! In the round, many other devilish couples were dancing, all kinds, all the fine personages who have done Jews the honor of appearing in our history . . . . As we danced past Ashmedai during the final figure, the sorceress gave me a yank, and, alas! For her sake, I bowed and gave him his sniff of incense! He became fresher, stronger, like an old codger after a whiff of snuff. He stamped his chicken-legs, chewed his tail, and *poof*! He jumped down from the platform, sneezing and gasping with joy.

I nearly fainted. I thought the same awful thing was about to happen to me that once happened to Joseph de la Reina. That pious soul had captured Samael and clapped him in chains. Samael begged him for a sniff of incense and so, taking pity, he gave him a sniff—which brought back Samael's strength. He flung off his chains and skedaddled. Whereupon Joseph de la Reina lost his mind . . . .

"Liven it up, everybody!" Ashmedai stirred them up. "C'mon, let the libations flow! Wine and whatever you like!"

And they rose like a tempest—devils, demons, of all shapes and sizes, big and little, young and old together. There was a chaos, a wild rush, on and on . . . . The ones with red noses and big mouths, a better sort, led the stampede, whistling, yelling, screaming, cheerful and merry and lively.

"Hurry, Izzy! Hurry over here! Just see and hear the great honor paid to me on earth," said Ashmedai, and he treated me to a sight by twisting and bending my head.

A wild hymn resounded from a thousand open mouths, a laughter, a smashing of glasses and bottles, a banging, breaking, broaching of barrels—and libations of brandy, and wine, and other liquors came pouring out. At the same time, I could hear a dreadful weeping, a wringing of hands, a sobbing, a moaning, from thousands of broken hearts—and libations of bitter tears came pouring out. There was a chaos of joy and wailing, a confusion of the strong and haughty and the weak and fallen—a clamor to the very heavens, fighting and backbiting, sneering, mockery, scandalmongering, and pointing fingers and nasty gestures.

It wasn't pretty, that hymn of the earth, a wild, raging hymn!

"Stop it! Stop it!" I shouted. "I've seen enough!"

There was no answer.

Ashmedai, I saw, was confused, and he had changed radically. His face was ruddy, his pupils were huge, his eyes were glassy and bulging, his head was swaying, he could barely move his wings. He was reeling dizzily through the air, about to crash like a rock at any moment—and I with him, and my bones would be scattered. Oh, how awful! I grabbed hold of him. Aha! His nose reeked of wine, brandy, hard liquor.

"So you're drunk, are you?" I chided, and pinched him with all my strength. "May you sweat and suffer for all that liquor and all that blood—but not now. Later, later. When I'm rid of you and when I'm out of your clutches, safe and sane."

I pinched him, I tried to revive him, but it was useless. "I'll have to call his witches," I thought to myself, "his cunning women." I looked around for them. They were all bombed, young and old, they were all smashed. There was no one I could talk to! . . . I felt like a man on a sinking ship.

In my despair, something bumped us from below. I leaped, and Ashmedai started.

"Ugh! Ugh!" he spit, glaring, and moving his lips in wordless confusion.

I looked and—oho! We were on a roof, by a skylight, which revealed a large hall.

"What? . . . Where are we? . . . A city hall! Hihihi!" blubbered Ashmedai, grinning drunkenly. He peeped down into the hall and nodded his head, as though greeting someone. "Ahhh! . . . Sholem-aleykhem, Lord Haman!"

"Haman! What are you talking about? Haman and his brats were hung thousands of years ago! You're talking like . . . excuse me . . . like a drunkard," was what I felt like saying, but I was too scared to come out with it.

"Jackass! 'If you need a thief, you cut him down from the gallows!' Who cares about the past! Do you hear, Izzy? It's Haman! All of his sons, too, down to the very last one."

Blabbering, he pushed my face against the skylight: "Do you see? Huh?"

"Yes," I said, biting my lips. "I can see stars!"

"Right!" Ashmedai praised me, pinching my cheek. "You're a fine astronomer! Indeed you are! Well, what else do you see?"

"The hall is packed. There's a man standing on the platform, and whenever he opens his mouth, he practically brings the house down."

"That's what I mean!" laughed Ashmedai, ducking my head and giving me another squeeze. "Can you hear the speech?"

"Ridiculous! There's nothing to hear!" I mumbled into my beard, resenting that squeeze.

"Nothing to hear!" he parroted me, sticking out his tongue. "That man's talking very clearly and plainly: 'There is a certain

people, scattered and dispersed, in all the lands...' Just listen to
what he says."

"Old stories!" I said, waving it off. "It turns my stomach listening
to this crap! C'mon! Let me off!"

"Too bad, really! What you just heard is only a drop in the
ocean. But it gives me heartburn, too. Ugh! I need a libation to so-
ber up .... C'mon, let's go to your people."

"For goodness' sake! Why *my* people?"

"They've got enough liquor to get the whole world drunk.
That's their business. The man who first gave me wine instead of
water and got me drunk—you know very well who that was ....
Solomon's adviser Benaiah. What? Isn't it true? Just ask your scholars. Listen to what your sages tell you!"

"We're damned if we do, and damned if we don't. There's no
pleasing you! If we give you water, you carry on something awful!
If we give you wine, you yell just as loud. So what can we do with
you? I've had it! My mind's gone! Please, please, it's enough! Let
me go!"

A witch suddenly appeared, curtsied, ran over to Ashmedai with a
sweet smile on her lips, and they whispered together for a good
long time. I looked. It was that beautiful sorceress I had danced
with earlier. She looked back at me, made eyes at me, flirted. I
have to admit I was strongly attracted, I felt like spending the rest
of my life with her.

"My precious friend, you've asked me to let you go," said Ashmedai, scanning every word, with a mischievous smirk.

I stood there bewildered, regretting what I had said. I didn't
know what to answer him.

"Well, where should I let you off? Tell me where you live. I
found you up in the air, after all."

I stood there like a golem, at a total loss for words, like a found-
ling who doesn't know where he comes from.

I stood there, and in my misery, I turned toward the east I
opened my mouth, and hot tears poured from my eyes.

"I can read your thoughts, Israel. I understand why you turned
toward the east with tears in your eyes. You're really asking a lot.
But your problem, Israel, is that you're not very practical. You're a
visionary. And not just a visionary: you split hairs and you chop
logic. You and your brethren can't see the forest for the trees,
whether you're in the marketplace or in the synagogue. Sophistry

warps your brains, it makes you overzealous, competitive, boastful. It causes hatred and rivalry, and fighting. It destroys brotherhood between you. You people split hairs, hold tirades—and don't accomplish a damn thing. Your sophistry prevents you all from getting together and working for the common good of your nation. You're a sophist, Israel, but you're not sophisticated. And I can only give you the same advice you gave the mare, about studying and understanding. Until you come to your senses and find your place in the sun, on the earth, you'll float in the air. The witch you see here is going to take care of you from now on. She wants to get to know you. Go with her."

I and my beauty looked at each other and bowed. At Ashmedai's order, Rohirot came along with a huge poker, and my beauty donned a bizarre headgear decorated with bats. She got astride the poker, and I mounted in back, holding on to her with both hands—and off we flew through the air, merry and excited.

CHAPTER TWENTY-THREE
*Israel Is Crowned as a Benefactor
and Put Astride the Mare*

If you've never ridden a poker through the air, as I have, then no words can possibly make you feel what it's like. You have to experience it yourself. And that was why I prayed fervently during my flight:

"O Lord! What did I, poor sinner, do to deserve this more than all other human beings, the children of Adam and Eve? What did I do to deserve this elevation and this flight under Your heavens, the way a bird doth fly through the air? O, Almighty God, make them, too, fly through the air, the people of this world, if not all, at least some of them, for the sake of Your truth and justice, O Father in heaven! If You have not graced them with wings, then let the devil take them and carry them on his wings, and let all of them fly through the air, old and young, men, women, and children. Let them know what it's like to soar through space."

I can't say for sure how long my air voyage lasted. All I know is that we flew and flew until at last we came to a huge and deep valley, far, far, away, between mountains that towered to the very clouds. I still shudder at the memory of that wild and deserted valley. There wasn't a sign of grass or trees. At every step of the way, there were only brambles and heaps of stones, with serpents, vipers, and lizards, darting and scuttling among them. There were ear-splitting shrieks from wild beasts and birds in their lairs, all kinds of dismal and weeping screams. Everything stank of sulphur and devil's dung. Here and there, clouds of smoke arose from the ground and spread everywhere like a fog. This was the valley that the devils had chosen for themselves, this was their home!

A gorge between rocks led to an enormous cavern, and words couldn't even begin to describe how dreadful it was. A river of black ink flowed through it. Forests of pens grew along its shores, teeming with hobgoblins, apelike creatures resembling humans. In the distance, I could see some of them ducking my poor mare, bathing and dunking her, until she emerged as black as a devil.

"This is my office!" said Ashmedai. "This river and the forests, which you see over there—I've prepared them for your brethren. My clerks will write and write about you people as long as there's ink in the wells and pens in the forests. Look! There are channels running from the inkhorns, inkducts leading to so many places— newspapers and offices. Pipe number nine hundred and ninety-nine thousand, nine hundred and ninety-nine, the one you're looking at now, runs into the inkwell of a journalist in Dnieprovitz. There's a sea of ink and pens, and there are as many writers as grains of sand on the beach."

He whistled, and the hobgoblins came swarming from the woods like flies. They lined up, each with a pen in his hand and a foolscap helmet on his head.

"These are my writers!" he exclaimed, smirking at me. He saluted his regiment of scribblers like a general. They cheered: "Hurray! Hurray!"

When they quieted down, he began drilling them. Their exercises consisted of sticking out their tongues, giving the finger, and guffawing. Next, he commanded in a loud voice:

"Present pens! Dunk!"

Then he let out a long, drawn-out call:

"Wriiiiiiiiiiiite!"

The regiment set about scribbling, almost all of them using the same topics and the same words. My hair stood on end when I read. Their words were barbed and pointed, they cut like spears. Hands were trembling, hearts pounding. These, as I found out later, belonged to recruits who had only just joined the regiment. They were still having a thorny time of it . . . . Others were working like firemen and simply slinging mud.

After this inspection, Ashmedai whistled again—and some devil walked in, a giant of a fellow, in full regalia. His head was hung with plumes, pens, and dusters.

"What have you done while I was gone? How's our business?" Ashmedai asked him. He also introduced us to one another: "This is my secretary Duke Lucifer, and this is Mr. Israel!"

Lucifer, the secretary, made a wry face and didn't even deign to glare at me. He took out his report and read:

"Your Ashmedaian Darkness! King of all devils and demons! Prince of all the hobgoblins, Duke of the seven chambers of Hell, Count of Sodom and Gomorrah, Archpastor of all scapegoats, etc., etc.

"Our agents, the do-gooders in all towns, have reported that thanks to their ubiquitous efforts in the proper places the tax on kosher meat has not been abolished."

Ashmedai was radiant with delight. "Thank you," he told his secretary. "I am grateful to Your Blackness, Duke Lucifer, for starting your report with this crucial matter." Then he said to me:

"Now that's what I call news! First of all, your brothers are going to eat crap instead of meat and be sickly all the time. They'll be ill, they'll fester and—to hell with them! Secondly, I need the kosher-meat tax for my business. That's how I can form my whole gang of do-gooders, who lead you around by the nose and never let you raise your heads. They provide my agents with salaries and a decent livelihood. And that's how all your hollow men get their hands on large sums of money to waste on unmentionable things. It's the best proof that with all your necessary community expenses, you're different from the Gentiles. That makes it impossible for you to join them in their feelings for the country. And so bad people will always have a rationale for attacking you.

"Your condition will be confused and chaotic. If I could only keep all other people on the same level as you! . . . Now do you see why that's good news for me? If, heaven forfend, the tax were abolished, then you'd be rid of all your troubles—may you live so long! Well, my agents know their politics. They deserve a bonus for their hard work.

"According to reliable intelligence," Lucifer went on, "a great many poor people have died. And generally, they're very badly off because of the benefits they get from the philanthropists."

"Great!" said Ashmedai. "Wonderful! The tax always shows what strength it has among the poor in a cholera epidemic. Just the other day, in some town, I read a notice on a house wall. It was signed in Hebrew: 'Those who wish the very best to our brethren, the nation of Israel.' The poster announced that because of the cholera epidemic it was absolutely essential for the Jews to eat meat, even on holidays when it was forbidden.

"I simply had to laugh when I read it. They advise eating meat 'for the good of our brethren, the good of our brethren!' And all the while, they've raised the prices!"

"Candidates for the office of philanthropist," Lucifer kept reading, "are to be found among people from all walks of life. There aren't even enough positions available, unless we give every assistant of a chief philanthropist a hundred subassistants, and they, in turn, will take care of tapping new sources for their salaries. A few of them have already submitted excellent projects on this score. I have turned the proposals over to a special committee consisting of Shenkhasai, Azael, Ahriman, Acheron, Typhon, Shiva, and Beelzebub.

"In the Dumbsville Hospital, things are going tolerably well, thanks to our agents. We've gotten quite a way with Dumbsville!

"As for recruits, three thousand, three hundred and thirty-three have come into the clerical regiments. They're still not properly trained, but Beelzebub is in charge of drilling them.

"In regard to ink, seven thousand, five hundred and ninety-nine buckets and one and a half quarts have been used since my last report."

"Is that all?" said Ashmedai, his face showing discontent.

Lucifer was about to explain, but just as he opened his mouth, a demon flew in with dispatches. Ashmedai motioned Lucifer to take the telegrams and read them.

"This wire is from Rumania," announced Lucifer. "They're frantic for ink. They promise to send us copies of everything they write, for our library. This other wire is from Austria. Congratulations on some good news, great Ashmedai!" said Lucifer, cheerily smiling and baring his sharp, canine fangs. "Cardinal Schwarzenberg is ordering a huge amount of ink for his gazette. He wants to do business with us. Aside from his own needs, he wants the concession for all the Catholic priests in Bohemia and Moravia who've started writing, some of them even at an advanced age."

"Long live my faithful disciples," said Ashmedai, his spirits soaring. "As long as their pulses keep throbbing, I don't have a thing to worry about. Lucifer! You'll have to add some of these substances to the ink to make it really effective: blood, venom, gall, scorpions, devil's dung, and so on."

"I've already done it on my own!" said Lucifer and began reading the rest of the telegrams. He perused the request from the editor of the *National Inquirer* in Galicia. Then, with a pitying expression, he waved his hand, saying: "Oh, this is from our man in Dnieprovitz! The poor guy's complaining that his inkhorn is almost dry. He has nothing to write, but he has to keep putting out issues on schedule. Isn't that sad?"

"Hurry! Open the spigots!" yelled Ashmedai.

A whole company of demons stormed the taps. The ink gushed through the conduits to various places.

All at once, a naked soul came flying in, fluttering up and down like a butterfly, beating its wings on the ground. Its wings were as blue as the flame of an alchohol lamp. It looked like a very thin, huge soap bubble, glittering with all sorts of lovely, attractive colors. Taking a close look, I could make out a shape of pure gas.

"Ahh!" screamed Ashmedai, grabbing his head when he saw it. "A noble philanthropist has passed away! A distinguished benefactor, one of my best agents! That's his soul. After death, it's come to me to live with the souls of all the other philanthropists."

I peered hard at the soul and recognized who it was. It was an enormously important benefactor in my home town.

"Weep and wail, Izzy!" said Ashmedai with a dismal voice. "Your native town has lost a great treasure, your community is bereft of a truly merciful human being, a rare gem! Oh, sob and lament, you devils, you demons! I, your king, have lost my finest counselor, my most devoted adviser. Without him, I am deprived of my right hand."

Throughout the cavern, throughout the valley, there was a hideous keening, a mixture of all kinds of wild sounds. There was a dreadful howling, like the nocturnal baying of a dog. There was a meowing, a caterwauling, like cats in heat. There was a melancholy dirge of owls, a cawing of ravens, a croaking of frogs. There was a hissing of serpents, a squeaking of rats, a bellowing of bulls, a growling of bears, a snarling of leopards. As though all the beasts were sobbing and grieving for such a fine philanthropist, such a pure soul. I nearly fainted, I practically turned deaf from that terrible mourning.

Ashmedai barely managed to restore peace and quiet. He caught the soul like a fly, and buried it deep in the earth, with these words:

"What's the use of weeping? Man is mortal! Sooner or later, the devil has to take you! So lie down six feet under and go to hell! I'll have to get along without you, somehow, and find another wretch to take your place . . . .

"Izzy, dear boy!" he turned to me after his eulogy. "You have no choice. You'll have to take his place as a benefactor in your home town."

"I won't, I can't!" I yelled in a fearful voice. "Have pity. Send someone else. There are so many people interested in the job, there are so many candidates. Send anyone you like, but please don't appoint me!"

"Now, now! Spare me your advice!" he replied. "I know what I'm doing."

"What do you see in me anyway?" I cried. "I'm all thumbs. I'm no good for that sort of thing. I can recommend people who are smarter, better, more experienced. Send Leybele, or Moyshe, or Treytel, or Fishke, or any one of their crowd. They all know what they're doing, and they do it so well. How can you compare me to them?"

"All these people are busy. They've all got jobs. It won't help, Izzy. I, Ashmedai, tell you again. Just hold your tongue, and don't be so stubborn if you want to keep living and if you don't want me to drive out your stubbornness forcibly. Don't say another word. Shush! Or else, I'll—"

He put on a horrid expression and shook his finger at me so hard that I felt goosebumps all over and fell as silent as the grave.

"That's how I like you, Izzy—silent," he said, with a mellow smirk, and he patted my cheek. "Ah, you're really nobody's fool, Izzy! I have to keep on my toes with you. I just know you'll do well, and in time you'll be a man of parts. But before I give you such an important office, I have to break you in a little and instruct you on how to act.

"Listen, my dear Izzy! *The town is—I!* The meaning of this is very simple. Do anything you like, and then say: 'That's what the people want.' There's no such thing as the community. You're all that exists. That's my first commandment.

"My second commandment is: *A God-fearing face!* Piety is a good cow for a smart man. You can milk her for all she's worth, like the best dairy cow. Such a marvelous animal has to be treated with kid gloves. You have to give her a bundle of ritual garments every so often, feed her on phylacteries, offer her a good sack with a prayer shawl, pages from the Bible and the Talmud, so that she'll spend several hours a day at the trough. You have to let her lick mezuzahs, suck the blood at a circumcision, water her with memorial drinks, a nip at the burial society, and so on and so forth. That's piety for you among my agents of the pious sort. My more secular agents also put on a devout face, but it's a different kind. They usually play the fool, try to get on well with everyone, smile pleasantly, turn their tongues this way and that, wear clothes that are neither new-fangeledly short nor old-fashionedly long. Their beards aren't quite all there, but they're not clean-shaven either. They turn every which way and try to get along with everyone.

"A few of them aren't all that pious. Their wisdom is in their strength, their power, their fists.... But there are very few. And these arrogant few are far from typical. Not every human being can attain this level.

"My third commandment is: *Compassion!* This means you can do any vile thing you like. You can fleece the living and the dead—and always say: 'What a pity!' In secret, you can pinch and bite and squeeze. But in front of others, you show concern, you moan, you pretend to be acting for the community.

"My fourth commandment is: *The common good!* This means, always make common cause with the stronger. Stick with the tax collector, for he is the Primal Cause, the source of all good, he is goodness in the flesh. Flesh of your flesh and bone of your bone. Therefore you shall leave father and mother and cleave unto the tax collector, and be of one body and soul with him. Let your will give way to his will, so that sometimes his will can give way to your will, so that you both shall rejoice and be glad.

"My fifth commandment is: *Demands!* This means: No matter how much you take on the sly, no matter how much you fleece and earn, keep complaining to people, grumble and grouse, make demands upon the town, say that you're losing money, that you're adding money of your own, that it's simply not worth running yourself ragged for the community.

"My sixth commandment is: *Lull!* It's as easy as pie. Just rock people to sleep, sing lullabies. People are such infants. All you have to do is sing them a lullaby, tell them a fairytale, and they'll shut their eyes and go to sleep. Just growl, and they'll think you're a bear. Whip them, and they'll kiss the lash. The best lullaby to cradle them to sleep is the old ditty about the little cash box. Then comes the song: 'Torah is the Highest Good.' Next the old story 'The Rabbi and His Wife,' the tale of the scamps, the wonder workers, and so on and so forth.

"My seventh commandment is: *My-oh-my!* The plain meaning of these noises is: In case the public, that silly little child, ever starts yelling and carrying on—then don't do a thing. The poor baby's probably got a bellyache, just let it suffer. My-oh-my! And don't say another word. Don't worry, the child will bawl its lungs out and then doze off again, and it will sleep even more soundly than before.

"My eighth commandment is: *Belittle!* This means: If someone starts asking questions, and says that this doesn't make sense or that doesn't make sense, then just belittle him. Say he's a heretic, a hooligan, a nobody, he's not worth talking to.

"My ninth commandment is: *Backbiting!* This means: If some poor wretch starts weeping and yelling bloody murder, 'They're squeezing me, they're fleecing me'—all you have to do is sic the gang on him: 'Ugh! What a crybaby! Tattletale, tattletale!'

"My tenth commandment is: *Home remedies!* When the child falls ill, gets in a wretched state, and is about to give up its soul, don't send for a doctor. It's better to resort to tried and tested home remedies. Go to charmers, gypsies, conjurors.

"And you shall keep these ten commandments. And thereby, you will please me, you will live in happiness and prosperity, you and your wife, and your children, and you will thus purchase the afterlife. And you will pay off others with the afterlife. Promise them meat and wine in the world to come, after they die. But you will eat meat and drink wine in this world, while you live."

I gaped, I gazed, I stared, like a golem, at hearing this decalogue.

"You've got to get going, Izzy!" said Ashmedai. "Your town is bereft of a benefactor. No good can come of that for me. I'll give you the mare. You can ride her."

"Oh, no!" I exclaimed at the word *mare*. "I can't. I don't know how to ride!"

"Nonsense!" he said. "You'll get the hang of it in no time! We'll teach you! The mare is very submissive. She's easy to ride. So what if she doesn't look so good! She's got other qualities. She comes from a fine background! You'll be satisfied with her, don't worry. In the end, you'll never want to let her go. Take my word for it!"

At his command, they dragged over the unhappy mare. She was heartbreaking to look at, wretched, lamentable. God only knew what the poor thing had endured from the hobgoblins. I hung my head in shame like a thief, I just couldn't look her in the eye. I burst into tears at the thought of having to ride her and get on her back like a massive load. I saw no way of getting out of it.

"Let's crown Izzy!" said Ashmedai. "Let's see what Izzy looks like dressed as a benefactor and riding the mare. C'mon gang, get to work!"

In the twinkling of an eye, his servants brought in a mass of clothes, all cuts and sizes. One of the servants, in charge of wardrobe and Ashmedai's valet de cham', took me in hand and dressed me. He arranged a lock on my head, smeared a pomade in my hair, cunningly did my beard, put a chemisette on me with mother-of-pearl buttons, a sateen cloth at my throat, then a pair of solid hobnailed boots, my goodness, a pair of woolen trousers that hung down like bags, a camlet jacket, an overcoat that reached down past my knees, and an artistically sewn cap on my head.

"Now what do we have here?" said Ashmedai, looking me over from head to foot. "This is the uniform of a community scribe! It's not the right thing for Izzy. Find something else."

The valet de cham' quickly changed my coiffure, trimmed my hair, straightened out my whiskers, put a different vest on me, satin I think, and buttoned up to my Adam's apple, a cotton overcoat with a split in the back and a hem reaching down much farther than the previous one, so that barely an inch or two of the trousers stuck out. And on my head, a worthy and dignified hat.

"Well, how do you look now?" said Ashmedai, inspecting me. "Ah, the uniform of a community deputy! The devil take them with their splits in back and their cavernous pockets. No. Izzy needs a different uniform entirely. Just look at his lamentable expression, and you'll understand what he ought to have."

The valet tried all sorts of uniforms on me. And while dressing me and combing me over and over again every minute, he tweaked and yanked and pulled my hair, bringing tears to my eyes. At long last, he cropped my hair, leaving me a pair of fine earlocks, stuck a skullcap on my pate, with a high fur hat over it, put a shirt on me with a huge turn-down collar, tied with ribbons and without a necktie, a long ritual four-colored garment, velvet breeches, shoes and stockings, a long satin gabardine with a belt, and a sheepskin overcoat. The valet looked me over, made a sour face, and stuck out his tongue.

"You're gorgeous, Izzy!" Ashmedai laughed joyously. "I'm absolutely delighted to see you in these clothes! Your face is as red as a carrot stew, you're sweating in that fur, and you're shining from underneath your fur hat like the radiant morning star. Sweat, sweat, Izzy. It's good for you! ... But there's something missing to make the uniform perfect," he went on, turning to the valet. "Do you remember how Yossel-Dintshes used to receive a new governor?"

"Right! Right!" the valet answered. "I completely forgot. Oh, yes! I'll do it in a jiffy!"

He shaved a pair of round spots on the back of my head, and stuck on cupping-glasses for a few minutes, for beauty's sake.

"Now Izzy's in full regalia," said Ashmedai. "And he can mount the mare."

With great pageantry, I was dragged over to the mare. "Ride, Izzy. Ride!" the devils sang. "How lucky you are that you're privileged to ride on such a mare, the mare of the world! Just climb up with your hands and feet, and ride on her, like a lord, ride till the end of your life, till the devil gets you and someone else takes your place!"

"Please forgive me, poor mare!" I begged, astride her back, my eyes weeping and my heart sorrowing. "What can I do, what can I say? The devils made me do it.... It's hideous for both of us! It's horrible for you because you're a mare and you have to carry me. And it's horrible for me, your friend, because I have to get on your back! What can we poor wretches do? We're in the same boat, and there's no way out!"

The devils lashed the mare so hard that she scurried off. There was a yelling and screaming! *Hurray! Hurray!* As she galloped, a deep sigh came from her heart. A sigh that cut me to the quick. I was so bewildered that I tumbled to the ground.

"Now, just don't let it get you down, Izzy! You'll make it!" Ashmedai laughed and plopped me back on the mare. "Don't delay, it's time to get going. Just repeat my ten commandments. Put your hands under my loins and swear you'll abide by them."

I sat there like a clay golem, not knowing what was happening.

"Don't dilly! Don't dally, Izzy!" said Ashmedai. "Do what you're told. Quick! Quick! Time's awasting!"

Willy-nilly, I reached out and put my hands under Ashmedai's loins. He motioned to his secretary, and Lucifer began reading a terrible oath.

"Cat's got your tongue, Izzy?" Ashmedai grumbled. "Why aren't you repeating the oath, word for word? Do you think I'll put up with tricks, qualms, and betrayals, the way you fine human beings do? No! I tell you. No reservations! Don't play the clown. It won't help! Just swear!"

"I can't swear," I replied in a trembling voice.

"What?!" Ashmedai screamed in rage, and the earth quaked beneath us.

The mare nodded her head as though to say: "Stick to your guns! Say, no, no, and no!"

"I can't swear!" I repeated, with greater courage.

"Swear!" yelled Ashmedai, angrier. Sparks flew from his eyes and smoke curled from his mouth.

My poor mare heaved a sigh. Her sigh reminded me of all she had gone through in her life. "Oh my!" I thought to myself. "The wretched creature suffers enough from others. Why should I add to her misery! Let come what may! I won't do such a thing! I have to resist temptation like a decent man."

"Absolutely not! I absolutely refuse to swear!" I answered Ashmedai coolly and pulled back my hand from under his loins. As I did so, I had the devilish misfortune to scratch him.

All hell broke loose! Ashmedai was terrifying to look at. With a fearful scream, he leaped into the air, stretched out terribly high, planted one foot on the earth, the other in the sky, grabbed me by my hair, and flung me away like a piece of wood.

I plunged like a bolt from the blue! As I plummeted, I heard taunts and laughter from all the demons at once. I saw the mare whooshing through the air, whirling and tumbling after me.

"We're falling, we're falling!" I barely managed to scream.

"Don't worry!" the mare yelled back. "When I fall, I either land on my feet, or else I get right back up again. I never bite the dust. I've had my share of falls, but none has ever spelled my downfall!"

I plunged and plunged, until at last I landed on my head, screaming in pain.

I felt hands taking hold of me. It was as if someone were weeping over me and hot tears were pouring onto my face.

CHAPTER TWENTY-FOUR
Goddamn Their Mothers!

Opening my eyes, I saw that I was lying on the floor next to my bed in my own room. My mother, in tears, was helping some people heave me up.

As I lay in bed, I began wondering what had happened. How had I suddenly ended up here? I felt my body all over and inspected it. I caught sight of the wonder worker again and the old witch, who were doing something and mumbling their spells. My mother touched my head and wept.

"Why are you crying, Mama?" I asked, and gave her a loving kiss.

"Oh, Izzy, Izzy!" she sobbed. "Oh what awful troubles I've had with you! Thank the Lord that you've opened your eyes. You really had a hard fall from your bed."

"Mama," I said. "What happened?"

"Oh, please don't ask, please don't ask! It's all because of your books."

"What do you mean my books?"

"Those silly stories you crammed into your head." My mother waved her hand. "Well, you absolutely insisted on studying medicine. What could I do? I had no choice. But what good are all those books, those tales, those nonsensical things? What do they have to do with medicine? If you want to be a doctor, well then study to your heart's content and learn anything you have to. You can get a diploma saying you can cure people, even if you don't know a word of those stories. They can't help you in the least. It seems to me that that's how it ought to be, at least according to my female way of thinking. But what did they say? What did they reply, when I ran to each one of them? They said: No! You might have a great mind! You might even become a great man, and a renowned physician. But if you're not well-versed in those tales, in . . . what they call 'histories,' then nothing can come of you. Oh, what suffering all those tales and stories brought me! Oh, Good Lord, if only the devil had taken them all, I would have been spared a lot of trouble!"

"What kind of trouble, Mama?"

"What kind of trouble! Izzy! Oh, what they did to me!"

And this is what my mother told me, weeping and wailing:

"You wrote me from Dnieprovitz, saying you hadn't done so well in the examinations on those stories, and that you had to give up studying medicine. I figured you'd soon be coming home. And then you'd throw over all your silly plans, and get married, as God commanded, and as Jews have to live.

"I waited for a week, but there was no sign of you. I waited another week, and still you didn't show up, and you didn't even write. I was worried sick, wondering what it was all about. I couldn't sleep. I couldn't find a moment's peace. I couldn't eat. You're my only child, after all, the apple of my eye. How can I go on living without you? Meanwhile, there was a lot of talk in town. Some people said you had died. Others—may their tongues rot—said you had converted to Christianity. And goodness only knows what else our enemies made up. I couldn't stand it any longer, so I went to Dnieprovitz.

"When I arrived, it was so awful. I found you in a wretched state! Your face was dark gray, you were all skin and bones, there wasn't an ounce of flesh on you. I asked you how you felt. And you gibbered something about castles in Spain. I tried to talk rationally to you, but you merely jabbered all sorts of nonsense.

"My heart bled for you. I felt like dying. People advised me to go to the teachers and beg them to overlook your mistakes.

Perhaps the good news would bring you to your senses. So I went, of course. I cried, I pleaded, but it was no use! They replied: No! Impossible!

"I hired a wagon and brought you home. Every day you got more and more despondent, you were always lost in thought. But the moment you started talking, you went on and on, a blue streak, cursing all the decent people, all the fine and upright men in town. It was a good thing—a miracle!—that I let no one in except for close friends. So people didn't hear the terrible things you were saying about them. You got sicker and sicker, and finally you took to your bed. You lay there in a coma, for about two weeks, never opening your eyes, practically without a sign of life, except that at times you ranted feverishly, raving about wild things.

"Oh, Izzy! My darling Izzy! What awful things your stories and books have done to us! Put an end to them! For goodness' sake! If only you had listened to your mother and gotten married. It's the way of the world. It's customary and traditional for us Jews. You would have spared us so much sorrow! Oh, Izzy! Your stories, your stories. Your histories, your histories! . . ."

"It all comes from *them*, from *them*, the evil spirits!" said the wonder worker. "Just the other day, I had the same sort of business with them. Our Christian friend here knows about it. Well, wasn't it a fine thing?" he asked the peasant woman.

"A fine thing indeed!" she replied with a yawn, absorbed in her spells. "He's right, he is. This is *their* doing. Goddamn their mothers!"

And On The Seventh Day

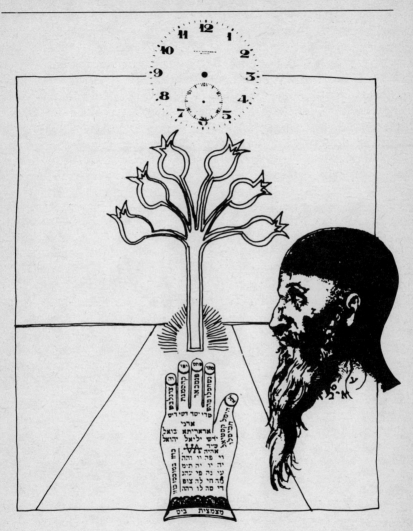

The Tale of the Seven Beggars

*I want to tell you
about a merry
time.*

1.

Once upon a time there was a king. And the king had an only son. Now the king wanted to give the prince his kingdom while he was still alive.

So he threw a grand ball.

And when the king throws a ball, why everything is gay and merry. And on this day, when he was giving the prince his kingdom while he was still alive, the joy was very great indeed.

All the lords of the realm were there, and all the dukes and earls; and they were all having a marvelous time at the ball.

The whole country was delighted that the king was giving the prince his kingdom while he was still alive. For this was a great honor from a king.

The rejoicing was great. There were all sorts of things for creating joviality, orchestras and plays and the like. Anything that could make for a celebration was there at the ball.

And when everyone was very merry, the king stood up and said to his son:

"I can read the stars, and I see that someday you will leave the kingdom, but make sure that you don't feel sad about leaving the kingdom, be cheerful. And if you're cheerful, then I'll be cheerful. But even if you're sad, I'll still be happy that you're not a king. For if you are the sort of man who cannot manage to be cheerful all the time, even when you leave the kingdom, then you're not fit to be king. However, if you're happy, then I'll be terribly happy."

The young king took over the kingdom in a high-handed fashion. He created dignitaries and dukes and earls and an army.

The young prince was extremely wise. He was very fond of wisdom, and he had many wise men around him. And any man who came to him with wisdom was greatly honored by him. And he would give him great honors and riches for his wisdom. Whatever the man wanted, the prince would give him. One man wanted money, so he gave him money. Another man wanted honor, so he gave him honor.

And since wisdom was so greatly honored at his court, the people all turned to wisdom.

The entire country was concerned only with wisdom. This man was concerned with wisdom because he wanted money, and that man was concerned with wisdom because he wanted honor.

And because they were all concerned only with wisdom, they forgot all about warfare and military matters.

They were all concerned only with wisdom, until all the men in the country became extraordinaily wise, and the unwisest man in the country was wiser than any wise man in another country.

Now because of their wisdom, the wise men in the country turned to heresy.

And they drew the prince into their doings. And he too became a heretic.

The common people, however, were not harmed. They didn't join the heresy. The wisdom of the wise men was so deep and subtle that the common people couldn't share it. Thus they remained unharmed and never turned to heresy. Only the wise man and the prince became heretics.

And the prince, having the basis of goodness, for he had been born with this basis of goodness, and had good and just traits in him, kept wondering every day: "Where am I in the world? What am I doing?"

And he would groan and sigh that he had yielded to such delusion and been led so far astray. And he would wonder: "What does it mean? Should I go astray in such things? What am I doing to myself?"

But as soon as he began using his mind, the wisdom of heresy became strong in him again.

And this kept happening all the time.

He would wonder where he was in the world, and groan and sigh. But then he would instantly start using his mind, and his heresy became strong in him once more.

One day there was a mass flight from the country.

Everyone fled. And while fleeing, they passed through a forest, where they lost two children, a male and a female.

One man lost a male child.

And one man lost a female child.

These children were still small, they were only four or five years old.

Now the children didn't have anything to eat. And they wept and wailed that they had no food.

Meanwhile, a beggar came along. He came to them with his sacks, in which he carried bread.

The children began to bother him and cling to him. So he gave them some bread. And they ate it.

He asked them: "Where do you come from?"

They replied: "We don't know."

For they were little children.

And he started to leave them.

They asked him to take them along.

He said to them: "I don't want you to come with me."

They looked at him closely: The beggar was blind.

They were amazed. If he was blind, how did he know the way?

And it was really amazing that this was a problem for the children. For they were still little, but they were smart, and they were amazed.

And the blind beggar blessed them so that they would be like him: "May you become as old as I."

He left them with some more bread and went away.

The children realized that the Good Lord was watching over them, and that He had sent them a blind beggar to give them food.

But then the bread was gone, and so once again they began shouting: "Food!"

Now the night came, and they went to sleep.

In the morning, they still didn't have anything to eat. So they wept and wailed.

Meanwhile, another beggar came over to them, and this one was deaf.

They began speaking to him.

He made signs with his hands and said: "I don't hear."

And the beggar also gave them bread and began to go away.

The children wanted him to take them along. But he didn't want to. He also blessed them: "May you become like me."

And he also left them some more bread and went away.

But then, after a while, this bread was also gone. And so they began weeping again.

Another beggar came over to them, and this one was slow of speech, he was a stammerer.

They began talking to him, and his tongue stammered. They didn't know what he was saying.

He did know what they were saying, but they didn't know what he was saying because his tongue stammered.

The beggar also gave them bread to eat.

He blessed them also so that they would become like him, and then he went away.

Then another beggar came over, and he had a crooked neck.

And the same thing happened as with the others.

Then came a beggar with a hunched back.

Then came a beggar without arms.

Then came a beggar without legs.

And each one of them gave the children bread and blessed them so that they would become like him.

Then, their bread was gone again.

They started walking to find people, and they came to a road. And they walked along this road until they came to a village.

There the children went into a house.

The people felt sorry for them and gave them some bread.

And thus they went from house to house. They saw that it was a good thing for them: People would give them bread.

The children agreed that they would always remain together.

They made big bags for themselves and then went from house to house. And they went to all the celebrations, to circumcisions and weddings.

They came to all kinds of little towns and went begging from house to house.

They also went to the county fairs and they would sit among the beggars, on the earthen seats around houses, holding their plates, until they became well known to all beggars. For all of them knew the children and had heard about their having been lost in the woods.

Now once there was a big fair in a big town. All the beggars went to the fair. And the children went too.

It occurred to the beggars to betroth the children and unite them in marriage.

And when several of the beggars began talking about this idea, they liked it very much.

So they made up their minds to betroth them.

But how could they celebrate a wedding?

They remembered that on a certain day the king would be giving a feast, for that was his birthday. All the beggars would go there and beg for meat and challah, enough for a wedding.

And that was what happened.

The beggars all went to the birthday feast, and managed to get meat and bread. And they gathered up the leftovers of the banquet: meat and challah.

Then they dug out a huge cave large enough for a hundred people, and they covered it with wood and soil and rubbish, and then they all went into it.

And there they celebrated the marriage of the children, and performed the ceremony with the wedding canopy, and they all had a marvelous time.

And the bride and groom were also very happy.

The bride and groom now began reminding the Hassids what the Good Lord had done for them when they were in the forest, and they wept longingly and bitterly:

"Where can we find the first beggar, the blind one, who brought bread to us in the forest?"

And as they were longing for the blind beggar, he suddenly called out:

"Here I am. I've come to your wedding, and I've brought you a wedding gift: May you become as old as I am. The first time, I merely wished that you would become as old as I, but today I'm giving it to you as a wedding present: May you live as long a life as I do.

"And you believe," he went on, "that I'm blind. I'm not the least bit blind. What is it then? All the time of all the world doesn't even amount to a moment for me."

And that was why he seemed blind, for he did not look upon the world. The entire existence of the world didn't even amount to a moment for him. So he couldn't even look at, or see, this world.

"And I am very old," he went on to say, "but nevertheless I'm still extremely young. And I haven't even begun to live, but nevertheless, I'm very old.

"And it's not just I who say so, I have the approval of the great eagle.

"Let me tell you a story."

The Blind Beggar's Story

Once upon a time, a whole bunch of people were sailing in ships on the sea. A gale arose and smashed the ships. But the passengers were saved.

They came to a tower. They climbed up the tower, and there they found all kinds of food and drink and clothing, and everything they needed, and all kinds of good things and all the delights of the world.

They decided that each one of them should tell an old tale, something he remembered from his earliest memory, from the time his memory first began.

Now there were old people and young people among them.

So they honored the eldest man among them, by asking him to tell the first tale.

And the eldest man spoke as follows:

"What shall I tell you? All I can remember is that they cut the apple off the branch."

No one understood what he was saying, but there were wise men present, and they said that this was really an old story.

Next they honored the next-eldest man, who was younger than the first, and they asked him to tell a tale.

The next-eldest man, who was not as old as the first, responded in a tone of amazement:

"That's an old story?! I remember it too. But I also remember that the candle was burning."

The others replied: "That story is even older than the first."

And they were surprised that the next-eldest was younger than the first one and yet remembered an older story.

Then they honored the third-eldest and asked him to tell a tale. And the third-eldest was even younger. And he replied:

"I can remember when the development of the fruit began, that is to say, when the fruit first started becoming a fruit."

The others replied: "That story is even older."

Then the fourth-eldest, who was even younger, said:

"I can remember how they brought the seed to plant the fruit."

Then the fifth-eldest, who was even younger, said:

"I can even remember the wise men who thought up the seed."

Then the sixth-eldest, who was even younger, said:

"I can remember the taste of the fruit before the taste even went into the fruit."

Then the seventh said:

"I can remember the fragrance of the fruit before it even went into the fruit."

Then the eighth said:

"I can remember the color of the fruit before it even came upon the fruit."

And I, the blind beggar, who am telling you all this, I was still a child then. I was present also. And I said:

"I remember all these tales, and I remember nothing."

To which they replied:

"That's a very old story—the oldest of all."

And they were surprised that the child remembered more than anyone else.

Meanwhile, a great eagle arrived, and he knocked on the tower and said to them:

"You are no longer poor! Return to your riches. Make use of your riches."

And he told them to leave the tower in order of age, each in turn, with the eldest going out first.

And he took them all out of the tower.

First he took out the child, for the truth was that the eldest of them was the child.

And thus he took each younger one out first, and didn't take out the eldest man until last.

For the younger any one of them was, the older he was, and the oldest of them was youngest of all.

And the great eagle said to them:

"I want to comment on all the tales that you all have told.

"For the man who told you that he remembers how they cut the apple off the branch means that he remembers how they cut his navel string, that is to say, even the things that happened to him when he was born, when they cut his navel string—he can remember all that.

"And the next one, who said he remembers that a candle was burning, means that when he crossed the high worlds, a candle was burning at his head.

"For it is written in the Talmud that when a child is in its mother's belly, a light burns at its head.

"And the one who said he remembers that he started to become a fruit—he means that he remembers the way his body started to develop when the child was first created.

"And the one who remembers when they brought the seed to plant the fruit, he means that he can still remember when the seed was sown in conjugal union.

"And the one who remembers the wise men who thought up the seed means that he remembers when the seed was still in the mind.

"And the one who remembers the taste—that is the *nefesh*, the lowest aspect of the soul, the animal aspect.

"And the fragrance is the *ruakh*, the moral element of the soul.

"And the color is the *neshamah*, the highest degree of the soul, corresponding to the intellectual world.

"And the child said he remembers nothing. For he is older than the others and he can even remember what there was before the *nefesh*, the *ruakh*, or the *neshamah*: the category of nothingness.

"That is why he said he remembers nothing. That is, he remembers that there was nothing. He even remembers what was happening then, and that is earlier than anyone else."

And now the great eagle said to them:

"Return to your ship: these are your bodies, which were smashed. They shall be rebuilt."

And he gave them his blessing.

And to me, the blind man, who was only a child then, and who is telling you all this now, to me the great eagle said:

"You, come with me. For you are like me. For you are very old and yet still very young. And you haven't even begun to live and yet you're already very old. And I am that way too. For I am very old and yet still very young."

Thus, I received the approval of the great eagle for being very old and yet still very young; and now I am giving you my long life as a wedding present, so that you may be as old as I.

And there was a great rejoicing and they were very happy.

2.

The second day of the wedding week, the young couple remembered the second beggar, the deaf one, who had nourished them by giving them bread.

And they missed him and wept for him: "Where can we find the deaf beggar who gave us nourishment?"

Meanwhile, as they wept for him, he came in and said: "Here I am."

And he fell upon them and kissed them and said to them:

"Today I'm giving you a present that you may be as I am, that you may live a good life as I do. Earlier, I gave you my blessing and now I'm giving you my present: my good life as a wedding gift. Now you think that I'm deaf. I'm not deaf at all, but the whole world isn't worth my hearing its defects. For all the noise in the world is merely the sounds of its defects. Each man yells about his defect, that is to say, whatever he is lacking. And all the rejoicings of the world are merely the joys of defects. For each man is overjoyed about having what he lacked. But as for me, the whole world isn't worth my hearing its faults, I live a good life with no lacks whatsoever. And I have approval to lead a good life in the land of riches."

And his good life consisted in his eating bread and drinking water.

And he told them the following story:

The Deaf Beggar's Story

There is a country where there are many rich men, they have great wealth. Now once, all these rich men gathered together, and each one started boasting about his good life, and each described the good life he was leading.

Then I spoke up and said to them:

"I live a good life that is much better than your good lives. The proof is that if you are living such good lives, then let me see whether you can help this country.

"For there is a country where there used to be a garden.

"And in that garden, there were fruits with all the tastes in the world. And there were also all the fragrances of the world, all the colors, all the hues, and all the blossoms of the worlds. Everything was there in that garden.

"And there was a gardener there, a man who tended the garden.

"And the people in that country lived a good life because of that garden.

"But then the gardener vanished.

"And everything that was in the garden was doomed, for the man who had taken care of it, the gardener, who had looked after it, was no longer there to tend it, to do all the things that needed to be done for the garden.

"Nevertheless, they could have lived from the things that grew by themselves, the things that sprouted from the fallings.

"But then a cruel king came to the country. And the king couldn't do anything to them.

"So he destroyed the good lives they were living because of the garden.

"And not only did he destroy the garden itself, he also left three companies of his men in the country and told them to carry out his orders.

"And thus they destroyed the sense of taste.

"And because of their action, each man who wanted to taste something, merely tasted carrion.

"And they also destroyed the sense of smell, so that all fragrance would smell like manure.

"And they also destroyed the sense of sight in carrying out the king's orders. For they made everything dark to the eyes as though the people were enveloped in clouds.

"All these things were done by the three companies of soldiers in that country.

"Now if you are living such good lives, let us see whether you can help these people!

"And I tell you," (the deaf beggar had gone on to say to the country of the wealthy men who had boasted of living good lives), "if you don't help them, then the destruction in that country will bring damage to you, the corruption of sight, taste, and smell will also happen to you."

The rich men got up and went to that country.

And I went along with them.

And on the way, each one of them lived his good life, for they were very wealthy.

When they came to that country, a corruption began of their taste and everything else, that is to say, taste, sight, and smell.

Whereupon I exclaimed:

"If you haven't entered the country and have already lost your taste and sight and smell, what's going to happen once you enter the country? And just how will you manage to help the people?"

I took my bread and my water and gave them to the rich men.

And in my bread and water they could taste all tastes and smell all smells, and their senses, which had been destroyed, were now mended again.

And the people of that country, where that garden was, and where the inhabitants had lost their sense of taste, began looking for a way to restore their lost sense of taste.

They remembered that there is a country of rich men, (that country where I, the beggar, had talked with the rich men) and their gardener, who had once caused them to have a good and wealthy life but had died, was of the same spiritual descent as those rich men who were also living a good life in their own country.

The people in the country with the garden liked the idea of sending for help to the country of rich men who were also living a good life.

And they did so.

They sent messengers to that country of rich men.

The messengers set out, and the two groups ran into one another, that is to say, the messengers ran into the rich men on the road. For the rich men had wanted to go to them and had sent messengers.

And they asked the messengers: "Where are you going?"

To which they replied:

"We're going to the country of the rich men to ask them for help."

The others exclaimed:

"Why, we're from the country of the rich men, and we're going to your country."

Then I, the deaf beggar, who am telling you all this, I said: "You ought to come to me, for you really can't go and help them. Stay here, and I'll go with the messengers to help them."

I went off with the messengers and arrived in the country.

When I entered a city, I saw people coming and telling jokes. Then they were joined by others, until there was a whole group of people telling jokes, and laughing and joking.

I listened to them: What were they saying? I discovered that they were telling obscenities. One was telling obscene jokes, the next person was more refined. He laughed, he was having a good time, the way people do.

Next I went to another city.

There I came upon two people arguing about some business deal. They went to court to litigate.

The court decided: "This man is innocent and this man is guilty."

The two men left the courthouse.

But then they had another quarrel. This time they said they wouldn't go to the same court but to another. And they picked another court for their litigation.

Then, one of these men had a fight with another man.

So they picked another court.

And thus the people kept fighting with one another, this one with that one, that one with this one, and each time they picked another court until the whole city was full of courts of justice.

I went to look, and I saw that this happened because there was no truth here. Today, the lower court was in session. The judge flattered a man and decided in his favor, and then that man in turn decided in *his* favor, and then that man in turn decided in *his* favor. For they took bribery and there was no truth in them.

Then I saw that they were really full of lechery and that there was so much lechery there that it became permissible.

So I said that this was why they had lost their taste and smell and eyesight. For the cruel king had left three companies of men with them, and these soldiers had spoiled the country. They had gone among the people and spoken obscenities. They had brought obscenities into the country. And these obscenities had destroyed the sense of taste, so that all things tasted like carrion.

They had also brought bribery into the country. This had darkened their eyes and destroyed their vision. For it is written: "Bribery blinds the eyes of sages."

And they also brought lechery into the country and it destroyed their sense of smell, for lechery destroys the sense of smell.

I said to the messengers.

"Thus you ought to free the country of these three sins and seek out the soldiers who brought in the three sins and drive them out. And when you have done away with these three sins, not only will your taste and vision and smell be restored, but even the gardener who disappeared will be found again."

And they did so.

They began to purge the country of the three sins and looked for the people responsible, the soldiers.

They would seize a person and ask him: "Where do you come from?" They did this until they had caught all the cruel king's men.

And they drove all those people out and purged the country of the sins.

Meanwhile, there was a commotion. Perhaps the madman who was going around, yelling that he was the gardener, and everyone thought he was crazy and threw stones at him and drove him away—perhaps he really *was* the gardener!

So they brought him before the men who had redeemed the country.

(And I, the beggar telling this story, I too was there.)

And I said:

"Of course, he is really and truly the gardener."

Thus, the country was saved because of me. And that is why I have approval from the country of the wealthy men, so that I live a good life, for I redeemed the corrupted country.

And today I give you, as a wedding present, my good life.

And there was great joy and merriment, and they were very happy.

And then all the beggars came to the wedding and gave them presents, the things they had wished them earlier that they might be like them.

The first beggar had given them long life and the second one gave them a good life.

3 .

The third day, the bride and groom recalled the beggars again and wept longingly and bitterly:

"Where can we find the third beggar, who was slow of speech?"

And along he came and said:

"Here I am."

And he embraced and kissed them, and he said:

"Earlier I blessed you that you might become like me. But today I am giving you as a wedding present that you may become like me.

"Now you think," he went on, "that I am slow of speech. However, I am not slow of speech. It is just that the words of this world that do not praise the Lord God have no perfection."

And thus he seemed slow of speech and stammering, for he did not wish to speak any word that did not laud God, for any word that does not laud God has no perfection. And that was why he stuttered . . . .

"In reality, I am not slow of speech. On the contrary, I am a wonderful orator, a fine speaker, and it is truly amazing that when I start speaking my poetry and my riddles there is not a creature in the world that will not listen. And my riddles and songs contain all wisdom. I have the approval for them from the great man who is known as the true Merciful Man.

"And there is a whole story to that."

The Stammering Beggar's Story

Once, all the wise men were sitting together, and each one boasted about his wisdom.

One sage boasted that with his wisdom he had brought iron into the world. That is to say, he had taught men how to make iron from the earth. He had brought that to the world. And another boasted that he had brought forth another kind of metal, tin or lead. And another boasted that with his wisdom he had brought forth silver, which is more important. And another boasted that he had found a way to make gold. Still another boasted that he had brought forth military weapons for waging war, muskets and cannon. And another boasted that he could make all these metals from other things than the ones they were usually made from. And another boasted about other wisdom, for there were many things that had been brought forth with wisdom, such as saltpeter and gunpowder and the like.

And thus each one of them boasted about his wisdom.

Now one of them spoke up and he said:

"I am wiser than all of you, for I am as wise as the day."

But they didn't understand what he was saying about being as wise as the day.

And he said to them that all their wisdom could be put together and it would not make more than an hour. For though each wisdom of theirs were taken from another day, according to the creation of that day, still all their wisdom was interwined, that is to say, a mixture of several things in one, to make a thing. That was why the wisdom was taken from the day of the creation containing the combination. Nevertheless, wisdom could intertwine all their wisdom, and it would be nothing more than an hour. "But I am as wise as a whole day."

That was how the lowest wise man boasted.

So I, the stammering beggar, spoke up:

"Which day are you as wise as?"

The wise man said:

"This man is wiser than I for he asks: 'Which day?' Well, I am as wise as any day you like."

And now the question is: "Why is he who asks 'Which day?' wiser than the wise man? After all, the wise man was wiser than any day you like.

Now there is a whole story to that. For this true Merciful Man is a very great man.

And I, the stutterer telling you all this, I go about and gather all the pious men and bring them to this Merciful Man. And the main thing, when the time comes, for time itself, that is to say, when there is the year and the day in the world, is a creation after all, and only through true Merciful Men. And so I go about and gather all the Merciful Men and bring them to the true Merciful Man.

And there is a mountain.

And there is a rock on this mountain.

And there is a spring that comes forth from this rock.

And every object has a heart.

And the world itself also has a heart.

And the heart of the world is a perfect human figure, with a face, arms, and legs. Only the nail on the foot of the heart of the world is heartier than any other heart.

And the mountain with the spring stands at one end of the world.

And the heart of the world is at the other end of the world.

And the heart is opposite the spring, and the heart yearns and longs to come to the spring.

And the yearning and longing of the heart for the spring is very wild. It always screams in great yearning to come to the spring.

And the spring yearns and longs for the heart.

And the heart has two ailments.

One ailment: Because the sun hurries after it and burns it for yearning and wanting to come to the spring.

And the other ailment attacks the heart because it always yearns and longs with all its might for the spring. It always remains opposite the spring and screams for help in its longing and yearning for the spring.

But when the heart has to rest a bit and breathe a bit, then a large bird comes flying and spreads its wings over the heart and conceals it from the sun.

Now the heart can rest a bit.

But even now, while resting, the heart looks at the spring and yearns for it.

Yet why doesn't the heart go to the spring if it yearns so deeply for it? For if the heart is opposite the mountain, it can see the tip of the slope of the mountain, where the spring is. But as soon as it tries to climb the mountain, it no longer sees the tip and it cannot look at the spring.

For such is the nature of a high mountain. If you stand far away, you can see the tip, but when you walk up to it, you can no longer see the tip.

And if the heart cannot look at the spring, then it will give up its soul, God forbid.

For its very life comes from that spring.

And if the heart were to perish, God forbid, then the world would go under.

For the heart contains in itself the life of every object, and how could the world go on without the heart?

And that is why the heart cannot go to the spring, but instead faces it and yearns for it and screams.

And the spring has no time whatsoever. For it does not live in time. It is beyond the time of the world. But how then can the heart be in the world? For in the world, no thing can be without time.

The time of the spring is only what the heart gives as a day.

And the time of this day comes, so that it may end and vanish, and when the day shall be gone, the spring shall have no more time: the spring will then pass away from the world. And when the spring is gone, the heart shall likewise perish, God forbid, and then all the world will pass away, God forbid. They start to take leave of one another, the heart and the spring, and they start telling riddles and songs to one another, wonderful riddles and songs, with great love and great yearning.

And that true Merciful Man is in charge of all this.

And when the day comes to its very end and is about to pass away, then the true Merciful Man comes and gives another day to the heart.

And the heart gives the day away to the spring.

And thus the spring once more has time.

And when the day comes from the place it comes from, it comes with riddles and wondrous songs containing all wisdom.

And there is a difference between the days.

For there is a day for Sunday and a day for Monday, and so on for all the days of the week. And likewise there are days for new moons and for holidays.

And whatever day it may be, those are the songs it brings.

And all the time that the true Merciful Man has comes from me, the stammerer, who is telling you all this.

For I go and gather all the true Merciful Men who come forth with time.

And that is why the stammerer is even wiser than the wise man who boasted that he was as wise as any day we like. For all time and all days only come forth through me, the stammerer, and I gather all the truly pious, whose time is there, and I bring them to the true Merciful Man, and he gives a day to the heart, and the heart gives the day to the spring, which lets the whole world go on living. And thus, everything, time, with the riddles and songs, and all the wisdom contained in them, all exist because of me, the stammerer.

Therefore, I have permission from the true Merciful Man to speak songs and riddles containing all wisdom, for all time, time, the poems and hymns are due to him.

And now I give you this, as a wedding present, that you may be as I.

When the stammerer had finished his story, there was great rejoicing and reveling.

When the merrymaking of that day was over, they slept all night, and in the morning they remembered and longed for the beggar with the crooked neck.

And along he came and said:

"Here I am. I once blessed you that you might become as I. Today, I shall give you as a present that you may become as I. Now you may think that I have a crooked neck. But my neck isn't crooked at all. On the contrary, it's very straight and very beautiful. But what is it then? There are so many foolish things in the world that I don't want to emit even one breath into the world.

"In reality, I have a very fine and very beautiful neck. For I have a very fine voice, and all the sounds and voices, even sounds that are merely sounds and not words—I can imitate them all with my voice. For I have a wondrous neck and a wondrous voice. And I have the agreement of that country.

The Story of the Beggar with the Crooked Neck

There is a country where all the people know the art of music, that is, the art of playing and singing. And all of them practice it. Even the little children. There isn't a child in all the country that cannot play some instrument.

And the very least man in this country would be the greatest musician in another country. And the musicians, and the king of this country, and the orchestras, are the greatest of musicians.

Now once the musicians of this country were sitting together, and each one boasted of his musicianship. One man boasted that he could play one instrument, and another boasted that he could play another instrument. And still another boasted that he could play several instruments. One boasted that his voice could imitate one instrument, and another boasted that his voice could imitate another instrument. And still another boasted that his voice could imitate several instruments. And another one boasted that his voice could imitate the beating of a drum. And still another boasted that he could imitate the booming of cannon.

And I, too, was sitting there, I, the man with the crooked neck, who am telling you all this.

So I spoke up and said to them:

"My voice is better than your voices.

"And here is the proof:

"If you are such great musicians, help those two countries. For there are two countries and they lie a thousand leagues apart. And there, in the two countries, no one can sleep when night comes. For when night comes, all begin moaning and lamenting, men, women, and children. If a rock stood there, it would melt away. For at night, you can hear a great wailing, and that is why all the people start lamenting.

"Now if you are really such great musicians, let us see whether you can help these two countries or at least imitate the wailing they can hear there."

And the musicians said to me, the man with the crooked neck:

"Will you take us there?"

So I said:

"Yes, I'll take you there."

And all of them agreed to go.

And they traveled and they came to one of the two countries.

And when they arrived and the night came, it was as it always was in that country, all the people began moaning. And the musicians also moaned. And thus they saw that they could not help this country.

And I, the man with the crooked neck, said to the musicians:

"At any rate, tell me where this lamenting comes from, which you can hear. Where does the sound come from?"

They said to me:

"Do you know?"

And I, the man with the crooked neck, said to the musicians:

"Of course, I know!

"For here are two birds.

"One is a male.

"And one is a female.

"And they are the only pair of these birds left in the world.

"And the female disappeared.

"And the male wandered about looking for her.

"And she looked for him.

"And they looked for one another for a long time and became gloomy when they saw they could not find one another.

"So they stopped where they were and each built a nest.

"The male built a nest not far from one of these two countries. And not quite near, but the voice of the bird makes him sound as if he were near. For, in this country, his voice can be heard from the place where he built his nest.

"And the female also built a nest not far from the other country. And not quite near, but her voice can be heard from there.

"And when the night comes, the two birds start lamenting in loud voices, for each is wailing for the beloved. He wails for her, and she wails for him. And that is the lamenting that can be heard in the two countries. And the people moan about the lament and they cannot sleep."

And that is what I told them, I, the man with the crooked neck.

But they wouldn't believe me, and they said:

"Will you take us there?"

"Yes," I said. "I can take you. But how will we get there? If you cannot bear the lament here, and all of you wail about it, then if you come there, then you certainly won't be able to stand the noise.

"We cannot get there by day, for we will not be able to endure the rejoicing.

"For by day, birds come flying to each of these birds, both to him and to her. And they comfort them and cheer them with their great rejoicing. They speak words of solace saying: 'It's still possible for you to find one another.' And they make them very cheerful.

"And by day it is not possible to endure the great rejoicing there.

"And the noise of the rejoicing birds cannot be heard. You can only hear it once you arrive. However, the lamenting of the bird can be heard from afar.

"That is why you cannot get there."

And so they said to me, the man with the crooked neck:

"Can you fix that?"

And I replied:

"Yes, I can fix it, for I can imitate any sound in the world. And I can also throw my voice, that is, I can throw any sound. And wherever I throw my voice, it will not be heard, but it can be heard far away. And so I can throw the voice of the birds, that is to say, I can throw her voice to him, the voice that I imitate will come close to him. And I can also throw his voice and bring it close to her, and in this way I can bring them together again, and everything will be all right."

But who would believe me?

And I led them into a forest.

And they heard someone opening a door and closing it with a bang of the latch, and then shooting a musket, and sending out the dog to bring back what was shot, and the dog ran and hopped about in the snow.

And the musicians heard this and looked about. But they didn't see anything, and they didn't hear anything. But I, the man with the crooked neck, threw my voice and made those sounds. And they saw that I could imitate all kinds of sounds and throw my voice.

Thus, I have the agreement of that country that I have a fine voice and can imitate all the sounds in the world, and now I give you this as a wedding present, that you may be as I am.

4.

On the fifth day, they also made merry.

Then the bridegroom remembered the beggar who had a hunched back.

And they longed for him: "Where can we find that beggar? If

he were here, we would be very merry, and the rejoicing would really be great!"

And along he came, and said:

"Here I am. I've come to your wedding."

And he hugged them and kissed them, and said to them:

"I once blessed you that you might become as I. Today, as a wedding present, I give you that you may be as I am. I am not hunchbacked. On the contrary, my back and shoulders are a little that contain a lot (as it is written in the Talmud). And I have approval."

The Hunchback's Story

Once, some people in a conversation were boasting about that very thing, for each of them was boasting that he had a little which contained a lot.

They all laughed at one of them. And the others, who boasted of having a little that contained a lot. But my category of a little that contains a lot is greater than all of them.

For one of them boasted that his brain is a little that contains a lot, for it carried tens of thousands of human beings with all their needs, their behaviors, their gestures and actions. His brain carried all these things. That was why he had a little that contained a lot. For it was something of a brain that could carry so many people with all their things.

And they laughed at him and said:

"You don't exist, and neither do your people."

And one of them spoke up and said:

"I once saw a little that contained a lot. For once I saw a mountain with a great deal of filth and dirt lying on top. I was very surprised. Where did all that filth and dirt come from. There was a man next to the mountain, and he said to me: 'It all comes from me.' For he sat next to the mountain and threw everything on top of it, his excrements and the garbage from his food and drink. And so much dirt and filth collected on the mountain. Thus, man is a little that contains a lot, for so much filth can come from one man. And that's how it is."

Another boasted that he had a little which contained a lot. For he had a bit of land that brought forth a great deal of fruit. If someone added up the fruits that the bit of land brought forth, he would see that bit of land could not have such an area as the total of the fruits. Hence, that was a little that contained a lot.

Everyone liked what he said, for this was really a little that contained a lot.

And one man said: "He has a garden, a lovely garden with fruit, and many people go there. For it is a very lovely garden. And when summer comes, many people travel to this garden and many noblemen, and they go strolling there. In reality, the area of the garden is not large enough to take in so many people. That is why it is a little that contains a lot."

And everyone liked what he said too.

And one man said that his speech was in the category of a little that contains a lot, for he was a keeper of secrets, the secretary of a great king: "And so many people came to the king. One man came with praises and another with favors, and the king cannot hear all of them. And so I gather all their words in just a few words, and I speak these few words to the king. And thus all their praises and favors are all taken together in these few words, which I speak to the king. Thus my speech is in the category of a little that contains a lot."

And one man said that his silence was in the category of a little that contains a lot. For there were many people who accused him, and slandered him, and informed on him. But no matter how many people accused him, and slandered him, and informed on him, he would merely respond with silence, and simply hold his tongue. Thus, his silence was a little that contained a lot.

Now one man said that he was in the category of a little that contains a lot. For there was a poor man, who was blind, and he was very tall. And he, the man talking and boasting, was very small—and he acted as a guide for the poor blind man, who was very tall. Thus, he was a little that contained a lot. For the blind man could easily slip and fall, but the small man, by guiding him, kept him on his feet. Thus, he was a little containing a lot, for he was small but held up the tall blind man.

And I, the hunchback telling you all this, was also there. And now I spoke:

"The truth is that you are all in the category of the little that contains a lot, and I know everything you meant. And the lowest among you, who boasted of guiding the tall blind man—he is greater than you all. But I am above and beyond any of you, for he who boasted of guiding the blind man meant the disk of the moon, that is to say, the lunar sky. For the moon is blind, for it has no eyesight. And he, the man who boasted of this, he guides the moon, even though he is small and the lunar sky is very large, and it is the existence of the world. For the world needs a moon. Thus, he is truly a little that contains a lot. But my way of being a little that contains a lot is higher than all others.

"Here is the proof:

"Once there was a sect which claimed that every beast has its shade in which it prefers to rest, and in no other shade and, likewise, every bird has its branch on which it prefers to rest, and on no other branch. Thus, the sect wondered if they could find a tree in whose shadow all beasts preferred to rest and on whose branches all birds preferred to rest.

"And they realized that such a tree did indeed exist.

"Now they wanted to go to that tree. For the delight of that tree was endless, since it had all beasts and all birds. And no beast hurt any other. And all the beasts were mingled together there. They played together there. And it was a great delight to be by that tree.

"So the members of the sect tried to figure out how to get to that tree.

"Now there was a difference of opinion on the matter and they couldn't settle it among them. For one man said they ought to go east. And another: They ought to go west. One said this way, and another said that way. None of them knew the right way to get to the tree.

"A wise man came and said: 'Why worry about how to get to the tree. First you have to think about which people can come to the tree! For not everyone can come to this tree, only those who have the qualities of the tree.

" 'For this tree has three roots. One root is *Faith*, one must believe in God, Blessed Be He. The second root is *Piety*, one must revere the Good Lord. And the third root is *Meekness*, one should not think too highly of oneself. And *Truth* is the body of the tree, that is to say, the tree itself is *Truth*. And branches grow out of it. And therefore, no one can come to the tree unless he has the qualities of the tree: *Faith*, he must believe in God, *Piety*, he must fear God, and *Meekness*, he mustn't think too highly of himself. And *Truth*.'

"That was what the wise man said to the sect.

"Now, not everyone in that sect had those qualities. Only some of them. But there was a great unity among them, they loved one another and held together. They didn't want to separate and have some of them, those with the qualities of the tree, go to the tree, while the rest stayed behind. They refused, because they were very close. So they agreed to wait until all of them had worked up to the qualities, so that all of them together might go to the tree.

"That was what they did, they worked and worked until all of them attained the necessary qualities, that is to say, they all had Faith and Piety. And when they acquired all the qualities, they all realized that they had agreed upon one path to get to the tree.

"And so they all went.

"And after walking for a time, they sighted the tree in the distance.

"They looked at it and saw that the tree was not standing in any place. For the tree had no place. And if it didn't have a place, how could anyone get to it?"

And I, the hunchback telling you all this, I was among them. And I said to them: "*I* can bring you to the tree. For this tree has no place whatsoever. It is completely beyond a place, that is to say, it is totally beyond the place of this world—it *has* no place. And the matter of the little that contains a lot is fully in this place. For even though it is a little that contains a lot, that is to say, a tiny place holds more than can be placed in it—nevertheless, it is still in the place. For it occupies some sort of place. And my category of the little that contains a lot is in the category of the total end of the place. For from there and higher, there is no place at all. Therefore, I can carry you all to the tree which is completely beyond all place."

And I took them and carried them to the tree.

Hence, I have the approval for having the highest category of the little that contains a lot.

And that is why I look like a hunchback, for I carry so much on myself, and therefore, I am a little that contains a lot.

"And now," said the hunchback to the bride and groom, "I give it to you as a wedding present, that you may be as I am."

And there was much joy and merriment.

6.

On the sixth day, they were also merry, and they yearned:

"Where can we find the beggar who had no arms?"

And at that moment, he came in and said:

"Here I am. I've come to your wedding."

And he said the same thing to them as the others. And he hugged and kissed them, and said:

"You think that I have no arms. But I am not crippled at all. I have powerful arms, but I do not use the power of my arms in this world. For I need the power for something else, and I have the agreement of the watercastle."

The Story of the Armless Beggar

Once, several of us were sitting together, and each man boasted of the power in his arms. One said he had enormous strength in his arms. And another said he had enormous strength in his arms. And thus each one boasted of the strength in his arms. Now one man boasted that the strength and power in his arms was such that when he shot an arrow into the air he could pull it back. For his arms were so powerful that when he shot the arrow they could simply turn it around and bring it back.

Then I, the armless man telling you all this, I asked:

"What kind of arrow can you pull back? For there are ten kinds of arrow, and there are ten kinds of poison to smear on arrows. One kind of poison can make an arrow harmful, and another kind can make it even more harmful. Altogether, there are ten kinds of poison, each one worse than the next, and more harmful. And that alone makes for ten kinds of arrow. For even though there is only one kind of arrow, if you smear any of the ten kinds of poison on them, you get ten different kinds of arrow.

"And that was why I asked you: What kind of arrow can you pull back?"

I also asked him whether he could pull back the arrow before it had hit someone, and could he pull it back after it hit someone.

And he replied that he could pull it back even after it had struck its victim. And in answer to the question as to what kind of arrow, he replied: "This arrow."

Whereupon I said:

"If that is so, then you cannot cure the princess. For if you can only pull back one kind of arrow, then you cannot heal the princess."

One man boasted that his arms were so powerful that whenever he took something, he really gave. That is to say: By taking something from someone, he would give them something. And this made him a charitable man.

So I asked him:

"What kind of charity do you give? For there are ten kinds of alms."

He replied that he gave a tithe.

To which I said:

"If that is so, then you cannot cure the princess, for you could not get to her place, because you only give a tithe. For you could only get through one wall to the place where the princess lives."

One man boasted that his hands had a great power. For there were rulers in the world, that is to say, men in charge of a town or country. Each ruler needed wisdom. "My arms are so powerful that I can give him wisdom by supporting him with my arms."

So I asked him:

"What kind of wisdom can you give with your arms? There are ten measures of wisdom, after all."

He replied: "One wisdom."

Whereupon I said to him:

"Then you cannot cure the princess. You cannot know her pulse, since you know only one kind of pulse. There are ten kinds of pulse, and you can know only one kind, for you know only one wisdom."

One man boasted that his arms were so powerful that when a tempest came he could hold it back with his arms. He could grab it and mold it down to a useful size.

I asked him:

"What kind of wind can you grab? For there are ten kinds of wind."

He replied: "One wind."

Whereupon I said to him:

"Then you cannot cure the princess. For you cannot play the tune for her. For the remedy for the princess is melodies, and there are ten kinds of melody. And you can play only one melody of the ten melodies."

"And what can *you* do?" they exclaimed.

I answered: "I can do what all of you cannot do. That is to say: All the nine parts that you cannot do, I *can* do. I can do everything.

"For there is a story: Once a king fell in love with a princess, so he used cunning until he finally managed to catch her. And he kept her with him.

"One night, he dreamt that the princess rose against him and murdered him.

"He awoke, but the dream had struck him to the quick. So he summoned all the dream interpreters, and they interpreted his dream and told him the meaning, saying it would come true and she would indeed murder him.

"The king didn't know what to do. If he killed her, he would be sorry. If he sent her away, he would be unhappy, for another would take her. He had worked so hard to get her, and now someone else would get her. And if he did send her away and she came to another man, then the dream could indeed come true. For she would be with someone else. On the other hand, if he kept her with him, he feared that the dream might also come true.

"And thus the king didn't know what to do with her.

"Meanwhile, his love for her was ruined little by little because of the dream, he no longer loved her as much as before. And the more his love was ruined, the more her love for him was ruined, until she despised him so much that she ran away from him.

"The king sent out men to find her.

"The men came and told him that she was near the watercastle. Now the watercastle had ten walls, each within the other. And all ten walls were of water. And the earth around the castle was also of water. And there were trees and fruits there—all of water. And the beauty of the castle and the wondrousness of the castle were beyond any telling. It was truly wondrous. For the entire castle was of water. And no one could enter the castle. For anyone trying to enter it would drown, for the castle was all of water.

"Now when the princess had run away, she had come to this castle. And she walked around the watercastle. So the king's men told him she was walking around there, all around the watercastle. Thereupon, the king rode out with his army to capture her.

"When the princess heard them, she decided to escape into the castle. For she would rather drown than be caught by the king and return to him. On the other hand, perhaps she might be saved and find refuge in the watercastle.

"When the king saw her running into the watercastle, he said it was so, and ordered his men to shoot her. If she died, then so be it.

"So they shot their arrows at her, and all ten kinds of arrow struck her, the ten kinds that were smeared with the ten kinds of poison.

"And the princess escaped into the castle and came into its interior. And she passed through the gates of the watery walls. For there were gates in the watery walls. And she passed through all the gates of the watery walls of the watercastle, until she came into the interior of the castle, and there she collapsed and lay in a faint. And I am healing her, I the armless man telling you all this."

For he who does not have in his hands all ten charities cannot pass through the walls of the watercastle. For he will drown in the water. And the king and his army chased after the princess and they all drowned in the water.

But I can pass through all ten walls of the watercastle.

And these walls of water—they are the waves of the sea, which stand like walls. And the winds raise up the waves of the sea and lift them high. And the waves which are the ten walls—they stand there forever. The winds hold them up and raise them aloft. And I can pass through the ten walls, and I can pull out all ten kinds of arrow from the princess. And I know all ten pulses through the ten fingers. For through each of the fingers, one can know another pulse of the ten pulses. And I can cure her, the princess, with all ten kinds of melody, and thus I cure her. And that is the great power in my arms.

And today, I give it to you as a wedding present.

And there was a great, great rejoicing, and everyone was very merry.

7.

But what about the seventh beggar?

That we do not know.

And we shall not know until the Messiah comes.

Yenne Velt

THE FIRST DAY
Ansky (pseudonym for S. Z. Rapoport) (1863–1920)

The Tower of Rome

Drawing on the Solomonic tales that date back to the Talmud, Ansky completely transformed the Jewish king into an anti-Semitic tyrant in order to weave a parable about political and worldly power versus the messianic aspirations of Judaism. The biblical diction, the use of magic, astrology, and symbolism places the story in a context that gives the Jewish religious strivings a mythic substance within an eschatological interpretation of Jewish history.

Mendele Moykher-Sforim (1836?–1917)
The Wandering of a Soul

Mendele's vicious satire (see *The Mare*, Vol. II, sixth day) reached a vitriolic peak in this laughable and pathetic adventure of a Jew who visits Heaven, only to be turned away because the Jewish quota is filled. This is the ultimate pessimism, born of the frustrations and deceptions of Jewish life in the nineteenth-century Pale of Settlement.

The Mayse-Book (1602)
The Rabbi Who Was Turned into a Werewolf

The Mayse-Book, a medieval collection of Yiddish stories, drew mainly on Talmudic material, but it also included tales from other, sometimes contemporary, sources. This tale about a rabbinical were-wolf is fairly similar to Marie de France's *Le Bisclavret. The Mayse-Book* version, however, made Jewish by turning the courtly gentle-man into a rabbi, is so much more misogynous as to make us wonder whether it might not almost function as a vicious attack on the posi-tion of women in a patriarchal culture. One can scarcely blame the rabbi's wife, who was left out of the male-bonding world of learning and friendship, for resenting her dreadful lot and taking appropriate revenge—like Shylock. The misogyny intermingles with a malaise about sex, thereby giving in to an equation of sex and sin as em-bodied by Eve or Lilith: salvation through study, virtue, and absten-tion as opposed to the worldly and carnal possibilities of human existence.

Der Nister (pseudonym for Pinhas Kahanovitch) (1884–1950)
At the Border

Der Nister gave himself a cabbalistic *nom de plume*, literally "The Arcane." His prose (before a conversion to soviet Socialist Realism) takes up cabbalistic energies, mythical material not always inherent to the Jewish tradition, and elements from Jewish folklore. The characters, however, tend not to be specifically Jewish, but, like many figures in fairytales, live in a timeless world beyond nationality and cultural specificity.

"At the Border," as well as his other stories in this anthology, are taken from his two-volume collection, *Gedakht (Spoken)*, published in Berlin in 1922. Setting up a mythical quest for redemption through national salvation, Der Nister curiously retains a reminiscence of a sense of Jewish life and survival as a route toward spiritual fulfill-ment. The nearly petrified waiting, the mystical yearning, the notion of an almost permanent quest on a superhuman level—create a private mysticism, self-enclosed and rarely admitting a lucid interpretation. Such absolute symbolism, easily traceable to the tales of Rabbi Nakhman (see below), and to cabbalism, evokes rather than ex-plains, and is perceptibly analogous to the poetic experimentation in European modernism. The language, an authentic, colloquial Yid-dish, alive with a hypnotic and mellow lyricism, flows along in strange, meandering sentences, with rhymes, repetitions, and peculiar rhythms. We are left on a hazy verge of something, a brink over-looking the ultimate reality, that we can only sense with the prera-tional strata of the mind, but cannot capture with logic or human discourse.

Y[itzok] L[eybesh] Peretz (1852–1915)
The Three Wedding Canopies

Taking the messianic yearnings of Eastern European Jewry and the dream of a political autonomy for Jews, Peretz wove this short novel of a quest for love as figuring the aspiration for harmonious earthly existence in both personal and political life. The un-answered question at the end is typical of a mootness in messianic hope: fulfillment just beyond our grasp. The novel is stylized with traditional fairytale material in a highly Germanicized Yiddish, betokening the powerful influence of the romantic *Kunstmärchen*. The glittering polish of the diction, the romantic trappings, the gentle irony coursing through the lyricism, create a nineteenth-century fairytale camp, that, for Peretz then, seemed the only way of expressing his dual attitude toward the two messianic strivings: the religious and the political one—parallel lines that could only meet in an infinity beyond literature and beyond history.

THE SECOND DAY

Ansky (See The First Day, *"The Tower of Rome,"* p. 3, and note, p. 347)
The Penitent

Ansky, deeply interested in Slavic folklore, translated this Russian folktale into Yiddish, totally preserving the Gentile world of the original, perhaps because he couldn't bring himself to present a Jewish robber and patricide. There is a curious kinship to the Lohengrin legend in the theme of penitence emblemized in the motif of a flowering staff as a sign of salvation and divine forgiveness.

Y. L. Peretz (1852–1915)
The Three Gifts

The theme of salvation endures a sardonic treatment here. Peretz's castigation of human mediocrity and pettiness is schematicized in the attempts of a thoroughly middling person to attain redemption. The depiction of the human condition as precisely balanced between good and evil is one of total mediocrity. The gifts themselves, apparently requisites of loftier action, bring salvation, but are waved off as petty trifles by the saints. The pessimism, measured and sarcastic, is more metaphysical than social.

Der Nister (See pp. 44, 246, and notes)
The Fool and The Forest Demon

Folk demonology was not always filled with sin and wickedness. There are oases, as in this lyrical pastoral that turns an apparently slight incident about release from servitude into bucolic tenderness and sensuality. Yet the motif of emancipation is crucial throughout Jewish history.

I. J. Trunk (1887–1961)
The Jewish Pope

Many of I. J. Trunk's writings were actually adaptations of older Jewish material such as the *Bovve Book*. His version of a medieval legend about a Jewish pope was taken from *The Mayse-Book* (1602). Greatly expanding the original tale into a parable of worldly ambition, he dwells on the historical condition of Jews as bearers of a national faith and ideology within a hostile, material world. Although there never was a pope from a Jewish background, the legend has nevertheless inspired literary and scholarly inquiry. Trunk's adaptation of the medieval tale is effective for its clear, linear plot, straightforward style, and pop schematicism of medieval color.

Moyshe Kulbak (1896–1940)
The Wind Who Lost His Temper

This fairytale for children is quite different from Kulbak's mystical novels and later soviet satires. The interest in nature was belated in Jewish life, and this anthropomorphic sympathy with natural forces ultimately domesticated by a child differs from Kulbak's other treatments. His kind optimism may have been dictated by his awareness of the juvenile audience.

Yudl Rosenberg
The Golem

Rosenberg brought out this pamphlet in 1909, passing it off as a translation from Hebrew. He actually wrote it himself in Yiddish, following the tradition of Hassidic hagiography, i.e., stories extolling the wondrous souls and feats of the great rabbis. Drawing on the old legend of a manmade humanoid, which tradition had somehow connected with the historical Rabbi Liva of Prague, Rosenberg produced a journalistic chronicle of adventures; primitive, schematic, and tendentious. His work was a striking example of Jewish pulp-writing for the masses, and yet it inspired Leivick's renowned drama *The Golem*, and was adapted into an episodic novel by Chaim Bloch (who never gave Rosenberg credit for supplying him with the contents of his book). The Blood Libels against Jews, accusing them of murdering Christians and using their blood to bake unleavened bread for Passover, were growing in force during the 1890s. It was this disastrous trend that Rosenberg attacked in his *vita* of Rabbi Liva. The one-dimensional pop quality of the writings, the intrusive journalese, the linear optimism contrast with more complex literary treatments of Jewish life in Eastern Europe. Conventions of pop and pulp tend to be ignored by historians and literati; and yet such grade-B Gothic is always widely disseminated, and captures a much greater segment of the popular imagination.

THE THIRD DAY

The Mayse-Book
The Conversation of Two Ghosts

Another (unfortunately) misogynous tale from the medieval collection (see p. 31, and note, p. 348). Pungent and anecdotal, the story derives from folk superstitions and mocks vanity and other supposedly feminine vices.

Ansky (See pp. 3,107, and notes, pp. 697, 699)

A Good Laugh

The Hassidic tradition of storytelling contributes both the theme and the structure of this tale. Hassidic stories tended to be hagiographic encomiums of guru-rebbes, and were told orally for the most part at a *farbrengen,* a get-together of the rebbe and his followers. The more conservative rabbinate thundered against such *maysenen* (storytelling) as sacrilegious, and the Hassidic narrator in this tale utters a reminiscence of that fear, when he points out that his stories might do his listeners more harm than good in drawing their attention away from the greatness of God. Ansky was interested in both the Hassidic substance of this narrative art and in the spiritual and intellectual atmosphere within which it developed. Thus, "A Good Laugh" is also about the intellectual and religious aesthetics behind *maysenen.*

The Mayse-Book (1602)

The Possession

This tale from the medieval *Mayse-Book* is probably the first Yiddish story about a possession, and begins a long tradition of dybbuk literature, the most famous example being Ansky's play, *The Dybbuk.* Although primitive in structure and rough in language, the story points out the ambiguous power of the possessed sinner to recognize evil in others, so that the dybbuk has the paradoxical function of rectifying evil before his own exorcism.

Dovid Bergelson

At Night (See Foreword)

Der Nister

In the Wine-Cellar

The cabbalistic and Hassidic forces in this story are concentrated in the enigmatic symbolism, the astrological lyricism, and the intricate convolutions of tales within tales. The material and structural peculiarities can easily be traced to Rabbi Nakhman's tales. The involved sentences, as usual in Der Nister (see pp. 44, 123), draw the action into a meandering flow outside the normal linear course of time.

Rabbi Nakhman of Bratslev

A Tale of a King and a Wise Man

(See pp. 349, 377, 687, and notes p. 703)

Moyshe Kulbak (1896–1940)

The Messiah of the House of Ephraim

The messianic yearning of the Jewish masses is expressed in a complex of legends concerning the Lamed-vovniks, the thirty-six hidden saints, who come from humble origins and carry on a tradition of silent virtue. Kulbak, writing in an earthy, colloquial Yiddish, blends together a number of folklore motifs, such as the figure of Lilith or the character of Simkhe Plakhte. At the same time, he draws on the apocalyptical intensity, the dramatic heightenings, and cinematic juxtapositions of German Expressionism to produce a mystical and lyrical novel. The plot disintegration of modern fiction becomes a structural parallel to a desperate chaos that seeks redemption in a vulnerable Savior, whose earthly fate is strongly Christological. Yet Kulbak, rejecting Christian possibilities, looks toward an ultimate Jewish salvation.

THE FOURTH DAY

Rabbi Nakhman of Bratslev (1772–1810)

A Tale of a Prince

The absolute symbolism forbids a rational unpeeling. When we remove the skin of the story, we find lyrical jewels. This poetic inner substance demands a nonrational, mystical response to an energy beyond verbalization. Only the poetry of modernism could teach us to experience literature on such levels. The ultimate shock, however, was the utterance of these mystical forces in Yiddish, the language of everyday life, rather than in the sacred tongue of Hebrew.

Ber Horovitz (1895–?)

The Dybbuk

Jewish folklore is rich in tales of wonder-rabbis and their exploits, which often included exorcisms. The sin and the guilt are here tied to illicit sexual thought, whose effects are as disastrous as those of deeds. Rectification of disorder leads to the confirmation of traditional values: family, religious study, etc. Morality is tied to conservative banalities that are never questioned even when flouted.

Y. L. Peretz

A Passion for Clothes

Unlike the sensuality that some Jewish writers saw as fulfillment in a pantheistic nature (see Der Nister), greed, the love of material things that are sharply divided from the spiritual, obsessed the Jewish imagination as much as it did the unhappy protagonist of Peretz's tale. Cut off, like all Jewish women, from the intellectual and spiritual world of men, she fails in her duties as wife and mother and has to endure the requisite punishment. Following Eve in succumbing to the Evil Spirit, she belatedly realizes her transgressions to become a didactic example.

The Mayse-Book

King Solomon and Ashmedai

Solomon was always an ambiguous figure in the Jewish tradition. This medieval tale, drawn from Talmudic material, naïvely and unwittingly presents a schizophrenic Solomon who, in the process of building the Temple (that spiritual center of all Jews) is confronted with his alter ego, Ashmedai, ruler of the demons. More cunning than the devil, Solomon is in many ways his moral inferior. After all, Ashmedai goes to heaven every day to study the holy texts, while the King devotes himself to worldly politics. The prophetic Ashmedai sounds almost like Solomon, paralleling his wisdom. Unhappily, Ashmedai's downfall is his sexuality, or rather, his transgression of Jewish sexual taboos, which Solomon, although the most powerful man in the world, would never flout. He leaves such sins to his darker alter ego, who has to take the consequences.

Rabbi Nakhman of Bratslev (1772–1810)

A Tale of a Rabbi and His Only Son

The Messiah will come when the world is totally good or totally evil. The polarities in this tale are kept in a negative dialectic: evil interferes with the fusion of good and good.

Y. L. Peretz

The Conjuror

Drawing on Jewish folklore, Peretz presents *Eli-Ha-Novi*—not Elijah, the formidable prophet of the Bible, but a friendly and lovable figure who wandered, anonymously poor, through Eastern Europe, helping Jews in moments of trouble. Above all, he reminds us that the Bible was often on a magnificent plane, its splendor far removed from the daily banalities of life. Of course, there was a sad side to Eli-Ha-Novi. His existence was limited to the Eastern Europe Diaspora. Ultimately, the land and the language of the Bible would have to be restored, and the awe-inspiring avatar, the Prophet Elijah, would have to loom over his folk alter ego.

A. B. Gotlober (1811–1899)

The Gilgul or The Transmigration

The Jewish Enlightenment, the Haskalah, turned its satirical venom on what is derided as superstition, mysticism, and degeneracy in Jewish life. Gotlober, using the folklore theme of reincarnation, viciously traces a series of lives through Jewish history, although obviously the conditions he describes were contemporary. Addressing the masses in their own language, and using popular motifs and material (a number of Hebrew books on the same theme preceded his short novel), he produced one of the most acute attacks on Hassidism and rabbinical corruption, as well as on the exploitive

Jews who added to the hardships of their vulnerable communities. Conversational in tone and structure, the story sums up much of the social and economic horrors of Jewish life, and paved the way for the ultimate vitriol of Mendele Moykher-Sforim (see Volume I: p. 21 and Volume II: p. 199).

THE FIFTH DAY

The Mayse-Book

Haninah and the Frog

This more universal story from the medieval *Mayse-Book* combines two fairytale complexes: the quest for the queen on the basis of a clue of hair *(Tristan and Isolde)*; and the ability to speak the languages of animals and employ them in time of trouble. The result seems almost like a weave of two stories, which possibly explains the author's callous treatment of Haninah's first wife, who conveniently dies so that he may wed the queen of the golden hair.

Rabbi Nakhman of Bratslev (1772–1810)

A Tale of a Menorah

The concept of imperfection and fragmentation are central to the aesthetics of Nakhman, the artist-rabbi, who deliberately truncated his tales, using the fragment as an allegorical figuration of human life, which find perfection only in the divine and the messianic. The young man who can show the faults in the craft of others is the rabbinical poet pointing out the imperfection of worldly existence.

Ber Horovitz

The Legend of the Madonna

Half-ecumenical, half-contemptuous of Christian hypocrisy, the author picks up a Christological motif that had become more and more frequent in Jewish writing: the attempt to re-Judaicize the New Testament figures. Humanizing them, and slyly making Christianity almost tempting, despite the horrors perpetrated in the name of the Church, Horovitz turns the Mariological miracles of medieval Christian literature into pro-Jewish feats that point out the superior force of true faith and piety.

Der Nister

A Tale of Kings

As in his other fiction, Der Nister draws on Rabbi Nakhman's tales within tales to produce a convoluted fairytale novella about a secular quest and salvation. The schematic and universal structure of the threefold problems to be solved by the hero before he attains the hand of the princess is thus refracted by a plot line that twists into and out of itself like a multidimensional Möbius strip. Stories told to the hero break up the irreversibility of time; prophecies described in detail and then realized in the same detail set up mirror images that once again slow down and splinter the movement of time. Bovve, a hero with no past but with a definite and timeless future of endless happiness, has to withstand the trials of earthliness in order to achieve that timeless redemption. Set in a world beyond the experience or possible reach of its readers, the long, meandering, lyrical story sets up an allegorical utopia beyond history. Bovve is the typical fairy-story self-made man, whose self-help nevertheless requires magical assistance from other sources, but whose courage and perseverance gain him the salvation that is neither religious nor worldly, but exists only within the private domain of fantasy.

THE SIXTH DAY

Mendele Moykher-Sforim (pseudonym for Sholem Yankev Abramovitch) (c. 1836–1917)

The Mare

He took the pen name of Mendele Moykher-Sforim, Mendele the Book Dealer, and employed this narrative persona in most of his fiction, which he wrote in both Yiddish and Hebrew. His subject was the life of Jews in Eastern Europe, and especially their double vulnerability—in the face of a hostile outer world and at the hands of their own exploiters within. His satire, armed with probably the most vicious irony since Fielding's *Jonathan Wild*, flayed the entire Jewish world of Eastern Europe, all classes of society, all the pleasures and frustrations, all types and characters.

Using the language of everyday life, Yiddish, he applied it with all the nuances at his disposal, all the colors and rhythms, the influences of Hebrew and Gentile culture. His style is a complex of subtleties, allusions, and playful twisting of language from mimetic realism to energies that make language an absolute power beyond its average use.

"The Mare" is an ambiguous title. The Yiddish word can mean a female horse (or donkey) or be a pejorative term for a "nag" or "dobbin," a broken-down horse, an old gray mare.

This intricate and didactic satire sets up a twofold allegory, in which the Jewish nation is split into Israel, Izzy, a young Jew striving to make something of himself in the misery of the Pale of Settlement, and the Mare, the representation of the Jewish people throughout history. Twice humiliated by being turned into an animal, and a female at that (the profoundly patriarchal structure dictated such a dehumanizing attitude toward women), the Mare engages in endless dialectics with Izzy, fashioning an inner Jewish struggle that plays on all the confusions and contradictions of Jewish history. Mendele, by resorting to the use of traditional folklore and Talmudic motifs, may have been giving in to a popular audience. But at the same time, he revealed the paradox of the Haskalah, the Jewish Enlightenment, which attacked what it called superstition and mysticism, and yet made use of this material in these very attacks. Mendele's works form a satirical *summa* of a devastating era in Jewish history. They look toward salvation as a historical development of human effort rather than as a messianic advent.

AND ON THE SEVENTH DAY

Rabbi Nakhman of Bratslev (1772–1810)

The Tale of the Seven Beggars

Hassidic stories usually extolled the wondrous doings of a rebbe. But here the rabbi became an artist and told an entirely different kind of story. Supposedly, Rabbi Nakhman of Bratslev, a great-grandson of the Baal Shem-Tov, told his tales to his disciples and dictated them to his scribe Nathan, who published them after the author's death. The book was bilingual, with the Yiddish versions filling out the bottom half of the page, and a Hebrew translation the top half. The symbolism of languages was obvious: Yiddish, the language of everyday life, of the earth and the Exile; Hebrew, the *loshen-(ha)koydesh*, the tongue of holiness and heaven. Nakhman had told his followers to pray in Yiddish, and he used it in his sermons. The long, rambling sentences of his stories twist and turn like existential dragons trying to shake off the categories of time and space. Repetitions, contradictions, puzzling symbols, tales within tales make for a mystical world that invites and yet defies rational analysis. The fragmentary character of the stories, often attacked by critics for "getting nowhere" (just as modernism is attacked for being fragmentary and anticlassical), actually emblemizes the unfulfillment and truncation of earthly life. The only way of completing these stories is in the messianic redemption; there is no earthly way of solving the puzzles or rounding out the fragments. That is why we not only never quite understand who the beggars are, but we never find out about the seventh beggar. Our ultimate Sabbath is still far away.